Turn the page for tips on finding help in *The St. Martin's Handbook*

# FINDING HELP IN
## *The St. Martin's Handbook*

The goal of the handbook is to help you become a more effective writer throughout and beyond your student years. Here are a few avenues for finding answers to your writing questions.

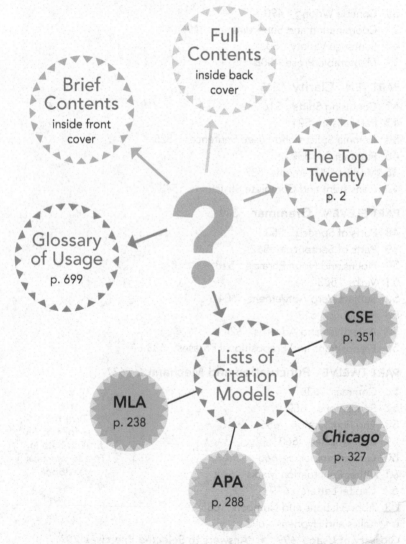

Full Contents
inside back cover

Brief Contents
inside front cover

The Top Twenty
p. 2

Glossary of Usage
p. 699

?

Lists of Citation Models

CSE
p. 351

MLA
p. 238

Chicago
p. 327

APA
p. 288

# The
# St. Martin's
# Handbook

NINTH EDITION

# The
# St. Martin's
# Handbook
## for South Dakota State University

**Andrea A. Lunsford**
Stanford University

*A section for multilingual writers and a section on genre with*

**Paul Kei Matsuda**
Arizona State University

**Christine M. Tardy**
University of Arizona

*A section on academic and professional writing with*

**Lisa Ede**
Oregon State University

bedford/st.martin's
Macmillan Learning

Boston | New York

## For Bedford/St. Martin's

*Vice President:* Leasa Burton
*Program Director:* Stacey Purviance
*Director of Content Development:* Jane Knetzger
*Senior Executive Editor:* Michelle M. Clark
*Assistant Editor:* Aislyn Fredsall
*Director of Media Editorial:* Adam Whitehurst
*Senior Media Editor:* Barbara G. Flanagan
*Marketing Manager:* Vivian Garcia
*Senior Director, Content Management Enhancement:* Tracey Kuehn
*Senior Managing Editor:* Michael Granger
*Senior Digital Content Project Manager:* Ryan Sullivan
*Senior Workflow Project Manager:* Lisa McDowell
*Production Supervisor:* Robin Besofsky
*Director of Design, Content Management:* Diana Blume
*Interior Design:* Claire Seng-Niemoeller
*Cover Design:* William Boardman
*Director of Rights and Permissions:* Hilary Newman
*Text Permissions Researcher:* Udayakumar Kannadasan, Lumina Datamatics, Inc.
*Photo Permissions Editor:* Angela Boehler
*Photo Researcher:* Sheri Blaney, Lumina Datamatics, Inc.
*Director of Digital Production:* Keri deManigold
*Senior Media Project Manager:* Allison Hart
*Copyeditor:* Christine Clark, Lumina Datamatics, Inc.
*Indexer:* Lumina Datamatics, Inc.
*Composition:* Lumina Datamatics, Inc.
*Printing and Binding:* BR Printers

*For information, write:* Macmillan Learning Curriculum Solutions, 14903 Pilot Drive, Plymouth, MI 48170 (macmillanlearning.com)

2    3    4    5    6        26        25   24   23   22   21

Printed in the United States of America.
Library of Congress Control Number: 2020944529

ISBN: 978-1-319-45916-1 (South Dakota State University Edition)

## Acknowledgments

*Text acknowledgments and copyrights appear at the back of the book on page 722, which constitutes an extension of the copyright page. Art acknowledgments and copyrights appear on the same page as the art selections they cover.*

# INTRODUCTION

# A Supplement for Students at South Dakota State University

# Objectives and Assessment Criteria

The English Department at SDSU offers a range of composition courses—from basic to advanced. While each serves a particular purpose within the curriculum, all promote critical thinking and the core principles of good prose that are essential to writing well at the college level and beyond. *The St. Martin's Handbook* provides excellent and ample advice about these and other topics—about the writing process, about argumentation, about research and documentation, and about grammar and mechanics. The purpose of this introduction, then, is not to say again what the *Handbook* already says well, but to describe briefly the objectives, assessment criteria, and policies concerning academic honesty common to the courses at SDSU for which this book is a required text.

## A-1 Objectives

While activities and assignments will vary from one composition course to the next, two closely related objectives are central to all such courses at SDSU. The first is that students will learn to think critically and to analyze the subjects they write about; the second, that students will learn to write well about those subjects.

### ☐ Critical thinking and analysis

*To think critically* is to wonder, to challenge received assumptions, to adopt multiple perspectives as a means of seeing issues and objects anew, and to seek and to create new knowledge. Such thinking is what your instructors hope to foster in your courses—as an applied skill, yes, but also as a habit of mind, as a way of being in the world. An effective writing course, after all, is not just about writing well but also about thinking well. It is about trying to discover the truth about a given subject and about trying to craft ever more accurate accounts and assessments of that subject. Good writing, in short, has style *and* substance. It weighs, considers, and questions. It takes chances. It broadens our perspective; it broadens—and improves—our understanding of the world.

Analysis is one means—perhaps the chief means—of demonstrating critical thinking in an essay. *To analyze* means to break something down into its constituent parts, to try to understand how those parts make up the whole so that the whole becomes newly visible, no longer obscured by the veneer of familiarity. In this way, new characteristics—flaws or perfections, contradictions or consistencies—come to light.

Unlike in a biology or a botany course in which you might analyze a living organism, in a composition course, concerned as it is with language and images, with forms of representation, you will examine not natural entities but fabricated or constructed ones—visual and print texts, for example, or the persona of a public figure, or events staged for the camera, or an article of clothing, or a theory, or even the self. And in ways that an organism, a bird or a tree, does not, each of these constructions vies for our attention. The form it assumes, in fact, is designed precisely for this purpose—to gain a hearing and, ultimately, to win admirers or adherents. An engineer—with, perhaps, a marketer's assistance—hopes to imbue an automobile with qualities that appeal to consumers; the writer of an editorial adopts a particular tone and style to sway readers; a political candidate or an entertainer creates a persona to court a wide audience. To analyze such tactics is to peek behind the curtain, to witness the grinding mechanism of calculated effect, to observe rhetoric at work. Analysis, in this regard, helps us to become thinking citizens, aware and, perhaps, wary of those who would influence us, and cognizant of the welter of shouts and pleas audible within the rhythms of daily life.

## ☐ Core principles of good prose

The principles of good prose noted here hardly constitute an exhaustive list, and your instructors, appropriately so, will add to them. At base, though, good prose in most circumstances will avoid the pitfalls and include the positive traits described below.

Note that each principle anticipates the expectations and needs of readers. This is most appropriate, for to communicate effectively—that is, to shape content into comprehensible and convincing form, to do more than just spill it out onto the page and hope readers will follow and credit what you say—you must take your readers into account. This means trying to anticipate their assumptions and views, of course, but it also means satisfying their expectation that you will abide by the conventions of formal discourse in regard to grammar, diction, syntax, and form.

### Good prose is clear.

As we well know, contemporary life places great demands upon our time, our attention, and our energies. When we read—at school, at home, at work—we expect that what we read will either inform us or in some way please or provoke us, and that it will do so fairly efficiently. Yet a text cannot fulfill these expectations if we cannot comprehend its grammar, diction, syntax, or form. Having to contend with error and confusion squanders our time, scatters our attention, and depletes our energies. We become frustrated and, in most cases, decide that the difficulty of deciphering the text is not worth the effort. We stop reading. But writing that is clear—writing that abides by the conventions of grammar, that presents the apt not the approximate word, that uses syntax to shape ideas and to signal the proper relation between them, and that conveys its content in coherent and unified fashion—enlivens and engages readers. It makes communication—the central purpose of all writing—possible.

### Good prose is concise.

Writing that is not clear confuses readers; writing that is not concise risks boring them. Redundancy, needless repetition, and wordy phrasing such as "due to the fact that" and "at this point in time" (rather than the more concise "because" and "now," respectively) all contribute to writing that uses more words than it needs to convey its meaning. Not only are such excesses tedious and potentially confusing to readers, but they also signal that the writer has not devoted sufficient time to revising and to editing a text—at readers' expense. Wordy prose can erode a writer's *ethos*—that good character so crucial to gaining readers' trust and securing readers' willingness to give the writer a full and fair hearing. Strive to write prose that is crisp, focused, and controlled—that respects readers' time and intelligence.

### Good prose is contextualized.

If you attend to it carefully, you will discover that much of the information we now receive via various electronic sources—radio, television, the Internet, text-messaging devices—is often brief, discontinuous, and devoid of context. Facts, testimonies, and accounts are often difficult for us to comprehend or credit because we receive them in disconnected bits, severed from the larger narratives and histories that give them meaning. Print texts, of course, can exhibit the same shortcomings—they can be as brief and as decontextualized as any electronic text—but they also, potentially, offer a more sustained form of discourse that can explain an issue in full rather than merely encapsulate it within the confines of a ten-second sound bite. Good writers know that they must provide background for the issues they discuss—that they must make clear to the reader what is at stake in their argument and how each of their claims advances that argument.

***Good prose is convincing.***

The ultimate measure of good prose is the degree to which it convinces its readers—to act, to consider or reconsider, to question, to accept, to affirm, or to follow, in any of a host of ways, the directives of a text. Following a tradition that dates back to Aristotle (384–322 BCE), writers historically have employed three means of appealing to an audience—through the logic of the text (*logos*), the character of the writer (*ethos*), and the emotions of the audience (*pathos*). What is important to remember is that these appeals are not givens, but potential features of a text that writers must *create*. A text's *logos* resides in the validity of its claims and in the valid sequencing of those claims; its *ethos*, in the clear, concise, contextualized prose and tempered, fair-minded approach that establish the writer as someone who is conscientious, competent, and knowledgeable; its *pathos*, in the articulation of what readers might feel, but also of what, perhaps, they should feel. In the end, of course, readers decide whether or not a text convinces them, but writers can do much to ensure that it does.

# A-2 Assessment criteria

Your instructors will assess each of your major essays upon quality of content (including use of source materials), clarity of form (including correct documentation), and clarity of style (including grammatical correctness). In determining a grade, they will apply criteria articulated in the following rubric.[1]

### The grade of "A" ("exceptional") designates:

- Fulfillment of the requirements and objectives of the assignment;
- An excellent, impressive command of content;
- A clear explanation, development, and application of ideas;
- Independent thought and analysis;
- Thorough and persuasive substantiation of claims;
- Clear and effective organization;
- Precise, fluent, and distinctive expression; and
- Correct grammar, punctuation, documentation, and format.

### The grade of "B" ("above average") designates:

- Fulfillment of most of the requirements and objectives of the assignment;

---

[1] A variant of this rubric appears in the *South Dakota State University General Catalog: Undergraduate Programs.*

- A competent command of content;
- Mostly clear explanation, development, and application of ideas;
- A capacity for independent thought and analysis, though it is not fully realized;
- Sufficient and mostly persuasive substantiation of claims;
- Mostly clear and effective organization;
- Mostly precise, fluent, and clear expression; and
- Mostly correct grammar, punctuation, documentation, and format.

## The grade of "C" ("average") designates:

- Fulfillment of the major requirements and objectives of the assignment, though minor ones are only partially fulfilled or unfulfilled;
- An adequate command of subject matter;
- Adequate explanation, development, and application of ideas, though lack of depth is evident;
- Lack of independent thought or sustained analysis;
- Inconsistent substantiation of claims;
- Adequate organization, though lapses are evident;
- Adequate expression, though lapses in precision, fluency, and clarity are evident; and
- Adequate grammar, punctuation, documentation, and format, though errors are evident.

## The grade of "D" ("lowest passing grade") designates:

- Insufficient fulfillment of the requirements and objectives of the assignment;
- An inadequate command of content;
- Insufficient explanation, development, and application of ideas;
- Unexamined, clichéd thinking and little analysis;
- Inadequate substantiation of claims;
- Inadequate organization, making the text hard to follow;
- Inadequate expression with significant lapses in precision, fluency, and clarity; and
- Numerous and significant errors in grammar, punctuation, documentation, and format.

## The grade of "F" ("failure") designates:

- A failure to follow or complete the assignment;
- A failure to control or comprehend the content;
- A failure to sufficiently explain, develop, or apply ideas;
- A failure to analyze;
- A failure to sufficiently substantiate claims;
- A failure to organize the content, making the text largely incoherent;
- A failure to write with any degree of precision, fluency, or clarity; and
- A failure to abide by the conventions of grammar, punctuation, documentation, or format.

# Policies and Resources

The following section covers policies and resources relevant to students in the composition program at South Dakota State University. Have a question about plagiarism? Refer to the policy below. Need help with your writing? Visit the Writing Center in 103 Briggs Library.

## B-1 Academic honesty

The English Department announces herewith that it will not tolerate plagiarism—representing another's work as one's own—in any form. Students must abide by the principles governing academic research and writing, the first and foremost of which is honesty. Students also must abide by the university's policies regarding academic integrity, set forth in Policy 2.4 of the *South Dakota State University Policy and Procedure Manual*. A summary of this policy, provided by the Office of the Provost, appears below.

> Student Academic Integrity and Appeals: The University has a clear expectation for academic integrity and does not tolerate academic dishonesty. University Policy 2.4 sets forth the definitions of academic dishonesty, which includes but is not limited to cheating, plagiarism, fabrication, facilitating academic dishonesty, misrepresentation, and other forms of dishonesty relating to academics. The Policy and its Procedures also set forth how charges of academic dishonesty are handled at the University. Academic dishonesty is strictly proscribed and if found may result in student discipline up to and including dismissal from the University.

If you have any questions about academic honesty, be sure to discuss them with your instructor or to review the full policy via the SDSU Web site. You should not hesitate to consult your instructor if you are feeling uncertain or anxious about an assignment or if you are unable to meet an approaching deadline. You will achieve a far better and more satisfying result if you seek assistance, which instructors are happy to provide, than if you resort to the drastic measures noted above.

## B-2 The Writing Center

For those who would like extra feedback on their drafts or assistance with generating ideas, developing and organizing those ideas, or expressing their meaning clearly and concisely, the English Department provides free tutoring in its Writing Center, located in 103 Briggs Library. This service is available to all students. To schedule an appointment, go to the Writing Center's Web site (sdstate.edu/writingcenter) or call (605) 688-6559. Depending upon availability of tutors, walk-ins are also welcome.

# Notes

# PREFACE

When I first began work on *The St. Martin's Handbook* in 1985, I could not have imagined the changes that would take place in our cultural and technological landscape. Could. Not. Imagine. What I did know, however, was that most writing reference books were based far more on what Steve North identified as "lore" than on current research. And in the case of one research-based text, the research had been carried out decades earlier and was clearly no longer current. It seemed to me that student writers would be best served by a reference book informed by significant research into student writing and its development — along with everything I knew about how to help students build on their strengths in writing. From my first research project on the most common errors in student writing to subsequent research on teachers' comments, teaching with technology, students' revising processes, multimodal composition, and translingual approaches in the classroom — every edition of *The St. Martin's Handbook* has been grounded in new and timely research with writers and with teachers of writing.

This ninth edition is no exception. But what kind of research would be most timely and important for student writers? Given the current state of public discourse — full of angry tweets, misinformation, and *us-versus-them* thinking, it seemed important to find out how student writers were feeling about how to communicate in such an atmosphere. In 2019, I surveyed students of writing across the country, asking them to identify examples of barriers that prevent people from reaching common ground on difficult topics and to articulate what benefits they see (if any) in being open-minded and respectful of those who hold views different from theirs or have backgrounds different from theirs. Students identified fear, stubbornness, ingrained cultural and religious beliefs, lack of knowledge, and stereotyping as major barriers to communication and understanding, some writing at length about how frustrated they feel and how often they simply withdraw rather than try to engage. Yet they also reported *wanting* to engage, saying over and over that getting to know people with differing views and life experience is necessary and desirable, that doing so helps broaden frames of reference and leads to emotional and intellectual growth as well as appreciation for diversity. Follow-up interviews with teachers underscored what students had told us and reinforced the view of today's composition classroom as a highly diverse space where students

> Every edition of *The St. Martin's Handbook* has been grounded in new and timely research with writers and with teachers of writing.

can learn to listen to and respect one another — even as they grow into communicators who can participate effectively in cross-cultural and translingual conversations. And recent events related to racial justice in the U.S. and the COVID-19 global health crisis have emphasized the need for respectful and informed communication. If ever there was a moment to say that writing, speaking, listening, and fact-finding can be matters of life or death, this is it.

The results of our 2019 research inform this edition in many ways. Throughout, *The St. Martin's Handbook* addresses students as learners who want to be open-minded and respectful and who want to have a global reach in their understanding of the world and their place in it. Chapter 2, "Expectations for College Writing," introduces the issue of engaging difference with respect and builds on student capacity to do just that, offering practical advice for overcoming some common barriers to communication. Chapter 14, "Evaluating Sources and Taking Notes," now focuses on how to balance fairness and open-mindedness with skepticism and introduces new information, now more important than ever, about fact-checking.

Chapter 33, "Language and Identity," is new to this edition and asks students to think about how language can be used for good — to shape or claim their own identity — or for ill — to label unfairly or assign a false identity. In the ninth edition, users will find carefully updated advice on pronoun use and on the use of singular *they* (Chapters 36, 52, and 53). And finally, I have substantially revised Chapter 34, "Language Varieties." *The St. Martin's Handbook* was the first such text to address this issue and to insist that all varieties of language — and indeed all languages — have their own validity and integrity. This new edition underscores this message and provides useful examples of translingualism in college writing. The student surveys I gathered show that students are indeed aware of these and other issues related to language and identity. I hope this new material — material that, according to one reviewer, "reassures students of their own value and history" — will help students engage with these important topics.

When I was a girl growing up in the foothills of Tennessee's Smoky Mountains, my grandmother — a farmer's wife who rose every day at 4:30, who made all our clothes, and who had one pair of black lace-up shoes to her name — sometimes surprised me with her very highest compliment: "Ah, Andrea, today you look as pretty as red shoes," her idea of the most fancy and beautiful thing imaginable. I have a collection of tiny red shoes in honor of my grandmother, and every once in a while I borrow her compliment. In this case, I say of this ninth edition of *The St. Martin's Handbook*, "Well, it is almost as pretty as red shoes." I hope you and your students will like it.

# New to this edition

*An emphasis on being an open-minded learner.* Based on new research with college writers and teachers of writing, a substantially revised Chapter 2, "Expectations for College Writing," provides a framework for developing the habits of open-minded readers, writers, listeners, and speakers. A new approach invites students to expect and engage difference and provides strategies for communicating respectfully with others and for stepping outside their social and ideological comfort zones. The ninth edition, featuring the voices of real students from across the country, helps writers think critically about the barriers to and benefits of openness — and better equips them for communicating in a global world.

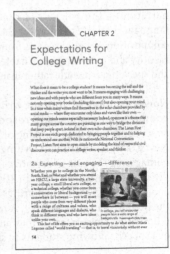

*New strategies for defensive reading, critical thinking, and fact-checking.* Writing with sources is a foundational skill for college, and too many students arrive with little experience in questioning the sources they read online and approaching them with skepticism. Revised advice for critical reading and evaluating (pp. 108–15) and new tips for fact-checking (p. 197) help students respond to the information and misinformation in news sources and in social media — and help them balance open-mindedness and skepticism as they evaluate sources.

*A broader presentation of language use.* Grounded in the argument that language is power, *The St. Martin's Handbook* coaches students in both following and experimenting with conventions. A new chapter on language and identity (Chapter 33) helps students think more openly and carefully about language we use to present ourselves and language used to label us and others. A new reading by Andrea Lunsford (Chapter 9) explores the theme of "narrative justice," the idea of giving people the opportunity to use their own language to control the narrative — the story — of their own experience. A revised chapter on language varieties (Chapter 34) fosters a new openness to translingual composition — with excerpts from student writing. Finally, attention to gender identity and pronoun use (Chapters 36 and 53) raises awareness about writing and speaking to include rather than exclude.

*New examples of student writing that emphasize narrative elements, combine languages, and respond to common assignments.* Some students come to college thinking of "academic writing" as boring and formulaic. New examples of student writing in the ninth edition defy that description, reimagining the role of narrative in argumentative and analytical writing (see the new rhetorical analysis in 10g and the new MLA research essay in 18e) and validating writing that brings in other languages for rhetorical effect (see the literacy narrative in 34e). A revised critical reading chapter (Chapter 9) follows two new writers as they annotate, summarize, and analyze a transcript of a speech, allowing students to see analysis as a process.

*Reorganized contents for academic writers.* The ninth edition groups argument, critical thinking, research, and documentation together (Parts 3, 4, and 5) so that the instruction at the heart of the composition course is centralized in the handbook. In addition, we've grouped the language and style chapters together (Parts 8 and 9) and have made the "Top Twenty" a new Part 1 to make it easier to find.

*More help with field research.* One way students can control the sources and data they use in their writing is to collect their *own* information with field research techniques such as polling, interviewing, and observing. The ninth edition includes new sample questions presented in visual format (13d).

*Up-to-date documentation help in four styles.* The St. Martin's Handbook, offering guidance for writing in MLA, APA, *Chicago,* and CSE styles, serves as a useful and valuable companion throughout college and across the disciplines. The ninth edition includes guidelines for the most recent Modern Language Association (2016), American Psychological Association (2020), University of Chicago (2017), and Council of Science Editors (2014) guidelines.

A Student's Companion
to Lunsford Handbooks

Bedford/St. Martin's

*An affordable resource in two formats.* Choose traditional paperback or go digital with a powerful e-book version of *The St. Martin's Handbook.*

*A new resource for developing college writers in co-requisite composition.* A new supplemental workbook for students in paired or co-requisite composition sections provides a wide range of activities to help students practice the skills and habits they need to be successful academic writers. *A Student's Companion to Lunsford Handbooks* is designed specifically to help underprepared students improve their reading and writing performance — with college success material on time management and etiquette, substantial coverage of reading strategies, graphic organizers for visual learners, and more than sixty exercises on writing, research, and grammar.

## What hasn't changed

*Rhetorical awareness as a writer's foundation.* The St. Martin's Handbook, although its roots are in the study of surface errors, is built on the idea that effective texts in every genre and medium follow conventions that depend — always — on purpose, audience, situation, and discipline. Strengthening writers' skills starts with creating an awareness of the choices they have and encouraging writers to reflect on the choices they make.

*Comprehensive coverage of critical reading, critical thinking, research, and argument.* As always, *The St. Martin's Handbook* provides students with strategies and examples that help them complete the most common types of assignments in the composition sequence.

*Plenty of practice with sentence, language, and writing skills.* A flexible resource that supports students before, during, and after class, the handbook includes 120 exercises and activities designed to offer skill-building, reinforcement, and low-stakes writing opportunities.

*Help for writing in the disciplines and succeeding in college.* The St. Martin's Handbook includes chapters on writing in the humanities, sciences, social sciences, and in professional situations. It also covers essay exams, portfolios, presentations, and multimodal composition strategies useful in any college course.

*Integrated advice about U.S. academic English.* Information for multilingual writers is integrated throughout the book and accessible to students from all language, cultural, and educational backgrounds. We acknowledge that international students and Generation 1.5 English speakers aren't the only students puzzled by English structures and academic expectations. Look for the multilingual icon ▣▣ and boxes called "Language, Culture, and Context."
Multilingual

## What *else* hasn't changed: Bedford/St. Martin's puts you first

From day one, our goal has been simple: to provide inspiring resources that are grounded in best practices for teaching reading and writing. For more than thirty-five years, Bedford/St. Martin's has partnered with the field, listening to teachers, scholars, and students about the support writers need. We are committed to helping every writing instructor make the most of our resources.

## How can we help you?

- Our editors can align our resources to your outcomes through correlation and transition guides for your syllabus. Just ask us.

- Our sales representatives specialize in helping you find the right materials to support your course goals.

- Our learning solutions and product specialists help you make the most of the digital resources you choose for your course.

- Our *Bits* blog on the Bedford/St. Martin's English Community (**community .macmillan.com**) publishes fresh teaching ideas weekly. Andrea Lunsford's "Teacher to Teacher" blog features hundreds of posts, including her popular "Multimodal Mondays" posts. You'll also find easily downloadable professional resources such as *Teaching with Lunsford Handbooks* and links to author webinars on our community site.

Contact your school's Bedford/St. Martin's sales representative or visit **macmillanlearning.com** to learn more.

## Ordering *The St. Martin's Handbook*

Choose the format that works best for your course, and ask about our packaging options that offer savings for students.

### Print

- *Paperback edition.* To order the traditional paperback edition, use ISBN 978-1-319-10753-6.

### Digital

- *Popular e-book formats.* For details about our e-book partners, visit **macmillanlearning.com/ebooks**.

- *Inclusive Access.* Enable every student to receive their course materials through your LMS on the first day of class. Macmillan Learning's Inclusive Access program is the easiest, most affordable way to ensure all students have access to quality educational resources. Find out more at **macmillanlearning.com/inclusiveaccess**.

## Your course, your way

No two writing programs or classrooms are exactly alike. Our Curriculum Solutions team works with you to design custom options that provide the resources your students need. Visit **macmillanlearning.com/curriculumsolutions**. (Options below require enrollment minimums.)

- *ForeWords for English.* Customize any print resource to fit the focus of your course or program by choosing from a range of prepared chapters, such as "Sentence Guides for Academic Writers."

- *Macmillan Author Program (MAP).* Add excerpts or package acclaimed works from Macmillan's trade imprints to connect students with prominent authors and public conversations. A list of popular examples or academic themes is available upon request.

- *Bedford Select.* Build your own print anthology from a database of more than 800 selections, and add your own materials to create your ideal text. Package with *The St. Martin's Handbook* for additional savings. Visit **macmillanlearning.com/bedfordselect**.

## Acknowledgments

*The St. Martin's Handbook* remains a collaborative effort in the best and richest sense of the word. For this edition, I am deeply grateful to Michelle Clark, editor extraordinaire, whose wisdom, clear-eyed judgment, efficiency, and great good humor sparkle on every page of this book: I am one very fortunate author to have had her guidance and her inspiration. I am also especially grateful to Aislyn Fredsall, whose editorial help with the art in the book, with permissions, with my weekly "Teacher to Teacher" blog posts, and with *Teaching with Lunsford Handbooks* repeatedly saved the day; to Barbara Flanagan for her knowledgeable and heroic work on handbook media; to Allison Hart for managing the endlessly multiplying media production tasks; to Claire Seng-Niemoeller and Diana Blume for their brilliant contributions to art and design; to William Boardman for another beautiful cover; to Christine Clark for her meticulous copyediting; and to Ryan Sullivan, the best content project manager ever — who manages to move a project from manuscript to bound book and e-book with skill and grace.

Many thanks, also, to the unfailingly generous and supportive members of the Bedford/St. Martin's team: Leasa Burton, Stacey Purviance, Vivian Garcia, Tracey Kuehn, Michael Granger, Elise Kaiser, Hilary Newman, Angie Boehler, Lisa McDowell, and Robin Besofsky. I will also always be grateful for the advice and counsel of Carolyn Lengel and Jimmy Fleming, who have added in so many ways to the effectiveness of my textbooks.

I am once again tremendously grateful to Paul Kei Matsuda and Christine Tardy for their helpful additions to the multilingual writer coverage of this book; to Laura Aull for her fascinating research with corpora linguistics and her useful advice on using these tools with students; and to Jeanne Bohannon for her fine work on *Teaching with Lunsford Handbooks*. I have also benefited greatly from the excellent advice of Tarez Samra Graban, who made time for conversations about translingual composition and about language and identity. I am indebted to the following fellow teachers for having conversations with me during a 2019 research project; they shared their experiences helping students step out of their comfort zones and embrace the social, cultural, and political differences among students in a typical composition course: Pamela Arlov, Middle Georgia State University; Sara Beam, University of Tulsa; Jeanne Bohannon, Kennesaw State University; Martina Clark, LaGuardia Community College; Jill Darley-Vanis, Clark College; Karen Keck, Texas Tech University; Maria Roberts, Northeastern Junior College; and Christopher Thurley, Gaston College.

I owe special thanks to the group of student writers whose work and voices appear in and enrich this book: Michelle Abbott, Carina Abernathy, Martha Bell, Deborah Burke, Tony Chan, Samyuktha Comandur, Justin Dart, Caroline Fairey, Paola García-Muñiz, Allyson Goldberg, Tara Gupta, Cameron Hauer, Joanna Hays, James Kung, Megan Lange, Emily Lesk, Nastassia Lopez, Alicia Michalski, Jenny Ming, Thanh Nguyen, Stephanie Parker, Rachel Quarta, Rachel Ramirez, Tawnya Redding, Amanda Rinder, Julia Sakowitz, David Sherman, Bonnie Sillay, Shuqiao Song, Nandita Sriram, Apeksha Vanjani, Caroline Warner, and Shravan Yandra.

Once again, I have been guided by a group of hardworking and meticulous reviewers, including E. Dominguez Barajas, Florida State University; Elliott Gruner, Plymouth State University; Deborah Hall, Valdosta State College; Paul Hauptmann, Palm Beach Atlantic University; Gwen K. Horsley, South Dakota State University; Debra Johanyak, Kent State University; Mamie L. Johnson, Norfolk State University; Michael Keller, South Dakota State University; Monica Norris, Texas Tech University; and J. Christian Tatu, Lafayette College.

Finally, and always, I continue to learn from students everywhere, who serve as the major inspiration for just about everything I do; from the extraordinary community of teacher-researchers at the Bread Loaf Teacher Network (BLTN); from the very best sisters, nieces, and nephews anyone has ever had; and from my beloved grandnieces, Audrey and Lila: this book is for all of you.

*Andrea A. Lunsford*

The
**St. Martin's
Handbook**

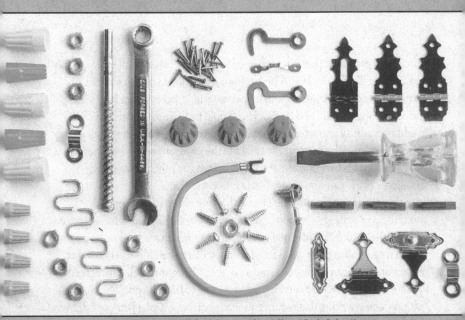

Photo by Mike Enright/www.menright.com. Photo styling by Barbara Lipp.

CHAPTER 1

# The Top Twenty

## A Quick Guide to Editing Your Writing

Mistakes in grammar, punctuation, word choice, and other small-scale matters don't always disturb readers. Whether your instructor marks an error in any particular assignment will depend on personal judgments about how serious and distracting it is and about what you should be focusing on in the draft. In addition, not all grammar and punctuation errors are consistently viewed as errors: some of the patterns identified in the research for this book are considered errors by some but as stylistic options by others. Moreover, so-called "errors" can sometimes create powerful effects.

Such differing opinions don't mean that there is no such thing as correctness in writing — only that *correctness always depends on some context*, on whether the choices a writer makes seem appropriate to readers.

All writers want to be considered competent and careful. You know that readers often judge you by your control of the conventions you have agreed to use, even if the conventions change from time to time. It's good news, then, that producing writing that is conventionally correct is a goal you can achieve. In fact, if you become familiar with the twenty most common error patterns among U.S. college students today, you will have taken care of many of the issues that instructors are concerned with. In this section, you'll find those twenty mistakes, listed in order of frequency (based on our findings from the research project in which we studied thousands of pieces of writing by first-year students), with brief explanations, examples of each, and cross-references to additional help in this book.

## 1 Wrong word

▶ **Religious texts, for some, take ~~prescience~~ precedence over other kinds of sources.**

*Prescience* means "foresight," and *precedence* means "priority."

▶ The child suffered from a severe ~~allegory~~ *allergy* to peanuts.

*Allegory* is a spell checker's replacement for a misspelling of *allergy*.

▶ The panel discussed the ethical implications ~~on~~ *of* the situation.

Wrong-word errors can involve using a word with the wrong shade of meaning, using a word with a completely wrong meaning, or using a wrong preposition or another wrong word in an idiom. Selecting a word from a thesaurus without knowing its meaning, or allowing a spell checker to correct spelling automatically, can lead to wrong-word errors, so use these tools with care. If you have trouble with prepositions and idioms, memorize the standard usage. See Chapter 37 on word choice and Chapter 55 on prepositions and idioms.

---

**QUICK HELP**

The Top Twenty

1. Wrong word   2
2. Missing comma after an introductory element   4
3. Incomplete or missing documentation   4
4. Vague pronoun reference   4
5. Spelling (including homonyms)   5
6. Mechanical error with a quotation   5
7. Unnecessary comma   5
8. Unnecessary or missing capitalization   6
9. Missing word   6
10. Confusing sentence structure   6
11. Missing comma with a nonrestrictive element   7
12. Unnecessary shift in verb tense   7
13. Missing comma in a compound sentence   7
14. Unnecessary or missing apostrophe (including *its/it's*)   8
15. Fused (run-on) sentence   8
16. Comma splice   8
17. Lack of pronoun-antecedent agreement   9
18. Poorly integrated quotation   9
19. Unnecessary or missing hyphen   10
20. Sentence fragment   11

## 2 Missing comma after an introductory element

▶ Determined to get the job done, we worked all weekend.
                              ^

▶ Although the study was flawed, the results may still be useful.
                              ^

Readers usually need a small pause — signaled by a comma — between an introductory word, phrase, or clause and the main part of the sentence. Use a comma after every introductory element. When the introductory element is very short, you don't always need a comma, but including it is never wrong. (See 56a.)

## 3 Incomplete or missing documentation

▶ Satrapi says, "When we're afraid, we lose all sense of analysis
  and reflection." *(263).*
                  ^

This quotation comes from a source with page numbers, so a page number is needed.

▶ Some experts agree that James Joyce wrote two of the five best novels of
       *("100 Best Novels").*
  all time.
          ^

The source of this information should be identified. The title is given for a source with no page numbers.

Cite each source you refer to in the text, following the guidelines of the documentation style you are using. (The preceding examples follow MLA style — see Chapter 18; for other styles, see Chapters 19–21.) Omitting documentation can result in charges of plagiarism (see Chapter 16).

## 4 Vague pronoun reference

POSSIBLE REFERENCE TO MORE THAN ONE WORD

▶ Transmitting radio signals by satellite is a way of overcoming the
                                         *the airwaves*
  problem of scarce airwaves and limiting how ~~they~~ are used.
                                            ^

In the original sentence, *they* could refer to the signals or to the airwaves.

REFERENCE IMPLIED BUT NOT STATED

                                *a policy*
▶ The company prohibited smoking, ~~which~~ many employees resented.
                                         ^

What does *which* refer to? The editing clarifies what employees resented.

A pronoun should refer clearly to the word or words it replaces (called the *antecedent*) elsewhere in the sentence or in a previous sentence. If more than one word could be the antecedent, or if no specific antecedent is present, edit to make the meaning clear. (See Chapter 53.)

## 5 Spelling (including homonyms)

▶ Ronald ~~Regan~~ Reagan won the election in a landslide.

▶ ~~Every where~~ Everywhere we went, we saw crowds of tourists.

The most common misspellings today are those that spell checkers cannot identify. The categories that spell checkers are most likely to miss include homonyms, compound words incorrectly spelled as separate words, and proper nouns, particularly names. After you run the spell checker, proofread carefully for errors such as these — and be sure to run the spell checker to catch other kinds of spelling mistakes.

## 6 Mechanical error with a quotation

▶ "I grew up the victim of a disconcerting confusion,", Rodriguez says (249).

The comma should be placed *inside* the quotation marks.

Follow conventions when using quotation marks with commas (56i), colons (61d), and other punctuation (60e). Always use quotation marks in pairs, and follow the guidelines of your documentation style for block quotations (60a). Use quotation marks for titles of short works (60b), but use italics for titles of long works (64a).

## 7 Unnecessary comma

BEFORE CONJUNCTIONS IN COMPOUND CONSTRUCTIONS THAT ARE NOT COMPOUND SENTENCES

▶ This conclusion applies to the United States, and to the rest of the world.

No comma is needed before *and* because it is joining two phrases that modify the same verb, *applies*.

**WITH RESTRICTIVE ELEMENTS**

▶ **Many parents, of gifted children, do not want them to skip a grade.**

No commas are needed to set off the restrictive phrase *of gifted children*, which is necessary to indicate which parents the sentence is talking about.

Do not use commas to set off restrictive elements that are necessary to the meaning of the words they modify. Do not use a comma before a coordinating conjunction (*and, but, for, nor, or, so, yet*) when the conjunction does not join parts of a compound sentence. Do not use a comma before the first or after the last item in a series, between a subject and verb, between a verb and its object or complement, or between a preposition and its object. (See 56k.)

## 8 Unnecessary or missing capitalization

▶ **Some T̶r̶a̶d̶i̶t̶i̶o̶n̶a̶l̶ Chinese M̶e̶d̶i̶c̶i̶n̶e̶s̶ containing E̶p̶h̶e̶d̶r̶a̶ remain legal.**
     *traditional*          *medicines*          *ephedra*

Capitalize proper nouns and proper adjectives, the first words of sentences, and important words in titles, along with certain words indicating directions and family relationships. Do not capitalize most other words. When in doubt, check a dictionary. (See Chapter 62.)

## 9 Missing word

▶ **The site foreman discriminated women and promoted men with less experience.**
     *against*

Proofread carefully for omitted words, including prepositions (55a), parts of two-part verbs (55b), and correlative conjunctions (48g). Be particularly careful not to omit words from quotations.

## 10 Confusing sentence structure

▶ **T̶h̶e̶ ̶i̶n̶f̶o̶r̶m̶a̶t̶i̶o̶n̶ ̶w̶h̶i̶c̶h̶ high school athletes are presented with m̶a̶i̶n̶l̶y̶ i̶n̶c̶l̶u̶d̶e̶s̶ information on what credits needed to graduate, a̶n̶d̶ ̶t̶h̶i̶n̶k̶i̶n̶g̶ a̶b̶o̶u̶t̶ ̶t̶h̶e̶ ̶c̶o̶l̶l̶e̶g̶e̶ which a̶t̶h̶l̶e̶t̶e̶s̶ ̶a̶r̶e̶ ̶t̶r̶y̶i̶n̶g̶ to play for, and apply.**
     *High*                    *they*
     *colleges to try*        *how to*

A sentence that starts out with one kind of structure and then changes to another kind can confuse readers. Make sure that each sentence contains a subject and a verb (49a), that subjects and predicates make sense together (47b), and that comparisons have clear meanings (47e). When you join elements (such as subjects or verb phrases) with a coordinating conjunction, make sure that the elements have parallel structures (see Chapter 43).

## 11 Missing comma with a nonrestrictive element

▶ **Marina, who was the president of the club, was first to speak.**

The clause *who was the president of the club* does not affect the basic meaning of the sentence: Marina was first to speak.

A nonrestrictive element gives information not essential to the basic meaning of the sentence. Use commas to set off a nonrestrictive element (56d).

## 12 Unnecessary shift in verb tense

▶ **Priya was watching the great blue heron. Then she <s>slips</s> and <s>falls</s> into the swamp.**

slipped    fell

Verbs that shift from one tense to another with no clear reason can confuse readers (42a).

## 13 Missing comma in a compound sentence

▶ **Meredith waited for Samir, and her sister grew impatient.**

Without the comma, a reader may think at first that Meredith waited for both Samir and her sister.

A compound sentence consists of two or more parts that could each stand alone as a sentence. When the parts are joined by a coordinating conjunction, use a comma before the conjunction to indicate a pause between the two thoughts (56c).

## 14 Unnecessary or missing apostrophe (including *its/it's*)

► Overambitious parents can be very harmful to a ~~childs~~ well-being.
  <sub>child's</sub>

► The car is lying on ~~it's~~ side in the ditch. ~~Its~~ a white 2020 Passat.
  <sub>its</sub>                                  <sub>It's</sub>

To make a noun possessive, add either an apostrophe and an *-s* (*Ed's book*) or an apostrophe alone (*the boys' gym*). Do not use an apostrophe in the possessive pronouns *ours, yours,* and *hers*. Use *its* to mean *belonging to it*; use *it's* only when you mean *it is* or *it has*. (See Chapter 59.)

## 15 Fused (run-on) sentence

► Klee's paintings seem simple, they are very sophisticated.
  <sub>but</sub>

► ~~She~~ doubted the value of meditation, she decided to try it once.
  <sub>Although she</sub>

A fused sentence (also called a *run-on*) joins clauses that could each stand alone as a sentence with no punctuation or words to link them. Fused sentences must either be divided into separate sentences or joined by adding words or punctuation. (See Chapter 44.)

## 16 Comma splice

► I was strongly attracted to her, she was beautiful and funny.
  <sub>for</sub>

► We hated the meat loaf, the cafeteria served ~~it~~ every Friday.
  <sub>that</sub>

A comma splice occurs when only a comma separates clauses that could each stand alone as a sentence. To correct a comma splice, you can insert a semi-colon or period, connect the clauses with a word such as *and* or *because,* or restructure the sentence. (See Chapter 44.)

## 17 Lack of pronoun-antecedent agreement

*its*
▶ Each of the proposals has ~~their~~ merits.

All students                                    uniforms.
▶ ~~Every student~~ must provide their own ~~uniform.~~

In formal academic writing, pronouns must agree with their antecedents both in gender (male or female) and in number (singular or plural). Traditionally, indefinite pronouns such as *every, everyone,* and *each* have been treated as singular antecedents and have required singular pronouns such as *his or her, his, her,* or *its.* Some writers choose to rewrite the sentence in plural, as in the second example above. However, the use of *they/their/them* is becoming increasingly acceptable with singular indefinite pronouns—to include people who do not identify as *he/his* or *she/her.* (See 53f.)

▶ Everyone should check their passport's expiration date before the trip.

When antecedents are joined by *or* or *nor,* the pronoun should always agree with the closer antecedent. A collective noun such as *team* can be either singular or plural, depending on whether the members are seen as a group or as individuals.

## 18 Poorly integrated quotation

showed how *color affects taste:*
▶ Schlosser cites a 1970s study that "Once it became apparent that

the steak was actually blue and the fries were green, some people

became ill" (565).

According to Lars Eighner,
▶ "Dumpster diving has serious drawbacks as a way of life" (~~Eighner~~ 383).

Finding edible food is especially tricky.

Quotations should fit smoothly into the surrounding sentence structure. They should be linked clearly to the writing around them (usually with a signal phrase) rather than dropped abruptly into the writing. (See Chapter 15.)

---

QUICK HELP

### Taking a writing inventory

One way to learn from your mistakes is to take a writing inventory. It can help you think critically and analytically about how to improve your writing skills.

1. Collect two or three pieces of your writing to which either your instructor or other students have responded.

2. Read through these writings, adding your own comments about their strengths and weaknesses. How do your comments compare with those of others?

3. Group all the comments into three categories—*broad content issues* (use of evidence and sources, attention to purpose and audience, and overall impression), *organization and presentation* (overall and paragraph-level organization, sentence structure and style, and formatting), and *surface errors* (problems with wrong words, spelling, grammar, punctuation, and mechanics).

4. Make an inventory of your own strengths in each category.

5. Study your errors. Mark every instructor and peer comment that suggests or calls for an improvement, and put all these comments in a list. Consult the relevant part of this book or speak with your instructor if you don't understand a comment.

6. Make a list of the top problem areas you need to work on. How can you make improvements? Then note at least two strengths that you can build on in your writing. Reflect on your findings in a writing log that you can add to as the class proceeds.

---

## 19 Unnecessary or missing hyphen

▶ **This paper looks at fictional and real⌃life examples.**

A compound adjective modifying a noun that follows it requires a hyphen.

▶ **The buyers want to fix⌃up the house and resell it.**

A two-word verb should not be hyphenated.

A compound adjective that appears before a noun needs a hyphen. However, be careful not to hyphenate two-word verbs or word groups that serve as subject complements. (See Chapter 64.)

## 20 Sentence fragment

NO SUBJECT

▶ Marie Antoinette spent huge sums of money on herself and her favorites.
Her extravagance
~~And~~ helped bring on the French Revolution.

NO COMPLETE VERB

▶ The old aluminum boat $\overset{was}{\wedge}$ sitting on its trailer.

BEGINNING WITH A SUBORDINATING WORD

▶ We returned to the drugstore $\overset{where}{,}$ ~~Where~~ we waited for our buddies.

A sentence fragment is part of a sentence that is written as if it were a complete sentence. Reading your draft out loud, backward, sentence by sentence, will help you spot sentence fragments. (See Chapter 45.)

# PART 2
# The Art and Craft of Writing

Photo by Mike Enright/www.menright.com. Photo styling by Barbara Lipp.

# CHAPTER 2

# Expectations for College Writing

What does it mean to be a college student? It means becoming the self and the thinker and the writer you most want to be. It means engaging with challenging new ideas and with people who are different from you in many ways. It means not only opening your books (including this one!) but also opening your mind. In a time when many writers find themselves in the echo chambers provided by social media — where they encounter only ideas and views like their own — opening our minds seems especially necessary. Indeed, openness is a theme that many groups across the country are pursuing as one way to bridge the divisions that keep people apart, isolated in their own echo chambers. The Listen First Project is one such group, dedicated to bringing people together and to helping us understand one another. With its nationwide National Conversation Project, Listen First aims to open minds by modeling the kind of respectful civil discourse you can practice as a college writer, speaker, and thinker.

## 2a  Expecting — and engaging — difference

Whether you go to college in the North, South, East, or West and whether you attend an HBCU, a large state university, a two-year college, a small liberal arts college, or a technical college, whether you come from a conservative or liberal background — or somewhere in between — you will meet people who come from very different places with a range of cultures and values, who speak different languages and dialects, who think in different ways, and who have ideas unlike your own.

*In college, you will encounter people from a wide range of backgrounds.* PeopleImages/E+/Getty Images

   This fact of life offers you an exciting opportunity to do what author Maria Lugones called "world traveling" — that is, to travel vicariously, without ever leaving your campus — to learn about cultures, languages, and ways of knowing practiced by people from other places, to listen and slowly understand, and to engage differences in an open and welcoming way.

But do college students today take advantage of such opportunities? How do students feel about engaging with people and ideas very different from their own? What do they see as barriers to such engagement, and what do they see as the benefits of overcoming or challenging those barriers? Those are questions I had in mind when I asked more than one hundred undergraduates from schools across the country to respond to a brief questionnaire.

Results indicate that these students want to be tolerant and open and to engage people who are different from them; they think that understanding others is important. In fact, one student summed up what others had said: they want to "be able to have a conversation with anyone, anywhere in the world, about any topic." Nearly half of the students said that they often talked to people who had different opinions from theirs and most said they "felt comfortable" doing so. And nearly all of them had a good friend who spoke a different language or came from a different cultural background.

---

### ◢ EXERCISE 2.1

Reflect on both the social and academic writing you have done in the past year. Identify a specific piece of writing that demonstrates your attempt to understand a point of view different from your own. Write a paragraph in which you explore why it was important for you to develop an understanding of another viewpoint.

---

## Understanding barriers to open engagement

Engaging differences in open-minded and fair ways is an ambitious goal. You may have witnessed disagreements or even closed-mindedness in your community or in your own family; certainly you have seen disagreement play out in your everyday life as well as in a number of ways in the national media. Have you ever wondered why it's so difficult to reach common ground? The college students in a survey conducted for this book listed a number of barriers that prevent people from reaching common ground on difficult issues and topics:

- fear (of being judged, of venturing out of comfort zones, of questioning beliefs)
- stubbornness
- ego ("my way or the highway" thinking)
- ingrained cultural and religious beliefs
- lack of knowledge, understanding, or willingness to listen
- name-calling and labeling
- stereotyping
- peer influence ("mob mentality")

*Those who disagree with one another often point fingers more than they listen.*
ANNA GASSOT/AFP/Getty Images

One student in the survey identified "language barriers" as an important consideration, saying that two people may "want the same thing" but "are describing it in different terms and thus cannot understand each other." Another says that the "most common disagreements" are ones based on "terminology: when we disagree about the definition of keywords, I find there is no common ground."

Some students spoke personally of how such barriers are affecting them, like a student who identifies as very conservative: "I know I'm in a minority at my school . . . [so] I tend to avoid controversial topics in public forums because it often proves to be fruitless, a waste of time. It typically ends in outrage." This student felt "there's a better chance of pigs falling out of the sky" than of being understood and accepted by classmates. This student is surely not alone in these feelings, indicating the very real need for others to listen respectfully and openly to their views.

This small study, then, suggests that many students feel a mismatch between the goals of openness, empathy, and understanding — and the harsh reality of barriers that prevent achieving these goals. For the writing and speaking you will be asked to do as a college student, try to commit yourself to overcoming such barriers and welcoming new ideas and different people.

## Seeing the benefits of welcoming difference

As a college student, you'll be expected to grapple with ideas and texts of increasing complexity. And you'll also be expected to write and speak in response to a world of ideas, even those you disagree with. In spite of barriers, students

I surveyed continue to recognize and applaud the benefits of being open-minded and respecting difference in their colleges and communities. "Being open-minded is like traveling," noted one student: "it allows you to experience more of life. Instead of just seeing a drawing, you get to see things in full color and with texture and sound. Even if you don't like it, you've experienced alternative possibilities." The students identified important personal and social benefits to being open-minded and engaging difference:

- learning, awareness
- expanding your experience
- self-knowledge, self-growth
- appreciation for the diversity and complexity of the human experience
- opportunity to explore ideas
- humanizing people who are different from you
- experiencing school as a safer environment (intellectually and physically)

In short, many or most of these students see college as a place to explore ideas and conduct research and see "being open-minded and respectful of other faiths/belief systems/ideas/research" as "essential." We certainly can't, and shouldn't, accept all ideas as equally valid, but each student member "deserves the right to study and consider ideas in a safe environment." Achieving such an environment seems absolutely essential, another student says, "if we want closed-mindedness to end." As you write in response to the ideas of others, reflect on what you see as the benefits of an open mind.

## Learning to balance emotion and inquiry

Students responding to this survey also recognized that emotions can sometimes carry them away in a discussion of a controversial or difficult topic, even when they believe they should be able to be "calm and reasonable." In heated conversations, for example, while 29 percent of the students said they feel "excitement" or "confidence" during such confrontations, the greatest number said they feel "annoyance" or "anxiety," while a few reported feeling "anger" or "hostility." Another student elaborated, saying that it's easy to see such instances as "contests, not conversations."

> People enter into a conversation with predetermined ideas of what is right and what is wrong (usually that they are right and the other person is wrong) instead of actually being open to understanding where the other person is coming from. I think people are hard-wired to do this, and getting away from this adversarial perspective is very emotionally taxing, which makes it rare.

Difficult conversations and deep inquiry often lead to growth and learning, but they can be "emotionally taxing." You may feel, as the students in the survey did, the need for a safe environment that lends itself to conversations rather than contests. Even when you are assigned academic writing that may not be based on personal experience, know that there is often an element of passion in the arguments you will read and make as a student.

If you are at least a little like the students who responded to these questions, you are well aware of the challenges involved in engaging differences respectfully and effectively while honoring your own convictions and values. However, you also know that part of your intellectual and emotional growth in college will depend on your taking opportunities to examine those convictions and perhaps even shifting or changing some of them. After all, that's what it means to learn and to grow.

### EXERCISE 2.2

In a 2019 survey, current college students were asked the following:

> When you are engaged in a heated conversation about a topic that's difficult or controversial, which one of these emotions do you feel most often: excitement, confidence, annoyance, anxiety, fear, anger, or hostility?

Take this opportunity to write your own response to the question, explaining your choice and reflecting on a particular conversation from your own experience. Would you change anything about your own approach to such conversations — ones with substantial differences of opinion?

## 2b Choosing openness and developing habits of mind

As this discussion of engaging difference points out, you may find yourself in classes or living in a dorm with people who hold opposing views on a range of topics, and you might have to work together to solve academic, social, and even professional challenges. While it's easy to diss — or dismiss — others in online settings, it's much harder to do so when the person is sitting right there with you. That's one reason your classes and other campus spaces are so important for learning: they put you face-to-face with others you may not agree with or understand and allow you to open your mind and your world — and invite them to do the same.

Openness is one way to get the most out of college and learn from others who are different from you. The authors of *The Framework for Success in Postsecondary Writing* identify eight key abilities — which they call "habits of mind" — that support success in college, and openness is one of them:

| | |
|---|---|
| curiosity | persistence |
| openness | responsibility |
| engagement | flexibility |
| creativity | metacognition |

It's worth noting that cultivating these habits of mind will help you to think *rhetorically* — that is, with careful attention to all the elements that make up any communication situation. Doing so is a major key to success in college and beyond.

Considering the full context of your college work also means considering what your instructors will most likely expect of you. Certainly they will expect you to be open to learning from and with people of widely different backgrounds and perspectives. They also will want you to think critically and rhetorically, reflect on and assess your own learning, consider ethical issues, identify and solve problems, do meaningful research, and present the knowledge you construct in a variety of genres and media. Your success will depend on communicating clearly, respectfully, and openly — and on making appropriate choices for your context and your audience.

## 2c  Using social media wisely

Social connections today involve so much writing that you probably write more out of class than in class. Writing on social media allows writers to reach large audiences and to get instant responses.

On Twitter, for example, you can compose short bursts of up to 280 characters, tagging content, tweeting at groups and individuals, and pointing toward links to start discussions, participate in ongoing conversations, and invite others to join you. But you can also encounter bots and trolls, mean-spirited "haters," and even stalkers. As Steve Kerr, head coach of the Golden State

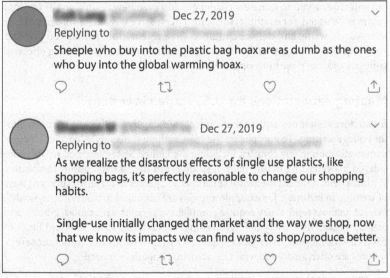

*Disagreements are common on social media; some users insult and point fingers while others use reason.*

Warriors, points out, social media writing "can come back and haunt you quickly." He suggests paying careful attention to what you write and to whom and always remembering that there's a person on the other side of that message. Further, you need to think twice about information you get from social media: spreading rumors and false information is as easy as a retweet. Keep in mind that being an effective writer, reader, and rhetorical thinker calls for both being responsible (one of those habits of mind!) for what you post and being skeptical of what you read on social media.

---

### EXERCISE 2.3

Choose a sample of your own informal writing from a social media site, blog, or your own text messages. What motivated you to write the post—curiosity, a hunch, anger? What did you assume about your readers, and why? Why did you choose the words, images, links, or other parts of the text, and how do these choices contribute to the way the writing comes across to an audience? Did you include any reposted material, and if so, can you vouch for its accuracy? Did the writing do what you wanted it to do? Why, or why not?

---

## 2d Positioning yourself as an academic writer

You probably have less familiarity with academic writing contexts than you do with informal social media writing. And you may not have written anything very lengthy or done extensive research. The full contexts for your college writing will require you to face new challenges and even new definitions of writing; you may be asked, for example, to create a persuasive website or infographic, or to research, write, and deliver a multimedia presentation. And if you grew up speaking and writing in other languages, the transition to producing effective college work can pose both opportunities and challenges.

### Meeting expectations for U.S. academic writing

Instructors sometimes assume that students are already familiar with expectations for college writing. To complicate the matter, there is no single "correct" style of communication in any country, including the United States. Further, what is considered good writing in one field of study is not necessarily "good" in another. Within a field, different rhetorical situations and genres may call for different ways of writing. In business, for example, memos are usually short and simple, while a market analysis report may require complex paragraphs with tables, graphs, and diagrams. Even the variety of English sometimes referred to as "standard English" covers a wide range of styles (see Chapter 34). In spite of this wide variation, several features are often associated with U.S. academic English in general:

- conventional grammar, spelling, punctuation, and mechanics
- organization that links ideas explicitly (Chapter 5)

- an easy-to-read type size and typeface, conventional margins, and double spacing
- explicitly stated claims supported by evidence (Chapter 11)
- careful documentation of all sources (Chapters 18–21)
- consistent use of an appropriate level of formality (Chapter 3)
- conventional use of idioms (Chapter 55)
- use of conventional academic formats (for literature reviews, research essays, lab reports, and research proposals)

Remember, though, that such conventions can and will change and that new contexts always require new conventions. As new genres appear, writers are experimenting in exciting ways and questioning old conventions, especially in terms of style. So academic writing itself is changing, opening up to new ways of approaching topics and new ways of getting points across (see 11g for a discussion of narrative elements in argument writing, for example). Keep this in mind as you approach your college writing assignments, and talk with instructors and fellow students about how you can make your academic writing fresh and exciting and sound like *you*.

## Establishing authority

In the United States, most college instructors expect student writers to begin to establish their own authority — to become constructive critics who can analyze and interpret the work of others. But what does establishing authority mean in practice?

- Assume that your informed opinions count and that your audience expects you to present them in a well-reasoned manner.
- Show your familiarity with the ideas and works of others, both from the assigned course reading and from points your instructor and classmates have made.

## Being direct and clear

Your instructors will often expect you to get to the point quickly and to be direct throughout an essay. Research for this book confirms that readers depend on writers to organize and present their material — using sections, paragraphs, sentences, arguments, details, and source citations — in ways that aid understanding. Good academic writing prepares readers for what is coming next, provides definitions, and includes topic sentences. (See 4e–f for a description of the organization that instructors often prefer in student essays.) To achieve directness in your writing, try the following strategies:

- State your main point early and clearly.
- Avoid hedging your statements. Instead of writing *I think the facts reveal*, come right out and say *The facts reveal* (see 11i).

---

**TALKING THE TALK | CONVENTIONS**

"Aren't conventions just rules with another name?" Not entirely. Conventions — agreed-on practices of grammar, punctuation, and style — convey shorthand information from writer to reader. But unlike hard-and-fast rules, conventions are flexible; a convention appropriate for one time or situation may be inappropriate for another. You may also choose to ignore conventions at times to achieve a particular effect. (Notice the sentence fragment *Not entirely* at the beginning of this box, for example.) As you become more experienced and confident in your writing, you will develop a sense of which conventions to apply in different writing situations.

---

- Use appropriate evidence, such as examples and concrete details, to support each point.
- Make transitions from point to point obvious and clear. The first sentence of a new paragraph should reach back to the preceding paragraph and then look forward to what is to come (see Chapter 5).
- Guide readers by using sentences that link together smoothly (see Chapter 5).
- Follow logical organizational patterns (see Chapter 4).
- Format the project appropriately for the audience and purpose you have in mind (see Chapter 3).

## 2e Reading and listening respectfully and actively

Your instructors expect you to be an active reader, one who brings an inquiring mind and talks back to texts and topics. You also need to be an active and attentive listener who respects the perspectives of others and is open to new and challenging ideas. And remember that stating your own informed opinions needn't be combative; just as you listen respectfully to others' opinions, so they should listen to yours.

### Reading and listening respectfully

One of the benefits of college is learning new things and encountering people and ideas that at first may seem completely foreign to you. While you may seek out only like-minded people on social media (but be careful of the effects of such echo chambers if you do!), in your college classes you will encounter a great diversity of perspectives. Psychologists find that engaging with such differences is actually good for us, helping us broaden our viewpoints and open our minds. Your instructors will expect you to bring such openness to class discussions and to the texts you read. Here are some tips for doing so.

**BEING AN OPEN-MINDED LEARNER**

- Understand what others are saying before drawing conclusions about what they have said. This requires careful and respectful listening and reading.

- Practice empathy by looking at the issue from the other person's or author's point of view, trying to understand where they are coming from and why they are making certain points.

- Try to be invitational rather than confrontational.

Then, when you feel you have a good understanding of the message or text, you can bring your full critical abilities to bear, making counterpoints or offering your own point of view, though always with fairness and respect.

## Reading and listening actively

The following strategies (and the detailed advice in Chapter 9) will help you read and listen *actively*. And remember that online, you may often need to read *defensively*. The following tips can help you do both.

**BEING AN ACTIVE READER AND LISTENER**

- Note the name of the author and the date and place of publication or presentation; these offer clues to the writer's or speaker's purpose and audience.

- Understand the overall content of a text or presentation well enough to summarize it (15d).

- Formulate critical questions, and bring these questions up in class.

- Understand each sentence, and make connections between sentences and paragraphs. Keep track of repeated themes or images and how they contribute to the entire piece.

- Note the author's attitude toward and assumptions about the topic. Then think about how the attitude and assumptions might affect the author's thinking.

- Read defensively as you note the author's sources: What evidence does the writer or speaker rely on, and why? Are the sources accurate and reliable? How can you tell?

- Distinguish between the author's stance, or position, and the author's reporting on the stances of others. Watch for phrases that signal an opposing argument: *while some have argued that . . .* , *in the past . . .* , and so on.

- Engage. If online readings allow you to post a comment, take advantage of the opportunity to get your voice into the conversation.

## Participating in class

Some cultures view speaking up in class as inappropriate or even rude. In U.S. colleges, however, doing so is expected and encouraged. Some instructors even assign credit for class participation. The challenge is to contribute without losing track of the overall aims of the class and without monopolizing the discussion. These guidelines can help.

**BEING AN ACTIVE CLASS PARTICIPANT**

- Be prepared by having completed the reading or writing homework.
- Listen purposefully, following the flow of the conversation closely and writing notes that can help you join in.
- Make your comments count by asking a key question to clarify a point, by taking the conversation in a more productive direction, or by analyzing or summarizing what has been said.
- Respond to questions or comments by others as specifically as possible (*The passage on p. 42 supports your point* rather than *I agree*).
- If you have trouble participating in class discussions, try making one comment a day. You might also ask your instructor for suggestions.

Remember that while there is no direct correlation between talking in class and being intellectually engaged (since many students *are* participating actively, whether or not they are speaking), participating actively in the conversation gives you a chance to get your own views considered and signal your engagement.

## 2f Planning research

One of the most exciting aspects of college is engaging in research that is important to you. You might start out just being curious about how many students on your campus are vegetarians, for example, and end up with a research project for a sociology class that then becomes part of a multimedia presentation about eating healthy foods that you present to your kid sister's third-grade class. Many of your writing assignments will require extensive formal research with a wide range of sources from various media as well as information drawn from observations, interviews, or surveys.

Research can help you access important information that you didn't know, even if you know a topic very well. And no matter what you discover, college research is an important tool for establishing credibility with your audience members and thus gaining their confidence. Often, what you write will be only as good as the research on which it is based. (For more on research, see Part 4.)

## 2g Using digital tools effectively

Your instructors will often expect you to communicate both in and out of class using a variety of media. You may be asked to post to course management systems, lists, blogs, and wikis, and you may respond to the work of others on such sites. In addition, you will probably contact your instructor and classmates using email and text messages. Because digital communication is so common, it's easy to fall into the habit of writing very informally. If you forget to adjust style and voice for different occasions and readers, you may undermine your own intentions.

## Using best practices for formal messages and posts

Email was once seen as highly informal, but you probably use it today mainly for more formal purposes, particularly to communicate for work and for school. When writing most academic and professional messages, then, or when posting to a public list that may be read by people you don't know well, follow the conventions of academic English, and be careful not to offend or irritate your audience. Remember that jokes may be read as insults and that ALL CAPS may look like shouting. Finally, proofread to make sure your message is clear and free of errors, and that it is addressed to your intended audience, before you hit SEND.

## Using best practices for informal situations

Sometimes audiences expect informality. When you write in certain situations — Twitter posts, for example, and most text messages — you can play with (or ignore) the conventions you would follow in formal writing. Most people receiving text messages expect shorthand such as *btw* for "by the way," but be cautious about using such shortcuts with an employer or instructor. You may want to stick to a more formal method of contact if your employer or instructor has not explicitly invited you to send text messages — or texted you first.

Even when you think a situation calls for an informal tone, be attuned to your audience's needs and your purpose for writing. And when writing for any online writing space that allows users to say almost anything about themselves or to comment freely on the postings of others, bear in mind that anonymity sometimes makes online writers feel less inhibited than they would be in a face-to-face discussion. Don't say anything you would want to remain private, and even if you disagree with another writer, avoid personal attacks.

▼ ▼ ▼ ▼ ▼ ▼ ▼ ▼ ▼ ▼ ▼ ▼ ▼ ▼ ▼ ▼ ▼ ▼ ▼ ▼ ▼ ▼ ▼

### THINKING CRITICALLY ABOUT YOUR EXPECTATIONS FOR COLLEGE WRITING

How do you define good college writing? Make a list of the characteristics you come up with. Then make a list of what you think your instructors' expectations are for good college writing and note how they may differ from yours. (Research for this book suggests that many students today define good writing as "writing that makes something happen in the world." Would that line up with your definition or that of your instructors?) What might account for the differences—and the similarities—in the definitions and lists? Do you need to alter your ideas about good college writing to meet your instructors' expectations? Why, or why not?

# CHAPTER 3

# Rhetorical Situations

What do a documented essay on environmental justice, a Facebook message objecting to the site's privacy breaches, a tweet to other students in your psychology class, a letter to the editor of your local newspaper, and a website devoted to women's health all have in common? To communicate effectively, the writers of these texts must analyze their particular situation and then respond to it in fair and honest ways that will connect to the intended audience and build common ground.

## 3a Making good choices for your rhetorical situation

If it is true that "no [one] is an island," then it is equally true that no piece of writing is an island, isolated and alone. Instead, writing is connected to a web of other writings as a writer extends, responds to, or challenges what others have said. All writing exists within a rich and broad context, and all writers listen and respond to others, even as they shape messages about particular topics and for their particular purposes and audiences.

A *rhetorical situation* is the full set of circumstances or the context surrounding any communication. When you communicate, whether you're posting on social media, creating a video, or writing an essay for a class, consider and make careful choices about all the elements of your situation.

### Seeing the big picture: Elements of the rhetorical situation

The rhetorical situation is often depicted as a triangle to present the idea that three important elements are closely connected — your *text*, including your topic and the message you want to convey (3b); your role as *communicator*, including your purpose and your stance,

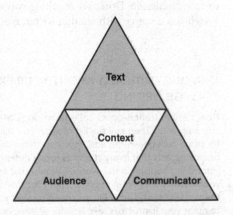

or attitude, toward the text and topic (3c); and your *audience* (3d). If all the pieces making up the larger triangle don't work together, the communication will not be effective. But important as these elements are, they are connected to a *context* that shapes all the angles of the triangle. Considering context fully requires you to consider other questions about the rhetorical situation, such as what kind of text you should create and what conventions you should follow to meet audience expectations about appearance and delivery (3e).

## Deciding to write

Because elements of the rhetorical situation are such important considerations in good writing, you should start thinking about them early on in any writing project — as soon as you decide to write. That decision is often made for you — an employer or instructor sets a deadline and you have to meet it. But even in those situations, consciously deciding to write is important: experienced writers report that making up their minds to begin a writing project represents a big step toward actually getting the job done.

## Understanding informal and formal rhetorical situations

Most people write in some rhetorical situations without analyzing them closely. When you post something on a friend's social media page, for example, you probably spend little time pondering what your friend values, how to phrase your message, which links or photos would best emphasize your point, or why you're taking the time to post. However, academic and other formal rhetorical situations may seem less familiar than the social writing you share with friends. Until you understand clearly what such situations call for, allow extra time to analyze the overall context, the topic and message, the purpose and stance, the audience, and other elements carefully.

## Seizing the opportune moment (*kairos*)

In ancient Greece, Kairos, the god of opportunity, was depicted as running, with a prominent lock of hair on his forehead but a bald head in back. Seizing the opportune moment meant grabbing the hair as Kairos approached; once he passed, the moment was gone. Considering rhetorical situations means thinking seriously about *kairos*, the appropriate time and the most opportune ways to get your point across. Take advantage of *kairos* to choose appropriate timing and current examples and evidence for your rhetorical situation. For example, students in 2019 who chose to write about the power of protest could draw on timely stories about the climate change movement and teen activist Greta Thunberg's call to action.

## 3b Planning your text's topic and message

An instructor or employer may tell you what topic to write about, but sometimes the choice will be yours. When the topic is left open, you may procrastinate because you can't decide what to choose. Experienced writers say that the best way to choose a topic is literally to let it choose you. Look to the topics that compel, confuse, or pose a problem for you: these are more likely to engage your interest and produce your best writing.

Deciding on a broad topic is an essential step before beginning to write, but you need to go further than that to decide what you want to say about one aspect of your topic and how you will shape what you want to say into a clear, powerful message.

## 3c Considering your purpose and stance as a communicator

Whether you choose to communicate for purposes of your own or have a purpose set for you by an instructor or employer, you should consider carefully the purpose for any communication. For the writing you do that is not connected to a class or work assignment, your reason for writing may be very clear to you: you may want to convince neighbors to support a community garden or tell blog readers what you like about your new phone. Even so, analyzing exactly what you want to accomplish and why can make you a more effective communicator.

### Considering purposes for academic assignments

An academic assignment may clearly explain why, for whom, and about what you are supposed to write. But some college assignments seem to come out of the blue, with no specific purpose, audience, or topic. Because comprehending the assignment is crucial to your success in responding to it, make an effort to understand what your instructor expects. Discuss any questions you have with your instructor or your classmates.

- What is the primary purpose of the piece of writing — to explain? to persuade? to entertain? to achieve some other purpose?
- What purpose did the instructor want to achieve — to make sure you have understood something? to evaluate your thinking and writing abilities?
- What are your own purposes in this piece of writing — to learn about a topic? to share your ideas? to express feelings? How can you achieve these goals?
- What, exactly, does the assignment ask you to do? Look for such words as *analyze, compare, describe, explain,* and *prove.* Remember that these words may differ in meaning from discipline to discipline.

## Considering stances for academic assignments

Thinking about your position as a communicator and your rhetorical stance — your attitude toward your text and topic — will help you to communicate effectively.

- Where are you coming from on this topic? What is your overall attitude toward your topic? How strong are your opinions?
- What social, political, religious, personal, or other influences account for your attitude? Will you need to explain any of these influences?
- What is most interesting to you about the topic? Why do you care about it?
- What conclusions do you think you might reach as you complete your text?
- How will you establish your credibility? How will you show you are knowledgeable and trustworthy?
- How will you convey your stance? Should you use words alone, combine words and images, include sound, or include something else?

 **EXERCISE 3.1**

The following assignment was given to an introductory business class: "Discuss in an essay the major contributions of the Apple and Microsoft companies to the personal computing industry." What would you need to know about the assignment to respond successfully? Using the questions in 3c, analyze this assignment.

**EXERCISE 3.2**

Consider a writing project that you are currently working on for a course. What can you tell about the purpose(s) of the project from reading the assignment? What is your purpose (or purposes) as the writer?

## 3d Analyzing your audience

Every communicator can benefit from thinking carefully about who the audience is, what the audience already knows or thinks, and what the audience needs and expects to find out. Effective communicators develop the ability to write for a variety of audiences, using language, style, and evidence appropriate to particular readers, listeners, or viewers. Even if your text can theoretically reach people all over the world, focus your analysis on those you most want or need to reach and those who are most likely to take an interest.

Thinking systematically about your audience can help you make decisions about writing projects. For example, it can help you decide what sort of organizational plan to follow, what information to include or exclude, and even what specific words to use. If you are writing an article for a journal for nurses about a drug that prevents patients from developing infections from feeding tubes, you will not need to give information about how such tubes work or to define many terms. But if you are writing about the same topic in a pamphlet for patients, you will have to give a lot of background information and define (or avoid) technical terms.

Research for this book shows that student writers today are aware of and concerned about being able to reach audiences, especially those who may not be in agreement with them. These students report that they want to reach out to very diverse audiences, but they fear being misunderstood — or misunderstanding those they are addressing. The questions below can help you get started in thinking about your entire audience, even those with whom you may not see eye to eye.

- What person or group do you most want to reach? Is the audience already knowledgeable about the topic?

- How much do you know about your audience? In what ways may its members differ from you or from one another? Consider education, geographic region, age, gender, occupation, social class, cultural heritage, politics, religion, sexual orientation, disabilities, and so on. (See Chapter 36.)

- What assumptions can you make about your audience members? What might they value — brevity, originality, conformity, honesty, wit, seriousness, generosity? What goals and aspirations do they have? Take special care to think about whether readers will understand your references, allusions, and so on.

- What do your audience members value? Do these values differ from yours? If so, how can you establish some common ground that will help you communicate effectively?

- What do members of the audience already know about your topic? What background information will they need to follow you?

- What kind of evidence will the audience find most compelling: quotations from experts? personal experience? photographs? statistics?

- What stance might your audience members have toward your topic?

- What is your relationship to the audience?

- What is your attitude toward the audience?

## Imagining informal and formal audiences

For some informal writing, you know exactly who your audience is, and communicating appropriately may be a simple matter. It's still worth remembering that when you post in a public space, you may not be aware of how large and varied your online audience can be. Can your friend's parents or your prospective employer see your social media posts? Who's reading your impassioned tweets?

Even if you write with ease in tweets and texts to friends, you may struggle when asked to write for an instructor or for a "general audience." You may wonder, for example, what a general audience might know about your topic, what they value, or what evidence they will find persuasive. When you are new to academic writing, making assumptions about such questions can be tricky. If you can identify samples of writing that appeal to a similar audience, look for clues about what that audience expects.

## Using appropriate language for an audience

If your readers can't understand what you mean, they're not likely to accept your points. Ask yourself whether the language of your text is as clear as it needs to be for your audience. For academic writing, consider whether to use any specialized varieties of English (see Chapter 34) along with academic English. How will these choices help you connect to your audience?

As you think about your audience, consider how you want them to respond to both the words and the images you use. And remember that sound and images can evoke very strong responses in your audience and can affect the tone of your writing, so choose them with special care.

In addition, pay special attention to your use of pronouns, which can include or exclude readers. When bell hooks says "The most powerful source any of us can have as we study and teach in university settings is full understanding and appreciation of the richness, beauty, and primacy of our familial and community backgrounds," she uses *us* and *we* to connect to her audience — those who "study and teach in university settings." Using *us* and *we* to speak directly to your audience, however, can sometimes be dangerous: those who do not see themselves as fitting into the "we" group can feel left out and they may resent it. (Also note that some disciplines may not want you to use first person *I, we,* or *us* at all.) Finally, remember that members of your audience may prefer pronouns other than the binary terms *he* and *she*. Some may prefer instead the use of singular *they* and *their*. Whenever possible, honor the pronoun preferences of your audience members (see 53f and g).

Finally, take a close look at your own assumptions about your audience and their views, and avoid language that may unintentionally exclude readers. Use words like *naturally* and *of course* carefully, for what seems "natural" to you may not seem natural at all to some members of your audience. Try to take nothing about the audience for granted.

CONSIDERING DISABILITIES | **YOUR WHOLE AUDIENCE**

Remember that considering your whole audience means thinking about members with varying abilities and special needs. Approximately one in five Americans lives with a disability. All writers need to think carefully about how their words connect with such diverse audiences.

**EXERCISE 3.3**

Describe one of your courses to three audiences: your best friend, your parents, and a group of high school students attending an open house at your college. How did the differences in audience affect the organization and wording of your descriptions?

# 3e  Thinking about genres and media

You may be familiar with the word *genre* as it applies to movies (comedy, action) or music (hip-hop, punk). But genre is also used to describe forms of writing, such as research essays and lab reports. Over time, genres develop conventions — such as the types of content, rhetorical strategies, and kinds of language used. Most audiences begin to expect those conventional features in the genre. But genres are flexible, not cookie-cutter templates. Genres can be produced in different media, such as digital or print forms. *Media* refers to how the text is delivered to its audience.

## Considering features of genres

If you are not sure what kind of text you are supposed to write, ask your instructor, classmates, or a writing center tutor for clarification and examples. Look carefully at the samples to make sure you understand the conventional expectations, and ask questions about the genre's typical features.

TALKING THE TALK | **GENRE NAMES**

"What does my instructor mean by *essay*?" Writing assignments often mention a specific genre, such as *essay* or *report*, but genre names can be confusing. The same genre may work differently in different contexts, or people may use the same term in various ways. Depending on the field, an essay might be a personal narrative, a critical analysis, or even a journal article. Even when the name of the genre sounds familiar to you, look for specific instructions for each assignment or analyze examples provided by the instructor.

- What does the genre look like? How is the text laid out? How are headings, sidebars, and other elements incorporated into the main text? Are its sections long or short? If visuals or media elements are included, how and why are they used? (See Chapter 22.)
- What topics are usually found in this genre? What type of content is rare?
- How does the text introduce the topic? Is the main point stated explicitly or implicitly?
- How are the key terms defined? What background information is provided?
- Are sentences short, long, simple, complicated? Is passive voice common?
- What is the level of formality? Does the text use contractions such as *he's* and *can't*? Does the text use technical jargon or slang?
- Does the text take a personal stance (*I, we*), address the audience directly (*you*), or talk about the subject without explicitly referring to the writer or the reader?
- Are sources used? How are they introduced and cited in the text?
- Who reads this genre, and why? Does the genre usually aim to inform, to persuade, to entertain, or to serve some other purpose?
- What medium is typically used for this genre? Are visual images or audio commonly used? If so, for what purposes?
- How much freedom do you have in stretching or ignoring the boundaries of the genre?

## Considering multimodal genres for academic work

Much college writing is still done in traditional print-based genres, but this is changing. You may have the option to create multimodal writing using audio, video, images, and words in combination. Make sure that your choices are appropriate for your topic, purpose, audience, and genre. You may start off planning to write a traditional academic essay and then discover as you proceed that a different genre or medium may offer more effective ways to communicate your point. One student, Will Rogers, who had been assigned to write an essay about something that most people take for granted, focused on a giant construction crane on campus. After he interviewed the crane's operator, who had left college after his first year to take this job, the student decided that his project would work better and be more powerful as a video. That way, viewers could actually see the crane operator and hear his voice as he described the decisions he had made.

You may be asked to create a work in one genre or medium, such as a print-based research project, and translate it to another type of composition, such as a multimedia presentation or podcast. Such translations may not be as straightforward as they seem. Just as filmmakers may streamline plot and conflate characters when they create a movie version of a book, developing a thesis and supporting it effectively may require different strategies if you are turning a print-based work into a digital form. You may need extra planning time.

**EXERCISE 3.4**

Consider some of the genres that you have encountered as a student, jotting down answers to the following questions and bringing them to class for discussion:

1. What are some genres that you read but don't usually write?
2. What are some genres that you write for instructors?
3. What are some genres that you use to write to or with other students?
4. What are some genres that you may encounter in your major or in your career?
5. How are some of the genres you listed different from those you encountered in high school?

**EXERCISE 3.5**

Consider a writing assignment you are currently working on. What is its genre? What medium or media does it use? How would you describe the style and tone? Finally, what visuals are you going to include, if any, and how well do they work to create the appropriate style and tone?

## 3f Considering language and style

Although most instructors still expect edited academic English for academic assignments, you may also need to use specialized occupational or professional varieties of English — those characteristic of medicine, say, or music. But you may also wish to use regional, communal, or other varieties of English to connect with certain audiences or to catch the sound of someone's spoken words. You may even need to use words from a language other than English — in quoting someone, perhaps, or capturing a cultural phenomenon. Think about what language varieties will be most appropriate for reaching your audience and accomplishing your purposes. (See Chapter 34.)

You will also want to think carefully about style: should you be casual and breezy, somewhat informal, formal, or extremely formal? Your style will be important in creating the tone you want — one that is appropriate to your assignment, audience, topic, purpose, and genre.

| LANGUAGE, CULTURE, AND CONTEXT | **BRINGING IN OTHER LANGUAGES** |

Even when you write in English, you may want or need to include words, phrases, or whole passages in another language. If so, consider whether your readers will understand that language and whether you need to provide a translation or more context. See 34e for more on bringing in other languages.

Remember that visual and audio elements can influence the tone of your writing. Such elements create associations in viewers' minds: one audience may react more positively than another to an element such as a rap or heavy metal soundtrack, for example. You can influence the way your work is perceived by analyzing your audience and choosing audio and visual elements that set a mood appropriate to your goals.

## 3g A sample rhetorical situation

Let's see how one writer analyzes a rhetorical situation. Emily Lesk, a student in a first-year English course, gets an assignment that asks her to "explore the ways in which one or more media have affected an aspect of American identity." (More examples of Emily's work appear in Chapter 6.) Because Emily is interested in advertising, she plans first to investigate how advertising might help shape American identity. Deciding that such a broad topic is not manageable in the time she has available, however, she shifts her focus to advertising for one company that seems particularly "American," Coca-Cola.

Since Emily's primary audience includes her instructor and her classmates, she needs to find ways to connect with them on an emotional as well as a logical level. She will do so, she decides, first by telling a story about being drawn into buying Coca-Cola products (even though she didn't really like the soft drink) because of the power of the advertising. She thinks that others in her audience may have had similar experiences. If you were to use the rhetorical triangle from 3a to map out Emily's writing situation, it might look like this:

TEXT (topic/message): Advertising is powerful and persuasive

AUDIENCE: Instructor and peers

CONTEXT: Brief academic essay for a writing class

COMMUNICATOR (purpose/stance): Reflect on a personal experience, draw audience in with story

Here is a portion of Emily's first draft and the visual she chose to illustrate her story:

Even before setting foot in the Promised Land three years ago, I knew exactly where I could find the Coke T-shirt. The shop in the central block of Jerusalem's Ben Yehuda Street did offer other shirt designs, but the one with the bright white "Drink Coca-Cola Classic" written in Hebrew cursive across the chest was what drew in most of the dollar-carrying tourists. While waiting almost twenty minutes for my shirt (depicted in fig. 1), I watched nearly everyone ahead of me say "the Coke shirt, *todah rabah* [thank you very much]."

At the time, I never thought it strange that I wanted one, too. Yet, I *had* absorbed sixteen years of Coca-Cola propaganda.

Fig. 1. Hebrew Coca-Cola T-shirt. Personal photograph by author.

Thinking about how she relates to her audience brings Emily to reflect more deeply on herself as the writer: Why has she chosen this topic? What does it say about her beliefs and values? What is her attitude toward her topic and toward her audience? What does she need to do to establish her credentials to write on this topic and to this audience?

Finally, Emily knows she will need to pay careful attention to the context in which she is writing: the assignment is due in two weeks, so she needs to work fast; the assignment calls for an essay written in academic English, though she plans to include some dialogue and a number of visuals to keep it lively; and since she knows she tends to sound like a know-it-all, she determines to work carefully on her tone and style.

▼ ▼ ▼ ▼ ▼ ▼ ▼ ▼ ▼ ▼ ▼ ▼ ▼ ▼ ▼ ▼ ▼ ▼ ▼ ▼ ▼ ▼ ▼ ▼ ▼

## THINKING CRITICALLY ABOUT RHETORICAL SITUATIONS

### Reading with an Eye for Purpose, Audience, and Context

Advertisements provide good examples of writing that is tailored carefully for specific audiences. Find two ads for the same product in contexts that suggest that the ads aim to appeal to different audiences — for example, men and women. What differences do you see in the messages and photography? What conclusions can you draw from this about ways of appealing to specific audiences?

### Thinking about Your Own Attention to Purpose, Audience, and Context

Analyze a text you have written or are working on right now for an academic course.

- Can you state its purpose(s) clearly? If not, what can you do to clarify its purpose(s)?
- What other purposes for this piece of writing can you imagine? How would fulfilling some other purpose change the writing?
- Can you tell from reading the piece who the intended audience is? If so, what in your text clearly relates to that audience? If not, what can you add that will strengthen your appeal to this audience?
- What other audiences can you imagine? How would the writing change if you were to address a different audience, such as people on social media?
- What changes would you have to make to create and deliver the work in a different genre or medium?
- Does your writing follow the conventions of academic English — and if not, should you revise it so that it will? Would the writing be more effective if you chose to use a dialect or other special variety of English?

# CHAPTER 4

# Exploring, Planning, and Drafting

Perhaps, like some writers, you just plunge right into your work, thinking about and developing ideas as you go along. Or perhaps you find that you can work more effectively by producing detailed blueprints or storyboards before you ever begin drafting. You may even draw pictures to help you find something new and compelling to say. If you haven't found an effective way to get started, you may want to try out different methods.

## 4a Exploring a topic

The point is so simple that it's easy to forget: you write best about topics you know well. One of the most important parts of the entire writing process, therefore, is choosing a topic that will engage your strengths and your interests, surveying what you know about it, and determining what you need to find out.

### Brainstorming

Used widely in business and industry, brainstorming involves listing your ideas — either orally or in writing — to discover new ways to approach a topic. You can brainstorm with others or by yourself.

1. Within five or ten minutes, list every word or phrase that comes to mind about the topic. Jot down key words and phrases, not sentences. No one has to understand the list but you. Don't worry about whether or not something will be useful — just list as much as you can in this brief span of time.

2. If little occurs to you, try calling out or writing down thoughts about the opposite side of your topic. If you are trying, for instance, to think of reasons to raise tuition and are coming up blank, try concentrating on reasons to reduce tuition. Once you start generating ideas in one direction, you'll find that you can usually move back to the other side fairly easily.

3. When the time is up, stop and read over the lists you've made. If anything else comes to mind, add it to the list. Then reread the list. Look for patterns of interesting ideas or for one central idea.

---

CONSIDERING DISABILITIES | **FREESPEAKING**

If you are better at talking out rather than writing out your ideas, try freespeaking. Begin by speaking into a recording device or into a computer with voice-recognition software, and just keep talking about your topic for at least seven to ten minutes. Say whatever comes to your mind, and don't stop talking. You can then listen to or read through the results of your freespeaking and look for an idea to pursue at greater length.

---

*Emily Lesk's brainstorming*

Emily Lesk, the student whose work appears in Chapters 3–6, did some brainstorming with her classmates on the general topic the class was working on: an aspect of American identity affected by one or more media. Here are some of the notes Emily made during the brainstorming session:

- "American identity" — Don't Americans have more than one identity?
- Picking a kind of media could be hard. I like clever ads. Maybe advertising and its influence on us?
- Wartime advertising; recruiting ads that promote patriotic themes.
- Look at huge American companies like Walmart and McDonald's and how their ads affect the way we view ourselves. Not sure what direction to take. . . .

## Freewriting and looping

Freewriting is a method of exploring a topic by writing about it for a period of time *without stopping*.

1. Write for ten minutes or so. Think about your topic, and let your mind wander freely. Write down everything that occurs to you — in complete sentences as much as possible — but don't worry about spelling or grammar. If you get stuck, write anything — just don't stop.

2. When the time is up, look at what you have written. Much of this material will be unusable, but you may still discover some important insights and ideas.

If you like, you can continue the process by looping: find the central or most intriguing thought from your freewriting and summarize it in a single sentence. Freewrite for five more minutes on the summary sentence, and then find and summarize the central thought from the second "loop." Keep this process going until you discover a clear angle or something about the topic that you can pursue.

*Emily Lesk's freewriting*

Here is a portion of the freewriting Emily Lesk did to focus her ideas after the brainstorming session:

> Media and effect on American identity. What media do I want to write about? That would make a big difference — television, radio, Internet — they're all different ways of appealing to Americans. TV shows that say something about American identity? What about magazine or TV advertising? Advertising tells us a lot about what it means to be American. Think about what advertising tells us about American identity. What ads make me think "American"? And why?

## Clustering

Clustering is a way of generating ideas using a visual scheme or chart. It is especially helpful for understanding the relationships among the parts of a broad topic and for developing subtopics. You may have a software program for clustering. If not, follow these steps:

1. Write your topic in the middle of a piece of paper and circle it.

2. In a ring around the topic circle, write what you see as the main parts of the topic. Circle each part, and draw a line from it to the topic.

3. Think of more ideas, examples, facts, or other details relating to each main part. Write each of these near the appropriate part, circle each one, and draw a line from each new idea to the part.

4. Repeat this process with each new circle until you can't think of any more details. Some trails may lead to dead ends, but you will still have many useful connections among ideas.

*Emily Lesk's Clustering*

When Emily Lesk asked herself what things made her think "American," one of her first answers was "Coca-Cola." So later in her planning and exploring process, she decided to work on the topic of Coca-Cola advertising and American identity (3g). After finding a large Coca-Cola advertising archive, Emily used clustering to help focus her emerging ideas. Her clustering appears here. (Remember that you may want to explore aspects of your ideas more than once — and exploring may be helpful at any stage as you plan and draft a piece of writing.)

**EMILY LESK'S CLUSTERING**

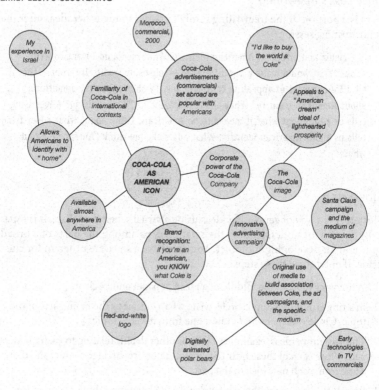

## Drawing or making word pictures

If you're someone who prefers visual thinking, you might either create a drawing about the topic or use figurative language — such as similes and metaphors — to describe what the topic resembles. Working with pictures or verbal imagery can sometimes also help illuminate the topic or uncover some of your unconscious ideas or preconceptions about it.

1. If you like to draw, try sketching your topic. What images do you come up with? What details of the drawing attract you most? What would you most like to expand on? A student planning to write an essay on her college experience began by thinking with pencils and pen in hand. Soon she found that she had drawn a vending machine several times, with different products and different ways of inserting money to extract them (one of her drawings appears here). Her sketches led her to think about what it might mean to

see an education as a product. Even abstract doodling can lead you to important insights about the topic and to focus your topic productively.

2. Look for figurative language — metaphors and similes — that your topic resembles. Try jotting down three or four possibilities, beginning with "My subject is _____" or "My subject is like _____." A student working on the subject of genetically modified crops came up with this simile: "Genetically modified foods are like empty calories: they do more harm than good." This exercise made one thing clear to this student writer: she already had a very strong bias that she would need to watch out for while developing her topic.

Play around a bit with your topic. Ask, for instance, "If my topic were a food (or a song or a movie or a video game), what would it be, and why?" Or make an Instagram post about your topic, or tweet a friend or an interested group saying why this topic appeals to you. Such exercises can get you out of the rut of everyday thinking and help you see your topic in a new light.

## Looking at images and videos

Searching images or browsing videos may spark topic ideas or inspire questions that you want to explore. If you plan to create a highly visual project — a video essay or slide presentation, for instance — you will probably need to decide what you want to show your audience before you plan the words that will accompany the images.

## Keeping a reflective journal or private blog

Writers often get their best ideas by jotting down or recording thoughts that come to them randomly. You can write in a notebook, record audio notes on a phone, store pictures and video files on a private blog — some writers even keep a marker and writing board on the shower wall so they can write down the ideas that come to them while bathing! As you begin thinking about your assignment, taking time to record what you know about your topic and what still puzzles you may lead you to a breakthrough or help you articulate your main idea.

## Asking questions

Another basic strategy for exploring a topic and generating ideas is simply to ask and answer questions. Here are several widely used sets of questions to get you started, either on your own or with one or two others.

### Questions to describe a topic

Originally developed by Aristotle, the following questions can help you explore a topic by carefully and systematically describing it:

- **What is it?** What are its characteristics, dimensions, features, and parts? What do your senses tell you about it?
- **What caused it?** What changes occurred to create your topic? How is it changing? How will it change?
- **What is it like or unlike?** What features differentiate your topic from others? What analogies can you make about your topic?
- **What larger system is the topic a part of?** How does your topic relate to this system?
- **What do people say about it?** What reactions does your topic arouse? What aspects of the topic cause those reactions?

### Questions to explain a topic

The well-known questions *who, what, when, where, why,* and *how,* widely used by news reporters, are especially helpful for explaining a topic.

- **Who** is doing it?
- **What** is at issue?
- **When** does it take place?
- **Where** is it taking place?
- **Why** does it occur?
- **How** is it done?

### Questions to persuade

When your purpose is to persuade or convince, the following questions, developed by philosopher Stephen Toulmin, can help you think analytically about your topic (10e and 11m):

- What **claim** are you making about your topic?
- What **good reasons** support your claim?
- What valid **underlying assumptions** support the reasons for your claim?
- What **evidence** can you find to back up your claim?
- What **refutations** of your claim should you anticipate?
- In what ways should you **qualify** your claim?

## Consulting sources

At the library and on the Internet, browse for a topic you want to learn more about. If you have a short list of ideas, follow links from one interesting article to another to see what you can find, or do a quick check of reference works to get overviews of the topics. You can begin with a general encyclopedia or a specialized reference work that focuses on a specific area, such as music or psychology. You can also use Wikipedia as a starting point: take a look at entries that relate to your topic, especially noting the sources they list. While you should not rely on Wikipedia alone, it is a highly accessible way to begin your research.

## Collaborating

As you explore your topic, remember that you can gain valuable insights from others. Many writers say that they get their best ideas in conversations with other people. If you talk with friends or roommates about your topic, at the very least you will hear yourself describe the topic and your interest in it; this practice will almost certainly sharpen your understanding of what you are doing. You can also seek out Facebook groups, online forums, or other networking sites as places to share your thinking on a topic and find inspiration.

 **EXERCISE 4.1**

Choose a topic that interests you, and explore it by using two of the strategies described in 4a. When you have generated some material, you might try comparing your results with those of other members of the class to see how effective or helpful each strategy was. If you have trouble choosing a topic, use one of the preliminary working thesis statements in Exercise 4.2.

## 4b Narrowing a topic

After exploring ideas, you may have found a topic that interests you and would be interesting to your audience. The topic, however, may be too large to be manageable. If this is the case, narrow your topic to focus on a more workable idea. You might consider your personal connections to the topic and why it interests you, or think about the most controversial or intriguing aspects of the topic. (For help crafting a thesis from your narrowed topic, see 4c.)

*Emily Lesk's work on narrowing her topic*

Emily Lesk planned to discuss how advertising affects American identity, but she knew that her topic was far too broad. She began to think about possible types of advertising and then about products that are pitched as particularly "American" in their advertising. When she got stuck, she posted a Facebook status update asking her friends to "name products that seem super-American." She quickly got seventeen responses with answers ranging from Hummers and Winchester rifles to "soft toilet paper," Spam, Wheaties, and maple syrup. One friend identified Pepsi-Cola, which made Emily recall an earlier idea of her own: Coca-Cola and its many memorable and well-documented advertising campaigns.

## 4c Drafting a working thesis statement

Academic and professional writing in the United States often contains an explicit thesis statement. The thesis functions as a promise to readers, letting them know what the writer will discuss. Your readers may (or may not) expect you to craft the thesis as a single sentence near the beginning of the text. If you want to suggest a thesis implicitly rather than stating one explicitly, if you plan to convey your main argument somewhere other than in your introduction, or if you prefer to make your thesis longer than a single sentence, consider whether the rhetorical situation allows such flexibility. For an academic project, also consult with your instructor about how to meet expectations.

Whether you plan to use an implicit or explicit thesis statement in your text, you should establish a tentative working thesis early in your writing process. The word *working* is important here because your thesis may well change as you write — your final thesis may be very different from the working thesis you begin with. Even so, a working thesis focuses your thinking and research and helps keep you on track.

A working thesis statement should have two parts: a topic, which indicates the subject matter the writing is about, and a comment, which makes an important point about the topic.

▶ **In the graphic novel *Fun Home*, illustrations and words combine to make meanings that are more subtle than either words alone or images alone could convey.**

A successful working thesis has three characteristics:

1. It is potentially *interesting* to the intended audience.
2. It is as *specific* as possible.
3. It limits the topic enough to make it *manageable*.

You can evaluate a working thesis by checking it against each of these characteristics, as in the following examples:

▶ **Graphic novels combine words and images.**

INTERESTING?   The topic of graphic novels could be interesting, but this draft of a working thesis has no real comment attached to it — instead, it states a bare fact, and the only place to go from here is to more bare facts.

▶ **In graphic novels, words and images convey interesting meanings.**

SPECIFIC?   This thesis is not specific. What are "interesting meanings," exactly? How are they conveyed?

▶ **Graphic novels have evolved in recent decades to become an important literary genre.**

MANAGEABLE?   This thesis would not be manageable for a short-term project because it would require research on several decades of history and on hundreds of texts from all over the world.

### Emily Lesk's working thesis

Emily Lesk wrote a preliminary thesis statement as she began to draft.

WORKING THESIS
Coca-Cola and Pepsi-Cola have shaped our national identity.

When she analyzed this thesis, she concluded that it was, indeed, interesting; however, she decided that the two brands were not trying to do exactly the same thing, so her thesis was probably not specific enough. In addition, both Coke and Pepsi had existed for over a century, and she realized that just investigating the advertising for the two brands would probably take more time than she had available — so the thesis was probably not manageable. After talking with her instructor, Emily decided to focus on a single advertising icon, the world-famous Coca-Cola logo.

REVISED THESIS
Coca-Cola is a cultural icon that shapes American identity.

For Emily Lesk's first draft, see 4g. For her final draft, see 6f.

LANGUAGE, CULTURE, | **STATING A THESIS EXPLICITLY**
AND CONTEXT

In some cultures, stating the main point explicitly or directly may be considered rude or inelegant. In U.S. academic and business practices, however, readers often expect the writer to make key points and positions explicit. Unless your main point is highly controversial or hard for the reader to accept (such as a rejection letter), state your main point early — before presenting the supporting details.

 **EXERCISE 4.2**

Choose one of the following preliminary working thesis statements, and after specifying an audience, evaluate the thesis in terms of its interest, specificity, and manageability. Revise the working thesis as necessary to meet these criteria.

1. The benefits of standardized testing are questionable.

2. Vaccinations are dangerous.

3. Too many American parents try to micromanage their children's college education.

4. Many people are afraid to fly in a plane, although riding in a car is statistically more dangerous.

5. An educated public is the key to a successful democracy.

 **EXERCISE 4.3**

Write a preliminary working thesis statement for your chosen topic. Evaluate the thesis in terms of its interest, specificity, and manageability. Revise it as necessary to create a satisfactory working thesis.

## 4d  Gathering information

Writing often calls for research. Your curiosity may be triggered by a found object or image that you want to learn more about. An assignment may specify that you conduct research on your topic and cite your sources. Even if you're writing about a topic on which you're an expert, you may find that you don't know enough about some aspect of the topic to write about it effectively without doing research.

You may need to do research at various stages of the writing process — early on, to help you understand or define your topic, and later on, to find additional examples and illustrations to support your thesis. Once you have developed a working thesis, consider what additional information, opinions, visuals, and media you might need.

You can do three kinds of research to support your thesis: *library research*, which gives you access not only to books and periodicals that are housed in the library but also to online databases the library subscribes to and which are available to you for free (and perhaps archives of other kinds of sources, such as music, films, posters, photographs, and so on); *Internet research*, which gives you access to texts, visuals, and media that are publicly available and searchable on the Internet; and *field research*, which includes personal observation, interviews, surveys, and other means of gathering information directly. (For more information on conducting research, see Chapter 13.)

# 4e Organizing verbal and visual information

While you're finding information on your topic, think about how you will group or organize that information to make it accessible and persuasive to readers. At the simplest level, writers most often group information in their writing projects according to four principles — space, time, logic, and association.

## Organizing spatially

Spatial organization of texts allows the reader to "walk through," beginning at one point and moving around in an organized manner — say, from near to far, left to right, or top to bottom. It can be especially useful when you want the audience to understand the layout of a structure or the placement of elements and people in a scene: texts such as a museum visitors' audio guide, a written description of a historic battlefield, or a video tour of a new apartment might all call for spatial organization. Remember that maps, diagrams, and other graphics may help readers visualize your descriptions more effectively.

## Organizing chronologically (by time)

Organization can also indicate *when* events occur, usually chronologically from first to last. Chronological organization is the basic method used in cookbooks, lab reports, instruction manuals, and many stories and narrative films. You may find it useful to organize information by describing or showing the sequence of events or the steps in a process.

## Organizing logically

Organizing according to logic means relating pieces of information in ways that make sense. Following is an overview of some of the most commonly used logical patterns: *illustration, definition, division and classification, comparison and contrast, cause and effect, problem and solution, analogy,* and *narration.* For examples of paragraphs organized according to these logical patterns, see 5c.

## Illustration

You will often gather examples to illustrate a point. If you write an essay discussing how one novelist influenced another, you might cite examples from the second writer's books that echo themes or characters from the first writer's works. For a pamphlet appealing for donations to the Red Cross, you might use photographs showing situations in which donations helped people in trouble, along with appropriate descriptions. For maximum effect, you may want to arrange examples in order of increasing importance unless your genre calls for an attention-grabbing initial illustration.

## Definition

Often a topic can be developed by definition — by saying what something is (or is not) and perhaps by identifying the characteristics that distinguish it from things that are similar or in the same general category. If you write about poverty in your community, for example, you would have to define very carefully what level of income, assets, or other measure defines a person, family, or household as "poor." In an essay about Pentecostalism, you might explain what characteristics separate Pentecostalism from related religious movements.

## Division and classification

Division means breaking a single topic into separate parts; classification means grouping many separate items of information about a topic according to their similarities. An essay about military recruiting policies might divide the military into different branches — army, navy, air force, and so on — and examine how each recruits volunteers. For a project on women's roles in the eighteenth century, you could organize your notes by classification: information related to women's education, occupations, legal status, and so on.

## Comparison and contrast

Comparison focuses on the similarities between two things, whereas contrast highlights their differences, but the two are often used together. If you were asked to analyze two case studies in an advertising text (one on Budweiser ads and the other on ads for the latest iPhone), you might well organize the response by presenting all the information on Budweiser advertising in one section and all on iPhone ads in another (block comparison) or by alternating between Budweiser and iPhone ads as you look at particular characteristics of each (alternating comparison).

## Cause and effect

Cause-effect analysis may deal with causes, effects, or both. If you examine why something happens or happened, you are investigating causes. If you explain what has occurred or is likely to occur from a set of conditions, you are discussing effects. An environmental-impact study of the probable consequences of building a proposed dam, for instance, would focus on effects. On the other hand, a video essay on the breakdown of authority in inner-city schools might begin with the effects of the breakdown and trace them back to their causes.

### Problem and solution

Moving from a problem to a solution is a natural way to organize certain kinds of information. For example, a student studying motorcycle parking on campus decided to organize his writing in just this way: he identified a problem (the need for more parking) and then offered two possible solutions, along with visuals to help readers imagine the solutions (his outline appears in 4f). Many assignments in engineering, business, and economics call for a similar organizational strategy.

### Analogy

An analogy establishes connections between two things or ideas. Analogies are particularly helpful in explaining something new in terms of something very familiar. Likening the human genome to a map, for example, helps explain the complicated concept of the genome to those unfamiliar with it.

### Narration

Narration involves telling a story. You might, for example, tell the story of how deer ravaged your mother's garden as a way of showing why you support population-control measures for wildlife. Narrating calls on the writer to set the story in a context readers can understand, providing any necessary background and descriptive details as well as chronological markers and transitions (*later that day, the following morning,* and so on) to guide readers through the story.

## Organizing by association

Some writers organize information through a series of associations that grow directly out of their own experiences and memories. In doing so, they may rely on a sensory memory, such as an aroma, a sound, or a scene. Thus, associational organization, in which the writer follows a chain of associations to render an experience vividly for readers, is common in personal narrative.

> Flying from San Francisco to Atlanta, I looked down to see the gentle roll of the Smoky Mountains begin to appear. Almost at once, I was transported back to my granny's porch, sitting next to her drinking iced tea and eating peaches. Those fresh-picked peaches were delicious — ripened on the tree, skinned, and eaten with no regard for the sticky juice trickling everywhere. And on special occasions, we'd make ice cream, and Granny would empty a bowl brimming with chopped peaches into the creamy dish. Now — that was the life!

---

QUICK HELP

Organizing visuals and media in academic writing

- Use video and still images to capture your readers' attention and interest in a vivid way, to emphasize a point you make in words, to present information that is difficult to convey in words, or to communicate with audiences with different language skills.
- Consider whether you want to use images alone to convey your message, or whether words are also needed in conjunction with the images to help readers understand.
- For presentations, consider what your audience should look at as they listen to you. Make sure that the visuals enhance rather than compete with what you say.
- If you are using visuals and words together, consider both the way each image or video works on its own and the way it works in combination with the words you use.
- If you are using visuals to illustrate a written-word text, place each visual as near as possible to the words it illustrates. Introduce each visual clearly (*As the map to the right depicts . . .*). Comment on the significance or effect of the visual (*Figure 1 corroborates the firefighters' statements . . .*). Label each visual appropriately, and cite the source. **(Chapters 18–21)**

---

## Combining organizational patterns

In much of your writing, you will want to use two or more principles of organization. You might, for example, combine several passages of narration with vivid examples to make a striking comparison, as one student did in an essay about the dramatic differences between her life in her Zuñi community and her life as a teacher in Seattle. In addition, you may want to include not only visuals but sound and other multimedia effects as well.

---

LANGUAGE, CULTURE, AND CONTEXT | **ORGANIZING INFORMATION**

You may know ways of organizing information that differ markedly from those discussed in this section. A Navajo teacher notes, for example, that explicit linear organization, through chronology or other strictly logical patterns, doesn't ever sound quite right to her. As she puts it, "In traditional Navajo, it's considered rude to get right to the point. Polite conversation or writing between two engaged people always takes a while to get to the point." Although effective organization depends largely on the reader's expectations, it may sometimes make sense to deviate from those expectations. If you choose to organize your writing differently from what your teacher or classmates might expect, consider explaining the reason for your choice — for example, in a cover letter or a footnote.

*Emily Lesk's organizational patterns*

Emily Lesk begins the final draft of her essay (6f) with what she calls a confession: *I don't drink Coke.* She follows this opening with an anecdote about a trip to Israel during which she nevertheless bought a T-shirt featuring the Coca-Cola logo. She goes on to explore what lies behind this purchase, relating it to the masterful advertising campaigns of the Coca-Cola Company and illustrating the way that the company's advertising "sells" a certain kind of American identity along with its products. She closes her draft by reflecting on the implications of this relationship between corporate advertising and national identity. Thus, her essay, which begins with a personal experience, combines the patterns of narrative with cause-effect and comparison.

**EXERCISE 4.4**

Identify the most effective means of organizing information for a project you are currently working on. Write a brief paragraph explaining why you chose this particular method (or these methods) of organization.

## 4f Planning

At this point, you will find it helpful to write out an organizational plan, outline, or storyboard. To do so, simply begin with your thesis; review your exploratory notes, research materials, and visual or multimedia sources; and then list all the examples and other good reasons you have to support the thesis. (For information on paragraph-level organization, see Chapter 5.)

### Creating an informal plan

One informal way to organize your ideas is to figure out what belongs in your introduction, body paragraphs, and conclusion. A student who was writing about solutions to a problem used the following plan:

**WORKING THESIS**

Increased motorcycle use demands the reorganization of campus parking lots.

**INTRODUCTION**

give background and overview (motorcycle use up dramatically), and include photograph of overcrowded lot

state purpose — to fulfill promise of thesis by offering solutions

BODY

*describe current situation (my research at area parking lots)*

*describe problem in detail (report on statistics; cars vs. cycles), and graph my findings*

*present two possible solutions (enlarge lots or reallocate space)*

CONCLUSION

*recommend against first solution because of cost and space*

*recommend second solution and summarize advantages*

## Writing a formal outline

Even if you have created an informal written plan before drafting, you may wish (or be required) to prepare a more formal outline, which can help you see exactly how the parts of your writing will fit together — how your ideas relate, where you need examples, and what the overall structure of your work will be. Even if your instructor doesn't ask you to make an outline or you prefer to use some other method of sketching out your plans, you may want to come back to an outline later: doing a retrospective outline — one you do after you've already drafted your project — is a great way to see whether you have any big logical gaps or whether parts of the essay are in the wrong place.

Most formal outlines follow a conventional format of numbered and lettered headings and subheadings, using roman numerals (I, II, III), arabic numerals (1, 2, 3), capital letters, and lowercase letters to show the levels of importance of the various ideas and their relationships. Each new level is indented to show its subordination to the preceding level. Here is a partial formal outline of student Julia Sakowitz's essay; you can read the entire essay in 18e.

SAMPLE FORMAL OUTLINE (PARTIAL)

**Thesis:** Although there is no simple solution for tourism in Harlem, small minority- and resident-owned businesses have the potential to more directly and widely benefit the community while causing fewer social and economic problems.

I. Economic development policy, particularly the Upper Manhattan Empowerment Zone (UMEZ), has played a major role in shaping tourism's growth in Harlem.

   A. The UMEZ specifically focuses on black and Latino cultural initiatives as a means of drawing tourism.

   B. Recent scholarship on tourism in Harlem suggests that marketing black and Latino culture is Harlem's golden ticket to escape economic marginalization.

    C.  Benefits of cultural tourism include revenue, cultural flourishing, community pride, tolerance, and destigmatization.

II.  Cultural tourism comes with significant complications for residents.

    A.  The power dynamic between tourists and residents is skewed in favor of the tourists, who can treat residents as "something to be consumed like a Broadway show."

    B.  Commercial gentrification stems from increased tourism.

    C.  Residential gentrification often follows commercial gentrification, leading to increased displacement of original Harlem residents.

III.  Small tour companies advertise authenticity as part of their appeal to tourists.

    A.  Welcome to Harlem (Johnson) features six different tours and workshops given by Harlem residents.

    B.  Many Harlem-based tour companies suffer from lack of visibility when hotels and tour companies recommend larger, outside tour companies that can afford to pay commission.

    C.  Authenticity and self-representation are extremely important to the success of Harlem-based tour companies.

## Making a storyboard

The technique of storyboarding — working out a narrative or argument in visual form — can be a good way to come up with an organizational plan, especially if you are developing a video essay, website, or other media project. You can find storyboard templates online to help you get started, or you can create your own storyboard by using note cards or sticky notes. Even if you're writing a more traditional word-based college essay, however, you may find storyboarding helpful: take advantage of different colors to keep track of threads of argument, subtopics, and so on. Flexibility is a strong feature of storyboarding: you can move the cards and notes around, trying out different arrangements, until you find an organization that works well for your writing situation. Here are some possible organizational patterns for a storyboard.

Use linear organization when you want readers to move in a particular order through your material. An online report might use the following linear organization:

**LINEAR ORGANIZATION**

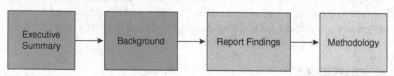

A hierarchy puts the most important material first, with subtopics branching out from the main idea. A website on dog-bite prevention might be arranged like this:

**HIERARCHICAL ORGANIZATION**

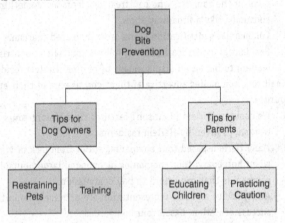

A spoke-and-hub organization allows readers to move from place to place in no particular order. Many portfolio websites are arranged this way:

**SPOKE-AND-HUB ORGANIZATION**

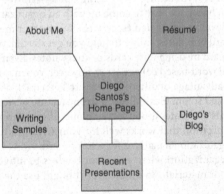

Whatever form your plan takes, you may want or need to change it along the way. Writing has a way of stimulating thought, and the process of drafting may generate new ideas. Or you may find that you need to reexamine some data or information or gather more material.

⬛ **EXERCISE 4.5**

Write out or sketch a plan for a piece of writing supporting your working thesis.

# 4g Drafting

In some sense, drafting begins the moment you start thinking about a topic. At some point, however, you attempt an actual written draft.

No matter how good your planning, investigating, and organizing have been, chances are you will need to return to these activities as you draft. The first principle of successful drafting is this: be flexible. If you see that your organizational plan is not working, alter it. If some information now seems irrelevant, leave it out, even if you went to great lengths to obtain it. Throughout the drafting process, you may need to refer to points you have already written about. You may learn that you need to do more research, that your whole thesis must be reshaped, or that your topic is still too broad and should be narrowed further.

---

**QUICK HELP**

Guidelines for drafting

- **Have all your information close at hand and arranged according to your organizational plan.** Stopping to search for a piece of information can break your concentration or distract you.
- **Try to write in stretches of at least thirty minutes.** Writing can provide momentum, and once you get going, the task becomes easier.
- **Keep track of any sources you plan to include.** Keep a working bibliography (14c), and make notes in your draft of any information that comes from your research. If you find useful information online, you can cut and paste it into a document to ensure that you have the information exactly as you found it; however, highlight or save it in a different color so that you don't mistakenly borrow writing that is not your own. **(Chapters 14–16)**
- **Don't let small questions bog you down.** Just make a note of them in brackets or in all caps—or make a tentative decision and move on.
- **Remember that first drafts aren't perfect.** Concentrate on getting all your ideas written down, and don't worry about anything else.
- **Stop writing at a place where you know exactly what will come next.** Doing so will help you start easily when you return to the draft.

---

**CONSIDERING DISABILITIES | A TALKING DRAFT**

Using a word processor with voice-recognition software will allow you to speak your ideas, which will then appear onscreen. A "talking" draft of this kind can be a very good way to get your initial draft done, especially if you have difficulty with the physical act of writing. If voice-recognition software isn't available, try to find another student who will work with you to produce talking drafts: as one of you talks, the other types what is being said. Your school's office of disability services should be able to provide scribes or notetakers as well.

*Emily Lesk's first draft*

Here is Emily Lesk's first draft. She uses [brackets] as she drafts to identify questions she is still pondering and sources she will need to cite.

All-Powerful Coke

STUDENT WRITING

I don't drink Coke. Call me picky for disliking the soda's saccharine aftertaste. Call me cheap for choosing a water fountain over a twelve-ounce aluminum can that costs nearly two dollars from a vending machine but only pennies to produce. Even call me unpatriotic for rejecting the potable god that over the last century has come to represent all the enjoyment and ease to be found in our American way of life. But don't call me a hypocrite when I admit that I still identify with Coke and the Coca-Cola culture.

I have a favorite T-shirt that says "Drink Coca-Cola Classic" in Hebrew. It's Israel's standard tourist fare, like little nested dolls in Russia or painted horses in Scandinavia, and before setting foot in the Promised Land three years ago, I knew where I could find one. The T-shirt shop in the central block of a Jerusalem shopping center did offer other shirt designs ("Maccabee Beer" was a favorite), but that Coca-Cola shirt was what drew in most of the dollar-carrying tourists. I waited almost twenty minutes for mine, and I watched nearly everyone ahead of me say "the Coke shirt" (and "thanks" in Hebrew).

At the time, I never asked why I wanted the shirt. I do know, though, that the reason I wear it often, despite a hole in the right sleeve, has to do with its power as a conversation piece. Few people notice it without asking something like, "Does that say Coke?" I usually smile and nod. They mumble a compliment and we go our separate ways. But rarely does anyone want to know what language the world's most famous logo is written in. And why should they? Perhaps because Coca-Cola is a cultural icon that shapes American identity.

Throughout the company's history, marketing strategies have centered on putting Coca-Cola in scenes of the happy, carefree American life we never stop striving for. What 1950s teenage girl wouldn't long to see herself in the soda shop pictured in a Coca-Cola ad appearing in a 1958 issue of *Seventeen* magazine? A clean-cut, handsome man flirts with a pair of smiling girls as they laugh and drink Coca-Colas. And any girls who couldn't put themselves in that perfect, happy scene could at least buy a Coke for consolation. The malt shop — complete with a soda jerk in a white jacket and paper hat — is a theme that, even today, remains a symbol of Americana. [Use ad? Source is *'50s American Magazine Ads edited by Ikuta.*]

But while countless campaigns with this general strategy have together shaped the Coca-Cola image, presenting a product as key to a happy life represents a fairly typical approach to advertising everything from Fords to Tylenol. Coca-Cola's advertising is truly unique, however, for the original way the beverage giant has utilized specific advertising media — namely magazines and television — to drive home this message.

One of the earliest and best-known examples of this strategy is artist Haddon Sundblom's masterpiece of Santa Claus. In December 1931, Coca-Cola introduced an advertising campaign featuring Sundblom's depiction of a jolly, Coke-drinking Santa. [Cite Coca-Cola website.] [Look for a picture of this original Coke Santa.] But the success of Santa Claus goes far beyond Sundblom's magazine advertisements depicting a warm, happy grandfather figure delighting in an ice-cold Coke after a tiring night of delivering presents. The way in which Coca-Cola advertisers presented that inviting image represents Coca-Cola's brilliant manipulation of the medium itself. [Need to cite Pendergrast book here.]

In today's world of CNN, e-journals, and *Newsweek.com*, it is often easy to forget how pervasive a medium the magazine was prior to the advent of television. Until the late 1950s, American households of diverse backgrounds and geographic locations subscribed loyally to general-subject weeklies and monthlies such as *Life* and the *Saturday Evening Post*. These publications provided a primary source of news, entertainment, and other cultural information to families nationwide. This large and constant group of subscribers enabled Coca-Cola to build a perennial Christmastime advertising campaign that used an extremely limited number of ads ["designs" better word?] [add source], which Americans soon came to look forward to and seek out each holiday season. The marketing strategy was not to capture consumers with a few color drawings, but rather to make them wait eagerly by the mailbox each December so that they could flip through the *Saturday Evening Post* to find the latest scene featuring Santa gulping a Coke. For this strategy to be successful, the advertisements had to be seen by many, but also be just hard enough to come by to be exciting. What better location for this than the December issue of an immensely popular magazine?

There is no denying that this strategy worked brilliantly, as this inviting image of Santa Claus graduated from the pages of the *Saturday Evening Post* to become the central figure of the most celebrated and beloved season of the year. Travel to any strip mall in the United States during December (or even November — that's how much we love Christmas!) and you will no doubt run into Santa clones left and right, punched out of cardboard and sculpted in tinsel hung atop lampposts, all in Coca-Cola red and white. And while, in today's nonmagazine world, Coca-Cola must celebrate Christmas with specially designed Diet Coke cans and television commercials, the Coca-Cola Santa Claus will forever epitomize the former power of magazine advertising in America. [Getting off track here?]

In other words, Coca-Cola has hammered itself into our perceptions — both conscious and subconscious — of an American cultural identity by equating itself with media that define American culture. When the omnipresent general magazine that marked the earlier part of the century fell by the wayside under television's power, Coke was there from the beginning. In its 1996 recap of the previous fifty years in industry history, the publication *Beverage Industry* [need to cite] cites Coca-Cola as a frontrunner in the very first form of television advertising: sponsorship of entire programs such as, in the case of Coke, *The Bob Dixon Show* and *The Adventures of Kit Carson*. Just as today we associate sports stadiums with their corporate sponsors, viewers of early television programs will forever equate them with Coke.

When networks switched from offering sponsorships to selling exclusive commercial time in short increments (a format modeled after magazine advertisements), Coca-Cola strove to distinguish itself again, this time by producing new formats and technologies for these commercials. [This sentence is way too long!] Early attempts at this — such as choppy "stop motion" animation, where photographs of objects such as Coke bottles move without the intervention of actors — attracted much attention, according to the Library of Congress Motion Picture Archives [need to cite]. Coca-Cola also experimented with color advertisements early enough that the excitement of color advertising technology drew additional attention to these commercials.

But the Coke advertising campaign that perhaps best illustrates the ability of Coca-Cola advertisers to equate their product with a medium/technology [reword!] did not appear until 1993. In the holiday Coke ad that year, completely digitally animated polar bears rolled, swam, snuggled, slid on ice, and gurgled about in a computerized North Pole and finished off the playful experience with a swig of Coke. This campaign captured America's attention and held it for six separate commercials, and not because or at least not just because the bears were cute and cuddly. Their main draw was the groundbreaking technology used to create them. In 1993, two years before the release of the first *Toy Story*, these were some of the very first widely viewed digital films [cite Library of Congress here]. With these bears, as with other campaigns, Coke didn't just utilize the latest technology — Coke *introduced* the latest technology.

As a result of this brilliant advertising, a beverage which I do not even let enter my mouth [reword!] is a significant part of my American cultural identity. That's why I spent thirty Israeli shekels and twenty minutes in a tourist trap I would ordinarily avoid buying my Hebrew Coca-Cola shirt. That shirt — along with the rest of the Coca-Cola collectibles industry — demonstrates the power of [something about Coke connecting itself with the American ideal of a life of diversion and lightheartedness]. Seeing the logo that embodies all of this halfway around the world gave me an opportunity to affirm a part of my American identity.

The red-and-white logo's ability to appeal to Americans even in such a foreign context speaks to Coke advertisers' success at creating this association. A 1999 American television commercial described by the Library of Congress archive [need to cite] as highly successful is set in Kenya, with dialogue in a local dialect and English subtitles. In it, two Kenyan boys taste their first Cokes and comment that the experience is much like the way they imagine kissing a girl will be. This image appeals to Americans because it enables us to use the symbol of Coca-Cola to make ourselves comfortable even in the most unfamiliar situations. And if that can't sell your product, nothing can.

(For the works-cited page that Emily Lesk submitted with her final paper, which includes the sources indicated in her notes in this draft, see 6f.)

▼ ▼ ▼ ▼ ▼ ▼ ▼ ▼ ▼ ▼ ▼ ▼ ▼ ▼ ▼ ▼ ▼ ▼ ▼ ▼ ▼ ▼ ▼ ▼ ▼

## THINKING CRITICALLY ABOUT YOUR WRITING PROCESS

Using the following guidelines, reflect on the process you went through as you pre-pared for and wrote your draft. Make your answers an entry in your writing log if you are keeping one.

1. When did you first begin to think about the assignment? How did you arrive at your specific topic?

2. What kinds of exploring or planning did you do? What kinds of research did you need to do?

3. How long did it take to complete your draft (including the time spent gathering information)? Where did you write your draft? Briefly describe the setting.

4. How did awareness of your audience help shape your draft?

5. What have you learned from your draft about your own rhetorical stance on your topic?

6. What did you learn about your ideas for this topic by exploring, planning, and talking with others about it?

7. What do you see as the major strengths of your draft? What is your favorite sentence, and why?

8. What do you see as the major weaknesses of your draft? What are you most worried about, and why?

9. How would you assess your introduction? Does it grab readers' attention and make them want to read on? How about the conclusion? Is it as powerful as it might be?

10. What would you like to change about your process of exploring, planning, and drafting?

# CHAPTER 5

# Developing Paragraphs

Paragraphs serve as signposts for your readers — pointers that anticipate what they need to know next and thus help guide them through a piece of writing. A look through a popular magazine will show paragraphs working this way: the first paragraph of an article almost always aims to get our attention and to persuade us to read on, and subsequent ones often indicate a new point or a shift in focus or tone. Put most simply, a paragraph is a group of sentences or a single sentence set off as a unit. All the sentences in a paragraph usually revolve around one main idea.

## 5a  Focusing on a main idea

An effective paragraph often focuses on one main idea. A good way to achieve such unity is to state the main idea clearly in one sentence (the topic sentence) and then relate all other sentences in the paragraph to that idea.

### Positioning a topic sentence

The following paragraph opens with a <u>clear topic sentence</u>, and the rest of the paragraph builds on the idea stated in that sentence:

> <u>Our friendship was the source of much happiness and many memories.</u>
> We grooved on every new recording from Jay-Z. We sweated together in the sweltering summer sun, trying to win the championship for our softball team. I recall the taste of pepperoni pizza as we discussed the highlights of our team's victory. Once we even became attracted to the same person, but luckily we were able to share his friendship.

But a topic sentence doesn't always appear at the beginning of a paragraph. When specific details lead up to a generalization, for example, putting the topic sentence at the end of the paragraph makes sense, as in the following paragraph from Alice Walker's "Everyday Use."

> During the visit, Dee takes the pictures, every one of them, including the one of the house that she used to live in and hate. She takes the churn top and dasher, both whittled out of a tree by one of Mama's uncles. She tries to take Grandma Dee's quilts. Mama and Maggie use these inherited items every day, not only

appreciating their heritage but living it too. <u>Dee, on the other hand, wants these items only for decorative use, thus forsaking and ignoring their real heritage.</u>

In still other instances, you may not want to state the topic sentence explicitly but rather leave it implied, especially if the main idea is so obvious that it doesn't need to be stated directly. Look at this paragraph from an essay about working as an airport cargo handler:

> In winter the warehouse is cold and damp. There is no heat. The large steel doors that line the warehouse walls stay open most of the day. In the cold months, wind, rain, and snow blow across the floor. In the summer, the warehouse becomes an oven. Dust and sand from the runways mix with the toxic fumes of fork lifts, leaving a dry, stale taste in your mouth. The high windows above the doors are covered with a thick, black dirt that kills the sun. The men work in shadows with the constant roar of jet engines blowing dangerously in their ears.
>
> —PATRICK FENTON, "Confessions of a Working Stiff"

Here, the implied topic sentence would be something like "Working conditions in the warehouse are uncomfortable, dreary, and hazardous to the workers' health." But the writer doesn't have to state this information explicitly because readers can easily infer it from the details provided.

## Developing other related sentences

Whether the main idea of a paragraph is stated in a topic sentence or is implied, make sure that all other sentences in the paragraph contribute to the main idea. In the preceding example about friendship, all of the sentences clearly relate to the point that is made in the first sentence. The result is a properly unified paragraph.

---

**QUICK HELP**

### Editing paragraphs

- What is the topic sentence of each paragraph? Is the main idea clear? **(5a)**
- Does the last sentence of each paragraph in some way conclude that paragraph's discussion? If not, does it need to?
- Within each paragraph, how does each sentence relate to the main idea? Revise or eliminate any that do not. **(5a)**
- How completely does each paragraph develop its main idea? What details and images are included? Are they effective? Do any paragraphs need more detail? **(5b)**
- What other methods of development might make the paragraph more effective? **(5c)**
- Within each paragraph, how well do transitions carry readers from one idea to the next? **(5d)**
- Are the paragraphs clearly linked? Do any links need to be added? Are any of the transitions from one paragraph to another artificial? **(5e)**
- How does the introductory paragraph catch readers' interest? How does the last paragraph draw the piece to a conclusion? **(5f)**

**EXERCISE 5.1**

Choose one of the following topic sentences, and spend some time exploring the topic. Then write a paragraph that includes the topic sentence. Make sure that each of the other sentences relates to it. Assume that the paragraph will be part of a letter you are writing to a friend.

1. I quickly discovered that college life was not quite what I had expected.
2. Being part of the "in crowd" used to be essential to me.
3. My work experience has taught me several important lessons.
4. Until recently, I never appreciated my parents fully.
5. One of my high school teachers helped prepare me for success in college.

# 5b Providing details

An effective paragraph develops its main idea by providing enough details, including visual details, to hold the reader's interest. Without such development, a paragraph may seem lifeless and abstract.

### A POORLY DEVELOPED PARAGRAPH

No such thing as human nature compels people to behave, think, or react in certain ways. Rather, from our infancy to our death, we are constantly being taught, by the society that surrounds us, the customs, norms, and mores of a distinct culture. Everything in culture is learned, not genetically transmitted.

This paragraph is boring! Although its main idea is clear, it fails to gain interest or hold readers' attention because it lacks any examples or details. Now look at the paragraph revised to include specific details.

### THE SAME PARAGRAPH, REVISED

A child in Los Angeles decorates a Christmas tree with shiny red ornaments and sparkling tinsel. A few weeks later, a child in Beijing celebrates the Chinese New Year with feasting, firecrackers, and gift money in lucky red envelopes. It is not by instinct that one child knows how to decorate the tree while the other knows how to celebrate the New Year. No such thing as human nature compels people to behave, think, or react in certain ways. Rather, from the time of our infancy to our death, we are constantly being taught, by the society that surrounds us, the customs, norms, and mores of one or more distinct cultures. Everything in culture is learned, not genetically transmitted.

Though both paragraphs present the same point, only the second one comes to life. It does so by bringing in specific details *from* life, including images that show readers what the paragraph describes. This paragraph appeals to our senses and our curiosity (*Why are red envelopes considered lucky?*).

*Cropping images may help your readers focus on a detail.* © Michael Enright/www.menright.com

## Considering details in visual texts

Details are important in both written and visual texts. If you decide to use an image because of a particular detail, make sure your readers will notice what you want them to see. Crop out any unnecessary information — making sure, however, not to distort the message by doing so — and clarify what's important about the image in your text or with a caption. If you are taking a photo to illustrate a blog post on street food, for example, you will need to decide whether you should crop the image to focus on the food or whether your discussion calls for the photo to include more of the surroundings. The photo on the left above is the original; the one on the right, used in a blog about street food, is cropped to focus on the sandwich.

# 5c Using effective methods of development

Writers can choose from among several patterns for developing paragraphs. Often in an essay, you will combine patterns as needed to achieve your purpose.

## Narrative

People almost always respond to stories, which can be used effectively in almost all kinds of writing. A narrative paragraph uses the chronological elements of a story to develop a main idea. The following is one student's narrative paragraph that tells a personal story to support a point about the dangers of racing bicycles with flimsy alloy frames:

> People who have been exposed to the risk of dangerously designed bicycle frames have paid too high a price. I saw this danger myself in last year's Putney Race. An expensive graphite frame failed, and the rider was catapulted onto Vermont pavement at fifty miles per hour. The pack of riders behind him was so dense that other racers crashed into a tangled, sliding heap. The aftermath: four hospitalizations. I got off with some stitches, a bad

road rash, and severely pulled tendons. My Italian racing bike was pretzeled, and my racing was over for that summer. Others were not so lucky. An Olympic hopeful, Brian Stone of the Northstar team, woke up in a hospital bed to find that his cycling was over — and not just for that summer. His kneecap had been surgically removed. He couldn't even walk.

## Description

A descriptive paragraph uses specific details to create a clear impression. See how the following paragraph includes details to describe the appearance of the skyscraper and its effect on those who see it.

The Chrysler Building, completed in 1930, still attracts the eyes of tourists and New Yorkers alike with its shiny steel exterior. The Chrysler cars of the era are incorporated into the design: the eagle-head gargoyles on the upper vertices of the building are shaped like the automobiles' hood ornaments, and winged details imitate Chrysler radiator caps. At night, an elaborate lighting scheme spotlights the sleek, powerful eagles from below — turning them into striking silhouettes — and picks out each of the upper stories' famed triangular windows, arching up into the darkness like the rays of a stylized sun.

## Definition

Often you may need to write an entire paragraph in order to define a word or concept, as in the following example:

Economics is the study of how people choose among the alternatives available to them. It's the study of little choices ("Should I take the chocolate or the strawberry?") and big choices ("Should we require a reduction in energy consumption in order to protect the environment?"). It's the study of individual choices, choices by firms, and choices by governments. Life presents each of us with a wide range of alternative uses of our time and other resources; economists examine how we choose among those alternatives. —TIMOTHY TREGARTHEN, *Economics*

## Example

One of the most common ways of developing a paragraph is by illustrating a point with one or more examples.

The Indians made names for us children in their teasing way. Because our very busy mother kept my hair cut short, like my brothers', they called me Short Furred One, pointing to their hair and making the sign for short, the right hand with fingers pressed close together, held upward, back out, at the height intended. With me this was about two feet tall, the Indians laughing gently at my abashed face. I am told that I was given a pair of small moccasins that first time, to clear up my unhappiness at being picked out from the dusk behind the fire and my two unhappy shortcomings made conspicuous. —MARI SANDOZ, "The Go-Along Ones"

## Division and classification

Division breaks a single item into parts. Classification groups many separate items according to their similarities. A paragraph evaluating a history course might divide the course into several segments — textbooks, lectures, assignments — and examine each one in turn. A paragraph giving an overview of many history courses might classify the courses in a number of ways — by time periods, by geographic areas, by the kinds of assignments, or by some other principle.

DIVISION

We all listen to music according to our separate capacities. But, for the sake of analysis, the whole listening process may become clearer if we break it up into its component parts, so to speak. In a certain sense, we all listen to music on three separate planes. For lack of a better terminology, one might name these: (1) the sensuous plane, (2) the expressive plane, (3) the sheerly musical plane. The only advantage to be gained from mechanically splitting up the listening process into these hypothetical planes is the clearer view to be had of the way in which we listen. —AARON COPLAND, *What to Listen for in Music*

CLASSIFICATION

Two types of people are seduced by fad diets. Those who have always been overweight turn to them out of despair; they have tried everything, and yet nothing seems to work. A second group of people to succumb appear perfectly healthy but are baited by slogans such as "look good, feel good." These slogans prompt self-questioning and insecurity — do I really look good and feel good? — and as a direct result, many healthy people fall prey to fad diets. With both types of people, however, the problems surrounding such diets are numerous and dangerous. In fact, these diets provide neither intelligent nor effective answers to weight control.

## Comparison and contrast

When you compare two things, you look at their similarities; when you contrast two things, you focus on their differences. You can structure paragraphs that compare or contrast in two basic ways. One way is to use the block method, presenting all the information about one item and then all the information about the other item, as in the following paragraph:

**BLOCK METHOD**

> You could tell the veterans from the rookies by the way they were dressed. The knowledgeable ones had their heads covered by kerchiefs, so that if they were hired, tobacco dust wouldn't get in their hair; they had on clean dresses that by now were faded and shapeless, so that if they were hired they wouldn't get tobacco dust and grime on their best clothes. Those who were trying for the first time had their hair freshly done and wore attractive dresses; they wanted to make a good impression. But the dresses couldn't be seen at the distance that many were standing from the employment office, and they were crumpled in the crush.  —MARY MEBANE, "Summer Job"

Or you can alternate between the two items, focusing on particular characteristics of each in turn.

**ALTERNATING METHOD**

> Malcolm X emphasized the use of violence in his movement and employed the biblical principle of "an eye for an eye and a tooth for a tooth." Martin Luther King Jr., on the other hand, felt that blacks should use nonviolent civil disobedience and employed the theme of "turning the other cheek," which Malcolm X rejected as "beggarly" and "feeble." The philosophy of Malcolm X was one of revenge, and often it broke the unity of black Americans. More radical blacks supported him, while more conservative ones supported King. King thought that blacks should transcend their humanity. In contrast, Malcolm X thought they should embrace it and reserve their love for one another, regarding whites as "devils" and the "enemy." The distance between King's thinking and Malcolm X's was the distance between growing up in the seminary and growing up on the streets, between the American dream and the American reality.

### EXERCISE 5.2

Reread the paragraph on Malcolm X and Martin Luther King Jr. above. Rewrite the paragraph using block organization—the first part of the paragraph devoted to King, the second to Malcolm X. Write a brief analysis of the two paragraphs, explaining which one you think seems more coherent and easier to follow and why.

## Analogy

Analogies, comparisons that explain an unfamiliar thing in terms of a familiar one, can also help develop paragraphs.

> Since the advent of Hollywood editing, back in the earliest days of cinema, the goal of filmmakers has been for us to feel the movement

of the camera but not to be aware of it, to look past the construction of the media, to ignore the seams in the material. Just as an Olympic diver smiles and hides the effort as she catapults skyward and manages to pull off multiple flips while seemingly twisting in both directions, good storytelling — whether oral, in print, or visual — typically hides the construction and the hard work that go into making it. Both the medal-winning dives and the best stories are more intricate than they appear.

—STEPHEN APKON, *The Age of the Image: Redefining Literacy in a World of Screens*

## Cause and effect

You can often develop paragraphs by explaining the causes of something or the effects that something brings about. The following paragraph discusses the causes that led pediatrician Phil Offit to study science and become a physician:

To understand exactly why Offit became a scientist, you must go back more than half a century, to 1956. That was when doctors in Offit's hometown of Baltimore operated on one of his legs to correct a club foot, requiring him to spend three weeks recovering in a chronic care facility with 20 other children, all of whom had polio. Parents were allowed to visit just one hour a week, on Sundays. His father, a shirt salesman, came when he could. His mother, who was pregnant with his brother and hospitalized with appendicitis, was unable to visit at all. He was five years old. "It was a pretty lonely, isolating experience," Offit says. "But what was even worse was looking at these other children who were just horribly crippled and disfigured by polio." That memory, he says, was the first thing that drove him toward a career in pediatric infectious diseases.

—AMY WALLACE, "An Epidemic of Fear"

## Process

Paragraphs that explain a process often use the principle of time or chronology to order the stages in the process.

In July of 1877, Eadweard Muybridge photographed a horse in motion with a camera fast enough to capture clearly the split second when the horse's hooves were all off the ground — a moment never before caught on film. His next goal was to photograph a sequence of such rapid images. In June of 1878, he set up twelve cameras along a track, each connected to a tripwire. Then, as a crowd watched, a trotting horse raced down the track pulling a two-wheeled carriage. The carriage wheels tripped each camera in quick succession, snapping a dozen photographs. Muybridge developed the negatives and displayed them to an admiring public that same morning. His technical achievement helped to pave the way for the first motion pictures a decade later.

## Problem and solution

Another way to develop a paragraph is to open with a topic sentence that states a problem or asks a question about a problem and then to offer a solution or answers in the sentences that follow — a technique used in this paragraph from a review of Ted Nordhaus and Michael Shellenberger's book *Break Through: From the Death of Environmentalism to the Politics of Possibility*:

> Unfortunately, at the moment growth means burning more fossil fuel. . . . How can that fact be faced? How to have growth that Americans want, but without limits that they instinctively oppose, and still reduce carbon emissions? [Nordhaus and Shellenberger's] answer is: investments in new technology. Acknowledge that America "is great at imagining, experimenting, and inventing the future," and then start spending. They cite examples ranging from the nuclear weapons program to the invention of the Internet to show what government money can do, and argue that too many clean-energy advocates focus on caps instead.
>
> —BILL McKIBBEN, "Can Anyone Stop It?"

## Reiteration

Reiteration is a method of development you may recognize from political speeches or some styles of preaching. In this pattern, the writer states the main point of a paragraph and then restates it, hammering home the point and often building in intensity as well. In the following passage from her speech at the 2019 World Economic Forum, environmental activist Greta Thunberg, a teen, reiterates her ideas about the size of the climate change crisis and her desire for adults to act:

> We are now at a time in history where everyone with any insight of the climate crisis that threatens our civilisation — and the entire biosphere — must speak out in clear language, no matter how uncomfortable and unprofitable that may be. We must change almost everything in our current societies. The bigger your carbon footprint is, the bigger your moral duty. The bigger your platform, the bigger your responsibility. Adults keep saying: "We owe it to the young people to give them hope." But I don't want your hope. I don't want you to be hopeful. I want you to panic. I want you to feel the fear I feel every day. And then I want you to act. I

Activist Greta Thunberg writes and speaks often about climate change.
picture alliance/Getty Images

want you to act as you would in a crisis. I want you to act as if our house is on fire. Because it is.

> — GRETA THUNBERG, from her 2019 speech at the World Economic Forum in Davos, Switzerland

## Combining Patterns

Most paragraphs actually combine patterns of development. See how the writer below begins with a topic sentence and then divides the topic into two subtopics before developing the second subtopic through examples and cause and effect:

> Most American companies have basically two accounting systems. One system summarizes the overall financial state to inform stockholders, bankers, and other outsiders. That system is not of interest here. The other option, called the managerial or cost accounting system, exists for an entirely different reason. It measures in detail all of the particulars of transactions between departments, divisions, and key individuals in the organization, for the purpose of untangling the interdependencies between people. When, for example, two departments share one truck for deliveries, the cost accounting system charges each department for part of the cost of maintaining the truck and driver, so that at the end of the year, the performance of each department can be individually assessed, and the better department's manager can receive a larger raise. Of course, all of this information processing costs money, and furthermore may lead to argument between the departments over whether the costs charged to each are fair.
>
> — WILLIAM OUCHI, "Japanese and American Workers: Two Casts of Mind"

---

**QUICK HELP**

### Determining paragraph length

Though writers must keep their readers' expectations in mind, paragraph length is determined primarily by content and purpose. Paragraphs should develop an idea, create any desired effects (such as suspense or humor), and advance the larger piece of writing. Fulfilling these aims sometimes requires short paragraphs, other times long ones. For example, if you are writing a persuasive essay, you may put all your evidence into a long paragraph to create the impression of a solid, convincing argument. In a narrative about an exciting event, on the other hand, a series of short paragraphs may create suspense, keeping the reader rushing from one paragraph to the next.

Just as timing is crucial in telling a joke, the pause signaled by a new paragraph helps readers anticipate what is to follow or think about what they've just read.

**REASONS TO START A NEW PARAGRAPH**

- to turn to a new idea
- to emphasize a point or example
- to encourage readers to pause
- to take up a subtopic
- to change speakers (in dialogue)
- to start the conclusion

### EXERCISE 5.3

Take an assignment you have written recently, and study the ways you developed each paragraph. For one of the paragraphs, write a brief evaluation of its development. How would you expand or otherwise improve the development?

## 5d  Making paragraphs flow

A paragraph has coherence — that is, it "flows" — if its details fit together clearly in a way that readers can easily follow. When you arrange information in a particular order, you help readers move from one point to another. Regardless of your organization, however, be aware of other ways to achieve paragraph coherence.

### Organizing ideas

When you arrange information in a particular order, you help readers move from one point to another. There are a number of ways to organize details — you might use spatial, chronological, or associational order (4e) or one or more logical patterns, such as illustration, definition, or comparison and contrast (5c). Two other patterns commonly used in paragraphs are general to specific and specific to general.

Paragraphs organized in a general-to-specific pattern usually open with a topic sentence that presents a <u>general idea</u>. The topic sentence is then followed by specific points that support the generalization. In the following paragraph, the topic sentence presents a general idea about the Black Death, which is then backed up by specific examples:

**GENERAL TO SPECIFIC**

<u>A massive epidemic, the Black Death of the fourteenth century, brought loss of life in the tens of millions of people and catastrophic debilitation to commerce and agriculture across Eurasia and North Africa.</u> The bubonic plague seems to have initially irrupted into Chinese populations beginning in the 1320s. It spread in many parts of China until the 1350s with great loss of life. At the same time, it appears to have been carried into Mongolia and across the steppes into Crimea. Two Central Asian areas, one inhabited by the Nestorian Christians and the other by the Uzbek Muslims, were devastated by the plague before it struck in Europe, Southwest Asia, and Northwest Africa. Travel along Chinese and Central Asian trade routes facilitated the spread of this deadly disease.

—LANNY B. FIELDS, RUSSELL J. BARBER, AND CHERYL A. RIGGS, *The Global Past*

Paragraphs can also follow a specific-to-general organization, first providing a series of specific examples or details and then tying them together with a topic sentence that provides a conclusion. The following paragraph begins with specific details about two people's reactions to an event and ends with a topic sentence:

SPECIFIC TO GENERAL

I remember one afternoon as I was sitting on the steps of our monastery in Nepal. The monsoon storms had turned the courtyard into an expanse of muddy water and we had set out a path of bricks to serve as stepping-stones. A friend of mine came to the edge of the water, surveyed the scene with a look of disgust, and complained about every single brick as she made her way across. When she got to me, she rolled her eyes and said, "Yuck! What if I'd fallen into that filthy muck? Everything's so dirty in this country!" Since I knew her well, I prudently nodded, hoping to offer her some comfort through my mute sympathy. A few minutes later, Raphaèle, another friend of mine, came to the path through the swamp. "Hup, hup, hup!" she sang as she hopped, reaching dry land with the cry "What fun!" Her eyes sparkling with joy, she added: "The great thing about the monsoon is that there's no dust." Two people, two ways of looking at things; six billion human beings, six billion worlds.
                                                              —MATTHIEU RICARD, *Happiness*

## Repeating key words and phrases

Weaving in repeated key words and phrases — or pronouns pointing to them — not only links sentences but also alerts readers to the importance of those words or phrases in the larger piece of writing. Notice in the following example how the repetition of key words helps hold the paragraph together:

Over the centuries, shopping has changed in function as well as in style. Before the Industrial Revolution, most consumer goods were sold in open-air markets, customers who went into a shop were expected to buy something, and shoppers were always expected to bargain for the best possible price. In the nineteenth century, however, the department store changed the relationship between buyers and sellers. Instead of visiting several market stalls or small shops, customers could now buy a variety of merchandise under the same roof; instead of feeling expected to buy, they were welcome to browse; and instead of bargaining with merchants, they paid a fixed price for each item. All of these changes helped transform shopping from serious requirement to psychological recreation.

## Using parallelism

Parallel structures can help connect the sentences within a paragraph. As readers, we feel pulled along by the force of the parallel structures in the following example:

William Faulkner's "Barn Burning" tells the story of a young boy trapped in a no-win situation. If he betrays his father, he loses his family. If he betrays justice, he becomes a fugitive. In trying to free himself from his trap, he does both.

## Using transitions

Transitions are words such as *so, however,* and *thus* that signal relationships between sentences and paragraphs. Transitions help guide the reader from one idea to another. To understand how important transitions are in directing readers, try reading the following paragraph, from which all transitions have been removed.

### A PARAGRAPH WITH NO TRANSITIONS

In "The Fly," Katherine Mansfield tries to show us the real personality of the boss beneath his exterior. The fly helps her to portray this real self. The boss goes through a range of emotions and feelings. He expresses these feelings to a small but determined fly, whom the reader realizes he unconsciously relates to his son. The author basically splits up the story into three parts, with the boss's emotions and actions changing quite measurably. With old Woodifield, with himself, and with the fly, we see the boss's manipulativeness. Our understanding of him as a hard and cruel man grows.

If we work at it, we can figure out the relationship of these sentences to one another, for this paragraph is essentially unified by one major idea. But the lack of transitions results in an abrupt, choppy rhythm; the paragraph lurches from one detail to the next, dragging the confused reader behind. See how much easier the passage is to read and understand with transitions added.

### THE SAME PARAGRAPH WITH TRANSITIONS

In "The Fly," Katherine Mansfield tries to show us the real personality of the boss beneath his exterior. The fly in the story's title helps her to portray this real self. In the course of the story, the boss goes through a range of emotions. At the end, he finally expresses these feelings to a small but determined fly, whom the reader realizes he unconsciously relates to his son. To accomplish her goal, the author basically splits up the story into three parts, with the boss's emotions and actions changing measurably throughout. First with old Woodifield, then with himself, and finally with the fly, we see the boss's manipulativeness. With each part, our understanding of him as a hard and cruel man grows.

---

**QUICK HELP**

Making connections with transitions

Writers use transitions to show a variety of relationships between ideas:

- to add an idea (*also, in addition*)
- to illustrate a point (*for example*)
- to compare (*in the same way, likewise, similarly*)
- to contrast (*on the other hand*)
- to put ideas in sequence (*first, next, finally*)
- to counter an idea (*however, nevertheless*)
- to show a causal relationship (*due to, as a result*)

## Making connections with transitions, continued

Professor Laura Aull's research shows that expert academic writers use a wider range and variety of transitions than student writers and that the transitions are closely tied to their purpose. Experts are most likely to use transitional markers to show contrast, sequence, addition, comparison, and illustration. Look closely at the transitional words and phrases in your writing. Is their purpose clear and appropriate? Overusing causal transitions can make your writing seem to jump to conclusions too quickly, while overusing countering transitions can make your writing seem more aggressive than you intend. Take a tip from expert writers and take particular care with transitions that show cause and effect and countering.

## Commonly used transitions

### TO SIGNAL SEQUENCE AND TIME

after a while, afterward, again, and then, as long as, as soon as, at last, at that time, before, besides, earlier, finally, first . . . second . . . third, immediately, in the meantime, in the past, last, lately, later, meanwhile, next, now, presently, simultaneously, since, so far, soon, still, then, thereafter, until, when

### TO ADD IDEAS

again, also, furthermore, in the same way, likewise, moreover, similarly, too

### TO SHOW CONTRAST OR COUNTERARGUMENT

although, but, despite, even though, however, in contrast, indeed, in spite of, instead, nevertheless, nonetheless, on one hand . . . on the other hand, on the contrary, regardless, still, though, while, yet

### TO SIGNAL EXAMPLES AND ILLUSTRATIONS

for example, for instance, in fact, of course, specifically, such as, the following example, to illustrate

### TO SIGNAL CAUSE AND EFFECT

accordingly, as a result, because, consequently, due to, hence, so, then, therefore, thereupon, thus, to this end

### TO SIGNAL PLACE

above, adjacent to, below, beyond, closer to, elsewhere, far, farther on, here, near, nearby, opposite to, there, to the left, to the right

### TO SIGNAL SUMMARY, REPETITION, OR CONCLUSION

as a result, as has been noted, as I have said, as mentioned earlier, as we have seen, in any event, in conclusion, in other words, in short, on the whole, therefore, to summarize

## 5e Linking paragraphs together

The same methods you use to link sentences and create coherent paragraphs can also link paragraphs themselves so that a whole piece of writing flows smoothly. You should include some reference to the previous paragraph, either explicit or implied, in each paragraph after the introduction. As with sentences, you can create this link by repeating or paraphrasing key words and phrases and by using parallel structures and transitional words or phrases.

#### REPEATING KEY WORDS

In fact, human offspring remain <u>dependent on their parents</u> longer than the young of any other species.

Children are <u>dependent on their parents</u> or other adults not only for their physical survival but also for their initiation into the uniquely human knowledge that is collectively called culture. . . .

#### USING PARALLEL STRUCTURES

John F. Kennedy made an effort to assure non-Catholics that he would respect the separation of church and state, and most of them did not seem to hold the religion against him in deciding how to vote. Since that election, <u>the church to which a candidate belongs</u> has become less important in presidential politics.

<u>The region from which a candidate comes</u> remains an important factor. . . .

#### USING TRANSITIONAL WORDS OR PHRASES

While the American Indian, in the character of Tonto, was more positively portrayed in *The Lone Ranger*, such a portrayal was more the exception than the rule.

<u>Moreover</u>, despite this brief glimpse of an American Indian as an ever-loyal sidekick, Tonto was never accorded the same stature as the man with the white horse and silver bullets. . . .

### ◢ EXERCISE 5.4

Look at a recent draft and identify the ways your paragraphs are linked together. Identify each use of repetition, parallel structures, and transitional expressions, and then evaluate how effectively you have joined the paragraphs.

## 5f Writing opening and closing paragraphs

Some types of paragraphs deserve special attention. Opening and closing paragraphs are two such types.

## Developing opening paragraphs

Especially today when we are bombarded by texts twenty-four hours a day, even a good piece of writing may remain unread if it has a weak opening paragraph. To get and hold the attention of your intended audience, your introductory paragraph needs not only to announce your topic clearly but also to engage readers' interest and focus their attention on what is to follow. One common kind of opening paragraph follows a general-to-specific sequence, in which a writer opens with a general statement and then gets more and more specific, concluding with the thesis. The following paragraph illustrates such an opening:

> The human organism is adapted to function in face-to-face encounters. We know that face-to-face is the most effective way to pitch woo. . . . And face-to-face is obviously the best way to transact an intimate relationship long term. But while we know this, there's much more to face-to-face interaction than meets the naked eye. And it is of grave importance. We risk losing a great deal in any heavy shift of social traffic onto exclusively electronic media. —MARIAM THALOS, "Why I Am Not a Friend"

In this paragraph, the opening sentence clearly presents a general subject, and the last sentence presents the thesis, which the rest of the essay will develop.

**OTHER EFFECTIVE WAYS OF OPENING**

- with a quotation

> There is a bumper sticker that reads, "Too bad ignorance isn't painful." I like that. But ignorance is. We just seldom attribute the pain to it or even recognize it when we see it. —NIKKI GIOVANNI, "Racism 101"

- with an anecdote

> Social networking pioneer Howard Rheingold begins his digital journalism course each year with a participatory experiment. Shut off your cell phones, he tells his students. Shut your laptop. Now, shut your eyes. —CATHY DAVIDSON, *Now You See It*

- with a question

> Why are Americans terrified of using nuclear power as a source of energy?

- with a strong opinion

> I have not always loved Dr. King. In the sixties I could not understand his reaching beyond race to stand on principle. I could not understand, or support, his own example of "nonviolence." There was so much I didn't know. —JUNE JORDAN, *Some of Us Did Not Die*

## Developing concluding paragraphs

A good conclusion wraps up a piece of writing in a satisfying and memorable way. A common and effective strategy for concluding is to restate the central idea (but not word for word), perhaps specifying it in several sentences, and then ending with a much more general statement.

> Lastly, and perhaps greatest of all, there was the ability, at the end, to turn quickly from war to peace once the fighting was over. Out of the way these two men [Generals Grant and Lee] behaved at Appomattox came the possibility of a peace of reconciliation. It was a possibility not wholly realized, in the years to come, but which did, in the end, help the two sections to become one nation again . . . after a war whose bitterness might have seemed to make such a reunion wholly impossible. No part of either man's life became him more than the part he played in this brief meeting in the McLean house at Appomattox. Their behavior there put all succeeding generations of Americans in their debt. Two great Americans, Grant and Lee — very different, yet under everything very much alike. Their encounter at Appomattox was one of the great moments of American history.
>
> —BRUCE CATTON, "Grant and Lee: A Study in Contrasts"

**OTHER EFFECTIVE WAYS OF CONCLUDING**

- with a quotation

> Despite the celebrity that accrued to her and the air of awesomeness with which she was surrounded in her later years, Miss Keller retained an unaffected personality, certain that her optimistic attitude toward life was justified. "I believe that all through these dark and silent years God has been using my life for a purpose I do not know," she said. "But one day I shall understand and then I will be satisfied."
>
> —ALDEN WHITMAN, "Helen Keller, June 1, 1880–June 1, 1968"

- with a question

> In the process of learning how to read, every literate person absorbs, at a young age, a broad and potentially confusing range of cultural, ethical, and social lessons. As much as gender, race, religion, class, or national identity, one's literacy defines one's place in society. But like these other givens, literacy need not mean only one thing. Just as one can be male, female, or transgendered, one race or multiracial, a member of more than one religion or ethnic identity, so also one can read in different ways. Why assume that literacy is the simple answer to a complex question?
>
> —WYN KELLEY AND HENRY JENKINS, *Reading in a Participatory Culture*

- with a vivid image

> At the time the Web was born, in the early 1990s, a popular trope was that a new generation of teenagers, reared in the conservative Reagan years, had turned out to be exceptionally bland. The members of "Generation X" were characterized as blank and inert. The anthropologist Steve Barnett saw in them the phenomenon of pattern exhaustion, in which a culture runs out of variations in their pottery and becomes less creative. A common rationalization in the fledgling world of digital culture back then was that we were entering a transitional lull before a creative storm — or were already in the eye of one. But we were not passing through a momentary calm. We had, rather, entered a persistent somnolence, and I have come to believe that we will escape it only when we kill the hive.
>
> —JARON LANIER, *You Are Not a Gadget*

- with a call for action

> To save ourselves, we don't need a new technology; we just need the political will to face up to our problems of population and the environment.　　　—JARED DIAMOND, "The Ends of the World as We Know Them"

- with a warning

> Because propaganda is so effective, it is important to track it down and understand how it is used. We may eventually agree with what the propagandist says because all propaganda isn't necessarily bad. . . . Even so, we must be aware that propaganda is being used. Otherwise, we will have consented to handing over our independence, our decision-making ability, and our brains.
>
> —ANN McCLINTOCK, "Propaganda Techniques in Today's Advertising"

## THINKING CRITICALLY ABOUT PARAGRAPHS

Examine two or three paragraphs you have written, using the guidelines in 5a to evaluate how unified, coherent, and developed each one is. Identify the topic of each paragraph, the topic sentence if one is stated explicitly, and all patterns of development and transitions. Decide whether or not each paragraph successfully guides your readers, and explain how you came to that conclusion. Then choose the paragraph you like best and revise it.

# Reviewing, Revising, and Editing

The Roman poet Horace once advised aspiring writers to get distance from their work by putting it away for nine years. Although impractical for college writers, to say the very least, Horace's advice holds some truth: putting your draft aside even for a short time can give you more objectivity about your writing.

Make time to review your work (by yourself or with others) and to revise, edit, and proofread. Reviewing calls for reading your draft with a critical eye and asking others to look over your work. Revising involves reworking your draft on the basis of the review, making sure the draft is clear, effective, complete, and well organized. Editing involves attending to sentence-level details.

## 6a Reviewing your writing

After giving yourself and your draft a rest, review the draft by rereading it carefully for meaning, recalling your purpose and audience, reconsidering your stance, and evaluating your organization and use of visuals.

### Reading for meaning

When you pick up the draft again, don't sweat the small stuff. Instead, concentrate on your message and on whether you have expressed it clearly. Note any places where the meaning seems unclear.

### Reflecting on your purpose

If you responded to an assignment, make sure that you have produced what was asked for. If you set out to prove something, have you succeeded? If you intended to propose a solution to a problem, have you set forth a well-supported solution rather than just an analysis of the problem?

### Considering your audience

How appropriately do you address your audience members, given their experiences and expectations? Will you catch their interest, and will they be able to follow your discussion? Is your language formal or informal enough for your readers? Have you defined any terms they may not know? What objections might they raise?

When Emily Lesk reread her draft (see 4g), she thought she sounded a little bit like a know-it-all, especially in the opening of her essay. After reflection, she decided that her tone was inappropriate, perhaps because she was trying too hard to get her audience's attention, and that she needed to work on tone in her revision.

## Thinking about your stance

Ask yourself one central question: where are you coming from in this draft? Consider whether your stance appropriately matches the stance you started out with or whether your stance has legitimately evolved.

## Checking your organization

One way to check the organization of your draft is to outline it. After numbering the paragraphs, read through each one, jotting down its main idea. Does the first sentence of each new paragraph relate clearly to the one that came before it? Do the main ideas clearly relate to the thesis? Can you identify any confusing leaps from point to point? Have you left out any important points? Do you have strong transitions from idea to idea?

## Thinking about genre and media

You decided to write in a particular genre, so think again about why you made that choice. Is writing in this genre the best way to achieve your purpose and reach your audience? Does the draft fulfill the requirements of the genre? Would any content in your draft be more effective presented in another genre — for example, as a print handout instead of a presentation slide? Should you consider "translating" your work into another medium? (See Chapters 23 and 24.) Look closely at any images, audio, and video you have chosen to use. How do they contribute to your draft? Make sure that all visuals and media files are labeled with captions and sources, and remember to refer to visuals and media and to comment on their significance to the rest of your text.

| LANGUAGE, CULTURE, AND CONTEXT | ASKING AN EXPERIENCED WRITER TO REVIEW YOUR DRAFT |
|---|---|

One good way to make sure that your writing is easy to follow is to have someone else read it. You might ask someone who is experienced in the kind of writing you are working on to read over your draft and to point out language or patterns that are unclear or ineffective.

**EXERCISE 6.1**

Take twenty to thirty minutes to look critically at a draft you have written recently. Reread it carefully, check to see how well the purpose is accomplished, and consider how appropriate the draft is for the audience. Then write a revision plan—a paragraph about how you would go about revising the draft.

 **EXERCISE 6.2**

To prepare for a peer review, write a description of your purpose, rhetorical stance, and audience for your reviewer(s) to consider. For example, student Emily Lesk might write, *I want to figure out why Coca-Cola seems so American and how the company achieves this effect. My audience is primarily college students like me, learning to analyze their own cultures. I want to sound knowledgeable, and I want this essay to be fun and interesting to read.* This type of summary statement can help focus your reviewers and help them keep your goals in mind as they give you feedback.

## 6b Getting the most from peer review

In addition to your own critical appraisal and that of your instructor (6d), you will probably want to get responses to your draft from friends, classmates, or colleagues. In a writing course, you may be part of a peer-review group in which you will respond to each other's work throughout the term.

### Understanding the role of peer reviewers

One of the main goals of a peer reviewer is to help a writer see a draft differently. When you review a draft, you want to show the writer what does and doesn't work about particular aspects of the draft — and where you are still curious or confused. Visually marking up the draft can help the writer absorb at a glance the revisions you suggest.

Peer review is important and helpful for several reasons. First, giving good, solid, concrete advice provides practice in critical thinking and also can get you started thinking in new ways about revising your own work. Second, peer review gives you a chance to work alongside writers who are different from you — they may be better at some things or worse at others. In any case, you can learn a lot from paying close attention to their writing. Finally, research shows that strong peer reviewing helps to improve the writing of the reviewer. It's a good idea, then, to tell writers what you learned from studying their drafts: as you articulate what you have learned, you'll be more likely to remember these lessons.

Different stages in the writing process call for a peer reviewer to have different strategies and focus areas.

| Early-stage drafts | Intermediate-stage drafts | Late-stage or final drafts |
|---|---|---|
| O Offer direction, options | O Say which parts of the draft are clear | O Help with first and last impressions |
| O Help the writer think of ways to expand ideas | O Say which parts of the draft confuse readers | O Help with sentence structure |
| O Ask questions | O Identify which claims lack sufficient evidence | O Suggest stronger word choice or a different tone |
| O Offer examples | O Tell the writer if their approach reaches or misses the target audience | O Say how the format can be improved |
| O Help the writer imagine the final draft | O Praise and offer constructive criticism | |
| O Don't focus on grammar | | |

## Marking up drafts

If you are reviewing a print copy of a draft, make sure that your handwriting is clear and legible. If you underline or use highlighting, explain what you mean by it. And don't forget to point out where the draft is effective or especially good.

It's more likely that you'll be responding to a digital draft. If so, save the document under a name you will recognize and then use Track Changes to add comments and suggestions. If you are using a file-sharing platform such as Google Docs, you can work alongside the writer and other reviewers. In either case, insert a comment to explain each suggestion or piece of advice you give. If your peer has impaired vision, you can offer audio comments. Your goal is to offer as much helpful advice as possible and for it to be fully accessible to the writer.

As you prepare a peer response, think about how you would react to the same markup comments in your own draft. Avoid an overwhelming number of comments or changes, for example, and don't highlight too extensively. And remember that your job is to point out the problems and to make suggestions about how to address them. It's a good idea, too, to aim for a balance between positive comments and criticism. If you think the author has stated something particularly well, say why you like it. If you have trouble understanding an idea, comment on what you think may be causing the problem. What follows are several examples of ways to frame effective comments in a peer response:

| Compliments | Constructive Criticism |
|---|---|
| • I'd never thought of it that way. Really smart insight.<br>• Your strongest evidence is _____.<br>• You got my attention here by _____.<br>• This example is great because _____.<br>• I like the way you use _____ to tie all these ideas together.<br>• I like this sentence because _____.<br>• I think this approach and your tone are perfect for the audience because _____. | • Here I expected _____ instead of _____.<br>• I think you need more evidence to support your claim that _____.<br>• You might consider adding _____.<br>• What about _____? There are other perspectives on this topic.<br>• I think you need to say this sooner.<br>• I had to read this sentence twice to get what you mean. Simplify it.<br>• Your tone shifts here. Try to sound more _____. |

Finally, consider writing a brief note or letter to the writer of the draft, summing up your overall response, noting the most important changes you suggest, and giving encouragement.

LANGUAGE, CULTURE, AND CONTEXT | **UNDERSTANDING PEER REVIEW**

If you are not used to giving or receiving criticisms directly, you may be uneasy with a classmate's challenges to your work. However, constructive criticism (saying how you might improve a draft) is appropriate to peer review. Your peers will expect you to offer your questions, suggestions, and insights.

**QUICK HELP**

Guidelines for peer review

The following questions may help you to respond to a peer's draft. As a way to focus your response, choose three to five sets of questions from below:

• **Initial thoughts.** What are the main strengths and weaknesses of the draft? What might confuse readers? What is the most important thing the writer says in the draft?

• **Assignment.** Does the draft carry out the assignment?

• **Title and introduction.** Do the title and introduction tell what the draft is about and create interest? How else might the draft begin?

Guidelines for peer review, continued

- **Thesis and purpose.** Paraphrase the thesis: *In this paper, the writer will . . .* Does the draft fulfill that promise?
- **Audience.** How does the draft interest and appeal to its audience?
- **Rhetorical stance.** Where does the writer stand? What words indicate the stance?
- **Supporting points.** List the main points and review them one by one. How well does each point support the thesis? Do any need more explanation? Do any seem confusing or boring?
- **Visuals, media, and design.** Do visuals, if any, add to the key points? Do media files play properly and serve their intended purpose? Is the design clear and effective?
- **Organization and flow.** Is the writing easy to follow? How effective are transitions between sentences and between paragraphs?
- **Paragraphs or sections.** Which paragraphs or sections are most clear and interesting? Which need further development, and how might they be improved?
- **Sentences.** Are any sentences particularly effective and memorable? Are any sentences weak—confusing, awkward, or uninspired? Are the sentences varied in length and structure? Are the sentence openings varied? **(Chapter 40)**
- **Words.** Which words draw vivid pictures or provoke a strong response? Which words are weak, vague, or unclear? Do any words need to be defined? Are the verbs active and vivid? (See Chapter 41.) Are any words potentially offensive?
- **Tone.** What dominant impression does the draft create—serious, humorous, persuasive, impartial and fair, or something else? Where, specifically, does the writer's attitude come through most clearly? Is the tone appropriate to the topic and the audience? Is it consistent throughout (6f)?
- **Conclusion.** Does the draft conclude memorably? Is there another way it might end?

## Reviews of Emily Lesk's draft

On the following pages are the first paragraphs of Emily Lesk's draft, as reviewed by two students, Beatrice Kim and Nastassia Lopez. Beatrice and Nastassia reviewed the draft separately and combined their comments on the draft they returned to Emily. As this review shows, Nastassia and Bea agreed on some of the major problems — and good points — in Emily's draft. Their comments on the draft, however, revealed some different responses. You, too, will find that different readers do not always agree on what is effective or ineffective. In addition, you may find that you simply do not agree with their advice. In examining responses to your writing, you can often proceed efficiently by looking first for areas of agreement (*everyone was confused by this sentence — I'd better revise it*) or strong disagreement (*one person said my conclusion was "perfect," and someone else said it "didn't conclude" — better look carefully at that paragraph again*).

## All-Powerful Coke

I don't drink Coke. Call me picky for disliking the soda's saccharine aftertaste. Call me cheap for choosing a water fountain over a twelve-ounce aluminum can that costs nearly two dollars from a vending machine but only pennies to produce. Even call me unpatriotic for rejecting the potable god that over the last century has come to represent all the enjoyment and ease to be found in our American way of life. But don't call me a hypocrite when I admit that I still identify with Coke and the Coca-Cola culture.

I have a favorite T-shirt that says "Drink Coca-Cola Classic" in Hebrew. It's Israel's standard tourist fare, like little nested dolls in Russia or painted horses in Scandinavia, and before setting foot in the Promised Land three years ago, I knew where I could find one. The T-shirt shop in the central block of a Jerusalem shopping center did offer other shirt designs ("Maccabee Beer" was a favorite), but that Coca-Cola shirt was what drew in most of the dollar-carrying tourists. I waited almost twenty minutes for mine, and I watched nearly everyone ahead of me say "the Coke shirt" (and "thanks" in Hebrew).

At the time, I never asked why I wanted the shirt. I do know, though, that the reason I wear it often, despite a hole in the right sleeve, has to do with its power as a conversation piece. Few people notice it without asking something like, "Does that say Coke?" I usually smile and nod. They mumble a compliment and we go our separate ways. But rarely does anyone want to know what language the world's most famous logo is written in. And why should they? Perhaps because Coca-Cola is a cultural icon that shapes American identity.

Throughout the company's history, marketing strategies have centered on putting Coca-Cola in scenes of the happy, carefree American life we never stop striving for. What 1950s teenage girl wouldn't long to see herself in the soda shop pictured in a Coca-Cola ad appearing in a 1958 issue of *Seventeen* magazine? A clean-cut, handsome man flirts with a pair of smiling girls as

---

**Comment (NL):** I'm not sure the title says enough about your argument.

**Comment (NL):** The first sentence is a good attention-getter.

**Comment (BK):** The beginning seems kind of abrupt.

**Comment (BK):** What does this mean? Will other readers know?

**Comment (NL):** The style of repeating "call me" is good, but I'm not sure the first three have much to do with the rest of the essay.

**Comment (NL):** Do you need these details? Will any of this be important later?

**Comment (NL):** One of what? A doll or a horse?

**Comment (BK):** Saying it in Hebrew would be cool here.

**Comment (NL):** This transition works really well. I wasn't sure where this was going, but here you are starting to clue the reader in.

**Comment (NL):** Good detail! Lots of people can relate to a "conversation piece" shirt.

**Comment (NL):** Good question! But I don't think the next sentence really answers it.

**Comment (BK):** Is this the thesis? It kind of comes out of nowhere.

**Comment (BK):** OK, here I am beginning to understand where your argument is going.

**Comment (NL):** Maybe this is a little too broad?

they laugh and drink Coca-Colas. And any girls who couldn't
put themselves in that perfect, happy scene could at least
buy a Coke for consolation. The malt shop — complete with
a soda jerk in a white jacket and paper hat — is a theme
that, even today, remains a symbol of Americana.

> **Comment (BK):** *Any girls? Really?*

 **EXERCISE 6.3**

Use the Quick Help guidelines in section 6b to analyze your own draft. Write notes
to yourself or make a revision plan.

## 6c Deciding which peer responses are most helpful

Remember that your reviewers should be acting as coaches, not judges, and
that their job is to help you improve your essay as much as possible. Listen to
and read their comments carefully. If you don't understand a particular suggestion, ask for clarification, ask for examples, or ask to have a conversation about
the draft. Remember, too, that reviewers are commenting on your *writing*, not
on you, so be open and responsive to what they recommend.

But you are the final authority on your essay, after all; you will decide which
suggestions to follow and which to disregard. Keep your purpose, audience,
and writing goals in mind as you review each suggestion from a peer. Also keep
the requirements of the assignment in mind. Sometimes reviewers make suggestions out of enthusiasm for the topic or the draft, but the suggestions could
possibly be beyond the scope of the assignment.

## 6d Learning from instructor comments

Instructor comments on your writing can help you identify mistakes, particularly ones that you make repeatedly, and can point you toward issues that prevent your writing from being as effective as it could be. Whether or not you
will have an opportunity to revise a particular piece of writing, you should look
closely at any comments your instructor provides and, if possible, schedule an
appointment to talk over those comments.

In responding to student writing, however, instructors still sometimes use
phrases or comments that are a kind of shorthand — comments that are perfectly
clear to the instructor but may be less clear to the students reading them. The
instructor comments in the following chart, gathered from over one thousand
first-year student essays, are among those you may find most puzzling. If your
essay includes a puzzling comment that is not listed here, be sure to ask your
instructor what the comment means and how you can address the problem.

| Instructor Comment | Actions to Take in Response |
|---|---|
| *thesis not clear* | Make sure that you have a main point, and state it directly. The rest of the paper will need to support the main point, too—this problem cannot be corrected by adding a sentence or two. (4c) |
| *trying to do too much*<br>*covers too much ground* | Focus your main point more narrowly (4b) so that you can explain your topic fully in a project of the assigned length. You may need to cut back on some material and then provide evidence and details to expand what remains. |
| *hard to follow*<br>*not logical*<br>*incoherent*<br>*jumps around*<br>*parts not connected*<br>*transition* | If overall organization is unclear, try mapping or outlining and rearranging your work. (4e) See if transitions and signals or additional explanation will solve the problem. |
| *too general*<br>*vague* | Use concrete language and details, and make sure that you have something specific and interesting to say. (Chapters 37, 38, and 41) If not, reconsider your topic. |
| *underdeveloped*<br>*thin*<br>*sparse* | Add examples and details, and be as specific as possible. You may need to do more research. (Chapters 12–14) |
| *what about the opposition?*<br>*one-sided* | Add information on why some people disagree with you, and represent their views fairly and completely before you refute them. Recognize that reasonable people may hold views that differ from yours. (11i) |
| *repetitive*<br>*you've already said this* | Revise any parts of your writing that repeat an argument or point; avoid using the same evidence over and over. |
| *awk*<br>*awkward* | Ask a peer or your instructor for suggestions about revising awkward sentences. |

| Instructor Comment | Actions to Take in Response |
|---|---|
| *syntax* <br> *awkward syntax* <br> *convoluted* | Read the sentence aloud to identify the problem; revise or replace the sentence. |
| *unclear* | Find another way to explain what you mean; add any background information or examples that your audience may need to follow your reasoning. |
| *tone too conversational* <br> *not an academic voice* <br> *too informal* | Consider your audience and genre, and revise material that may suggest that you are not serious about the topic, audience, or assignment. (6f) |
| *pompous* <br> *stilted* <br> *stiff* | Make sure you understand the connotations of the words that you use. Revise material that adds nothing to your meaning, no matter how impressive it sounds. (37a and b) |
| *set up quotation* <br> *integrate quotation* | Read the sentence containing the quotation aloud; revise it if it does not make sense as a sentence. Introduce every quotation with information about the source. Explain each quotation's importance to your work. (15b) |
| *your words?* <br> *source?* <br> *cite* | Mark all quotations clearly. Cite paraphrases and summaries of others' ideas. Give credit for help from others, and remember that you are responsible for your own work. (Chapters 15 and 16) |

## 6e Revising globally

Approach comments from peer reviewers or from your instructor in several stages. First, read straight through the comments. Take a few minutes to digest the feedback and get some distance from your work. Then make a revision plan — as elaborate or as simple as you want — that prioritizes the changes needed in your next draft.

If you have comments from more than one reviewer, you may want to begin by making two lists: (1) areas in which reviewers agree on needed changes, and (2) areas in which they disagree. You then have to choose which advice to take and which to ignore from both lists. Next, rank the suggestions you've chosen to address.

Focus on comments about your purpose, audience, stance, thesis, and support. Leave any changes to sentences, words, punctuation, and format for later in the process; your revision of bigger-picture issues comes first.

Be prepared to revise heavily, if necessary; if comments suggest that your thesis isn't working, for example, you may need to change the thesis or the entire direction of your text. Heavy revision is not a sign that there's something wrong with your writing; on the contrary, major revision is a common feature of serious, goal-oriented writing.

Once you are satisfied that the revisions adequately address your major concerns, make corrections to sentences, words, and punctuation.

## Reviewing your thesis statement

Make sure that your thesis states the topic clearly and comments on what is particularly significant about the topic (4c). In addition, ask yourself whether the thesis statement is narrowed and focused enough to be thoroughly supported. If not, take time now to refine or limit your thesis further. When you revise your thesis, remember also to revise the rest of the draft accordingly.

## Reviewing your support

Make sure that each paragraph relates to or supports the thesis statement and that each paragraph has sufficient detail to support the point it is making. Eliminate unnecessary material and identify sections that need further details or examples. Student writer Emily Lesk found, for example, that an entire paragraph in her draft did nothing to support her thesis, so she deleted it during revision.

## Reviewing your organization

Should any sections or paragraphs be moved to clarify your point or support your thesis statement more logically? Are there any paragraphs or parts of paragraphs that don't fit with the essay now or that are unnecessary? Have you left out any important points? Look for confusing leaps or gaps, and identify places where transitions would make the writing easier to follow.

## Writing an engaging title

A good title gives readers information, draws them into the piece of writing, and may indicate the writer's view of the topic. The title of Emily Lesk's draft, "All-Powerful Coke," did not provide the link Emily wanted to establish between Coca-Cola and American identity. During the review process, she titled her new draft "Red, White, and Everywhere." This title piques readers' curiosity and suggests that the familiar "red, white, and blue" would be linked to something that is everywhere — in this case, Coca-Cola.

## Writing an effective introduction

A good introduction accomplishes two important tasks: first, it attracts readers' interest, and, second, it presents the topic and makes some comment on it. It contains, in other words, a strong lead or hook and often an explicit thesis as well. Many introductions open with a general statement about the topic and then go into more detail, leading up to a specific thesis. You can also begin effectively with a vivid statement of a problem that led to the thesis or with an intriguing quotation, an anecdote, a question, or a strong opinion (see 5f).

In some cases, especially if you begin with a quotation or an anecdote, the introduction consists of two or three paragraphs: the first provides the hook, while the next paragraph or two explain the significance of the hook. Emily Lesk used this pattern in her introduction. Her first paragraph begins with a strong lead or hook, followed by a two-paragraph narrative anecdote about a trip to Israel that links Coca-Cola advertising and Americans' sense of identifying with the product. After considering the responses of her peers and analyzing her opening, however, Emily decided that the introduction took too long to get to the point and didn't lead to a clear thesis. She decided to shorten the introduction and make her thesis more detailed and explicit.

## Writing an effective conclusion

You want your conclusion to leave readers satisfied that a full and fair discussion has taken place and perhaps fired up to take some action. Many conclusions begin by restating or echoing the thesis and summing up its significance. You may also use a provocative question or quotation, a vivid image, or a warning to conclude effectively. Because readers notice beginnings and endings more than other parts of a piece of writing, pay special attention to how you introduce and conclude your work (see 5f).

## Reviewing visuals, media, and design

As you check what you've written about your topic, you also need to take a close look at the way your text looks and works. Do your visuals, audio, and video (if any) help you make your points? How can you make this content more effective? Do you use design effectively for your genre and medium? Is your text readable and inviting?

Before you produce a copy for final proofreading, reconsider one last time the format and the "look" you want your text to have. This is one last opportunity to think carefully about the visual appearance of your final draft. For more on document design, see Chapter 22. For more on the design conventions of different disciplines, see Chapters 18 (MLA), 19 (APA), 20 (*Chicago*), or 21 (CSE).

---

**TALKING THE TALK | REVISION**

"I thought I had revised my assignment, but my instructor said I'd just corrected the typos." It's always a good idea to clarify what revision means with a particular instructor. Generally, though, when a writing instructor asks for a revision, minor corrections will not be enough. Plan to review your entire draft, and be prepared to make major changes if necessary. Look for sentence-level errors and typos later, during the editing stage, since these may disappear or change as you revise.

---

*Emily Lesk's visuals and media*

Emily Lesk originally planned to include an early Coca-Cola ad or the original Coca-Cola Santa Claus in her draft, and in fact, she did so. But then she wanted to post her essay on a class website that was open to the public, which meant that she would have to obtain permission to use those images. She tried to contact the copyright holder but had quite a bit of trouble connecting, and her time was running out. As a result, she looked for other images. Her peer reviewers had asked if she could include a photo of her T-shirt, so she took their advice and included that photo in her draft. She also decided to include links to some of her web sources in the version she posted online.

## 6f Editing sentences, words, and tone

Once you have revised a draft for content and organization, look closely at your sentences and words. Turning a "blah" sentence into a memorable one (see Chapter 41) — or finding exactly the right word to express a thought — can result in writing that is really worth reading. As with life, variety is the spice of sentences. You can add variety to your sentences by looking closely at their length, structure, and opening patterns.

### Reviewing sentence length

Too many short sentences, especially one following another, can sound like a series of blasts on a car horn, whereas a steady stream of long sentences may tire or confuse readers. Most writers aim for some variety in the length of their sentences (see Chapter 40).

Emily Lesk found that all the sentences in one paragraph were fairly long:

> In other words, Coca-Cola has hammered itself into our perceptions — both conscious and subconscious — of an American cultural identity by equating itself with media that define American culture. When the omnipresent general magazine that marked the earlier part of the century fell by the wayside under television's power, Coke was there from the beginning. In its 1996 recap of the previous fifty years in industry history, the publication

*Beverage Industry* cites Coca-Cola as a frontrunner in the very first form of television advertising: sponsorship of entire programs such as, in the case of Coke, *The Bob Dixon Show* and *The Adventures of Kit Carson*. Just as today we associate sports stadiums with their corporate sponsors, viewers of early television programs will forever equate them with Coke.

## Reviewing sentence structure

Using only simple sentences can make your writing sound choppy, but overusing compound sentences can result in a singsong rhythm, and strings of long complex sentences may sound — well, overly complex. Try to vary your sentence structure (see Chapter 40).

In an early revision of her draft, Emily decided to <u>shorten the second sentence</u>, thereby inserting a short, easy-to-read sentence between two long sentences:

> In other words, Coca-Cola has hammered itself into our perceptions — both conscious and subconscious — of an American cultural identity by equating itself with media that define American culture. <u>As the print magazine gave way to television, Coke was there.</u> In its 1996 recap of the previous fifty years in industry history, the publication *Beverage Industry* cites Coca-Cola as a frontrunner in the very first form of television advertising: sponsorship of entire programs such as, in the case of Coke, *The Bob Dixon Show* and *The Adventures of Kit Carson*. Just as we now associate sports stadiums with their corporate sponsors, viewers of early television programs will forever equate them with Coke.

## Reviewing sentence openings

Most sentences in English follow subject-predicate order and hence open with the subject of an independent clause, as does the sentence you are now reading. But opening sentence after sentence this way results in a jerky, abrupt, or choppy rhythm. You can vary sentence openings by beginning with a dependent clause, a phrase, an adverb, a conjunctive adverb, or a coordinating conjunction (see Chapter 40).

Emily Lesk's second paragraph tells the story of how she got her Coke T-shirt in Israel. Before she revised her draft, every sentence in this paragraph opened with the subject: *I have a favorite T-shirt, It's Israel's standard tourist fare, I waited. . . .* In her revision, Emily deleted some examples and <u>varied her sentence openings</u> for a dramatic and easy-to-read paragraph:

> <u>Even before</u> setting foot in Israel three years ago, I knew exactly where I could find the Coke T-shirt. The tiny shop in the central block of Jerusalem's

Ben Yehuda Street did offer other designs, but the one with a bright white "Drink Coca-Cola Classic" written in Hebrew cursive across the chest was what drew in most of the dollar-carrying tourists. <u>While waiting</u> almost twenty minutes for my shirt, I watched nearly every customer ahead of me ask for "the Coke shirt, todah rabah [thank you very much]."

## Recasting sentences beginning with *it* and *there*

As you go over the opening sentences of your draft, look especially at those beginning with *it* or *there*. Sometimes these words can create a special emphasis, as in *It was a dark and stormy night*. But they can also appear too often. Another, more subtle problem with these openings is that they may be used to avoid taking responsibility for a statement. The following sentence can be improved by editing:

▶ ~~It is necessary to~~ raise student fees.
  The university must

## Reviewing tone

Tone refers to the attitude a writer's language conveys toward the topic and the audience. In examining the tone of your draft, think about the topic, your own attitude toward it, and that of your intended audience. Does your language create the tone you want to achieve (humorous, serious, impassioned, and so on), and is that tone appropriate, given your audience and topic?

Although Emily Lesk's peer reviewers liked the overall tone of her draft, one of them found her opening sentence abrupt and slightly off-putting. To make her tone friendlier, she decided to preface *I don't drink Coke* with another clause, resulting in *America, I have a confession to make: I don't drink Coke*. She also shortened her first paragraph considerably, in part to eliminate the "know-it-all" attitude she herself had detected.

## Examining word choice

Word choice — or diction — offers writers an opportunity to put their personal stamp on a piece of writing. Becoming aware of the kinds of words you use should help you get the most mileage out of each word. Check for connotations, or associations, of words and make sure you consider how any use of slang, jargon, or emotional language may affect your audience. (See Chapter 37.)

In addition, consider the following questions:

- Do you use mostly abstract and general nouns rather than concrete and specific ones?

- Are there too many nouns in relation to the number of verbs? In the sentence *The effect of the overuse of nouns in writing is the placing of too much strain on the inadequate number of verbs and the resulting prevention of movement of the thought,* the verb *is* carries the entire weight of all those nouns. The result: a heavy, deadly boring sentence. Why not say this instead: *Overusing nouns places a big strain on the verbs and slows down the prose.*

- How many verbs are forms of *be* — *be, am, is, are, was, were, being, been*? If *be* verbs account for more than about a third of your total verbs, you are probably overusing them and producing weak prose.

- Are most of your verbs active rather than passive? Although the passive voice has many uses (51g), your writing will generally be stronger and more energetic if you use active verbs.

- Are your words appropriate? Check to make sure they are not too fancy or too casual for your audience and purpose.

Emily Lesk made a number of changes in word choice. She decided to change *Promised Land* to *Israel* since some of her readers might not regard these two as the same. She also made her diction more lively, changing *from Fords to Tylenol* to *from Allstate to Ziploc bags* to take advantage of the A to Z reference.

### EXERCISE 6.4

Find a paragraph in your own writing that lacks variety in sentence length, sentence openings, or sentence structure. Then write a revised version.

## Proofreading the final draft

Take time for one last, careful proofreading, which means reading to correct any errors or other inconsistencies in spelling and punctuation. To proofread most effectively, read through the copy aloud, making sure that you've used punctuation marks correctly and consistently, that all sentences are complete, unless you are using a fragment or run-on for special effect, and that no words are missing. Then go through the copy again, this time reading backward so that you can focus on each word and its spelling.

### A student's revised draft

You have already seen and read about a number of the revisions student writer Emily Lesk made to her draft. On the following pages, you will see the edited and proofread version she turned in to her instructor. If you compare this final draft with her first one (4g), you will notice a number of additional changes she made in editing and proofreading.

**STUDENT WRITER**
Emily Lesk

Emily Lesk
Professor Arraéz
Electric Rhetoric
November 15, 2018

### Red, White, and Everywhere

America, I have a confession to make: I don't drink Coke. But don't call me a hypocrite just because I am still the proud owner of a bright red shirt that advertises it. Just call me an American.

Even before setting foot in Israel three years ago, I knew exactly where I could find the Coke T-shirt. The tiny shop in the central block of Jerusalem's Ben Yehuda Street did offer other designs, but the one with a bright white "Drink Coca-Cola Classic" written in Hebrew cursive across the chest was what drew in most of the dollar-carrying tourists. While waiting almost twenty minutes for my shirt (depicted in fig. 1), I watched nearly every customer ahead of me ask for "the Coke shirt, *todah rabah* [thank you very much]."

At the time, I never thought it strange that I wanted one, too. After having absorbed sixteen years of Coca-Cola propaganda through everything from NBC's Saturday morning cartoon lineup to the concession stand at Camden Yards (the Baltimore Orioles' ballpark), I associated the shirt with singing along to the "Just for the Taste of It" jingle and with America's favorite pastime, not with a brown fizzy beverage I refused to consume. When I later realized the immensity of Coke's corporate power, I felt somewhat manipulated, but that didn't stop me from wearing the shirt. I still don it often, despite the growing hole in the right sleeve, because of its power as a conversation piece. Few Americans notice it without asking something like "Does that say Coke?" I usually smile and nod. Then they mumble a one-word compliment, and we go our separate ways. But rarely do they want to know what language the internationally recognized logo is written in. And why should they? They are interested in what they can relate to as Americans: a familiar red-and-white logo, not a foreign language. Through nearly a century of brilliant advertising strategies, the Coca-Cola Company has given Americans not only a thirst-quenching beverage but a cultural icon that we have come to claim as our own.

Throughout the company's history, its marketing strategies have centered on putting Coca-Cola in scenes of the happy, carefree existence Americans are supposedly striving for. What 1950s teenage girl, for example, wouldn't long to see herself in the Coca-Cola ad that appeared in a 1958 issue of *Seventeen* magazine? A clean-cut, handsome man flirts with a pair of smiling girls as they laugh and

Fig. 1. Hebrew Coca-Cola T-shirt. Personal photograph by author.

drink Cokes at a soda-shop counter. Even a girl who couldn't picture herself in that idealized role could at least buy a Coke for consolation. The malt shop, complete with a soda jerk in a white jacket and paper hat and a Coca-Cola fountain, is a theme that, even today, remains a piece of Americana (Ikuta 74).

But while countless campaigns with this general strategy have together shaped the Coca-Cola image, presenting a product as key to a happy life is a fairly typical approach to advertising everything from Allstate insurance to Ziploc bags. Coca-Cola's advertising strategy is unique, however, for the original way the beverage giant has used the specific advertising media of magazines and television to drive home this message. As a result, Coca-Cola has become associated not only with the images of Americana portrayed in specific advertisements but also with the general forms of advertising media that dominate American culture.

One of the earliest and best-known examples of this strategy is artist Haddon Sundblom's rendering of Santa Claus. Using the description of Santa in Clement Moore's poem "A Visit from St. Nicholas" — and a friend's rosy-cheeked face as a model — Sundblom contributed to the round, jolly image of this American icon, who just happens to delight in an ice-cold Coke after a tiring night of delivering presents ("True"). Coca-Cola utilized the concept of the magazine to present this inviting image in a brilliant manipulation of the medium (Pendergrast 181).

Today, it's easy to forget how pervasive a medium the magazine was before television became readily available to all. Well into the 1960s, households of diverse backgrounds all across America subscribed loyally to general-subject weeklies and monthlies such as *Life* and the *Saturday Evening Post*, which provided news and entertainment to families nationwide. This large and constant group of subscribers enabled Coca-Cola to build an annual Christmastime campaign that used an extremely limited number of advertisements. According to the Coca-Cola Company's website, Sundblom created only around forty images of Santa Claus during the campaign's duration from 1931 to 1964 ("True"). As a result, Americans soon began to seek out the ads each holiday season. The marketing strategy was to make consumers wait eagerly by the mailbox each December to see the latest *Saturday Evening Post* ad featuring Santa gulping a Coke. For this strategy to succeed, the advertisements had to be seen by many, but they also had to be just hard enough to come by to seem special. What better way to achieve these goals than to place an advertisement in the December issue of an immensely popular magazine?

Effective magazine advertising is just one example of the media strategies Coca-Cola has used to encourage us to equate Coke with the "happy life" element of American identity. As the print magazine gave way to television, Coke was there. In its 1996 recap of the previous fifty years in industry history, the publication *Beverage Industry* cites Coca-Cola as a frontrunner in the very first form of television advertising: sponsorship of entire programs such as *The Bob Dixon Show* and *The Adventures of Kit Carson* ("Fabulous" 16). Just as we now associate sports stadiums with their corporate sponsors, viewers of early television programs will forever equate those programs with Coke.

When networks switched from offering sponsorships to selling exclusive commercial time in short increments, Coca-Cola strove to distinguish itself once again, this time by experimenting with new formats and technologies for those commercials. Early attempts — such as choppy "stop motion" animation, where photographs of objects such as Coke bottles move without the intervention of actors — attracted much attention, according to the Library of Congress Motion Picture Archives website. Coca-Cola was also a pioneer in color television; after a series of experimental reels, the company produced its first color commercial in 1964 ("Highlights"). While the subject matter of these original commercials was not particularly memorable (Coca-Cola cans and bottles inside a refrigerator), the hype surrounding the use of new technologies helped draw attention to the product.

But the advertising campaign that perhaps best illustrates the ability of Coca-Cola advertisers to tie their product to a groundbreaking technology did not appear until 1993. For the 1994 Winter Olympics, Coke created six television commercials featuring digitally animated polar bears rolling, swimming, snuggling, and sliding about in a computerized North Pole — and finishing off the playful experience with a swig of Coke. In 1993, two years before the release of *Toy Story*, these commercials were some of the very first widely viewed digital films ("Highlights"). As with Sundblom's Santa Clauses, television viewers looked forward to their next sighting of the cute, cuddly, cutting-edge bears, who created a natural association between Coca-Cola and digital animation. Once again, Coke didn't just use the latest technology — Coke defined it.

As a result of all of this brilliant advertising, a beverage I never even drink is a significant part of my American cultural identity. That's why I spent thirty Israeli shekels and twenty minutes in a tourist trap I would ordinarily avoid buying my Hebrew Coca-Cola shirt. That shirt, along with the rest of the enormous Coca-Cola collectibles industry, demonstrates Coke's power to identify itself with the American ideal of a lighthearted life of diversion and pleasure. Standing in line halfway around the world for the logo that embodies these values gave me an opportunity to affirm a part of my American identity.

## Works Cited

"The Fabulous Fifties." *Beverage Industry*, vol. 87, no. 6, June 1996, pp. 16+.

*Fifty Years of Coca-Cola Television Advertisements: Highlights from the Motion Picture Archives at the Library of Congress, Motion Picture, Broadcasting, and Recorded Sound Division*, 29 Nov. 2000, memory.loc.gov/ammem/ccmphtml/indsthst.html.

Hebrew Coca-Cola T-shirt. Personal photograph by the author, 8 Nov. 2018.

"Highlights in the History of Coca-Cola Television Advertising." *Fifty Years of Coca-Cola Television Advertisements: Highlights from the Motion Picture Archives at the Library of Congress, Motion Picture, Broadcasting, and Recorded Sound Division*, 29 Nov. 2000, memory.loc.gov/ammem/ccmphtml/colahist.html.

Ikuta, Yasutoshi, editor. *'50s American Magazine Ads*. Graphic-Sha, 1987.

Pendergrast, Mark. *For God, Country, and Coca-Cola: The Definitive History of the Great American Soft Drink and the Company That Makes It*. 2nd ed., Basic Books, 2000.

"The True History of the Modern-Day Santa Claus." *The Coca-Cola Company: Holidays*, 1 Jan. 2012, www.coca-colacompany.com/stories/coke-lore-santa-claus/.

# CHAPTER 7

# Reflecting on Your Writing

Research shows that there's a strong connection between careful reflection and learning: thinking back on and articulating what you've learned, and then assessing it, help make the learning really stick. This research led leaders of first-year writing programs to make *metacognition* — reflecting on your own thought processes or, in other words, really thinking about your own thinking! — one of the eight key "habits of mind" for student success in college (see Chapter 2). As a result, first-year college writing courses are increasingly encouraging students to take time for such reflection.

Whether or not your instructor asks you to produce formal reflective essays, letters, or voice recordings, it's worth it to take some time to step back and reflect on a writing experience and see what lessons you can learn from it.

## 7a Reflecting to learn

You can learn a great deal about yourself as a writer by thinking critically about your reviewing and revising processes. Try to make time to think about questions like these after every important piece of writing you do — either for school or for other purposes.

- How has writing about this topic helped you clarify your thinking about it, extend your knowledge about it, or deepen your understanding? Has writing about it changed your mind in any way?
- How did you begin reviewing your draft?
- What kinds of comments on or responses to your draft did you have? How helpful were they, and why?
- How long did the revising take? How many drafts did you produce?
- What kinds of changes did you make — and why?

- What gave you the most trouble as you were revising?
- What pleased you most about your revision? What are you most proud of? What is your favorite sentence or passage, and why?
- What would you want to change about your process of revising?

## 7b Reflecting to improve and transfer skills

Careful reflection turns out to be a key element in the move from writing for social reasons to writing for a wider public to accomplish bigger goals. When you reflect on your writing, you help ensure that what you have learned *transfers* — that is, you will be able to use what you've learned in other disciplines and situations. Without time for reflection, you may feel like you are plunging from one assignment to the next, trying desperately to keep ahead of the syllabus, without being able to meaningfully note the ways in which you've improved as a writer.

You may be asked to write a reflective statement to capture your thinking about the work you've done on a particular assignment or in the course as a whole. The following questions might guide you in writing such a statement for your course:

- How can you sum up the takeaways from writing an individual essay — or from the entire course?
- How can you apply what you've learned to the work you are doing for other classes — or on the job?
- What about this piece (or these pieces) of writing do you feel most confident and like the best — and why?
- What aspects of your writing or writing process do you feel you still need to work on?
- What goals do you have now for your writing?

### EXERCISE 7.1

Write a brief response in which you identify four to five specific skills or habits you are hoping will transfer from your writing course to other courses you will take or that will transfer from the writing that you do for school to the writing that you do in your job or your community.

## 7c  A student's reflective statement

Here is a reflective letter that James Kung wrote at the end
of his writing course. In it, he reflects on the process of
writing a research-based argument, one piece in a larger
collection of writing he produced during a semester.

**STUDENT WRITER**
James Kung

December 6, 2018

Dear Professor Ashdown:

"Writing is difficult and takes a long time." This simple yet powerful
statement has been uttered so many times in our class that it has essentially
become our motto. During this class, my persuasive writing skills have
improved dramatically, thanks to many hours spent writing, revising,
polishing, and thinking about my topic. The various drafts, revisions, and
other materials in my portfolio show this improvement.

I entered this first-quarter Writing and Rhetoric class with both strengths
and weaknesses. I have always written fairly well-organized essays. However,
despite this strength, I struggled throughout the term to narrow and define
the various aspects of my research-based argument.

The first aspect of my essay that I had trouble narrowing and defining was
my major claim, or my thesis statement. In my "Proposal for Research-Based
Argument," I proposed to argue about the case of Wen Ho Lee, the Los Alamos
scientist accused of copying restricted government documents. I stated, "The
Wen Ho Lee incident deals with the persecution of not only one man, but a
whole ethnic group." You commented that the statement was a "sweeping
claim" that would be "hard to support."

I spent weeks trying to rework that claim. Finally, as seen in my "Writer's
Notebook 10/16/18," I realized that I had chosen the Lee case because of my
belief that the political inactivity of Asian Americans contributed to the case
against Lee. Therefore, I decided to focus on this issue in my thesis. Later, I
once again revised my claim, stating that the political inactivity did not cause
but rather contributed to racial profiling in the Wen Ho Lee case.

I also had trouble defining my audience. I briefly alluded to the fact that
my audience was a "typical American reader." However, I later decided to
address my paper to an Asian American audience for two reasons. First, it

would establish a greater ethos for myself as a Chinese American. Second, it would enable me to target the people the Wen Ho Lee case most directly affects: Asian Americans. As a result, in my final research-based argument, I was much more sensitive to the needs and concerns of my audience, and my audience trusted me more.

I hope to continue to improve my writing of research-based arguments.

Sincerely,

*James Kung*

James Kung

▼ ▼ ▼ ▼ ▼ ▼ ▼ ▼ ▼ ▼ ▼ ▼ ▼ ▼ ▼ ▼ ▼ ▼ ▼ ▼ ▼ ▼ ▼ ▼ ▼

## THINKING CRITICALLY ABOUT YOUR REVIEWING AND REVISING PROCESS

Using some of the questions in 7b, write a reflection paragraph that describes your own reviewing and revising process, noting especially what you believe works well for you and what you would most want to improve in the future.

## CHAPTER 8

# Working with Others

In a memorable statement, philosopher Hannah Arendt confirms what many people feel about collaboration: "For excellence, the presence of others is always required." The old maxim that two heads are better than one seems to be especially true in today's world of digital communication, Wikipedia, and crowdsourcing. Feedback is more visible than ever; today's writers expect and want reactions to their posts, messages, and updates. And thanks to collaborative tools that allow writers anywhere to work on a single document, working on a group project has never been more feasible. Still, successful collaboration requires special attention.

## 8a Collaborating in college

Although you will find yourself working together with many people on or off campus, your most immediate collaborators will probably be the members of your writing class. You can learn a great deal by comparing ideas with these classmates and by using them as a first audience for your writing (3d). As one student put it, "There's a lot of brains around here, and I try to take advantage of that!" As you talk and write, you will find the ideas you get from others contribute to your writing, and your ideas to theirs. In short, the texts you write are shaped in part by conversations with others. This exchange is one reason citing sources and help from others is so important.

In online communication especially, the roles of "writer" and "reader" and "text" are often interchangeable, as readers become writers and then readers again, and texts constantly change as multiple voices contribute to them. A blog post, for example, may carry with it a long discussion that has accumulated as people have replied to one another in the comments section. Or a document being drafted in Google Drive or another program designed to facilitate collaboration will carry the voices of multiple authors. These examples paint a portrait of how meaning is almost always made collaboratively.

> **TALKING THE TALK | COLLABORATING—OR CHEATING?**
>
> "When is asking others for help and opinions acceptable, and when is it cheating?" In academic work, the difference between collaborating and cheating depends almost entirely on context. There will be times — during exams, for example — when instructors will expect you to work alone. At other times, working with others — for a team project, perhaps, or peer review — may be required, and getting others' opinions on your writing is always a good habit. You should draw the line, however, at having another person do your work for you. Submitting material under your name that you did not write is unacceptable in college writing. But collaboration is a key fact of life in today's digital world, so it's important to think carefully about how to collaborate both effectively and ethically.

# 8b Working on group projects

You may often be asked to work as part of a team to produce a group project such as a print report, an oral presentation, or a web document or site. Since group projects are collaborative from the outset, they require additional planning and coordination.

## Planning a collaborative project

Planning goes a long way toward making any group collaboration work well. Although you will probably do much of your group work online, keep in mind that face-to-face meetings can accomplish some things that virtual meetings cannot.

Most college instructors now routinely integrate online work into their classes. If your course has a website, it probably offers space for extending the collaborative work of the classroom. Your writing class may already have a discussion list, chat space, blog, or wiki; if not, you may want to set up such a space for yourself and your collaborators. You may also want to use a space such as Google Drive or Dropbox to create a collaborative project; if so, make sure that every member of your group knows where to find the project and has the appropriate level of access — the ability to edit, for example — to any document posted there.

---

**QUICK HELP**

Guidelines for group projects

- Establish a regular meeting time and space (whether in person or online), and exchange contact information.
- During your first meeting, discuss the overall project and establish ground rules. For example, you might agree that everyone has a responsibility to participate and to meet deadlines and that all members will be respectful toward others in the group.

Guidelines for group projects, continued

- Establish clear duties for each participant.
- With final deadlines in mind, create an overall agenda to organize the project. At each group meeting, take turns writing up notes on what was discussed and review them at the end of the meeting.
- Use group meetings to work together on difficult problems. If an assignment is complex, have each member explain one section to the others. Check with your instructor if part of the task is unclear or if members don't agree on what is required.
- Express opinions clearly and politely. If disagreements arise, try paraphrasing to see if everyone is hearing the same thing.
- Remember that the goal is not for everyone just to get along; constructive conflict is desirable. Get a spirited debate going, and discuss all available options.
- If your project requires a group-written document, assign one member to get the writing project started. Set deadlines for each part of the project. Come to an agreement about how you will edit and change each other's contributions to avoid offending any member of the group.
- Assess the group's effectiveness periodically. Should you make changes as you go forward? What has been accomplished? What has the group done best? What has it done less successfully? What has each member contributed? What have you learned about how to work more effectively with others on future projects?

## Considering models for collaboration

Experienced collaborative writers often use one of three models for setting up the project: an expertise model, a division-of-labor model, or a process model.

### Expertise model

This model plays to the strengths of each team member. The person who knows the most about graphics and design, for example, takes on all jobs that require those skills, while the person who knows the most about the topic takes the lead in drafting.

### Division-of-labor model

In this model, each group member becomes an expert on one aspect of the project. For example, one person might agree to do Internet research, while another searches library resources, and still another conducts interviews. This model is particularly helpful if a project is large and time is short.

### Process model

You can also divide up the project in terms of its chronology: one person gets the project going, presenting an outline for the group to consider and carrying out any initial research; then a second person takes over and begins a draft for the group to review; a third person designs and illustrates the project; and another person takes the job of revising and editing. This model can work well if members are unable to participate equally throughout the entire project. Once the project is completely drafted, however, the whole group needs to work together to create a final version.

---

CONSIDERING DISABILITIES | **ACCOMMODATING DIFFERENCES**

When you are working with other members of your class to share files for peer review or other group activities, remember to consider differences group members may have. Think of such differences not only in terms of computer compatibility but also in terms of the sensory, physical, or learning abilities of yourself and your classmates. You may have colleagues who wish to receive printouts in a very large type size, for example, in order to read them with ease. Similarly, you may have a peer who prefers to share files early to read the material or avoid the stress of last-minute preparation. You may have a peer who uses a voice screen reader. Help your group get off to a good start by making a plan to accommodate everyone's needs.

---

LANGUAGE, CULTURE, AND CONTEXT | **CONSTRUCTIVE CRITICISM**

When you collaborate with your peers, criticizing each other's work is often necessary, but remember that different cultures have different ways of expressing criticisms that are appropriate. Observe how your peers communicate their suggestions and comments and how others respond to them. If you feel uncomfortable with strong criticisms from your peers, you can ask them to "put it more gently."

---

### EXERCISE 8.1

Write a brief response in which you answer these questions: Which of the collaboration models do you have experience with (expertise model, division-of-labor model, process model)? Is there one that you prefer over the others? In what assignment situations might one be more useful than another?

---

## 8c Making presentations

Some collaborative projects may call for oral or multimedia presentations. If your group is to make such a presentation, follow these guidelines:

- Find out exactly how much time you will have for the presentation, and stick to that time limit.
- Divide the preparatory work fairly. For example, who will revise the written text for an oral presentation? Who will prepare the slides or other visuals? Who will do the necessary research?
- Decide how each group member will contribute to the presentation. Make sure that everyone has an obvious role.

- Leave time for at least two practice sessions. During the first session, time yourselves carefully, and make a video or sound recording of the presentation. Then view or listen to the recording, and make any necessary adjustments. If you can't make a video of your group presentation, then practice it in front of several friends: feedback is very important, so ask them to summarize what they got out of the presentation and to comment on how easy it was to understand the major points, how effective body language and eye contact were, and how well you used visual or multimedia support.

- If your presentation will be available online, remember that it's very hard to know who may see it. Try for a presentation that will be easily understood by people beyond your own class or university — or even your own culture. Also, remember that you *must* label all visuals and cite their sources.

- Make sure that your audience will be able to read any accompanying handouts, slides, or posters, and revise any that fail this test. Use your visuals as you rehearse, and try to do so in a room similar in size and lighting to the room in which you will make the presentation.

- After your presentation, try to have a debriefing with your instructor so that you can get pointers on improving future presentations.

For more on oral and multimedia presentations, see Chapter 23.

▼ ▼ ▼ ▼ ▼ ▼ ▼ ▼ ▼ ▼ ▼ ▼ ▼ ▼ ▼ ▼ ▼ ▼ ▼ ▼ ▼ ▼ ▼ ▼

### THINKING CRITICALLY ABOUT YOUR COLLABORATIVE WORK

Begin by making a list of all the ways in which you collaborate with others. Then reflect on the kinds of collaboration you find most effective. Finally, take an example of a recent collaboration you have been part of, and examine how well it worked by answering the following questions: What did I contribute to the collaboration? What worked well, and what did not work well? What could I have done to improve the collaboration?

# PART 3
# Critical Thinking and Argument

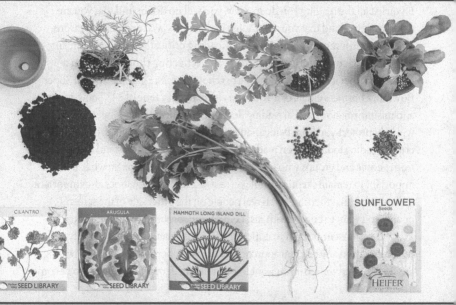

CILANTRO · SEED LIBRARY

ARUGULA · SEED LIBRARY

MAMMOTH LONG ISLAND DILL · SEED LIBRARY

SUNFLOWER Seeds · HEIFER

Photo by Mike Enright/www.menright.com. Photo styling by Barbara Lipp.

CHAPTER 9

# Reading Critically

If you list all the reading you do in a day, you will no doubt find that you are reading a lot — and that you are reading in different ways for different reasons, and using different tools and media. Reading critically has always meant questioning, commenting, analyzing, and reflecting thoughtfully on a text — whether it's a white paper for a psychology class, a graphic novel, a Super Bowl ad, a business email, or a YouTube video. But in a time of 24/7 newsfeeds and misinformation, critical reading demands *defensive* reading strategies that will help protect you from being manipulated by the texts you read. In addition, critical reading today calls on readers to engage with and understand messages from people and groups who may be very different from them. So while it's important to remain skeptical until you're sure a text is accurate, it's also important to remember that there are often real people on the other side of the screen, people you want to engage with respectfully and responsibly (see 10b and 11i). In any case, most important to critical reading is *attention*: focusing intently and purposefully on any text you approach. And remember that reading and writing are closely intertwined: if you want to become a better writer, you need to become a better reader.

## 9a Reading print and digital texts

You're probably used to reading a lot onscreen — posting and responding to updates in your social networks, checking email, browsing the web, and so on. Onscreen reading is often social and collaborative, allowing you to connect with other readers, discuss what you've read, and thus turn reading into writing. Reading online is one way to find information — and make sure it is reliable — quickly. But research shows that all onscreen readers tend to take shortcuts, scanning and skimming and jumping from link to link, and that's basically a good thing because it allows us to read laterally, checking sources and accumulating solid information. But current research also suggests that when the stakes are high (you must master a difficult essay to do well on an exam, for example), reading printed text is still preferred. When you really need to absorb and remember information, it still makes sense to read a hard copy. If you have a choice of media when you're asked to read a text, then consider whether reading onscreen or in print will work better for your purposes. And if you *must* read a complex text onscreen rather than in print, be aware that you must try harder than usual to focus. That may well mean closing all other windows and shutting down social media until you've had time to read and understand the text you're working on. Get in the habit of working through the steps described in this chapter — previewing (9c), annotating (9d), summarizing (9e), and analyzing (9f and g) — to ensure that you are reflecting and making appropriate connections, whether you're reading a printed page or a digital text.

## 9b  Reading collaboratively

Especially for difficult or high-stakes reading, there's nothing better than tackling the task with others. Research shows, in fact, that if you read and take notes on an assigned reading in small groups, understanding of the text improves, as do test scores based on the material.

**TIPS FOR EFFECTIVE COLLABORATIVE READING**

- Join two or three classmates to form a reading group; make sure you all know what the specific reading assignment is and when it is due. Trade contact information.

- Decide whether you will proceed in person or online. If in person, find a convenient time to meet; if online, set a deadline by which each member will have participated.

- Professor of history Aiala Levy asks her students to set up a shared folder on Google Drive and then use a Google Doc to share their notes as they read, annotate, and respond to assigned texts. Exchanging views on a text in this way helps you see perspectives or points of view you might not have considered and gives you a chance to test out your own ideas about what you are reading.

- Use differences of opinion on the text's ideas and meanings to sharpen your thinking.

## 9c  Previewing a text; considering the source

Find out all you can about a text before beginning to look closely at it, considering its context, author or sponsor, subject, genre, and design.

### PREVIEWING THE CONTEXT

- Where have you encountered the work? Are you encountering the work in its original context? For example, an essay in a collection of readings may have been previously published in a magazine; a speech you watch on YouTube may have been delivered originally to a live or televised audience.

- Is there reason to suspect the work is fake? For example, a retweet you receive from someone you don't know may have been taken out of context or be false, or a photo you find in a blog post may have been altered from its original.

- What can you infer from the original or current context of the work about its intended audience and purpose?

### LEARNING ABOUT THE AUTHOR OR SPONSOR

- What information can you find about the author or sponsor of the text?

- What purpose, expertise, values, and possible agenda might you expect this person or sponsor to have? What assumptions do you think the author or sponsor holds? How trustworthy is this person or persons and how do you know?

### PREVIEWING THE SUBJECT

- What do you know about the subject of the text?

- What do you expect the main point to be? Why?

- What opinions might you already have about the subject?

- What unspoken assumptions underlie your opinions: that is, where do your opinions come from and how informed and reasonable are they?

- What would you like to learn about the subject?

### CONSIDERING THE TITLE, MEDIUM, GENRE, AND DESIGN

- What does the title (or caption or other heading) indicate?

- In what medium (or media) does the work appear? Is it a video on YouTube? a printed advertising brochure? a podcast on Spotify? an animated cartoon on television? some combination of media? What role does the medium play in achieving the purpose and connecting to the audience?

- What is the genre of the text — and what can it help illuminate about the intended audience or purpose? Why might the authors or creators have chosen this genre?

- How is the text presented? What do you notice about its formatting, use of color, visuals or illustrations, overall design, general appearance, and other design features?

*Student preview of an assigned text*

STUDENT WRITER
Samyuktha Comandur

STUDENT WRITER
Caroline Fairey

Samyuktha Comandur and Caroline Fairey, students in a first-year writing class, read and analyzed "The Challenge of (Re)Inventing Stories," by Andrea A. Lunsford. Some of the preview notes they made before reading the text appear below. (See 9d–f for both the text and the additional steps in the critical reading process from these students.)

**PREVIEW OF ANDREA LUNSFORD'S TEXT, "THE CHALLENGE OF (RE)INVENTING STORIES"**

- The text is a speech delivered on July 1, 2018, to members of the Bread Loaf Teacher Network (BLTN), a community of teachers of writing. Andrea Lunsford has been a part of the BLTN for many years — she is speaking to an audience of her peers.

  *Information on context*

- This version of the speech is a transcript — a reader might interpret certain phrases differently than someone who listened to the live speech. Look out for rhetorical devices that work best orally!

- Searched Google for Lunsford's credentials. She's a professor of writing and rhetoric at Stanford, and has over 9,000 books, chapters, essays, studies, and articles credited to her on Google Scholar. She is also author of the textbook that our school uses in its first-year writing program.

  *About the author*

- The genre is a persuasive speech. Lunsford wants her audience to be inspired to take action after hearing her evidence.

  *Note about the genre*

- Includes lots of references to current social media movements and even some hashtags. Even a reader who wasn't sure about the date of this speech could easily identify it as contemporary.

- The word "reinventing" in the title is formatted unusually. I wonder if Lunsford will talk about "inventing," "reinventing," or both?

  *Note about the formatting of the title*

- The main topic will probably be something about seeing stories differently. Since the speech is persuasive, Lunsford also includes a call to action at the end, which suggests a specific course of action for her audience to take.

  *A prediction*

◢ **EXERCISE 9.1**

During a 2017 music festival, a screenshot of what appeared to be a news article from the BBC about Radiohead popped up on social media, posted by "Dave the Merciless."

**NEWS**

Home   UK   World   Business   Politics   Tech   Science   Health   Education   Enter

Entertainment & Arts

## Radiohead crowd left red-faced after applauding three minute guitar tuning, mistaking it for new song

🕐 3 minutes ago   Entertainment & Arts                    f  🐦  💬  ✉  ≪ Share

**Tens of thousands of Radiohead fans embarrassed themselves at Glastonbury festival this evening after mistaking the band tuning their guitars for new material.**

Many tweets were sent from members of the crowd during the incident, some claiming it to be the band's best work since OK Computer. One fan described it as "minimalist, but also complex, emotionally raw, but still able to push the boundaries of what music can be."

More to follow.

Look closely at the "news" article and, working with a friend or classmate, first ask yourselves how likely it is that thousands of fans would mistake tuning for a new song. Then check out the format of BBC News and see whether this article follows it precisely. Then check to see if the headline appears in the BBC News site files—or anywhere on Radiohead's artist pages. Also see if you can find any other news organizations reporting on such an incident. If you turn up empty-handed, the "news" article is almost surely fake. In fact, you can read what the BBC really had to say about Radiohead right here: www.bbc.com/news/entertainment-arts-40389552. Reflect on the experience with your partner.

## 9d Annotating and responding to a text

After you've carefully previewed a text, you're ready to read it — with pen or mouse in hand. So while you are reading, you will also be writing: making notes in margins or on sticky notes, raising questions, marking confusing passages, and so on. As you do so, you'll be paying very close attention to the content of the text and to the points the author is making, as well as to the intended audience, the genre and design of the piece, the context in which it was written, and the author's stance and tone. Pay attention to the key terms and ideas and the author's use of evidence. After your first reading, does the text leave questions unanswered?

*Student annotation of an assigned text*

Following is an excerpt from "The Challenge of (Re)Inventing Stories," a presentation delivered by Andrea A. Lunsford at a teachers' workshop, with annotations made by students Samyuktha ("Samyu") Comandur and Caroline Fairey.

## The Challenge of (Re)Inventing Stories

**ANDREA A. LUNSFORD**

Bread Loaf / BLTN / 2018

Why is it important to me to think of rhetorical traditions, and of the work we do as teachers of writing and rhetoric, in terms of narrative, of story? In the most simple terms, because story is the universal genre, because stories lie at the base of all cultures, because our lives are attempts to tell particular stories that can guide us, and because, in Anne Haas Dyson and Celia Genishi's telling book title, we have a *Need for Story*.

> **Caroline Fairey:** The speaker uses repetition ("because . . . because . . . because . . .") as a device for emphasis and to respond to her own opening question.

I want to argue not only that it is important to understand, challenge, explore, and remake the stories we tell about rhetoric, its origins, principles, and practices—but also because it is important to take on the *responsibility* for story, for narrative, and for the way stories shape our experience of the world. Along with Lyotard and scholars in many other disciplines, we have interrogated and rejected the master narratives that have held enormous power over our lives. We know in our bones what Nigerian writer Chimamanda Ngozi Adichie calls "The Danger of a Single Story," what happens when whole groups of richly complex people are reduced to a single narrative. In her remarkable 2009 TED talk of that title, Adichie tells about her life as a child in Nigeria, growing up reading British and American stories and writing her own stories with characters that all had "fair hair and blue eyes." That was a single story that shaped her way of reading and writing. In her talk, she says it's fairly simple to create a single story: just "show people as one thing and one thing only, over and over again, and that is what they will become." Adichie notes that stories are enmeshed in structures

> **Samyu Comandur:** This example is aimed at people who keep up with the scholarly community, but it may be unfamiliar to students like me who are not aware of Lyotard's work as a 20th-century philosopher. References to other scholars and thinkers help us see Lunsford's credibility.

> **Caroline Fairey:** Lunsford uses "we" here to remind the audience that she is a part of their peer group, not a distant authority.

of power, that how they are told, when they are told, how many are told are all dependent on power, and the ultimate power is to tell the story of another person—but to make it THE definitive story of that person. Or that people. Or that culture.

Perhaps all times have been defined by struggles over stories—who gets to tell them and who has the power to create and reify them. But certainly our own time is rife with the struggle over stories, over narratives. In early 2018, even military officials in this country were talking about a "war of narratives." And we have witnessed attempts to create a "single story" of past American greatness and the steps some see as "necessary" to recapture it.

On a more hopeful note, of course, we have only to think of #OccupyWallSt, #BlackLivesMatter, #MeToo, #TimesUp, #indigenouswomenrise, #lagenteunida, and many others, to see efforts to create narratives that can displace a single story about groups of people and cultures. In a recent issue of *Anthropology News*, Anna Babel traces the forces at work in the discourse of #MeToo and shows how they create a story that has had effects internationally. As she says in "The Invisible Walls of the Whisper Network,"

> **Samyu Comandur:** To make her message more relatable, the speaker uses a variety of social media movements that a younger audience might be familiar with.

> #MeToo does not *create* a community; it opens an existing community to public discussion. The #MeToo hashtag asks people to open their eyes and ears to stories they may have once been able to ignore. It might be easy to ignore or dismiss one woman, but can you discount the stories of nearly every woman you know?

I want all of us to take on the project not only of examining and challenging stories that crush dreams and choke freedoms, but also to work hard at creating and maintaining stories that are worthy of our best vision of ourselves. What I want is for us to pursue what I am calling *narrative justice*. Because I don't see how we can ever achieve social justice, for

> **Caroline Fairey:** These verbs, "crush" and "choke," conjure images of violence, even though the nouns are abstract. It definitely helps the audience feel the weight of these words and think about what's at stake.

example, when the narratives in which people are trapped and silenced simply will not allow for it. Hence the need for *just narratives*, which can then lay the groundwork for social justice.

> **Samyu Comandur:** The speaker uses these examples because she seems confident that her audience will agree that these narratives are dangerous.

I believe our work can stand as testimony to a future in which scholars and teachers and practitioners of rhetoric will continue to broaden and deepen the scope of rhetoric, that we will link hands, and stories, with rhetors around the globe, to listen carefully and respectfully to those

> **Caroline Fairey:** Or was this list written to make them examine their own "single-narrative" beliefs?

who argue for single narratives, but then to resist the dangerous narratives we hear daily: "only guns can keep us safe," "immigrants are criminals," "climate change is a hoax." We ignore or dismiss such stories at our peril. Instead, we need to listen to them, to understand them, to trace the roots of their power, and then work to check them. Against them, we are already at work creating inclusive and respectful stories that reflect our best selves, our best values.

### ◢ EXERCISE 9.2

Following is the full text of Abraham Lincoln's Gettysburg Address, delivered in 1863 to dedicate the Soldiers' National Cemetery at the site of the Battle of Gettysburg. Using the guidelines in 9c, preview the speech to understand the context. Then use the guidelines in 9d to read and annotate Lincoln's speech.

> Four score and seven years ago our fathers brought forth on this continent a new nation, conceived in Liberty, and dedicated to the proposition that all men are created equal.
>
> Now we are engaged in a great civil war, testing whether that nation, or any nation so conceived and so dedicated, can long endure. We are met on a great battlefield of that war. We have come to dedicate a portion of that field, as a final resting place for those who here gave their lives that that nation might live. It is altogether fitting and proper that we should do this.
>
> But, in a larger sense, we can not dedicate—we can not consecrate—we can not hallow—this ground. The brave men, living and dead, who struggled here, have consecrated it, far above our poor power to add or detract. The world will little note, nor long remember what we say here, but it can never forget what they did here. It is for us the living, rather, to be dedicated here to the unfinished work which they who fought here have thus far so nobly advanced. It is rather for us to be here dedicated to the great task remaining before us—that from these honored dead we take increased devotion to that cause for which they gave the last full measure of devotion—that we here highly resolve that these dead shall not have died in vain—that this nation, under God, shall have a new birth of freedom—and that government of the people, by the people, for the people, shall not perish from the earth.          —ABRAHAM LINCOLN, *Gettysburg Address*

## 9e Summarizing main ideas

When you feel that you have read and thoroughly understood a text, try to summarize the content in your own words. A summary *briefly* captures the main ideas of a text and omits information that is less important. Try to identify the key points in the text, find the essential evidence supporting those points, and explain the contents concisely and fairly, so that a reader unfamiliar with the original can make sense of it all. Deciding what to leave out can make summarizing a tricky task — but mastering this skill can serve you well in all the reading you do in your academic, professional, and civic life. To test your understanding — and to avoid unintentional plagiarism — it's wise to put the text aside while you write your summary. (For more information on writing a summary, see 15d.)

## TALKING THE TALK | CRITICAL THINKING

"Are criticizing and thinking critically the same thing?" *Criticize* can sometimes mean "find fault with," but you don't have to be negative to think critically. Instead, critical thinking means asking good questions — and not simply accepting what you see at first glance. By asking not only what words and images mean, but also how meaning gets across, critical thinkers consider why a text makes a particular claim, what writers may be leaving out, and how to tell whether evidence is accurate and believable. If you're considering questions like these, then you're thinking critically.

*Student summary of an assigned text*

Students Samyuktha Comandur and Caroline Fairey, whose critical reading notes appear in this chapter, summarized the "Challenge" speech that is printed in 9d. Here is Samyu's summary:

> In "The Challenge of (Re)Inventing Stories," a speech given at a teacher's conference, Andrea Lunsford argues for the examination and rejection of the single, simplistic stories that describe human experience. Lunsford uses the occasion of speaking to a group of educators as a powerful call to action, and she references philosophers, literary figures, and linguists to help her do so. The social consequences of falling prey to simplistic narratives are made clear; Lunsford suggests that if we do not pursue "narrative justice" and give individuals and groups the opportunity to voice their experiences, they will not be heard and will be unlikely to grow beyond the circumstances and stories that now trap them. According to Lunsford, all immigrants, for example, might continue to be labeled as "criminals." This speech highlights the responsibility of the educators, scholars, and speakers to create more inclusive environments for stories to be told and to question power structures that allow single narratives to define whole groups of people.

# 9f Analyzing and reflecting on a text

When you feel that you understand the meaning of a text, move on to your analysis — your overall interpretation of the text or some aspect of it — by asking additional questions about the text.

## ANALYZING IDEAS AND EXAMPLES

- What are the main points in this text? Are they implied or explicitly stated?
- Which points do you agree with? Which do you disagree with? Why?
- Does anything in the text surprise you? Why, or why not?
- What kinds of examples does the text use? What other kinds of evidence does the text offer to back up the main points? Can you think of other examples or evidence that should have been included?
- How does the text get its meaning across?
- Are viewpoints other than those of the author or creator included and treated fairly?
- How trustworthy and valid are the sources the text cites or refers to?
- What assumptions does the text make? Are those assumptions valid?

## ANALYZING FOR OVERALL IMPRESSION

- Do the authors achieve their purpose? Why, or why not?
- What intrigues, puzzles, or irritates you about the text? Why?
- What else would you like to know?

### Student analysis of an assigned text

After previewing, reading, annotating, and summarizing the text, students Samyuktha Comandur and Caroline Fairey analyzed the text. Here is Caroline's analysis:

In "The Challenge of (Re)Inventing Stories," Andrea Lunsford, Stanford University professor and long-time member and teacher with the Bread Loaf Teacher Network, turns a scholarly topic into a compelling call-to-action. She pairs powerful word choice and inclusive rhetoric with established, well-known sources, and engages in a long-standing tradition of storytelling practices. Ultimately, she is able to lead her audience to an effective and surprising conclusion.

Captures the presenter's purpose

Student writer's thesis

As a presenter at a conference for teachers of writing and rhetoric, Lunsford already possesses authority, but she builds her credibility through referencing the authority of others. The audience of this speech — teachers of writing and rhetoric from around the country—would no doubt be familiar with the content of Adichie's famous TED talk. Both the TED stage and popular magazines like *Anthropology Now*, which Lunsford references later, toe the line between scholarly and popular. The speaker's references to current popular social media movements show the audience that she is also tuned in to popular interpretations of storytelling and rhetoric as well as academic ones.

*Notes how the presenter is in tune with her audience*

Lunsford uses several other rhetorical techniques to win the favor of her audience. The repeated use of the first-person plural pronoun, "we," emphasizes both the connection among teachers of writing and rhetoric from all backgrounds and the speaker's own inclusion in the peer group that she is addressing. She also repeatedly uses parallelism and repetition to drive her strongest points home. Repetition and parallel structures can make any piece of writing more powerful, but they are particularly effective with speeches because they remind the audience of the important points and slow down the delivery for emphasis.

*Notes effect of specific strategies the presenter uses*

In a sense, Lunsford supports her main argument through what she is doing even more than what she is saying. She uses more than one story (Adichie, Babel) to inform the audience of the importance of multiple points of view. She also adapts some of the elements of a good story—the very narrative elements that inform every aspect of our lives, according to this speech—to create the speech itself. The third and fourth paragraphs, specifically, feature the appearance of conflict, escalation, and hope in the face of a great danger. The first-person plural and word choice also play a role in creating a sense of story throughout the speech; the "we" becomes a united front not just in understanding, but in joining forces to combat the "single story." Choosing phrases like "crush dreams," "choke freedoms," and "resist dangerous narratives" gives a sense of urgency, of the real threat that single stories pose.

*References to specific passages strengthen the analysis*

Lunsford's speech ends with a surprising call to action. Instead of calling for the eradication of the single story, she asks her audience to consider where such stories come from and to work with empathy, not force, to dismantle them. If she had started out with this idea of "listening carefully and respectfully to those who argue for single narratives," the argument might have been ineffective with an audience of her peers. But since the speaker prefaced her final point with both credible sources and compelling, familiar narrative structures, the point is likely received by the audience as both a well-thought-out scholarly reaction and a viable way of inspiring her audience to seek narrative justice.

## 9g  Thinking critically about visual texts

You can use the steps given in 9c–f to read any kind of text, from a scholarly article for a research project to an Instagram image. You may be at least as accustomed to reading visual texts as you are to reading words, whether or not you take time to make a formal analysis of what you see. But pausing to look closely and reflect on how a visual text works can make you more aware of how visuals convey information and provoke thought or action.

On the following page, a Pulitzer Prize–winning photograph (by Craig F. Walker of the *Denver Post*) appears with its caption. This image appeared as part of a series documenting the experiences of a Colorado teenager, Ian Fisher, who joined the U.S. Army to fight in Iraq.

TALKING THE TALK | **VISUAL TEXTS**

"How can an image be a text?" In its traditional sense, a *text* involves words on paper. But now we spend at least as much time reading and analyzing images — including moving images — as we spend on printed words. So it makes sense to broaden the definition of *text* to include anything that sends a message. That's why images, ads, videos, films, and the like are often called *visual texts*.

*During a weekend home from his first assignment at Fort Carson, Colorado, Ian walked through a Denver-area mall with his new girlfriend, Kayla Spitzlberger, on December 15, 2007, and asked whether she wanted to go ring shopping. She was excited, but working out the financing made him nervous. They picked out the engagement ring in about five minutes, but Ian wouldn't officially propose until Christmas Day in front of her family. The couple had met in freshman math class but never really dated until now. The engagement would end before Valentine's Day.* Craig F. Walker/Denver Post/Getty Images

An analysis of this photograph made the following points:

The couple are in the center of the photo — and at the center of our attention. But at this moment of choosing an engagement ring, they do not look "engaged" with each other. Kayla looks excited but uncertain, as if she knows that Ian feels doubts, but she hopes he will change his mind. She is looking right at him, with her body leaning toward him but her head leaning away: she looks very tentative. Ian is looking away from Kayla, and the expression on his face suggests that he's already having second thoughts about the expense of the ring (we see his wallet on the counter by his elbow) and perhaps even about asking Kayla to marry him. The accompanying caption helps us interpret the image, telling us about the couple's brief history together and noting that the engagement will last less than two months after this moment. But the message comes through pretty clearly without words.

> Notes what is foregrounded in image and relates it to "main point" of visual

> Analyzes why they "do not look 'engaged' with each other"

> Shows how caption underscores image's main point

Ian and Kayla look as if they're trying on roles in this photograph. She looks ready to take the plunge, and he is resisting. These attitudes conform to stereotypical gender roles for a man and woman considering marriage (or going shopping, for that matter). The woman is expected to want the marriage and the ring; the man knows that he shouldn't show too much enthusiasm about weddings and shopping. It's hard for the reader to tell whether Ian and Kayla really feel that they are making good or careful choices for their situation at this moment or whether they're just doing what they think they're supposed to do under the circumstances.

*Analysis suggests that people in the image conform to stereotypical gender roles*

The reader also can't tell how the presence of the photographer, Craig F. Walker, affected the couple's actions. The photo is part of a series of images documenting Ian Fisher's life after joining the military, so Walker had probably spent a lot of time with Ian before this photo was taken. Did Ian want to give a particular impression of himself on this day? Were he and Kayla trying on "adult" roles in this situation? Were they feeling pressure to produce a memorable moment for the camera? And what was Walker thinking when he accompanied them to the mall and took this photograph? Did he foresee the end of their engagement when he captured this revealing moment? What was his agenda?

*Notes that photographer's perspective may affect readers' understanding of image*

*Raises questions for further analysis*

**EXERCISE 9.3**

Write a two- to three-paragraph analysis of an image or text you have seen or read.

## 9h  A student's critical reading of a text

**STUDENT WRITER**
Shuqiao Song

Following is an excerpt of a student essay written by Shuqiao Song, based on her critical reading of Alison Bechdel's graphic novel *Fun Home: A Family Tragicomic*. Shuqiao's critical reading involved looking closely at the words, at the images, and at how the words and images together create a very complex story. For more on Shuqiao Song's slide presentation of this essay, see 23b and c.

Shuqiao Song

Dr. Andrea Lunsford

English 87N

13 March 2018

### Residents of a DysFUNctional HOME

  In a 2008 online interview, comic artist Alison Bechdel remarked, "I love words, and I love pictures. But especially, I love them together—in a mystical way that I can't even explain" ("Stuck"). Indeed, in her graphic novel memoir, *Fun Home: A Family Tragicomic,* text and image work together in a mystical way: text *and* image. But using both image and text results not in a simple summation but in a strange relationship—as strange as the relationship between Alison Bechdel and her father. These strange pairings have an alluring quality that makes Bechdel's *Fun Home* compelling; for her, both text and image are

necessary. As Bechdel tells and shows us, alone, words can fail; alone, images deceive. Yet her life story ties both concepts inextricably to her memories and revelations such that only the interplay of text and image offers the reader the rich complexity, honesty, and possibilities in Bechdel's quest to understand and find closure for the past.

  The idea that words are insufficient is not new—certainly we have all felt moments when language simply fails us and we are at a loss for words, moments like being "left . . . wordless" by "the infinite gradations of color in a fine sunset" (Bechdel, *Fun* 150). In those wordless moments, we strain to express just what we mean. Writers are especially aware of what is lost between word and meaning; Bechdel's comment on the translation of Proust's *À la Recherche du Temps Perdu* is a telling example of the troubling gap:

> After Dad died, an updated translation of Proust came out.
> *Remembrance of Things Past* was retitled *In Search of Lost Time.*
> The new title is a more literal translation of *À la Recherche . . .*

Song 3

    The Bechdels' elaborately restored house is the gilded, but tense, context of young Alison's familial relationships and a metaphor for her father's deceptions. "He used his skillful artifice not to make things, but to make things appear to be what they were not," Bechdel notes alongside an image of her father taking a photo of their family, shown in fig. 1 (*Fun* 16). The scene represents the nature of her father's artifice; her father is *posing* a photo, an image of their family.

First example in support of thesis

Fig. 1. Alison's father posing a family photo (Bechdel, *Fun* 16).

    In that same scene, Bechdel also shows her own sleight of hand; she manipulates the scene and reverses her father's role and her own to show young Alison taking the photograph of the family and her father posing in Alison's place (fig. 2). In the image, young Alison symbolizes Bechdel in the present — looking back through the camera lens to create a portrait of her family. But unlike her father, she isn't using false images to deceive. Bechdel overcomes the treason of images by confessing herself as an "artificer" to her audience (*Fun* 16). Bechdel doesn't . . .

Second example in support of thesis

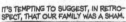

Fig. 2. Alison and her father trade places (Bechdel, *Fun* 17).

Song 8

### Works Cited

Bechdel, Alison. *Fun Home: A Family Tragicomic.* Houghton Mifflin, 2006.

---. "An Interview with Alison Bechdel." Interview by Hillary Chute. *MFS Modern Fiction Studies,* vol. 52, no. 4, Winter 2006, pp. 1004–13. *Project Muse,* doi:10.1353/mfs.2007.0003.

---. "Stuck in Vermont 109: Alison Bechdel." Interview by Eva Sollberger. *YouTube,* 13 Dec. 2008, www.youtube.com/watch?v=nWBFYTmpC54.

Chabani, Karim. "Double Trajectories: Crossing Lines in *Fun Home.*" *GRAAT,* no. 1, Mar. 2007, pp. 1–14.

Gardner, Jared. "Autography's Biography, 1972–2007." *Biography,* vol. 31, no. 1, Winter 2008, pp. 1–26. *Project Muse,* doi:10.1353/bio.0.0003.

Magritte, René. *The Treachery of Images.* 1929, Los Angeles County Museum of Art, collections.lacma.org/node/239578.

*Uses MLA style appropriately*

## THINKING CRITICALLY ABOUT READING

Choose a text you have been assigned to read for a class. Read it over carefully, annotating the material, and then write a one- or two-paragraph summary of the contents. Then analyze your summary. Did your annotations help you summarize? Why, or why not? Does your summary interpret the material or aim for an objective stance? What does your summary omit from the original material, and how did you decide what to leave out?

# CHAPTER 10

# Analyzing Arguments

In one sense, all language has a slant, or what you might call an argumentative edge. When you greet friends, you are indirectly convincing them that you're glad to see them. When you tell a bedtime story to a child, you're subtly arguing that it's time to sleep. Even news reporting that strives for objectivity and evenhandedness has clear argumentative overtones: when a news outlet highlights a particular story, for example, the editors are arguing that this subject is more important than others that it did not highlight. Since argument is so pervasive, you need to be able to recognize and use it effectively — and to question your own arguments as well as those of others.

But just what do we mean by "argument"? "Argument" does not only mean trying to win out over someone else. Of course, getting others to accept our point of view and in that sense "winning" is one reason for argument, but by no means is it the only one or even the most important. Today, writers argue for other important reasons: to join in exploration of an important issue; to explain something to ourselves and others, often using storytelling to add to understanding; to help make important decisions; even to meditate. Keep this in mind as you read and analyze arguments: they may have goals that go far beyond simply "winning."

Emily Lesk's primary purpose in her essay "Red, White, and Everywhere" is not to "win" but to reflect on her own identification with one particular American icon, Coca-Cola (6f). But her essay clearly has an argumentative edge, asking readers to examine their cultural identifications and to understand the power of advertising in creating and sustaining such identifications.

It's possible, then, to read any message or text, verbal or visual, as an argument, even if argument is not its primary purpose. In much academic writing, however, argument is more narrowly defined as a text that makes a claim (usually in the form of an arguable statement) and supports it fully.

# 10a  Thinking critically about argument

Critical thinking is a crucial component of argument, for it guides you in both examining and forming arguments. Here are some ways to think critically about argument:

- **Check understanding.**  First, understand what is being argued and why. If you need to find out more about an unfamiliar subject to grasp the argument, do the research. And remember that reading and note-taking with others can help you with understanding.

- **Play the believing — and the doubting — game.**  Begin by playing the *believing game*: put yourself in the position of the person creating the argument to see the topic from that person's point of view as much as possible. Once you have given the argument sympathetic attention, play the *doubting game*: look skeptically at each claim, and examine each piece of evidence to see how well (or poorly) it supports the claim.

- **Ask pertinent questions.**  Whether you are thinking about others' ideas or your own, you should question unstated purposes and assumptions, the writer's qualifications, the context, the goal of the argument, and the evidence. What objections might be made to the argument?

- **Interpret and assess information.**  All information that comes to you has a perspective — a spin. Your job is to identify the perspective and assess it, examining its sources and finding out what you can about its context.

- **Assess your own arguments.**  The ultimate goal of all critical thinking is to reach your own conclusions. These, too, you must question and assess.

---

**QUICK HELP**

Analyzing an argument

Here are some questions that can help you judge the effectiveness of an argument:

- What is the overall purpose of the argument? How do you know?
- What conclusions about the argument can you reach by playing both the believing and the doubting game, by saying "yes" or "maybe" before saying "no"? **(10a)**
- What cultural contexts inform the argument, and what do they tell you about where the writer is coming from? **(10b)**
- What emotional, ethical, and logical appeals is the writer making in support of the argument? **(10c)**
- How has the writer established credibility to write about the topic? **(10c)**
- What is the claim (or arguable statement)? Is the claim qualified in any way? **(10e)**
- What reasons and assumptions support and underlie the claim? **(10e)**
- What evidence backs up the assumptions and claim? How current and trustworthy or accurate are the sources? **(10e)**

Analyzing an argument, continued

- How and why does the writer use visuals or other media to support the argument? **(10c)**
- What fallacies can you identify, and what effect do they have on the argument's persuasiveness? **(10f)**
- What overall impression do you get from analyzing the argument? Are you convinced?

## 10b Considering cultural contexts

To understand as fully as possible the arguments of others, pay attention to clues about cultural context and to how that context may affect the writer's or creator's ideas and beliefs. Put yourself in that person's position and read openly and respectfully before looking skeptically at every claim and examining the evidence. Above all, watch out for your own assumptions as you analyze what you read or see: just because you assume that statistics count more than, say, precedent drawn from religious belief, don't assume that all writers agree with you. Take a writer's cultural beliefs into account before you analyze an argument.

## 10c Identifying an argument's basic appeals

Aristotle categorized argumentative appeals into three types: emotional appeals that speak to readers' hearts and values (*pathos*), ethical appeals that support the writer's character (*ethos*), and logical appeals that use facts and evidence (*logos*).

### Emotional appeals

Emotional appeals stir your feelings and remind you of deeply held values. When politicians argue that the country needs more tax relief, they almost always use examples of one or more families they have met, stressing the concrete ways in which a tax cut would improve the quality of their lives. Doing so creates a strong emotional appeal. Some have criticized the use of emotional appeals in argument, claiming that they manipulate the audience. Emotional appeals can certainly do that, but nonetheless they are an important part of almost every argument. Critical readers are perfectly capable of "talking back" to such appeals by analyzing them, deciding which are acceptable and which are not. As part of an argument for action on climate change, the accompanying photo (see p. 128) shows a lonely polar bear, helpless on an ice floe where an ice field used to be. To what emotions is the photographer appealing here? Do you find the appeal effective, manipulative, or both?

*Emotional appeals can be seen as effective, manipulative, or both.*
Jan Martin Will/Shutterstock

## Ethical appeals

Ethical appeals support the credibility, moral character, and goodwill of the argument's creator. We may admire an athlete, for example, but should we hire the insurance company the athlete promotes? To identify ethical appeals in arguments, ask yourself these questions: How do the creators of the argument demonstrate knowledge and credibility on the subject? What sort of character do they build, and how? More important, is that character trustworthy? How can you tell whether the creator of the argument has the best interests of the audience in mind? Do those interests match your own, and, if not, how does that alter the effectiveness of the argument? Try to identify the ethical appeals that documentary filmmaker Joshua Oppenheimer makes in this excerpt from his "Director's Statement" for *The Act of Killing*, a film in which the perpetrators of massacres in the 1960s in Indonesia reenact the murders they committed:

> When I began developing *The Act of Killing* in 2005, I had already been filming for three years with survivors of the 1965–66 massacres. I had lived for a year in a village of survivors in the plantation belt outside Medan. I had become very close to several of the families there. During that time, Christine Cynn and I collaborated with a fledgling plantation workers' union to make *The Globalization Tapes*, and began production on a forthcoming film about a family of survivors that begins to confront (with tremendous dignity and patience) the killers who murdered their son. Our efforts to record the survivors' experiences — never before expressed publicly — took place in the shadow of their torturers, as well as the executioners who murdered their relatives — men who, like Anwar Congo, would boast about what they did.
> —JOSHUA OPPENHEIMER

## Logical appeals

Logical appeals are often viewed as especially trustworthy: "The facts don't lie," some say. Of course, facts are not the only type of logical appeals, which also include firsthand evidence drawn from observations, interviews, surveys, experiments, and personal experience. Facts also include secondhand evidence drawn from authorities, the testimony of others, and reported data. Critical readers need to examine logical appeals just as carefully as emotional and ethical ones. What is the source of the appeal — and is that source trustworthy, or might the "facts" have been made up? Are all terms clearly defined? Has the logical evidence presented been taken out of context, and, if so, does that change its meaning? Look, for example, at the following brief passage:

> [I]t is well for us to remember that, in an age of increasing illiteracy, 60 percent of the world's illiterates are women. Between 1960 and 1970, the number of illiterate men in the world rose by 8 million, while the number of illiterate women rose by 40 million.[1] And the number of illiterate women is increasing.
> —ADRIENNE RICH, "What Does a Woman Need to Know?"

As a critical reader, you would question these facts and hence check the footnote to discover the source, which in this case is the *UN Compendium of Social Statistics*. At this point, you might accept this document as authoritative — or you might look further into the United Nations' publications policy, especially to find out how that body defines *illiteracy*. You would also no doubt wonder why Rich chose the decade from 1960 to 1970 for her example and, as a result, check to see when this essay was written. As it turns out, the essay was written in 1979, so the most recent data available on literacy would have come from the decade of the sixties. That fact might make you question the timeliness of these statistics: Are they still meaningful more than forty years later? How might these statistics have changed?

If you attend closely to the emotional, ethical, and logical appeals in any argument, you will be on your way to analyzing the argument.

## Appeals in a visual argument

The following poster, from TurnAround, a group that helps victims of domestic violence, is intended to strike a chord with abusers as well as their victims.

| LANGUAGE, CULTURE, AND CONTEXT | **RECOGNIZING APPEALS IN VARIOUS SETTINGS** |
| --- | --- |

You may be familiar with emotional, ethical, or logical appeals that are not discussed in this chapter. If so, consider describing them — and how they work — to your class. Doing so would deepen the entire class's understanding of what appeals carry the most power in particular settings.

The dramatic combination of words and image builds on an analogy between a child and a target and makes strong emotional and ethical appeals.

The bull's-eye that draws your attention to the center of the poster is probably the first thing you notice. Then you may note that the "target" is a child's body with arms, legs, and a head. The caption "A child is not a target" reinforces the connection.

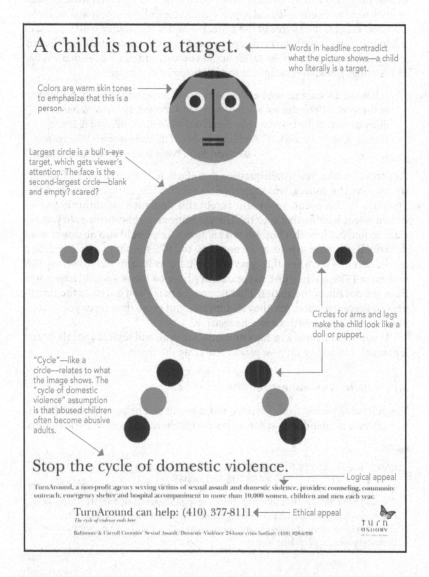

This poster's stark image and headline appeal to viewers' emotions, offering the uncomfortable reminder that children can be victims of domestic violence. The design causes viewers to see a target first and only afterward recognize that the target represents a child — an unsettling experience. But the poster also offers ethical appeals ("TurnAround can help") to show that the organization is credible and that it supports the worthwhile goal of ending "the cycle of domestic violence" by offering counseling and other support services. Finally, it uses the logical appeal of a statistic, noting that TurnAround has served "more than 10,000 women, children and men each year" and giving specific information about where to get help.

## 10d  Recognizing the use of stories in argument

The TurnAround poster makes an argument, but it also tells a story about a child who is being set up like a target for assault. In fact, narrative — someone's story — is often a major part of the arguments you will view and read and analyze, and with good reason: in every culture, stories play a key role in communicating and creating knowledge.

You can see narrative arguments at work in most movies today: think of *Coco* or *Black Panther*, for instance, both movies that use stories to make an overall argument about the crucial importance of family remembrance or the revisioning of African American history.

You will also see stories or narratives featured in written arguments. Rachel Carson's book *Silent Spring*, which argued successfully that the use of pesticides was destroying our environment, opens with a story. Here's an excerpt of the first paragraph:

> There was once a town in the heart of America where all life seemed to be in harmony with its surroundings. The town lay in the midst of a checkerboard of prosperous farms, with fields of grain and hillsides of orchards. . . . The countryside was, in fact, famous for the abundance and variety of its bird life, and when the flood of migrants was pouring through in spring and fall, people came from great distances to observe them. Other people came to fish streams, which flowed clear and cold out of the hills and contained shady pools where trout lay. So it had been from the days, many years ago, when the first settlers raised their houses, sank their wells, and built their barns.

Carson continues the story, noting that now the trees and grasses are withered, the fish and birds are dead — and the cause of this devastation has been human activity. This story introduces and frames her entire argument against the use of pesticides.

You can also see stories at work in student essays in this book: Julia Sakowitz's argument about tourism in Harlem (see Chapter 18) opens with a narrative about her own experiences of and interest in Harlem, a story that gets readers' attention and leads them to the heart of her argument. And Cameron Hauer's argument about threats to public lands in the United States (see 10g) begins with a story about his skiing and hiking as a teen in the Pacific Northwest. Be sure to watch out for how writers use stories in their essays and arguments, and take some tips on how you might use them in your own work.

### EXERCISE 10.1

Read through some magazines, newspapers, or online publications, looking for those in which the authors use stories or narratives to help get their points across. Then, using the guidelines presented in this chapter, analyze how effectively the narrative connects with an audience.

## 10e Understanding Toulmin's elements of argument

In philosopher Stephen Toulmin's framework for analyzing arguments, most arguments contain common features: a *claim* or *claims*; *reasons* for the claim; *assumptions*, whether stated or unstated, that underlie the argument (Toulmin calls these *warrants*); *evidence* or *backing*, such as facts, authoritative opinions, examples, and statistics; and *qualifiers* that limit the claim in some way.

### Claims

Claims, or arguable statements, are statements that a writer wants to convince a reader to accept or consider. Longer essays may include a series of linked claims or several separate claims that you need to analyze before you agree to

**ELEMENTS OF TOULMIN ARGUMENT**

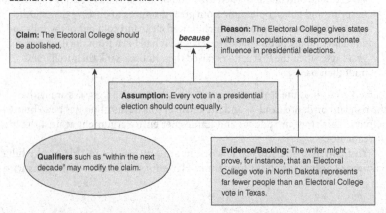

**Claim:** The Electoral College should be abolished.

*because*

**Reason:** The Electoral College gives states with small populations a disproportionate influence in presidential elections.

**Assumption:** Every vote in a presidential election should count equally.

**Qualifiers** such as "within the next decade" may modify the claim.

**Evidence/Backing:** The writer might prove, for instance, that an Electoral College vote in North Dakota represents far fewer people than an Electoral College vote in Texas.

accept them. Claims worthy of arguing are those that are debatable: to say "Ten degrees Fahrenheit is cold" is a claim, but it is probably not debatable — unless you are describing northern Alaska, where ten degrees might seem balmy. In the example on the previous page, the claim that the Electoral College should be abolished is certainly arguable; a web search will turn up numerous arguments for and against this claim.

## Reasons

A claim is only as good as the reasons attached to it. If a student claims that course portfolios should be graded pass or fail because so many students in the class work full-time jobs, critical readers may question whether that reason is sufficient to support the claim. In the preceding example, the writer gives a reason — that states with small populations have too much influence over the Electoral College — to support the claim of abolishing the institution. As you analyze claims, test each reason by asking how directly it supports the claim, how timely it is, and what counter-reasons you could offer to question it.

## Assumptions

Putting a claim and reasons together often results in what Aristotle called an *enthymeme*, an argument that rests on an assumption the writer expects the audience to hold. These assumptions (which Toulmin calls *warrants*) that connect claim and reasons are often the hardest to detect in an argument, partly because they are often unstated, sometimes masking a weak link. As a result, it's especially important to identify the assumptions in arguments you are analyzing. Once the assumption is identified, you can test it against evidence and your own experience before accepting it. If a writer argues that the Electoral College should be abolished because states with small populations have undue influence on the outcome of presidential elections, what is the assumption underlying this claim and reason? It is that *presidential elections should give each voter the same amount of influence*. As a critical reader, remember that such assumptions are deeply affected by culture and belief: ask yourself, then, what cultural differences may be at work in your response to any argument.

## Evidence or backing

Evidence, which Toulmin calls *backing*, also calls for careful analysis. In an argument about abolishing the Electoral College, the writer may offer as evidence a statistical analysis of the number of voters represented by an Electoral College vote in the least populous states and in the most populous states, a historical discussion of why the Founders developed the Electoral College system, or studies showing that voters in states where one political party dominates feel disengaged from presidential elections. As a critical reader, you must evaluate all evidence the writer offers, asking how it relates to the claim, whether it is appropriate and timely, and whether it comes from a credible source.

## Qualifiers

Qualifiers offer a way of limiting or narrowing a claim so that it is as precise as possible. Words or phrases that signal a qualification include *many, sometimes, in these circumstances,* and so on. Claims having no qualifiers can sometimes lead to overgeneralizations. For example, the statement *The Electoral College should be abolished* is less precise than *The Electoral College should be abolished by 2028.* Look carefully for qualifiers in the arguments you analyze, since they will affect the strength and reach of the claim.

## Elements of a visual argument

Visual arguments can also be analyzed using these Toulmin methods. Look closely at the advertisement on this page. If you decide that this advertisement is claiming that people should adopt shelter pets, you might word a reason like this: *Dogs and cats need people, not just shelter.* You might note that the campaign assumes that people make pets happier (and that all pets deserve happiness) — and that the image backs up the overall message that this inquisitive, well-cared-for dog is happier living in a home with a human than in a shelter. Considering unstated qualifiers (should *every* person consider adopting a shelter pet?) and thinking about

potential evidence for the claim would help you complete an analysis of this visual argument.

# 10f Identifying fallacies

Fallacies, instances of false logic, have traditionally been viewed as serious flaws that damage the effectiveness of an argument. But arguments are often complex in that they always occur in some specific rhetorical situation and in some particular place and time; thus what looks like a fallacy in one situation may appear quite different in another. The best advice is to learn to identify fallacies but also to be cautious in jumping to conclusions about them. Rather than thinking of them as errors you can use to discredit an arguer, you might think of them as barriers to common ground and understanding, since they often shut off rather than facilitate debate.

## Verbal fallacies

### Ad hominem

Ad hominem charges make a personal attack rather than focusing on the issue at hand.

▶ **Who cares what that fat loudmouth says about the health care system?**

### Guilt by association

Guilt by association attacks someone's credibility by linking that person with a person or activity the audience considers suspicious or untrustworthy.

▶ **She does not deserve reelection; her husband had extramarital affairs.**

### False authority

False authority is often used by advertisers who show famous actors or athletes testifying to the greatness of a product about which they may know very little.

▶ **He's today's greatest NASCAR driver — and he banks at National Mutual!**

### Bandwagon appeal

Bandwagon appeal suggests that a great movement is under way and the reader will be a fool or a traitor not to join it.

▶ **This new phone is everyone's must-have item. Where's yours?**

### Flattery

Flattery tries to persuade readers by suggesting they are thoughtful, intelligent, or perceptive enough to agree with the writer.

▶ **You have the taste to recognize the superlative artistry of Bling diamond jewelry.**

### Paralipsis—saying what you say you won't

Paralipsis occurs when speakers or writers say they will *not* talk about something, thus doing the very thing they say they're not going to do, as does Robert Downey Jr.'s character in *Iron Man 2*.

▶ **I'm not saying I'm responsible for this country's longest run of uninterrupted peace in 35 years! . . . It's not about me!**

## Veiled threat

Veiled threats try to frighten readers into agreement by hinting that they will suffer adverse consequences if they don't agree.

▶ **If Public Service Electric Company does not get an immediate 15 percent rate increase, its services to you may be seriously affected.**

## False analogy

False analogies make comparisons between two situations that are not alike in important respects.

▶ **The volleyball team's sudden descent in the rankings resembled the sinking of the *Titanic*.**

## Begging the question

Begging the question is a kind of circular argument that treats a debatable statement as if it had been proved true.

▶ **Television news covered that story well; I learned all I know about it by watching TV.**

## Post hoc fallacy

The post hoc fallacy (from the Latin *post hoc, ergo propter hoc*, which means "after this, therefore caused by this") assumes that just because B happened *after* A, it must have been *caused* by A.

▶ **We should not rebuild the town docks because every time we do, a hurricane comes along and damages them.**

## Non sequitur

A non sequitur (Latin for "it does not follow") attempts to tie together two or more logically unrelated ideas as if they were related.

▶ **If we can send a spaceship to Mars, then we can discover a cure for cancer.**

## Either-or fallacy

The either-or fallacy insists that a complex situation can have only two possible outcomes.

▶ **If we do not build the new highway, businesses downtown will be forced to close.**

*Hasty generalization*

A hasty generalization bases a conclusion on too little evidence or on misunderstood evidence.

▶ **I couldn't understand the lecture today, so I'm sure this course will be impossible.**

*Oversimplification*

Oversimplification claims an overly direct relationship between a cause and an effect.

▶ **If we prohibit the sale of alcohol, we will get rid of binge drinking.**

*Straw man*

A straw-man argument misrepresents the opposition by pretending that opponents agree with something that few reasonable people would support.

▶ **My opponent believes that we should offer therapy to the terrorists. I disagree.**

## Visual fallacies

Fallacies can also take the form of misleading images. The sheer power of images can make them especially difficult to analyze — people tend to believe what they see. Nevertheless, photographs and other visuals can be manipulated to present a false impression.

*Misleading photographs*

Faked or altered photos are, unfortunately, fairly common. In 2018, *Teen Vogue* ran a story that featured Emma González, Parkland shooting survivor and gun control activist, tearing a target shooting poster in half. A quick Internet search will show you an altered image of González tearing the U.S. Constitution in half — an image that was posted on Gab, a social media platform with a conservative audience. See the images on the following page.

*Original photo* *Altered photo*

Today's technology makes such photo alterations easier than ever, if also easier to detect with a reverse image search using Google or Tin Eye. But photographs need not be altered to try to fool viewers. Think of all the photos that make a politician look misleadingly bad or good. In these cases, you should closely examine the motives of those responsible for publishing the images.

### Misleading charts and graphs

Facts and statistics, too, can be presented in ways that mislead readers. On page 139, the bar graph on the left attempts to deliver an argument about how differently Democrats, on the one hand, and Republicans, on the other, felt about a particular issue. Look closely and you'll see a visual fallacy: the vertical axis starts not at zero but at 53 percent, so the visually large difference between the groups is misleading. In fact, a majority of all respondents agree about the issue, and only eight percentage points separate Democrats from Republicans (in a poll with a margin of error of +/- seven percentage points). Look at the bar graph on the right; the vertical axis begins at zero and the data is presented more accurately.

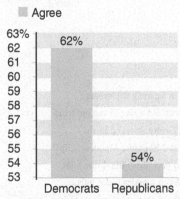

DATA PRESENTED
MISLEADINGLY

■ Agree

TELEPHONE POLL RESULTS BY PARTY
SAMPLING ERROR: +/− 7% pts

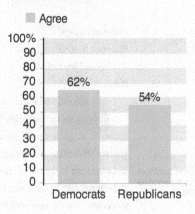

DATA PRESENTED
MORE ACCURATELY

■ Agree

---

**◢ EXERCISE 10.2**

For a reading or visual text you have been assigned, carry out an analysis of the argument. Begin with identifying the audience and the author's purpose, and move to identifying the claim, reason(s), assumption(s), evidence, and qualifiers (if any). As you work, be sure also to identify the emotional, ethical, and logical appeals as well as any fallacies put forward by the author.

---

# 10g A student's rhetorical analysis

STUDENT WRITER
Cameron Hauer

For a class assignment, Cameron Hauer was asked to analyze the emotional, ethical, and logical appeals in a *New York Times* op-ed article in which Nicholas Kristof argues that America's public lands are being threatened.

Hauer 1

Cameron Hauer

Professor Walters

Writing and Rhetoric 1

March 7, 2019

Appeal, Audience, and Narrative in Kristof's Wilderness

Growing up in the Pacific Northwest instilled a love of the outdoors in me. As an adolescent, I spent practically every weekend in the pristine wilderness of Washington, Idaho, and Montana. Alpine ski trips and weeklong backpacking treks were a big part of my life. I owe a lot of personal development and fond memories to America's vast public wilderness, the value of which Nicholas Kristof captures stirringly in his *New York Times* op-ed column, "Fleeing to the Mountains." He warns, however, that America's wilderness is under attack.

To strengthen his case for the specialness of America's wildlands, Kristof relies on ethical and emotional appeals: a lively account of his family's backpacking trips and the ways they free people from the buzz and hum of modern life. Kristof's style here ranges from breezy and playful (the wilderness is "heaven with blisters") to awestruck and reverent (it is "our inheritance and shared playground"). He also offers personal testimony; having spent time in wild places, Kristof is well positioned to describe their virtues. He invites readers to share this ethic, to see the joy of open spaces, and to regard them as a sacred inheritance.

Halfway through the column, Kristof shifts his focus to address threats facing our wilderness. He lays blame on those in power, like members of the current administration, who, Kristof alleges, "see this heritage as an opportunity for development" and are "systematically handing over America's public lands for private exploitation in ways that will scar the land forever." He moves to using logos rather than the ethos and pathos of the earlier sections. Whereas earlier he tries to evoke a particular feeling and ethic, his present goal is to marshal facts — including the administration's lifting of a moratorium on new mining leases and the opening up of new lands to fossil fuel extraction — to convince readers that public lands in the U.S. are

*Marginal annotations:*

Uses personal experience to help establish ethos

Provides succinct overview of Kristof's argument

States Kristof's claims

Transitions to Kristof's discussion of threats to wilderness

Focuses on Kristof's use of appeals

Shows how Kristof engages his audience

under threat. Kristof lessens the abruptness of this shift in appeal by maintaining his narrative of wilderness as an inheritance.

Several elements of Kristof's argument give insight into his context and audience. The place of Trump in Kristof's narrative is significant. The policies Kristof describes are simply the implementation of long-standing Republican priorities and have little to do with Trump himself. But in Kristof's rhetorical context — a left-of-center newspaper in 2017 — choosing Trump as an anti-environmental symbol is a strong, if obvious, rhetorical move. The mention of the sitting president invites Kristof's liberal readership to adopt a pro-wilderness platform as one plank of a broader anti-Trump agenda.

*Analyzes Kristof's intended audience*

There are some notable omissions in Kristof's argument. In his framing, wildlands are either public and devoted to use by the people or privatized for resource extraction and for "ranches for the rich." To a liberal already inclined to value publicly owned resources, this framework may be convincing, but conservatives often view public ownership of natural resources with suspicion. Kristof portrays public ownership as a means of providing equal access for all Americans, but rural conservatives may view it as a way that valuable resources are turned into playgrounds for yuppies. They may also resist Kristof's portrayal of private ownership as promoting degradation and waste, viewing it instead as a way for hardworking people to make a living off the land.

*Practices critical reading to point out Kristof's omissions*

*Considers opposing viewpoints*

Another evasion in Kristof's argument, one that may stand out sharply to left and right, is his characterization of public lands as "a bastion of equality." This is true in a sense — most public lands are open to everyone, free of charge; but in practical terms, access to wilderness requires a salary and paid time off, among other things. In a country where millions struggle to make ends meet, frequent recreational use of America's wildlands remains out of reach.

*Questions Kristof's assumption that wilderness is accessible to all*

These evasions and omissions may indicate Kristof's biases and his own rhetorical stance, but they are not damning. An op-ed article is, after all, crafted for a particular audience. To address the concerns of staunch conservatives would require Kristof to adopt different rhetorical strategies. Kristof's readers are likely a self-selected group

Hauer 3

Underscores
Kristof's major
purpose

of liberal-minded people already sympathetic to his views. His rhetorical
goal is not to convince a group of adversaries of his position but to
persuade a group of amenable readers that this particular issue — and
this particular ethic — is one that they should adopt as their own.

Hauer 4

Work Cited

Follows MLA
style

Kristof, Nicholas. "Fleeing to the Mountains." *New York Times,* 12 Aug.
2017, www.nytimes.com/2017/08/12/opinion/sunday/hiking
-pacific-crest-trail.html.

### EXERCISE 10.3

Working with one or two classmates, analyze a brief argumentative text—an essay,
an advertisement, or an editorial cartoon—by playing the believing and doubting
game; identifying emotional, ethical, and logical appeals; and listing claims, reasons,
assumptions, evidence, and qualifiers. Then work together to create a collaborative
critical response to the text you've chosen.

## THINKING CRITICALLY ABOUT OTHERS' ARGUMENTS

In the following brief review of *SGN,* a webcast created in response to the corona-
virus emergency, a student writer argues about factors contributing to the show's
success. What central claim(s) does the writer make? What emotional, ethical, and
logical appeals does he present in support of his claim(s), and how effective are
these appeals?

# Good News in a Bad Time

The first weeks of the COVID-19 pandemic had everyone glued to the news and numbers — obsessively tracking the rise in positive cases and trying hard to follow recommendations from governors and doctors like Birx and Fauci. But then, we began to go a little stir-crazy. The internet gave us daily tallies and cautions, but we needed — really needed! — some humor to balance the growing horror show. Enter John Krasinski and *SGN* (#SomeGoodNews), a multi-episode YouTube show dedicated to good news. In a time of great challenges, Krasinski's show succeeded because it was a celebration of everyday moments in everyday life: cooking a meal, having a birthday, finishing chemo, checking the weather, and putting on a prom gown.

There is no doubt that *Some Good News* was a success. Its March 2020 Episode 1 was viewed more than 16 million times in the first six weeks of the U.S. lockdown. The success of *SGN*, modeled after *SNL*'s "Weekend Edition," was due to a combination of three factors. First, the show had a relatable host in John Krasinski, a celebrity in his own right (famous for roles in *The Office* and *Jack Ryan*); but Krasinski's celebrity took a back seat to his self-deprecating humor and regret about roles he didn't get (Captain America) and stuff he's not good at (commencement speeches, homeschooling a six-year-old). Second, the show featured other celebrities — and not all from music and movies. Viewers loved hearing from Chance the Rapper, Steven Spielberg, Billie Eilish, Oprah, and Brad Pitt, among others, but they also got important messages from activist Malala Yousafzai and the U.S. astronauts aboard the International Space Station. Of course, other celebrity events were created during the pandemic to raise money and entertain — the Disney Sing-A-Long broadcast, for example, and the Together at Home virtual concert series — and they certainly entertained. But the focus of those events was the star-powered talent. The third factor in *SGN*'s success was the necessary presence of the regular people whose tweets at #johnkrasinski and #somegoodnews provided the show's content. Celebrities appeared in the service of regular people like Coco, Ben, Aubrey, Yael, and Tom. They became the "stars" whose inspiring lives and accomplishments Krasinski was more than happy to narrate.

Will Krasinski profit from the *SGN* endeavor? Yup. Post-pandemic projects will no doubt come his way because of his efforts. Will we resent him for it? Nope. And here's why: In a moment when we felt panicked by fear and uncertainty, John Krasinski gave us the boost we needed on the platform that celebrates everyday humans. To balance mounting bad news, he produced a show to highlight good sense, good humor, good people, and good news.

# CHAPTER 11

# Constructing Arguments

You see and respond to arguments all the time. When you see a stop sign and come to a halt, you've accepted the argument that stopping at such signs is a sensible thing to do. But constructing an effective argument of your own isn't as easy as putting up a stop sign — or obeying its command. Creating a thorough and convincing argument requires careful reasoning and appropriate attention to your audience, purpose, and other aspects of the rhetorical situation. It also calls for remembering *kairos* — recognizing the most suitable time and place for making your argument and for the most opportune way to make it.

Sometimes instructors will assign an argument on a specific topic; other times, you may have a choice. In either case, remember that these assignments belong to you and that they offer opportunities to explore new ideas, to test the limits of your thinking, to do research that will allow you to gain expertise, and to make your voice heard on issues that are important to you. If the topic is assigned, look for ways to shape it to your own interests; if it is an open inquiry, think about what you want to make happen as a result of your argument. What you discover may be of lasting importance to you and, perhaps, to others.

## 11a  Understanding contexts for arguments

Remember that writing in general, and arguments in particular, exist in relationship to a larger conversation that surrounds the topic or subject and helps create the context for a particular argument. When you begin to think about making an argument of your own, then, it's important to see what other people are saying and thinking about the topic. Doing so often means doing some early research about your topic and learning how others have approached the topic and what they have contributed to it. Then you can consider how your argument fits into this larger conversation and how it can make its own distinct contributions to it. You can then put your argument out in the world and see how others will respond — and how you might become a part of an ongoing intellectual conversation.

# 11b  Understanding purposes for argument

While winning is an important purpose of argument, it is by no means the only one.

## Arguing to win

The most traditional purpose of academic argument, arguing to win, is common in campus debating societies, in political debates, in trials, and often in business. The writer or speaker aims to present a position that will prevail over some other position. Presidential debates and trials, for example, focus most often not on changing an opponent's mind but on defeating the opponent in order to appeal to someone else — the voting public, the judge, and so on.

## Arguing to convince

Often, out-and-out defeat of another's position is not only unrealistic but also undesirable. Instead, the goal might be to convince others to change their minds. Doing so calls on a writer to provide *compelling reasons* for an audience to accept some or all of the writer's conclusions. Such is the goal of advocates of assisted suicide: they well know that they cannot realistically hope to defeat or conquer those who oppose such acts. Rather, they understand that they must provide reasons compelling enough to change people's minds.

## Arguing to understand

A writer often enters into a conversation with others to seek the best understanding of a problem, explore all approaches, and choose the best options. Argument to understand does not seek to conquer others or even to convince them. A writer's purpose in many situations — from trying to decide which job to pursue to exploring the best way to care for an elderly relative — will be to share information and perspectives in order to make informed political, professional, and personal choices.

## Arguing to change yourself

Sometimes you will find yourself arguing primarily with yourself, and those arguments often take the form of intense meditations on a theme, or even of prayer. In such cases, you may be hoping *to transform something in yourself* or to reach peace of mind on a troubling subject. If you know a familiar mantra or prayer, for example, think of what it "argues" for and how it uses quiet meditation to help achieve that goal.

---

**QUICK HELP**

Reviewing your argument

- What is the context of your argument? How much do you know about other arguments related to the one you are making? **(11a)**
- What is the purpose of your argument—to win? to convince others? to explore an issue? **(11b)**
- Is the point you want to make arguable? **(11c)**
- Have you formed a strong working thesis with a clear claim and good reasons? **(11d)**
- Have you considered your audience sufficiently in shaping your appeals? **(11f)**
- Have you considered using stories or narratives in your argument? **(11g)**
- How have you fully established your own credibility in the argument? **(11i)**
- How have you used logical and emotional appeals in your argument? **(11j and k)**
- If you use sources, how effectively are they integrated into your argument? **(11l)**
- How is your argument organized? **(11m)**

## 11c Determining whether a statement can be argued

At school, at home, or on the job, you will often need to convince someone or decide something. To do so, start with an arguable statement, which should meet three criteria:

1. It attempts to convince readers of something, change their minds about something, or urge them to do something — or it explores a topic in order to make a wise decision.

2. It addresses a problem for which no easily acceptable solution exists or asks a question to which no absolute answer exists.

3. It presents a position that readers might realistically have varying perspectives on.

---

TALKING THE TALK | **ARGUMENTS**

"Argument seems so negative — I don't want to attack anybody or contradict what someone else says." In some times and places — law courts, for example — argument may call for attacking the credibility of the opponent. Or you may have used the word *argument* in childhood to describe a conversation in which you voiced nothing more than "I did not!" or "You did too!" But in college writing, you have a chance to reject this narrow definition and to use argument in a much broader way. Instead of attacking or contradicting, you will be expected to explore ideas and to work toward convincing yourself as well as others that these ideas are valuable.

UNARGUABLE STATEMENT   Women's magazines earn millions of dollars every year from advertising.

This statement does not present a position; it states a fact that can easily be verified and thus offers a poor basis for argument.

ARGUABLE STATEMENT   Advertisements in women's magazines contribute to the poor self-image that afflicts many young women.

This statement seeks to convince, addresses a problem — poor self-image among young women — that has no clear-cut solution, and takes a position many could disagree with.

### EXERCISE 11.1

Using the three characteristics listed in 11c, decide which of the following statements are arguable and which are not.

1. Alfonso Cuaron's *Roma* is the best movie of the last decade.
2. The climate of the earth is gradually warming.
3. The United States must further reduce social spending in order to balance the budget.
4. Shakespeare died in 1616.
5. President Roosevelt knew that the Japanese were planning to bomb Pearl Harbor in December 1941.
6. Water boils at 212 degrees Fahrenheit.
7. LeBron James, and not Michael Jordan, is the best NBA player of all time.
8. The incidence of breast cancer has risen in the last ten years.
9. The Federal Emergency Management Agency's response to disasters must be radically improved.
10. A fifty-five-mile-per-hour speed limit lowers accident rates.

## 11d Making a claim and drafting a working thesis statement

Once you have an arguable statement, you need to develop it into a working thesis (4c). One way to do so is to identify the elements of an argument (10e): the claim or arguable statement; one or more reasons for the claim; and assumptions, sometimes unstated, that underlie the claim and reasons.

To turn a claim into a working thesis for an argument, include at least one good reason to support the arguable statement.

| REASON | Pesticides endanger the lives of farmworkers. |
| WORKING THESIS (CLAIM WITH REASON ATTACHED) | Because they endanger the lives of farmworkers, pesticides should be banned. |

## 11e Examining your assumptions

Once you have a working thesis, examine your assumptions to help test your reasoning and strengthen your argument. Begin by identifying underlying assumptions that support the working thesis.

| WORKING THESIS | Because they endanger the lives of farmworkers, pesticides should be banned. |
| ASSUMPTION 1 | Workers have a right to a safe working environment. |
| ASSUMPTION 2 | Substances that endanger the lives of workers deserve to be banned. |

It's worth considering your unspoken assumptions carefully: What evidence do you have to support them? What values do they reflect and where did those values come from? Learning to think critically about your own assumptions can help you identify biases that may color your thinking. Once you have a working thesis, you may want to use qualifiers to make it more precise and thus less susceptible to criticism. The preceding thesis might be qualified in this way:

▶ **Because they *often* endanger the lives of farmworkers, *most* pesticides should be banned.**

 **EXERCISE 11.2**

Find or create two arguable statements. Then form two working thesis statements, identifying the claim, reason(s), and assumption(s) for each.

 **EXERCISE 11.3**

For two of the following general topics, write an arguable statement and then draft a working thesis:

1. U.S. immigration policy
2. anti-bullying education in public schools
3. lowering college tuition
4. reinstatement of a U.S. military draft
5. privacy on social media sites

Working with two other members of your class, find two current advertisements you consider particularly eye-catching and persuasive. Then work out what central claim each ad is making, and identify reasons and assumptions in support of the claim. Finally, prepare a brief collaborative report of your findings for the class.

## 11f Shaping your appeal to your audience

Arguments and the claims they make are effective only if they appeal to the appropriate audience. For example, let's say you want to argue for increased lighting in parking garages on campus. You might appeal to an audience of fellow students with one kind of evidence; however, if your audience is school administrators, you may find you need to change your approach.

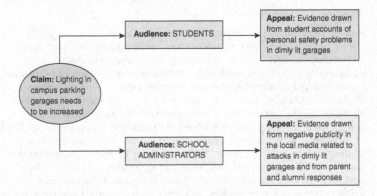

## 11g Considering the use of narratives or stories

Because storytelling is such a common way of communicating, *narratives* can be very persuasive in helping readers understand and possibly accept an argument. You might decide to open an argument with a vivid story that embodies the major point you want to make: opening an argument essay on the devastating effects of global climate change, for example, might begin with the story of an Alaskan village that is now under so much water that it must be abandoned. In fact, it may be helpful to think of your entire argument as following a *narrative arc*, from a dramatic and vivid opening story through other stories that provide evidence for the points you are making, to a conclusion that says "the end." Narratives that use video and audio to capture the faces and voices of the people involved are often particularly compelling.

Stories drawn from your own experience can also be very effective, for they help make your point in true-to-life terms and help readers relate to you and your experiences. Note that in such cases the use of first-person (*I*) is appropriate.

When you include stories in an argument, ask the following questions:

- Does the narrative support your thesis or major point?
- Does the narrative reflect the values you truly hold?
- Will the story's significance to the argument be clear to readers?
- Is the story one of several good reasons or pieces of evidence — or does it have to carry the main burden of the argument?

For examples of academic arguments that begin with narratives, see Cameron Hauer's rhetorical analysis (10g) and Julia Sakowitz's research essay (Chapter 18).

---

**QUICK HELP**

Showing certainty in an argument

How much certainty should you show when you're making an arguable claim? You may know that it's safer to say "*most* students believe" than "*all* students believe," but think carefully about when you should qualify or downplay a claim and when you can show greater confidence. Research conducted by Professor Laura Aull shows that expert academic writers in all disciplines tend to qualify their claims by using "hedges" —words such as *seems*, *might*, *generally*, *relatively*, *some*, or *likely*—and that expert writers are less likely to use intensifiers or "boosters" that show a high level of certainty—words such as *clearly*, *always*, *never*, and *must*. In contrast, student writers use many more "boosters" than "hedges." Learn from the experts: guard against overconfidence and aggressive critique of others' perspectives. Overstating the truth of your claim can make you seem unfair or less credible to readers. Academic claims usually make room for alternative points of view, and they are more often qualified and cautious than absolutely certain.

---

## 11h Finding and developing good reasons

In his *Rhetoric*, Aristotle discusses various ways that one can support a claim. Torture, he notes, makes for a very convincing argument but not one that reasonable people will resort to. In effecting real changes in minds and hearts, we need instead to rely on *good reasons* — reasons that establish our credibility, that appeal to logic, and that appeal to emotion (10e). You can use these appeals to analyze the arguments of others (10c) as well as to construct arguments of your own.

# 11i Establishing credibility through ethical appeals

To make your argument convincing, you must first gain the respect and trust of your readers, or establish credibility with them. In general, writers can establish credibility by making ethical appeals in four ways.

## Knowledge

Writers and speakers can establish credibility first by showing that they know what they're talking about. To decide whether you know enough to argue an issue credibly, consider the following questions:

- Can you provide information about your topic from sources other than your own knowledge?
- How reliable are your sources? (See 14e on spotting misinformation and fake news.)
- If sources contradict one another, can you account for or resolve the contradictions?
- Would a personal experience relating to the issue help support your claim?

These questions may well show that you must do more research, check sources, resolve contradictions, refocus your working thesis, or even change your topic.

## Common ground

Some arguments are doomed before they even begin because the two sides never even listen to one another. One way to get beyond such an impasse is to listen openly and respectfully to the perspectives of others and, if possible, to find some common ground. The following questions can help you find common ground in presenting an argument:

- What are all the differing perspectives on this issue (including those that differ from your own)? Where might they overlap?
- What common ground can all sides agree on?
- How can you show that standing on this common ground will be of benefit to everyone involved?
- How can you use language — word choice, analogies or other figures of speech, varieties of English, or languages other than English (see Chapter 34) — to establish common ground with your audience?

---

**QUICK HELP**

**Building *ethos* through careful restatement**

Expert writers, says linguist Laura Aull, use "reformulation" or restatement to help build credibility and signal their own take on the evidence they're presenting. Phrases like *in other words*, *that is to say*, and *to be precise* show that a writer is interpreting information for the reader; *especially* or *in particular* emphasize what the writer finds particularly important; *in fact* or *indeed* show that a writer is contrasting an existing view. Expert writers use such phrases to restate and underscore their interpretation and introduce their own voices into their writing far more often than student writers do. Like transitions, these restatements help showcase the writer's reason for organizing the text in a particular way or emphasize the relation between ideas or parts of a text. How can you use restatement to build your *ethos*, or credibility? Look for—and ask peer reviewers to point out—opportunities to restate others' ideas.

## Fairness

In arguing a position, the most effective writers deal fairly with alternative or opposing arguments (often called counterarguments). After all, people are more inclined to listen to writers who seem to consider other views fairly than to those who ignore or distort such views. The following questions can help you make sure you are being open-minded:

- How can you show that you are considering and respecting all significant points of view?

- How can you demonstrate that you understand and empathize with points of view other than your own?

- What can you do to show that you have considered evidence carefully, even when it does not support your position?

Some writers, instead of demonstrating fairness, may make unjustified attacks on an opponent's credibility. Avoid such attacks in your writing.

## Visuals that make ethical appeals

In arguments and other kinds of writing, visuals can combine with text to present a writer or an organization as trustworthy and credible. Like businesses, many institutions and individuals are using logos and other images to brand themselves as they wish the public to see them. The Sustainable Food Laboratory logo, seen on
this page, suggests that the organization is concerned about both food production and the environment.

---

LANGUAGE, CULTURE, AND CONTEXT | **COUNTING YOUR OWN EXPERIENCE**

You may have been told that personal experience doesn't count in making academic arguments. If so, reconsider this advice. Showing an audience that you have relevant experience with a topic can carry strong persuasive appeal with English-speaking readers.

---

Visuals that make ethical appeals add to your credibility as a writer. Just as you consider the impression your social media profile photo makes on your audience, you should think about what kind of case you're making for yourself when you choose images and design elements for your argument.

### EXERCISE 11.5

List the ways in which the Sustainable Food Laboratory's logo demonstrates knowledge, establishes common ground, and shows fairness. Do you think the visual is helpful in convincing you of the organization's credibility? Why, or why not?

### EXERCISE 11.6

Using a working thesis you have drafted, write a paragraph or two describing how you would go about establishing your credibility in arguing that thesis.

---

## 11j Using effective logical appeals

Credibility alone cannot and should not carry the full burden of convincing readers. The logic of the argument, the reasoning behind it, is as important as its ethos.

### Examples and precedents

Just as an authentic picture can sometimes be worth a thousand words, so can a well-conceived example be valuable in arguing a point. Examples are used most often to support generalizations or to bring abstractions to life. In making the general statement that popular media send the message that a woman must be thin to be attractive, you might include these examples:

> At the supermarket checkout, a tabloid publishes unflattering photographs of a young singer and comments on her apparent weight gain in shocked captions that ask "What happened?!?" Another praises a star for quickly shedding "ugly pounds" after the recent birth of a child. The cover of

*Cosmopolitan* features a glamorously made-up and airbrushed actress in an outfit that reveals her tiny waist and flat stomach. Every woman featured in the magazine's ads is thin — and the context makes it clear that readers are supposed to think that these women are beautiful.

*Precedents* are examples taken from the past. If, as part of a proposal for making the engineering library more accessible by adding an additional wheel-chair ramp, you point out that the university has added such ramps to three other libraries on campus, you are arguing on the basis of precedent.

The following questions can help you check any use of example or precedent:

- How representative are the examples?

- Are the examples sufficient in strength or number to lead to a generalization?

- In what ways do they support your point?

- How closely does a precedent relate to your point? Are the situations really similar?

- How timely is the precedent? (An example from 1985 may not apply today.)

In research writing, remember to identify your sources for any examples or precedents not based on your own knowledge or research.

## Authority and testimony

Another way to support an argument logically is to cite an authority. The use of authority figured prominently in the controversy over smoking. Following the U.S. surgeon general's 1964 announcement that smoking is hazardous to health, millions of Americans quit smoking, largely persuaded by the authority of the scientists offering the evidence. Today, authorities are making similar arguments about vaping.

Ask the following questions to be sure you are using authorities effectively:

- Is the authority a "real" authority — or are credentials false or overstated?

- Is the authority *timely*?

- Is the authority *qualified* to judge the topic at hand?

- Is the authority likely to be *known and respected* by readers?

- Are the authority's *credentials* clearly stated and verifiable?

Testimony — the evidence that an authority presents in support of a claim — is a feature of much contemporary argument. If testimony is timely, accurate, representative, and provided by a respected authority, then it, like authority itself, can add powerful support.

In research writing, you should cite your sources for authority and for testimony not based on your own knowledge.

## Causes and effects

Showing that one event is the cause or the effect of another can help support an argument. Suppose you are trying to explain, in a petition to change your grade in a course, why you were unable to take the final exam. You might trace the causes of your failure to appear — your illness or the theft of your car, perhaps — so that the committee reading the petition would reconsider the effect — your not taking the exam.

Tracing causes often lays the groundwork for an argument, particularly if the effect of the causes is one we would like to change. In an environmental science class, for example, a student may argue that a law regulating smokestack emissions from utility plants is needed because (1) acid rain on the East Coast originates from emissions at utility plants in the Midwest, (2) acid rain kills trees and other vegetation, (3) utility lobbyists have prevented Midwestern states from passing laws controlling emissions, and (4) if such laws are not passed, acid rain will soon destroy most eastern forests. In this case, the fourth point ties all of the previous points together to provide an overall argument from effect: if X, then Y.

## Inductive and deductive reasoning

Traditionally, logical arguments are classified as using either inductive or deductive reasoning; in practice, the two often work together. Inductive reasoning is the process of making a generalization based on a number of specific instances. If you are ill on ten occasions after eating seafood, for example, you might draw the inductive generalization that seafood makes you ill. You may not be certain that seafood is to blame, but the probability lies in that direction.

Deductive reasoning, on the other hand, reaches a conclusion by assuming a general principle (the major premise) and then applying that principle to a specific case (the minor premise). In practice, this general principle is usually derived from induction. The inductive generalization *Seafood makes me ill*, for instance, could serve as the major premise for the deductive argument *Since all seafood makes me ill, the shrimp on this buffet is certain to make me ill.*

Deductive arguments have traditionally been analyzed as syllogisms: reasoning that contains a major premise, a minor premise, and a conclusion.

| | |
|---|---|
| MAJOR PREMISE | All people die. |
| MINOR PREMISE | I am a person. |
| CONCLUSION | I will die. |

Syllogisms, however, are too rigid to serve in arguments about questions that have no absolute answers, and they often lack any appeal to an audience. Aristotle's more flexible alternative, the enthymeme, asks the audience to supply the implied major premise. Consider the following example:

Because they harm other children, bullies should be disciplined by schools.

You can analyze this enthymeme by restating it in the form of two premises and a conclusion.

| | |
|---|---|
| MAJOR PREMISE | Students who harm other children should be disciplined by schools. |
| MINOR PREMISE | Bullies harm other children. |
| CONCLUSION | Bullies should be disciplined by schools. |

Note that the major premise is one the writer can count on an audience agreeing with or supplying: safety and common sense demand that schools should discipline children who harm other students. By implicitly asking the audience to supply this premise to the argument, the writer engages the audience's participation.

Toulmin's system (10e) looks for claims, reasons, and assumptions instead of major and minor premises.

| | |
|---|---|
| CLAIM | Bullies should be disciplined by schools. |
| REASON(S) | Bullies harm other children. |
| ASSUMPTION | Students who harm other children should be disciplined by schools. |

Note that in this system the assumption — which may be unstated — serves the same function as the assumed major premise in an enthymeme.

Whether it is expressed as a syllogism, an enthymeme, or a claim, a deductive conclusion is only as strong as the premise or reasons on which it is based.

### EXERCISE 11.7

The following sentences contain deductive arguments based on implied major premises. Identify each of the implied premises.

1. The use of marijuana for medical purposes should be legal if it is regulated the same way alcoholic beverages are.

2. Women soldiers should not serve in combat positions because doing so would expose them to a much higher risk of death.

3. Animals can't talk; therefore, they can't feel pain as humans do.

## Visuals that make logical appeals

Visuals that make logical appeals can be especially useful in arguments, since they present factual information that can be taken in at a glance. The U.S. Census Bureau used this simple chart to make a statement about disaster preparedness. Consider how long it would take to explain all the information in the following chart with words alone.

### ◢ EXERCISE 11.8

Write a paragraph describing the logical appeals you would use to support the thesis of a project you are working on.

# 11k Using appropriate emotional appeals

Most successful arguments appeal to our hearts as well as to our minds — as is vividly demonstrated by the debate over whether aid to Puerto Rico was sufficient after Hurricane Maria devastated the island in 2017. Facts and figures (logical appeals) convince us that the problem is real and serious. What elicits an outpouring of support, however, is the arresting emotional power of stories and images of people affected by the disaster. But credible writers take care when they use emotional appeals; audiences can easily begin to feel manipulated when an argument tries too hard to appeal to their pity, anger, or fear.

## Concrete descriptive details

Like photographs, vivid words can bring a moving immediacy to any argument. A student may amass facts and figures, including diagrams and maps, to illustrate the problem of wheelchair access to the library. But only when the student asks a friend who uses a wheelchair to accompany her to the library does the student writer discover the concrete details necessary to move readers. The student can then write, "Manisha inched her heavy wheelchair up the entrance ramp, her arms straining, her face pinched with effort."

## Figurative language

Figures of speech are the special effects of language: they can paint a detailed and vivid picture by making striking comparisons between something you are writing about and something else that helps a reader visualize, identify with, or understand it (37a). As such they are not "decoration" but crucial elements in human communication.

Figures of speech include metaphors, similes, and analogies. Most simply, metaphors compare two things directly:

Serena Williams, the trailblazer

old age, the evening of life

Similes make comparisons using *like* or *as*:

Serena Williams is like a trailblazer.

Old age is like the evening of life.

Analogies are extended metaphors or similes that compare an unfamiliar concept or process to a more familiar one. For more about these special effects of language, see Chapter 41.

## Visuals that make emotional appeals

Visuals that make emotional appeals can also add substance to your argument. To make sure that such visual appeals will enhance your argument, test them out with several potential readers to see how they interpret the appeal. Consider, for example, this photograph depicting a Boston rally of gun-rights advocates. The image includes a group of protesters, one of whom is holding a sign say-

ing "More gun laws will not stop mad men from killing," with a large yellow "Don't Tread on Me" flag in the foreground. Readers who generally oppose laws regulating gun ownership in the United States may feel very differently about this image than readers who tend to support restrictions.

### ◢ EXERCISE 11.9

Make a list of common emotions that might be attached to the following topics, and suggest appropriate ways to appeal to those emotions in a specific audience:

1. binge drinking on campus
2. airport security
3. birth control
4. health care reform
5. the opioid crisis

### ◢ EXERCISE 11.10

Using a working thesis you have formulated, make a list of the emotional appeals most appropriate to your topic and audience. Then spend ten to fifteen minutes brainstorming, looking for descriptive and figurative language as well as images to carry out the appeals.

# 11l Using sources in an argument

Academic arguments almost always call for using sources. The key to persuading people to accept your argument is providing good reasons; even if your assignment doesn't specify it, consulting reliable sources is often the most effective way of finding and establishing these reasons. Accurate, reliable, and truthful sources can help you to do the following:

- provide background information on your topic
- demonstrate your knowledge of the topic to readers
- cite authority and testimony in support of your thesis
- discover and consider opinions that differ from yours and thus sharpen your thinking, qualify your thesis if necessary, and demonstrate fairness to opposing arguments

For a more thorough discussion of finding and evaluating sources, see Chapters 13 and 14.

## 11m  Organizing your argument

Once you have assembled good reasons and evidence in support of an argumentative thesis, you must organize your material to present the argument convincingly. Although there is no universally favored, one-size-fits-all organizational framework, you may want to use one of the following patterns.

### The classical system

The system of argument often followed by ancient Greek and Roman orators is now referred to as *classical*. You can adapt the ancient format to written arguments as follows:

1. Introduction
   - Gain readers' attention and interest.
   - Establish your qualifications to write about your topic.
   - Establish common ground with readers.
   - Demonstrate fairness.
   - State or imply your thesis.

2. Background: Present any necessary background information, including relevant personal narrative.

3. Lines of argument
   - Present good reasons (including logical and emotional appeals) in support of your thesis.
   - Present reasons in order of importance, with the most important ones generally saved for last.
   - Demonstrate ways your argument may be in readers' best interest.

4. Alternative arguments
   - Examine alternative points of view.

- Note advantages and disadvantages of alternative views.
- Explain why one view is better than other(s).

5. Conclusion
   - Summarize the argument if you choose.
   - Elaborate on the implication of your thesis.
   - Make clear what you want readers to think or do.
   - Reinforce your credibility.

## The Toulmin system

This simplified form of the Toulmin system (10e and 11j) can help you organize an argumentative essay:

1. Make your claim (arguable statement).

   ▶ **The federal government should ban smoking.**

2. Qualify your claim if necessary.

   ▶ **The ban would be limited to public places.**

3. Present good reasons to support your claim.

   ▶ **Smoking causes serious diseases in smokers.**

   ▶ **Nonsmokers are endangered by others' smoke.**

4. Explain the assumptions that underlie your claim and your reasons. Provide additional explanations for any controversial assumptions.

   | ASSUMPTION | The Constitution was established to "promote the general welfare." |
   |---|---|
   | ASSUMPTION | Citizens are entitled to protection from harmful actions by others. |
   | ADDITIONAL EXPLANATION | The United States is based on a political system that is supposed to serve the basic needs of its people, including their health. |

5. Provide additional evidence to support your claim (such as facts, statistics, testimony, and other logical, ethical, or emotional appeals).

   | STATISTICS | Cite the incidence of deaths attributed to secondhand smoke. |
   |---|---|
   | FACTS | Cite lawsuits won against large tobacco companies, including one that awarded billions of dollars to states in reparation for smoking-related health care costs. |
   | FACTS | Cite bans on smoking already imposed on indoor public spaces in many cities. |
   | AUTHORITY | Cite the surgeon general. |

6. Acknowledge and respond to possible counterarguments.

COUNTER-ARGUMENT   Smokers have rights, too.

RESPONSE   The suggested ban applies only to public places; smokers are free to smoke in private.

7. Finally, state your conclusion in the strongest way possible.

## Rogerian and invitational argument

The psychologist Carl Rogers argued that people should not enter into disputes until they can thoroughly and fairly understand the other person's (or persons') perspectives. From Rogers's theory, rhetoricians Richard Young, Alton Becker, and Kenneth Pike adapted a four-part structure that is now known as Rogerian argument:

1. The introduction describes the issue, problem, or conflict in enough detail to demonstrate that the writer fully grasps and respects alternative points of view.

2. The writer then fairly describes the contexts in which such alternative positions might be valid.

3. The writer offers his or her position on the issue and explains in what circumstances and why that position would be valid.

4. Finally, the writer explains how those who hold alternative positions can benefit from adopting the writer's position.

Like Rogerian argument, invitational rhetoric, first proposed by Sonja Foss and Cindy Griffin, has as its goal getting people to work together effectively, to listen respectfully, and to identify with each other; it aims for connection and collaboration. Such arguments call for structures that are closer to good two-way conversations or freewheeling dialogues than a linear march from thesis to conclusion. If you use such an organizational plan, you might

• begin with an introduction that recognizes varying positions and perspectives on the topic and makes it clear that the major goal is understanding

• describe each perspective fairly and respectfully, if possible using the words of those who advocate the perspectives

• conclude by identifying and exploring common ground and what it might lead to

If you try developing such a conversational structure, you may find that it opens up a space in your argument for new perceptions and fresh ideas.

# 11n Considering design and delivery

Asked to name the three most important parts of rhetoric, the ancient orator Demosthenes said: *delivery, delivery, delivery.* In short, while what speakers said was important, the way they said it was of even greater importance. Today, we live in a time of information overload, when many powerful messages are vying for our attention. Getting and keeping an audience's attention is all about delivery. Figuring out the medium of delivery (print? digital? in-person?) and the appropriate genre is also important, as is designing the argument to appeal to your audience.

- What medium will best get and hold your audience's attention? print? video? in-person presentation? social media post? Choosing just the right one is important to your success.
- What genre is most appropriate for your message? a report? a narrative? an essay? a brochure?
- What word choice, style, and tone will be most successful in delivering your message?
- What visual style will appeal to your intended readers, set a clear tone for your argument, and guide readers through your text?
- Are visual and media elements clearly integrated into your argument? Place images close to the text they illustrate, and label each one clearly. Make sure that audio and video files appear in appropriate places and are identified for users.

**EXERCISE 11.11**

Using the guidelines in this chapter, draft an argument in support of the working thesis for a project you are working on.

# 11o A student's argument essay

STUDENT WRITER
Benjy Mercer-Golden

In this argument essay, Benjy Mercer-Golden argues that socially conscious businesses and traditional for-profit businesses can learn from each other in ways that benefit businesses, consumers, and the environment. His essay has been annotated to point out the various parts of his argument as well as his use of good reasons, evidence, and appeals to logic and emotion.

Mercer-Golden 1

Benjy Mercer-Golden

Professor Sood

English 102

22 November 2019

Lessons from Tree-Huggers and Corporate Mercenaries:

A New Model of Sustainable Capitalism

**Provocative word choice for title**

Televised images of environmental degradation — seagulls with oil coating their feathers, smokestacks belching gray fumes — often seem designed to shock, but these images also represent very real issues: climate change, dwindling energy resources like coal and oil, a scarcity of clean drinking water. In response, businesspeople around the world are thinking about how they can make their companies greener or more socially beneficial to ensure a brighter future for humanity. But progress in the private sector has been slow and inconsistent. To accelerate the move to sustainability, for-profit businesses need to learn from the hybrid model of social entrepreneurship to ensure that the company is efficient and profitable while still working for social change, and more investors need to support companies with long-term, revolutionary visions for improving the world.

**Emotional appeals through use of vivid imagery**

**Thesis establishing purpose**

In fact, both for-profit corporations and "social good" businesses could take steps to reshape their strategies. First, for-profit corporations need to operate sustainably and be evaluated for their performance with long-term measurements and incentives. The conventional argument against for-profit companies deeply embedding environmental and social goals into their corporate strategies is that caring about the world does not go hand in hand with lining pockets. This morally toxic case is also problematic from a business standpoint. A 2012 study of 180 high-profile companies by Harvard Business School professors Robert G. Eccles and George Serafeim and London Business School professor Ioannis Ioannou

**Claim related to thesis**

**Opposing viewpoint to establish writer's credibility**

**Response to counterargument**

shows that "high sustainability companies," as defined by environmental and social variables, "significantly outperform their counterparts over the long term, both in terms of stock market and accounting performance." The study argues that the better financial returns of these companies are especially evident in sectors where "companies' products significantly depend upon extracting large amounts of natural resources" (Eccles et al.).

Such empirical financial evidence to support a shift toward using energy from renewable sources to run manufacturing plants argues that executives should think more sustainably, but other underlying incentives need to evolve in order to bring about tangible change. David Blood and Al Gore of Generation Investment Management, an investment firm focused on "sustainable investing for the long term" ("About"), wrote a groundbreaking white paper that outlined the perverse incentives company managers face. For public companies, the default practice is to issue earnings guidances — announcements of projected future earnings — every quarter. This practice encourages executives to manage for the short term instead of adding long-term value to their company and the earth (Gore and Blood). Only the most uncompromisingly green CEOs would still advocate for stricter carbon emissions standards at the company's factories if a few mediocre quarters left investors demanding that they be fired. Gore and Blood make a powerful case against requiring companies to be subjected to this "What have you done for me lately?" philosophy, arguing that quarterly earnings guidances should be abolished in favor of companies releasing information when they consider it appropriate. And to further persuade managers to think sustainably, companies need to change the way the managers get paid. Currently, the CEO of ExxonMobil is rewarded for a highly profitable year but is not held accountable for depleting

*(margin annotations)*

Transition referring to ideas in previous paragraph

Details of claim

Logical appeals using information and evidence in white paper

Ethical appeal to companies

Partial solution proposed

Mercer-Golden 3

nonrenewable oil reserves. A new model should incentivize thinking for the long run. Multiyear milestones for performance evaluation, as Gore and Blood suggest, are essential to pushing executives to manage sustainably.

**Claim extended to socially responsible businesses**

But it's not just for-profit companies that need to rethink strategies. Social good–oriented leaders also stand to learn from the people often vilified in environmental circles: corporate CEOs. To survive in today's economy, companies building sustainable products must operate under the same strict business standards as profit-driven companies. Two social enterprises, Nika Water and Belu, provide perfect examples. Both sell bottled water in the developed world with the mission of providing clean water to impoverished communities through their profits. Both have visionary leaders who define the lesson that all environmental and social entrepreneurs need to understand: financial pragmatism will add far more value to the world than idealistic dreams. Nika Water founder Jeff Church explained this in a speech at Stanford University:

**Logical appeals**

> Social entrepreneurs look at their businesses as nine parts cause, one part business. In the beginning, it needs to be nine parts business, one part cause, because if the business doesn't stay around long enough because it can't make it, you can't do anything about the cause.

**Additional logical appeals**

When U.K.-based Belu lost £600,000 ($940,000) in 2007, it could only give around £30,000 ($47,000) to charity. Karen Lynch took over as CEO, cutting costs, outsourcing significant parts of the company's operations, and redesigning the entire business model; the company now donates four times as much to charity (Hurley). The conventional portrayal of do-gooders is that they tend to be terrible businesspeople, an argument often grounded in reality. It is easy to criticize the Walmarts of the world for caring little about sustainability or social good, but the idealists with big

Mercer-Golden 4

visions who do not follow through on their promises because
their businesses cannot survive are no more praiseworthy.
Walmart should learn from nonprofits and social enterprises on
advancing a positive environmental and social agenda, but
idealist entrepreneurs should also learn from corporations about
building successful businesses.

The final piece of the sustainable business ecosystem is the
investors who help get potentially world-changing companies
off the ground. Industries that require a large amount of money
to build complex products with expensive materials, such as solar
power companies, rely heavily on investors — often venture
capitalists based in California's Silicon Valley (Knight). The problem
is that venture capitalists are not doing enough to fund truly
groundbreaking companies. In an oft-cited blog post titled "Why
Facebook Is Killing Silicon Valley," entrepreneur Steve Blank argues
that the financial returns on social media companies have been
so quick and so outsized that the companies with the really big
ideas — like providing efficient, cheap, scalable solar power — are not
being backed: "In the past, if you were a great [venture capitalist],
you could make $100 million on an investment in 5–7 years. Today,
social media start-ups can return hundreds of millions or even billions
in less than 3 years." The point Blank makes is that what is earning
investors lots of money right now is not what is best for the United
States or the world.

There are, however, signs of hope. PayPal founder Peter
Thiel runs his venture capital firm, the Founders Fund, on the
philosophy that investors should support "flying cars" instead of new
social media ventures (Packer). While the next company with
the mission of making photo-sharing cooler or communicating with
friends easier might be both profitable and valuable, Thiel and a

*Marginal annotations:*

Return to thesis: businesses should learn from one another

Transition to second part of thesis signaled

Problem explained

Reasons in support of claim

Transition signaling reason for optimism

Mercer-Golden 5

Reason
presented

select few others fund technology that has the potential to solve the
huge problems essential to human survival.

The world's need for sustainable companies that can build
products from renewable energy or make nonpolluting cars will
inevitably create opportunities for smart companies to make
money. In fact, significant opportunities already exist for
venture capitalists willing to step away from what is easy today
and shift their investment strategies toward what will help us
continue to live on this planet tomorrow — even if seeing strong
returns may take a few more years. Visionaries like Blank and
Thiel need more allies (and dollars) in their fight to help produce
more pioneering, sustainable companies. And global warming

Emotional
appeal

won't abate before investors wise up. It is vital that this shift
happen now.

Logical
appeal

When we think about organizations today, we think about
nonprofits, which have long-term social missions, and corporations,
which we judge by their immediate financial returns like quarterly

Thesis
revisited

earnings. That is a treacherous dichotomy. Instead, we need to see the
three major players in the business ecosystem — corporations, social
enterprises, and investors — moving toward a *single* model of long-
term, sustainable capitalism. We need visionary companies that not
only set out to solve humankind's biggest problems but also have the
business intelligence to accomplish these goals, and we need investors
willing to fund these companies. Gore and Blood argue that "the

Quotation,
restatement
of thesis, and
emotional
appeal close
argument

imperative for change has never been greater." We will see this change
when the world realizes that sustainable capitalism shares the same goals
as creating a sustainable environment. Let us hope that this realization
comes soon.

### Works Cited

"About Us." *Generation*, 2012, www.generationim.com/about/.

Blank, Steve. "Why Facebook Is Killing Silicon Valley." *Steveblank
    .com*, 21 May 2012, steveblank.com/2012/05/21/why
    -facebook-is-killing-silicon-valley/.

Church, Jeff. "The Wave of Social Entrepreneurship." Entrepreneurial
    Thought Leaders Seminar, NVIDIA Auditorium, Stanford, 11 Apr.
    2012. Lecture.

Eccles, Robert G., et al. "The Impact of a Corporate Culture of
    Sustainability on Organizational Process and Performance."
    *Working Knowledge*, Harvard Business School, 14 Nov. 2011,
    hbswk.hbs.edu/item/the-impact-of-corporate-sustainability-on
    -organizational-process-and-performance.

Gore, Al, and David Blood. "Sustainable Capitalism." *Generation*, 15
    Feb. 2012, www.generationim.com/media/pdf-generation
    -sustainable-capitalism-v1.pdf.

Hurley, James. "Belu Boss Shows Bottle for a Turnaround." *Daily
    Telegraph*, 28 Feb. 2012, www.telegraph.co.uk/finance/
    businessclub/9109449/Belu-boss-shows-bottle-for-a
    -turnaround.html.

Knight, Eric R. W. "The Economic Geography of Clean Tech Venture
    Capital." Oxford University Working Paper Series in Employment,
    Work, and Finance, 13 Apr. 2010. *Social Science Research
    Network*, doi:10.2139/ssrn.1588806.

Packer, George. "No Death, No Taxes: The Libertarian Futurism of a
    Silicon Valley Billionaire." *The New Yorker*, 28 Nov. 2011, www
    .newyorker.com/magazine/2011/11/28/no-death-no-taxes.

▼ ▼ ▼ ▼ ▼ ▼ ▼ ▼ ▼ ▼ ▼ ▼ ▼ ▼ ▼ ▼ ▼ ▼ ▼ ▼ ▼ ▼ ▼

## THINKING CRITICALLY ABOUT CONSTRUCTING ARGUMENTS

Using the checklist in section 11b, analyze a draft of an argument you've recently written. Decide what you need to do to revise your argument, and write out a brief plan for revision.

# PART 4
# Doing Research and Using Sources

Photo by Mike Enright/www.menright.com. Photo styling by Barbara Lipp.

# Preparing for a Research Project

Your employer asks you to recommend the best software for a particular project. You want to curate a podcast lineup for spring break. You dream of starting a community garden. Once you begin to think about it, you'll find that many of your day-to-day activities call for research. Preparing to do research means taking a long look at what you already know, the best way to proceed, and the amount of time you have to find the information you need.

## 12a Considering the research process

If you have little experience doing research for academic projects, you may feel some anxiety about a major research assignment. Bear the following tips in mind to turn yourself into an expert researcher:

- **You already know something about doing research.** You act as a researcher whenever you try to find out more about anything that interests you. If you are researching coffee options, you may look up information online about the trade practices of coffee suppliers or talk with friends about coffee shops with the best atmosphere, the lowest prices, or the tastiest coffee.

- **Research projects that interest you are easier and more enjoyable to complete.** Researchers usually seek out information and opinions for a reason. Your main purpose in college research may be to fulfill an assignment, but if you can also find a purpose with which you make a personal connection, your research task will be more rewarding.

- **Research rarely progresses in a neat line from start to finish.** When you begin any research, you don't know exactly what you will discover. You begin with a question that may lead you to other sources. Additional research may narrow your idea — or cause you to change directions entirely. If you set out to find information on the development of the multiplayer online game *Overwatch* and end up interested in how players work together to succeed in the game, your new purpose will require you to take another look at the research you need to do.

- **Good research calls for careful reflection.** While you may often begin research by skimming to identify useful sources, once you have found key sources, stop skimming! Read carefully, taking notes and reflecting on the reliability of the source and its usefulness for your argument.

- **Good research can make you a genuine expert.** If you approach your research seriously and follow all the leads that you can, you may eventually become an expert on a topic that interests you — Korean films, homeopathic allergy treatments, or low-cost early childhood services in your neighborhood.

College research may range from a couple of hours spent gathering background information on a topic for a brief essay to weeks or months of full-scale exploration for a term project.

## 12b Analyzing the assignment

In an introductory writing course, you might receive an assignment like this one:

Choose a subject of interest to you, and use it as the basis for a research essay of approximately 2,500 words that makes and substantiates a claim. You should use a minimum of five to eight credible, authoritative sources.

### Considering requirements and limits

Before you begin any research assignment, make sure you understand what you need to do.

- How many sources should you use?
- Does your instructor require certain kinds of sources? If so, what kinds?
- What genre and medium will be appropriate for this project? Are you expected to write a traditional print essay or slide presentation? Should you consider another genre or medium, such as a blog post or video essay?
- Will you use images, sound, or video in your assignment?
- Should you work independently or collaborate with others on the project?
- What kind of documentation style is required? (See Chapters 18–21.)
- Do you understand what your instructor expects? If not, ask for clarification.

### Considering the rhetorical situation

Be sure to consider the rhetorical situation of any research project (p. 174).

*Purpose*

- If you can choose the purpose, what would you like to accomplish?
- What do you need to do in this project — explain a situation? weigh opposing viewpoints and make a claim about which is correct? convince the audience to do something? explore causes or effects? Your purpose will affect the kinds of sources you need to find.
- If you have been assigned a specific research project, keep in mind the key words in that assignment. Does the assignment ask that you *describe, survey, analyze, persuade, explain, classify, compare,* or *contrast*?

*Audience*

- Who will be the audience for your research project (3d, 11f)?
- What do you know about their backgrounds? What assumptions might they hold about the topic? What do they already know, and what do they need to know?
- What genre and medium will be the best way to reach your audience (3e, 11f)?
- What response do you want to elicit from them?
- What kinds of evidence will you need to convince them?
- How can you be sure to respect differences among your various audiences and between you and your audience?

*Rhetorical stance*

- What is your attitude or stance toward your topic (3c)?
- Are you curious about it? critical of it? Do you like it? dislike it? find it confusing?
- What influences have shaped your stance?

*Scope*

- How long is the project supposed to be? Base your research and writing schedule on the scale of the finished project (brief vs. long paper or presentation, a simple vs. complex website) and the amount of time you have to complete it.
- How many and what kind(s) of sources should you use (12f)? What kind(s) of visuals—charts, maps, photographs, and so on—will you need? Will you use sound or video files? What field research might you do—interviewing, surveying, or observing (13d)?

## Deadlines

When is the project due? Are any drafts or outlines required before the due date? Here is a sample schedule for a research project.

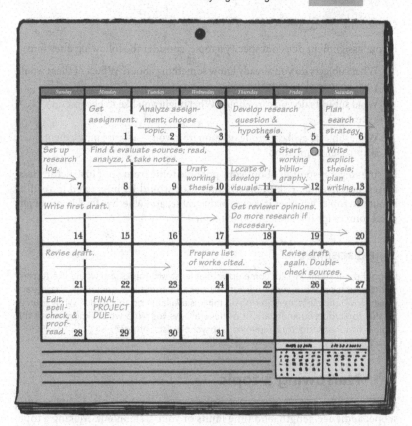

| Sunday | Monday | Tuesday | Wednesday | Thursday | Friday | Saturday |
|---|---|---|---|---|---|---|
| | Get assignment. 1 | Analyze assignment; choose topic. 2 | 3 | Develop research question & hypothesis. 4 | 5 | Plan search strategy. 6 |
| Set up research log. 7 | Find & evaluate sources; read, analyze, & take notes. 8 | 9 | Draft working thesis 10 | Locate or develop visuals. 11 | Start working bibliography. 12 | Write explicit thesis; plan writing. 13 |
| Write first draft. 14 | 15 | 16 | 17 | Get reviewer opinions. Do more research if necessary. 18 | 19 | 20 |
| Revise draft. 21 | 22 | 23 | Prepare list of works cited. 24 | 25 | Revise draft again. Double-check sources. 26 | 27 |
| Edit, spell-check, & proofread. 28 | FINAL PROJECT DUE. 29 | 30 | 31 | | | |

---

## TALKING THE TALK | **REACHING AN AUDIENCE**

"Isn't my audience just my teacher?" To write effectively, you must think of your writing as more than just an assignment you go through to get a grade. After all, depending on how you share your work, your research has the potential to reach a much wider audience. Recognize that you have something to say — and that to get others to pay attention, you have to think about who they are and how to reach them. Of course, your instructor is part of your audience. But who else will be interested in your topic and the unique perspective you bring to it?

## Choosing a topic

If your assignment does not specify a topic, consider the following questions:

- What subjects do you already know something about? Which of them would you like to explore more fully?
- What subjects do you care about? What might you like to become an expert on?
- What subjects evoke a strong reaction from you — intense puzzlement, skepticism, affirmation?

Be sure to get responses about your possible topic from your instructor, classmates, and friends. Ask them whether they would be interested in reading about the topic, whether it seems manageable, and whether they know of any good sources for information on the topic.

### EXERCISE 12.1

Using the questions in 12b, come up with at least two topics you would like to carry out research on. Then write a brief response to some key questions about each topic: How much information do you think is available on this topic? What sources on this topic do you know about or have access to? Who would know about this topic—historians, doctors, filmmakers, psychologists, others?

## 12c Narrowing a topic

Any topic you choose to research must be manageable — it should suit the scope, audience, length, and time limits of your assignment. Making a topic manageable often requires narrowing it, but you may also need to find a particular slant and look for a question to guide your research. To arrive at such a question, you might first generate a series of questions about your topic. You can then evaluate them and choose one or two that are both interesting and manageable.

## 12d Moving from research question to hypothesis

Once you have analyzed your task, chosen your topic, and narrowed it (see 4b), formulate a research question that you can tentatively answer with a hypothesis. The hypothesis, a statement of what you anticipate your research will show, needs to be manageable, interesting (see 4c), and debatable.

Julia Sakowitz, the student whose research paper appears in Chapter 18, made the following move from general topic to a narrowed topic and then to a research question and hypothesis:

| TOPIC | How tourism affects residents/neighborhoods |
|---|---|
| NARROWED TOPIC | How tourism in Harlem affects its residents |
| ISSUE | Many types of tourism businesses are operating in the historic Harlem neighborhood, but not all bring benefits for residents. |
| RESEARCH QUESTION | Which type of tourism business is more beneficial to the residents of Harlem, a small local and minority-owned business or an outside tour company? |
| HYPOTHESIS | Small, local, minority-owned tour businesses seem to benefit the residents of Harlem more than those businesses that come in from outside Harlem. |

## 12e Determining what you know

Once you have formulated a hypothesis, determine what you already know about your topic. Here are some strategies for doing so:

- **Brainstorming.** Take five minutes to list everything you think of or wonder about your hypothesis (4a). You may find it helpful to do this in a group with other students.

- **Freewriting about your hypothesis.** For five minutes, write about every reason for believing your hypothesis is true. Then for another five minutes, write down every argument you can think of, no matter how weak, that someone opposed to your hypothesis might make.

- **Freewriting about your audience.** Write for five minutes about your readers, including your instructor. What do you think they currently believe about your topic? What sorts of evidence will convince them to accept your hypothesis? What sorts of sources will they respect?

- **Tapping your memory for sources.** List everything you can remember about *where* you learned about your topic: websites, emails, books, magazines, courses, conversations, television. What you know comes from somewhere, and that "somewhere" can serve as a starting point for research.

### EXERCISE 12.2

Using the tips in 12e, write down as much as you can about a topic that interests you. Then take some time to reread your notes, and jot down the questions you still need to answer as well as the sources you need to find.

## 12f Making a preliminary research plan

Once you've considered what you already know about your topic, you can develop a research plan. To do so, answer the following questions:

- What kinds of sources (books, journal articles, databases, websites, government documents, reference works) and how many sources will you need to consult?
- How current do your sources need to be?
- How can you determine the location and availability of the kinds of sources you need?

One goal of your research plan is to begin building a strong working bibliography (see 14c). Carrying out systematic research and keeping careful notes on your sources will make developing your works-cited list or bibliography (Chapters 18–21) easier later on.

Finally, setting up a *research log*—a physical notebook, digital file, or Google Doc in which you record ideas about sources and keep track of what you read and find—will make writing and documenting your sources efficient and accurate.

## 12g Moving from hypothesis to working thesis statement

As you gather more information and begin reading and evaluating sources, you will probably refine your research question and change your hypothesis significantly. You may find that your interest shifts, that a whole line of inquiry is unproductive, or that your hypothesis is simply wrong. In each case, the process of research pushes you to learn more about your hypothesis, to make it more precise, and to become an expert on your topic. Only after you have explored your hypothesis, tested it, and sharpened it by reading, writing, and talking with others does it become a working thesis statement.

---

CONSIDERING DISABILITIES | **DICTATION**

If you have difficulty taking notes either on a computer or in a notebook, consider dictating your notes. You might dictate into a handheld recorder for later playback, into a word processor with voice-recognition capability, or into a phone for podcasting on a website.

## Julia Sakowitz's working thesis statement

Student writer Julia Sakowitz, a native New Yorker, researched tourism in Harlem, focusing first on the policies that led to change in Harlem over three decades, which she learned about through traditional library and online sources. When she started to interview Harlem residents and local business owners, she shifted her attention to the effects of tourism on members of the community and developed a new working thesis: "Tour businesses owned by Harlem residents benefit the mostly minority local community better than businesses owned by those who come from outside of Harlem." For Sakowitz's research essay, see Chapter 18.

▼ ▼ ▼ ▼ ▼ ▼ ▼ ▼ ▼ ▼ ▼ ▼ ▼ ▼ ▼ ▼ ▼ ▼ ▼ ▼ ▼ ▼ ▼ ▼ ▼ ▼ ▼

### THINKING CRITICALLY ABOUT YOUR OWN RESEARCH

If you have done research for an essay or research project before, go back and evaluate the work you did as a researcher and as a writer in light of the principles in this chapter. What was the purpose of the research? Who was your audience? How did you narrow and focus your topic? What kinds of sources did you use? Did you use a research log? What about your research and your essay pleased you most? What pleased you least? What would you do differently?

# CHAPTER 13

# Conducting Research

Whether you are researching Heisenberg's uncertainty principle or haircuts, you need to be familiar with the kinds of sources you are likely to use, the searches you are likely to perform, and the three main types of research you will most often be doing: library, Internet, and field research.

## 13a Understanding different kinds of sources

Sources can include data from interviews and surveys, books and articles in print and online, websites, films, video and audio content, images, and more.

### Using primary and secondary sources

Primary sources provide firsthand knowledge; secondary sources report on or analyze the research of others. Primary sources are basic sources of raw information, including your own field research; films, works of art, or other objects you examine; literary works you read; and eyewitness accounts, photographs, news reports, and historical documents such as letters and speeches.

Secondary sources are descriptions or interpretations of primary sources, such as researchers' reports, reviews, biographies, and encyclopedia articles. Often what constitutes a primary or secondary source depends on the purpose of your research. A critic's review of a film, for instance, serves as a secondary source if you are writing about the film but as a primary source if you are studying the critic's writing.

### Using scholarly and popular sources

While nonacademic sources can help you get started on a research project, you will usually want to depend on authorities in a field, whose work generally appears in scholarly journals. The following list will help you distinguish scholarly and popular sources:

SCHOLARLY

POPULAR

| SCHOLARLY | POPULAR |
|---|---|
| • Title often contains the word *Journal* | • *Journal* usually does not appear in title |
| • Available mainly through libraries and library databases | • Available outside of libraries (at newsstands or from a home Internet connection) |
| • Few commercial advertisements | • Many advertisements |
| • Authors identified with academic credentials | • Authors are usually journalists or reporters hired by the publication, not academics or experts |
| • Summary or abstract appears before beginning of article; articles are fairly long | • No summary or abstract; articles are fairly short |
| • Articles cite sources and provide bibliographies | • Articles may include quotations but do not cite sources or provide bibliographies |
| • Examples: *Public Opinion Research Quarterly, Journal of the American Medical Association, Ecology and Society* | • Examples: *Time, The New Yorker, Salon* |

Many (but not all) scholarly sources are *peer reviewed*, which means that experts in the discipline read and approve every article before it is published in the journal.

## Using older and more current sources

Most projects can benefit from both older, historical sources and more current ones. Some older sources are classics in their fields, essential for understanding the scholarship that follows them. Others are simply dated, though even these works can be useful to researchers who want to see what people wrote and read about a topic in the past. Depending on your purpose, you may rely primarily on recent sources (for example, if you are writing about a new scientific discovery), primarily on historical sources (for instance, if your project discusses a nineteenth-century industrial accident), or on a mixture of both. Whether a source appeared hundreds of years ago or this morning, evaluate it carefully to determine how useful it will be for you (Chapter 14).

## 13b Using web and library resources

To find scholarly, popular, primary, secondary, traditional, and multimedia sources, you will most often turn to the web or to your college library.

### Starting with online searches

Many writers begin doing research by turning to Google. The number of results, however, can be overwhelming, giving you much more than you could possibly evaluate or, eventually, use. Nevertheless, doing a quick Google search can give you an overview of what's out there. Wikipedia also offers a good place to begin research, though most instructors warn against citing an article from Wikipedia because many of its authors are often unknown and Wikipedia information may not be entirely credible. But the entries are relatively short, clearly written, and well organized; they can point to themes or issues you can then pursue on trusted sites such as Google Scholar.

Unlike Google, which captures (nearly) everything related to your topic, Google Scholar filters a search, pulling up only articles from scholarly sources. And with Google Scholar, you can pull up a full text rather than simply an abstract or an excerpt from an article.

### Finding authoritative sources on the open web

You can find many sources online that are authoritative and reliable. For example, the Internet enables you to enter virtual libraries that allow access to some collections in libraries other than your own. Online collections housed in government sites can also be reliable and useful sources. The following have useful online collections of articles:

The Library of Congress (www.loc.gov)

National Institutes of Health (www.nih.gov)

U.S. Census Bureau (www.census.gov)

For current national news, consult online versions of reputable newspapers such as the *Washington Post* or the *Chicago Tribune* or sites like C-SPAN.org.

Some scholarly journals (such as those from Berkeley Electronic Press) and general-interest magazines (including *Slate* and *Salon*) are published only on the web, and many other publications, like *Newsweek*, the *New Yorker*, and the *New Republic*, make at least some of their contents available online for free.

## 13c Consulting your library's staff, databases, and other resources

You may have gotten a good start by using Google, Wikipedia, and filtered searches like those from Google Scholar, but you can capitalize on that good start by turning now to the sources available to you for free through your college library.

### Reference librarians

The staff of your library, especially reference librarians, will willingly help you access and use the many databases the library subscribes to. If your writing instructor does not schedule a library orientation, it's worth making an appointment to talk with a librarian about your research project and get specific recommendations about databases and other helpful places to continue your research. To get the most helpful advice, whether online or in person, pose *specific* questions — not "Where can I find information about computers?" but "Where can I find information on the history of messaging technologies?"

### Catalogs and databases

Your library's computers hold many resources not available on the web or not accessible to students except through the library's system. One of these resources is the library's own catalog, but most libraries also subscribe to a large number of databases — digital collections of information, such as indexes to journal and magazine articles, texts of news stories and legal cases, lists of sources on particular topics, and compilations of statistics — that have been vetted by scholars and that students can access for free. Your library may also have software that allows you to search several databases at once.

Many library search engines offer a variety of search options to help you combine keywords (*sleep deprivation* AND *college*), search for an exact phrase (*sleep habits of college students*), or exclude items containing particular keywords (*sleep deprivation* NOT *new parents*). Often they can limit your search in other ways as well, such as by date or language. Look for a "refine your search" box or consider checking "full text" and "scholarly peer review" to make sure you will get relevant, complete, and authoritative texts for your project.

## General and specialized indexes

Different indexes cover different groups of periodicals; articles written before 1990 may be indexed only in a print volume. General indexes of periodicals list articles from general-interest magazines (such as *Time*), newspapers, and perhaps some scholarly journals. General indexes are useful for finding current sources on a topic. Specialized indexes, which tend to include mainly scholarly periodicals, may focus on one discipline (as the education index ERIC does) or on a group of related disciplines (as Social Sciences Abstracts does).

## Full text and abstracts

Be sure not to confuse an abstract with a complete article. Full-text databases can be extremely convenient — you can read and print out articles directly from the computer without the extra step of tracking down the periodical in question. However, if you limit yourself to full-text databases you may miss out on graphics and images that appeared in the print version of the periodical. You can also take advantage of abstracts, which give you a very brief overview of the article's contents so you can decide whether you need to spend time finding and reading the full text.

To locate a promising article that is not available in a full-text digital version, check to see whether a print version is available in your library's periodicals room.

## Books

Libraries categorize books by the *author's name*, by the *title*, and by one or more *subjects*. If you can't find a particular source under any of these headings, you can search by using a combination of subject headings and keywords. Such searches may turn up other useful titles as well. Catalog entries for print books may indicate whether a book has been checked out and, if so, when it is due.

## Bibliographies

Look at any bibliographies (lists of sources) in books or articles you are using for your research; they can lead you to other valuable resources. In addition, check with a reference librarian to find out whether your library has more extensive bibliographies devoted to the area of your research.

## Other library resources

In addition to books and periodicals, libraries give you access to many other useful materials that might be appropriate for your research.

---

CONSIDERING DISABILITIES | **WEBSITE ACCESSIBILITY**

While the Americans with Disabilities Act stipulates that all government websites must be accessible to those with disabilities, these rules now cover educational and other websites as well. If you encounter sites that are not accessible to you, ask a reference librarian to help you identify similar sites that may be more accessible. Also consider clicking on the CONTACT US button, if there is one, and letting the sponsors of the site know that some potential users can't access the information.

---

- **Special collections and archives.** Your library may house archives and other special materials that are often available to student researchers. One student, for example, learned that her university owned a vast collection of twentieth-century posters. With help from a librarian, she was able to use some of these posters as primary sources for her research project on German culture after World War II.

- **Audio, video, multimedia, and art collections.** Many libraries have areas devoted to media and art, where they collect films, videos, paintings, and sound recordings.

- **Government documents.** Many libraries have collections of historical documents produced by local or state government offices. Check with a librarian if government publications would be useful sources for your topic. You can also look at the online version of the U.S. Government Printing Office at www.govinfo.gov for electronic versions of government publications.

- **Interlibrary loans.** To borrow books, videos, or audio materials from another library, use an interlibrary loan. You can also request copies of journal articles from other libraries.

---

TALKING THE TALK | **WIKIS AS SOURCES**

"Why doesn't my instructor want me to use Wikipedia as a source?" Wikis are sites that users can edit as they see fit; as a result, their contents are not always completely reliable for research. It's true that Wikipedia has such a large and enthusiastic audience that editors and users are likely to catch mistakes and remove deliberately false information fairly quickly. But you can never be certain that a wiki entry has not been tampered with. The best advice is to use wikis as sources for preliminary research — Wikipedia's bibliography entries are often a good place to start — and then to make sure that you double-check any information you find there.

# 13d Conducting field research

Many research topics that interest you may call for you to collect field data. The "field" may be many things — a classroom, a church, a laboratory, or a social media site. As a field researcher, you will need to discover *where* you can find relevant information, *how* to gather it, and *who* might be your best providers of information. Also remember that carrying out research on people ("human subjects") may require permission from your college Institutional Review Board, the group that ensures research will not result in harm to people. Observing whether and when motorcycle riders are able to find parking space in the campus lots will probably not require permission, but observing kindergarten students in a local classroom probably will. Talk with your instructor about whether or not you may need such permission.

## Interviews

Some information is best obtained by interviewing — asking direct questions of other people, as Julia Sakowitz did. If you can talk with an expert in person, on the phone, or online, you might get information you could not have obtained through any other kind of research.

Your first step is to find interview subjects. Has your research generated the names of people you might contact directly? Brainstorm for additional names, looking for authorities on your topic and people in your community, and then write, call, or email them to try to arrange an interview.

When you have identified someone to interview, prepare several kinds of questions. Questions about facts and figures (*How many employees do you have?*) elicit specific answers and don't invite expansion or opinion. You can lead the interviewee to think out loud and to give additional details by asking open-ended questions: *How do you feel now about deciding to enlist in the military after 9/11?*

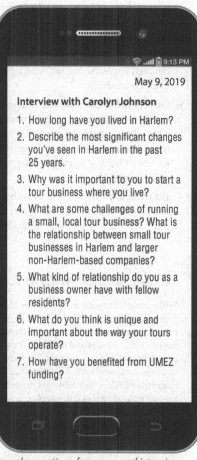

May 9, 2019

**Interview with Carolyn Johnson**

1. How long have you lived in Harlem?
2. Describe the most significant changes you've seen in Harlem in the past 25 years.
3. Why was it important to you to start a tour business where you live?
4. What are some challenges of running a small, local tour business? What is the relationship between small tour businesses in Harlem and larger non-Harlem-based companies?
5. What kind of relationship do you as a business owner have with fellow residents?
6. What do you think is unique and important about the way your tours operate?
7. How have you benefited from UMEZ funding?

*Sample questions for a personal interview*

Avoid questions that would encourage vague answers (*What do you think of youth today?*) or yes/no answers (*Should laws governing student loans be changed?*). Instead, ask questions that must be answered with supporting details (*Why should laws governing student loans be changed?*).

Student writer Julia Sakowitz wrote seven questions in preparation for her interview with a small business owner in her native Harlem.

---

**QUICK HELP**

Conducting an interview

- Determine your exact purpose, and be sure it relates to your research question and hypothesis. Make sure you know enough about your topic to ask intelligent and useful questions.
- Set up the interview early in your research process. Specify how long it will take, and if you wish to record the session, ask permission.
- Prepare a written list of factual and open-ended questions. If the interview proceeds in a direction that seems fruitful, do not feel that you have to ask all of your prepared questions.
- Record the subject, date, time, and place of the interview.
- Even if you are recording, take notes. Ask your interviewee for permission to use video, audio, or quotations in your project.
- Always thank those you interview, both in person and in a letter or email.
- After the interview, check facts and other information you gained, especially anything that seems questionable. You may want to interview other people who can confirm or discredit such information.

---

## Observations

Before you conduct any observation, decide exactly what you want to find out, and anticipate what you are likely to see. Are you going to observe an action repeated by many people (such as pedestrians crossing a street), a sequence of actions (such as a medical procedure), or the interactions of a group (such as a church congregation)? Also decide exactly what you want to record and how. And keep in mind that just as a photographer has a particular angle on a subject, so an observer always has an angle on what he or she is looking at.

## Surveys

To do survey research, you need a representative sample of people (a subset of a group that matches the characteristics of the whole group) and a questionnaire that will elicit the information you need.

On any questionnaire, the questions should be clear and easy to understand and designed so that you will be able to analyze the answers easily. Questions that ask respondents to say yes or no or to rank items on a five-point scale are particularly easy to tabulate. And leaving room for "other" or "additional information" may help you get information that a simple yes/no misses.

Because tabulating the responses takes time and because people sometimes resent answering long questionnaires, limit the number of questions to no more than twenty.

---

**QUICK HELP**

### Conducting an observation

- Determine the purpose and method of the observation, and be sure it relates to your research question and hypothesis.
- Determine whether you will need permission to conduct the observation, record the observation, and take photos. If necessary, make appointments to conduct the observations.
- Brainstorm about what you are looking for, but don't be rigidly bound to your expectations.
- Decide what materials or equipment you may need and make sure it works.
- Develop a system for recording data. Consider using a "split" notebook or screen: on one side, record your observations directly; on the other, record your thoughts and interpretations either during or after the observation.
- Record the date, time, and place of the observation.
- Trust your instincts: you may observe something you weren't looking for but strikes you as interesting and important. Make a note of it.
- Go back over your notes, looking for recurring actions and other patterns, and make a note to come back to them when you begin to analyze your data.

---

## Analyzing and interpreting data

To make sense of the information you have gathered, first try to find a focus, since you can't pay equal attention to everything. This step is especially important in analyzing results from observations or survey questionnaires.

Go back over your notes and results, looking for patterns or trends. In an observation of motorcycle riders looking for parking, you may note a pattern related to the time of day that is busiest, or a certain part of the parking lot that seems to be favored. In your survey results, you may note that women tend to answer one way, men another. You're looking for all such patterns that will help you interpret your findings. Remember to identify quotations you may want to use later; these can help illustrate the points you make.

Next, synthesize the data by looking for recurring words or ideas that fall into patterns. Establish a system for coding your information, labeling each pattern you identify — a plus sign for every positive response on a questionnaire, for example. If you ask classmates to review your notes or data, they may notice other patterns.

---

QUICK HELP

Designing a survey questionnaire

- Write out your purpose, and review your research question and hypothesis to determine the kinds of questions to ask.
- Figure out how to get a representative sample of the group you want to survey and decide how to reach them—by written survey through email or an online survey tool such as Google Forms or SurveyMonkey? By phone or face-to-face?
- Decide what kind of survey questions to use:

  MULTIPLE CHOICE
  Please choose your favorite site for studying:
  _____ dorm
  _____ library
  _____ writing center
  _____ campus café
  _____ outdoor spot

  LEVEL OF AGREEMENT
  Please indicate how much you agree with this statement: *I have a favorite place to study.*
  _____ strongly agree
  _____ agree
  _____ disagree
  _____ strongly disagree

  OPEN-ENDED
  Where on campus do you most like to study?
  _____
  _____

- Draft questions that call for short, specific answers.
- Test the questions on several people, and then revise any questions that seem unfair, ambiguous, too hard to answer, or too time consuming.
- Draft an invitation that introduces the survey. Be sure to state your deadline.
- If you are using a print questionnaire, make sure to leave adequate space for answers.
- Proofread the questionnaire carefully.
- Record the responses you receive, using a blank survey to tally responses or creating a spreadsheet to track findings.

Finally, interpret your data by summing up the meaning of what you have found and articulating insights. Why are the patterns you've identified important? What is the significance of your findings? Be careful not to make large generalizations.

▼ ▼ ▼ ▼ ▼ ▼ ▼ ▼ ▼ ▼ ▼ ▼ ▼ ▼ ▼ ▼ ▼ ▼ ▼ ▼ ▼ ▼ ▼ ▼ ▼

## THINKING CRITICALLY ABOUT CONDUCTING RESEARCH

Begin to analyze the research project you are now working on by examining the ways in which you conducted your research: What use did you make of primary and secondary sources? What library, online, and field research did you carry out? What aspect of the research process was most satisfying? What was most disappointing or irritating? How could you do research more efficiently? Bring your answers to these questions to class.

# CHAPTER 14

# Evaluating Sources and Taking Notes

With most topics, your problem will not be so much finding sources as figuring out *which* sources to consult in the limited time you have available. The difference between a useful source and a poor one depends to a great extent on your topic, purpose, and audience. Learning how to tell which sources are best for you allows you to use your time wisely. Once you've found good sources, taking effective notes allows you to use the insights you find to your greatest advantage.

## 14a Using sources for a purpose

Why do writers decide to use one source rather than another? Sources serve different purposes, so part of evaluating sources involves deciding what you need the source to provide for your research project:

- background information or context that your audience will need to follow your writing
- explanations of concepts unfamiliar to your audience
- verbal and visual emphasis for your points
- authority or evidence for your claims, which can help you create your own authority
- other perspectives on your topic
- counterexamples or counterevidence that you need to consider

As you begin to work with your sources, make notes in your research log about why you plan to use a particular source. At the same time, you should also begin your working bibliography (14c).

## 14b Moving beyond previewing a source

Researchers examining research writing by first-year college students report that student writers often seem to use a quotation or paraphrase from the very beginning of a source — and then set that source aside and go on to something else. By skimming or even skipping the rest of the source, such writers may miss information that could be useful to them. In addition, this research project strongly suggests that student writers often have not read a source carefully, or have misinterpreted or misunderstood it. Again, once you identify a source that seems useful to you, read it carefully — and make sure that you have grasped its meaning. That means reading most or all of the source, not just the first page.

## 14c Keeping a working bibliography

A working bibliography is a list of sources that you may ultimately use for your project. As you find and begin to evaluate research sources — articles, books, websites, and so on — you should record information that will allow you to find the source again and cite it correctly. The emphasis here is on *working* because the list will probably include materials that end up not being useful. For this reason, you don't absolutely need to put all entries into the documentation style you will use (see Chapters 18–21). If you do follow the required documentation style, however, that part of your work will be done when you prepare the final draft.

The following chart will help you keep track of the sorts of information you should try to find:

| Type of Source | Information to Collect (if applicable) |
|---|---|
| Online/digital source | Author(s), title of document, title of site, editor(s) of site, sponsor of site, publication information for print version of source, name of database or online service, date of electronic publication or last update, date you accessed the source, URL or DOI or other stable locator |
| Print article | Call number of publication, author(s) of article, title of article, name of periodical, volume number, issue number, date of issue, inclusive page numbers for article |
| Print book | Library call number, author(s) and/or editor(s), title and subtitle, place of publication, publisher, year of publication, any other information (translator, edition, volume) |
| Part of a book | Call number, author(s) of part, title of part, author(s) or editor(s) of book, title of book, place of publication, publisher, year of publication, inclusive page numbers for part |

For other kinds of sources (films, recordings, visuals), you should also list the information required by the documentation style you are using (see Chapters 18–21) and note where you found the information.

## Creating an annotated bibliography

You might want (or be assigned) to annotate your working bibliography to include a summary of the source's contents as well as publishing information because annotating can help you understand and remember what the source says. Your instructor might also ask you to evaluate the source by noting its strengths or weaknesses (14d) or by commenting on the usefulness of the source to your project.

The following single entry shows a student's annotation for one source.

**SAMPLE ANNOTATED BIBLIOGRAPHY ENTRY (MLA STYLE)**

Dávila, Arlene. "Empowered Culture? New York City's Empowerment Zone and the Selling of El Barrio." *The Annals of the American Academy of Political and Social Science,* vol. 594, no. 1, July 2004, pp. 49–64. *JSTOR,* www .jstor.org/stable/4127693.

> NYU sociology professor Arlene Dávila explains that programs designed to stimulate tourism in Harlem have largely ignored Latino/a residents of East Harlem, known as *El Barrio*. Rather than blaming leaders of Harlem's black neighborhoods, which she suggests are seen as more marketable to tourists, she questions the anti-Latino bias of the economic policies of the Upper Manhattan Empowerment Zone. Dávila calls for debate about the problems that come with treating culture as a commodity. Although the article is older, Dávila's argument is a valuable one. She provides a counterpoint to the idea that economic initiatives adopted since the 1990s have benefited all Harlemites. I can also use her analysis of culture as a product to set up my conclusion.

In this annotated bibliography entry for an article Julia Sakowitz used in her essay on tourism in Harlem (see Chapter 18), she opens by summarizing Dávila's argument in the first three sentences and then explains why the source is useful to her in the last three sentences, thus combining description and evaluation in her bibliographical note.

# 14d Evaluating usefulness and credibility

Since you want the information and ideas you glean from sources to be reliable and persuasive, you must evaluate each potential source carefully. Doing so is especially important because false information can circulate widely, especially

TALKING THE TALK | **RESEARCH WITH AN OPEN MIND**

"What's wrong with looking for sources that back up what I want to say?" When you start researching a topic, keep an open mind: investigate every important source, even if you think you won't agree with it. If all your sources take the same position you take, you may be doing some pretty selective searching — and you may be missing a big part of the picture. Who knows? You may change your position after learning more about the topic. Even if you don't, ignoring counterarguments and other points of view harms your credibility, suggesting that you haven't done your homework.

online. (See 9c and 14e for more on identifying false and misleading sources.) Use these guidelines to help you assess the sources you are considering:

- **Your purpose.** What will this source add to your research project? Does it help you support a major point, demonstrate that you have thoroughly researched your topic, or help establish your own credibility through its authority?

- **Relevance.** How closely related is the source to the narrowed topic you are pursuing? You may need to read beyond the title and opening paragraph to check for relevance.

- **Level of specialization and audience.** General sources can be helpful as you begin your research, but you may then need the authority or currency of more specialized sources. On the other hand, specialized works may be hard to understand. Who was the source originally written for — the general public? experts in the field? advocates or opponents? How does this fit with your concept of your own audience?

- **Credentials of the publisher or sponsor.** What can you learn about the publisher or sponsor of the source you are using? For example, is it a major newspaper known for integrity in reporting, or is it an amateur's blog? Is it sponsored by a professional or government organization or academic institution or by a questionable group you've never heard of?

- **Credentials of the author.** As you do your research, note names that come up from one source to another, since these references may indicate that the author is influential in the field. An author's credentials may also be presented in the article, book, or website, or you can search the Internet for information about the author. In U.S. academic writing, experts and those with significant experience in a field have more authority on the subject than others.

- **Date of publication.** Recent sources are often more useful than older ones, particularly in the sciences or other fields that change rapidly. However, in some fields — such as the humanities — the most authoritative works may be older ones.

- **Accuracy of the source.** How accurate and complete is the information in the source? How thorough is the bibliography or list of works cited that accompanies the source? Can you find other sources that corroborate what your source is saying? If not, be skeptical.

- **Stance of the source.** Identify the source's point of view or rhetorical stance, and scrutinize it carefully. Does the source present facts, or does it interpret or evaluate them? If it presents facts, what is included and what is omitted, and why? If it interprets or evaluates information that is not disputed, the source's stance may be obvious, but at other times, you will need to think carefully about the source's goals (14e). What does the author or sponsoring group want? to convince you of an idea? sell you something? call you to action in some way?

- **Cross-references to the source.** What do other sources or sites have to say about the source? If you see your source cited by others, notice how they cite it and what they say about it to find additional clues to its credibility. This is called *lateral reading*.

For more on evaluating web sources and periodical articles, see the source maps in 14e.

---

### EXERCISE 14.1

Choose two sources that seem well suited to your topic, and evaluate their usefulness and credibility using the criteria presented in this chapter. If possible, analyze one print source and one digital source. Bring the results of your analysis to class for discussion.

---

## 14e Reading sources critically

For those sources that you want to analyze more closely, reading with a critical eye can make your research process more efficient. Use the following tips to guide your critical reading.

### Keeping your research question in mind

With your research question in mind, determine how the source material supports or refutes your hypothesis and whether any quotations or data from the source help you answer your research question.

### Previewing a source before you commit

Looking quickly at the various parts of a source can provide useful information and help you decide whether to explore that particular source more thoroughly.

- *Basic elements* such as title and subtitle, copyright page, home page, table of contents, index, footnotes, and bibliography provide critical information.

- *Abstracts* routinely precede journal articles and offer a summary of the discussion.

- A *preface* or *foreword* generally discusses both the writer's purpose and thesis.

- *Subheadings* can alert you to how much detail is given on a topic.

- A *conclusion* or *afterword* may summarize or draw the strands of an argument together.

- For a digital source, click on some of the *links* to see if they're useful, and see if the overall *design* of the site is easy to navigate.

## Considering the argument and evidence

Every piece of writing takes a position. Even a scientific report implicitly "argues" that we should accept it and its data as reliable. As you read, look for the main point or the main argument the author is making. Try to identify the reasons the author gives to support his or her position. Then try to determine *why* the author takes this position.

- What is the author's main point, and what evidence supports it?

- How persuasive is the evidence? Can you think of a way to refute it?

- Can you detect any questionable logic or fallacious thinking (10f)?

- Does this author disagree with arguments you have read elsewhere? If so, what causes the disagreements — differences about facts or about how to interpret facts?

For more on argument, see Chapters 10–11.

## Checking the author's stance and tone

Read with an eye for the author's perhaps unstated overall rhetorical stance, or perspective, as well as for facts or explicit opinions. Also pay attention to the author's tone—the way that attitude toward the topic and audience is conveyed. The following questions can help:

- Is the author a strong advocate or opponent of something? a skeptical critic? a specialist in the field? Are there any clues to why the author takes this stance?

- How does this stance affect the author's presentation and your reaction to it?

- What facts does the author include? Can you think of any important information that is left out — and why the author may have done so?

- What is the author's tone? Is it cautious, angry, flippant, serious, impassioned? What words indicate this tone?

## Guidelines for checking facts

Begin to practice what media analyst Howard Rheingold calls "crap detection," which means reading defensively and identifying information that is false or deceptive. The following tips can help you to become a good fact-checker:

• Identify the information that is presented as *fact* in a source. Ask questions: Does this information seem accurate? complete? trustworthy? Check to see if the source presents a bibliography or list of works cited.

• Search for other credible sources (Rheingold suggests three) that corroborate the facts you are checking. If you can't find sources that verify a fact, be suspicious.

• Use nonpartisan fact-checkers such as the following:

  PolitiFact.com (and related PunditFact)

  Snopes.com

  FactCheck.org

  FlackCheck.org

  AmericanPressInstitute.org

  Hoaxy (sponsored by Indiana University)

  Snopes.com is useful for fact-checking general rumors and memes. Hoaxy is useful for checking and tracking social media claims.

• Be on the lookout for clickbait headlines and titles—that is, those that say "click me, click me."

• Watch for sites with nonstandard URLs. The site NYTimes.com.co, for example, posts fake news articles that it hopes readers take as true because they think a reputable news outlet is the source. Watch for ".co" at the end of a news URL.

• Pay attention to the tone with which facts are presented. If the tone is sensational or highly exaggerated, take care that the facts are not also exaggerated.

# Evaluating Web Sources

## Is the sponsor credible?

1. Who is the **sponsor or publisher** of the source? See what information you can get from the URL. The domain names for government sites may end in *.gov* or *.mil* and for educational sites in *.edu*. The ending *.org* may—but does not always—indicate a nonprofit organization. If you see a tilde (~) or percent sign (%) followed by a name, or if you see a word such as *users* or *members*, the page's creator may be an individual, not an institution. In addition, check the header and footer, where the sponsor may be identified. The web page shown here comes from a site sponsored by the nonprofit Nieman Foundation for Journalism at Harvard University.

2. Look for an ***About* page** or a link to a home page for background information on the sponsor. Is a mission statement included? What are the sponsoring organization's purpose and point of view? Does the mission statement seem balanced? What is the purpose of the site (to inform, to persuade, to advocate for a cause, to advertise, or something else)? Does the information on the site come directly from the sponsor, or is the material reprinted from another source? If it is reprinted, check the original.

## Is the author credible?

3. What are the **author's credentials**? Look for information accompanying the material on the page. You can also run a search on the author to find out more. Does the author seem qualified to write about this topic?

## Is the information credible and current?

4. When was the information **posted or last updated**? Is it recent enough to be useful?

5. Does the page document sources with **footnotes or links**? If so, do the sources seem credible and current? Does the author include any additional resources for further information? Look for ways to corroborate the information the author provides.

## In addition, consider the following questions:

- What is the source's stance or point of view? What are the author's goals? What does the author want you to know or believe?

- How does this source fit in with your other sources? Does any of the information it provides contradict or challenge other sources?

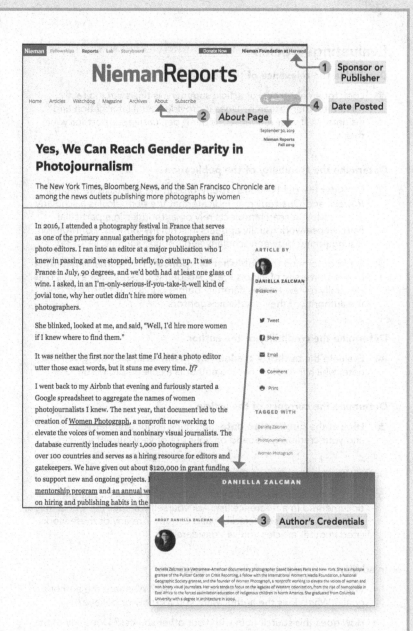

**1** Sponsor or Publisher

**4** Date Posted

**2** About Page

# Yes, We Can Reach Gender Parity in Photojournalism

The New York Times, Bloomberg News, and the San Francisco Chronicle are among the news outlets publishing more photographs by women

In 2016, I attended a photography festival in France that serves as one of the primary annual gatherings for photographers and photo editors. I ran into an editor at a major publication who I knew in passing and we stopped, briefly, to catch up. It was France in July, 90 degrees, and we'd both had at least one glass of wine. I asked, in an I'm-only-serious-if-you-take-it-well kind of jovial tone, why her outlet didn't hire more women photographers.

She blinked, looked at me, and said, "Well, I'd hire more women if I knew where to find them."

It was neither the first nor the last time I'd hear a photo editor utter those exact words, but it stuns me every time. *If?*

I went back to my Airbnb that evening and furiously started a Google spreadsheet to aggregate the names of women photojournalists I knew. The next year, that document led to the creation of Women Photograph, a nonprofit now working to elevate the voices of women and nonbinary visual journalists. The database currently includes nearly 1,000 photographers from over 100 countries and serves as a hiring resource for editors and gatekeepers. We have given out about $120,000 in grant funding to support new and ongoing projects. [...] mentorship program and an annual we[...] on hiring and publishing habits in the [...]

ARTICLE BY

**DANIELLA ZALCMAN**
@dzalcman

- Tweet
- Share
- Email
- Comment
- Print

TAGGED WITH

Daniella Zalcman

Photojournalism

Women Photograph

**DANIELLA ZALCMAN**

ABOUT DANIELLA ZALCMAN

**3** Author's Credentials

Daniella Zalcman is a Vietnamese-American documentary photographer based between Paris and New York. She is a multiple grantee of the Pulitzer Center on Crisis Reporting, a fellow with the International Women's Media Foundation, a National Geographic Society grantee, and the founder of Women Photograph, a nonprofit working to elevate the voices of women and non-binary visual journalists. Her work tends to focus on the legacies of Western colonization, from the rise of homophobia in East Africa to the forced assimilation education of indigenous children in North America. She graduated from Columbia University with a degree in architecture in 2009.

# Evaluating Articles

**Determine the relevance of the source.**

**1** Look for an **abstract**, or article summary. Is this source directly related to your research? Does it provide useful information and insights? Will your readers consider it persuasive support for your thesis?

**Determine the credibility of the publication.**

**2** Consider the publication's **title**. Words in the title such as *Journal*, *Review*, and *Quarterly* may indicate that the periodical is a scholarly source. Most research projects rely on authorities in a particular field, whose work usually appears in scholarly journals. For more on distinguishing between scholarly and popular sources, see 13a.

**3** Try to determine the **publisher or sponsor**. This journal is published by the University of Illinois Press. Academic presses such as this one generally review articles carefully before publishing them and bear the authority of their academic sponsors.

**Determine the credibility of the author.**

**4** Evaluate the **author's credentials**. In this case, they are given in a note, which indicates that the author is a college professor.

**Determine the currency of the article.**

**5** Look at the **publication date**, and think about whether your topic and your credibility depend on your use of very current sources.

**Determine the accuracy of the article.**

**6** Look at the **sources cited** by the author of the article. Here, they are documented in a reference list. Ask yourself whether the works the author has cited seem credible and current. Are any of these works cited in other articles you've considered?

**In addition, consider the following questions:**

- What is the article's stance or point of view? What are the author's goals? What does the author want you to know or believe?

- How does this source fit in with your other sources? Does any of the information it provides contradict or challenge other sources?

Elizabeth Tucker

Changing Concepts of Childhood:
Children's Folklore Scholarship
since the Late Nineteenth Century

**1** Abstract

407

*This essay examines children's folklore scholarship from the late nineteenth century to the present, tracing key concepts from the Gilded Age to the contemporary era. These concepts reflect significant social, cultural, political, and scientific changes. From the "savage child" to the "secret-keeping child," the "magic-making child," the "cerebral child," the "taboo-breaking child," the "monstrous child," and others, scholarly representations of young people have close connections to the eras in which they developed. Nineteenth-century children's folklore scholarship relied on evolutionism; now evolutionary biology provides a basis for children's folklore research, so we have re-entered familiar territory.*

Hall" (1968), which mentions

Jay Mechling's and my studies ...ed Child." Although my word ...ognize the impact on children

...randall (2009).

SINCE 1977, WHEN THE American Folklore Society decided to form a new section for scholars interested in young people's traditions, I have belonged to the Children's Folklore Section. It has been a joy to contribute to this dynamic organization, which

...re Genres, ed. Dan Ben-Amos,

Anglund, Joan Walsh. 2003. *Little Angels' Alphabet of Love*. New York: Simon and Schuster.

Ariès, Philippe. 1962. *Centuries of Childhood: A Social History of Family Life*. New York: Vintage.

Beresin, Anna R. 2010. *Recess Battles: Playing, Fighting, and Storytelling*. Jackson: University Press of Mississippi.

Berres, Allen. 2002. "Everybody Is Their Enemy": Goths, Spooky Kids, and the American School Shooting Panic. *Children's Folklore Review* 24(1–2):43–54.

Blake, William. 1901. *Songs of Innocence and Experience*. London: Knight and Millet.

Blank, Trevor J. 2010. "Cheeky Behavior": The Meaning and Function of 'Fartlore' in Childhood and

Before ...ing concepts of chi...ood that folklo...s have develope... ...of-fer a working definition of this life stage and briefly explain the beginning of childhood studies. I will also summarize the Children's Folklore Section's work during the past thirty-four years. According to the *Oxford English Dictionary*, childhood consists of "the state or stage of life of a child; the time during which one is a child; the time from birth to puberty" (2011). Scholars of childhood tend to draw ...

k: Bradbury Press.

Press, 1970.

New York: D. Appleton.

... *Narratives*. Salt Lake City:

**2** Title of Publication ...gins at puberty and follows pre-adol...

...gust House.

Elizabeth Tucker is Professor of English at Binghamton University

**4** Author's Credentials

*Journal of American Folklore* 125(498):389–410
Copyright © 2012 by the Board of Trustees of the University of Illinois

...tary. *Children's Folklore Review*

...nerican Folklore Society. *Children's Folklore Review* 26(1–2):37–...

**3** Publisher

———. 2002. Introduction: Folklore Responds to Columbine and Adolescence. *Children's Folklore Review* ...2):7–20.

**5** Publication Date

———. 2011a. *Explaining Traditions: Folk Behavior in Modern Culture*. Lexington: University Press of Kentucky.

———. 2011b. Framing Violence and Play in American Culture. *Journal of Ritsumeikan Social Sciences and Humanities* 3:145–60.

Carpenter, Carole H. 2011. Why Children's Studies? *Centre for Research in Young People's Texts and Cultures*. crytc.uwinnipeg.ca/pdf/papers/Carole.Carpenter.pdf.

Chamberlain, Alexander Francis. 1896. *The Child and Childhood in Folk-Thought*. New York: Macmillan.

**6** Sources Cited ...line, Foster W., and Jim Fay. 1990. *Parenting with Love and Logic: Teaching Children Responsibility*. Colorado Springs, CO: Pinon Press.

Conrad, JoAnn. 2002. The War on Youth: A Modern Oedipal Tragedy. *Children's Folklore Review* 24(1–2):33–42.

Crandall, Bryan Ripley. 2009. *Cow Project*. bryanripleycrandall.files.wordpress.com/2009/05/slbscow-project.pdf.

**201**

# 14f Synthesizing sources

When you read and evaluate a source — for example, when you consider its purpose and relevance, its author's credentials, its accuracy, and the kind of argument it is making — you are analyzing the source. Analysis requires you to take apart something complex (such as an article in a scholarly journal) and look closely at the parts to understand the whole better. For academic writing, you also need to *synthesize* — group similar pieces of information together and look for patterns — so you can put your sources (and your own knowledge and experience) together in an original argument. Synthesis is the flip side of analysis: you already understand the parts, so your job is to assemble them into a new whole.

To synthesize sources for a research project, try the following tips:

- **Read the material carefully.** Don't just grab a quotation and move on — make sure you really understand. For tips on reading with a critical eye, see Chapter 9.

- **Understand the purpose of each source.** Make sure the source is relevant and necessary to your argument.

- **Determine the important ideas in each source.** Take notes on each source (14g). Identify and summarize the key ideas of each piece.

- **Formulate a position.** Review the key ideas of each source and figure out how they fit together. Look for patterns: discussions of causes and effects, specific parts of a larger issue, background information, and so on. Be sure to consider the complexity of the issue, and demonstrate that you have considered more than one perspective.

- **Summon evidence to support your position.** You might use paraphrases, summaries, or direct quotations from your sources as evidence (15b–d), or your personal experience or prior knowledge. Integrate your quotations properly (see Chapter 15), and keep your ideas central to the piece of writing.

- **Deal with counterarguments.** You don't have to use every idea or every source available — some will be more useful than others. However, ignoring evidence that opposes your position makes your argument weaker. You should fairly consider the valid opinions that differ from yours, and try to explain why they may be misguided or incomplete.

- **Combine your source materials effectively.** Be careful to avoid simply summarizing or listing information from your sources. You also need to comment on the sources, showing how they support and fit into the points you are making. If possible, weave the various sources together rather than discussing your sources one by one.

Using sources effectively can pose challenges (14b). Even after you have evaluated a source, take time to look at how well it works in your specific situation. And if you change the focus of your work after you have begun doing research, be especially careful to check whether your sources still fit.

*A student's synthesis project*

STUDENT
WRITING
Caroline
Warner

In this excerpt from her full research essay, "Hydration and Sports Drinks in Competitive Cycling," Caroline Warner identifies important ideas from her research on hydration for athletes, formulates a position, and supports her argument, effectively synthesizing her sources.

There is little controversy as to the seriousness of dehydration. However, experts recommend varied methods for dealing with it. The *British Journal of Sports Medicine* outlines two general approaches. One method is for athletes to hydrate, using only water, whenever they are thirsty during exercise. The athlete, after his workout, is then free to use sports drinks for recovery and electrolyte replacement. While this method does result in some degree of dehydration, exercise-associated hyponatremia (EAH) — overdrinking — is no longer a danger, and this method may better prepare athletes for any competitive situation in which they will not be able to rehydrate until after performing. This method has been adopted by USA Track & Field, as well as the International Marathon Medical Directors Association. The other approach to hydration maintains that an athlete should attempt to replace 100 percent of body weight lost during exercise. The athlete should drink every fifteen to twenty minutes, preferably consuming supplemental sodium like that found in sports drinks; the sodium allows the athlete to retain water and allows for better nervous system communication. In this scenario, the athlete does not wait to become thirsty (the assumption is that a thirsty athlete is already dehydrated); instead, he drinks small amounts consistently, and his body weight losses are less than 1 percent.

> Source identifies two main methods of hydration for athletes

Summary of
journal source

Reasons
for cyclists'
preference for
second method

Synthesis of
findings from
a number of
sources that
establish a
clear pattern in
favor of appeal

This approach has been adopted by the American College of Sports Medicine as well as the National Athletic Trainers Association (Beltrami, Hew-Butler, and Noakes).

Most cyclists are believers in the second method. In a sport that both requires alertness and demands performance for extended amounts of time, it makes sense to stay up on hydration. As for what to drink, online communities at both www.bikeforums.com and www.cyclingforums .com are filled with advocates for sports drinks rather than water. There is some debate over which drink is most effective — Heed, Cytomax, Pro-Opti, Accelerade, GU20, and Gatorade are among the most popular — and over how much to use (many people dilute or mix their drinks), but everyone seems to advocate one drink or another. Arielle Filiberti, a three-time junior national champion cyclist and the favorite for women's U23s this year, says that her most horrific crash came at the end of a long ride when she ran out of both water and her preferred energy drink. Filiberti had been experiencing dizziness and light-headedness for some time, and as she was rounding a corner, she misjudged the turn and swung out too far into the road. She then swerved to avoid oncoming traffic, lost her balance, and skidded sideways off the road. Doctors found that Filiberti had lost about 3.5 percent of her body weight over a four-hour ride — almost five pounds of water. Furthermore, her reflexes were slow and she was unable to focus her eyes either close up or far away — a result of electrolyte and sodium loss. She was put on a saline drip and hospitalized overnight (Filiberti). This kind of story is much more common than is safe or necessary. Thus for the competitive cyclist, it makes most sense to hydrate continuously through training.

Note the way Caroline identifies important information from a journal and expands on the significance of the information in her discussion of sources from two websites for cyclists and a personal interview. All of these sources are synthesized to support her own claim that continuous hydration with sports drinks is the best way for cyclists to combat the threat of dehydration. (For more on synthesizing sources, see Chapter 15 and 17.)

## 14g Taking notes and annotating sources

Note-taking methods vary greatly from one researcher to another, so you may decide to use a digital file, a notebook, or index cards. Regardless of the method, however, you should (1) record enough information to help you recall the major points of the source; (2) put the information in the form in which you are most likely to incorporate it into your research essay, whether a summary, a paraphrase, or a quotation; and (3) note all the information you will need to cite the source accurately, including the author's name, the shortened title, and, for print sources, the page number(s) on which the quoted material appears. Make sure you have a corresponding working-bibliography entry with complete source information (14c).

The following example shows the major items a note should include:

**ELEMENTS OF AN ACCURATE NOTE**

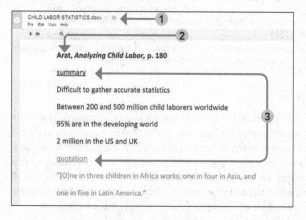

1. **Use a subject heading.** Label or title each note with a brief, descriptive heading so that you can group similar subtopics together.

2. **Identify the source.** List the author's name and a shortened title of the source, and a page number, if available. Your working-bibliography entry (14c) for the source will contain the full bibliographic information, so you don't need to repeat it in each note.

3. **Indicate whether the note is a direct quotation, paraphrase, or summary.** Make sure quotations are copied accurately. Put square brackets around any change you make, and use ellipses if you omit material.

Taking complete notes will help you digest the source information as you read and incorporate the material into your text without inadvertently plagiarizing the source (see Chapter 16). Be sure to reread each note carefully, and recheck it against the source to make sure quotations, statistics, and specific facts are accurate. (For more information on working with quotations, paraphrases, and summaries, see Chapter 15.)

## Using quotations

Some of the notes you take will contain quotations, which give the *exact words* of a source.

---

**QUICK HELP**

Guidelines for quotation notes

- Copy quotations carefully, with punctuation, capitalization, and spelling *exactly* as in the original.
- Use quotation marks; don't rely on your memory to distinguish your own words from those of the source. Identify the note as a quotation.
- Use square brackets if you introduce words of your own into a quotation or make changes in it, and use ellipses if you omit material. If you later incorporate the quotation into your essay, copy it faithfully—brackets, ellipses, and all. **(15b)**
- If the quotation appears on more than one page of a print source, use a slash ( / ) to indicate where one page ends and another begins.

---

## Using paraphrases

A paraphrase accurately states all the relevant information from a passage *in your own words and sentence structures,* without any additional comments or elaborations. A paraphrase is useful when the main points of a passage, their order, and at least some details are important but — unlike passages worth quoting — the particular wording is not. Unlike a summary, a paraphrase always restates *all* the main points of a passage in the same order and often in about the same number of words. See 15c for examples of acceptable and unacceptable paraphrases.

---

**QUICK HELP**

Guidelines for paraphrase notes

- Include all main points and any important details from the original source, in the same order in which the author presents them.
- State the meaning in your own words and sentence structures (without looking at the original). If you want to include especially memorable language from the original, enclose it in quotation marks. Identify your work as a paraphrase.
- Save your comments, elaborations, or reactions on another note.
- Represent the author's ideas in a way that shows you understand the ideas.
- Cite the source even if you have paraphrased it and have not used any exact language.

## Using Summaries

A summary is a significantly shortened version of a passage or even of a whole chapter or work that captures main ideas *in your own words*. Unlike a paraphrase, a summary uses just the main points of a source. Your goal is to keep the summary as brief as possible without distorting the author's meaning. See 15d for a sample summary.

---

**QUICK HELP**

### Guidelines for summaries

- To summarize a short passage, read it carefully and, without looking at the text, write a one- or two-sentence summary.
- To summarize a long passage or an entire chapter, start with a careful read, and then go back to skim the headings and topic sentences, making notes; then write your summary in a paragraph or two. For a whole book, you may want to refer to the preface and introduction as well as chapter titles, headings, and topic sentences—and your summary may take a page or more. In general, try to identify the thesis or claim being made, and then look for the subtopics or supports for that claim.
- Include just enough information to recount the main points you want to cite. A summary is usually far shorter than the original.
- Use your own words. If you include any language from the original, enclose it in quotation marks.
- Represent the author's ideas in a way that shows you understand the ideas.
- Cite the source even if you have summarized it without exact words.

---

## Taking other kinds of notes

Many researchers take notes that don't fall into the categories of quotations, paraphrases, or summaries. Those who work with media sources, especially, need alternatives. Some researchers take key-term notes, which might include the topic addressed in the source along with names or short statements to jog their memories when they begin drafting. Others record personal or critical notes — questions, criticisms, or other ideas that come to mind as they read. Student writer Julia Sakowitz annotated screenshots of sightseeing photos she found online as part of her research about tourism in Harlem (see Chapter 18).

In fact, an exciting part of research occurs when the materials you are reading spark new ideas in your mind, ideas that may become part of your thesis or argument. Don't let them get away. While you may later decide not to use these ideas, you need to make notes about them just in case. Whatever form your notes take, be sure to list the source's title, author, and a way to find the information again, such as page number(s), links, or time codes. In addition, check that you have carefully distinguished your own thoughts and comments from those of the source itself.

## Annotating source material

Sometimes you may scan or print out a source you intend to use. In such cases, you can annotate the scans or printouts with your thoughts and questions and highlight interesting quotations and key terms. You can also use video or audio annotation tools to take notes on media sources.

If you take notes in a computer file, you may be able to copy online sources electronically, paste them into the file, and annotate them there. Try not to rely too heavily on copying or printing out whole pieces, however; you still need to read the material very carefully. Also resist the temptation to treat copied material as notes, an action that could lead to inadvertent plagiarizing. (In a computer file, using a different color for text pasted from a source will help prevent this problem.)

### EXERCISE 14.2

Choose an online source you are sure you will use in your research project. Then download and print out the source, record all essential publication information for it, and annotate it as you read it.

▼ ▼ ▼ ▼ ▼ ▼ ▼ ▼ ▼ ▼ ▼ ▼ ▼ ▼ ▼ ▼ ▼ ▼ ▼ ▼ ▼ ▼ ▼ ▼ ▼

## THINKING CRITICALLY ABOUT YOUR EVALUATION OF SOURCES

Take a careful look at the sources you have gathered for your research project. How many make points that support your point of view? How many provide counter-arguments to your point of view? Which sources are you relying on most—and why? Which sources seem most credible to you—and why? Which sources, if any, are you suspicious of or worried about? Bring the results of this investigation to class for discussion.

# CHAPTER 15

# Integrating Sources

The process of absorbing your sources and then integrating them gracefully into your own writing is one of the challenges but also the pleasures of successful research. When you integrate sources appropriately into your work, they don't take over your writing or drown out your voice. Instead, they work in support of your own good ideas.

## 15a Deciding whether to quote, paraphrase, or summarize

When you write, decisions about when and where to use exact language from a source or whether to paraphrase or summarize ideas from a source are yours to make. The following guidelines can help you decide whether to quote, paraphrase, or summarize.

---

**QUICK HELP**

Deciding to quote, paraphrase, or summarize

**QUOTE**

- wording that is so memorable or powerful, or expresses a point so perfectly, that you cannot change it without weakening the meaning
- authors' opinions you wish to emphasize
- authors' words that show you are considering varying perspectives
- respected authorities whose opinions support your ideas
- authors whose opinions challenge or vary greatly from those of others in the field

**PARAPHRASE**

- passages in which the details, but not the exact words, are important to your point

**SUMMARIZE**

- long passages in which the main point is important to your point but the details are not

---

## 15b Working with quotations

Quoting involves using a source's exact words. You might use a direct quotation to catch readers' attention or make an introduction memorable. Quotations from respected authorities can help establish your credibility by showing that you've sought out experts in the field. In addition, quoting authors who disagree with your opinions helps demonstrate your fairness (11f, 11i).

Finally, well-chosen quotations can broaden the appeal of your project by drawing on emotion as well as logic (10c and 11g–k). A student writing on the ethics of bullfighting, for example, might quote Ernest Hemingway's striking comment that "the formal bullfight is a tragedy, not a sport, and the bull is certain to be killed."

Although quotations can add interest and authenticity to an essay, be careful not to overuse them: your research project is primarily your own work, meant to showcase your ideas and your argument.

### Integrating brief quotations

Short prose quotations should be run in with your text, enclosed in quotation marks that mark where someone else's words begin and end. When you include such quotations — or other source material — use both signal phrases and parenthetical references or notes, depending on the requirements of the documentation style you are using (see Chapters 18–21). Signal phrases introduce the material, often including the author's name. Parenthetical references and notes direct your readers to full bibliographic entries included elsewhere in your text.

The following brief quotation uses Modern Language Association (MLA) style:

> In Miss Eckhart, Welty recognizes a character who shares with her "the love of her art and the love of giving it, the desire to give it until there is no more left" (10).

In this example, the signal phrase that introduces the quotation (*In Miss Eckhart, Welty recognizes*) includes the author's name, so MLA style requires only the page number in parentheses for this print source.

---

LANGUAGE, CULTURE, AND CONTEXT | **IDENTIFYING SOURCES**

While some language communities and cultures expect audiences to recognize the sources of important documents and texts, thereby eliminating the need to cite them directly, conventions for writing in North America call for careful attribution of any quoted, paraphrased, or summarized material. When in doubt, explicitly identify your sources.

## Integrating long quotations

If you are following MLA style, set off a prose quotation longer than four lines. If you are following the style of the American Psychological Association (APA), set off a quotation of forty or more words or more than one paragraph. If you are following *Chicago* style, set off a quotation of more than one hundred words or more than one paragraph. Begin such a quotation on a new line. For both MLA and APA style, indent every line one-half inch; for *Chicago* style, indent the text one-half inch or use a smaller font (check your instructor's preference). Quotation marks are unnecessary. Introduce long quotations with a signal phrase or a sentence followed by a colon.

The following long quotation follows MLA style:

> A good seating arrangement can prevent problems; however, "withitness," as defined by Woolfolk, works even better:
>> Withitness is the ability to communicate to students that you are aware of what is happening in the classroom, that you "don't miss anything." With-it teachers seem to have "eyes in the back of their heads." They avoid becoming too absorbed with a few students, since this allows the rest of the class to wander. (359)
>
> This technique works, however, only if students actually believe that their teacher will know everything that goes on.

Note that the parenthetical citation comes after the period at the end of the quotation and does not have a period after it.

Though long quotations are often necessary in research projects, use them cautiously. Too many of them may make your writing seem choppy — or suggest that you have not relied enough on your own thinking.

## Using signal phrases

Carefully integrate quotations into your text so that they flow smoothly and clearly into the surrounding sentences by using a signal phrase or signal verb.

**QUICK HELP**

### Signal verbs

| | | | |
|---|---|---|---|
| acknowledges | concludes | emphasizes | remarks |
| advises | concurs | explains | replies |
| agrees | confirms | expresses | reports |
| allows | criticizes | interprets | responds |
| answers | declares | lists | reveals |
| asserts | describes | objects | says |
| believes | disagrees | observes | states |
| charges | discusses | offers | suggests |
| claims | disputes | opposes | writes |

Remember that the signal verb must be appropriate to the idea you are expressing. In the following example, the verb *notes* tells us that the writer probably agrees with what Welty is saying. If that were not the case, the writer might have chosen a different verb, such as *asserts* or *contends*.

> As Eudora Welty notes, "learning stamps you with its moments. Childhood's learning," she continues, "is made up of moments. It isn't steady. It's a pulse" (9).

In the next example, the signal phrase *Some instructors claim* indicates that other authorities might disagree with the teacher's opinion or that the writer of this example disagrees. To support a point, the writer might have used entirely different wording, such as *Many instructors agree*.

> Some instructors claim that the new technology damages students' ability to compose academic work. "Abbreviations commonly used in online instant messages are creeping into formal essays that students write for credit," says Debbie Frost, who teaches language arts and social studies to sixth-graders ("Young").

Notice that these examples also feature neutral signal verbs — *continues* and *says* — where appropriate. The signal verbs you choose allow you to characterize the author's viewpoint or perspective as well as your own, so choose them with care.

## Marking changes with brackets and ellipses

Sometimes you may wish to alter a direct quotation in some way — to make a verb tense fit smoothly into your text, to replace a pronoun with a noun, to eliminate unnecessary detail, or to change a capital letter to lowercase or vice versa. Enclose any changed or added words or letters in square brackets, and indicate any deletions with ellipsis points (see Chapter 61). Do not use ellipses at the beginning or end of a quotation unless the last sentence as you cite it is incomplete.

Here are two examples of quotations that have been altered with bracketed information or ellipsis points and integrated smoothly into the surrounding text.

> "There is something wrong in the [Three Mile Island] area," one farmer told the Nuclear Regulatory Commission after the plant accident ("Legacy" 33).

The brackets indicate that this information was added by the writer and is not part of the original quotation.

> Economist John Kenneth Galbraith pointed out that "large corporations cannot afford to compete with one another. . . . In a truly competitive market someone loses" (qtd. in Key 17).

TALKING THE TALK | **COMMENTING ON OR EVALUATING YOUR SOURCE MATERIAL**

Your choice of signal verbs often reveals your attitude toward or relationship to your sources. Signal verbs like *proves, demonstrates, shows,* or *establishes* suggest that you take a positive view of the information in the source, while signal verbs like *fails, lacks, refuses, overlooks,* or *ignores* suggest that you take a critical view. In between are more neutral verbs (*argues, indicates, suggests, notes*) indicating an objective relationship to the source material. Professor Laura Aull's research shows that advanced academic writers favor neutral signal verbs, which build the writer's ethos as fair and evenhanded. She also finds that these expert writers rarely use verbs associated with opinions or feelings (*feels, believes, thinks*), while student writers use them a great deal. You can learn from the experts to look very closely at the verbs you choose when you are reporting what your sources say.

Whenever you change a quotation, be careful not to alter its meaning. In addition, use brackets and ellipses sparingly; too many of them make for difficult reading and might suggest that you have removed some of the context for the quotation.

**EXERCISE 15.1**

Take a source-based piece of writing you have done recently or a research project you are working on now, and examine it to see how successfully you have integrated quotations. Have you used accurate signal verbs and introduced the sources of the quotations? Have you used square brackets and ellipses accurately to indicate changes in quotations?

## 15c Paraphrasing

A paraphrase accurately states all the relevant information from a passage *in your own words and sentence structures,* without any additional comments or elaborations. A paraphrase is useful when the main points of a passage, their order, and at least some details are important but the exact wording is not. Unlike a summary, a paraphrase always restates *all* the main points of a passage in the same order and often in about the same number of words.

ORIGINAL

Language play, the arguments suggest, will help the development of pronunciation ability through its focus on the properties of sounds and sound contrasts, such as rhyming. Playing with word endings and decoding the syntax of riddles will help the acquisition of grammar. Readiness to play with words and names, to exchange puns and to engage in nonsense talk, promotes links with semantic development. The kinds of dialogue interaction illustrated above are likely to have consequences for the development of conversational skills. And language play, by its nature, also contributes greatly to what in recent years has been called *metalinguistic awareness*, which is turning out to be of critical importance in the development of language skills in general and of literacy skills in particular.

—DAVID CRYSTAL, *Language Play* (180)

The following paraphrase starts off well enough, but it moves away from paraphrasing the original to inserting the writer's own ideas; Crystal says nothing about learning new languages or pursuing education.

### UNACCEPTABLE PARAPHRASE: STRAYING FROM THE AUTHOR'S IDEAS

Crystal argues that playing with language — creating rhymes, figuring out how riddles work, making puns, playing with names, using invented words, and so on — helps children figure out a great deal about language, from the basics of pronunciation and grammar to how to carry on a conversation. Increasing their understanding of how language works in turn helps them become more interested in learning new languages and in pursuing education (180).

Because the underlined phrases below are either underlined{borrowed from the original} without quotation marks or underlined{changed only superficially} in language and structure, these paraphrases plagiarize the original.

### UNACCEPTABLE PARAPHRASE: USING THE AUTHOR'S WORDS

Crystal suggests that language play, including rhyme, helps children improve underlined{pronunciation ability}, that looking at underlined{word endings and decoding the syntax of riddles} allows them to understand grammar, and that other underlined{kinds of dialogue interaction} teach conversation. Overall, language play may underlined{be of critical importance in the development of language and literacy skills} (180).

### UNACCEPTABLE PARAPHRASE: USING THE AUTHOR'S SENTENCE STRUCTURES

Language play, Crystal underlined{suggests, will improve} pronunciation by zeroing in on sounds underlined{such as} rhymes. underlined{Having fun with} word endings underlined{and analyzing} riddle structure underlined{will help} a person acquire grammar. underlined{Being prepared to play with language, to use puns and talk} nonsense, improves the ability to use semantics. underlined{These} playful methods of communication underlined{are likely to} influence a person's ability to talk to others. underlined{And language play} inherently underlined{adds enormously to what has} recently underlined{been} known as *metalinguistic awareness*, a concept underlined{of great magnitude in developing speech abilities generally and literacy abilities particularly} (180).

Here is a paraphrase of the original passage that expresses the author's ideas accurately and acceptably:

**ACCEPTABLE PARAPHRASE: IN THE STUDENT WRITER'S OWN WORDS**

Crystal argues that playing with language—creating rhymes, figuring out riddles, making puns, playing with names, using invented words, and so on—helps children figure out a great deal, from the basics of pronunciation and grammar to how to carry on a conversation. This kind of play allows children to understand the overall concept of how language works, a concept that is key to learning to use—and read—language effectively (180).

Notice that the writer uses a signal phrase — "Crystal argues" — to introduce the source's ideas smoothly into her own text. The verb *argues* shows the writer communicating a neutral relationship to the source material.

Also notice that the student writer cites the source by last name and page number even though no exact language from the original appears in the paraphrase.

## 15d Summarizing

A summary is a significantly shortened version of a passage or even of a whole chapter or work that captures main ideas *in your own words*. Unlike a paraphrase, a summary uses just enough information to record the main points you wish to emphasize. Introduce summaries clearly, usually with a <u>signal phrase</u> that includes the author of the source, as the underlined words preceding the summary in this example indicate:

Professor of linguistics Deborah <u>Tannen says</u> that she offers her book *That's Not What I Meant!* to those wanting to strengthen communication between women and men. Tannen <u>goes on to illustrate</u> how communication breaks down <u>and then to suggest</u> that a full awareness of what she calls "genderlects" can improve relationships (297).

## 15e Integrating visuals and media effectively and ethically

Choose visuals and media wisely, whether you use video, audio, photographs, illustrations, charts and graphs, or other kinds of images. Integrate all visuals and media smoothly into your text.

- **Does each visual or media file make a strong contribution to the message?** Tangential or purely decorative visuals and media may weaken the power of your writing.

- **Are you sure that the work is accurate and credible?** Could the visual have been altered in some way?

- **Is each visual or media file appropriate and fair to your subject?** An obviously biased perspective may misrepresent the subject you are writing about.

- **Is each visual or media file appropriate for and fair to your audience?** Visuals and media should appeal to various members of your likely audience.

Whenever you post documents containing visuals or media online, make sure you check for copyright information. While it is considered "fair use" to use such materials in an essay or other project for a college class, once that project is published on the web, you might infringe on copyright protections if you do not ask the copyright holder for permission to use the visual or media file. If you have questions, ask your instructor for help.

Like quotations, paraphrases, and summaries, visuals and media need to be introduced and commented on in some way.

- Refer to the visual, audio, or video in the text *before* it appears. See student writer Julia Sakowitz's essay in 18e. She refers to a photograph with the reference *seen in fig. 1.*

- Explain or comment on the relevance of the visual or media file. This can appear *after* the visual or media file.

- Check the documentation system you are using to make sure you label visuals and media appropriately; MLA, for instance, asks that you number and title tables and figures (*Table 1: Average Amount of Rainfall by Region*).

---

TALKING THE TALK | **SAYING SOMETHING NEW**

"What can I say about my topic that experts haven't already said?" All writers — no matter how experienced — face this problem. As you read more about your topic, you will see areas of disagreement among experts, who may not be as expert as they first appear. Notice what your sources say and what they don't say. Consider how your own experiences give you a unique perspective on the topic. In time, you will identify a claim that you can make, one related to what others say but taking a new angle.

# 15f Checking for excessive use of source material

Your text needs to synthesize your research in support of your own argument; it should not be a patchwork of quotations, paraphrases, and summaries from other people. You need a rhetorical stance that represents you as the author. If you cite too many sources, your own voice will disappear, a problem the following passage demonstrates:

> The United States is one of the countries with the most rapid population growth. In fact, rapid population increase has been a "prominent feature of American life since the founding of the republic" (Day 31). In the past, the cause of the high rate of population growth was the combination of large-scale immigration and a high birth rate. As Day notes, "Two facts stand out in the demographic history of the United States: first, the single position as a receiver of immigrants; second, our high rate of growth from natural increase" (31).
>
> Nevertheless, American population density is not as high as in most European countries. Day points out that the Netherlands, with a density of 906 persons per square mile, is more crowded than even the most densely populated American states (33).

Most readers will think that the source is much too prominent here and that the author of the essay is only secondary. The quotations and paraphrases overwhelm the writer's voice and may leave readers wondering what the writer's own argument is.

▼ ▼ ▼ ▼ ▼ ▼ ▼ ▼ ▼ ▼ ▼ ▼ ▼ ▼ ▼ ▼ ▼ ▼ ▼ ▼ ▼ ▼ ▼ ▼ ▼

## THINKING CRITICALLY ABOUT YOUR INTEGRATION OF SOURCES

From a research project you have finished or are drafting now, choose three passages that cite sources. Then examine how well these sources are integrated into your text. Consider how you can make that integration smoother, and try your hand at revising one of them.

CHAPTER 16

# Acknowledging Sources and Avoiding Plagiarism

Whatever writing you do has in some way been influenced by what you have already read and experienced and is part of a much larger conversation that includes other writers and thinkers. As a writer, you need to understand current definitions of plagiarism, which have changed over time and vary from culture to culture, as well as the concept of intellectual property — works protected by copyright or by alternatives such as a Creative Commons license — so you can give credit where credit is due. An age of instant copying and linking may someday lead to revised understandings about who can "own" a text. But in college today, you should cite your sources carefully and systematically to avoid plagiarism, the use of someone else's words and ideas as if they were your own.

## 16a  Understanding reasons to acknowledge sources

Acknowledging, or citing, sources says to your reader that you have done your homework, that you have gained expertise on your topic, and that you are credible. Acknowledging your sources can also demonstrate fairness and open-mindedness when you have considered several points of view. In addition, recognizing your sources can help provide background for your research by placing it in the context of other thinking. Most of all, you should acknowledge sources to help your readers follow your thoughts, understand how your ideas relate to the thoughts of others, and know where to go to find more information.

Acknowledging sources fully and generously, then, is a way to establish your trustworthiness as a researcher. Failure to credit sources can destroy both your own credibility and that of your research.

---

Avoiding plagiarism

- Maintain an accurate and thorough working bibliography. **(14c)**
- Establish a consistent note-taking system, listing sources and page numbers and clearly identifying all quotations, paraphrases, summaries, statistics, and visuals. **(14g)**
- Identify all quotations with quotation marks—both in your notes and in your essay. **(15b)**
- Be sure your paraphrases and summaries use your own words and sentence structures. **(15c–d)**
- Give a citation or note for each quotation, paraphrase, summary, arguable assertion or opinion, statistic, and visual from a source, including an online source. **(To understand what sources to cite, see 16b; for in-text documentation, see 18b, 19b, 20b, or 21b.)**
- Prepare an accurate and complete list of sources cited according to the required documentation style. **(18d, 19d, 20c, or 21c)**
- Plan ahead on writing assignments so that you can avoid the temptation to take shortcuts.

# 16b Knowing which sources to acknowledge

You should understand the distinction between source materials that require acknowledgment (using in-text citations, footnotes or endnotes, or entries in a works-cited list or bibliography) and those that do not. Now that huge amounts of reliable information are available online, conventions regarding acknowledgment, fair use, and source citation are shifting. It is still important, however, to be as careful as possible in providing citations so that your readers will know where you got your information.

## Materials that do not require acknowledgment

- **Common knowledge.** If most readers know a fact, you probably do not need to cite a source for it. You do not need to credit a source to say that Barack Obama was reelected president in 2012, for example.
- **Facts available in a wide variety of sources.** If a number of encyclopedias, almanacs, or textbooks include a certain piece of information, you usually need not cite a specific source for it. For instance, you would not need to cite a source if you write that the Japanese bombed Pearl Harbor on December 7, 1941.
- **Findings from field research.** If you conduct observations or surveys, announce your findings as your own. Acknowledge people you interview as individuals rather than as part of a survey.

If you are not sure whether a fact, an observation, or a piece of information requires acknowledgment, err on the side of safety, and cite the source.

## Materials that require acknowledgment

For material that does not fall under the preceding categories, credit sources as fully as possible.

- **Quotations, paraphrases, and summaries.** Whenever you use another person's words, ideas, or opinions, credit the source. Even though the wording of a paraphrase or summary is your own, you should still acknowledge the source (15b–d).

- **Facts that aren't widely known or claims that are arguable.** If your readers would be unlikely to know a fact, or if an author presents as fact a claim that may or may not be true, cite the source. If you are not sure whether a fact will be familiar to your readers or whether a statement is arguable, cite the source.

- **Visuals from any source.** Credit all visual and statistical material not derived from your own field research, even if you create your own graph or table from the data provided in a source.

- **Help provided by others.** If an instructor gave you a good idea or if friends responded to your draft or helped you conduct surveys, give credit.

Here is a quick-reference chart to guide you in deciding whether or not you need to acknowledge a source:

| NEED TO ACKNOWLEDGE | DON'T NEED TO ACKNOWLEDGE |
|---|---|
| • quotations | • your own ideas expressed in your own words |
| • paraphrases or summaries of a source | |
| • ideas you glean from a source | • your own observations, surveys, and findings from field research you conduct yourself |
| • little-known or disputed facts | |
| • graphs, tables, and other statistical information from a source | • common knowledge — facts known to most readers |
| • photographs, visuals, video, or sound taken from sources | • drawings and other visuals, audio recordings, video, and any other materials you create on your own ▶ |
| • experiments conducted by others | |

| NEED TO ACKNOWLEDGE | DON'T NEED TO ACKNOWLEDGE |
|---|---|
| • interviews that are not part of your own field research | • facts available in many reliable sources, whether or not they are common knowledge |
| • organization or structure taken from a source | |
| • help or advice from an instructor or another student | |

## 16c Recognizing patchwriting

Integrating sources into your writing can be a significant challenge. In fact, as a beginning researcher, you might do what Professor Rebecca Howard calls "patchwriting"; that is, rather than integrate sources smoothly and accurately, you patch together words, phrases, and even structures from sources into your own writing, sometimes without citation. The author of this book remembers doing such "patchwriting" for a middle-school report on her hero, Dr. Albert Schweitzer. Luckily, she had a teacher who sat patiently with her, showing her how to paraphrase, summarize, and quote from sources correctly and effectively. So it takes time and effort — and good instruction — to learn to integrate sources appropriately rather than patchwriting, which is sometimes considered plagiarism even if you didn't mean to plagiarize.

## 16d Adapting structures and phrases from a genre without plagiarizing

Multilingual

If you are not accustomed to writing in a particular academic genre, you may find it useful to borrow and adapt transitional devices and pieces of sentence structure from other people's writing in the genre or discipline you are working in. Be careful to borrow only structures that are generic and not ideas or sentences that come from a particular, identifiable writer. You should not copy any whole sentences or sentence structures verbatim, or your borrowing may seem plagiarized.

| ORIGINAL ABSTRACT FROM A SOCIAL SCIENCE PAPER | EFFECTIVE BORROWING OF STRUCTURES FROM A GENRE |
|---|---|
| <u>Using the</u> interpersonal communications <u>research of</u> J. K. Brilhart and G. J. Galanes, and W. Wilmot and J. Hocker, along with T. Hartman's personality assessment, <u>I observed and</u> | <u>Drawing on the research</u> of Deborah Tannen on men's and women's conversational styles, <u>I analyzed</u> the conversational styles of six first-year students at DePaul University. <u>Based on</u> ▶ |

**ORIGINAL ABSTRACT FROM A SOCIAL SCIENCE PAPER**

analyzed the leadership roles and group dynamics of my project collaborators in a communications course. Based on results of the Hartman personality assessment, I predicted that a single leader would emerge. However, complementary individual strengths and gender differences encouraged a distributed leadership style, in which the group experienced little confrontation and conflict. Conflict, because it was handled positively, was crucial to the group's progress.

**EFFECTIVE BORROWING OF STRUCTURES FROM A GENRE**

Tannen's research, I expected that the three men I observed would use features typical of male conversational style and the three women would use features typical of female conversational style. In general, these predictions were accurate; however, some exceptions were also apparent.

The example above illustrates effective borrowing. The student writer borrows phrases (such as "drawing on" and "based on") that are commonly used in academic writing in the social sciences to perform particular functions. Notice how the student also modifies these phrases to suit her needs.

## 16e Maintaining academic integrity and avoiding plagiarism

Effective writing always involves trust between writers and their audiences: in putting your name on something, you are saying to your readers, "you can trust that what I say here is accurate and that I am responsible for its contents." While there are many ways to destroy that trust and damage academic integrity, two that are especially important are the inaccurate or incomplete acknowledgment of sources — also called unintentional plagiarism — and plagiarism that is deliberately intended to pass off one writer's work as another's.

Whether intentional or not, plagiarism can bring serious consequences. At some colleges, students who plagiarize fail the course automatically; at others, they are expelled. Academics who plagiarize, even inadvertently, have had their degrees revoked and their books withdrawn from publication. And outside academic life, eminent political, business, and scientific leaders have been stripped of candidacies, positions, and awards because of plagiarism.

## Avoiding inaccurate or incomplete citation of sources

If your paraphrase is too close to the original wording or sentence structure of the source (even if you identify the source); if you do not identify the source of a quotation (even if you include the quotation marks); or if you fail to indicate clearly the source of an idea that you obviously did not come up with on your own, you may be accused of plagiarism even if your intent was not to plagiarize. Inaccurate or incomplete acknowledgment of sources often results either from carelessness or from not learning how to borrow material properly in the first place.

Academic integrity calls for you to be faithful not only to the letter of the material you are drawing on but also to its spirit: you need to honor the intention of the original source. For example, if your source says that an event *may* have happened in a particular way, then it isn't ethical to suggest that the source says that the event *absolutely* happened that way.

Because the costs of even unintentional plagiarism can be severe, it's important to understand how it can happen and how you can guard against it. In a January 2002 article published in *Time* magazine, historian Doris Kearns Goodwin explains how she made acknowledgment errors in one of her books. The book in question, nine hundred pages long and with thirty-five hundred footnotes, took Goodwin ten years to write. During this time, she says, she took most of her notes by hand, organized them, and later checked her sources to make sure all the material she was using was correctly cited. "Somehow in this process," Goodwin goes on to say, "a few books were not fully rechecked," and thus she omitted some acknowledgments and some quotation marks by mistake. Discovering such carelessness in her own work was very troubling to Goodwin since, as she puts it, "the writing of history is a rich process of building on the work of the past. . . . Through footnotes [and citations] you point the way to future historians."

Goodwin certainly paid a steep price for her carelessness: she had to leave Harvard's Board of Overseers and also resigned from the committee that awards Pulitzer Prizes. In addition, she was put on indefinite leave from a television program to which she had contributed regularly, was asked not to give a planned commencement address at the University of Delaware, and had to negotiate at least one settlement with a person whose work she had used without proper citation. Perhaps most seriously, this event called into question all of Goodwin's work.

As a writer of academic integrity, you will want to take responsibility for your research and for acknowledging all sources accurately. One easy way to keep track is to keep photocopies, printouts, or unaltered digital copies of every source as you conduct your research; then you can identify needed quotations by highlighting them on each source.

## Avoiding deliberate plagiarism

Deliberate plagiarism — handing in an essay written by a friend or downloaded from an essay-writing company; copying and pasting passages directly from source materials without acknowledgment; failing to credit the source of an idea or concept in your text — is what most people think of when they hear the word *plagiarism*. This form of plagiarism is particularly troubling because it represents dishonesty and deception: those who intentionally plagiarize present the hard thinking and hard work of someone else as their own, and they deceive readers by claiming knowledge they don't really have.

Deliberate plagiarism is also fairly simple to spot: your instructor will be well acquainted with your writing and likely to notice any sudden shifts in the style or quality of your work. In addition, by typing a few words from an essay into a search engine, your instructor can identify "matches" very easily.

### EXERCISE 16.1

Read the brief original passage that follows, and then look closely at the five attempts to quote or paraphrase it. Decide which attempts are acceptable and which plagiarize, prepare notes on what supports your decision in each case, and bring your notes to class for discussion.

> The strange thing about plagiarism is that it's almost always pointless. The writers who stand accused, from Laurence Sterne to Samuel Taylor Coleridge to Susan Sontag, tend to be more talented than the writers they lift from.
> — MALCOLM JONES, "Have You Read This Story Somewhere?"

1. According to Malcolm Jones, writers accused of plagiarism are always better writers than those they are supposed to have plagiarized.

2. According to Malcolm Jones, writers accused of plagiarism "tend to be more talented than the writers they lift from."

3. Plagiarism is usually pointless, says writer Malcolm Jones.

4. Those who stand accused of plagiarism, such as former vice president Joseph Biden, tend to be better writers than those whose work they use.

5. According to Malcolm Jones, "plagiarism is . . . almost always pointless."

LANGUAGE, CULTURE, | **PLAGIARISM AS A CULTURAL CONCEPT**
AND CONTEXT

Many cultures do not recognize Western ideas about plagiarism, which rest on a belief that language and ideas can be owned by writers. Indeed, in many countries other than the United States, and even within some communities in the United States, using the words and ideas of others without attribution is considered a sign of deep respect as well as an indication of knowledge. In academic writing in the United States, however, you should credit all materials except those that are common knowledge, that are available in a wide variety of sources, or that are your own creations (photographs, drawings, and so on) or your own findings from field research.

# 16f Considering your intellectual property

Although you may not have thought too much about it, all of your work in college — including all the research and writing you do, online and off — represents a growing bank of intellectual property. In fact, such original work is automatically copyrighted, even if it lacks the © symbol. But remember that the open source movement is gaining momentum and that sharing your ideas and writing freely with others is a way to perpetuate them and to gain an audience for your views.

For work that you want to protect, here are some tips for making sure that others respect your intellectual property just as you respect theirs:

- Realize that your text and email messages, blog posts and comments, and posts to social networking sites and discussion groups are essentially public. If you don't want your thoughts and ideas repeated or forwarded, keep them offline. Let recipients know specifically when you do not want your email messages passed on to any third parties. In turn, remember that you should not use material from email, discussion groups, or other online forums without first asking for permission.

- Be careful with your passwords, and use a secure storage method so that only you can give someone access to your work.

- Save all your drafts and notes so that you can show where your work has come from, should anyone ask you.

# 16g Collaborating

With so much focus on plagiarism and with the advent of online essay archives, you may feel reluctant to share or discuss your work with anyone else. That would be a very unfortunate result, however, since much of our knowledge comes from talking with and learning from others. Indeed, many college projects now require some form of collaboration or teamwork, whether it involves commenting on someone else's draft, preparing a group presentation of research findings, or composing a text with many others on a wiki or on Google Drive.

Collaborative writing projects call for the same kind of acknowledgments you use in a paper or other project you prepare by yourself. In general, cite all sources used by the group, and acknowledge all assistance provided by others. In some cases, you may decide to do this in an endnote rather than in your bibliography or list of works cited.

▼ ▼ ▼ ▼ ▼ ▼ ▼ ▼ ▼ ▼ ▼ ▼ ▼ ▼ ▼ ▼ ▼ ▼ ▼ ▼ ▼ ▼ ▼ ▼ ▼ ▼

## THINKING CRITICALLY ABOUT YOUR OWN ACKNOWLEDGMENT OF SOURCES

Look at a recent piece of your writing that incorporates material from sources, and try to determine how completely and accurately you acknowledged them. Did you properly cite every quotation, paraphrase, and summary? every opinion or other idea from a source? every source you used to create visuals? Did you unintentionally plagiarize someone else's words or ideas? Make notes, and bring them to class for discussion.

# CHAPTER 17

# Writing a Research Project

When you are working on an academic research project, there comes a time to draw the strands of research together and articulate your conclusions in writing.

## 17a Refining your plans

You should by now have notes containing facts, opinions, paraphrases, summaries, quotations, and other material; you probably have images or media to integrate as well. You may also have ideas about how to synthesize these many pieces of information. And you should have some sense of whether your hypothesis has sufficient support. Now is the time to reconsider your purpose, audience, stance, and working thesis.

- What is your central purpose? What other purposes, if any, do you have?
- What is your stance toward your topic (3c)? Are you an advocate, a critic, a reporter, an observer?
- What audience(s) are you addressing (3d and 11f)?
- How much background information or context does your audience need?
- What supporting information will your readers find most convincing?
- Should your tone be that of a colleague, an expert, a friend?
- How can you establish common ground with your readers and show them that you have considered points of view other than your own? (See 11f and Chapter 36.)
- What is your working thesis trying to establish? Will your audience accept it?

### Moving from working thesis to explicit thesis

Writing out an explicit, or direct, thesis statement allows you to articulate your major points and to see how well they carry out your purpose and appeal to your audience. Depending on the purpose, audience, and genre of your project, you may or may not decide to include the explicit thesis in your final draft — but developing your working thesis into an explicit statement can still be very useful.

Julia Sakowitz, the student whose research essay appears in Chapter 18, developed the following explicit thesis statement:

> Although there is no simple solution for tourism in Harlem, small minority- and resident-owned tour businesses have the potential to more directly and widely benefit the community while causing fewer social and economic problems.

## Asking questions about your thesis

Although writing out an explicit thesis will often confirm your research, you may find that your hypothesis is invalid, inadequately supported, or insufficiently focused. In such cases, you need to rethink your original research question and perhaps do further research. To test your thesis, consider the following questions:

- How can you state your thesis more precisely or more clearly (4c)? Should the wording be more specific? Could you use more specific, concrete nouns (Chapter 37) or stronger verbs (Chapter 41)? Should you add qualifying adjectives or adverbs (Chapter 54)?

- In what ways will your thesis interest your audience? What can you do to increase that interest (3d)?

- Will your thesis be manageable, given your limits of time and knowledge? If not, what can you do to make it more manageable?

- What evidence from your research supports each aspect of your thesis? What additional evidence do you need?

### EXERCISE 17.1

Take the thesis from your current research project, and test it against the questions provided in 17a. Make revisions if your analysis reveals weaknesses in your thesis.

## Planning design

As you move toward producing a draft, take some time to think about how you want your research project to look. What font will you use? Should you use color? Do you plan to insert text boxes and visuals? Will you need headings and subheadings? Will you incorporate audio, video, or other media? (For more on design, see Chapter 22.)

LANGUAGE, CULTURE, | **ASKING EXPERIENCED WRITERS**
AND CONTEXT | **TO REVIEW A THESIS**

If you speak two or more languages, you might find it helpful to ask one or two classmates who have more experience with the particular type of academic writing to look at your explicit thesis. Ask if the thesis is as direct and clear as it can be, and revise accordingly.

## 17b Organizing information

Experienced writers differ considerably in the ways they go about organizing ideas and information, and you will want to experiment until you find a method that works well for you. (For more on organizational strategies, see 4e.) This section will discuss two organizing strategies — grouping material by subject and outlining.

### Grouping by subject

You may find it useful to have physical notes to arrange — note cards or sticky notes, for example, or printouts of your slides or of notes you have been keeping online that you mark in some way to make the subject categories easy to identify. You can group the pieces around subject headings and reorder the parts until they seem to make sense. Shuqiao Song, the student who wrote the critical analysis in 9h, organized the plans for her PowerPoint presentation (Chapter 23) by moving sticky notes around on her window.

Grouping your notes will help you see how well you can support your thesis and help you see if you have missed any essential points. Do you need to omit any ideas or sources? Do you need to find additional evidence for a main or supporting point? Once you have gathered everything together and organized your materials, you can see how the many small pieces of your research fit together. Make sure that your evidence supports your explicit thesis; if not, you may need to revise it or do additional research — or both.

Once you have established initial groups, skim through the notes and look for ways to organize your draft. Figure out what background your audience needs, what points you need to make first, how much detail and support to offer for each point, and so on.

### Making an outline

You can use outlines in various ways and at various stages. Some writers group their notes, write a draft, and then outline the draft to study its tentative structure. Others develop an informal working outline from their notes and revise it as they go along. Still other writers prefer to plot out their organization early on in a formal outline. (For more on outlines, see 4f.)

Student writer Julia Sakowitz drew up a working outline of her ideas as she was conducting research about tourism in Harlem. She thought this simple structure would help her focus on the information she still needed to find.

**SAMPLE WORKING OUTLINE**

Tourism growth
- Description of Upper Manhattan Empowerment Zone (UMEZ)
- How has UMEZ encouraged tourism in Harlem?

Benefits and disadvantages of tourism
- Economic benefits (statistics)
- Research "gentrification"

Tour companies
- Harlem-based vs. outside tour companies
- Interviews with company owners

# 17c Drafting

For most college research projects, drafting should begin *at least* two weeks before the instructor's deadline in case you need to gather more information or do more drafting. Set a deadline for having a complete draft, and structure your work with that date in mind. Gather your notes, outline, and sources, and read through them, getting involved in your topic. Most writers find that some sustained work (two or three hours at a time) pays off at this point. Begin drafting a section that you feel confident about. For example, if you are not sure how you want to introduce the draft but do know how you want to approach a particular point, begin with that, and return to the introduction later. The most important thing is to get started.

The drafting process varies considerably among researchers (4g), and no one else can determine what will work best for you. No matter what approach you take, remember to include sources (for quotations, paraphrases, summaries, and media) as you draft; doing so will save time later and help you produce your list of works cited.

## Creating a working title and introduction

The title and introduction (5f) play special roles, for they set the context for what is to come. Ideally, the title announces your subject in an intriguing or memorable way. To accomplish these goals, Emily Lesk, the student writer whose work appears in Part 2, revised the title of her essay from "All-Powerful Coke" to "Red, White, and Everywhere" (6f). Julia Sakowitz began with the title "Tourism in Harlem," but she later moved that to the subtitle and focused on an intriguing quote from her field research as the title: "We're a Lot More Than Gospel Singing."

The introduction should draw readers in and provide any background they will need to understand the discussion. Here are some tips for drafting an introduction to a research project:

- You may want to open with a *question*, especially your research question, or with a *strong or arresting statement* of some kind. Next, you might explain what you will do to answer the question or to elaborate on the statement. For academic projects, instructors may expect you to end with your *explicit thesis statement*—in essence, the answer to the question or the response to the strong statement.

- Help readers get their bearings by *forecasting your main points*.

- *Establish your own credibility* by revealing how you have become knowledgeable about your topic.

- You may use a *quotation* to get attention, but singling out one source in this way may give that source too much emphasis.

Julia Sakowitz's introduction is more extensive than usual, because she uses it to link her own experience to the issues she addresses (18e). She begins on a personal note, as a native of New York City, to engage her readers, establish her connection to the topic she will pursue, and create a narrative frame for the entire essay. She then provides necessary details and background information to introduce her readers to the topic, tourism in Harlem, noting that the current surge in tourism has brought with it both benefits and problems, before presenting her explicit thesis statement.

## Crafting a conclusion

A good conclusion helps readers know what they have learned (5f). Its job is not to persuade—the body of the essay or project should already have done that—but to contribute to the overall effectiveness of your writing. The following strategies may be helpful:

- Refer to your thesis, and then expand to a more general conclusion that reminds readers of the significance of your discussion.

- If you have covered several main points, you may want to remind readers of them. Be careful, however, to provide more than a summary.

- Try to end with something that will have an impact—a provocative quotation or question, a vivid image, a call for action, or a warning. But guard against sounding preachy.

In her conclusion, Julia Sakowitz sums up the major points of her argument and reiterates her thesis. See her full research essay in 18e.

## 17d Incorporating source materials

When you reach the point of drafting your research project, a new task awaits: weaving your source materials into your writing. The challenge is to use your sources yet remain the author — to quote, paraphrase, and summarize other voices while remaining the major voice in your work. (Because learning how to effectively integrate source material is so important, Chapter 15 is devoted entirely to this process.)

## 17e Reviewing and getting responses to your draft

Because a research project involves a complex mix of your thoughts and materials from outside sources, it calls for an especially careful review. You should examine the draft yourself as well as seek the comments of other readers. Ask friends and classmates to read and respond to your draft, and get a response from your instructor if possible.

### Reviewing your own draft

As with most kinds of writing, taking a break after drafting is important so that when you reread the draft, you can bring a fresh eye to the task. When you do return to the draft, read it straight through without stopping. Then read the draft again slowly, reconsidering your purpose, audience, stance, thesis, and support.

- From your reading of the draft, what do you now see as its *purpose*? How does this compare with your original purpose? Does the draft do what your assignment requires?
- What *audience* does your essay address?
- What is your *stance* toward the topic?
- What is your *thesis*? Is it clearly stated?
- What *evidence* supports your thesis? Is the evidence sufficient?

Answer these questions as best you can, since they are the starting point for revision. If you notice a problem but are unsure how to solve it, write down your concerns so that you can ask readers if they notice the same problem and have ideas about solving it.

## Outlining your draft

You might find that outlining your draft helps you analyze it at this point: an outline will reveal the bare bones of your argument and help you see what may be missing or out of place. See 4f for the formal outline that Julia Sakowitz prepared to show the skeleton of her argument about tourism businesses in Harlem.

## Seeking responses from peers

You should seek responses from friends and classmates as your draft evolves. Your reviewers will be best prepared to give you helpful advice and to ask questions specific to your project if they have background information about your writing task.

Tell your reviewers the purpose of your draft, the assignment's criteria, and your target audience. Ask them to explain their understanding of your stance on the topic. Also ask for feedback on your thesis and its support. If you are unsure about whether to include a particular point, how to use a certain quotation, or where to add more examples, ask your reviewers specifically what they think you should do. You should also ask them to identify any parts of your draft that confuse them. Even if you are writing to a target audience with more expertise in the topic than your peer reviewers, you should carefully consider revising the parts they identify as confusing: you may be making too many assumptions about what concepts need to be explained. (For more on peer review, see 6b.)

# 17f Revising and editing

When you have considered your reviewers' responses and your own analysis, you can turn to revising and editing.

---

QUICK HELP

Guidelines for revising a research project

- **Take responses into account.** Look at specific problems that reviewers think you need to solve or strengths you might capitalize on. For example, if they showed great interest in one point but no interest in another, consider expanding the first and deleting the second.
- **Reconsider your original purpose, audience, and stance.** Have you achieved your purpose? How well have you appealed to your readers? Make sure you satisfy any special concerns of your reviewers. If your rhetorical stance toward your topic has changed, does your draft need to change, too?
- **Assess your research.** Think about whether you have investigated the topic thoroughly and consulted materials with more than one point of view. Have you left out any important sources? Are the sources you use reliable and appropriate for your topic? Have you synthesized your research findings and drawn warranted conclusions?

▶

Guidelines for revising a research project, continued

- **Assess your use of visuals and media.** Make sure that each one supports your argument, is clearly labeled, and is cited appropriately.
- **Gather additional material.** If you need to strengthen any points, first check your notes to see whether you already have the necessary information. In some instances, you may need to do more research.
- **Decide what changes you need to make.** List everything that you must do to strengthen your draft. With your deadline in mind, plan your revision.
- **Rewrite your draft.** However you revise, be sure to save copies of each draft. Begin with the major changes, such as adding content or reorganizing. Then turn to sentence-level problems and word choice. Can you sharpen the work's dominant impression?
- **Reevaluate the title, introduction, and conclusion.** Is your title specific and engaging? Does the introduction capture readers' attention and indicate what the work discusses? Does your conclusion help readers see the significance of your argument?
- **Check your documentation.** Make sure you've included a citation in your text for every quotation, paraphrase, summary, visual, and media file you incorporated, and that you've followed your documentation style consistently.
- **Edit your draft.** Check grammar, usage, spelling, punctuation, and mechanics. Consider the advice of computer spell checkers and grammar checkers carefully before accepting it.

## 17g Preparing a list of sources

Once your final draft and source materials are in place, you are ready to prepare a list of sources. Follow the guidelines for your documentation style carefully (see Chapters 18–21), creating an entry for each source used. Double-check your work to make sure that you have listed every source mentioned in your draft and (unless you are listing all the sources you consulted) that you have not listed any sources not cited.

## 17h Proofreading your final copy

Your final rough draft may look very rough indeed, so your next step is to create a final, perfectly clean copy. You will submit this version, which represents all your work and effort, to your instructor. At this point, run the spell checker but do not stop there. To make sure that this final version puts your best foot forward, proofread extremely carefully. Read the copy aloud for content and for the flow of the argument, making sure you haven't mistakenly deleted words, lines, or whole sections. Then read the copy backward from the last sentence to the first, looking for small mistakes such as punctuation problems or missing words. If you are keeping an editing checklist, look for the types of editing problems you have had in the past.

Once you are sure your draft is free of errors, check the design one last time to be sure you are using effective margins, type size, color, boldface and italics, headings, and so on. You want your final copy to be as readable as possible (see Chapter 22).

After your formatting and proofreading are complete, celebrate your achievement: your research and hard work have produced a project that you can, and should, take pride in.

▼ ▼ ▼ ▼ ▼ ▼ ▼ ▼ ▼ ▼ ▼ ▼ ▼ ▼ ▼ ▼ ▼ ▼ ▼ ▼ ▼ ▼ ▼ ▼

## THINKING CRITICALLY ABOUT RESEARCH PROJECTS

Reflect on the research project you have completed. How did you go about organizing your information? What would you do to improve this process? What problems did you encounter in drafting? How did you solve these problems? How many quotations did you use, and how did you integrate them into your text? When and why did you use summaries and paraphrases? If you used visuals, how effective were they in supporting your points? What did you learn from revising?

# PART 5
# Documenting Sources

Photo by Mike Enright/www.menright.com. Photo styling by Barbara Lipp.

# List of Examples

## In-text citations in MLA style (18c)

## Works-cited entries in MLA style (18d)

### Guidelines for author listings

### Print books

### Print periodicals

# MLA Style

Different rhetorical situations call for different approaches to citing sources — that is, for different ways of answering the question "Says who?" If you're reading a popular magazine, you probably won't expect the writer to provide careful source citations or a list of references at the end of an article. If you're posting material on a blog, you might follow conventions for citation by simply linking to the material you're talking about. But in other situations, including most academic writing, you will be expected to follow a more rigorous system for citing the information you use. Many courses in English ask writers to follow MLA style, the system developed by the Modern Language Association. This chapter includes guidelines adapted from the *MLA Handbook,* Eighth Edition (2016).

## 18a Understanding the basics

When you are assigned to use MLA style for a research project, it is helpful to think through your responsibilities as an academic writer: What do your readers need from you? What are the elements of an MLA citation? How do in-text citations connect to entries in the works-cited list? And is there any need for explanatory notes for your reader?

### Thinking about what readers need from you

Why does academic work call for very careful citation practices when writing for the general public might not? The answer is that readers of your academic work expect to get certain information from source citations:

- Source citations demonstrate that you've done your homework on your topic and that you are a part of the conversation surrounding it. Careful citation shows your readers what you know, where you stand, and what you think is important.

- Source citations show that you understand the need to give credit when you use someone else's intellectual property. Especially in academic writing, when it's better to be safe than sorry, include a citation for any source you think you might need to cite. (See Chapter 15 for details.)

- Source citations give explicit directions to guide readers who want to look for themselves at the works you're using.

The guidelines for MLA style help you with this last purpose, giving you instructions on exactly what information to include in your citation and how to format that information.

## Identifying elements of MLA citations

New kinds of sources crop up regularly. As the *MLA Handbook* confirms, there are often several "correct" ways to cite a source, so you will need to think carefully about *your own context* for using the source so you can identify the pieces of information that you should emphasize or include and any other information that might be helpful to your readers. The first step is to identify elements that are commonly found in most works writers cite.

### AUTHOR AND TITLE

The first two elements, both of which are needed for many sources, are the author's name and the title of the work. Each of these elements is followed by a period.

**Author. Title.**

Even in these elements, your context is important. The author of a novel may be obvious, but who is the "author" of a television episode? The director? The writer? The show's creator? The star? The answer may depend on the focus of your own work. If an actor's performance is central to your discussion, then MLA guidelines ask you to identify the actor as the author. If the plot is your focus, you might name the writer of the episode as the author.

### CONTAINER

The next step is to identify elements of what the MLA calls the "container" for the work. The context in which you are discussing the source and the context in which you find the source will help you determine what counts as a container in each case. If you watch a movie in a theater, you won't identify a separate container after the film title. But if you watch the same movie as part of a box set of the director's work, the container title is the name of the box set. If you read an article in a print journal, the first container will be the journal that the article appears in. If you read it online, the journal may also be part of a second, larger container, such as a database. Thinking about a source as nested in larger containers may help you to visualize how a citation works.

The elements you may include in the "container" part of your citation include the following, in this order: the title of the larger container, if it's different from the title of the work; the names of any contributors such as editors or translators; the version or edition; the volume and issue numbers; the publisher or sponsor; the date of publication; and a location such as the page numbers, DOI, permalink, or URL. These elements are separated by commas, and the end of the container is marked with a period.

> **Author. Title. Container title, contributor names, version or edition, volume and issue numbers, publisher, date, location.**

Most sources won't include all these pieces of information, so include only the elements that are available and relevant to create an acceptable citation. If you need a second container — for instance, if you are citing an article from a journal you found in a database — you simply add it after the first one, beginning with the container title and including as many of the same container elements as you can find. The rest of this chapter offers many examples of how elements and containers are combined to create citations.

One student researching messaging technologies found a potentially useful journal article by searching a library database, Academic Search Premier, through his library's website. The journal is the first container of the article, and the database is the second container.

> Counts, Scott, and Karen E. Fisher. "Mobile Social Networking as Information Ground: A Case Study." *Library and Information Science Research*, vol. 32, no. 2, Apr. 2010, pp. 98–115. *Academic Search Premier,* doi:10.1016/j.lisr.2009.10.003.

Notice that the first container includes just four relevant elements — the journal title, number (here, that means the volume and issue numbers), date, and page numbers; and the second container includes just two — the database title and location.

### Types of sources

Refer to the List of Examples at the beginning of this chapter to locate guidelines on citing various types of sources, including print books, print periodicals (journals, magazines, and newspapers), digital written-word sources, and other sources (films, artwork) that consist mainly of material other than written words. A digital version of a source may include updates or corrections that the print version of the same work lacks, so MLA guidelines ask you to indicate where you found the source. If you can't find a model exactly like the source you've selected, see the Quick Help list on page 251.

## Planning and connecting your citations

MLA citations appear in two connected parts — the brief in-text citation, usually in parentheses in the body of your written text, and the full citation in the list of works cited, to which the in-text citation directs your readers. The most straightforward in-text citations include the <u>author's name</u> and the <u>page number</u>, but many variations on this basic format are discussed in 18c.

In the text of her research essay (see 18e), Julia Sakowitz paraphrases material from a journal article by anthropologist Arlene Dávila. As shown, she cites the article page on which the original information appears in a parenthetical reference that points readers to the entry for "Dávila, Arlene" in her list of works cited. She also cites portions of a personal interview she has conducted with Seth Kamil, which has no page numbers. These examples show just two of the many ways to cite sources using in-text citations and a list of works cited. You'll need to make case-by-case decisions based on the types of sources you include.

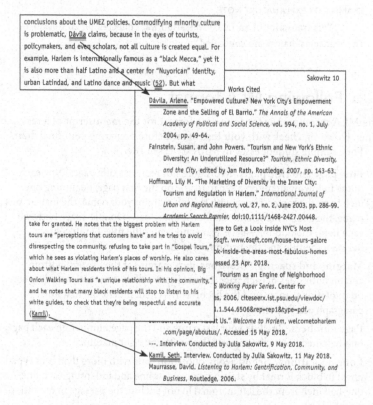

conclusions about the UMEZ policies. Commodifying minority culture is problematic, <u>Dávila</u> claims, because in the eyes of tourists, policymakers, and even scholars, not all culture is created equal. For example, Harlem is internationally famous as a "black Mecca," yet it is also more than half Latino and a center for "Nuyorican" identity, urban Latinidad, and Latino dance and music (<u>52</u>). But what

Sakowitz 10

Works Cited

Dávila, <u>Arlene</u>. "Empowered Culture? New York City's Empowerment Zone and the Selling of El Barrio." *The Annals of the American Academy of Political and Social Science*, vol. 594, no. 1, July 2004, pp. 49-64.

Fainstein, Susan, and John Powers. "Tourism and New York's Ethnic Diversity: An Underutilized Resource?" *Tourism, Ethnic Diversity, and the City*, edited by Jan Rath, Routledge, 2007, pp. 143-63.

Hoffman, Lily M. "The Marketing of Diversity in the Inner City: Tourism and Regulation in Harlem." *International Journal of Urban and Regional Research*, vol. 27, no. 2, June 2003, pp. 286-99. *Academic Search Premier*, doi:10.1111/1468-2427.00448.

take for granted. He notes that the biggest problem with Harlem tours is "perceptions that customers have" and he tries to avoid disrespecting the community, refusing to take part in "Gospel Tours," which he sees as violating Harlem's places of worship. He also cares about what Harlem residents think of his tours. In his opinion, Big Onion Walking Tours has "a unique relationship with the community," and he notes that many black residents will stop to listen to his white guides, to check that they're being respectful and accurate (<u>Kamil</u>).

...ere to Get a Look Inside NYC's Most ...*6sqft*. www.6sqft.com/house-tours-galore ...bk-inside-the-areas-most-fabulous-homes ...essed 23 Apr. 2018.

..."Tourism as an Engine of Neighborhood ...*S Working Paper Series*. Center for ...es, 2006, citeseerx.ist.psu.edu/viewdoc/ ...1.1.544.6506&rep=rep1&type=pdf.

...t Us." *Welcome to Harlem*, welcometoharlem .com/page/aboutus/. Accessed 15 May 2018.

---. Interview. Conducted by Julia Sakowitz, 9 May 2018.

<u>Kamil, Seth</u>. Interview. Conducted by Julia Sakowitz, 11 May 2018.

Maurrasse, David. *Listening to Harlem: Gentrification, Community, and Business*, Routledge, 2006.

## Including notes as needed

MLA citation style asks you to include explanatory notes for information or comments that don't readily fit into your text but are needed for clarification or further explanation. In addition, MLA permits bibliographic notes for offering information about or evaluation of a source, or to list multiple sources that relate to a single point. Use superscript numbers in the text to refer readers to the notes, which may appear as endnotes (under the heading *Notes* on a separate page immediately before the list of works cited) or as footnotes at the bottom of each page where a superscript number appears.

**EXAMPLE OF SUPERSCRIPT NUMBER IN TEXT**

Although such communication relies on the written word, many messagers disregard standard writing conventions. For example, here is a snippet from an IM conversation between two teenage girls:[1]

**EXAMPLE OF EXPLANATORY NOTE**

1. This transcript of an IM conversation was collected on 20 Nov. 2014. The teenagers' names are concealed to protect privacy.

## 18b Following MLA format

The MLA recommends the following format for the manuscript of a research paper. However, check with your instructor before preparing your final draft.

For a sample student essay in MLA style, see 18e.

- **First page and title page.** MLA does not require a title page. Type each of the following items on a separate line on the first page, beginning one inch from the top and flush with the left margin: your name, the instructor's name, the course name and number, and the date. Double-space between each item; then double-space again and center the title. Double-space between the title and the beginning of the text.

- **Margins and spacing.** Leave one-inch margins at the top and bottom and on both sides of each page. Double-space the entire text, including set-off quotations, notes, and the list of works cited. Indent the first line of a paragraph one-half inch.

- **Page numbers.** Include your last name and the page number on each page, one-half inch below the top and flush with the right margin.

- **Long quotations.** Set off a long quotation (one with more than four typed lines) in block format by starting it on a new line and indenting each line one-half inch from the left margin. Do not enclose the passage in quotation marks (15b).

- **Headings.** MLA style allows, but does not require, headings. Many students and instructors find them helpful.

- **Visuals.** Place tables, photographs, drawings, charts, graphs, and other figures as near as possible to the relevant text. (See 15e for guidelines on incorporating visuals into your text.) Tables should have a label and number

(*Table 1*) and a clear caption. The label and caption should be aligned on the left, on separate lines. Give the source information below the table. All other visuals should be labeled *Figure* (abbreviated *Fig.*), numbered, and captioned. The label and caption should appear on the same line, followed by the source information. Remember to refer to each visual in your text, indicating how it contributes to the point you are making.

# 18c Creating MLA in-text citations

In MLA style, a citation in the text of an essay is required for every quotation, paraphrase, summary, or other material requiring documentation (see Chapter 15). In-text citations document material from other sources with both signal phrases and parenthetical references. Parenthetical references should include the information your readers need to locate the full reference in the list of works cited at the end of the text (18d). An in-text citation in MLA style aims to give the reader two kinds of information: (1) it indicates *which source* on the works-cited page the writer is referring to, and (2) it explains *where in the source* the material quoted, paraphrased, or summarized can be found, if the source has page numbers or other numbered sections.

The basic MLA in-text citation includes the <u>author's last name</u> either in a signal phrase introducing the source material (15b) or in parentheses at the end of the sentence. For sources with stable page numbers, it also includes the <u>page number</u> in parentheses at the end of the sentence.

**SAMPLE CITATION USING A SIGNAL PHRASE**

In his discussion of Monty Python routines, <u>Crystal</u> notes that the group relished "breaking the normal rules" of language (<u>107</u>).

**SAMPLE PARENTHETICAL CITATION**

A noted linguist explains that Monty Python humor often relied on "bizarre linguistic interactions" (<u>Crystal</u> <u>108</u>).

(For digital sources without stable page numbers, see model 2.)

Note in the examples on the following pages where punctuation is placed in relation to the parentheses. We have used underlining in some examples only to draw your attention to important elements. Do not underline anything in your own citations.

*1. Basic format for a quotation*   The MLA recommends using the <u>author's name</u> in a signal phrase (15b) to introduce the material and citing the <u>page number(s)</u> in parentheses.

<u>Lee</u> claims that his comic-book creation, Thor, was "the first regularly published superhero to speak in a consistently archaic manner" (<u>199</u>).

When you do not mention the author in a signal phrase, include the author's last name before the page number(s), if any, in the parentheses. Use no punctuation between the author's name and the page number(s).

> The word *Bollywood* is sometimes considered an insult because it implies that Indian movies are merely "a derivative of the American film industry" (Chopra 9).

*2. Digital or nonprint source*   Give enough information in a signal phrase or in parentheses for readers to locate the source in your list of works cited. Many works found online or in electronic databases lack stable page numbers; you can omit the page number in such cases. However, if you are citing a work with stable pagination, such as an article in PDF format, include the page number in parentheses.

**DIGITAL SOURCE WITHOUT STABLE PAGE NUMBERS**

> As a *Slate* analysis explains, "Prominent sports psychologists get praised for their successes and don't get grief for their failures" (Engber).

**DIGITAL SOURCE WITH STABLE PAGE NUMBERS**

> According to Whitmarsh, the British military had experimented with using balloons for observation as far back as 1879 (328).

If the source includes numbered sections, paragraphs, or screens, include that number preceded by the abbreviation *sec., par.,* or *scr.* in parentheses.

*3. Two authors*   Use both authors' last names in a signal phrase or in parentheses.

> Gilbert and Gubar point out that in the Grimm version of "Snow White," the king "never actually appears in this story at all" (37).

*4. Three or more authors*   Use the first author's name and *et al.* ("and others") in parentheses. Give the first author's name followed by *and others* in a signal phrase.

> Similarly, as Belenky and others assert, examining the lives of women expands our understanding of human development (7).

*5. Organization as author*   Give the group's full name in a signal phrase; in parentheses, abbreviate any common words (such as *Corporation, Association*) in the name.

> Any study of social welfare involves a close analysis of "the impacts, the benefits, and the costs" of its policies (Social Research Corp. iii).

*6. Unknown author*   Use the full title, if it is brief, in your text — or a shortened version of the title in parentheses.

> One analysis defines *hype* as "an artificially engendered atmosphere of hysteria" (*Today's* 51).

*7. Author of two or more works cited in the same project*   If your list of works cited has more than one work by the same author, include the title of the work you are citing in a signal phrase or a shortened version of the title in parentheses to prevent reader confusion.

> Gardner shows readers their own silliness in his description of a "pointless, ridiculous monster, crouched in the shadows, stinking of dead men, murdered children, and martyred cows" (*Grendel* 2).

*8. Two or more authors with the same last name*   Include the author's first *and* last names in a signal phrase or first initial and last name in a parenthetical reference.

> Children will learn to write if they are allowed to choose their own subjects, James Britton asserts, citing the Schools Council study of the 1960s (37–42).

*9. Multivolume work*   In a parenthetical reference, note the volume number first and then the page number(s), with a colon and one space between them.

> Modernist writers prized experimentation and gradually even sought to blur the line between poetry and prose, according to Forster (3: 150).

If you name only one volume of the work in your list of works cited, include only the page number in the parentheses.

*10. Literary work*   Because literary works are usually available in many different editions, cite the page number(s) from the edition you used followed by a semicolon, and then give other identifying information that will lead readers to the passage in any edition. Indicate the act and/or scene in a play (37; sc. 1). For a novel, indicate the part or chapter (175; ch. 4).

> In utter despair, Dostoyevsky's character Mitya wonders aloud about the "terrible tragedies realism inflicts on people" (376; bk. 8, ch. 2).

For a poem, cite the part (if there is one) and line(s), separated by a period. If you are citing only line numbers, use the word *line(s)* in the first reference (*lines* 33–34).

> Whitman speculates, "All goes onward and outward, nothing collapses, / And to die is different from what anyone supposed, and luckier" (6.129–30).

For a verse play, give only the <u>act, scene, and line numbers</u>, separated by periods.

> The witches greet Banquo as "lesser than Macbeth, and greater" (<u>1.3.65</u>).

**11.** *Work in an anthology or collection* For an essay, short story, or other piece of prose reprinted in an anthology, use the name of the <u>author</u> of the work, not the editor of the anthology, but use the <u>page number(s)</u> from the anthology.

> Narratives of captivity play a major role in early writing by women in the
> United States, as demonstrated by <u>Silko</u> (<u>219</u>).

**12.** *Sacred text* To cite a sacred text such as the Qur'an or the Bible, give the <u>title of the edition</u> you used, the <u>book</u>, and the <u>chapter and verse</u> (or their equivalent) separated by a period. In your text, spell out the names of books. In parenthetical references, use abbreviations for books with names of five or more letters (*Gen.* for *Genesis*).

> He ignored the admonition "Pride goes before destruction, and a haughty
> spirit before a fall" (<u>*New Oxford Annotated Bible*</u>, <u>Prov. 16.18</u>).

**13.** *Encyclopedia or dictionary entry* An entry from a reference work — such as an encyclopedia or a dictionary — without an author will appear on the works-cited list under the entry's title. Enclose the <u>entry title</u> in quotation marks, and place it in parentheses. Omit the page number for print reference works that arrange entries alphabetically.

> The term *prion* was coined by Stanley B. Prusiner from the words
> *proteinaceous* and *infectious* and a suffix meaning *particle* (<u>"Prion"</u>).

**14.** *Government source with no author named* Because entries for sources authored by government agencies will appear on your list of works cited under the name of the country (see 18d, model 63), your in-text citation for such a source should include the name of the <u>country</u> as well as the name of the <u>agency</u> responsible for the source.

> To reduce the agricultural runoff into the Chesapeake Bay, the <u>United States
> Environmental Protection Agency</u> has argued that "[h]igh nutrient loading
> crops, such as corn and soybean, should be replaced with alternatives in
> environmentally sensitive areas" (2–26).

**15. Entire work**   Include the reference in the text, without any page numbers.

Krakauer's *Into the Wild* both criticizes and admires the solitary impulses of its young hero, which end up killing him.

**16. Indirect source (author quoting someone else)**   Use the abbreviation *qtd. in* to indicate that you are quoting from someone else's report of a source.

As Arthur Miller says, "When somebody is destroyed everybody finally contributes to it, but in Willy's case, the end product would be virtually the same" (qtd. in Martin and Meyer 375).

**17. Two or more sources in one citation**   List the authors in alphabetical order and separate the information with semicolons.

Economists recommend that *employment* be redefined to include unpaid domestic labor (Clark 148; Nevins 39).

**18. Visual**   When you include an image in your text, number it (*Fig. 2*) and include a parenthetical reference (*see fig. 2*). Number figures (photos, drawings, cartoons, maps, graphs, and charts) and tables separately. Each visual should include a caption with the figure or table number and information about the source — either a complete citation or enough information to direct readers to the works-cited entry.

This trend is illustrated in a chart that includes data distributed by the ACT as part of its 2018 analysis (see fig. 1).

Soon after the preceding sentence, readers find the following figure and a caption referring them to the entry in the list of works cited:

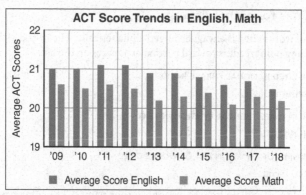

Fig. 1. Downward trend in ACT scores in English and math (2009–2018). Data source: Catherine Gewertz, "Math Scores Slide to a 20-Year Low on ACT," *Education Week*, 17 October 2018.

An image that you create might appear with a caption like this:

Fig. 4. Young women reading magazines. Personal photograph by author.

# 18d Preparing an MLA list of works cited

A list of works cited is an alphabetical list of the sources you have referred to in your essay. (If your instructor asks you to list everything you have read as background, call the list *Works Consulted*.)

## Formatting a list of works cited

- Start your list on a separate page after the text of your document and any notes.
- Center the heading *Works Cited* (not italicized or in quotation marks) one inch from the top of the page. See the example in 18e.
- Begin each entry flush with the left margin, but indent subsequent lines of each entry one-half inch. Double-space the entire list.
- List sources alphabetically by the first word. Start with the author's name, if available, or the editor's name. If no author or editor is given, start with the title.
- List the author's last name first, followed by a comma and the first name. If a source has two authors, the second author's name appears first name first (see model 2).
- Capitalize every important word in titles and subtitles. Italicize titles of books and long works, but put titles of shorter works in quotation marks.

## Guidelines for author listings

The list of works cited is always arranged alphabetically. The in-text citations in your writing point readers toward particular sources on the list.

**NAME CITED IN SIGNAL PHRASE IN TEXT**

Crystal explains . . .

**NAME IN PARENTHETICAL CITATION IN TEXT**

. . . (Crystal 107).

**BEGINNING OF ENTRY ON LIST OF WORKS CITED**

Crystal, David.

Models 1–5 explain how to arrange author names. The information that follows the name depends on the type of work you are citing. Consult the List of Examples at the beginning of Chapter 18 and choose the model that most closely resembles the source you are using.

---

Citing sources that don't match any model exactly

What should you do if your source doesn't match any of the models exactly? Suppose, for instance, your source is a translated essay appearing in the fifth edition of an anthology.

• Identify a basic model to follow. For example, if you decide that your source looks most like an essay in an anthology, start with a citation like model 9.

• After listing author and title information (if given), enter as many of the elements of the container as you can find (see 18a): title of the larger container, if any; other contributors, such as editor or translator; version or edition; volume; publisher; date; and page numbers or other location information such as a URL or DOI. End the container with a period. If the container is nested in a larger container, collect the information from the second container as well.

• If you aren't sure which model to follow or how to create a combination model with multiple containers, ask your instructor or a consultant in the writing center.

*1. One author*  Put the last name first, followed by a comma, the first name (and middle name or initial, if any), and a period.

Crystal, David.

*2. Multiple authors*  For two authors, list the first author with the last name first. Follow this with a comma, the word *and*, and the name of the second author with the first name first.

Gilbert, Sandra M., and Susan Gubar.

For three or more authors, list the first author followed by a comma and *et al.* ("and others") or list all authors.

Belenky, Mary Field, et al.

Belenky, Mary Field, Blythe McVicker Clinchy, Nancy Rule Goldberger, and Jill Mattuck Tarule.

*3. Organization or group author*  Give the name of the group, government agency, corporation, or other organization listed as the author.

Getty Trust.

United States. Government Accountability Office.

*4. Unknown author*  When the author is not identified, begin the entry with the title, and alphabetize by the first important word. Italicize titles of books and long works, but put titles of articles and other short works in quotation marks.

*New Concise World Atlas.*

"California Sues EPA over Emissions."

*5. Two or more works by the same author*    Arrange the entries alphabetically by title. Include the author's name in the first entry, but in subsequent entries, use three hyphens followed by a period.

> Chopra, Anupama. "Bollywood Princess, Hollywood Hopeful." *The New York Times*, 10 Feb. 2008, nyti.ms/1QEtNpF.
>
> ---. *King of Bollywood: Shah Rukh Khan and the Seductive World of Indian Cinema*. Warner Books, 2007.

**Note:** Use three hyphens only when the work is by *exactly* the same author(s) as the previous entry.

## Print books

*6. Basic format for a book*    Begin with the author name(s). (See models 1–5.) Then include the title and subtitle, the publisher, and the year of publication. The source map on pp. 254–55 shows where to find this information in a typical book.

> Roiphe, Katie. *The Power Notebooks*. Free Press, 2020.

*7. Author and editor both named*

> Bangs, Lester. *Psychotic Reactions and Carburetor Dung*. Edited by Greil Marcus, Alfred A. Knopf, 1988.

**Note:** To cite the editor's contribution, begin with the editor's name.

> Marcus, Greil, editor. *Psychotic Reactions and Carburetor Dung*. By Lester Bangs, Alfred A. Knopf, 1988.

*8. Editor, no author named*

> Wall, Cheryl A., editor. *Changing Our Own Words: Essays on Criticism, Theory, and Writing by Black Women*. Rutgers UP, 1989.

*9. Selection in an anthology or chapter in a book with an editor*    List the author(s) of the selection; the selection title, in quotation marks; the title of the book, italicized; the words *edited by* and the name(s) of the editor(s); the publisher; the year; and the abbreviation *pp.* with the selection's page numbers.

> Bird, Gloria. "Autobiography as Spectacle: An Act of Liberation or the Illusion of Liberation?" *Here First: Autobiographical Essays by Native Americans*, edited by Arnold Krupat and Brian Swann, Random House, 2000, pp. 63–74.

**Note:** To provide original publication information for a reprinted selection, use the <u>original publication information</u> as a second container (see 18a):

> Byatt, A. S. "The Thing in the Forest." *The O. Henry Prize Stories 2003*, edited by Laura Furman, Anchor Books, 2003, pp. 3–22. <u>Originally published in</u> *The New Yorker*, 3 June 2002, pp. 80–89.

**10. Two or more items from the same anthology**   List the anthology as one entry. Also list each selection separately with a cross-reference to the anthology. In the example below, the first two citations are for the selections used and the third is for the <u>anthology</u>.

> Estleman, Loren D. "Big Tim Magoon and the Wild West." <u>Walker</u>, pp. 391–404.

> Salzer, Susan K. "Miss Libbie Tells All." <u>Walker</u>, pp. 199–212.

> Walker, Dale L., editor. *Westward: A Fictional History of the American West.* Forge Books, 2003.

**11. Translation**

> Bolaño, Roberto. *2666*. <u>Translated by</u> Natasha Wimmer, Farrar, Straus and Giroux, 2008.

If the book has an editor and a translator, list both names after the title, in the order they appear on the title page.

> Kant, Immanuel. *"Toward Perpetual Peace" and Other Writings on Politics, Peace, and History*. <u>Edited by</u> Pauline Kleingeld, <u>translated by</u> David L. Colclasure, Yale UP, 2006.

If different translators have worked on various parts of the book, identify the translator of the part you are citing.

> García Lorca, Federico. "The Little Mad Boy." <u>Translated by</u> W. S. Merwin. *The Selected Poems of Federico García Lorca,* <u>edited by</u> Francisco García Lorca and Donald M. Allen, Penguin, 1969, pp. 51–53.

**12. Book in a language other than English**   Include a translation of the title in brackets, if necessary.

> Benedetti, Mario. *La borra del café [The Coffee Grind]*. Editorial Sudamericana, 2000.

## Books

Take information from the book's title page and copyright page (on the reverse side of the title page), not from the book's cover or a library catalog.

1. **Author.** List the last name first. End with a period. For variations, see models 2–5.

2. **Title.** Italicize the title and any subtitle; capitalize all major words. End with a period.

3. **Publisher.** Identify the publisher's name as given on the book's title page. If more than one publisher appears on the title page, separate the names with a slash, leaving a space before and after the slash. If no publisher is listed on the title page, check the copyright page. Abbreviate *University* and *Press* as *U* and *P* (*Oxford UP*). Omit terms such as *Company* and *Incorporated*. Follow the publisher's name with a comma.

4. **Year of publication.** If more than one copyright date is given, use the most recent one. End with a period.

**A citation for the book shown on the next page would look like this:**

Patel, Raj. *The Value of Nothing: How to Reshape Market Society and Redefine Democracy*. Picador, 2009.

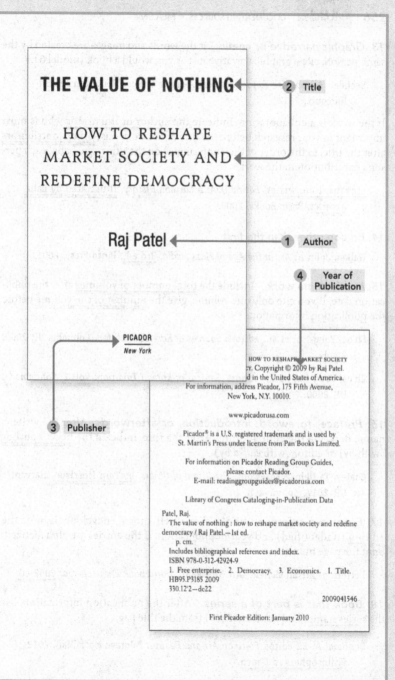

# THE VALUE OF NOTHING

**2** Title

## HOW TO RESHAPE MARKET SOCIETY AND REDEFINE DEMOCRACY

## Raj Patel

**1** Author

**4** Year of Publication

PICADOR
*New York*

**3** Publisher

www.picadorusa.com

Picador® is a U.S. registered trademark and is used by
St. Martin's Press under license from Pan Books Limited.

For information on Picador Reading Group Guides,
please contact Picador.
E-mail: readinggroupguides@picadorusa.com

Library of Congress Cataloging-in-Publication Data

Patel, Raj.
   The value of nothing : how to reshape market society and redefine
democracy / Raj Patel.—1st ed.
      p. cm.
   Includes bibliographical references and index.
   ISBN 978-0-312-42924-9
   1. Free enterprise.   2. Democracy.   3. Economics.   I. Title.
HB95.P3185 2009
330.12′2—dc22

                                                                2009041546

First Picador Edition: January 2010

*13. Graphic narrative or comic* If the words and images are created by the same person, cite a graphic narrative just as you would a book (model 6).

> Bechdel, Alison. *Are You My Mother? A Comic Drama.* Houghton Mifflin
> Harcourt, 2012.

If the work is a collaboration, indicate the author or illustrator who is most important to your research before the title of the work. List other contributors after the title, in the order of their appearance on the title page. Label each person's contribution to the work.

> Stavans, Ilan, writer. *Latino USA: A Cartoon History.* Illustrated by Lalo
> Arcaraz, Basic Books, 2000.

*14. Edition other than the first*

> Walker, John A. *Art in the Age of Mass Media.* 3rd ed., Pluto Press, 2001.

*15. Multivolume work* Include the total number of volumes after the publication date. If you cite only one volume, give the number of the volume before the publication information.

> Ch'oe, Yong-Ho, et al., editors. *Sources of Korean Tradition.* Columbia UP, 2000.
> 2 vols.

> Ch'oe, Yong-Ho, et al., editors. *Sources of Korean Tradition.* Vol. 2, Columbia
> UP, 2000. 2 vols.

*16. Preface, foreword, introduction, or afterword* After the writer's name, describe the contribution. After the title, indicate the book's author (with *by*) or editor (with *edited by*).

> Coates, Ta-Nehisi. Foreword. *The Origin of Others*, by Toni Morrison, Harvard
> UP, 2017, pp. vii–xvii.

*17. Entry in a reference book* For a well-known encyclopedia, note the edition (if identified) and year of publication. If the entries are alphabetized, omit the page number.

> Kettering, Alison McNeil. "Art Nouveau." *World Book Encyclopedia,* 2002 ed.

*18. Book that is part of a series* After the publication information, list the series name (and number, if any) from the title page.

> Denham, A. E., editor. *Plato on Art and Beauty.* Palgrave Macmillan, 2012.
> Philosophers in Depth.

**19. Republication (modern edition of an older book)**   Indicate the original publication date after the title.

>   Austen, Jane. *Sense and Sensibility.* 1813. Dover, 1996.

**20. More than one publisher's name**   If the title page gives two publishers' names, separate them with a slash. Include spaces on both sides of the slash.

>   Hornby, Nick. *About a Boy.* Riverhead / Penguin Putnam, 1998.

**21. Book with a title within the title**   Do not italicize the title of a book or other long work within an italicized book title. For an article title within a title, italicize as usual and place the article title in quotation marks.

>   Masur, Louis P. *Runaway Dream:* Born to Run *and Bruce Springsteen's American Vision.* Bloomsbury, 2009.

>   Lethem, Jonathan. *"Lucky Alan" and Other Stories.* Doubleday, 2015.

**22. Sacred text**   To cite any individual published editions of sacred books, begin the entry with the title.

>   *Qur'an: The Final Testament (Authorized English Version) with Arabic Text.* Translated by Rashad Khalifa, Universal Unity, 2000.

## Print periodicals

Begin with the author name(s). (See models 1–5.) Then include the article title, the title of the periodical, the volume and issue information, the date of publication, and the page numbers. The source map on pp. 258–59 shows where to find information in a typical periodical.

>   Altschuler, Sari. "The Gothic Origins of Global Health." *American Literature,* vol. 89, no. 3, Sept. 2017, pp. 557–90.

**23. Article in a print journal**   Include the volume number, the issue number, and the date.

>   Beckwith, Sarah. "Reading for Our Lives." *PMLA,* vol. 132, no. 2, Mar. 2017, pp. 331–36.

**24. Article in a print magazine**   Provide the date from the magazine cover instead of volume or issue numbers.

>   Surowiecki, James. "The Stimulus Strategy." *The New Yorker,* 25 Feb. 2008, p. 29.

>   Tran, Diep. "Wide Awake in America." *American Theatre,* Nov. 2017, pp. 26–28.

## Articles in Print Periodicals

**1**   **Author.** List the last name first. End with a period. For variations, see models 2–5.

**2**   **Article title.** Put the title and any subtitle in quotation marks; capitalize all major words. Place a period inside the closing quotation mark.

**3**   **Periodical title.** Italicize the title; capitalize all major words. End with a comma.

**4**   **Volume and issue.** For journals, give the abbreviation *vol.* and the volume number, and the abbreviation *no.* and the issue number, if the journal provides them. Put commas after the volume and issue. (Do not include volume and issue for magazines or newspapers.)

**5**   **Date of publication.** List day (if given), month (abbreviated except for May, June, and July), and year, or season and year, of publication. Put a comma after the date.

**6**   **Page numbers.** Give the abbreviation *p.* (for "page") or *pp.* (for "pages") and the inclusive page numbers. If the article skips pages, put the first page number and a plus sign. End with a period.

**A citation for the article shown on the next page would look like this:**

Quart, Alissa. "Lost Media, Found Media: Snapshots from the Future of Writing." *Columbia Journalism Review*, May/June 2008, pp. 30–34.

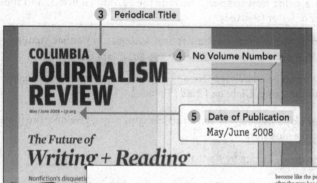

**3** Periodical Title

**COLUMBIA JOURNALISM REVIEW**

May / June 2008 • cjr.org

**4** No Volume Number

**5** Date of Publication
May/June 2008

The Future of
**Writing + Reading**

Nonfiction's disquieti...

**2** Article Title

## Lost Media, Found Media

*Snapshots from the future of writing*

BY ALISSA QUART

**1** Author
ALISSA QUART

If there were an ashram for people who worship contemplative long-form journalism, it would be the Nieman Conference on Narrative Journalism. This March, at the Sheraton Boston Hotel, hundreds of journalists, authors, students, and aspirants came for the weekend event. Seated on metal chairs in large conference rooms, we learned about muscular storytelling (the Q-shaped narrative structure—who knew?). We sipped cups of coffee and ate bagels and heard about reporting history through letters and public documents and how to evoke empathy for our subjects, particularly our most marginal ones. As we listened to reporters discussing great feats—exposing Walter Reed's fetid living quarters for wounded soldiers, for instance—we also renewed our pride in our profession. In short, the conference exemplified the best of the older media models, the ones that have so recently fallen into economic turmoil.

Yet even at the weekend's strongest lectures on interview techniques or the long-form profile, we couldn't ignore the digital elephant in the room. We all knew as writers that the kinds of pieces we were discussing require months of work to be both deep and refined, and that we were all hard-pressed for the time and the money to do that. It was always hard for nonfiction writers, but something seems to have changed. For those of us who believed in the value of the journalism and literary nonfiction of the past, we had

become like the people at the ashram after the guru has died.

Right now, journalism is more or less divided into two camps, which I will call Lost Media and Found Media. I went to the Nieman conference partially because I wanted to see how the forces creating this new division are affecting and afflicting the Lost Media world that I love best, not on the institutional level, but for reporters and writers themselves. This world includes people who write for all the newspapers and magazines that are currently struggling with layoffs, speedups, hiring freezes, buyouts, the death or shrinkage of film- and book-review sections, limits on expensive investigative work, the erasure of foreign bureaus, and the general narrowing of institutional ambition. It includes freelance writers competing with hordes of ever-younger competitors willing to write and publish online for free, the fade-out of established journalistic career paths, and, perhaps most crucially, a muddled sense of the meritorious, as blogs level and scramble the value and status of print publications, and of professional writers. The glamour and influence once associated with a magazine elite seem to have faded, becoming a sort of pastiche of winsome articles about yearning and boxers and dinners at Elaine's.

Found Media-ites, meanwhile, are the bloggers, the contributors to Huffington Post-type sites that aggregate blogs, as well as other work that somebody else paid for, and the new nonprofits and pay-per-article schemes that aim to save journalism from 20 percent profit-margin demands. Although these elements are often disparate, together they compose the new media landscape. In economic terms, I mean all the outlets for nonfiction writing that seem to be thriving in the new era or striving to fill niches that Lost Media is giving up in a new order. Stylistically, Found Media tends to feel spontaneous, almost accidental. It's a domain dominated by the young, where writers get points not for following traditions or burnishing them but for amateur and hybrid vigor, for creating their own venues and their own genres. It is about public expression and community—not quite John Dewey's Great Community, which the critic Eric Alterman alluded to in a recent *New Yorker* article on newspapers, but rather a fractured form of Dewey's ideal: call it Great Communities.

To be a Found Media journalist or pundit, one need not be elite, expert, or trained; one must simply produce punchy intellectual property that is in conversation with groups of

*Illustration by Tomer Hanuka*

Text: Alissa Quart

**6** Page Numbers
30–34

259

**25. Article in a print newspaper**   Include the edition (if listed) and the section number or letter (if listed).

> Fackler, Martin. "Japan's Foreign Minister Says Apologies to Wartime Victims
>     Will Be Upheld." *The New York Times,* 9 Apr. 2014, late ed., p. A6.

**Note:** For locally published newspapers, add the city in brackets after the name if it is not part of the name: *Globe and Mail [Toronto].*

**26. Article that skips pages**   When an article skips pages, give only the first page number and a plus sign.

> Tyrnauer, Matthew. "Empire by Martha." *Vanity Fair,* Sept. 2002, pp. 364+.

**27. Editorial or letter to the editor**   Include the writer's name, if given, and the title, if any. Then end with the label *Editorial* or *Letter.*

> "California Dreaming." *The Nation,* 25 Feb. 2008, p. 4. Editorial.

> MacEwan, Valerie. *The Believer,* vol. 12, no. 1, Jan. 2014, p. 4. Letter.

**28. Review**

> Nussbaum, Emily. "Change Agents: Review of *The Americans* and *Silicon
>     Valley.*" *The New Yorker,* 31 Mar. 2014, p. 68.

> Schwarz, Benjamin. Review of *The Second World War: A Short History*, by
>     R. A. C. Parker, *The Atlantic Monthly,* May 2002, pp. 110–11.

## Digital written-word sources

Digital sources such as websites differ from print sources in the ease with which they can be changed, updated, or eliminated. The most commonly cited electronic sources are documents from websites and databases.

**29. Work from a database**   For an article that is available in print but that you access in an online database such as Academic Search Premier, begin with the name(s) of the author(s), the title of the work, the title of the periodical, volume/issue, and date of the publication of the print version of the work. Give page numbers for the print version. Then give the name of the online database and the location — a DOI or other stable link. The source map on pp. 262–63 shows where to find information for a work from a database.

> Reich, Elizabeth. "The Power of Black Film Criticism." *Film Criticism,* vol. 40,
>     no. 1, Jan. 2016, pp. 1–3. *Omnifile Full Text Select*, doi:10.3998/
>     fc.13761232.0040.126.

**30. Article from a journal on the web**  Begin an entry for an online journal article as you would one for a print journal article (see model 23). End with the online location (permalink, DOI, or URL) and a period.

> Clark, Msia Kibona. "Hip Hop as Social Commentary in Accra and Dar es Salaam." *African Studies Quarterly,* vol. 13, no. 3, Summer 2012, asq.africa.ufl.edu/files/Clark-V131s3.pdf.

---

**QUICK HELP**

### Citing works from websites

When citing online sources, give as many of the following elements as you can find:

1. **Author.** Provide the author of the work, if you can find one. End with a period.
2. **Title.** Give the title of the work you are citing, ending with a period. If the work is part of a larger container (such as a video on YouTube), put the title in quotation marks.
3. **Website title.** If the title that you have identified is not the name of the website itself, list the website title, in italics, followed by a comma.
4. **Publisher or sponsor.** If the site's publisher or sponsor is different from the title of the site, identify the publisher or sponsor, followed by a comma. If the name is very similar to the site title, omit the publisher.
5. **Date of publication.** Give the date of publication or latest update, followed by a comma.
6. **DOI, permalink, or URL.** Give a DOI or permalink (if you can find one) or URL. End with a period. If you have to break a DOI or URL across lines, break it before a period or hyphen or before or after any other mark of punctuation.
7. **Date of access.** If the work does not include any date, add "Accessed" and the day, month (abbreviated, except for May, June, and July), and year you accessed the source. End with a period. If you provided a date before the DOI or URL, omit the access date.

---

**31. Article in a magazine on the web**  List the author, the article title, and the name of the magazine. Then identify the date of publication, and provide a permalink or DOI, if one is available, or a URL.

> Landhuis, Esther. "Is Dementia Risk Falling?" *Scientific American,* 25 Jan. 2016, www.scientificamerican.com/article/is-dementia-risk-falling/.

## Articles from Databases

Library subscriptions provide access to huge databases of articles, such as Academic Search Premier, ProQuest, and JSTOR.

**1** **Author.** List the last name first. End with a period. For variations, see models 2–5.

**2** **Article title.** Enclose the title and any subtitle in quotation marks. End with a period.

**3** **Periodical title.** Italicize it. Follow it with a comma.

**4** **Volume and issue.** For journal articles, list the volume and issue number, if any, separated by commas. Use the abbreviations *vol.* and *no.*

**5** **Date of publication.** Include the day (if given), month or season, and year, in that order. Add a comma.

**6** **Page numbers.** Give the inclusive page numbers from the print version, using the abbreviations *p.* or *pp.* End with a period.

**7** **Database name.** Italicize the name of the database. End with a period.

**8** **Location.** Give the DOI or other permalink. If neither is available, give the URL for the home page of the database, omitting the protocol *http://.*

**A citation for the article shown on the next page would look like this:**

Kirkpatrick, Ellen, and Suzanne Scott. "Representation and Diversity in Comics Studies." *Cinema Journal*, vol. 55, no. 1, Fall 2015, pp. 120+. *ProQuest Arts and Humanities Database*, www.proquest.com/products -services/Arts_and_Humanities.html.

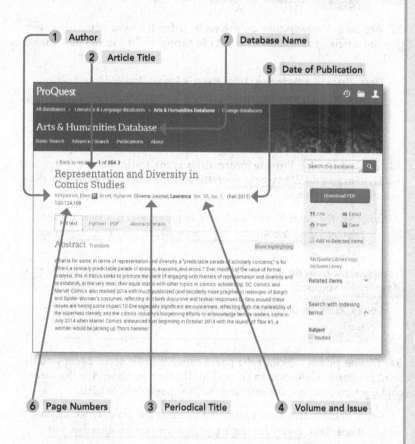

1. Author
2. Article Title
7. Database Name
5. Date of Publication

**ProQuest**

All databases > Literature & Language databases > **Arts & Humanities Database** > Change databases

# Arts & Humanities Database

Basic Search   Advance Search   Publications   About

‹ Back to results  1 of 354 ›

## Representation and Diversity in Comics Studies

Kirkpatrick, Ellen  Scott, Suzanne. **Cinema Journal; Lawrence** Vol. 55, Iss. 1, (Fall 2015): 120-124,168.

Full text    Full text - PDF    Abstract/Details

Abstract  Translate                                              Show highlighting

What is for some, in terms of representation and diversity, a "predictable parade of scholarly concerns," is for others a similarly predictable parade of elisions, evasions, and errors.7 Ever mindful of the value of formal analysis, this In Focus seeks to promote the merit of engaging with matters of representation and diversity and to establish, at the very least, their equal status with other topics in comics scholarship. DC Comics and Marvel Comics also marked 2014 with much publicized (and decidedly more pragmatic) redesigns of Batgirl and Spider-Woman's costumes, reflecting that both discursive and textual responses by fans around these issues are having some impact.10 One especially significant announcement, reflecting both the malleability of the superhero identity, and the comics industry's burgeoning efforts to acknowledge female readers, came in July 2014 when Marvel Comics announced that beginning in October 2014 with the launch of Thor #1, a woman would be picking up Thor's hammer.

Search this database

Download PDF

Cite        Email
Print       Save

Add to Selected items

McQuade Library logo
McQuade Library

Related items

Search with indexing terms

Subject
Studies

6. Page Numbers
3. Periodical Title
4. Volume and Issue

**32. Article in a newspaper on the web**   After the name of the newspaper, give the article's publication date and the permalink (if you can find one) or URL.

> Hirsh, Marc. "Pop Perfection: What Makes a Song a Classic?" *Boston Globe*,
>    10 Nov. 2017, www.bostonglobe.com/arts/music/2017/11/09/pop
>    -perfection-what-makes-song-classic/2SPDGw5PgQty1lPyeTKYRN/
>    story.html.

**33. Digital book**   Provide information as for a print book (see models 6–22); then give the digital container title and any other relevant information, including the location.

> Euripides. *The Trojan Women*. Translated by Gilbert Murray, Oxford UP, 1915.
>    *Internet Sacred Text Archive*, 2011, www.sacred-texts.com/cla/eurip/
>    trok_w.htm.

If you read the book on an e-reader such as a Kindle or Nook, specify the type of reader file you used.

> Schaap, Rosie. *Drinking with Men: A Memoir*. Riverhead / Penguin, 2013.
>    Kindle.

**34. Online poem**   Include the poet's name, the title of the poem, and the print publication information (if any) for the first container. For the second container, give the title, the date, and the DOI, permalink, or URL.

> Geisel, Theodor. "Too Many Daves." *The Sneetches and Other Stories,* Random
>    House, 1961. *Poetry Foundation,* 2015, www.poetryfoundation.org/
>    poem/171612.

**35. Online editorial or letter to the editor**   Include the author's name (if given) and the title (if any). Follow the appropriate model for the type of source you are using. (Check the List of Examples at the beginning of Chapter 18.) End with the label *Editorial* or *Letter*.

> "Migrant Children Deserve a Voice in Court." *The New York Times,* 8 Mar. 2016,
>    www.nytimes.com/2016/03/08/opinion/migrant-children-deserve-a
>    -voice-in-court.html. Editorial.

> Starr, Evva. "Local Reporting Thrives in High Schools." *The Washington Post,*
>    4 Apr. 2014, wpo.st/7hmJ1. Letter.

**36. Online review** Cite an online review as you would a print review (see model 28). End with the name of the website, the date of publication, and the URL or permalink.

> O'Hehir, Andrew. "Aronofsky's Deranged Biblical Action Flick." *Salon,* 27 May 2014, www.salon.com/2014/03/27/noah_aronofskys_deranged_biblical _action_flick/.

**37. Entry in an online reference work or wiki** Begin with the title unless the author is named. (A wiki, which is collectively edited, will not include an author.) Include the title of the entry; the name of the work, italicized; the sponsor or publisher; the date of the latest update; and the location (permalink or URL). Before using a wiki as a source, check with your instructor.

> Cartwright, Mark. "Apollo." *Ancient History Encyclopedia,* 18 May 2012, www .ancient.eu/apollo/.

> "Gunpowder Plot." *Wikipedia,* 4 Mar. 2016, en.wikipedia.org/wiki/ Gunpowder_Plot.

**38. Short work from a website** To cite a work on a website that is not part of a regularly published journal, magazine, or newspaper, include all of the following elements that are available: the author, the title of the work, the title of the website, the publisher or sponsor, the date of publication or latest update, and the URL. If the site is undated, include "Accessed" and the date you visited the site. The source map on pp. 266–67 shows where to find information for a work from a website.

> Bali, Karan. "Kishore Kumar." *Upperstall.com,* upperstall.com/profile/kishore -kumar/. Accessed 2 Mar. 2019.

> "Our Mission." *Trees for Life International,* 2011, www.treesforlife.org/our -work/our-mission.

**39. Entire website** Follow the guidelines for a work from the web, beginning with the name of the author or editor (if any), followed by the title of the website, italicized; the name of the sponsor or publisher (if different from the name of the site); the date of publication or last update; and the location.

> Glazier, Loss Pequeño, director. *Electronic Poetry Center.* State U of New York Buffalo, 1994–2016, epc.buffalo.edu/.

> *Weather.com.* Weather Channel Interactive, 1995–2016, weather.com/.

For a personal website, include the name of the person who created the site as you would with a site's author or editor. If the site is undated, end with your date of access.

> Enright, Mike. *Menright.com.* www.menright.com. Accessed 30 Mar. 2019.

# Works from Websites

1.  **Author.** List the last name first. End with a period. If no author is given, begin with the title. For variations, see models 2–5.

2.  **Title of work.** Enclose the title and any subtitle of the work in quotation marks.

3.  **Title of website.** Give the title of the entire website, italicized. Follow it with a comma.

4.  **Publisher or sponsor.** Look for the sponsor's name at the bottom of the home page. If the sponsor's name is roughly the same as the site title, omit the sponsor. Follow it with a comma.

5.  **Date of publication or latest update.** Give the most recent date, followed by a comma.

6.  **Location.** Give the DOI or permalink, if you can find one, or the site's URL, followed by a period.

7.  **Date of access.** If the site is undated, end with *Accessed* and the date you accessed the site.

**A citation for the website shown on the next page would look like this:**

Tønnesson, Øyvind. "Mahatma Gandhi, the Missing Laureate." *Nobelprize.org*, 2015, www.nobelprize.org/nobel_prizes/themes/peace/gandhi/.

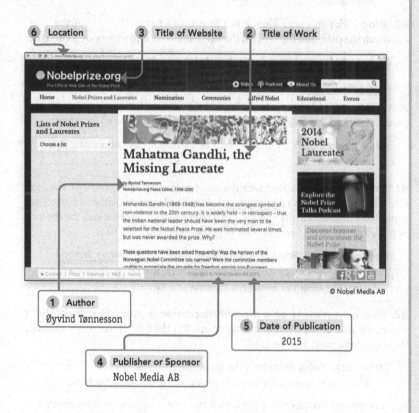

**6** Location

**3** Title of Website

**2** Title of Work

**1** Author
Øyvind Tønnesson

**5** Date of Publication
2015

**4** Publisher or Sponsor
Nobel Media AB

© Nobel Media AB

*40. Blog* For an entire blog, give the author's name; the title of the blog, italicized; the date; and the URL. If the site is undated, end with your access date.

> Levy, Carla Miriam. *Filmi Geek*. 2006–2015, www.filmigeek.com.

> *Little Green Footballs*. littlegreenfootballs.com. Accessed 4 Mar. 2019.

**Note:** To cite a blogger who writes under a pseudonym, begin with the pseudonym and then put the writer's real name (if you know it) in parentheses.

> Atrios (Duncan Black). *Eschaton*. www.eschatonblog.com. Accessed 8 Mar.
> 2019.

*41. Online interview* Start with the name of the person interviewed. Give the title, if there is one. Give a descriptive label such as *Interview*, neither italicized nor in quotation marks, and the interviewer, if relevant; the title of the site; the sponsor or publisher (if there is one); the date of publication; and the URL.

> Bigelow, Kathryn. "New Again: Kathryn Bigelow." Interview by Victoria
> Hamburg. *Interview Magazine*, 14 July 2017, www.interviewmagazine
> .com/film/new-again-kathryn-bigelow.

*42. Post or comment on a blog or discussion group* Give the author's name; the title of the post, in quotation marks; the title of the site, italicized; the date of the post; and the URL.

> Edroso, Roy. "Going Down with the Flagship." *Alicublog,* 24 Feb. 2016,
> alicublog.blogspot.com/2016/02/going-down-with-flagship.html.

For a comment on an online post, give the writer's name or screen name; a label such as *Comment on*, not italicized; the title of the article commented on; and the label *by* and the article author's name. End with the citation information for the type of article.

> JennOfArk. Comment on "Going Down with the Flagship," by Roy Edroso.
> *Alicublog,* 24 Feb. 2016, alicublog.blogspot.com/2016/02/going-down
> -with-flagship.html#disqus_thread.

*43. Posting on a social networking site* To cite a posting on Facebook, Instagram, or another social networking site, include the writer's name; up to 140 characters of the posting, in quotation marks (or a description such as *Photograph*, not italicized and not in quotation marks, if there's no text); the name of the site, italicized; the date of the post; and the location of the post (URL).

> Cannon, Kevin. "Portrait of Norris Hall in #Savannah, GA — home (for a few
> months, anyway) of #SCAD's sequential art department." *Instagram,* Mar.
> 2014, www.instagram.com/p/lgmqk4i6DC/.

*44. Email or message*   Include the writer's name; the subject line, in quotation marks, if one is provided, or a descriptive message such as *Text message*; Received by (not italicized or in quotation marks) followed by the recipient's name; and then the date of the message.

> Carbone, Nick. "Screen vs. Print Reading." Received by Karita dos Santos,
>     17 Apr. 2016.

*45. Tweet*   Begin with the writer's Twitter handle, and put the real name, if known, in parentheses. Include the entire tweet, in quotation marks. Give the site name in italics (*Twitter*), the date and time of the message, and the tweet's URL. When alphabetizing in the list of works cited, ignore the @ symbol and alphabetize using the first few letters.

> @LunsfordHandbks (Andrea A. Lunsford). "Technology & social media have
>     changed the way we write. That doesn't mean literacy has declined."
>     *Twitter*, 24 Feb. 2016, 10:17 a.m., twitter.com/LunsfordHandbks/
>     status/702512638937460736.

## Visual, audio, multimedia, and live sources

*46. Film (theatrical, DVD, or other format)*   If you cite a particular person's work, start with that name. If not, start with the title of the film; then name the film's director, distributor, and year of release. Other contributors, such as writers or performers, may follow the director. If you cite a feature from a disc, treat the film as the first container and the disc as the second container.

> Bale, Christian, performer. *Vice*. Directed by Adam McKay, Annapurna
>     Pictures, 2018.

> Lasseter, John. Introduction. *Spirited Away*, directed by Hayao Miyazaki,
>     2001. Walt Disney Video, 2003, disc 1.

*47. Online video*   Cite an online video as you would a short work from a website (see model 38).

> Nayar, Vineet. "Employees First, Customers Second." *YouTube*, 9 June 2015,
>     www.youtube.com/watch?v=cCdu67s_C5E.

**48. Television (broadcast or on the web)**  For a show broadcast on television, begin with the title of the program, italicized (for an entire series), or the title of the episode, in quotation marks. Then list important contributors (writer, director, actor); season and episode number (for a specific episode); the network; the local station and city, if the show appeared on a local channel; and the broadcast date(s). For a show accessed on a network website, include the URL after the date of posting.

> *The Marvelous Mrs. Maisel.* Created by Amy Sherman-Palladino, performances by Rachel Brosnahan, Alex Borstein, and Jane Lynch, Prime Video, 2017–2020.

> "Time Zones." *Mad Men,* written by Matthew Weiner, directed by Scott Hornbacher, season 7, episode 1, AMC, 13 Apr. 2014, www.amc.com/shows/mad-men/season-7/episode-01-time-zones.

**49. Radio (broadcast or on the web)**  If you are citing a particular episode or segment, cite a radio broadcast as you would a television episode.

> "Tarred and Feathered." *This American Life,* narrated by Ira Glass, WNYC, 11 Apr. 2013.

For a show or segment accessed on the web, follow the date of posting with the website title, a comma, the URL, and a period.

**50. Television or radio interview**  List the person interviewed and then the title, if any. If the interview has no title, use the label *Interview* and the name of the interviewer, if relevant. Then identify the source. End with information about the program and the interview date(s). (For an online interview, see model 41.)

> Russell, David O. Interview by Terry Gross. *Fresh Air,* WNYC, 20 Feb. 2014.

**51. Personal interview**  List the person who was interviewed; the label *Telephone interview,* *Personal interview,* or *Email interview;* and the date the interview took place.

> Freedman, Sasha. Personal interview. 10 Nov. 2020.

**52. Sound recording**  List the name of the person or group you wish to emphasize (such as the composer, conductor, or band); the title of the recording or composition; the artist, if appropriate; the manufacturer; and the year of issue. If you are citing a <u>particular song or selection</u>, include its title, in quotation marks.

> <u>Bach, Johann Sebastian</u>. *Bach: Violin Concertos*. Performances by Itzhak Perlman and Pinchas Zukerman, English Chamber Orchestra, EMI, 2002.

> <u>Rihanna</u>. "<u>Work</u>." *Anti*, Roc Nation, 2016.

**Note:** If you are citing instrumental music that is identified only by <u>form, number, and key</u>, do not underline, italicize, or enclose it in quotation marks.

> Grieg, Edvard. <u>Concerto in A minor, op. 16</u>. Conducted by Eugene Ormandy, Philadelphia Orchestra, RCA, 1989.

*53. Musical composition*   When you are not citing a specific published version, first give the composer's name, followed by the title.

> Mozart, Wolfgang Amadeus. *Don Giovanni*, K527.

> Mozart, Wolfgang Amadeus. Symphony no. 41 in C major, K551.

**Note:** Cite a published score as you would a book. If you include the date that the composition was written, do so immediately after the title.

> Schoenberg, Arnold. *Chamber Symphony No. 1 for 15 Solo Instruments, Op. 9*. 1906. Dover, 2002.

*54. Video game*   Start with the <u>developer or author</u> (if any). After the title, give the <u>distributor</u> and the date of publication.

> <u>Mojang</u>. *Minecraft Dungeons*. <u>Xbox Game Studios</u>, 2020.

*55. Lecture or speech*   For a live lecture or speech, list the <u>speaker</u>; the title (if any), in quotation marks; the <u>sponsoring institution or group</u>; the place; and the date. Add the label *Lecture* or *Speech* after the date if readers will not otherwise be able to identify the work.

> <u>Eugenides, Jeffrey</u>. <u>Portland Arts and Lectures</u>. Arlene Schnitzer Concert Hall, Portland, OR, 30 Sept. 2003.

For a lecture or speech on the web, cite as you would a short work from a website (see model 38).

Burden, Amanda. "How Public Spaces Make Cities Work." *TED.com,* Mar. 2014,
www.ted.com/talks/amanda_burden_how_public_spaces_make_cities
_work.

**56. Live performance**   List the title, the appropriate names (such as the
writer or performer), the place, and the date.

*The Sea Ranch Songs.* By Aleksandra Vrebalov, performed by the Kronos
Quartet, White Barn, The Sea Ranch, CA, 23 May 2015.

**57. Podcast**   Cite a podcast as you would a short work from a website (see
model 38).

Fogarty, Mignon. "Begs the Question: Update." *QuickandDirtyTips.com,*
Macmillan, 6 Mar. 2014, www.quickanddirtytips.com/education/grammar/
begs-the-question-update.

**58. Work of art or photograph**   List the artist's or photographer's name;
the work's title, italicized; and the date of composition. Then cite the name of
the museum or other location and the city. To cite a reproduction in a book,
add the publication information. To cite online artwork, add the title of the
database or website, italicized, and the URL or permalink.

Bronzino, Agnolo. *Lodovico Capponi.* 1550–55, Frick Collection, New York.

*General William Palmer in Old Age.* 1810, National Army Museum, London.
*White Mughals: Love and Betrayal in Eighteenth-Century India,* by William
Dalrymple, Penguin Books, 2002, p. 270.

Hura, Sohrab. *Old Man Lighting a Fire.* 2015, *Magnum Photos,* pro
.magnumphotos.com/Asset/-2K1HRG6NSSEE.html.

**59. Map or chart**   Cite a map or chart as you would a short work within a
longer work. For an online source, include the location. End with the label *Map*
or *Chart* if needed for clarity.

"Australia." *Perry-Castaneda Library Map Collection,* U of Texas, 1999, www.lib
.utexas.edu.maps.australia_pol99.jpg.

*California.* Rand McNally, 2002. Map.

**60. Cartoon or comic strip**   List the artist's name; the title of the cartoon or
comic strip, in quotation marks; and the publication information. You may end
with a label (*Cartoon* or *Comic strip*) for clarity.

Flake, Emily. *The New Yorker,* 13 Apr. 2015, p. 66. Cartoon.

Munroe, Randall. "Heartbleed Explanation." *xkcd.com,* xkcd.com/1354/. Comic strip.

**61. Advertisement** Include the label *Advertisement* at the end of the entry.

Ameritrade. *Wired,* Jan. 2014, p. 47. Advertisement.

Lufthansa. *The New York Times,* 16 Apr. 2014, www.nytimes.com. Advertisement.

## Other sources (including digital versions)

If an online version is not shown in this section, use the appropriate model for the source and then end with a DOI, permalink, or URL.

**62. Report or pamphlet** Follow the guidelines for a print book (models 6–22) or a digital book (model 33).

Rainie, Lee, and Maeve Duggan. *Privacy and Information Sharing.* Pew Research Center, 14 Jan. 2016, www.pewinternet.org/files/2016/01/ PI_2016.01.14_Privacy-and-Info-Sharing_FINAL.pdf.

**63. Government publication** Begin with the author, if identified. Otherwise, start with the name of the government, followed by the agency. For congressional documents, cite the number, session, and house of Congress; the type (*Report, Resolution, Document*); and the number. End with the publication information. For online versions, follow the models for a short work from a website (model 38) or an entire website (model 39).

Gregg, Judd. *Report to Accompany the Genetic Information Act of 2003.* US 108th Congress, 1st session, Senate Report 108-22, Government Printing Office, 2003.

United States, Department of Health and Human Services, National Institutes of Health. *Keep the Beat Recipes: Deliciously Healthy Dinners.* Oct. 2009, healthyeating.nhlbi.nih.gov/pdfs/Dinners_Cookbook_508-compliant.pdf.

**64. Published proceedings of a conference** Cite the proceedings as you would a book.

Cleary, John, and Gary Gurtler, editors. *Proceedings of the Boston Area Colloquium in Ancient Philosophy 2002.* Brill Academic Publishers, 2003.

**65. Dissertation**   Italicize the title and add the year the work was accepted, the institution, and a description of the type of degree.

> Thompson, Brian. *I'm Better Than You and I Can Prove It: Games, Expertise,*
> *and the Culture of Composition*. 2015. Stanford U, PhD dissertation.

**66. Dissertation abstract**   Cite the abstract as you would an unpublished dissertation, and add the label *Abstract* after the year. For an abstract that uses *Dissertation Abstracts International*, include the volume, year, and page number.

> Huang-Tiller, Gillian C. *The Power of the Meta-Genre: Cultural, Sexual, and*
> *Racial Politics of the American Modernist Sonnet*. 2000. U of Notre Dame,
> PhD dissertation. Abstract. *Dissertation Abstracts International*, vol. 61,
> 2000, p. 1401.

> Moore, Courtney L. *Stress and Oppression: Identifying Possible Protective*
> *Factors for African American Men*. 2016. Chicago School of Professional
> Psychology, PsyD dissertation. Abstract. *ProQuest Dissertations and*
> *Theses,* search.proquest.com/docview/1707351557.

**67. Letter**   Cite a published letter as a work in an anthology (see model 9). If the letter is unpublished, follow this form:

> Anzaldúa, Gloria. Letter to the author. 10 Sept. 2002.

**68. Manuscript or other unpublished work**   List the author's name; the title (if any) or a description of the material; any identifying numbers; and the name of the library or research institution housing the material, if applicable.

> Woolf, Virginia. "The Searchlight." 1902–56. Papers of Virginia Woolf, Smith
> College, Northampton, MA, series III, box 4, item 184.

**69. Legal source**   To cite a court case, give the name of the court; the first plaintiff and defendant, italicized; the year; and the publication information. To cite an act, give the legislative body, the act's Public Law number, and the publication information.

> United States, Supreme Court. *Citizens United v. FEC*. 2010. *Legal*
> *Information Institute*, Cornell U Law School, www.law.cornell.edu/supct/
> pdf/08-205P.ZS.

> United States, Congress. Public Law 116–136. "H.R. 748—CARES Act."
> *Congress.gov*, 27 Mar. 2020, congress.gov/bill/116th-congress/
> house-bill/748/text.

**Note:** You do not need an entry on the list of works cited when you cite articles of the U.S. Constitution.

## 18e  A student research essay, MLA style

**STUDENT WRITER**
Julia Sakowitz

A research-based argument by Julia Sakowitz appears on the following pages. Julia followed the MLA guidelines described in 18a–d.

Sakowitz 1

Name, instructor, course, and date aligned at left

Julia Sakowitz

Professor Yamboliev

PWR 1

21 May 2019

Title centered

"We're a Lot More Than Gospel Singing":

Tourism in Harlem

Connects her personal experience to the topic of the essay, establishing a narrative frame

As a New York City resident of the new millennium, I grew up barely aware that Harlem had ever been a *no-go* zone and couldn't understand why people of the older generation, my parents included, were afraid to venture uptown. I knew nothing about the heroin and crack epidemics of the 1960s, 70s, and 80s and in general was accustomed to a New York City that was safer than it had been in years.

Provides background information on problems in Harlem and responses to them

Harlem has changed rapidly over the past several decades. As problems with crime and drug abuse in the storied New York neighborhood decreased in the 1980s and 1990s, new government-sponsored and privately funded economic initiatives like the Upper Manhattan Empowerment Zone (UMEZ) pushed for outside investment and economic development (Hoffman 288; Zukin et al.). In a recent interview, Carolyn Johnson, owner of "Welcome to Harlem," a boutique tour company, recalled that "[Harlem] went from 0 to 100 in a short period of time," to the point that even Harlem residents themselves weren't aware of new businesses in their neighborhood. Tourism in Harlem clearly played a central role in this process, both responding to and creating social and economic change. By 2000, more than 800,000 people were visiting Harlem each year (Hoffman 288).

Introduces a key area of debate

It's clear that Harlem's surge in tourism is good for the city. But an equally important and more complex question is whether tourism benefits Harlem residents or sells them short. Close examination of current policy and tour business in Harlem reveals problems that come with tourism, such as cultural commodification and commercial gentrification, which are made worse by an Empowerment Zone program that favors only the most socioeconomically advantaged residents and outsiders. Although there is no simple solution for tourism in Harlem, small minority- and resident-owned tour businesses have the potential to more directly and widely benefit the community while causing fewer social and economic problems.

Economic development policy, particularly the UMEZ, has played a major role in shaping tourism's growth. Founded in 1994, the organization operates programs targeting business investment, loans to small businesses, grants for arts and culture, and employment and business training for residents (UMEZ). But promoting tourism is one of its most important aims.

The UMEZ especially focuses on cultural initiatives as a means of drawing tourism, sponsoring a "Catalyst Fund" specifically to "build cultural tourism," funding marketing and publicity for "UMEZ- eligible cultural organizations" (UMEZ). This cultural marketing approach to Harlem tourism is not unique to the UMEZ. Recent scholarship on tourism in Harlem concludes that marketing black and Latino culture is Harlem's golden ticket to escape economic marginalization. Scholar Lily Hoffman identifies black culture as the driving force that increased tourism to Harlem, claiming that for visitors, Harlem is the embodiment of "Black America and its music and entertainment traditions" (288). In Hoffman's eyes, "capitalizing on ethnic culture" for tourism not only generates revenue but also promotes cultural flourishing and instills community pride (297). Other scholars echo these sentiments, emphasizing that "diversity" or minority culture is Harlem's major and perhaps only asset and that "cultural tourism" has the additional benefit of promoting tolerance and de-stigmatization (Fainstein and Powers; Huning and Novy). But although it seems reasonable to assume that most tourists come to

Writer's last name and page number appear on every page

Presents explicit thesis statement at the end of introductory paragraphs

Provides detailed discussion of the UMEZ organization and its effects in Harlem

When the author is mentioned in a signal phrase, only a page number is needed in the parenthetical citation for a source with page numbers

Uses a semicolon to separate information about two sources in one citation

Sakowitz 3

Harlem expecting to experience black culture, significant cultural complications still stand.

Cultural tourism comes with problems. The power dynamic between a tourist with means and mobility, and Harlem residents, who might lack both, is skewed. One of the most obvious dangers is that visitors will disrespect Harlem and the people who live there, participating in "negative sightseeing" or treating locals as if they're "put on exhibit" (Fainstein and Powers 14). In the popular Lonely Planet guide to New York City, there are hints of a clash between tourists and locals over cultural tourism: "Many locals are upset by visitors [to Harlem churches] who chat during sermons, leave in the middle of services or show up in skimpy attire," Lonely Planet warns. "Plus, for some, there's the uncomfortable sense that African American spirituality is something to be consumed like a Broadway show" (St. Louis and Bonnetto 254).

Another, equally important issue stemming from tourism is commercial gentrification, the phenomenon of large chain stores and boutiques replacing stores that serve the poor (Zukin et al. 48). Such changes have long been viewed as positive. A low-income neighborhood often lacks necessary retail infrastructure, instead featuring businesses like used merchandise outlets, check cashing operations, liquor stores, or job training and family services (Hoffman 288). Tourism can encourage middle-class economic activity like supermarkets, commercial banks, and legal and accounting services, which are as much needed by low-income residents as wealthier ones (Hoffman 288). But boutique stores and chain stores, seen in fig. 1, can replace services that might still be needed by the poor, leaving low-income residents feeling unwelcome (Zukin et al. 48). Economic gain from new businesses also bypasses most Harlem residents: fewer than half of new retail entrepreneurs are residents, according to Zukin and others, and even

---

**Margin notes:**

Defines a key term ("gentrification") and shows how it relates to tourism and affects the community

Refers to visual in the text of the essay

Sakowitz 4

COURTESY OF GRAY LINE CITYSIGHTSEEING NEW YORK

Fig. 1. This photo shows a typical tour bus passing Harlem's historic Apollo Theater, which now sits amid chain stores such as Banana Republic and GameStop (City Sightseeing New York).

Provides figure number, explanatory caption, and source information for a visual

those entrepreneurs who are residents overwhelmingly come from the newly arrived middle class (59).

Commercial gentrification can feed into residential gentrification as the neighborhood becomes attractive to new middle-class residents. These might be any of a variety of races and nationalities, including African and African American, but tend to be better educated, have more money, and come from outside New York City (Zukin et al. 59). In fact, tourism itself can facilitate residential gentrification, sometimes overtly through real estate tours much like the Harlem "brownstone tours" that first occurred in the 1980s ("House Tours Galore"; Sandford 103). Today, this kind of "neighborhood-shopping" continues. Non-Harlemite New Yorkers, visitors, and even real estate moguls will often visit Harlem with Big Onion Walking Tours to ask pointed questions about whether Harlem is a friendly and safe place to live (Kamil).

Sakowitz 5

Both commercial and residential gentrification favor outsiders and newcomers. While it is possible for tourism to economically empower Harlem and its residents, in reality the greatest economic gains bypass low-income residents completely.

In this context, Carolyn Johnson, Harlem resident and founder of "Welcome to Harlem," a self-described "certified minority and women-owned visitor center and boutique-tour company," is a unique player ("About Us"). In the early 2000s, Johnson realized her neighborhood was changing rapidly and started the website "Welcome to Harlem" in 2004 as an informational tool for the community, so residents could learn about Harlem's new businesses and venues. In 2008, Johnson decided to branch out into tourism. Seeing outsiders coming to Harlem to give bus and walking tours, she decided to complete a short tour guide training program and start leading tours herself (Interview). "Welcome to Harlem" now features six different tours, including jazz tours, food-tasting tours, and historic tours, as well as "music programs and workshops" ("About Us").

> Includes two personal interviews as field research

For Johnson, running her own business can be an economic challenge, but another, equally serious problem is developing a trustworthy reputation to attract clients. She says she struggled to get recognition outside the community, noting it was more common for hotels and tour agencies to recommend large non-Harlem-based tour companies, which might be able to pay a sizeable commission. Visibility is a common problem for Harlem-based tour companies. Almost half of the listed businesses resulting from a Google search for "Harlem tour" are not Harlem-based businesses, but larger outside companies, like "New York Visions," "Free Tours by Foot," and "Big Onion Walking Tours."

In the tour business, which aims to represent a neighborhood for outsiders, issues of cultural representation are important. For Harlem-based entrepreneurs, offering tours can be a means of self-representation. Johnson's own identity as a Harlem resident motivates her to create tours that disprove negative stereotypes. "Most people think that Harlem is just Sylvia's, the Apollo, and gospel on Sunday," Johnson says. She wants to show that Harlem is a self-contained community, "a lot more than just gospel singing" (Interview).

This point of "authenticity" is so important that Harlem-based companies compete with even more exclusive definitions. The "Welcome to Harlem" website states, "Our tours are led by true Harlemites (those who grew up here or live here) which allows for an authentic and personal experience." According to Seth Kamil, owner of "Big Onion Walking Tours," "authenticity" is not an asset at all. Kamil, who founded his business 25 years ago as a graduate student at Columbia University, believes that living in a certain place is no qualification for leading tours, and that the best tours are strongly academic, offering historical fact. Kamil employs mainly graduate students as guides, and his Harlem guides are neither African American nor necessarily Harlem locals. In a recent interview, Kamil questioned the motives of tourists seeking a minority or Harlemite guide and suggested that there is a "subtle racism" that drives tourists to request a minority guide in Harlem, but not in other economically challenged minority neighborhoods like Chinatown. He stated simply, "We don't play that game" (Kamil).

But at the same time, much like "Welcome to Harlem" or Harlem Heritage Tours, Kamil is concerned about representing Harlem fairly and dispelling stereotypes. In addition to focusing on history, his tours aim to express the struggles of living in Harlem because of its continued lack of infrastructure that many middle-class New Yorkers take for granted. He notes that the biggest problem with Harlem tours are "perceptions that customers have" and he tries to avoid disrespecting the community, refusing to take part in "Gospel Tours," which he sees as violating Harlem's places of worship. He also cares

*Right margin annotations:*

Demonstrates the benefits of having a Harlem resident represent the community in all its richness

Presents an opposing point of view

Sakowitz 7

about what Harlem residents think of his tours. In his opinion, Big Onion Walking Tours has "a unique relationship with the community," and he notes that many black residents will stop to listen to his white guides, to check that they're being respectful and accurate (Kamil).

Kamil seemed to view "cultural" tours as, at worst, empty and unethical, and, at best, self-commodifying. Could he be partially right? Is Harlem-based tour companies' heavy-handed advertising of "authenticity" based on minority status and Harlem residence demeaning for Harlem residents?

Coming at this same question of cultural commodification from a different perspective is Arlene Dávila, a scholar whose focus on Latino issues in East Harlem, or El Barrio, led her to surprising conclusions about the UMEZ policies. Commodifying minority culture is problematic, Dávila claims, because in the eyes of tourists, policymakers, and even scholars, not all culture is created equal. For example, Harlem is internationally famous as a "black Mecca," yet it is also more than half Latino and a center for "Nuyorican" identity, urban Latindad, and Latino dance and music (52). But what happens when visitors' needs and residents' reality just don't align? Dávila writes:

> By limiting East Harlem's funding eligibility to certain sections
> and imposing requirements that only institutionalized cultural
> industries could meet, EZ virtually guaranteed that cultural
> institutions in Central and West Harlem, which are the most
> established cultural institutions in Upper Manhattan, would be
> most prominently featured in EZ-sponsored tourist promotional
> materials and the ones eligible for the largest amounts of
> funding. (51)

When Latino cultural initiatives have applied for UMEZ funding, the UMEZ board has questioned the appeal of Latino culture, in one instance rejecting a salsa museum's application because it doubted

*Introduces a third important voice in the debate*

*Block format for a quotation of more than four lines; quotation marks are not needed*

*Note that the parenthetical citation comes after the period that ends the sentence*

Sakowitz 8

the international popularity of salsa and the museum's ability to
create at least five jobs (Dávila 59). The results of such policy for El
Barrio are dramatic: Dávila estimates that as little as 6% of the UMEZ
cultural funding was given to Latino initiatives (51).

But Latino Harlemites aren't the only ones who suffer from
the UMEZ policies. Even though the UMEZ funding of tourism and
cultural initiatives is supposed to be an equalizing force that
elevates those with few resources, its economic prerequisites favor
those with money and education (Dávila 58). Harlem residents echo
these sentiments. Deborah Faison, a Harlem resident, commented
that the technical training the UMEZ provides is "by itself . . . not
enough" and that it's necessary to be "in a strong position already
to participate" in the program (qtd. in Maurrasse 164). Carolyn
Johnson, who receives funding for "Welcome to Harlem" through
the UMEZ, believes that UMEZ doesn't do enough for small business
and the "people who have been here" (Interview). The ultimate
result of the UMEZ's supposedly equal-access programs of economic
empowerment through culture is that the "largest beneficiaries under
the EZ were developers and outside visitors" (Dávila 61).

If tourism is going to be a means of economic empowerment for
Harlem, there's an urgent need to revise UMEZ policy. For example,
when allocating funding, the UMEZ should focus less on the revenue
and jobs a cultural initiative will create and more on its cultural
value to the community. Harlem's cultural life is as important
as its economic life, *especially* from the perspective of tourism,
because cultivating genuine culture that comes from and serves the
community keeps Harlem authentically itself, which is what draws
tourists in the first place. Doing otherwise sells the soul of the
neighborhood, turning it into a hollow Disneyland version of itself.
The UMEZ also needs to take civic participation and empowerment
more seriously. Instead of providing sparse job training and business
skills classes, it should take steps to organize community meetings

Transition to
final point

Includes
"qtd. in"
to indicate
an indirect
quotation
(source
quoted in
another source)

Writer
proposes
a policy
change
and gives
examples

Sakowitz 9

and start more comprehensive programs that would create a genuine sense of resident involvement and power.

Finally, the UMEZ can't remain socioeconomically blind. Doing so benefits those who have economic or social advantage, enabling commercial gentrification rather than uplifting the community. The organization should develop a policy of need-based preference, giving special consideration to long-term residents, minorities, and economically disadvantaged entrepreneurs. Instead of selecting businesses based on how accomplished they seem already, the UMEZ should award grants based on their potential to grow.

Conclusion sums up writer's argument and reiterates thesis

With these changes to the UMEZ, Harlem entrepreneurs will be able to receive funding and compete on an even playing field with outside companies like Big Onion Walking Tours without having to sell their identity. Small business will be able to flourish, and Harlem will remain resilient and diverse, a wonderful place to live and a wonderful place to visit.

Sakowitz 10

Works Cited

Dávila, Arlene. "Empowered Culture? New York City's Empowerment Zone and the Selling of El Barrio." *The Annals of the American Academy of Political and Social Science,* vol. 594, no. 1, July 2004, pp. 49–64.

Fainstein, Susan, and John Powers. "Tourism and New York's Ethnic Diversity: An Underutilized Resource?" *Tourism, Ethnic Diversity, and the City,* edited by Jan Rath, Routledge, 2007, pp. 143–63.

Hoffman, Lily M. "The Marketing of Diversity in the Inner City: Tourism and Regulation in Harlem." *International Journal of Urban and Regional Research,* vol. 27, no. 2, June 2003, pp. 286–99. *Academic Search Premier,* doi:10.1111/1468-2427.00448.

"House Tours Galore: Where to Get a Look inside NYC's Most Fabulous Homes." *6sqft.* www.6sqft.com/house-tours-galore -where-to-get-a-look-inside-the-areas-most-fabulous-homes -and-gardens/. Accessed 23 Apr. 2019.

Huning, S., and J. Novy. "Tourism as an Engine of Neighborhood Regeneration?" *CMS Working Paper Series.* Center for Metropolitan Studies, 2006, citeseerx.ist.psu.edu/viewdoc/download? doi:10.1.1.544.6506&rep=rep1&type=pdf.

Johnson, Carolyn. "About Us." *Welcome to Harlem,* welcometoharlem .com/page/aboutus/. Accessed 15 May 2019.

---. Interview. Conducted by Julia Sakowitz, 9 May 2019.

Kamil, Seth. Interview. Conducted by Julia Sakowitz, 11 May 2019.

Maurrasse, David. *Listening to Harlem: Gentrification, Community, and Business,* Routledge, 2006.

Sandford, Mariellen R. "Tourism in Harlem: Between Negative Sightseeing and Gentrification." *The Journal of American Culture,* vol. 10, no. 2, Summer 1987, pp. 99–105. *Wiley Online Library,* doi:10.1111/j.1542-734X.1987.1002_99.x.

St. Louis, Regis, and Cristian Bonnetto. "Harlem and Upper Manhattan." *Lonely Planet New York City.* Lonely Planet, 2014.

Heading centered

Print journal article

Chapter in a book with an editor

Article found in a database

Information from a website

Online report

Personal interview

Print book

Second and subsequent lines of each entry are indented

Upper Manhattan Empowerment Zone (UMEZ). "Upper Manhattan
Empowerment Zone: Who We Are." Upper Manhattan
Empowerment Zone Development Corporation, 2016, umez.org.

*Uptown Tour*. 2016. City Sightseeing New York, www
.citysightseeingnewyork.com/nyc-bus-tours/uptown-treasures
-harlem-tour-plus.html. Photograph.

Zukin, Sharon, et al. "New Retail Capital and Neighborhood Change:
Boutiques and Gentrification in New York City." *City &
Community*, vol. 8, no. 1, Mar. 2009, pp. 47–64.

Photograph

# CHAPTER 19

# APA Style

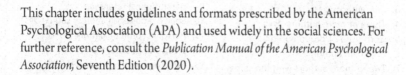

This chapter includes guidelines and formats prescribed by the American Psychological Association (APA) and used widely in the social sciences. For further reference, consult the *Publication Manual of the American Psychological Association,* Seventh Edition (2020).

## 19a Understanding the basics

When you are assigned to use APA style for a research project, it is helpful to think through your responsibilities as an academic writer: What do your readers need from you? What are the elements of an APA citation? How do in-text citations connect to entries in the reference list? And is there any need for explanatory notes for your readers?

### Thinking about what readers need from you

Why does academic work call for very careful citation practices when writing for the general public might not? The answer is that readers of your academic work expect source citations for a number of reasons:

- Source citations demonstrate that you've done your homework on your topic and that you are a part of the conversation surrounding it.
- Source citations show that you understand the need to give credit whenever you use someone else's intellectual property. (See Chapter 15 for details.)
- Source citations give explicit directions to guide readers who want to look for themselves at the works you're using.

The guidelines for APA style tell you exactly what information to include in your citation and how to format that information.

# List of Examples

## In-text citations in APA style (19c)

## References in APA style (19d)

### Guidelines for author listings

### Print books

### Print periodicals

A List of Examples for **MLA style** is on page 238.

A List of Examples for **CMS (*Chicago*) style** is on page 327.

A List of Examples for **CSE style** is on page 351.

## Identifying elements of APA citations

As a researcher, you're responsible for knowing which elements to gather for creating APA citations. A basic APA-style reference consists of four parts:

- the **author**'s (or authors') name(s)
- the **date** of publication
- the **title** of the work
- the **source** of the work

In general, the first two elements — author and date of publication — appear in both in-text citations and reference list entries. In general, the title and source information appear only in the reference list entry. The author is the person or people most responsible for the work. For a book or article, the author is the person who wrote it; for a movie, treat the director as the author; for a government report, the author is the specific agency or department that created the report, such as the Department of Agriculture. The publication date is expressed as a year for books and scholarly journals but is typically more specific for other sources. The title is the name of the work. And the source refers to information readers would need to locate the information that you have used in your project. Source information can include publisher name and pages for printed works, URLs and DOIs for digital works, and locator information such as time stamps and paragraph numbers for sources without page numbers.

## Identifying the type of source you are using

Before you can decide how to cite your source following APA guidelines, you need to determine what kind of source you're using.

### Types of sources

Refer to the List of Examples at the beginning of this chapter to locate guidelines on citing various types of sources — print books (or parts of print books), print periodicals (journals, magazines, and newspapers), and digital written-word sources (an online article or a book on an e-reader). A digital version of a source may include updates that the print version lacks, so it's important to provide the correct information for readers. For sources that consist mainly of material other than written words — such as a film, song, or artwork — consult the "other sources" section of the directory. If you can't find a model exactly like the source you've selected, see the Quick Help box on page 306.

### A note about articles from web and database sources

You need a subscription to look through most databases, so individual researchers almost always gain access to articles in databases through a library. The easiest way to tell whether a source comes from a database, then, is that its information is *not* generally available for free. Many databases are digital collections of articles that originally appeared in edited print periodicals, ensuring that an authority has vouched for the accuracy of the information. Such sources often have more credibility than free material available on the web.

## Planning and connecting your citations

APA citations appear in two connected parts of your text — a brief in-text citation in the body of your written text and a full citation in the list of references, to which the in-text citation directs readers. The most straightforward in-text citations include the <u>author's name</u>, the publication <u>year</u>, and the page number, but many variations on this basic format are discussed in 19c.

In the text of her research essay (see 27c), Tawnya Redding includes a paraphrase of material from an online journal that she accessed through the publisher's website. She cites the authors' names and the year of publication in a parenthetical reference, pointing readers to the entry for "Baker, F., & Bor, W. (2008)" in her references list, shown below.

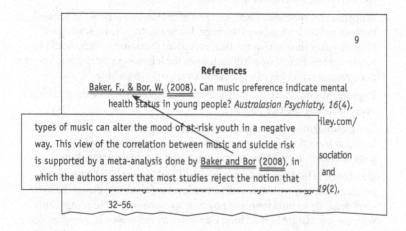

9

**References**

<u>Baker, F., & Bor, W.</u> <u>(2008)</u>. Can music preference indicate mental
health status in young people? *Australasian Psychiatry, 16*(4),
…iley.com/

types of music can alter the mood of at-risk youth in a negative
way. This view of the correlation between music and suicide risk
is supported by a meta-analysis done by <u>Baker and Bor</u> <u>(2008)</u>, in
which the authors assert that most studies reject the notion that

sociation
and
*19*(2),
32–56.

## Including notes as needed

APA style allows you to use content notes, either at the bottom of the page or on a separate page at the end of the text, to expand or supplement your text. Indicate such notes in the text by superscript numerals ([1]). Single-space all entries. Indent the first line of each note one-half inch, but begin subsequent lines at the left margin.

### SUPERSCRIPT NUMBER IN TEXT

The age of the children involved in the study was an important factor in the selection of items for the questionnaire.[1]

FOOTNOTE
   [1] Marjorie Youngston Forman and William Cole of the Child Study
Team provided great assistance in identifying appropriate items for the
questionnaire.

## 19b Following APA format

The following formatting guidelines are adapted from the APA recommendations for undergraduate student papers. However, you may want to check with your instructor before preparing your final draft.

For a sample student essay in APA style, see 19e.

- **Title page.** A few double-spaced lines from the top margin, center the title of the paper in bold font. After one blank double-spaced line, include the following details on separate lines: your name, the department and school in which the course is offered, the course number and name, the instructor's name, and the assignment due date.

- **Margins and spacing.** Leave margins of at least one inch at the top and bottom and on both sides of the page. Do not justify the right margin. Double-space throughout the text, except for footnotes, which should be single-spaced. Indent one-half inch from the left margin for the first line of a paragraph and all lines of a quotation over forty words long.

- **Page numbers.** Place the page number in the upper-right corner of each page, including the title page.

- **Long quotations.** For a quotation of forty or more words, indent it one-half inch from the left margin, and do not use quotation marks. Place the page reference in parentheses one space after the final punctuation.

- **Headings.** Headings are frequently used within the text of APA-style projects. In a text with only one or two levels of headings, center the first-level headings in bold font, and position any second-level headings flush with the left margin in bold font. Capitalize all major words; however, do not capitalize any articles, short prepositions, or coordinating conjunctions unless they are the first word or follow a colon.

- **Visuals.** Tables should be labeled "Table" and numbered in bold font. All other visuals (such as charts, graphs, photographs, and drawings) should be labeled "Figure" and numbered in bold font. Both tables and figures should have a title in italics on the line below the label. Provide any source information in a note below the table or figure. Begin with the word "Note," italicized and followed by a period. Remember to refer to each visual in your text, stating how it contributes to the point(s) you are making. Tables and figures should generally appear after the paragraph in which they are called out.

## 19c Creating APA in-text citations

An in-text citation in APA style always indicates which source on the references page the writer is referring to, and it explains in what year the material was published; for quoted material, the in-text citation also indicates where in the source the quotation can be found.

Note that APA style generally calls for using the past tense or present perfect tense for signal verbs: "Baker (2018) showed" or "Baker (2018) has shown." Use the present tense only to discuss results ("the experiment demonstrates") or widely accepted information ("researchers agree").

We have used underlining in some examples only to draw your attention to important elements. Do not underline anything in your own citations.

*1. Basic format for a quotation*  Generally, use the author's name in a signal phrase to introduce the cited material, and place the date, in parentheses, immediately after the author's name. The page number, preceded by "p.," appears in parentheses after the quotation.

> Gitlin (2001) pointed out that "political critics, convinced that the media are rigged against them, are often blind to other substantial reasons why their causes are unpersuasive" (p. 141).

If the author is not named in a signal phrase, place the author's name, the year, and the page number in parentheses after the quotation: (Gitlin, 2001, p. 141). For a long, set-off quotation (more than forty words), place the page reference in parentheses one space after the final quotation.

For quotations from works without page numbers, include other information from the source, such as a section heading, a paragraph number, a figure number, or a time stamp, to help readers find the cited passage.

> Driver (2007) has noticed "an increasing focus on the role of land" in policy debates over the past decade (para. 1).

*2. Basic format for a paraphrase or summary*  Include the author's last name and the year as in model 1. A page number is not required for a summary or a paraphrase, but include one if it would help readers find the material in a long work.

> Gitlin (2001) has argued that critics sometimes overestimate the influence of the media on modern life (p. 141).

*3. Two authors* Use both names in all citations. Use "and" in a signal phrase, but use an ampersand (&) in parentheses.

Babcock and Laschever (2003) have suggested that many women do not negotiate their salaries and pay raises as vigorously as their male counterparts do.

A recent study has suggested that many women do not negotiate their salaries and pay raises as vigorously as their male counterparts do (Babcock & Laschever, 2003).

*4. Three or more authors* Use only the first author's name and "et al." in a signal phrase or in parentheses.

As Soleim et al. (2017) demonstrated, advertising holds the potential for manipulating "free-willed" consumers.

A recent study has demonstrated that advertising holds the potential for manipulating "free-willed" consumers (Soleim et al., 2017).

*5. Corporate or group author* If the name of the organization or corporation is long, spell it out the first time you use it, followed by an abbreviation in brackets. In later references, use the abbreviation only.

FIRST CITATION   The national conversation about bullying has changed recently to include the dangers of social media (Centers for Disease Control and Prevention [CDC], 2018).

LATER CITATIONS   Though bullying is defined by some as a form of "youth violence," current social media channels offer evidence that social bullying is not restricted to youth (CDC, 2018).

*6. Unknown author* Use the title or its first few words in a signal phrase or in parentheses. A book's title is italicized, as in the following example; an article's title is placed in quotation marks.

The employment profiles for this time period substantiated this trend (*Federal Employment*, 2001).

*7. Two or more authors with the same last name* Include the authors' initials in each citation.

S. Bartolomeo (2000) conducted the groundbreaking study on teenage childbearing.

*8. Two or more works by an author in a single year*   Assign <u>lowercase letters</u> ("a," "b," and so on) alphabetically by title, and include the letters after the year.

> Gordon (<u>2017b</u>) examined this trend in more detail.

*9. Two or more sources in one parenthetical reference*   List any sources by different authors in alphabetical order by the authors' last names, separated by semicolons: (Cardone, 2018; Lai, 2014). List works by the same author in chronological order, separated by commas: (Lai, 2014, 2017).

*10. Source reported in another source*   Use the phrase "as cited in" to indicate that you are reporting information from a secondary source. Name the <u>original source</u> in a signal phrase or in parentheses, and list the <u>secondary source</u> in parentheses and in your list of references.

> <u>Amartya Sen</u> developed the influential concept that land reform was necessary for "promoting opportunity" among the poor (<u>as cited in Driver</u>, 2007, para. 2).

*11. Personal communication*   Cite any personal letters, email messages, electronic postings, telephone conversations, or interviews as shown. Do not include personal communications in the reference list.

> R. Tobin (personal communication, November 4, 2006) supported his claims about music therapy with new evidence.

*12. Electronic source*   Cite a web or electronic source as you would a print source, using the author's <u>name</u> and <u>date</u>.

> <u>Link and Phelan</u> (<u>2005</u>) argued for broader interventions in public health that would be accessible to anyone, regardless of individual wealth.

The APA recommends the following for electronic sources without names, dates, or page numbers:

**AUTHOR UNKNOWN**

Use a shortened form of the title in a signal phrase or in parentheses (see model 6). If an organization is the author, see model 5.

**DATE UNKNOWN**

Use the abbreviation "n.d." (for "no date") in place of the year: (Hopkins, n.d.).

**NO PAGE NUMBERS**

If a source lacks stable page numbers, include <u>paragraph numbers</u>, <u>section headings</u>, or both. If a source lacks numbered paragraphs or headings, count the paragraphs manually. If you shorten a long heading, place it in quotation marks: ("What Is It" section). When quoting audio or video sources, use a time stamp to indicate the start of the quotation. Do not include location numbers for sources in e-book format.

> Jacobs and Johnson (2007) have argued that "the South African media is still highly concentrated and not very diverse in terms of race and class" (<u>South African Media After Apartheid section</u>, <u>para. 3</u>).

*13. Table or figure reproduced in the text*   Number figures (graphs, charts, illustrations, and photographs) and tables separately.

For both tables and figures, place the label ("Table 1") and an informative heading ("Hartman's Key Personality Traits") above the table or figure; below, provide information about its source. Begin with the word "Note," italicized and followed by a period.

**Table 1**

*Hartman's Key Personality Traits*

| Trait category | Color | | | |
|---|---|---|---|---|
| | Red | Blue | White | Yellow |
| Motive | Power | Intimacy | Peace | Fun |
| Strengths | Loyal to tasks | Loyal to people | Tolerant | Positive |
| Limitations | Arrogant | Self-righteous | Timid | Uncommitted |

*Note.* Adapted from *The Hartman Personality Profile,* by N. Hayden (http://students.cs.byu.edu/~nhayden/Code/index.php).

If you do not cite the source of the table or figure elsewhere in your text, you do not need to include the source in your list of references.

# 19d Preparing an APA list of references

The alphabetical list of the sources cited in your document is called "References." If your instructor asks that you list everything you have read — not just the sources you cite — call the list "Bibliography."

All the entries in this chapter of the book use hanging indent format, in which the first line aligns on the left and the subsequent lines indent one-half inch or five spaces. This is the customary APA format.

## Guidelines for author listings

List authors' last names first, and use only initials for first and middle names. The in-text citations in your text point readers toward particular sources in your list of references (see 19c).

**NAME CITED IN SIGNAL PHRASE IN TEXT**

Lapowsky (2017) has noted . . .

**NAME IN PARENTHETICAL CITATION IN TEXT**

. . . (Lapowsky, 2017).

**BEGINNING OF ENTRY IN LIST OF REFERENCES**

Lapowsky, I. (2017).

Models 1–5 explain how to arrange author names. The information that follows the name of the author depends on the type of work you are citing — a book (models 6–14), a print periodical (models 15–21), a digital written-word source (models 22–31), or another kind of source (models 32–47).

*1. One author*   Give the last name, a comma, the initial(s), and the date in parentheses.

Zimbardo, P. G. (2009).

*2. Multiple authors*   List up to twenty authors, last name first, with commas separating authors' names and then an ampersand (&) before the last author's name.

Walsh, M. E., & Murphy, J. A. (2003).

**Note:** For a work with more than twenty authors, list the first nineteen, then an ellipsis (. . .), and then the final author's name.

---

## Formatting a list of references

- Start your list on a new page after the text of your document but before appendices or notes. Continue consecutive page numbers.
- Center the heading "References" in bold one inch from the top of the page.
- Begin each entry flush with the left margin, but indent subsequent lines one-half inch or five spaces. Double-space the entire list.
- List sources alphabetically by author's last name. If no author is given, alphabetize the source by the first word of the title other than "A," "An," or "The." If the list includes two or more works by the same author, list them in chronological order.
- Italicize titles and subtitles of books and periodicals. Do not italicize titles of articles, and do not enclose them in quotation marks.
- For titles of books and articles, capitalize only the first word of the title and the subtitle and any proper nouns or proper adjectives.
- For titles of periodicals, capitalize all major words.

---

*3. Corporate or group author*

Resources for Rehabilitation. (2016).

*4. Unknown author*    Begin with the work's title. Italicize the titles of works that are a stand-alone item, such as a novel, a movie, a one-time TV special (such as the 2020 Grammy Awards), or a podcast series. Do not italicize titles of works that are part of a larger whole, such as an article in a journal, a chapter in a book, or an episode of a TV or podcast series. Capitalize only the first word of the title and subtitle (if any) and proper nouns and proper adjectives.

*Safe youth, safe schools.* (2009).

*5. Two or more works by the same author*    List works by the same author in chronological order. Repeat the author's name in each entry.

Goodall, J. (2009).

Goodall, J. (2013).

If the works appeared in the same year, list them alphabetically by title, and assign lowercase letters ("a," "b," etc.) after the dates.

Shermer, M. (2002a). On estimating the lifetime of civilizations. *Scientific American, 287*(2), 33.

Shermer, M. (2002b). Readers who question evolution. *Scientific American, 287*(1), 37.

If the works appeared in the same year but use a more specific date that includes the month or month and day, list the works in chronological order.

---

QUICK HELP

### Combining parts of models

What should you do if your source doesn't match the model exactly? Suppose, for instance, that your source is a translation of a republished book with an editor.

- Identify a basic model to follow. If you decide that your source looks most like a republished book, for example, start with a citation that looks like model 13.
- Look for models that show additional elements in your source. For this example, you would need elements of model 9 (for the translator) and model 7 (for the editor).
- Add new elements from other models to your basic model in the order that makes the most sense to you.
- If you still aren't sure how to arrange the pieces to create a combination model, ask your instructor or a consultant in the writing center.

## Print books

*6. Basic format for a book*   Begin with the <u>author name(s)</u>. (See models 1–5.) Then include the <u>publication year</u>, title and subtitle, and the publisher. The source map on pp. 300–301 shows where to find information in a typical book.

> <u>Kahneman, D.</u> (<u>2011</u>). *Thinking fast and slow.* Farrar, Straus and Giroux.

*7. Editor*   For a book with an editor but no author, list the source under the <u>editor's name</u>, followed by the abbreviation "Ed." in parentheses and a period.

> <u>Schwartz, R. G. (Ed.).</u> (2009). *Handbook of child language disorders.* Psychology Press.

To cite a book with an author and an editor, place the editor's name, with a comma and the abbreviation "Ed.," in parentheses after the title.

> Austin, J. (1995). *The province of jurisprudence determined* (<u>W. E. Rumble, Ed.</u>). Cambridge University Press.

*8. Selection in a book with an editor*

> Pettigrew, D. (2018). The suppression of cultural memory and identity in Bosnia and Herzegovina. In J. Lindert & A. T. Marsoobian (Eds.), *Multidisciplinary perspectives on genocide and memory* (pp. 187–198). Springer.

*9. Translation*

> Calasso, R. (2019). *The unnamable present* (<u>R. Dixon, Trans.</u>). Farrar, Straus and Giroux. (Original work published 2017)

## Books

Take information from the book's title page and copyright page, not from the book's cover or a library catalog.

1. **Author.** List all authors' last names first, and use only initials for first and middle names. For more about citing authors, see models 1–5.

2. **Publication year.** Enclose the year of publication in parentheses.

3. **Title.** Italicize the title and any subtitle. Capitalize only the first word of the title and the subtitle and any proper nouns or proper adjectives.

4. **Publisher.** List the publisher's name, dropping any terms that indicate corporate structure, such as "Inc." or "Ltd."

**A citation for the book shown on the next page would look like this:**

Tsutsui, W. (2004). *Godzilla on my mind: Fifty years of the king of monsters.*
Palgrave Macmillan.

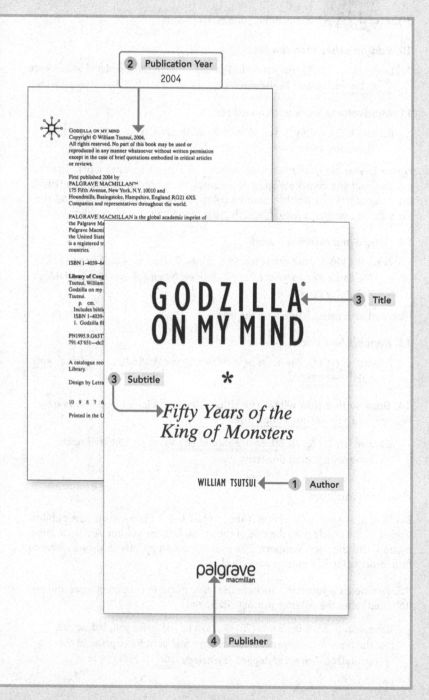

**2 Publication Year**

2004

First published 2004 by
PALGRAVE MACMILLAN™
175 Fifth Avenue, New York, N.Y. 10010 and
Houndmills, Basingstoke, Hampshire, England RG21 6XS.
Companies and representatives throughout the world.

PALGRAVE MACMILLAN is the global academic imprint of
the Palgrave Ma
Palgrave Macmill
the United State
is a registered tr
countries.

ISBN 1-4039-6

**Library of Cong**
Tsutsui, William
Godzilla on my
Tsutsui.
  p.  cm.
  Includes bibli
  ISBN 1-4039-
  1. Godzilla fi

PN1995.9.G63T
791.43'651—dc2

A catalogue rec
Library.

Design by Letra

10 9 8 7 6

Printed in the U

**3 Title**

# GODZILLA®
# ON MY MIND

**3 Subtitle**

*

*Fifty Years of the
King of Monsters*

WILLIAM TSUTSUI     **1 Author**

palgrave
macmillan

**4 Publisher**

*10. Edition other than the first*

Berger, K. S. (2018). *The developing person through childhood and adolescence* (11th ed.). Worth Publishers.

*11. Multivolume work with an editor*

Barnes, J. (Ed.). (1995). *Complete works of Aristotle* (Vols. 1–2). Princeton University Press.

**Note:** If you are citing just one volume of a multivolume work, list that volume, not the complete span of volumes, in parentheses after the title. If the volume has its own title, insert a colon following the series title and then the volume number, a period, and the title of the volume, all in italics.

*12. Article in a reference work*

Dean, C. (1994). Jaws and teeth. In S. Jones, R. Martin, & D. Pilbeam (Eds.), *The Cambridge encyclopedia of human evolution* (pp. 56–59). Cambridge University Press.

If no author is listed, begin with the title.

*13. Republished book*

Fremlin, C. (2017). *The hours before dawn*. Dover Publications. (Original work published 1958)

*14. Book with a title within the title*    Do not italicize or enclose in quotation marks a title within a book title.

Klarman, M. J. (2007). Brown v. Board of Education *and the civil rights movement*. Oxford University Press.

## Print periodicals

Begin with the author name(s). (See models 1–5.) Then include the publication date, the article title, the title of the periodical, the volume and issue information, and the page numbers. The source map on pp. 304–5 shows where to find information in a sample periodical.

*15. Article in a journal*    Include the issue number (in parentheses and not italicized) after the volume number (italicized).

Ganegoda, D. B., & Bordia, P. (2019). I can be happy for you, but not all the time: A contingency model of envy and positive empathy in the workplace. *Journal of Applied Psychology, 104*(6), 776–795.

*16. Article in a magazine*    Include the <u>month (and day</u>, if given).

Solomon, A. (<u>2014, March 17</u>). The reckoning. *The New Yorker, 90*(4), 36–45.

*17. Article in a newspaper*

Finucane, M. (2019, September 25). Americans still eating too many low-quality carbs. *The Boston Globe,* B2.

*18. Editorial or letter to the editor*    Add an identifying <u>label</u>.

Doran, K. (2019, October 12). Homeless who look like grandma or grandpa [<u>Letter to the editor</u>]. *The New York Times,* A22.

*19. Unsigned article*

Annual meeting announcement. (2003, March). *Cognitive Psychology, 46,* 227.

*20. Review*    Identify the <u>work reviewed</u>.

Douthat, R. (2019, October 14). A hustle gone wrong [<u>Review of the film *Hustles,* by L. Scafaria, Dir.</u>]. *National Review, 71*(18), 47.

*21. Published interview*    For an interview published in print, begin with the <u>interviewer</u>. If the interviewee is not named in the title of the work, as in this example, include the interviewee's name in a signal phrase.

<u>Tracy, A.</u> (2019, December). The super Speaker. *Vanity Fair,* (712), 96–103.

## Digital written-word sources

---

**QUICK HELP**

Citing digital sources

When citing sources accessed online, include as many of the following elements as you can find:

- **Author.** Give the author's name, if available.
- **Publication date.** Include the date of electronic publication or of the latest update, if available. When no publication date is available, use "n.d." ("no date").
- **Title.** If the source is not from a larger work, italicize the title.
- **Print publication information.** For articles from online journals, magazines, or reference databases, give the publication title and other publishing information as you would for a print periodical (see models 15–21).
- **Retrieval information.** If a DOI (digital object identifier) is available, include it after the publication information with no period at the end. If there is no DOI, include a URL for the article except if the article is from a database (see model 23). If a DOI or URL is long, you can include a shortened form by using a site like shortdoi.org or bitly.com.

# Articles from Print Periodicals

1. **Author.** List all authors' last names first, and use only initials for first and middle names. For more about citing authors, see models 1–5.

2. **Publication date.** Enclose the date in parentheses. For journals, use only the year. For magazines and newspapers, use the year, a comma, the month (spelled out), and the day, if given.

3. **Article title.** Do not italicize or enclose article titles in quotation marks. Capitalize only the first word of the article title and subtitle and any proper nouns or proper adjectives.

4. **Periodical title.** Italicize the periodical title (and subtitle, if any), and capitalize all major words. Follow the periodical title with a comma.

5. **Volume and issue numbers.** Give the volume number (italicized) and, without a space in between, the issue number (if given) in parentheses. Follow with a comma.

6. **Page numbers.** Give the inclusive page numbers of the article. End the citation with a period.

**A citation for the article shown on the next page would look like this:**

Etzioni, A. (2006). Leaving race behind: Our growing Hispanic population creates a golden opportunity. *The American Scholar*, *75*(2), 20–30.

**2** Publication Date

**4** Periodical Title

**5** Volume and Issue Numbers

*The* AMERICAN
SCHOLAR

Spring 2006 | Vol. 75, No. 2

*The* AMERICAN
SCHOLAR

**3** Article Title

# Leaving Race Behind

*Our growing Hispanic population creates a golden opportunity*

AMITAI ETZIONI ◀ **1** Author

Some years ago the United States government asked me what my race was. I was reluctant to respond because my 50 years of practicing sociology—and some powerful personal experiences—have underscored for me what we all know to one degree or another, that racial divisions bedevil America, just as they do many other societies across the world. Not wanting to encourage these divisions, I refused to check off one of the specific racial options on the U.S. Census form and instead marked a box labeled "Other." I later found out that the federal government did not accept such an attempt to de-emphasize race, by me or by some 6.75 million other Americans who tried it. Instead the government assigned me to a racial category, one it chose for me. Learning this made me conjure up what I admit is a far-fetched association. I was in this place once before. When I was a Jewish child in Nazi Germany in the early 1930s, many Jews who saw themselves as good Germans wanted to "pass" as Aryans. But the Nazi regime would have none of it. Never mind, they told these Jews, *we determine* who is Jewish and who is not. A similar practice prevailed in the Old South, where if you had one drop of African blood you were a Negro, disregarding all other facts and considerations, including how you saw yourself.

You might suppose that in the years since my little Census-form protest

◥ Amitai Etzioni is University Professor at George Washington University and the author of *The Monochrome Society*.

20

**6** Page Numbers

Reprinted from *The American Scholar*, Volume 75, No. 2, Spring 2006

Citing sources without models in APA style

You may need to cite a source for which you cannot find a model in APA style. If so, collect as much information as you can find about the creator, title, sponsor, date, and so on, with the goal of helping readers find the source for themselves. Then look at the models in this chapter to see which one most closely matches the type of source you are using.

In an academic project, before citing an electronic source for which you have no model, ask your instructor's advice.

**22. Article from an online periodical**   Give the author, date, title, and publication information as you would for a print document. Include both the volume and issue numbers for all journal articles. If the article has a digital object identifier (DOI), include it. If there is no DOI, include the URL for the article instead.

> Bruns, A. (2017). Consequences of partner incarceration for women's employment. *Journal of Marriage and Family, 79*(5), 1331–1352. https://doi.org/10.1111/jomf.12412

> Srinivasan, D. (2019, June 4). How digital advertising markets really work. *The American Prospect.* https://prospect.org/article/how-digital-advertisingmarkets-really-work

**23. Article from a database**   For an article that is available in print but that you access in an online database, provide the author(s), date, title of the work, the title of the periodical, and volume/issue information. Give page numbers for the print version. Then give the DOI. If there is no DOI, do not include a URL. The source map on pp. 308–9 shows where to find information for a typical article from a database.

> Hazleden, R. (2003). Love yourself: The relationship of the self with itself in popular self-help texts. *Journal of Sociology, 39*(4), 413–428. https://doi.org/10.1177/0004869003394006

**24. Abstract for an online article**   Include a label.

> Gudjonsson, G. H., & Young, S. (2010). Does confabulation in memory predict suggestibility beyond IQ and memory? [Abstract]. *Personality & Individual Differences, 49*(1), 65–67. https://doi.org/10.1016/j.paid.2010.03.014

**25. Comment on an online article**   Give the writer's real name (if known) or screen name. Use up to the first twenty words of the comment in the title position. Add the label "Comment on the article" and then the title of the article in quotation marks. Provide a URL to the comment (if available) or to the article.

> lollyl2. (2019, September 25). My husband works in IT in a major city down South. He is a permanent employee now, but for years [Comment on the article "The Google workers who voted to unionize in Pittsburgh are part of tech's huge contractor workforce"]. *Slate*. https://fyre.it/0RT8HmeL.4

**26. Report or document from a website**   Include all of the following information that you can find: the author, the publication date or "n.d." if no date is given, the title of the work, the name of the website if different from the author, and the URL. The source map on pp. 310–11 shows where to find information for a typical report or document from a website.

> Tahseen, M., Ahmed, S., & Ahmed, S. (2018). *Bullying of Muslim youth: A review of research and recommendations*. The Family and Youth Institute. http://www.thefyi.org/wp-content/uploads/2018/10/FYI-Bullying-Report.pdf

**27. Online book**   Give the original print publication date, if different.

> Russell, B. (2008). *The analysis of mind*. Project Gutenberg. http://www.gutenberg.org/files/2529/2529-h/2529-h.htm (Original work published 1921)

**28. Email or private message**   Do not include entries for email messages or any postings that are private and cannot be retrieved by readers. Instead, cite these sources in your text as forms of personal communication (see item 11 in 19c).

**29. Posting on public social media**   List an online posting in the references list only if it is retrievable by readers. Provide the author's name, if given, followed by the screen name in brackets. If only the screen name is known, provide it without brackets. Include the date of posting and up to the first twenty words of the post. List any attachments, such as images, videos, or links, and include a descriptive label, such as "[Tweet]" or "[Status update]," in separate brackets. Provide the website or app name and the URL for the post.

> National Science Foundation [@NSF]. (2019, October 13). *Understanding how forest structure drives carbon sequestration is important for ecologists, climate modelers and forest managers, who are working on* [Thumbnail with link attached] [Tweet]. Twitter. https://twitter.com/NSF/status/1183388649263652864

## Articles from Databases

1. **Author.** Include the author's name as you would for a print source. List all authors' last names first, and use initials for first and middle names. For more about citing authors, see models 1–5.

2. **Publication date.** Enclose the date in parentheses. For journals, use only the year. For magazines and newspapers, use the year, a comma, the month, and the day if given.

3. **Article title.** Capitalize only the first word of the article title and the subtitle and any proper nouns or proper adjectives.

4. **Periodical title.** Italicize the periodical title.

5. **Volume and issue numbers.** For journals and magazines, give the volume number (italicized) and the issue number (in parentheses).

6. **Page numbers.** Give inclusive page numbers.

7. **Retrieval information.** If the article has a DOI (digital object identifier), include it after the publication information; do not include the name of the database. If there is no DOI, do not include a URL. Do not add a period after the DOI.

**A citation for the article shown on the next page would look like this:**

Knobloch-Westerwick, S., & Crane, J. (2012). A losing battle: Effects of

prolonged exposure to thin-ideal images on dieting and body satisfaction.

*Communication Research, 39*(1), 79–102. https://doi.org/10.1177/

0093650211400596

**3** Article Title

**4** Periodical Title

**6** Page Numbers

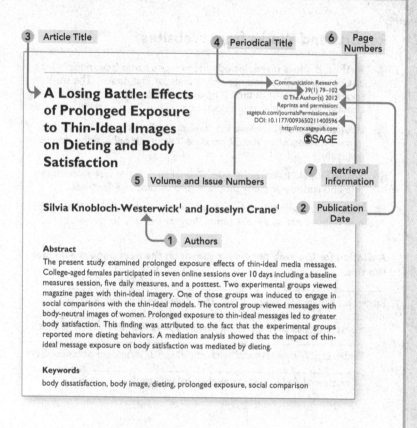

Communication Research
39(1) 79–102
© The Author(s) 2012
Reprints and permission:
sagepub.com/journalsPermissions.nav
DOI: 10.1177/0093650211400596
http://crx.sagepub.com
⑤SAGE

# A Losing Battle: Effects of Prolonged Exposure to Thin-Ideal Images on Dieting and Body Satisfaction

**5** Volume and Issue Numbers

**7** Retrieval Information

Silvia Knobloch-Westerwick[1] and Josselyn Crane[1]

**2** Publication Date

**1** Authors

**Abstract**

The present study examined prolonged exposure effects of thin-ideal media messages. College-aged females participated in seven online sessions over 10 days including a baseline measures session, five daily measures, and a posttest. Two experimental groups viewed magazine pages with thin-ideal imagery. One of those groups was induced to engage in social comparisons with the thin-ideal models. The control group viewed messages with body-neutral images of women. Prolonged exposure to thin-ideal messages led to greater body satisfaction. This finding was attributed to the fact that the experimental groups reported more dieting behaviors. A mediation analysis showed that the impact of thin-ideal message exposure on body satisfaction was mediated by dieting.

**Keywords**

body dissatisfaction, body image, dieting, prolonged exposure, social comparison

# Reports and Works from Websites

**1** **Author.** If one is given, include the author's name (see models 1–5). List last names first, and use only initials for first names. The site's sponsor may be the author. If no author is identified, begin the citation with the title of the document.

**2** **Publication date.** Enclose the date of publication or latest update in parentheses. Use "n.d." ("no date") when no publication date is available.

**3** **Title of work.** Italicize the title. Capitalize only the first word of the title and subtitle and any proper nouns or proper adjectives.

**4** **Retrieval information.** Include the website name unless the author and website name are the same. Provide the URL to the work.

**A citation for the web document shown on the next page would look like this:**

Parker, K., & Wang, W. (2013, March 14). *Modern parenthood: Roles of moms and dads converge as they balance work and family.* Pew Research Center. http://www.pewsocialtrends.org/2013/03/14/modern-parenthoodroles-of-moms-and-dads-converge-as-they-balance-work-and-family/

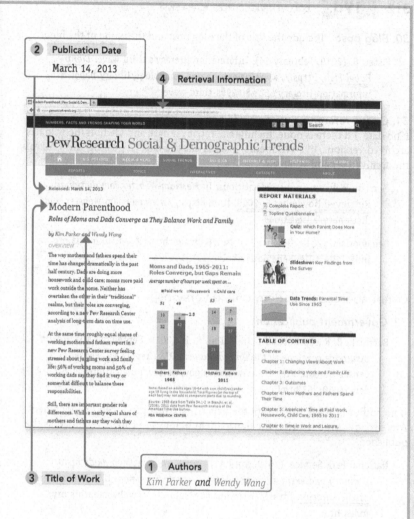

**30.** *Blog post*    Include the title of the blog post and the name of the blog.

> Fister, B. (2019, February 14). Information literacy's third wave. *Library Babel Fish*. https://www.insidehighered.com/blogs/library-babel-fish/ information-literacy%E2%80%99s-third-wave

**31.** *Online reference work or wiki entry*    Use the date of posting, or "n.d." ("no date") if there is none. Include the retrieval date and URL. If the wiki has archived versions, like Wikipedia, instead use the date of posting and URL of the archived version you read.

> Merriam-Webster. (n.d.). Adscititious. In *Merriam-Webster.com dictionary*. Retrieved November 5, 2019, from https://www.merriam-webster.com/ dictionary/adscititious

> Behaviorism. (2019, October 11). In *Wikipedia*. https://en.wikipedia.org/w/ index.php?title=Behaviorism&oldid=915544724

## Other sources (including online versions)

**32.** *Government publication*

> Berchick, E. R., Barnett, J. C., & Upton, R. D. (2019, September 10). *Health insurance coverage in the United States: 2018* (Report No. P60-267). U.S. Census Bureau. https://www.census.gov/library/publications/2019/ demo/p60-267.html

If no author is listed, begin with the department that produced the document. Any broader organization the department belongs to can be included as the publisher.

> National Park Service. (2019, April 11). *Travel where women made history: Ordinary and extraordinary places of American women*. U.S. Department of the Interior. https://www.nps.gov/subjects/travelwomenshistory/ index.htm

**33.** *Data set or graphic representation of data (chart, graph)*

> Reid, L. (2019). *Smarter homes: Experiences of living in low carbon homes 2013–2018* [Data set]. UK Data Service. https://doi.org/10.5255/ UKDA-SN-853485

> Centers for Disease Control and Prevention. (2020, May 9). *New cases by day* [Chart]. U.S. Department of Health & Human Services. https://www.cdc.gov/ coronavirus/2019-ncov/cases-updates/cases-in-us.html

*34. Dissertation*   If you retrieved the dissertation from a database, include the <u>granting university</u> in brackets after the title. Do not include a URL.

> Bacaksizlar, N. G. (2019). *Understanding social movements through simulations of anger contagion in social media* (Publication No. 13805848) [Doctoral dissertation, <u>University of North Carolina at Charlotte</u>]. ProQuest Dissertations & Theses.

If you retrieve a dissertation from a website, provide the URL.

> Degli-Esposti, M. (2019). *Child maltreatment and antisocial behaviour in the United Kingdom: Changing risks over time* [Doctoral dissertation, University of Oxford]. Oxford University Research Archive. https://ora.ox.ac.uk/objects/uuid:6d5a8e55-bd19-41a1-8ef5-ef485642af89

*35. Technical or research report*   Give the <u>report number</u>, if available, in parentheses after the title.

> McCool, R., Fikes, R., & McGuinness, D. (2003). *Semantic web tools for enhanced authoring* (<u>Report No. KSL-03-07</u>). Knowledge Systems, AI Laboratory. http://www.ksl.stanford.edu/KSL_Abstracts/KSL-03-07.html

*36. Conference proceedings*

> Robertson, S. P., Vatrapu, R. K., & Medina, R. (2009). YouTube and Facebook: Online video "friends" social networking. In *Conference proceedings: YouTube and the 2008 election cycle* (pp. 159–176). ScholarWorks@UMass Amherst. http://scholarworks.umass.edu/jitpc2009

*37. Paper presented at a meeting or symposium, unpublished*   Include the <u>dates of the entire meeting</u> or symposium, even if the paper presentation occurred on a specific day.

> Vasylets, O. (<u>2019, April 10–13</u>). *Memory accuracy in bilinguals depends on the valence of the emotional event* [Paper presentation]. XIV International Symposium of Psycholinguistics, Tarragona, Spain. https://psico.fcep.urv.cat/projectes/gip/files/isp2019.pdf

*38. Poster session*

> Wood, M. (2019, January 3–6). *The effects of an adult development course on students' perceptions of aging* [Poster session]. Forty-First Annual National Institute on the Teaching of Psychology, St. Pete Beach, FL, United States. https://nitop.org/resources/Documents/2019%20Poster%20Session%20II.pdf

*39. Presentation slides*

> Mader, S. (2007, March 27). *The Zen aesthetic* [Presentation slides].
>    SlideShare. http://www.slideshare.net/slmader/the-zen-aesthetic

*40. Film*    Begin with the director and include the <u>production company</u> after the title.

> Peele, J. (Director). (2017). *Get out* [Film]. <u>Universal Pictures</u>.

Separate multiple production companies with semicolons. If the film is a <u>special version</u>, like an extended cut, include that information in brackets after the title. Always include the <u>original release year</u>.

> Hitchcock, A. (Director). (<u>1959</u>). *The essentials collection: North by northwest*
>    [Film; <u>five-disc special ed. on DVD</u>]. Metro-Goldwyn-Mayer; Universal
>    Pictures Home Entertainment.

*41. Online video*    Think of the author of an online video or audio file as the person or organization that posted it. For a TED Talk, for example, the presenter is the author if the video was accessed on the TED website. However, if the TED Talk was accessed on YouTube, then TED becomes the author because the TED organization posted the video.

> Wray, B. (2019, May). *How climate change affects your mental health* [Video].
>    TED Conferences. https://www.ted.com/talks/britt_wray_how_climate_
>    change_affects_your_mental_health

> TED. (2019, September 20). *Britt Wray: How climate change affects
>    your mental health* [Video]. YouTube. https://www.youtube.com/
>    watch?v=IlDkCEvsYw

When deciding whether to italicize the title of the video or audio file, consider whether it is part of a series (regular font) or a stand-alone item (italics).

> BBC. (2018, November 19). Why do bad managers flourish? [Audio]. In
>    *Business Matters*. https://www.bbc.co.uk/programmes/p06s8752

> The New York Times. (2018, January 9). *Taking a knee and taking
>    down a monument* [Video]. YouTube. https://www.youtube.com/
>    watch?v=qY34DQCdUvQ

*42. Television program, single episode*

> Imperioli, M. (Writer), & Buscemi, S. (Director). (2002, October 20). Everybody
>    hurts (Season 4, Episode 6) [TV series episode]. In D. Chase (Executive
>    Producer), *The Sopranos*. Chase Films; Brad Grey Television; HBO.

43. *Television series*

Waller-Bridge, P., Williams, H., & Williams, J. (Executive Producers). (2016–2019). *Fleabag* [TV series]. Two Brothers Pictures; BBC.

44. *Podcast episode*

West, S. (Host). (2018, July 27). Logical positivism (No. 120) [Audio podcast episode]. In *Philosophize this!* https://philosophizethis.org/logical-positivists/

45. *Podcast series*

Abumrad, J., & Krulwich, R. (Hosts). (2002–present). *Radiolab* [Audio podcast]. WNYC Studios. https://www.wnycstudios.org/podcasts/radiolab/podcasts

46. *Recording*

Carlile, B. (2018). The mother [Song]. On *By the way, I forgive you*. Low Country Sound; Elektra.

47. *Photograph*

McHardy, Amanda. (2018). *Art of the self portrait* [Photograph]. https://amandamchardyphotos.wordpress.com/portfolio/#jp-carousel-148

## 19e  A student research essay, APA style

STUDENT WRITER
Martha Bell

On the following pages is a paper by Martha Bell that conforms to the APA guidelines described in this chapter.

Page number appears flush right on first line of every page

Title (boldface), writer's name, department and school, course number and title, professor, and date centered and double-spaced

1

**The Mystery of Post-Lyme Disease Syndrome**

Martha Bell

Department of Language and Literature,

Eastern Mennonite University

WRIT 130C: College Writing

Professor Eads

October 29, 2014

Annotations indicate effective choices or APA-style formatting.

2

# The Mystery of Post-Lyme Disease Syndrome

The Centers for Disease Control and Prevention (CDC) estimates a total of 300,000 cases of Lyme disease annually. Many medical professionals believe Lyme disease can be cured in a matter of weeks with a simple antibiotic treatment. In some cases, however, patients develop post-Lyme disease syndrome, sometimes called "chronic Lyme disease," exhibiting persistent symptoms of Lyme after initial treatment is completed. The scientific community, divided over the causes of post-Lyme disease syndrome, cannot agree on the best treatment for the syndrome. Although Lyme disease is preventable, people are still vulnerable to infection; consequently, there is a need for more research and collaboration with a focus on developing the technology to perform replicable studies, which may subsequently lead to an effective treatment algorithm for post-Lyme disease syndrome.

## Prevention

Ixodes ticks, also known as blacklegged and deer ticks, are infected with the bacterium *Borrelia burgdorferi,* responsible for Lyme disease (Hawker et al., 2012). Since being bitten by an infected tick is the only known way of contracting Lyme disease, evading Ixodes ticks is an effective measure. According to M'ikanatha et al. (2013), "Lyme disease is acquired peridomestically and the risk is highest in residential settings abutting areas with forests, meadows, and high prevalence of deer" (p. 168). While adult ticks are more active in the cooler months, developing Ixodes ticks, called nymphs, feed the most during the spring and summer months (Centers for Disease Control and Prevention [CDC], 2014d). Therefore, avoiding areas such as meadows and grasslands in the spring and summer seasons aids in preventing Lyme disease.

Using permethrin repellent on clothes and 20 to 30 percent DEET insect repellent on the skin also keeps ticks away (Brody, 2013). Other measures include wearing light-colored clothing to make ticks

Full title boldface and centered

Introduction provides background information

Boldface centered headings help organize review

Reference to work with more than two authors uses "et al."

First reference to organization gives abbreviation for later references

3

more visible, wearing long sleeves and long pants, tucking shirts into pants and pants into socks, and taping closed open areas of clothing when spending time outdoors in areas where ticks are prevalent (Hawker et al., 2012). Additionally, individuals should keep yards and houses clean to avert mammals, such as deer and rodents, that carry Ixodes ticks, and should check pets for ticks.

Though all of these measures greatly reduce the chance of receiving a tick bite, they are not foolproof. The bacterium *B. burgdorferi* takes approximately 36 to 48 hours to become infectious after the tick has bitten an individual (Hawker et al., 2012). A bull's-eye rash called erythema migrans is the only unique symptom of Lyme disease. It appears 3 to 32 days after infection (Hawker et al., 2012). According to one study, only 70 to 80 percent of Lyme disease victims develop erythema migrans; therefore, other symptoms must be assessed (Steere & Sikand, 2003, p. 2472). Other characteristics of Lyme disease include fevers, headaches, stiff neck, swollen lymph nodes, body aches, fatigue, facial palsy, polyarthritis, aseptic meningitis, peripheral root lesions, radiculopathy, and myocarditis (CDC, 2014c; Hawker et al., 2012).

On average, it takes a few weeks for infected individuals to produce antibodies against *B. burgdorferi* (CDC, 2014a). Consequently, most cases of Lyme disease have better outcomes and recovery rates when antibiotics are administered quickly (CDC, 2014e). Administered in the beginning stages of Lyme disease, antibiotics help speed recovery and prevent more serious symptoms, such as heart and nervous system problems, from developing (Lantos, 2011, Introduction section).

Erythema migrans is not always present, and other symptoms of Lyme disease are similar to those of other illnesses. Therefore, Lyme disease may be misdiagnosed and untreated. Stricker (2007) explained that "in the absence of typical features of Lyme disease, patients may go on to develop a syndrome with multiple nonspecific

*Transition sentence moves readers from one idea to the next*

*Multiple citations in parentheses listed alphabetically and separated by semicolon*

4

symptoms that affect various organ systems, including the joints, muscles, nerves, brain, and heart" (p. 149). Conversely, even when patients receive proper antibiotic treatment for two to four weeks, they can continue to experience symptoms.

Parenthetical citation for quotation includes page number

### Post-Lyme Disease Syndrome

The majority of Lyme disease patients are cured after multiple weeks of antibiotics; however, 10 to 15 percent of patients acquire relapsing nonspecific symptoms such as fatigue, arthritis, and short-term memory problems that can persist for months or even years (Brody, 2013). When there is no other possible origin of the nonspecific symptoms, and the individual has had proper treatment for Lyme disease, the patient is classified as having post-Lyme disease syndrome (Lantos, 2011). Marques (2008) explained, "The appearance of post-Lyme disease symptoms seems to correlate with disseminated diseases, a greater severity of illness at presentation, and delayed antibiotic therapy, but not with the duration of the initial antibiotic therapy" (p. 343). The medical community is unsure of how to treat the nonspecific symptoms or what causes them (Lantos, 2011, "A Clinical Approach" section).

### Possible Sources of Post-Lyme Disease Syndrome

Scientists are unable to identify the exact source of post-Lyme disease syndrome for several reasons. Identifying patients is difficult because of the general nature of the symptoms. Several surveys demonstrate that a relatively high percentage of the overall population reports nonspecific symptoms, such as fatigue, chronic pain, or cognitive dysfunction after a tick bite (Lantos, 2011, Post-Lyme Disease Syndromes section). In addition, researchers struggle to find participants for their studies (Marques, 2008, p. 342). Study participants must have previous documentation of contracting Lyme disease, which significantly diminishes the testing population (Lantos, 2011).

Scientists and physicians suspect the source of post-Lyme disease syndrome to be multifactorial. Plausible causes of reoccurring

5

nonspecific symptoms include "persistent infection of *B. burgdorferi*, other tick-borne infections, part of the expected resolution of symptoms after treatment, postinfective fatigue syndrome, autoimmune mechanisms, and intercurrent conditions" (Marques, 2008, p. 343). Nevertheless, only a few ideas have been thoroughly explored thus far by the scientific community. The majority of scientists believe remaining damage to tissue and the immune system from the infection causes post-Lyme disease syndrome; however, some believe persistent infection of the bacteria is the source (CDC, 2014b).

Despite complications, a majority of the medical community considers persistent symptoms to be a result of residual damage to the tissues and the immune system that occurred during the infection. These "autoimmune" reactions, which the body uses against foreign elements, occur in infections similar to Lyme disease such as campylobacter, chlamydia, and strep throat (CDC, 2014b). Patients report their nonspecific symptoms improving over time after the typical antibiotic treatment (Marques, 2008, p. 342). Physicians who followed their patients with post-Lyme disease syndrome for extended times also see nonspecific symptoms resolve without further antibiotic treatment (Marques, 2008, p. 347). Consequently, post-Lyme disease syndrome may be a natural evolution of the body healing after an intense infection.

A smaller portion of the medical community considers persistent infection of the microorganism *B. burgdorferi* as the cause of post-Lyme disease syndrome. Recently published studies performed on animals show signs of ongoing infection of the bacterium. One scientific study infected mice with *B. burgdorferi* and gave them intense treatment of antibiotics that should have wiped out the bacterium (Bockenstedt et al., 2012). Bockenstedt et al. (2012) observed the mice over a period of time and found "that infectious spirochetes are rapidly eliminated after institution of antibiotics, but inflammatory *B. burgdorferi* antigens persist adjacent

6

to cartilage and in the enthuses" (p. 2652). This is one of the first
studies to show continuous effects of the harmful microorganism
in post-Lyme disease syndrome (Embers et al., 2012, Discussion
section). Another scientific study was conducted on nonhuman
primates, rhesus macaques. Once again the scientists infected
the animals with *B. burgdorferi* and then four to six months later
administered an antibiotic treatment to half of the monkeys (Embers
et al., 2012). Their results also confirmed that *B. burgdorferi* could
withstand antibiotic treatment in rhesus macaques and proceed to
cause post-Lyme disease syndrome (Embers et al., 2012, Discussion
section). Nonetheless, these results showing perpetual infection as
the cause of post-Lyme disease syndrome have yet to be replicated in
humans.

    In contrast, many studies over the years contradict the theory of
ongoing infection, though these studies have not been confirmed true
in humans. Lantos (2011) clarified that "no adequately controlled,
hypothesis-driven study using a repeatable method has demonstrated
that viable *B. burgdorferi* is found in patients with persistent post-
Lyme symptoms any more frequently than in those with favorable
outcomes" (Biological Plausibility section). Most scientific studies
trying to prove persistent infection of *B. burgdorferi* have not been
replicated because their procedures and techniques are at fault. The
problem derives from the technology that detects the microorganism
(Lantos, 2011, Biological Plausibility section).

    PCR and *B. burgdorferi* culture are commonly used to find evidence
of the bacteria in the body; however, both have "low sensitivity in most
body fluids from patients with Lyme disease" (Marques, 2008, p. 353).
Even though other methods, such as finding antibodies in immune
complexes, changes in C6 antibody levels, and PCR in urine samples,
have been tried, none prove helpful (Marques, 2008, p. 353). Therefore,
the persistent infection of *B. burgdorferi* has not yet successfully been
proven as the cause of post-Lyme disease syndrome.

Presents
opposing
studies and
points of view

7

### Post-Lyme Disease Syndrome Treatment

Since the cause of post-Lyme disease syndrome is controversial, treatment for the infection varies from patient to patient and physician to physician. Treatment is still in the experimental stages, meaning no set treatment algorithm currently exists. Numerous patients rely on long-term antibiotic medication, despite the overwhelming defying scientific evidence against this treatment (CDC, 2014b). The research studies that focus on prolonged antibiotic treatment observe no dramatic difference in benefits or recoveries of those who had the treatment and those who did not (Marques, 2008, p. 353). On the contrary, many long-term antibiotic research studies found that post-Lyme disease syndrome patients develop harmful side effects. These adverse health effects include "catheter-associated venous thromboembolism, catheter-associated septicemia, allergic reactions and ceftriaxone-induced gallbladder toxicity" (Lantos, 2011, "Extended Antibiotics" section). Therefore, most of the scientific community considers long-term antibiotic treatment for chronic Lyme disease a harmful, risky, and unbeneficial plan.

Most of the scientific community advises against the use of long-term antibiotics because of potential adverse effects. Nevertheless, a small minority of physicians have observed improvements with long-term antibiotics. Because numerous studies show a lack of benefit to long-term antibiotics, these hopeful patients may be experiencing a placebo effect, which occurs when patients improve because they believe they are receiving an effective treatment (Marques, 2008, p. 356).

### Solving the Mystery

Individuals can take various simple preventive measures to avoid contracting Lyme disease. If the infection is contracted, those who seek prompt treatment increase the chance of full recovery and decrease the chance of developing post-Lyme disease syndrome. However, these steps do not guarantee complete avoidance of post-

*Shortened section heading in quotation marks*

8

Lyme disease syndrome. Finding the source of post-Lyme disease
syndrome will lead to a specific treatment plan that effectively heals
patients. Many scientists deem the source of post-Lyme disease syndrome
to be a natural autoimmune reaction; conversely, a few other scientists
consider persistent infection as the cause. Both theories, however, need
better technology to prove their accuracy. Since scientists disagree about
the source of post-Lyme disease syndrome, a variety of experimental
treatments have arisen. Replicable studies are needed so that an
effective treatment for post-Lyme disease syndrome can be found.

Conclusion indicates need for further research

9

**References**

Bockenstedt, L., Gonzalez, D., Haberman, A., & Belperron, A. (2012). Spirochete antigens persist near cartilage after murine Lyme borreliosis therapy. *The Journal of Clinical Investigation, 122*(7), 2652–2660. https://doi.org/10.1172/JCI58813

Brody, J. (2013, July 8). When Lyme disease lasts and lasts. *The New York Times.* https://well.blogs.nytimes.com/2013/07/08/when-lyme-disease-lasts-and-lasts

Centers for Disease Control and Prevention. (2014a). *Diagnosis and testing.* https://www.cdc.gov/lyme/diagnosistesting/index.html

Centers for Disease Control and Prevention. (2014b). *Post-treatment Lyme disease syndrome.* https://www.cdc.gov/lyme/postlds/index.html

Centers for Disease Control and Prevention. (2014c). *Signs and symptoms of untreated Lyme disease.* https://www.cdc.gov/lyme/signs_symptoms/index.html

Centers for Disease Control and Prevention. (2014d). *Transmission.* https://www.cdc.gov/lyme/transmission/index.html

Centers for Disease Control and Prevention. (2014e). *Treatment.* https://www.cdc.gov/lyme/treatment/index.html

Embers, M. E., Barthold, S. W., Borda, J. T., Bowers, L., Doyle, L., Hodzic, E., Jacobs, M. B., Hasenkampf, N. R., Martin, D. S., Narasimhan, S., Phillippi-Falkenstein, K. M., Purcell, J. E., Ratterree, M. S., & Philipp, M. T. (2012). Persistence of *Borrelia burgdorferi* in rhesus macaques following antibiotic treatment of disseminated infection. *PLoS ONE, 7*(1). https://doi.org/10.1371/journal.pone.0029914

Hawker, J., Begg, N., Blair, L., Reintjes, R., Weinberg, J., & Ekdahl, K. (2012). *Communicable disease control and health protection handbook* (3rd ed.). John Wiley & Sons.

Lantos, P. (2011). Chronic Lyme disease: The controversies and the science. *Expert Review of Anti-Infective Therapy, 9*(7), 787–797. https://doi.org/10.1586/eri.11.63

References begin on a new page; heading is centered and boldface

Article from an online newspaper

Two or more works by the same author in the same year arranged alphabetically by title; letters added after year

All authors up to twenty listed

Print book

Journal article with DOI

10

Marques, A. (2008). Chronic Lyme disease: A review. *Infectious Disease Clinics of North America, 22*(2), 341–360. https://doi.org/10.1016/j.idc.2007.12.011

M'ikanatha, N. M., Lynfield, R., Van Beneden, C. A., & de Valk, H. (2013). *Infectious disease surveillance* (2nd ed.). John Wiley & Sons.

Steere, A., & Sikand, V. (2003). The presenting manifestations of Lyme disease and the outcomes of treatment [Letter to the editor]. *The New England Journal of Medicine, 348*(24), 2472–2474. https://doi.org/10.1056/NEJM200306123482423

Stricker, R. (2007). Counterpoint: Long-term antibiotic therapy improves persistent symptoms associated with Lyme disease. *Clinical Infectious Diseases, 45*(2), 147–157. https://doi.org/10.1086/518853

Letter to the editor

# CHAPTER 20

# *Chicago* Style

The style guide of the University of Chicago Press has long been used in history as well as in other areas of the arts and humanities. The Seventeenth Edition of *The Chicago Manual of Style* (2017) provides a complete guide to *Chicago* style, including two systems for citing sources. This chapter presents the notes and bibliography system. For easy reference, examples of notes and bibliographic entries are shown together in 20c.

## 20a Understanding the basics

When you are assigned to use *Chicago* style for a research project, it is helpful to think through your responsibilities as an academic writer: What do your readers need from you? What are the parts of a *Chicago*-style citation? And how do notes in the text connect to entries in the bibliography?

### Thinking about what readers need from you

Why does academic work call for very careful citation practices when writing for the general public may not? The answer is that readers of academic work expect source citations for several reasons:

- Source citations demonstrate that you've done your homework on your topic and that you are a part of the rich conversation surrounding it.
- Source citations show that you understand the need to give credit when you use someone else's intellectual property. (See Chapter 15 for more details.)
- Source citations give explicit directions to guide readers who want to look for themselves at the works you're using.

Guidelines from *The Chicago Manual of Style* will tell you exactly what information to include in your citation and how to format that information.

### Types of sources

Refer to the List of Examples on page 327 to locate guidelines for citing sources in *Chicago* style. You will need to be careful to tell your readers whether you read a print version or a digital version of a source. Digital magazine and newspaper

# List of Examples

## Notes and bibliographic entries in *Chicago* style (20c)

📖 Print and digital books

📄 Print and digital periodicals

💻 Online sources

➕ Other sources

A List of Examples for **MLA style** is on page 238.

A List of Examples for **APA style** is on page 288.

A List of Examples for **CSE style** is on page 351.

articles may include updates or corrections that the print version lacks; digital books may not number pages or screens the same way the print book does. If you are citing a source with media elements — such as a film, song, or artwork — consult the "other sources" section of the examples. And if you can't find a model exactly like the source you've selected, see the box in 20c.

### Articles from web and database sources

You need a subscription to look through most databases, so individual researchers almost always gain access to articles in databases through a school or public library that pays to subscribe. The easiest way to tell whether a source comes from a database, then, is that its information is *not* generally available free to anyone with an Internet connection. Many databases are digital collections of articles that originally appeared in edited print periodicals, ensuring that an authority has vouched for the accuracy of the information. Such sources may have more credibility than free material available on the web.

## Planning and connecting your citations

Citations in *Chicago* style will appear in three places in your text — a note number in the text marks the material from the source, a footnote or an endnote includes information to identify the source (or information about supplemental material), and the bibliography provides the full citation.

Chicago is a city for the working man. Nowhere is this more evident than in its architecture. David Garrard Lowe, author of *Lost Chicago*, notes that early Chicagoans "sought reality, not fantasy, and the reality of America as seen from the heartland did not include the pavilion of princes or the castles of kings."² The inclination toward unadorned, sturdy buildings began in the late nineteenth century.

Bibliography

Bluestone, Daniel. *Constructing Chicago*. New Haven: Yale
*the City*. Chicago:

Notes

1. Tracie Rozhon, "Chicago Girds for Big Battle over Its Skyline," *New York Times*, November 12, 2000, Academic Search Premier.

*ndfill*. Chicago:
2000.

2. David Garrard Lowe, *Lost Chicago* (New York: Watson-Guptill Publications, 2000), 123.

*cago Tribune*, March

Lowe, David Garrard. *Lost Chicago*. New York: Watson-Guptill Publications, 2000.

## 20b Following *Chicago* format

The *Chicago Manual of Style* recommends the following format for the manuscript of a research paper. However, check with your instructor before preparing your final draft.

For a sample student essay in *Chicago* style, see 20d.

- **Title page.** About halfway down the title page, center the full title of your project and your name. Unless otherwise instructed, at the bottom of the page also list the course name, the instructor's name, and the date submitted. Do not type a number on this page.

- **Margins and spacing.** Leave one-inch margins at the top, bottom, and sides of your pages. Double-space the entire text, including block quotations and between entries in the notes and bibliography.

- **Page numbers.** Number all pages (except the title page) in the upper-right corner. Also use a short title or your name before page numbers. Check to see if your instructor has a preference on whether to count the title page as part of the text (if so, the first text page will be page 2) or as part of the front matter (if so, the first text page will be page 1).

- **Long quotations.** For a long quotation, indent one-half inch (or five spaces) from the left margin and do not use quotation marks. *Chicago* defines a long quotation as one hundred words or eight lines, though you may set off shorter quotes for emphasis (60a).

- **Headings.** *Chicago* style allows, but does not require, headings. Many students and instructors find them helpful.

- **Visuals.** Visuals (photographs, drawings, charts, graphs, and tables) should be placed as near as possible to the relevant text. (See 15e for guidelines on incorporating visuals into your text.) Tables should be labeled *Table*, numbered, and captioned. All other visuals should be labeled *Figure* (abbreviated *Fig.*), numbered, and captioned. Remember to refer to each visual in your text, pointing out how it contributes to the point(s) you are making.

### Notes

Notes can be footnotes (each one appearing at the bottom of the page on which its citation appears) or endnotes (in a list on a separate page at the end of the text). (Check your instructor's preference.) Indent the first line of each note one-half inch and begin with a number, a period, and one space before the first word. All remaining lines of the entry are flush with the left margin. Single-space footnotes and endnotes, with a double space between each entry.

Use underlined superscript numbers ([1]) to mark citations in the text. Place the superscript number for each note just after the relevant quotation, sentence, clause, or phrase. Type the number after any punctuation mark except the dash, and do not leave a space before the superscript. Number citations sequentially throughout the text. When you use signal phrases to introduce source material, note that *Chicago* style requires you to use the present tense (*citing Bebout's studies, Meier argues . . .*).

**IN THE TEXT**

Thompson points out that African American and Puerto Rican prisoners at Attica were more likely than white prisoners to have their mail censored and family visits restricted.[19]

**IN THE FIRST NOTE REFERRING TO THE SOURCE**

   19. Heather Ann Thompson, *Blood in the Water: The Attica Prison Uprising of 1971 and Its Legacy* (New York: Pantheon Books, 2016), 13.

After giving complete information the first time you cite a work, shorten additional references to that work: list only the author's last name, a shortened version of the title, and the page number. If the second reference to the work immediately follows the first reference, list only the author's name and the page number.

**IN FIRST AND SUBSEQUENT NOTES**

   19. Heather Ann Thompson, *Blood in the Water: The Attica Prison Uprising of 1971 and Its Legacy* (New York: Pantheon Books, 2016), 13.

   20. Thompson, 82.

   21. Julia Sweig, *Inside the Cuban Revolution* (Cambridge, MA: Harvard University Press, 2002), 21.

   22. Thompson, *Blood in the Water,* 304.

## Bibliography

Begin the list of sources on a separate page after the main text and any endnotes. Continue numbering the pages consecutively. Center the title *Bibliography* (without underlining, italics, or quotation marks) one inch below the top of the page. Double-space, and then begin each entry at the left margin. Indent the second and subsequent lines of each entry one-half inch, or five spaces.

List sources alphabetically by authors' last names or by the first major word in the title if the author is unknown. See 20d for an example of a *Chicago*-style bibliography.

In the bibliographic entry, include the same information as in the first note for that source; in the case of books and other long works, you'll omit the page reference. Give the first author's last name first, followed by a comma and the first name; separate the main elements of the entry with periods rather than commas; and do not enclose the publication information for books in parentheses.

**IN THE BIBLIOGRAPHY**

Thompson, Heather Ann. *Blood in the Water: The Attica Prison Uprising of 1971 and Its Legacy*. New York: Pantheon Books, 2016.

## 20c Preparing *Chicago* notes and bibliographic entries

The following examples demonstrate how to format both notes and bibliographic entries according to *Chicago* style. The note, which is numbered, appears first; the bibliographic entry, which is not numbered, appears below the note. We have used underlining in some examples only to draw your attention to important elements. Do not underline anything in your own citations.

### Print and digital books

The note for a book typically includes five elements: author's name, title and subtitle, city of publication and publisher, year, and page number(s) or electronic locator information for the information in the note. The bibliographic entry usually includes all these elements but the page number (and does include a URL or other locator if the book is digitally published), but it is styled differently: commas separate major elements of a note, but a bibliographic entry uses periods. The author's name is first name first in the note but last name first in the bibliography. For multiple authors, invert just the first author's name in the bibliography.

---

**QUICK HELP**

Citing sources without models in *Chicago* style

To cite a source for which you cannot find a model, collect as much information as you can find—about the creator, title, date of creation or update, and location of the source—with the goal of helping your readers find the source for themselves, if possible. Then look at the models in this chapter to see which one most closely matches the type of source you are using.

In an academic writing project, before citing an electronic source for which you have no model, also be sure to ask your instructor's advice.

---

*1. One author*

1. Nell Irvin Painter, *The History of White People* (New York: W. W. Norton, 2010), 119.

Painter, Nell Irvin. *The History of White People*. New York: W. W. Norton, 2010.

## 2. Multiple authors

2. Mark Littman and Fred Espenak, *Totality: The Great American Eclipses of 2017 and 2024* (New York: Oxford University Press, 2017), 35.

Littman, Mark, and Fred Espenak. *Totality: The Great American Eclipses of 2017 and 2024*. New York: Oxford University Press, 2017.

With four or more authors, you may give the first-listed author followed by *et al.* in the note. In the bibliography, list all the authors' names.

2. Stephen J. Blank et al., *Conflict, Culture, and History: Regional Dimensions* (Miami: University Press of the Pacific, 2002), 276.

Blank, Stephen J., Lawrence E. Grinter, Karl P. Magyar, Lewis B. Ware, and Bynum E. Weathers. *Conflict, Culture, and History: Regional Dimensions*. Miami: University Press of the Pacific, 2002.

## 3. Organization as author

3. World Intellectual Property Organization, *Intellectual Property Profile of the Least Developed Countries* (Geneva: World Intellectual Property Organization, 2002), 43.

World Intellectual Property Organization. *Intellectual Property Profile of the Least Developed Countries*. Geneva: World Intellectual Property Organization, 2002.

## 4. Unknown author

4. *Broad Stripes and Bright Stars* (Kansas City, MO: Andrews McMeel, 2002), 10.

*Broad Stripes and Bright Stars*. Kansas City, MO: Andrews McMeel, 2002.

## 5. Online book

5. Dorothy Richardson, *Long Day: The Story of a New York Working Girl, as Told by Herself* (New York: Century, 1906; UMDL Texts, 2010), 159, http://quod.lib.umich.edu/cgi/t/text/text-idx?c=moa;idno=AFS7156.0001.001.

Richardson, Dorothy. *Long Day: The Story of a New York Working Girl, as Told by Herself*. New York: Century, 1906. UMDL Texts, 2010. http://quod.lib.umich.edu/cgi/t/text/text-idx?c=moa;idno=AFS7156.0001.001.

## 6. Electronic book (e-book)

6. Atul Gawande, *Being Mortal: Medicine and What Matters in the End* (New York: Metropolitan, 2014), chap. 3, Nook.

Gawande, Atul. *Being Mortal: Medicine and What Matters in the End*. New York: Metropolitan, 2014. Nook.

### 7. Book with an editor

> 7. Leopold von Ranke, *The Theory and Practice of History*, ed. Georg G. Iggers (New York: Routledge, 2010), 135.

> von Ranke, Leopold. *The Theory and Practice of History*. Edited by Georg G. Iggers. New York: Routledge, 2010.

If an edited book has no author, put the editor's name first.

> 7. James H. Fetzer, ed., *The Great Zapruder Film Hoax: Deceit and Deception in the Death of JFK* (Chicago: Open Court, 2003), 56.

> Fetzer, James H., ed. *The Great Zapruder Film Hoax: Deceit and Deception in the Death of JFK*. Chicago: Open Court, 2003.

### 8. Selection in an anthology or chapter in a book with an editor

> 8. Denise Little, "Born in Blood," in *Alternate Gettysburgs*, ed. Brian Thomsen and Martin H. Greenberg (New York: Berkley Publishing Group, 2002), 245.

Give the inclusive page numbers of the selection or chapter in the bibliographic entry.

> Little, Denise. "Born in Blood." In *Alternate Gettysburgs*. Edited by Brian Thomsen and Martin H. Greenberg, 242–55. New York: Berkley Publishing Group, 2002.

### 9. Introduction, preface, foreword, or afterword

> 9. Ta-Nehisi Coates, foreword to *The Origin of Others*, by Toni Morrison (Cambridge, MA: Harvard University Press, 2017), xi.

Give the inclusive page numbers of the section cited in the bibliographic entry.

> Coates, Ta-Nehisi. Foreword to *The Origin of Others*, by Toni Morrison, vii–xvii. Cambridge, MA: Harvard University Press, 2017.

### 10. Translation

> 10. Suetonius, *The Twelve Caesars*, trans. Robert Graves (London: Penguin Classics, 1989), 202.

> Suetonius. *The Twelve Caesars*. Translated by Robert Graves. London: Penguin Classics, 1989.

### 11. Edition other than the first

11. Dee Brown, *Bury My Heart at Wounded Knee: An Indian History of the American West,* 4th ed. (New York: Owl Books, 2007), 12.

Brown, Dee. *Bury My Heart at Wounded Knee: An Indian History of the American West,* 4th ed. New York: Owl Books, 2007.

### 12. Multivolume work

12. John Watson, *Annals of Philadelphia and Pennsylvania in the Olden Time,* vol. 2 (Washington, DC: Ross & Perry, 2003), 514.

Watson, John. *Annals of Philadelphia and Pennsylvania in the Olden Time.* Vol. 2. Washington, DC: Ross & Perry, 2003.

### 13. Work with a title within the title   Use quotation marks around any title within a book title.

13. John A. Alford, *A Companion to "Piers Plowman"* (Berkeley: University of California Press, 1988), 195.

Alford, John A. *A Companion to "Piers Plowman."* Berkeley: University of California Press, 1988.

### 14. Sacred text   Include sacred texts in notes but not the bibliography.

14. Luke 18:24–25 (New International Version).

14. Qur'an 7:40–41.

### 15. Source quoted in another source   Identify both the original and the secondary source.

15. Frank D. Millet, "The Filipino Leaders," *Harper's Weekly,* March 11, 1899, quoted in Richard Slotkin, *Gunfighter Nation: The Myth of the Frontier in Twentieth-Century America* (New York: HarperCollins, 1992), 110.

Millet, Frank D. "The Filipino Leaders." *Harper's Weekly,* March 11, 1899. Quoted in Richard Slotkin, *Gunfighter Nation: The Myth of the Frontier in Twentieth-Century America* (New York: HarperCollins, 1992), 110.

## Print and digital periodicals

The note for an article in a periodical typically includes the author's name, the article title, and the periodical title. The format for other information, including the volume and issue numbers (if any) and the date of publication, as well as the page number(s) to which the note refers, varies according to the type of periodical and whether you consulted it in print, on the web, or in a database.

In a bibliographic entry for a journal or magazine article from a database or a print periodical, also give the inclusive page numbers.

### 16. Article in a print journal

16. Catherine Bishop and Angela Woollacott, "Business and Politics as Women's Work: The Australian Colonies and the Mid-Nineteenth-Century Women's Movement," *Journal of Women's History* 28, no. 1 (2016): 87.

Bishop, Catherine, and Angela Woollacott. "Business and Politics as Women's Work: The Australian Colonies and the Mid-Nineteenth-Century Women's Movement." *Journal of Women's History* 28, no. 1 (2016): 84–106.

### 17. Article in an online journal
Give the DOI, preceded by *https://doi.org/*. If there is no DOI, include the article URL. If page numbers are provided, include them as well.

17. Jeffrey J. Schott, "America, Europe, and the New Trade Order," *Business and Politics* 11, no. 3 (2009), https://doi.org/10.2202/1469-3569.1263.

Schott, Jeffrey J. "America, Europe, and the New Trade Order." *Business and Politics* 11, no. 3 (2009). https://doi.org/10.2202/1469-3569.1263.

### 18. Article from a database
Give the name of the author followed by the article title and title of the periodical. After volume and issue information and date, list the page(s). For the note, give the page where the information is found; in the bibliographic entry, give the entire page range. End with retrieval information. The source map and additional examples on pp. 336–37 show where to find information for a typical article from a database.

18. Elizabeth Tucker, "Changing Concepts of Childhood: Children's Folklore Scholarship since the Late Nineteenth Century," *Journal of American Folklore* 125, no. 498 (2012): 399, https://doi.org/10.5406/jamerfolk.125.498.0389.

Tucker Elizabeth. "Changing Concepts of Childhood: Children's Folklore Scholarship since the Late Nineteenth Century." *Journal of American Folklore* 125, no. 498 (2012): 389–410. https://doi.org/10.5406/jamerfolk.125.498.0389.

### 19. Article in a print magazine

19. Terry McDermott, "The Mastermind: Khalid Sheikh Mohammed and the Making of 9/11," *New Yorker*, September 13, 2010, 42.

McDermott, Terry. "The Mastermind: Khalid Sheikh Mohammed and the Making of 9/11." *New Yorker*, September 13, 2010, 38–51.

## Articles from Databases

1. **Author.** In a note, list the author(s) first name first. In the bibliographic entry, list the first author last name first, comma, first name; list other authors first name first.

2. **Article title.** Enclose the title and subtitle (if any) in quotation marks, and capitalize major words. In the notes section, put a comma before and after the title. In the bibliography, put a period before and after the title.

3. **Periodical title.** Italicize the title and subtitle, and capitalize all major words. For a magazine or newspaper, follow with a comma.

4. **Volume and issue numbers (for journals) and date.** For journals, follow the title with the volume number, a comma, the abbreviation *no.*, and the issue number; enclose the publication year in parentheses and follow with a colon. For other periodicals, give the month and year or month, day, and year, not in parentheses, followed by a colon.

5. **Page numbers.** In a note, give the page where the information is found. In the bibliographic entry, give the page range.

6. **Retrieval information.** Provide the article's DOI, if one is given, the name of the database, or a stable URL for the article. Because you provide stable retrieval information, you do not need to identify the electronic format of the work (e.g., PDF). End with a period.

**Citations for the article shown on the next page would look like this:**

ENDNOTE

1. Deborah R. Coen, "Big Is a Thing of the Past: Climate Change and Methodology in the History of Ideas," *Journal of the History of Ideas* 77, no. 2, April 2016: 310, OmniFile Full Text Select.

BIBLIOGRAPHIC ENTRY

Coen, Deborah R. "Big Is a Thing of the Past: Climate Change and Methodology in the History of Ideas." *Journal of the History of Ideas* 77, no. 2, April 2016: 305–21. OmniFile Full Text Select.

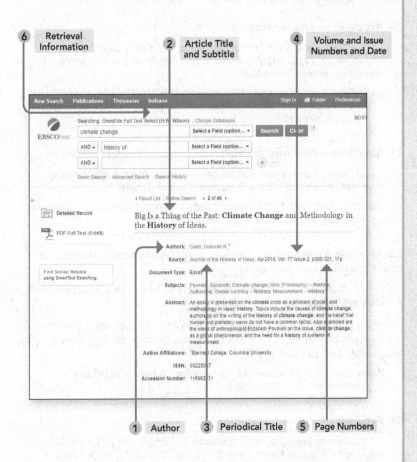

**6** Retrieval Information

**2** Article Title and Subtitle

**4** Volume and Issue Numbers and Date

New Search   Publications   Thesaurus   Indexes                                      Sign In    📁 Folder   Preferences

EBSCO*host*   Searching: OmniFile Full Text Select (H.W. Wilson) | Choose Databases                              BOS⁻

climate change                                    Select a Field (option... ▾)   Search   Clear   ?

AND ▾   history of                                Select a Field (option... ▾)

AND ▾                                             Select a Field (option... ▾)   ⊕ ⊖

Basic Search   Advanced Search   Search History

‹ Result List | Refine Search   ‹ 2 of 46 ›

Detailed Record

PDF Full Text (516KB)

Big Is a Thing of the Past: **Climate Change** and Methodology in the **History** of Ideas.

Find Similar Results using SmartText Searching.

Authors: Coen, Deborah R. [1]

Source: Journal of the History of Ideas, Apr2016, Vol. 77 Issue 2, p305-321, 17p

Document Type: Essay

Subjects: Povinelli, Elizabeth; Climate change; Idea (Philosophy) -- History; Authorship; Global warming -- History; Measurement -- History

Abstract: An essay is presented on the **climate** crisis as a problem of scale and methodology in ideas' history. Topics include the causes of **climate** change, authorship on the writing of the history of **climate** change, and the belief that human and planetary views do not have a common factor. Also examined are the views of anthropologist Elizabeth Povinelli on the issue, **climate change** as a global phenomenon, and the need for a **history** of systems of measurement.

Author Affiliations: [1] Barnard College, Columbia University

ISSN: 00225037

Accession Number: 115962131

**1** Author

**3** Periodical Title

**5** Page Numbers

### 20. Article in an online magazine

20. Tracy Clark-Flory, "Educating Women Saves Kids' Lives," *Salon,* September 17, 2010, http://www.salon.com/life/broadsheet/2010/09/17 /education_women/index.html.

Clark-Flory, Tracy. "Educating Women Saves Kids' Lives." *Salon,* September 17, 2010. http://www.salon.com/life/broadsheet/2010/09/17/education _women/index.html.

### 21. Magazine article from a database

21. Sami Yousafzai and Ron Moreau, "Twisting Arms in Afghanistan," *Newsweek,* November 9, 2009, 8, Academic Search Premier.

Yousafzai, Sami, and Ron Moreau. "Twisting Arms in Afghanistan." *Newsweek,* November 9, 2009, 8, Academic Search Premier.

### 22. Article in a newspaper   Do not include page numbers for a newspaper article, but you may include the section, if any.

22. Caroline E. Mayer, "Wireless Industry to Adopt Voluntary Standards," *Washington Post,* September 9, 2003, sec. E.

*Chicago* recommends that newspaper articles appear in the notes section only, not in the bibliography. Check your instructor's preference. A bibliography entry would look like this:

Mayer, Caroline E. "Wireless Industry to Adopt Voluntary Standards." *Washington Post,* September 9, 2003, sec. E.

### 23. Article in an online newspaper

23. Somini Sengupta, "How a Seed Bank, Almost Lost in Syria's War, Could Help Feed a Warming Planet," *New York Times,* October 13, 2017, https:// www.nytimes.com/2017/10/13/climate/syria-seed-bank.html.

Sengupta, Somini. "How a Seed Bank, Almost Lost in Syria's War, Could Help Feed a Warming Planet." *New York Times,* October 13, 2017. https://www .nytimes.com/2017/10/13/climate/syria-seed-bank.html.

### 24. Newspaper article from a database

24. Demetria Irwin, "A Hatchet, Not a Scalpel, for NYC Budget Cuts," *New York Amsterdam News,* November 13, 2008, Academic Search Premier.

Irwin, Demetria. "A Hatchet, Not a Scalpel, for NYC Budget Cuts." *New York Amsterdam News,* November 13, 2008. Academic Search Premier.

*25. Book review*   Give the name of the reviewer and title of the review, if any, followed by information about the book. End with publication information for the source.

25. Roderick MacFarquhar, "China's Astounding Religious Revival," review of *The Souls of China: The Return of Religion after Mao,* by Ian Johnson, *New York Review of Books,* June 8, 2017, http://www.nybooks.com /articles/2017/06/08/chinas-astounding-religious-revival/ .

MacFarquhar, Roderick. "China's Astounding Religious Revival." Review of *The Souls of China: The Return of Religion after Mao,* by Ian Johnson. *New York Review of Books,* June 8, 2017. http://www.nybooks.com /articles/2017/06/08/chinas-astounding-religious-revival/.

## Online sources

Notes and bibliographic entries for online sources typically include the author; the title of the work; the name of the site; the sponsor of the site, if different from the name of the site or name of the author; the date of publication or most recent update; and a URL. If the online source does not indicate when it was published or last modified, include your date of access.

*26. Work from a website*   See the source map on pp. 340–41.

26. Rose Cohen, "My First Job," Remembering the 1911 Triangle Factory Fire, Cornell University ILR School, accessed October 13, 2017, http://trianglefire.ilr.cornell.edu/primary/testimonials/ootss_RoseCohen .html?sto_sec=sweatshops.

Cohen, Rose. "My First Job." Remembering the 1911 Triangle Factory Fire. Cornell University ILR School. Accessed October 13, 2017. http:// trianglefire.ilr.cornell.edu/primary/testimonials/ootss_RoseCohen .html?sto_sec=sweatshops.

*27. Entire website*   For clarity, you may add the word *website* in parentheses after the title.

27. Rutgers School of Arts and Sciences, Rutgers Oral History Archive (website), 2017, http://oralhistory.rutgers.edu/.

Rutgers School of Arts and Sciences. Rutgers Oral History Archive (website). 2017. http://oralhistory.rutgers.edu/.

*28. Online reference work*   In a note, give the title of the work and the heading of the section in which the information appears. Use *s.v.* (*sub verbo* is Latin for "under the word") before the heading. Include the date the entry was posted, last modified, or accessed. Do not list reference works such as encyclopedias or dictionaries in your bibliography.

28. *Encyclopedia Britannica,* s.v. "Monroe Doctrine," accessed October 12, 2017, https://www.britannica.com/event/Monroe-Doctrine.

# Works from Websites

1. **Author.** In a note, list the author(s) first name first. In a bibliographic entry, list the first author last name first, comma, first name; list additional authors first name first.

2. **Document title.** Enclose the title in quotation marks, and capitalize all major words. In a note, put a comma before and after the title. In the bibliography, put a period before and after the title.

3. **Title of website.** Capitalize all major words. Italicize the website title only if it is an online book or periodical. In the notes section, put a comma after the title. In the bibliography, put a period after the title.

4. **Sponsor of site.** If the sponsor is the same as the author or site title, you may omit it. End with a comma (in the note) or a period (in the bibliography).

5. **Date of publication or last modification.** If a time stamp is given, include it. If no date is available, include your date of access. End with a comma (in the note) or a period (in the bibliography).

6. **Retrieval information.** Give the URL for the work and end with a period.

**Citations for the website shown on the next page would look like this:**

ENDNOTE

1. Evan Haefeli, "Liberty, Diversity, and Slavery: The Beginnings of American Freedom," Preserving American Freedom: The Evolution of American Liberties in Fifty Documents, Historical Society of Pennsylvania, accessed October 13, 2017, https://digitalhistory.hsp.org/pafrm/essay/liberty-diversity-and-slavery-beginnings-american-freedom.

BIBLIOGRAPHIC ENTRY

Haefeli, Evan. "Liberty, Diversity, and Slavery: The Beginnings of American Freedom." Preserving American Freedom: The Evolution of American Liberties in Fifty Documents. Historical Society of Pennsylvania. Accessed October 13, 2017. https://digitalhistory.hsp.org/pafrm/essay/liberty-diversity-and-slavery-beginnings-american-freedom.

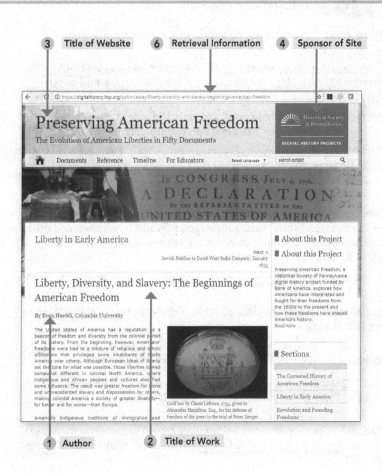

**3** Title of Website     **6** Retrieval Information     **4** Sponsor of Site

← → C ⓘ https://digitalhistory.hsp.org/pafrm/essay/liberty-diversity-and-slavery-beginnings-american-freedom

# Preserving American Freedom

The Evolution of American Liberties in Fifty Documents

Historical Society
of Pennsylvania

**DIGITAL HISTORY PROJECTS**

🏠   Documents   Reference   Timeline   For Educators    Select Language ▼    search exhibit 🔍

IN CONGRESS, JULY 4, 1776.
A DECLARATION
BY THE REPRESENTATIVES OF THE
UNITED STATES OF AMERICA

Liberty in Early America

Next »
Jewish Petition to Dutch West India Company, January
1655

## Liberty, Diversity, and Slavery: The Beginnings of American Freedom

By Evan Haefeli, Columbia University

The United States of America has a reputation as a beacon of freedom and diversity from the colonial period of its history. From the beginning, however, Americans' freedoms were tied to a mixture of religious and ethnic affiliations that privileged some inhabitants of North America over others. Although European ideas of liberty set the tone for what was possible, those liberties looked somewhat different in colonial North America, where indigenous and African peoples and cultures also had some influence. The result was greater freedom for some and unprecedented slavery and dispossession for others, making colonial America a society of greater diversity—for better and for worse—than Europe.

America's indigenous traditions of immigration and

Gold box by Clares LeRoux, 1735, given to
Alexander Hamilton, Esq., for his defense of
freedom of the press in the trial of Peter Zenger.

■ About this Project

■ About this Project

Preserving American Freedom, a
Historical Society of Pennsylvania
digital history project funded by
Bank of America, explores how
Americans have interpreted and
fought for their freedoms from
the 1600s to the present and
how these freedoms have shaped
America's history.
*Read more*

■ Sections

The Contested History of
American Freedom

Liberty in Early America

Revolution and Founding
Freedoms

**1** Author       **2** Title of Work

*29. Blog post* Treat a <u>blog</u> post as a short work from a website (see model 26).

> 29. Jai Arjun Singh, "On the Road in the USSR," *Jabberwock* (<u>blog</u>), November 29, 2007, http://jaiarjun.blogspot.com/2007/11/on-road-in-ussr .html.

*Chicago* recommends that blog posts appear in the notes section only, not in the bibliography. Check your instructor's preference. A bibliography reference would look like this:

> Singh, Jai Arjun. "On the Road in the USSR." *Jabberwock* (blog). November 29, 2007. http://jaiarjun.blogspot.com/2007/11/on-road-in-ussr.html.

*30. Email, social media messages, and other personal communications* Cite email messages, social media messages, personal interviews, and other personal communications, such as letters and telephone calls, in the text or in a note only; do not cite them in the bibliography.

> 30. Kareem Adas, <u>Facebook private message to author</u>, February 11, 2018.

*31. Social media post* In place of a title, include the <u>text of the post</u>, up to the first 160 characters.

> 31. NASA (@nasa), <u>"This galaxy is a whirl of color,"</u> Instagram photo, September 23, 2017, https://www.instagram.com/p/BZY8adnnZQJ/.

> NASA. <u>"This galaxy is a whirl of color."</u> Instagram photo, September 23, 2017. https://www.instagram.com/p/BZY8adnnZQJ/.

*32. Podcast* Treat a podcast as a short work from a website (see model 26). Include the <u>type of podcast or file format</u> (if downloadable), the <u>time stamp</u>, and the URL.

> 32. Toyin Falola, "Creativity and Decolonization: Nigerian Cultures and African Epistemologies," Episode 96, November 17, 2015, in *Africa Past and Present*, African Online Digital Library, <u>podcast, MP3 audio</u>, <u>43:44</u>, http://afripod.aodl.org/2015/11/afripod-96/.

> Falola, Toyin. "Creativity and Decolonization: Nigerian Cultures and African Epistemologies." Episode 96, November 17, 2015. *Africa Past and Present*. African Online Digital Library. <u>Podcast, MP3 audio</u>. <u>43:44</u>. http://afripod .aodl.org/2015/11/afripod-96/.

*33. Online audio or video* Treat an online audio or video source as a short work from a website (see model 26). If the source is downloadable, give the medium or file format before the URL.

33. Alyssa Katz, "Did the Mortgage Crisis Kill the American Dream?" YouTube video, 4:32, posted by NYCRadio, June 24, 2009, http://www.youtube.com/watch?v=uivtwjwd_Qw.

Katz, Alyssa. "Did the Mortgage Crisis Kill the American Dream?" YouTube video, 4:32. Posted by NYCRadio. June 24, 2009. http://www.youtube.com/watch?v=uivtwjwd_Qw.

## Other sources

### 34. Published or broadcast interview

34. David O. Russell, interview by Terry Gross, *Fresh Air*, WNYC, February 20, 2014.

Russell, David O. Interview by Terry Gross. *Fresh Air*. WNYC, February 20, 2014.

Interviews you conduct are considered personal communications (see model 30).

### 35. DVD or Blu-ray   Include both the date of the original release and the date of release for the format you are citing.

35. *American History X,* directed by Tony Kaye (1998; Los Angeles: New Line Studios, 2002), DVD.

Kaye, Tony, dir. *American History X.* 1998; Los Angeles: New Line Studios, 2002. DVD.

### 36. Sound recording

36. "Work," MP3 audio, track 4 on Rihanna, *Anti*, Roc Nation, 2016.

Rihanna. "Work." *Anti*. Roc Nation, 2016, MP3 audio.

### 37. Work of art   Works of art usually can be mentioned in the text rather than cited in a note or bibliography entry. Check your instructor's preference.

37. Hope Gangloff, *Vera*, 2015, acrylic on canvas, Kemper Museum of Contemporary Art, Kansas City, MO.

Gangloff, Hope. *Vera*. 2015. Acrylic on canvas. Kemper Museum of Contemporary Art, Kansas City, MO.

If you refer to a reproduction, give the publication information.

37. Mary Cassatt, *The Child's Bath,* 1893, oil on canvas, *Art Access*, The Art Institute of Chicago, accessed October 13, 2017, http://www.artic.edu/aic/collections/exhibitions/Impressionism/Cassatt.

Cassatt, Mary. *The Child's Bath*. 1893. Oil on canvas. *Art Access*. The Art Institute of Chicago. Accessed October 13, 2017. http://www.artic.edu/aic/collections/exhibitions/Impressionism/Cassatt.

*38. Pamphlet, report, or brochure*  Information about the author or publisher may not be readily available, but give enough information to identify your source.

> 38. International Monetary Fund, *Western Hemisphere: Tale of Two Adjustments,* World Economic and Financial Surveys (Washington, DC: International Monetary Fund, 2017), 29.

> International Monetary Fund. *Western Hemisphere: Tale of Two Adjustments.* World Economic and Financial Surveys. Washington, DC: International Monetary Fund, 2017.

*39. Government document*

> 39. U.S. House Committee on Ways and Means, *Report on Trade Mission to Sub-Saharan Africa,* 108th Cong., 1st sess. (Washington, DC: Government Printing Office, 2003), 28.

> U.S. House Committee on Ways and Means. *Report on Trade Mission to Sub-Saharan Africa.* 108th Cong., 1st sess. Washington, DC: Government Printing Office, 2003.

# 20d An excerpt from a student research essay, *Chicago* style

**STUDENT WRITER**
Amanda Rinder

On the following pages is an excerpt from an essay by Amanda Rinder that conforms to the *Chicago* guidelines described in this chapter.

Sweet Home Chicago: Preserving the Past,
Protecting the Future of the Windy City

Title announces topic clearly and succinctly

Amanda Rinder

Title and writer's name centered

Twentieth-Century U.S. History
Professor Goldberg
November 27, 2006

Course title, instructor's name, and date centered at bottom of title page

Annotations indicate effective choices or *Chicago*-style formatting.

First page of
body text is
p. 2

Paper refers to
each figure by
number

Thesis
introduced

Double-spaced
text

Source
cited using
superscript
numeral

Figure
caption
includes
number, short
title, and
source

Only one city has the "Big Shoulders" described by Carl Sandburg: Chicago (fig. 1). So renowned are its skyscrapers and celebrated building style that an entire school of architecture is named for Chicago. Presently, however, the place that Frank Sinatra called "my kind of town" is beginning to lose sight of exactly what kind of town it is. Many of the buildings that give Chicago its distinctive character are being torn down in order to make room for new growth. Both preserving the classics and encouraging new creation are important; the combination of these elements gives Chicago architecture its unique flavor. Witold Rybczynski, a professor of urbanism, told Tracie Rozhon of the *New York Times*, "Of all the cities we can think of . . . we associate Chicago with new things, with building new. Combining that with preservation is a difficult task, a tricky thing. It's hard to find the middle ground in Chicago."[1] Yet finding a middle ground is essential if the city is to retain the original character that sets it apart from the rest. In order to maintain Chicago's distinctive identity and its delicate balance between the old and the new, the city government must provide a comprehensive urban plan that not only

Fig. 1. Chicago skyline, circa 1940s. (Postcard courtesy of Minnie Dangburg.)

Rinder 3

directs growth, but calls for the preservation of landmarks and historic districts as well.

Opening paragraph concludes with formal thesis statement

Chicago is a city for the working man. Nowhere is this more evident than in its architecture. David Garrard Lowe, author of *Lost Chicago*, notes that early Chicagoans "sought reality, not fantasy, and the reality of America as seen from the heartland did not include the pavilions of princes or the castles of kings."[2] The inclination toward unadorned, sturdy buildings began in the late nineteenth century with the aptly named Chicago School, a movement led by Louis Sullivan, John Wellborn Root, and Daniel Burnham and based on Sullivan's adage, "Form follows function."[3] The early skyscraper, the very symbol of the Chicago style, represents the triumph of function and utility over sentiment, America over Europe, and perhaps, as Daniel Bluestone argues, even the frontier over the civilization of the East Coast.[4] These ideals of the original Chicago School were expanded upon by architects of the Second Chicago School. Frank Lloyd Wright's legendary organic style and the famed glass and steel constructions of Mies van der Rohe are often the first images that spring to mind when one thinks of Chicago.

Second paragraph provides background

Yet the architecture that is the city's defining attribute is being threatened by the increasing tendency toward development. The root of Chicago's preservation problem lies in the enormous drive toward economic expansion and the potential in Chicago for such growth. The highly competitive market for land in the city means that properties sell for the highest price if the buildings on them can be obliterated to make room for newer, larger developments. Because of this preference on the part of potential buyers, the label "landmark" has become a stigma for property owners. "In other cities, landmark status is sought after — in Chicago, it's avoided at all costs," notes Alan J. Shannon of the *Chicago Tribune*. Even if owners wish to keep their property's original structure, designation as a landmark is still undesirable as it limits the renovations that can be made to a building and thus decreases its value . . .

Clear transition from previous paragraph

Rinder 9

Notes

1. Tracie Rozhon, "Chicago Girds for Big Battle over Its Skyline," *New York Times,* November 12, 2000, Academic Search Premier.

2. David Garrard Lowe, *Lost Chicago* (New York: Watson-Guptill, 2000), 123.

3. *Columbia Encyclopedia,* 6th ed. (2000), s.v. "Louis Sullivan."

4. Daniel Bluestone, *Constructing Chicago* (New Haven: Yale University Press, 1991), 105.

5. Alan J. Shannon, "When Will It End?" *Chicago Tribune,* September 11, 1987, quoted in Karen J. Dilibert, *From Landmark to Landfill* (Chicago: Chicago Architectural Foundation, 2000), 11.

6. Steve Kerch, "Landmark Decisions," *Chicago Tribune,* March 18, 1990, sec. 16.

7. John W. Stamper, *Chicago's North Michigan Avenue* (Chicago: University of Chicago Press, 1991), 215.

8. Alf Siewers, "Success Spoiling the Magnificent Mile?" *Chicago Sun-Times,* April 9, 1995.

9. Paul Gapp, "McCarthy Building Puts Landmark Law on a Collision Course with Developers," *Chicago Tribune,* April 20, 1986, quoted in Karen J. Dilibert, *From Landmark to Landfill* (Chicago: Chicago Architectural Foundation, 2000), 4.

10. Gapp, 4.

11. Rozhon, "Chicago Girds for Big Battle."

12. Kerch, "Landmark Decisions."

13. Robert Bruegmann, *The Architects and the City* (Chicago: University of Chicago Press, 1997), 443.

Bibliography

Bluestone, Daniel. *Constructing Chicago*. New Haven: Yale University Press, 1991.

Bruegmann, Robert. *The Architects and the City*. Chicago: University of Chicago Press, 1997.

Dilibert, Karen J. *From Landmark to Landfill*. Chicago: Chicago Architectural Foundation, 2000.

Kerch, Steve. "Landmark Decisions." *Chicago Tribune,* March 18, 1990, sec. 16.

Lowe, David Garrard. *Lost Chicago*. New York: Watson-Guptill, 2000.

Rozhon, Tracie. "Chicago Girds for Big Battle over Its Skyline." *New York Times,* November 12, 2000. Academic Search Premier.

Siewers, Alf. "Success Spoiling the Magnificent Mile?" *Chicago Sun-Times,* April 9, 1995.

Stamper, John W. *Chicago's North Michigan Avenue*. Chicago: University of Chicago Press, 1991.

Bibliography starts on new page

Print book

Pamphlet

Newspaper article

Article from database

Bibliography entries use hanging indent and are not numbered

# CHAPTER 21

# CSE Style

Writers in the physical sciences, the life sciences, and mathematics often use the documentation style set forth by the Council of Science Editors (CSE). Guidelines for citing print sources can be found in *Scientific Style and Format: The CSE Manual for Authors, Editors, and Publishers,* Eighth Edition (2014).

## 21a Following CSE format

*Title page*    Center the title of your paper. Beneath it, center your name. Include other relevant information, such as the course name and number, the instructor's name, and the date submitted.

*Margins and spacing*    Leave standard one-inch margins at the top and bottom and on both sides of each page. Double-space the text and the references list.

*Page numbers*    Type a short version of the paper's title and the page number in the upper-right corner of each page. Omit the page number on the title page and number the first page of text as page 2.

*Abstract*    CSE style frequently calls for a one-paragraph abstract. The abstract should be on a separate page, right after the title page, with the title *Abstract* centered one inch from the top of the page.

*Headings*    Use headings when possible to help readers quickly find the contents of a section of the paper.

*Tables and figures*    Tables and figures must be labeled *Table* or *Figure* and numbered separately, one sequence for tables and one for figures. Give each table and figure a short, informative title. Be sure to introduce each table and figure in your text, and comment on its significance.

*List of references*    Start the list of references on a new page at the end of the paper, and continue to number the pages consecutively. Center the title *References* one inch from the top of the page, and double-space before beginning the first entry.

# List of Examples

## References in CSE style

A List of Examples for **MLA style** is on page 238.

A List of Examples for **APA style** is on page 288.

A List of Examples for **CMS (*Chicago*) style** is on page 327.

## 21b Creating CSE in-text citations

In CSE style, citations within the text follow one of three formats:

- The *citation-sequence format* calls for a superscript number or a number in parentheses after any mention of a source. The sources are numbered in the order they appear. Each number refers to the same source every time it is used. The first source mentioned in the paper is numbered 1, the second source is numbered 2, and so on.

- The *citation-name format* also calls for a superscript number or a number in parentheses after any mention of a source. The numbers are added *after* the list of references is completed and alphabetized, so that the source numbered 1 is alphabetically first in the list of references, 2 is alphabetically second, and so on.

- The *name-year format* calls for the last name of the author and the year of publication in parentheses after any mention of a source. If the last name appears in a signal phrase, the name-year format allows for giving only the year of publication in parentheses.

Before deciding which system to use, ask your instructor's preference.

*1. In-text citation using citation-sequence or citation-name format*

VonBergen[12] provides the most complete discussion of this phenomenon.

For the citation-sequence and citation-name formats, you would use the same superscript ([12]) for each subsequent citation of this work by VonBergen.

*2. In-text citation using name-year format*

VonBergen (2003) provides the most complete discussion of this phenomenon.

Hussar's two earlier studies of juvenile obesity (1995, 1999) examined only children with diabetes.

The classic examples of such investigations (Morrow 1968; Bridger et al. 1971; Franklin and Wayson 1972) still shape the assumptions of current studies.

If a work has three or more authors, use the first author's name and *et al.* in the in-text citation.

## 21c Preparing a CSE list of references

The citations in the text of a paper correspond to items on a list titled *References*, which starts on a new page at the end of the paper. Continue to number the pages consecutively, center the title *References* one inch from the top of the page, and double-space before beginning the first entry. Start each entry flush left and indent subsequent lines one-quarter inch.

The order of the entries depends on which format you follow:

- **Citation-sequence format:** number and list the references in the order they are first cited in the text.
- **Citation-name format:** list and number the references in alphabetical order.
- **Name-year format:** list the references, unnumbered, in alphabetical order.

In the following examples, you will see that both the citation-sequence and citation-name formats call for listing the date after the publisher's name in references for books and after the periodical name in references for articles. The name-year format calls for listing the date immediately after the author's name in any kind of reference.

CSE style also specifies the treatment and placement of the following basic elements in the list of references:

- **Author.** List all authors last name first, and use only initials for first and middle names. Do not place a comma after the author's last name, and do not place periods after or spaces between the initials. Use a period after the last initial of the last author listed.

- **Title.** Do not italicize titles and subtitles of books and titles of periodicals. Do not enclose titles of articles in quotation marks. For books and articles, capitalize only the first word of the title and any proper nouns or proper adjectives. Abbreviate and capitalize all major words in a periodical title.

As you refer to these examples, pay attention to how publication information (publishers for books, details about periodicals for articles) and other specific elements are styled and punctuated. We have used underlining in some examples only to draw your attention to important elements. Do not underline anything in your own citations.

## Books

For the basic format for citing a print book, see the source map on pp. 354–55.

### 1. One author

CITATION-SEQUENCE AND CITATION-NAME

1. Tyson ND. Astrophysics for people in a hurry. New York (NY): Norton; 2017.

NAME-YEAR

Tyson ND. 2017. Astrophysics for people in a hurry. New York (NY): Norton.

### 2. Two or more authors.

List all authors up to ten. If there are more than ten authors, follow the tenth with the abbreviation *et al.*

CITATION-SEQUENCE AND CITATION-NAME

2. Wojciechowski BW, Rice NM. Experimental methods in kinetic studies. 2nd ed. St. Louis (MO): Elsevier Science; 2003.

NAME-YEAR

Wojciechowski BW, Rice NM. 2003. Experimental methods in kinetic studies. 2nd ed. St. Louis (MO): Elsevier Science.

### 3. Organization as author

CITATION-SEQUENCE AND CITATION-NAME

3. World Health Organization. The world health report 2002: reducing risks, promoting healthy life. Geneva (Switzerland): The Organization; 2002.

Place the organization's underline{abbreviation} at the beginning of the name-year entry, and use the abbreviation in the corresponding in-text citation. Alphabetize the entry by the underline{first word} of the full name, not by the abbreviation.

NAME-YEAR

[WHO] World Health Organization. 2002. The world health report 2002: reducing risks, promoting healthy life. Geneva (Switzerland): The Organization.

# Books

Note that, depending on whether you are using the citation-sequence
or citation-name format or the name-year format, the date placement
will vary.

**1** **Author.** List author(s) last name first, and use initials for first and
middle names, with no periods or spaces. Use a period only after the
last initial of the last author.

**2** **Publication year.** In name-year format, put the year of publication
immediately after the author name(s). In citation-sequence or citation-
name format, put the year of publication after the publisher's name.

**3** **Title.** Do not italicize or put quotation marks around titles and
subtitles of books. Capitalize only the first word of the title and any
proper nouns or proper adjectives. If an edition number is given, list it
after the title.

**4** **City of publication and publisher.** List the city of publication (and
the country or state abbreviation for unfamiliar cities) followed by a
colon. Give the publisher's name. In citation-sequence or citation-
name format, follow with a semicolon. In name-year format, follow
with a period.

**A citation for the book shown on the next page would look like this:**

CITATION-SEQUENCE OR CITATION-NAME FORMAT

1. Creighton TE. Proteins: structures and molecular properties. 2nd ed.
New York (NY): WH Freeman; 1993.

NAME-YEAR FORMAT

Creighton TE. 1993. Proteins: structures and molecular properties. 2nd ed.
New York (NY): WH Freeman.

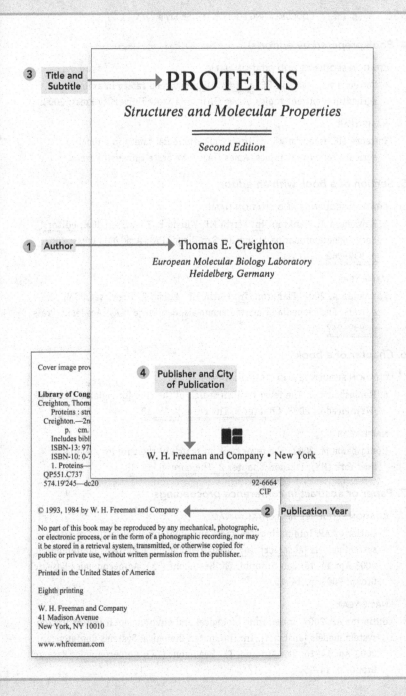

**3** Title and Subtitle →

# PROTEINS

*Structures and Molecular Properties*

*Second Edition*

**1** Author →

Thomas E. Creighton

*European Molecular Biology Laboratory*
*Heidelberg, Germany*

Cover image prov

**Library of Cong**
Creighton, Thoma
   Proteins : str
Creighton.—2n
      p.   cm.
   Includes bibl
   ISBN-13: 97
   ISBN-10: 0-7
   1. Proteins—
QP551.C737
574.19′245—dc20

**4** Publisher and City of Publication ↓

W. H. Freeman and Company • New York

92-6664
CIP

Printed in the United States of America

Eighth printing

W. H. Freeman and Company
41 Madison Avenue
New York, NY 10010

www.whfreeman.com

## 4. Book prepared by editor(s)

CITATION-SEQUENCE AND CITATION-NAME

4. Torrence ME, Isaacson RE, editors. Microbial food safety in animal agriculture: current topics. Ames (IA): Iowa State University Press; 2003.

NAME-YEAR

Torrence ME, Isaacson RE, editors. 2003. Microbial safety in animal agriculture: current topics. Ames (IA): Iowa State University Press.

## 5. Section of a book with an editor

CITATION-SEQUENCE AND CITATION-NAME

5. Kawamura A. Plankton. In: Perrin MF, Wursig B, Thewissen JGM, editors. Encyclopedia of marine mammals. San Diego (CA): Academic Press; 2002. p. 939–942.

NAME-YEAR

Kawamura A. 2002. Plankton. In: Perrin MF, Wursig B, Thewissen JGM, editors. Encyclopedia of marine mammals. San Diego (CA): Academic Press. p. 939–942.

## 6. Chapter of a book

CITATION-SEQUENCE AND CITATION-NAME

6. Honigsbaum M. The fever trail: in search of the cure for malaria. New York (NY): Picador; 2003. Chapter 2, The cure; p. 19–38.

NAME-YEAR

Honigsbaum M. 2003. The fever trail: in search of the cure for malaria. New York (NY): Picador. Chapter 2, The cure; p. 19–38.

## 7. Paper or abstract in conference proceedings

CITATION-SEQUENCE AND CITATION-NAME

7. Gutierrez AP. Integrating biological and environmental factors in crop system models [abstract]. In: Integrated Biological Systems Conference; 2003 Apr 14–16; San Antonio, TX. Beaumont (TX): Agroeconomics Research Group; 2003. p. 14–15.

NAME-YEAR

Gutierrez AP. 2003. Integrating biological and environmental factors in crop system models [abstract]. In: Integrated Biological Systems Conference; 2003 Apr 14–16; San Antonio, TX. Beaumont (TX): Agroeconomics Research Group. p. 14–15.

## Periodicals

Provide volume and issue numbers for journals. For magazines, include the month and year or the month, day, and year. For newspaper articles, include the section designation and column number, if any, and the date. For all periodicals, give inclusive page numbers. For rules on abbreviating journal titles, consult the CSE manual or ask an instructor.

### 8. Article in a journal

CITATION-SEQUENCE AND CITATION-NAME

8. Citrin DE. Recent developments in radiotherapy. New Engl J Med. 2017;377(11):1065–1075.

NAME-YEAR

Citrin DE. 2017. Recent developments in radiotherapy. New Engl J Med. 377(11):1065–1075.

### 9. Article in a magazine

CITATION-SEQUENCE AND CITATION-NAME

9. Livio M. Moving right along: the accelerating universe holds secrets to dark energy, the Big Bang, and the ultimate beauty of nature. Astronomy. 2002 Jul:34–39.

NAME-YEAR

Livio M. 2002 Jul. Moving right along: the accelerating universe holds secrets to dark energy, the Big Bang, and the ultimate beauty of nature. Astronomy. 34–39.

### 10. Article in a newspaper

CITATION-SEQUENCE AND CITATION-NAME

10. Kolata G. Bone diagnosis gives new data but no answers. New York Times (National Ed.). 2003 Sep 28;Sect. 1:1 (col. 1).

NAME-YEAR

Kolata G. 2003 Sep 28. Bone diagnosis gives new data but no answers. New York Times (National Ed.). Sect. 1:1 (col. 1).

## Digital sources

These examples use the citation-sequence or citation-name system. To adapt them to the name-year system, delete the note number and place the update date immediately after the author's name.

# Articles from Databases

Note that date placement will vary depending on whether you are using the citation-sequence or citation-name format or the name-year format.

**1** **Author.** List author(s) last name first, and use only initials for first and middle names.

**2** **Publication date.** For name-year format, put publication date after author name(s). In citation-sequence or citation-name format, put it after periodical title. Use year only (for journals) or year month day (for other periodicals).

**3** **Article title.** Capitalize first word and proper nouns/adjectives.

**4** **Periodical title.** Capitalize major words. Abbreviate journal titles.

**5** **Date of access.** In brackets, write *accessed* and the year, month, and day. End with a semicolon.

**6** **Publication information for article.** Give volume number, issue number (in parentheses), and a colon.

**7** **Page numbers.** Give page range. End with a period.

**8** **Name of database.** End with a period.

**9** **Web address and document number.** Include the brief URL, then *Document no.* and the identifying number.

**A citation for the article shown on the next page would look like this:**

CITATION-SEQUENCE OR CITATION-NAME FORMAT

1. Miller AL. Epidemiology, etiology, and natural treatment of seasonal affective disorder. Altern Med Rev. 2005 [accessed 2014 25 May]; 10(1): 5–13. Academic Search Premier. http://www.ebscohost.com. Document No.: 16514813.

NAME-YEAR FORMAT

Miller AL. 2005. Epidemiology, etiology, and natural treatment of seasonal affective disorder. Altern Med Rev. [accessed 2014 25 May]; 10(1): 5–13. Academic Search Premier. http://www.ebscohost.com. Document No.: 16514813.

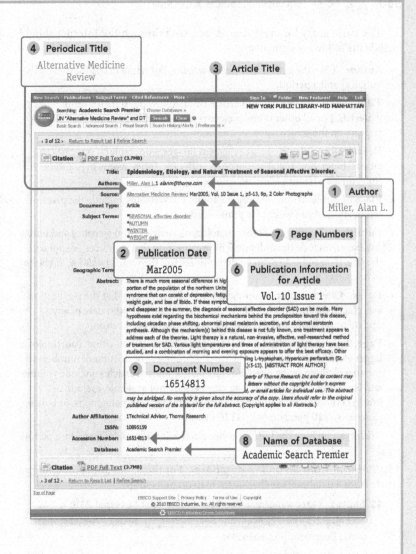

**4 Periodical Title**
Alternative Medicine Review

**3 Article Title**

New Search · Publications · Subject Terms · Cited References · More ·    Sign In · Folder · New Features! · Help · Exit

Searching: **Academic Search Premier** | Choose Databases »    NEW YORK PUBLIC LIBRARY–MID MANHATTAN
JN "Alternative Medicine Review" and DT | Search | Clear ·
Basic Search | Advanced Search | Visual Search | Search History/Alerts | Preferences »

‹ 3 of 12 › · Return to Result List | Refine Search

Citation · PDF Full Text (3.7MB)

| | |
|---|---|
| **Title:** | **Epidemiology, Etiology, and Natural Treatment of Seasonal Affective Disorder.** |
| **Authors:** | Miller, Alan L.1 *alanm@thorne.com* |
| **Source:** | Alternative Medicine Review; Mar2005, Vol. 10 Issue 1, p5-13, 9p, 2 Color Photographs |
| **Document Type:** | Article |
| **Subject Terms:** | *SEASONAL affective disorder |
| | *AUTUMN |
| | *WINTER |
| | *WEIGHT gain |

**1 Author**
Miller, Alan L.

**7 Page Numbers**

**2 Publication Date**
Mar2005

**6 Publication Information for Article**
Vol. 10 Issue 1

**Geographic Term**

**Abstract:** There is much more seasonal difference in hig... portion of the population of the northern Unite... syndrome that can consist of depression, fatigu... weight gain, and loss of libido. If these sympto... and disappear in the summer, the diagnosis of seasonal affective disorder (SAD) can be made. Many hypotheses exist regarding the biochemical mechanisms behind the predisposition toward this disease, including circadian phase shifting, abnormal pineal melatonin secretion, and abnormal serotonin synthesis. Although the mechanism(s) behind this disease is not fully known, one treatment appears to address each of the theories. Light therapy is a natural, non-invasive, effective, well-researched method of treatment for SAD. Various light temperatures and times of administration of light therapy have been studied, and a combination of morning and evening exposure appears to offer the best efficacy. Other ...ing L-tryptophan, Hypericum perforatum (St. ...):5-13). [ABSTRACT FROM AUTHOR]

**9 Document Number**
16514813

...perty of Thorne Research Inc and its content may ... listserv without the copyright holder's express ...d, or email articles for individual use. This abstract may be abridged. No warranty is given about the accuracy of the copy. Users should refer to the original published version of the material for the full abstract. (Copyright applies to all Abstracts.)

| | |
|---|---|
| **Author Affiliations:** | 1Technical Advisor, Thorne Research |
| **ISSN:** | 10995199 |
| **Accession Number:** | 16514813 |
| **Database:** | Academic Search Premier |

**8 Name of Database**
Academic Search Premier

Citation · PDF Full Text (3.7MB)

‹ 3 of 12 › · Return to Result List | Refine Search

Top of Page

EBSCO Support Site | Privacy Policy | Terms of Use | Copyright
© 2010 EBSCO Industries, Inc. All rights reserved.
EBSCO Publishing Green Initiatives

The basic entry for most sources accessed through the Internet should include the following elements:

- **Author.** Give the author's name, if available, last name first, followed by the initial(s) and a period.

- **Title.** For book, journal, and article titles, follow the style for print materials. For all other types of electronic material, reproduce the title that appears on the screen.

- **Description.** Identify sources such as images, infographics, podcasts, videos, blogs, and social media posts with descriptive words in brackets: *[infographic]*, *[video]*, *[podcast, episode 12]*.

- **Place of publication.** For online books and websites, include the place of publication as you would for print sources.

- **Publisher.** For material other than journal articles from websites and online databases, include the individual or organization that produces or sponsors the site. If no publisher can be determined, use the words *publisher unknown* in brackets.

- **Dates.** Cite three important dates if possible: the date that the publication was placed on the Internet or the copyright date; the latest date of any update or revision; and the date you accessed the publication.

- **Page, document, volume, and issue numbers.** When citing a portion of a larger work or site, list the inclusive page numbers or document numbers of the specific item being cited. For journals or journal articles, include volume and issue numbers. If exact page numbers are not available, include in brackets the approximate length in computer screens, paragraphs, or bytes: *[2 screens]*, *[10 paragraphs]*, *[332K bytes]*.

- **Address.** Include the URL or other electronic address, followed by a period.

*11. Material from an online database*   For the basic format for citing an article from a database, see the source map on pp. 358–59.

> 11. Shilts E. Water wanderers. Can Geographic. 2002 [accessed 2010 Jan 27];122(3):72–77. <u>Academic Search Premier</u>. http://www.ebscohost .com/. Document No.: 6626534.

*12. Article in an online journal*

> 12. Perez P, Calonge TM. Yeast protein kinase C. <u>J Biochem</u>. 2002 Oct [accessed 2008 Nov 3];132(4):513–517. http://edpex104.bcasj.or.jp/jb-pdf/132-4 /jb132-4-513.pdf.

*13. Article in an online newspaper*

> 13. Gorman J. Trillions of flies can't all be bad. New York Times. 2017 Nov 13 [accessed 2017 Dec 1]. https://nyti.ms/2hwjhw0.

### 14. Online book

14. Patrick TS, Allison JR, Krakow GA. Protected plants of Georgia. Social Circle (GA): Georgia Department of Natural Resources; c1995 [accessed 2010 Dec 3]. http://www.georgiawildlife.com/content/displaycontent .asp?txtDocument=89&txtPage=9.

To cite a portion of an online book, give the name of the part after the publication information: *Chapter 6, Encouraging germination.* See model 6.

### 15. Website

15. Geology and public policy. Boulder (CO): Geological Society of America; c2010 [updated 2010 Jun 3; accessed 2010 Sep 19]. http://www.geosociety .org/geopolicy.htm.

### 16. Government website

16. Health disparities in cancer: reducing health disparities in cancer. Atlanta (GA): Centers for Disease Control and Prevention (US); 2012 Nov 14 [updated 2014 Jul 21; accessed 2017 Nov 13]. http://www.cdc.gov/cancer /healthdisparities/basic_info/disparities.htm.

# 21d An excerpt from a literature review, CSE style

STUDENT
WRITER
Joanna
Hays

The following excerpt from a literature review by Joanna Hays for a biology class conforms to the name-year format in the CSE guidelines described in this chapter.

Running head has short title, page number

## Overview

Niemann-Pick Disease (NP) occurs in patients with deficient acid sphingomyelinase (ASM) activity as well as with the lysosomal accumulation of sphingomyelin. It is an autosomal recessive disorder (Levran et al. 1991). As recently as 1991, researchers had classified two major phenotypes: Type A and Type B (Levran et al. 1991). In more recent studies several more phenotypes have been identified, including Types C and D. Each type of NP has distinct characteristics and effects on the patient. NP is distributed worldwide, but is closely associated with Ashkenazi Jewish descendants. Niemann-Pick Disease is relevant to the molecular world today because of advances being made in the ability to identify mutations, to trace ancestry where the mutation may have originated, and to counsel patients with a high potential of carrying the disease. Genetic counseling primarily consists of confirmation of the particular disease and calculation of the possible future reappearance in the same gene line (Brock 1974). The following discussion will summarize the identification of mutations causing the various forms of NP, the distribution of NP, as well as new genotypes and phenotypes that are correlated with NP.

Overview provides key background information

Headings organize project

## Mutations Causing NP

Levran et al. (1991) inform readers of the frequent identification of missense mutations in the gene associated with Ashkenazi Jewish persons afflicted by Type A and Type B NP. This paper identifies the mutations associated with NP and the beginning of many molecular techniques to develop diagnoses. Greer et al. (1998) identify a new mutation that is specifically identified to be the cause of Type D. NP in various forms is closely associated with the founder effect caused by a couple married in the early 1700s in what is now Nova Scotia. Simonaro et al. (2002) discuss the distribution of Type B NP as well as new phenotypes and genotypes. All three of these papers identify . . .

Annotations indicate effective choices or CSE-style formatting.

Niemann-Pick Disease 9

### References

Brock DJH. 1974. Prenatal diagnosis and genetic counseling. J Clin Pathol Suppl. (R Coll Path.) 8:150–155.

Greer WL, Ridell DC, Gillan TL, Girouard GS, Sparrow SM, Byers DM, Dobson MJ, Neumann PE. 1998. The Nova Scotia (type D) form of Niemann-Pick disease is caused by a $G_{3097} \rightarrow T$ transversion in NPC1. Am J Hum Genet 63:52–54.

Levran O, Desnick RJ, Schuchman EH. 1991. Niemann-Pick disease: a frequent missense mutation in the acid sphingomyelinase gene of Ashkenazi Jewish type A and B patients. P Natl Acad Sci USA 88:3748–3752.

Simonaro CM, Desnick RJ, McGovern MM, Wasserstein MP, Schuchman EH. 2002. The demographics and distribution of type B Niemann-Pick disease: novel mutations lead to new genotype/phenotype correlations. Am J Hum Genet 71:1413–1419.

Alphabetical by name

# PART 6
# Designing and Performing Writing

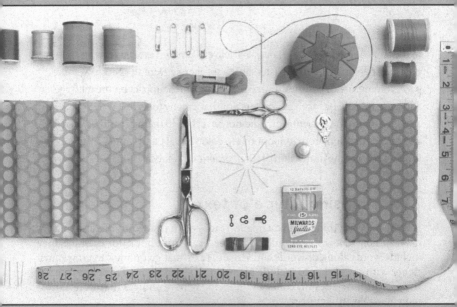

Photo by Mike Enright/www.menright.com. Photo styling by Barbara Lipp.

# CHAPTER 22

# Design for Print and Digital Writing

In the ancient Greek world, a speaker's delivery (known as *actio*) was an art every educated person needed to master: how a speaker delivered a speech — tone, pace, volume, use of gestures, and so on — had a great impact on the message and how it would be received. Writers now have many tools that writers and speakers in the ancient world did not have to help them get and hold an audience's attention, from font options to color, visuals, and sound. All these tools help bring the dimension of *visual rhetoric* to today's writing.

## 22a Choosing a type of text

A text can be anything that you might "read" — not just words but also images, data, audio, video, or combinations of media. A print book, for example, may include words alone or words and visuals. Texts that go online can grow much richer with the ability to include animations, video, audio, links, and interactive features. As a result, college writers today have choices that were almost unimaginable until quite recently.

### Considering the rhetorical context for your design

Ultimately, the organization and look of any text you design should depend on your rhetorical situation. You should make decisions about layout, formatting, color, fonts (for written words), elements such as images or video, and other aspects of design based on rhetorical needs — your audience, purpose, topic, stance, genre conventions, and so on — and on practical constraints, such as the time and tools available.

### Making design choices for different genres

While you might still be assigned to compose traditional texts such as academic essays, you may also be asked to create coursework in other genres. Research conducted for this textbook found that today's students are encountering assignments that range from newsletters, infographics, and poster presentations to PechaKuchas, podcasts, and video essays — and that multimodal assignments are increasingly characteristic of first-year writing courses. Whatever genre you choose for your assignment, familiarize yourself with conventions of design for that genre, and think carefully about the most appropriate and compelling design choices for your particular context.

### Choosing print or digital delivery

One of your first design decisions will be determining whether you'll deliver your text digitally, in print, or both ways. In general, print documents are portable, easy to read without online access or technical assistance, and relatively fast to produce. Digital texts, on the other hand, can include sound, animation, and video; updates are easy to make; distribution is fast and efficient; and feedback can be swift. Design decisions may have similar goals, such as clarity and readability, no matter what medium you are working in, but the specific choices you make to achieve those goals may differ in print and digital texts.

## 22b Planning a visual structure

Today, all writers need to think carefully about the look of any text they create and plan a visual structure for it. The design decisions you make will help guide readers by making the texts easier on the eyes and easier to understand.

### Following design principles

Designer Robin Williams, in her *Non-Designer's Design Book*, points out four simple principles for designing effective texts — contrast, alignment, repetition, and proximity. These principles are illustrated on page 368 with the familiar Wikipedia page design.

#### Contrast

Contrast attracts your eye to elements on a page and guides you around it, helping you follow an argument or find information. You may achieve contrast through the use of color, icons, boldface or large type size, headings, and so on. Begin with a focus point — the dominant point, image, or words where you want your reader's eye to go first — and structure the flow of your visual information from this point.

#### Alignment

Alignment refers to the way visuals and text on a page are lined up, both horizontally and vertically. The overall guideline is not to mix alignments arbitrarily. That is, if you begin with a left alignment, stick with it for the major

*Chances are that most readers will look first at either the heading or the images on this Wikipedia page. The site uses large black type against a white background for the title of each page at the upper left. On this page, color images of molecular models also draw the eye.*

parts of your page. The result will be a cleaner and more organized look. For example, the title, text, and subheadings of a Wikipedia article align with the left margin, and images align with the right margin.

### Repetition

Readers are guided by the repetition of key words and elements. Use a consistent design throughout your document for such elements as color, typeface, and images. Every Wikipedia page uses the same fonts and the same layout, so readers know what to expect.

### Proximity

Parts of a text that are closely related should appear together (proximate to one another). Your goal is to position related points, text, and visuals near one another and to use clear headings to identify these clusters, as the Wikipedia page does.

*Consistent overall impression*

Aim for a visual structure and design that create the appropriate overall impression or mood for your text. For an academic essay, whether print or digital, you will probably make conservative choices that strike a serious scholarly note. In a newsletter for a campus group, you might choose attention-getting images. In a website designed to introduce yourself to future employers, you might favor a mix of material drawn from your current résumé, including writing, embedded video or links to digital content that relates to your skills and career goals, and at least one image of yourself — all in a carefully organized and easy-to-comprehend structure.

## Using templates

If designing your writing yourself seems intimidating, consider using a template. Templates are basic models that show you how to lay out a particular type of text. You may have used templates in a word-processing program to create a document such as a memo or report, in presentation software to create slides, or in a blog-publishing service to design your content. Before you create a text in a genre that is new to you, it's a good idea to look for available design templates. You can use them to familiarize yourself with conventional elements and layouts for the genre, even if you decide not to follow the template's settings for color, fonts, and other details of formatting.

# 22c Formatting print and digital texts

With so many options available, you should always spend some time thinking about appropriate formatting for elements of your text. Although the following guidelines often apply, remember that print documents, web pages, slide shows, videos, and so on all have their own formatting conventions. (To learn more about formatting requirements for academic essays in MLA style, see 18b; in APA style, see 19b; in *Chicago* style, see 20b; in CSE style, see 21a.)

---

**LANGUAGE, CULTURE, AND CONTEXT** | **READING PATTERNS**

In documents written in English and other Western languages, information tends to flow from left to right and top to bottom — since that is the way English texts are written and read. In some languages, which may be written from right to left or vertically, documents may be arranged from top right to bottom left. Understanding the reading patterns of the language you are working in will help you design your documents most effectively.

## Using white space (negative space)

The parts of a page or screen left intentionally blank are called *white space* or *negative space*, and they emphasize content and direct readers' eyes. Too little white space makes a page look crowded, while too much can make it seem empty or unfinished. Think about the amount of white space at the page level (top and side margins), paragraph level (the space between paragraphs), and sentence level (the space between sentences). Aim for consistency. Within the page, you can also use white space around particular content, such as an image, an embedded video, or a list, to make it stand out.

## Using color

As you design your documents, keep in mind that some colors can evoke powerful responses, so take care that the colors you use match the message you are sending. Color can enliven texts that are mainly alphabetic, but using color poorly can also make a text seem less readable and inviting. If you decide to use color in a document, keep your color palette, or range of colors, fairly limited to avoid a jumbled look. Use the following tips to carry readers through your document:

- Use color to draw attention to elements you want to emphasize: headings, text boxes, or graphs, for example.
- Be consistent in your use of color; use the same color for all of your subheads, for example, or the same background color for all of your presentation slides.
- Choose color combinations that are easy to read. Ask a few peers or friends whether your text is legible against the background before presenting, submitting, or posting your work.
- Make sure all visuals and text are legible in the setting in which they will be read. Colors can be sharper on a computer monitor than in a print document, and slides may look different when you project them.

---

CONSIDERING DISABILITIES | **COLOR FOR CONTRAST**

Remember when you are using color that not everyone will see it as you do. Some individuals do not perceive color at all; others perceive color in a variety of ways, especially colors like blue and green, which are close together on the color spectrum. You can learn more at colourblindawareness.org.

## Choosing type sizes and fonts

For words in the body of a traditional report, essay, or web posting, an 11- or 12-point type size is conventional.

Choose a readable font, either a serif font (used in this sentence) or a sans serif font (used in headings on this page). Although unusual fonts might seem attractive at first glance, readers may find such styles distracting and hard to read over long stretches of material. Remember that fonts help you create the tone of a document, so consider your audience and purpose when selecting type.

*Different fonts convey different feelings.*
**Different fonts convey different feelings.**
DIFFERENT FONTS CONVEY DIFFERENT FEELINGS.
Different fonts convey different feelings.

Most important, be consistent in the size and style of typeface you use, especially for the main part of your text. Unless you are striving for some special effect, shifting sizes and fonts within a document can give an appearance of disorderliness. But purposeful use of special fonts can signal imagination, humor, and even spontaneity.

## Using margin and line spacing

For traditional print projects, you will probably use a single column of text with standard one-inch margins for your writing, but many other kinds of projects call for text columns of variable widths or for multiple columns. Both very short and very long text lines can be difficult to read. Online readers generally prefer short, manageable chunks of text rather than long paragraphs; consider breaking up a long online piece with headings or visuals.

By using buttons like those shown here, you can decide whether or not you want left and right margins justified, or squared off — as they are on typical book pages (including this one). Readers will often expect you to align the left margin, except in posters and other texts where you are trying *left align, center, right align, justify* to achieve a distinctive visual effect. However, most readers — and many instructors — prefer the right margin to be "ragged," or unjustified, as it is in the Wikipedia entry in 22b.

For college writing assignments, you will usually use double-spaced type with the first line of each paragraph indented one-half inch. Letters, memos, and online texts are usually single-spaced and may use spaces between paragraphs instead of paragraph indentation. Look for samples of texts in the genre, or ask about your instructor's preference.

## Using headings

For brief essays and reports, you may need no headings at all. For longer texts, however, headings help readers understand the organization. Headings can also help break long web texts into the short, manageable chunks that online readers expect. Some kinds of reports require conventional headings (such as *Abstract* and *Summary*), which writers must provide.

You can distinguish headings by type size and font as well as by color, as this book does. Position each level of heading consistently throughout the text. And remember that headings need to appear above the text they introduce; be careful, for example, not to put a heading at the bottom of a printed page.

For formal academic work, look for the most succinct, informative, and consistent way to word headings. Choose all nouns, for example, or all questions.

| | |
|---|---|
| NOUN | Toxicity |
| NOUN PHRASE | Levels of toxicity |
| GERUND (-*ING*) PHRASE | Measuring toxicity |
| QUESTION | How can toxicity be measured? |
| COMMAND/IMPERATIVE | Measure the toxicity. |

## 22d Considering visuals and media

Choose visuals and other media that will help make a point more vividly and succinctly than written words alone. In some cases, visuals and media may even be your primary text.

---

QUICK HELP

### Using visuals and media effectively

- Choose visual and media elements that will make your text more effective for your audience.
- Consider design principles for placement of visual and media files within a text, and aim to make your media files accessible to as many readers as possible. **(22b)**
- Tell the audience explicitly what a visual demonstrates, especially if it presents complex information. Do not assume readers will "read" the visual the way you do; your commentary on it is important.
- Follow established conventions for documenting visual and media sources. See 18b (MLA), 19b (APA), 20b (*Chicago*), or 21a (CSE). Ask permission for use if someone else controls the rights. **(Chapter 16)**
- Get responses to your visuals and media in an early draft. If readers can't follow them or are distracted by them, revise accordingly.
- If you alter or edit visuals, audio, or video to include them in your writing, be sure to do so ethically. **(15e)**

## Selecting visuals and media

Consider carefully what you want visuals, audio, or video to do for your writing. What will your audience want or need you to show? Try to choose visuals and media that will enhance your credibility, allow you to make your point more emphatically, and clarify your overall text. Note that different visuals work best for different situations. Tables, for example, help make detailed numerical information easier to read; a diagram can illustrate the parts of an object or process; and a photograph can capture something meaningful about an event, object, or person.

### Sample Table

| | United States | | |
|---|---|---|---|
| **SCHOOL ENROLLMENT** | Estimate | Percent | Percent margin of error |
| Population 3 years and older enrolled in school | 82,148,370 | — | — |
| Nursery/preschool | 4,959,823 | 6.0 | +/−0.1 |
| Kindergarten | 4,181,764 | 5.1 | +/−0.1 |
| Elementary school (grades 1–8) | 32,831,750 | 40.0 | +/−0.1 |
| High school (grades 9–12) | 16,985,786 | 20.7 | +/−0.1 |
| College or graduate school | 23,189,247 | 28.2 | +/−0.1 |

U.S. Census Bureau

### Sample Diagram

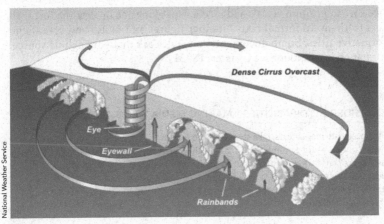

National Weather Service

## Sample Photograph

Libby Welch/Alamy Stock Photo

Effective media content can be your own work or materials created by others. If you are using media from another source, be sure to give appropriate credit and to get permission before making it available to the public as part of your work. Note how credit lines are placed next to the photos in this chapter.

### Positioning and identifying visuals and media

Make sure to position visuals and media clips alongside or after the text that refers to them. In formal texts, number figures and tables and give them informative titles. Some documentation styles ask that you include source information in a caption (see Chapters 18–21).

---

**CONSIDERING DISABILITIES | MAKING MEDIA TEXTS ACCESSIBLE**

As you create media texts, take steps to make sure that all your readers can access your content — for example, by providing alternative text for all visuals so that they will make sense when read by a screen reader, and by providing captions for sound files and transcripts of longer audio content. For details on designing accessible texts, visit the Americans with Disabilities Act site at www.ada.gov, and click on "Design Standards."

## Using visuals and media ethically

Technical tools available to writers and designers today make it relatively easy to manipulate and edit visuals, audio, and video. As you would with any source material, carefully assess any visuals you find for effectiveness, appropriateness, and validity, and identify the source for any media files you use that you have not created yourself.

- Check the context in which the visual, video, or audio appears. Is it part of an official government, school, or library site or otherwise from a credible source (14d)?
- If the visual is a photograph, is the information in the photo believable? Could it have been altered or "doctored" (10f)?
- If the visual is a chart, graph, or diagram, are the numbers and labels explained? Are the sources of the data given? Will the visual representation help readers make sense of the information, or could it mislead them (10e and f)?
- Can you find contact information for the creator or rightsholder?

At times, you may make certain changes to visuals that you use, such as cropping an image to show the most important detail, digitally brightening a dark image, or using a short clip from a longer audio or video file. You can make digital changes as long as you do so ethically, making no attempt to mislead readers.

### EXERCISE 22.1

Take an essay or other writing assignment you have done recently, one that makes little use of the design elements discussed in this chapter. Reevaluate the effectiveness of your text, and make a note of all the places where visuals and other design elements (color, different type size, and so on) would help you get your ideas across more effectively.

▼ ▼ ▼ ▼ ▼ ▼ ▼ ▼ ▼ ▼ ▼ ▼ ▼ ▼ ▼ ▼ ▼ ▼ ▼ ▼ ▼ ▼ ▼ ▼

## THINKING CRITICALLY ABOUT DESIGN FOR WRITING

Look at a print text you have recently completed. Using the advice in this chapter, assess your use of visual structure, consistent use of conventions for guiding readers through your text, and use of visuals. Then take a look at an online text that you have composed—a web page or a blog posting or an invitation or announcement of some kind—and make the same kind of assessment. Then write a brief analysis of how well each text is designed and how you could improve either or both.

# CHAPTER 23

# Presentations

When the Gallup Poll reports on what U.S. citizens say they fear most, the findings are often the same from year to year: public speaking is apparently even scarier than an attack from outer space. Nevertheless, many writing courses may require you not only to compose written texts but also to give presentations in front of an audience, and it's safe to say that most jobs require you to present information orally in front of audiences of all kinds. People who are successful presenters point to four elements crucial to their effectiveness:

- a thorough knowledge of the subject at hand
- careful attention to the interactive nature of speaking and thus to the needs of the audience
- careful integration of verbal and visual information
- practice, practice, and more practice

## 23a Considering assignment, purpose, and audience for presentations

You'll be wise to begin preparing for a class presentation as soon as you get the assignment. Think about how much time you have to prepare; how long the presentation is to be; whether you will use written-out text or note cards or some other kind of cue; what kind of posters, handouts, slides, or other materials you may need; and what equipment you will need. If you are making a group presentation, you will need time to divide duties and practice (8b). Make sure that you understand how the presentation will be graded or assessed.

Consider the purpose of your presentation (3c). Are you expected to lead a discussion? teach a lesson? give a report? engage a group in an activity? Also consider the audience (3d). If your instructor is a member of the audience, what will he or she expect you to do — and do well? What do audience members know about your topic? What do they need to know to follow your presentation and perhaps accept your point of view? If your presentation will be posted online, is there any reason to limit the audience who will have access to it? Finally, consider your own stance toward your topic and audience. Are you an expert? novice? well-informed observer?

QUICK HELP

Guidelines for presentations

- Check to make sure your presentation accomplishes the goals of the assignment.
- Be sure you are achieving your intended purpose.
- Consider your audience's expectations and knowledge about the subject. Provide any background information necessary to help your audience follow your line of reasoning and your major points.
- Use a clear and straightforward organizational structure for your presentation.
- Check for signposts that can guide listeners, including explicit transitions and the repetition of key words and ideas.
- Rely mostly on easy-to-understand and straightforward sentences. Consider revising any long or complicated sentences to make your presentation easier to follow. Use concrete language.
- Consider marking your notes for pauses and emphasis. Also note material that you can skip if you find yourself short of time.
- Make sure that your slides and media contribute clearly to your presentation.
- Review your visuals to make sure they follow principles of good design.
- Prepare a list of sources to accompany your presentation.
- Practice your presentation so that you will appear confident and knowledgeable—and then practice it again!

*Shuqiao Song's analysis of a presentation assignment*

Student writer Shuqiao Song got a two-part assignment for her writing class on graphic narratives: she had to write a researched argument, and then she had to turn that information into a script for a twelve-minute oral presentation with slides. After some brainstorming and talking with her instructor, Shuqiao chose her favorite graphic memoir, Alison Bechdel's *Fun Home*, as her topic.

As she thought about her assignment and topic, Shuqiao realized that she had more than one purpose. Certainly she wanted to do well on the assignment and receive a good grade. But she also wanted to convince her classmates that Bechdel's book was a complex and important one and that its power lay in the relationship of words and images. She also had to admit to at least one other purpose: it would be great to turn in a truly *impressive* performance.

## 23b Writing to be heard and remembered

Getting and keeping the attention of listeners may require you to use different strategies than the ones you generally employ when writing for a reading audience. To be *remembered* rather than simply heard, consider these features of memorable presentations.

## Including stories

There's nothing like a good story to get and hold audience attention. In fact, presentation expert Nancy Duarte found that stories were at the heart of hundreds of great speeches she analyzed, whether they were informative or argumentative. Many speakers prefer to use personal stories that are witty and memorable. Andrew Linderman, a storytelling coach, says that the best ones are "honest and personal . . . without emoting too much or going off the rails." But a good presentation story may also be about someone else. Shuqiao Song used several stories from the graphic narrative *Fun Home* to help make her argument.

## Planning your introduction and conclusion

Remember that listeners, like readers, tend to remember beginnings and endings most readily, so work extra hard to make these elements memorable. Consider, for example, using a startling statement, opinion, or question; a dramatic anecdote; a powerful quotation; or a vivid image. Shifting language, especially into a variety of language that your audience will identify with, is another effective way to catch their attention (see Chapter 34). Whenever you can link your subject to the experiences and interests of your audience, do so.

### Shuqiao Song's introduction

Shuqiao Song began her presentation this way:

> Welcome, everyone. I'm Shuqiao Song and I'm here today to talk about residents of a dys*FUN*ctional *HOME*.
>
> We meet these residents in a graphic memoir called *Fun Home*.

---

### CONSIDERING DISABILITIES | **ACCESSIBLE PRESENTATIONS**

Remember that some members of your audience may have trouble seeing or hearing your presentation, so do all you can to make your presentation accessible.

- Be sure to face any audience members who rely on lip-reading to understand your words. For a large audience, request an ASL (American Sign Language) interpreter.
- Do not rely on color or graphics alone to get across information.
- For presentations you publish online, provide brief textual descriptions of your visuals.
- If you use video, provide labels for captions to explain any sounds that won't be audible to some audience members, and embed spoken captions to explain images to those who cannot see them. Be sure that the equipment is caption capable.
- Provide a transcript for audio or video elements for those who need it.

To start, Shuqiao showed a three-second video clip of author Alison Bechdel saying, "I love words, and I love pictures. But especially, I love them together — in a mystical way that I can't even explain."

> That was Alison Bechdel, author of *Fun Home*. In that clip, she conveniently introduces the topics of my presentation today: Words. Pictures. And the mystical way they work together.

Note that this presentation opened with a play on words ("dys*FUN*ctional *HOME*"), to which Shuqiao returned later on, and with a short, vivid video clip that perfectly summed up the main topic of the presentation. Also note the use of short sentences and fragments, special effects that act like drumbeats to get and hold the attention of the audience.

## Using signpost language

Organize your presentation clearly and carefully, and give an overview of your main points toward the beginning of your presentation. (You may wish to recall these points again toward the end of the talk.) Throughout your presentation, pause between major points, and use signpost language as you move from one topic to the next. Such signposts act as explicit transitions in your talk and should be clear and concrete: *The second crisis point in the breakup of the Soviet Union occurred hard on the heels of the first* instead of *The breakup of the Soviet Union came to another crisis point*. In addition to such explicit transitions (5d) as *next*, *on the contrary*, and *finally*, you can offer signposts to your listeners by carefully repeating key words and ideas as well as by sticking to concrete topic sentences to introduce each new idea.

### Shuqiao Song's signpost language

At the end of Shuqiao's introduction, she set forth the structure of her presentation in a very clear, straightforward, and simple way to help her audience follow what came next:

> So, to outline the rest of my presentation: <u>first,</u> I'll show how *text* is insufficient — but also why it is necessary to Bechdel's story. <u>Second,</u> I'll show how *images* can't be trusted, but again, why they are still necessary for Bechdel's purposes. <u>Third and finally,</u> I'll show how the interplay of text and image in *Fun Home* creates a more complex and comprehensive understanding of the story.

## Using simple syntax and memorable language

Avoid long, complicated sentences, and use straightforward sentence structure (subject-verb-object) as much as possible. Listeners prefer action verbs and concrete nouns to abstractions. You may need to deal with abstract ideas, but try to provide concrete examples for them (37c). Memorable presentations

*In a presentation on* Fun Home, *Shuqiao Song uses a Magritte painting as evidence to show that "images can't be trusted."*

often call on the power of figures of speech and other devices of language, such as careful repetition, parallelism, and climactic order.

### Shuqiao Song's example

Shuqiao Song's presentation script included the following example:

> Now, to argue my second point, I'll begin with an image. This is a René Magritte painting. The text means, *"This is not a pipe."* Is this some surrealist Jedi mind trick? Not really. Now listen to the title of the painting to grasp Magritte's point. The painting is called *The Treason of Images.* Here Magritte is showing us that "this is not a pipe" because it is an *image* of a pipe.

Shuqiao's short sentences, vivid word choice ("surrealist Jedi mind trick"), and straightforward subject-verb-object syntax all help to make the passage easy on listeners.

## Turning writing into a script

Even though you will probably rely on some written material, you will need to adapt it for speech. Depending on the assignment, the audience, and your personal preferences, you may even speak from a full script. If so, double- or triple-space it, and use fairly large print so that it will be easy to refer to. Try to end each page with the end of a sentence so that you won't have to pause while you turn a page. In addition, you may decide to mark spots where you want to pause and to highlight words you want to emphasize.

*A paragraph from Shuqiao Song's print essay*

> Finally, we can see how image and text function together. On the one hand, image and text support each other in that each highlights the subtleties of the other; but on the other hand, the more interesting interaction comes when there is some degree of distance between what is written and what is depicted. In *Fun Home*, there is no one-to-one closure that mentally connects text and image. Rather, Bechdel pushes the boundaries of mental closure between image and text. If the words and pictures match exactly, making the same point, the story would read like a children's book, and that would be too simple for what Bechdel is trying to accomplish. However, text and image can't be so mismatched that meaning completely eludes the readers.

*Shuqiao Song's paragraph revised for oral presentation*

Note that the revised paragraph presents the same information, but this time it is written to be heard. The revision uses helpful signpost language, some repetition, simple syntax, and informal varieties of English to help listeners follow along and keep them interested.

> Finally, image and text can work together. They support each other: each highlights the subtleties of the other. But they are even more interesting when there's a gap — some distance between the story the words tell and the story the pictures tell. In *Fun Home*, text and image are never perfectly correlated. After all, if the words and pictures matched up exactly, the story would read like a kids' book. That would be way too simple for Bechdel's purposes. But we wouldn't want a complete disconnect between words and images either, since we wouldn't be able to make sense of them.

## Speaking from notes

If you decide to speak from notes rather than from a full script, here are some tips for doing so effectively:

- In general, use one note card for each point in your presentation.
- Number the cards.
- On each card, include the major point you want to make in large bold text and any subpoints in a bulleted list.
- Include signpost language (*another benefit is . . .*) on each note.
- Practice your presentation using the notes at least twice.
- Time your presentation. Use color or brackets to mark material in your notes that you can skip if you are running too long.

## 23c Creating a presentation

Visuals are often an integral part of a presentation, carrying a lot of the message the speaker wants to convey. So think of your visuals not as add-ons but as a major means of getting your points across. Many speakers use slides created in presentation software to help keep themselves on track and to guide the audience. In addition, posters, flip charts, chalkboards, or interactive whiteboards can also help you make strong visual statements.

Presentation tools such as PowerPoint, Google Slides, or Prezi allow you to prepare slides you want to display and even to enhance the images with sound. To choose among them, consider what the tool allows you to do and how much time you will need to learn to use it effectively. For more on design principles, see Chapter 22.

---

**QUICK HELP**

Guidelines for slide presentations

- Audiences can't read and listen to you at the same time, so make the slides support what you are saying as clearly and visually as possible. Just one or two words—or a visual without words—may be more effective than a list of bullet points.
- Avoid reading from your slides. Your audience can read faster than you can talk, and you are guaranteed to bore them with this technique.
- Use your media wisely, and respect your audience's time. If you feel that you need to include more than three or four bullet points (or more than fifty words of text) on a slide, you may be trying to convey too much information and may need to rethink your presentation.
- Make sure text is large enough to read, and create a clear contrast between text or illustration and background. In general, light backgrounds work better in a darkened room, and dark backgrounds in a lighted one.
- Choose visuals that will reproduce sharply, and make sure they are large enough to be clearly visible.
- Make sure that sound or video clips are audible and that they relate directly to your topic.
- Although there are no firm rules about how many slides you should use or how long each slide should be made visible, plan length and timing with your audience's needs and your purpose in mind.
- Most important, make sure your slides engage and help your listeners rather than distract them from your message.

---

*Shuqiao Song's slides*

For her presentation, "Residents of a DysFUNctional HOME: Text and Image," Shuqiao Song developed a series of very simple slides aimed at underscoring her points and keeping her audience focused on them. She began by introducing the work, showing the book cover on an otherwise black slide. Throughout the presentation, she used very simple visuals — a word or two, or a large image

*In her presentation, Shuqiao uses simple visuals to focus her audience on her analysis.*

from the book she was discussing — to keep her audience focused on what she was saying.

## 23d Practicing the presentation

In oral presentations, as with many other things in life, practice makes perfect. Prepare a draft of your presentation and slides or other media far enough in advance to allow you to seek feedback from friends or classmates — just as you would with an essay. If possible, make a video of yourself, and then examine the video in detail. You can also practice in front of a mirror or in front of friends. Do whatever works for you — just as long as you practice!

If you are using slides or other visuals to accompany your presentation (and most students do so), make sure your use of the visuals is smooth and on track with your script.

Also, make sure you can be heard clearly. If you are soft-spoken, concentrate on projecting your voice. If your voice tends to rise when you are in the spotlight, practice lowering your pitch. If you speak rapidly, practice slowing down and enunciating words clearly. Remember that tone of voice affects listeners, so aim for a tone that conveys interest in and commitment to your topic and listeners.

Once you are comfortable giving the presentation, make sure you will stay within the allotted time. One good rule of thumb is to allow roughly two and a half minutes per double-spaced page of text. The only way to be sure about your time, however, is to time yourself as you practice. Knowing that your presentation is neither too short nor too long will help you relax and gain self-confidence; and when the members of your audience sense your self-confidence, they will become increasingly open to your message.

## 23e Delivering the presentation

Experienced speakers always expect to feel at least some anxiety before delivering a presentation — and they develop strategies for dealing with it. Remember that a little nervousness can act to your advantage: adrenaline, after all, can help you perform well.

Having confidence in your own knowledge will help to make you a confident presenter. In addition to doing your homework, however, you may be able to use the following strategies to good advantage:

- Consider how you will dress and how you will move around. In each case, your choices should be appropriate for the situation. Most experienced speakers like to dress simply and comfortably for easy movement. But dressing up a little signals your pride in your appearance and your respect for your audience.

- Go over the scene of your presentation in your mind, and think it through completely, in order to feel more comfortable during it. In addition, check out the presentation room and double-check to make sure you have all the equipment you might need.

- If you are using handouts, decide when to distribute them. Unless they include material you want your audience to use while you speak, distribute them after the presentation.

Pause before you begin your presentation, concentrating on your opening lines. During your presentation, interact with your audience as much as possible. You can do so by facing the audience at all times and making eye contact as often as possible; avoid staring just at your laptop or at the screen behind you. Allow time for the audience to ask questions. Try to keep your answers short so that others may participate in the conversation. When you conclude, remember to thank your audience.

### EXERCISE 23.1

Attend a lecture or watch a presentation online (such as a TED Talk) and analyze its effectiveness. How does the speaker capture and hold your interest? What signpost language and other guides to listening can you detect? How well are visuals integrated into the presentation? How do the speaker's tone of voice, dress, and eye contact affect your understanding and appreciation (or lack of it)? What is most memorable about the presentation, and why? Bring your analysis to class and report your findings.

## 23f  Considering other kinds of presentations

You may want or need to think about other kinds of presentations for school or work, including poster presentations, online presentations, or PechaKuchas.

### Giving a poster presentation

Many college courses and conferences now call on students to make *poster presentations*. During the class or conference session, the presenter uses a poster board as background while talking through the presentation and answering questions. Poster presentations give you a chance to demonstrate your knowledge about a subject "on your feet," answering questions and interacting with those who attend the class or session. If you are preparing for a poster presentation, remember to make sure the information on the poster can be easily seen and read and is simply and clearly organized.

### Presenting online

You may also have an opportunity to make presentations online, in your classes, or in your job. A webcast, for example, is a presentation that is broadcast on the Internet, using streaming media to distribute the presentation to viewers who might be anywhere in the world. As you prepare for an online presentation, you will want to develop a clear script as well as a set of slides or other visuals. Remember that you probably won't be able to make eye contact with your audience; you'll need to speak into the camera — as if you are speaking directly to them.

### Presenting a PechaKucha

PechaKucha — from Japanese: ペチャクチャ, for "chit chat" — is a special form of presentation with a set structure: twenty slides, each of which advances automatically after twenty seconds, for a total time of 6:40. Astrid Klein and Mark Dytham, architects in Tokyo, invented PechaKucha in 2003 because they felt that "architects talk too much" about their own work; they wanted to design a way to keep the presentations succinct and crisp. From this professional presentation format grew "PechaKucha nights" where people can share their work in a relaxed and supportive, if sometimes also competitive, atmosphere. Some college instructors are now inviting students to try their hands at constructing a PechaKucha as a way of presenting ideas to classmates.

For any of these presentation types — posters, online webcasts, or PechaKuchas — remember to consider your purpose carefully and to make sure that your presentation will appeal to the audience you have chosen.

▼ ▼ ▼ ▼ ▼ ▼ ▼ ▼ ▼ ▼ ▼ ▼ ▼ ▼ ▼ ▼ ▼ ▼ ▼ ▼ ▼ ▼ ▼ ▼ ▼ ▼ ▼ ▼

## THINKING CRITICALLY ABOUT ORAL AND MULTIMODAL PRESENTATIONS

Study the text of an oral or multimodal presentation you've prepared or given. Using the advice in this chapter, see how well your presentation appeals to your audience. Look in particular at how well you catch and hold their attention. How effective is your use of signpost language or other structures that help guide your listeners? How helpful are the visuals (slides, posters) in conveying your message? What would you do to improve this presentation?

# CHAPTER 24

# Communicating in Other Media

Writing instructors across the country are assigning not just slide presentations but also annotated playlists, blogs, comics, live tweets, podcasts, video essays, wikis, and more. Student writers seem to like and appreciate such multimodal assignments, saying that they provide room for creative control, self-expression, and, in some cases, interaction. As communicating with media becomes more common and even more necessary in your life, it's important to think carefully about your goals and your audiences — as well as about how to accomplish and reach them most effectively, no matter what kind of project you are creating.

## 24a Considering your rhetorical context

As with any college assignment, you will want to make sure you consider time and technical constraints. Many online projects take much more time than a traditional writing assignment: one student, for example, told us that she spent ninety hours creating a three-minute animated video. So you need to plan carefully to make sure you have both the access to any tools you will need and the time to carry out the project (and to learn about the tools, if necessary).

As with any writing project, you will want to think about rhetorical concerns, such as your purpose for creating the text, the needs of your audience, and the main point or message you want to get across.

---

**QUICK HELP**

Rhetorical contexts for multimodal writing

- Why are you creating this text, document, or project? How do you want viewers to use it? Considering purpose will help you determine what features you want to highlight.
- What potential audience(s) can you identify? Thinking about the audience for your project will help you make strong rhetorical choices about tone, word choice, graphic style and design, level of detail, and many other factors. If your intended audience is limited to people you know (such as a wiki for members of your class), you may be able to make some assumptions ▶

---

Rhetorical contexts for multimodal writing, continued

about their background, knowledge, and likely responses. Plan your project to appeal to readers you expect—but remember that an online text may reach other, unanticipated audiences.

• What is the subject or topic of your project? The topic will certainly affect the content and design of the project. If you want to focus on the latest Hong Kong film releases, for example, you might create a blog that always places your most recent posts at the top; if you want to explore the works of 1940s detective writers, you might produce a website with pages devoted to particular writers or themes. If you prefer to show information on your topic, you might consider creating an infographic or a video essay that you can post to an existing site.

• How do you relate to your subject matter? Your rhetorical stance determines how your audience will see you. Will you present yourself as an expert? a fan? a novice seeking input from others? What information will make you seem credible and persuasive to your audience(s)?

# 24b Planning web-based texts

Use organization, interactivity, and links to make your multimodal text work as effectively as possible.

## Organizing content

Whether you are creating a layout for a web page or storyboarding a video essay, you should develop a clear structure for your text. Some types of online texts are organized in standard ways — most blogs and social media sites, for example, put the newest posts at the top. Others allow you to make choices about how to arrange materials. Choose a structure that makes sense for your purpose, audience, topic, and rhetorical stance. Arrange your text to allow readers to find what they are looking for as quickly and intuitively as possible. (For more on organizing and planning your text, see 4e and f.)

## Allowing interaction

The possibility of interaction with readers is one of the great opportunities of online writing, but you can consider different levels of interactivity. While wikis are full-scale collaborative efforts and frequently allow contribution from users, you might also include something as simple as a thumbs-up / thumbs-down or LIKE button to allow users to register their reaction to a text. Online texts can incorporate polls, comments, and links for contacting writers.

## Linking

Academic and formal writing follows guidelines that tell readers the sources of other people's ideas and research through notes and bibliographic references.

Some less formal online writing includes links to external sites. You can also link to content that helps prove a point — complex explanations, supporting statistics, bibliographies, referenced websites, or additional readings. Links also help readers navigate from one part of a text to another.

Each link should have a clear rhetorical purpose and be in an appropriate location. If you put a link in the middle of a paragraph, be aware that readers may go to the linked content before finishing what's before them — and if that link takes them to an external site, they may never come back! If it's important for users to read the whole paragraph, you may want to move the link to the end of it.

## 24c Creating different types of multimodal texts

Among the common types of multimodal assignments in college writing courses are websites and web pages, blogs, microblogs, wikis, audio and video projects, and nondigital multimodal projects like comics. The following table presents six kinds of assignments that call for multimodal work, along with characteristics and questions you should ask yourself as you undertake such assignments.

**Common Multimodal Assignments**

| Type | Characteristics | Rhetorical Considerations |
|------|-----------------|---------------------------|
| Website | Websites allow a writer to organize elements as a cluster of associations. Each page may cover a single aspect of a larger topic. A menu on the page typically lets readers find related information on the site. | • What decisions will you make about layout?<br>• How do you want visitors to navigate your site? |
| Blog | Blogs function like an online journal or column. Individual posts can be short or long, formal or informal—and the content can be on a single topic or a variety of topics. Bloggers often invite commentary. | • How do you want to represent yourself to readers?<br>• How often will readers expect you to post? |

| Type | Characteristics | Rhetorical Considerations |
|---|---|---|
| Microblog (Twitter, for example) | Microblogs allow users to post brief updates and comments about a variety of topics. Users can hold individual accounts or can write officially for a company, organization, or government agency. | • What labels will you add to your posts to help readers find them?<br>• What are expectations and conventions around sharing other people's posts? |
| Wiki | Wikis are online texts that empower all users to contribute content. Wikis create communities where all content is evaluated by other members; they draw on the collective knowledge of many contributors. | • How will you identify your sources of information?<br>• What responsibilities do you have to others in your community? |
| Audio/ Video | Audio and video content can vary as widely as the content found in written-word media. Writers who create podcasts (which can be downloaded for playback) and streaming media (which can be played without downloading) may produce episodic content united by a common host or theme. | • Will you embed your file in another type of document, such as a website or slide presentation?<br>• What technical help do you need to achieve your purpose and reach your viewers or listeners? |
| Nondigital multimodal project | Projects like comics, posters, and scrapbooks offer creative ways to reach audiences without having to use digital tools. | • How will you share your work?<br>• Why is a nondigital project right for your writing situation? |

## CONSIDERING DISABILITIES | **ACCESSIBLE WEB TEXTS**

Much on the web remains hard to access and read for persons with disabilities. The website for the Americans with Disabilities Act provides guidelines on designing accessible sites, which include offering textual descriptions of any visuals and captions for any sound files. For details, visit www.ada.gov, and click on "Design Standards."

### EXERCISE 24.1

Use a search engine to find a website that you haven't visited before but that addresses a topic you know something about. What is the purpose of the text? Who is its intended audience? What rhetorical stance does it take? How credible is the information on the site? What overall impression does the text create—and how does it do so?

▼ ▼ ▼ ▼ ▼ ▼ ▼ ▼ ▼ ▼ ▼ ▼ ▼ ▼ ▼ ▼ ▼ ▼ ▼ ▼ ▼ ▼ ▼ ▼ ▼

## THINKING CRITICALLY ABOUT MULTIMODAL TEXTS

Take some time to reflect on a multimodal text you have created, whether it's an assignment posted to a course website, a blog post or comment, a YouTube video, or a poster presentation. Evaluate the work you've created. For what purpose did you create the text? Did you achieve your goals? What audience did you anticipate, and did that audience see your work? Who else saw it? What was your topic, and what stance did you take? Finally, what kind of feedback did you get? Conclude by drawing up a list of tips for making future online texts, noting what aspects of your text were successful and what you would do differently.

# PART 7
# Academic, Professional, and Public Writing

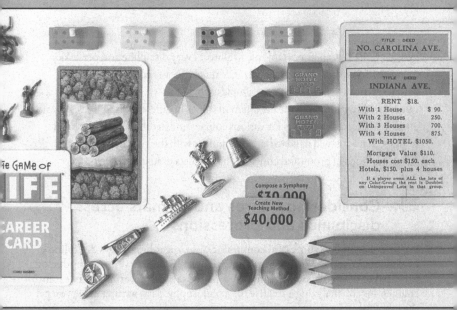

Photo by Mike Enright/www.menright.com. Photo styling by Barbara Lipp.

# CHAPTER 25

# Writing Well in Any Discipline or Profession

Writing well plays an important role in almost every discipline and profession. As one MBA wrote, "Those who advance quickly in my company are those who write and speak well — it's as simple as that." But while writing is always a valuable skill, writing well means different things in different disciplines. As you prepare written assignments for various courses and in different professional settings, then, you will need to become familiar with the genres, vocabularies, styles, methods of proof, and conventional formats used in each field.

## 25a Considering genres and formats across disciplines and professions

Writing is central to successful communication, regardless of the discipline or profession. Whether you are explaining the results of a survey you conducted for a psychology class, working on a proposal for material sciences and engineering, or analyzing a treatise for a philosophy class, writing helps you get the job done.

One good way to learn to write well in a discipline or profession is to think carefully about the *genres,* or kinds of writing, aimed at achieving a particular goal for a particular audience. Like popular genres (think of sci-fi movies, for instance, or hip-hop music), academic and professional genres share characteristic features and conventions — but they are not lockstep, fill-in-the-blank forms. Rather, they are flexible and adaptable to different audiences and rhetorical situations. In addition, genres evolve in response to shifting linguistic and cultural contexts. For centuries, letters followed conventions established in the medieval era (they were very formal, for one thing), but more recently they evolved to include lots of subgenres (thank-you letters, rejection letters, cover letters) before shading into email and text messages and adapting to online environments.

Sometimes you will be assigned to write in a particular genre — a rhetorical analysis in first-year writing, for example, or care notes for your internship at a nursing home. You may also be expected to follow certain formats, such as the IMRAD — introduction, methods, results, and discussion — typically used in much science writing. If so, look for examples of these genres and formats, and study them to see how they work and what their features are. Whether or not you are assigned a genre or format, you will profit by thinking carefully about genre before beginning to write. Here are some ways to begin:

- **Think about the discipline or profession the assignment is for.** If you are writing about sustainable agriculture for a human biology class, you may be expected to write an argument presenting the debate around sustainability and offering a solution. If you're sharing results of an interview you conducted as part of your work for a nonprofit organization, you will probably choose to follow the conventions of a report.

- **Ask: Who is the audience?** If you are writing about sexual harassment policies on campus and your audience is the first-year class, you might use a narrative or story; while writing about the same subject for a presentation to the student governing body, you might use the features of a resolution.

- **Determine the best medium to use.** For a presentation on climate change in a political science class, you might choose to create an infographic, following the characteristic features of that genre. You might choose to distribute the infographic as a print document or, if you've built links into the data, you may find that digital distribution works better for your purposes.

---

### EXERCISE 25.1

Do some investigation related to the field you plan to major or minor in. Set up a time to interview a member of the faculty in that department or a member of the staff in your school's writing center. Ask a few questions such as the following.

- What genres are typically assigned or expected in this field?
- Does each genre have a typical audience? Which genres are likely to be aimed at an expert audience? Which are more often aimed at a general audience?
- Which types of documents in this field are typically delivered in print form, if any?

## 25b Reading in any discipline

As you already know, reading isn't a "one size fits all" activity: you need to adjust your reading strategies to fit the task at hand (see Chapter 9). Most instructors probably won't give you specific instruction in how to read texts; they will simply assume that you know how.

The more you read in any discipline, the easier you will find it to understand — and to write in that discipline. So read a lot, and pay attention to the texts you are reading. To get started, choose an article in an important journal in the field you plan to major in and then answer the following questions:

- How does a journal article in this discipline begin?

- How is the article organized? Does it have specific sections with subheads?

- What sources are cited, and how are they used — as backup support, as counterexamples, or as an argument to refute?

- What audience does the text seem to address? Is it a narrow technical or disciplinary audience, or is it aimed at a broader reading public? Is it addressed to readers of a specific journal? Is it published in print, online, or both? Is it intended for an international readership?

- How is the text formatted, and what citation style does it use?

- How are visuals such as charts or graphs used?

Finally, make sure you know whether articles you are reading are from peer-reviewed (sometimes called "juried") journals (13a). Peer-reviewed journals use panels of expert readers to analyze proposed articles and recommend publication (or not) to the journal editor, so articles in juried journals have been examined and accepted by experts in the field. Non-peer-reviewed journals can also offer valuable information, but they may bear the stamp of the editor and that person's biases more strongly than a peer-reviewed journal would.

## 25c Considering expectations for academic assignments

When you receive an assignment, your first job is to be sure you understand what that assignment is asking you to do. Some assignments may be as vague as "Write a five-page essay on one aspect of the Civil War." Others may be fairly specific: "Collect, summarize, and interpret data drawn from a sample of letters to the editor published in two newspapers, one in a small rural community and one in an urban community, over a period of three months." Whatever the assignment, use the questions in this section to analyze it.

---

**QUICK HELP**

Analyzing an assignment

- **What is the purpose of the assignment?** Are you expected to join a discussion, demonstrate your mastery of the topic in writing, or something else?
- **Who is the audience?** The instructor will be one audience, but are there others? If so, who are they?
- **What does the assignment ask of you?** Look for key terms such as *summarize, explain, evaluate, interpret, illustrate,* and *define.*
- **Do you need clarification of any terms?** If so, ask your instructor.
- **What do you need to know or find out to complete the assignment?** You may need to do background reading, develop a procedure for analyzing or categorizing information, or carry out some other kind of preparation.
- **What does the instructor expect in a written response?** How will you use sources? What kinds of sources should you use? How should you organize and develop the assignment? What is the expected format and length?
- **Can you locate a model of an effective response to a similar assignment?**
- **What do other students think the assignment requires?** Talking over an assignment with classmates is one good way to test your understanding.

---

**EXERCISE 25.2**

Analyze the following assignment from a communications course.

Assignment: Distribute a questionnaire to twenty people (ten male, ten female) asking these four questions: (1) What do you expect to say and do when you meet a stranger? (2) What don't you expect to say and do when you meet a stranger? (3) What do you expect to say and do when you meet a very close friend? (4) What don't you expect to say and do when you meet a very close friend?

When you have collected your twenty questionnaires, read them over and answer the following questions:

- What, if any, descriptions were common to all respondents' answers?
- How do male and female responses compare?
- What similarities and differences did you find between the responses to the stranger and to the very close friend?
- What factors (environment, time, status, gender, and so on) do you think had an impact on these responses?

Discuss your findings, using concepts and theories explained in your text.

## 25d Learning specialized vocabulary

As philosopher Kenneth Burke has noted, entering into an academic discipline is like going to a party where you do not know anyone. At first you feel like an outsider, and you may not understand much of what you hear or see. Before you enter the conversation, you have to listen and observe carefully. Eventually, however, you will be able to join in — and if you stay long enough, participating in the conversation becomes easy and natural.

To learn the routines, practices, and ways of knowing in a new field, you must also make an effort to enter into the conversation. One good way to get started is to study the vocabulary of the field you are most interested in.

Highlight the key terms in your reading or notes to learn how much specialized or technical vocabulary you will be expected to know. If you find only a small amount of specialized vocabulary, try to master the new terms quickly by reading your textbook carefully, looking up key words or phrases, and asking questions. If you find a great deal of specialized vocabulary, however, you may want to familiarize yourself with it methodically. Any of the following procedures may help:

- Keep a log of unfamiliar or confusing words *in context*. Check definitions in your textbook's glossary or index, and study pertinent sections to master the terms.

- Consult a specialized dictionary for definitions.

- Try to use and work with key concepts. Even if they are not yet entirely clear to you, working with them will help you understand them. For example, in a statistics class, try to work out (in words) how to do an analysis of *covariance*, step by step, even if you are not sure of the precise definition of the term. And don't forget that you can ask a tutor, TA, or instructor to help you understand the concept.

- Take special note of the ways technical language or disciplinary vocabulary is used in online information related to a particular field.

## 25e Following disciplinary style

Another important way to learn about disciplinary and professional writing is to look closely at stylistic features. Study some pieces of writing in the field with the following in mind:

- **Overall tone.** How would you describe the tone of the writing? (See 6f.)

- **Titles.** Are titles generally descriptive ("Findings from a Double-Blind Study of the Effect of Antioxidants"), persuasive ("Antioxidants Proven Effective"), or something else? How do each of the titles shape your expectations?

- **Stance.** To what extent do writers in the field strive for distance and objectivity? What strategies help them to achieve this stance? (See 3c.)

TALKING THE TALK | **THE FIRST PERSON**

"Is it true that I should never use *I* in college writing?" In much writing in college, using the first-person *I* is perfectly acceptable to most instructors. As always, think about the context — if your own experience is relevant to the topic, you are better off saying *I* than trying too hard not to. But don't overdo it, especially if the writing isn't just autobiographical. And check with your instructor if you aren't sure: in certain academic disciplines, using *I* may be seen as inappropriate.

- **Sentence length.** Are sentences long and complex? simple and direct?
- **Voice.** Are verbs generally active or passive? Why? (See 51g.)
- **Point of view.** Do writers use the first-person *I* or third-person terms such as *the investigator*? What is the effect of this choice?
- **Visuals.** Do writers typically use elements such as graphs, tables, maps, or photographs? How are visuals integrated into the text? What role, if any, do headings and other formatting elements play in the writing? (See Chapter 22.)
- **Documentation style.** Do writers use MLA, APA, *Chicago*, or CSE style? (See Chapters 18–21.) Are sources cited in some other way?

## 25f Using appropriate evidence

As you grow familiar with an area of study or a professional position, you will develop a sense of what it takes to prove a point in that field or role. You can speed up this process, however, by investigating and questioning. The following questions will help you think about the use of evidence in materials you read:

- How do writers in the field use precedent and authority? What or who counts as an authority in this field? How are the credentials of an authority established? (See 11i.)
- What kinds of quantitative data (countable or measurable items) are used, and for what purposes? How are the data gathered and presented?
- How are qualitative data (systematically observed items) used?
- How are statistics used and presented? Are tables, charts, graphs, or other visuals important, and why?
- How is logical reasoning used? How are definition, cause and effect, analogy, and example used?
- Do writers in the field include any personal information, use first person, or provide evidence intended to stir emotions?

- How does the field use primary and secondary sources? (See 13a.) What are the primary and secondary materials? How is each type of source presented?

- What kinds of textual evidence are cited?

- How are quotations and other references to sources used and integrated into the text? (See Chapter 15.)

In addition to carrying out your own investigation, ask your instructor how you can best go about making a case in this field.

 **EXERCISE 25.3**

Read a few journals associated with your prospective major or a discipline of particular interest to you, using the preceding questions to study the use of evidence in that discipline. If you are keeping a writing log, make an entry summarizing what you have learned.

## 25g Using conventional patterns and formats

To produce effective writing in a discipline, you need to know the field's generally accepted formats for organizing and presenting evidence. A typical laboratory report, for instance, follows a fairly standard organizational framework and usually has a certain look (see 28c for an example). A case study in sociology or education or anthropology likewise follows a typical organizational plan.

Ask your instructor to recommend some excellent examples of the kind of writing you will do in the course. Then analyze these examples in terms of format and organization. You might also look at major scholarly journals in the field to see what types of formats seem most common and how each is organized. Consider the following questions about organization and format:

- What types of articles, reports, or documents are common in this field? What is the purpose of each?

- What can a reader expect to find in each type of writing? What does each type assume about its readers?

- Do articles or other documents typically begin with an abstract? If so, does the abstract describe the parts of the article to come, or does it provide substantive information such as findings or conclusions? (See 27c.)

- How is each type of text organized? What are its main parts? How are they labeled?

- How does a particular type of essay, report, or document show the connections among ideas? What assumptions does it take for granted? What points does it emphasize?

Remember that there is a close connection between the writing patterns and formats a particular area of study uses and the work that scholars in that field undertake.

## 25h Making ethical decisions

Writers in all disciplines face ethical questions. Those who plan and carry out research on living people, for example, must be careful to avoid harming their subjects. Researchers in all fields must be scrupulous in presenting data to make sure that others can replicate research and test claims. In whatever discipline or field you are working, you should take into consideration your own interests, those of your collaborators, and those of your employers — but you must also responsibly safeguard the interests of the general public as well as any people you are interviewing, surveying, or otherwise using in your research.

Fortunately, a growing number of disciplines have adopted guidelines for ethics. The American Psychological Association has been a pioneer in this area, and many other professional organizations and companies have their own codes or standards of ethics. These guidelines can help you make decisions about day-to-day writing. Even so, you will no doubt encounter situations where the right or ethical decision is murky at best. In such situations, consult your own conscience first and then talk your choices over with colleagues you respect before coming to a decision on how to proceed.

## 25i Collaborating and communicating

In academic and professional environments, working with others is not just a highly valued skill — it is a necessity. Such collaboration happens when peers work together on a shared document, when classmates divide research and writing duties to create a multimedia presentation, when reviewers share advice on a draft, or when colleagues in an office offer their views on appropriate revisions for a companywide document.

Because people all over the world now have the ability to research, study, write, and work together, you must be able to communicate effectively within and across cultures. Conventions for academic writing (or for forms of digital communication) can vary from culture to culture, from discipline to discipline, and from one form of English to another. What is considered polite in one culture may seem rude in another, so those who communicate globally must take care to avoid giving offense — or taking it where none was intended. (For more information on writing across cultures, see Chapter 35.)

▼ ▼ ▼ ▼ ▼ ▼ ▼ ▼ ▼ ▼ ▼ ▼ ▼ ▼ ▼ ▼ ▼ ▼ ▼ ▼ ▼ ▼ ▼ ▼ ▼ ▼ ▼ ▼

## THINKING CRITICALLY ABOUT READING AND WRITING IN A DISCIPLINE

### Thinking about your own writing in a discipline

Choose a piece of writing you have produced for a class in a particular discipline—a blog or discussion post, a laboratory report, a review of the literature, or any other written assignment. Examine your writing closely for its use of that discipline's vocabulary, style, methods of proof, and conventional formats. How comfortable are you writing a piece of this kind? In what ways are you using the conventions of the discipline easily and well? What conventions give you difficulty, and why? You might talk with an instructor in this field about the conventions and requirements for writing in the discipline. Make notes about what you learn about being a better writer in the field.

# CHAPTER 26

# Writing in the Humanities

In humanities disciplines, the nature of texts can vary widely, from poems and plays to novels, articles, philosophical treatises, films, advertisements, paintings, and so on. But whether the text being studied is ancient or modern, literary or historical, verbal or visual, you can expect critical reading and textual analysis to play important roles in humanities courses.

## 26a  Reading texts in the humanities

To read critically in the humanities, you will need to pose questions and construct hypotheses as you read. You may ask, for instance, why a writer might make some points or develop some examples but omit others. Rather than finding meaning only in the surface information that texts or artifacts convey, you should use your own questions and hypotheses to create fuller meanings and make claims about the significance of what you read.

To successfully engage texts, you must recognize that you are not a neutral observer, not an empty cup into which the meaning of a work is poured. If such were the case, writing would have exactly the same meanings for all of us, and reading would be a fairly boring affair. If you have ever gone to see a movie with a friend and each come away with a completely different understanding or response, you already have ample evidence that a text never has just one meaning.

Nevertheless, you may in the past have been willing to accept the first meaning to occur to you — to take a text at face value. Most humanities courses, however, will expect you to exercise your interpretive powers. The following guidelines can help you build your strengths as a close reader of humanities texts.

---

**QUICK HELP**

Guidelines for reading texts in the humanities

- **Determine the purpose of the text.** The two most common purposes for works in the humanities are to provide information and to argue for a particular interpretation. Pay attention to whether the text presents opinions or facts, to what is included and omitted, and to how facts are presented to the audience. **(14d)** ▶

Guidelines for reading texts in the humanities, continued

- **Get an overall impression.** What does the work make you think about—and why? What is most remarkable or memorable? What confuses you?
- **Annotate the text.** Be prepared to "talk back," ask questions, note emerging patterns or themes, and point out anything out of place or ineffective. **(Chapter 9)**
- **Look at the context.** Consider the time and place represented in the work as well as when and where the writer lived. You may also consider social, political, or personal forces that may have affected the writer.
- **Think about the audience.** Who are the readers or viewers the writer seems to address? Do they include you?
- **Pay attention to genre.** What category does the work fall into (graphic novel, diary, political cartoon, sermon, argumentative essay, Hollywood western)? What is noteworthy about the form? How does it conform to, stretch, or even subvert your expectations about the genre? **(3e)**
- **Pay attention to visual elements and design.** How does the text look? What visual elements does it include? What contribution do these make to the overall effect or argument?
- **Note the point of view.** Whose point of view is represented? How does it affect your response?
- **Notice the major themes.** Are specific claims being advanced? How are these claims supported?
- **Understand the difference between primary and secondary sources.** Primary sources provide firsthand knowledge, while secondary sources report on or analyze the research of others. **(13a)**

## 26b Writing texts in the humanities

As a writer in the humanities, you will use the findings from close examination of a text or artifact to develop an argument or to construct an analysis.

### Understanding assignments

Common assignments that use the skills of close reading, analysis, and argument include summaries, personal responses, position papers, critical analyses of primary and secondary sources, and research-based projects. In philosophy, for example, you might need to summarize an argument, critique a text's logic and effectiveness, or discuss a moral issue from a particular philosophical perspective. A literature assignment may ask you to look very closely at a particular text ("Examine the role of chocolate in Toni Morrison's *Tar Baby*") or to go well beyond a primary text ("Discuss the impact of agribusiness on modernist novels"). Other disciplines may ask you to write articles, primary source analyses, or research papers.

For texts in literature, modern languages, and philosophy, writers often use the documentation style of the Modern Language Association; see Chapter 18 for advice on using MLA style. For projects in history and other areas of the humanities, writers often use the documentation style of the University of Chicago Press; see Chapter 20 for advice on using *Chicago* style.

## Developing a critical stance

To analyze a text, you need to develop a critical stance — the approach you will take to the work — that can help you develop a thesis or major claim (see 4c and 11d). To evaluate the text and present a critical response to it, you should look closely at the text itself, including its style; at the context in which it was produced; and at the audience the text aims to reach, which may or may not include yourself.

To look closely at the text itself, consider its genre, form, point of view, and themes, and look at the stylistic features, such as word choice, use of imagery, visuals, and design. Then consider context: ask why the text was created, note its original and current contexts, and think about how attitudes and ideas of its era may have influenced it. Consider who the intended audience might be, and think about how people outside this intended group might respond to the text. Finally, think about your personal response to the text as well.

Carrying out these steps should provide you with plenty of material to work with as you begin to shape a critical thesis and write your analysis. You can begin by grounding your analysis in one or more important questions you have about the work.

## Writing a literary analysis

When you analyze or interpret a literary work, think of your thesis as answering a question about some aspect of the work. The guiding question you bring to the literary work will help you decide on a critical stance toward the work. For example, a student writing about Shakespeare's *Macbeth* might find her curiosity piqued by the many comic moments that appear in this tragedy. She might turn the question of why Shakespeare uses so much comedy in *Macbeth* into the following thesis statement, which proposes an answer.

**QUESTION**        What role does comedy play in *Macbeth*, one of
                    Shakespeare's most widely read tragedies?

**THESIS STATEMENT**  The many unexpected comic moments in *Macbeth*
                    emphasize how disordered the world becomes for
                    murderers like Macbeth and his wife.

# 26c A student's close reading of poetry

Following is an excerpt from student Bonnie Sillay's close reading of two poems by E. E. Cummings. This essay follows MLA style (see Chapter 18). Bonnie is creating her own interpretation, so the only works she cites are the poems she analyzes.

**STUDENT WRITER**
Bonnie Sillay

1"

Sillay 1

Name,
instructor,
course, date on
left margin

Bonnie Sillay

Instructor Angela Mitchell

English 1102

December 4, 2010

Title centered

"Life's Not a Paragraph"

Present tense
used to discuss
poetry

Foreshadows
discussion of
work to come

Introductory
paragraph ends
with thesis
statement

Throughout his poetry, E. E. Cummings leads readers deep into a
thicket of scrambled words, missing punctuation, and unconventional
structure. Within Cummings's poetic bramble, ambiguity leads the reader
through what seems at first a confusing and winding maze. However, this
confusion actually transforms into a path that leads the reader to the
center of the thicket where Cummings's message lies: readers should not
allow their experience to be limited by reason and rationality. In order to
communicate his belief that emotional experience should triumph over
reason, Cummings employs odd juxtapositions, outlandish metaphors, and
inversions of traditional grammatical structures that reveal the illogic of
reason. Indeed, by breaking down such formal boundaries, Cummings's
poems "since feeling is first" and "as freedom is a breakfastfood" suggest
that emotion, which provides the compositional fabric for our experience
of life, should never be defined or controlled.

Quotation cited
parenthetically

Double spacing
throughout

In "since feeling is first," Cummings urges his reader to reject
attempts to control emotion, using English grammar as one example of
the restrictive conventions present in society. Stating that "since feeling
is first / who pays any attention / to the syntax of things" (lines 1–3),
Cummings suggests that emotion should not be forced to fit into some
preconceived framework or mold. He carries this message throughout the
poem by juxtaposing images of the abstract and the concrete — images
of emotion and of English grammar. Cummings's word choice enhances
his intentionally strange juxtapositions, with the poet using grammatical
terms that suggest regulation or confinement. For example, in the line
"And death i think is no parenthesis" (16), Cummings uses the idea that
parentheses confine the words they surround in order to warn the reader
not to let death confine life or emotions.

Annotations indicate **effective choices** or MLA-style formatting.

Sillay 4

### Works Cited

Cummings, E. E. "as freedom is a breakfastfood." *E. E. Cummings: Complete Poems 1904–1962*, edited by George J. Firmage, Liveright, 1991, p. 511.

---. "since feeling is first." *E. E. Cummings: Complete Poems 1904–1962*, edited by George J. Firmage, Liveright, 1991, p. 291.

Second work by same author uses three hyphens in place of name

▼ ▼ ▼ ▼ ▼ ▼ ▼ ▼ ▼ ▼ ▼ ▼ ▼ ▼ ▼ ▼ ▼ ▼ ▼ ▼ ▼ ▼ ▼

## THINKING CRITICALLY ABOUT WRITING IN THE HUMANITIES

Choose at least two projects or assignments you have written for different disciplines in the humanities—say, history and film. Reread these papers with an eye to their similarities. What features do they have in common? Do they use similar methods of analysis and value similar kinds of evidence, for instance? In what ways do they differ? Based on your analysis, what conclusions can you draw about these two disciplines?

# CHAPTER 27

# Writing in the Social Sciences

The social sciences share with the humanities an interest in what it means to be human. But the social sciences also share with the sciences the goal of engaging in a systematic, observable study of human behavior. When you write in the social sciences, you will attempt to identify, understand, and explain patterns of human behavior.

## 27a Reading texts in the social sciences

When you read in the social sciences, you ask questions, analyze, and interpret as you read, whether you are reading an academic paper that sets forth a theory and defends it, a case study that describes a particular case and draws out inferences and implications from it, or a research report that presents the results of an investigation into an important question in the field. Most of what you read in the social sciences will attempt to prove a point, and you will need to evaluate how well that point is supported.

The social sciences, like other disciplines, often use specialized vocabulary as shorthand for complex ideas that otherwise would take paragraphs to explain.

### Understanding qualitative and quantitative studies

Different texts in the social and natural sciences may call for different methods and strategies. Texts that report the results of *quantitative* studies collect data represented with numerical measurements drawn from surveys, polls, experiments, and tests. For example, a study of voting patterns in southern states might rely on quantitative data such as statistics. Texts that report the results of *qualitative* studies rely on non-numerical methods such as interviews and observations to reveal social patterns. A study of the way children in one kindergarten class develop rules of play, for instance, would draw on qualitative data — observations of social interaction, interviews with students and teachers, and so on. Of course, some work in the social and behavioral sciences combines quantitative and qualitative data and methods: an educational report might begin with statistical data related to a problem and then move to a qualitative case study to exemplify what the statistics reveal.

In the social sciences, both quantitative and qualitative researchers must determine what they are examining and measuring in order to get answers to research questions. A researcher who studies childhood aggression must first define and measure *aggression*. If the research is qualitative, a researcher may describe types of behavior that indicate aggression and then discuss observations of children and interviews with teachers and peers about those behaviors. A quantitative researcher, on the other hand, might design an experiment that notes how often children hit a punching bag or that asks children to rate their peers' aggression on a scale of one to ten.

Be sure to recognize that both quantitative and qualitative studies have points of view, and that researchers' opinions influence everything from the hypothesis and the design of the research study to the interpretation of findings. You must consider whether researchers' views are sensible and solidly supported by evidence, and you must pay close attention to the kind of data the writer is using and what those data can — and cannot — prove. For example, if researchers of childhood aggression define *aggression* in a way that you find unpersuasive, or if they observe behaviors that you consider playful rather than aggressive, then you will likely not accept their interpretation of the findings.

### Recognizing conventional formats

Use conventional disciplinary formats to help guide your reading in the social sciences. Many such texts conform to the format and documentation style of the American Psychological Association (APA). In addition, articles often include standard features — an abstract that gives an overview of the findings, followed by an introduction, review of literature, methods, results, discussion, and references. Become familiar with standard formats so that you can easily find the information you need. (For more on APA style, see Chapter 19.)

## 27b Writing texts in the social sciences

Perhaps because the social sciences share concerns with both the humanities and the sciences, the forms of writing within the social sciences are particularly varied. Assignments in social science classes can often be organized under five main categories:

- Writing that encourages student learning, such as reaction pieces and position papers
- Writing that demonstrates student learning, such as summaries, abstracts, and research papers

- Writing that requires students to analyze and evaluate the writings of others, such as literature reviews, book reviews, and briefs

- Writing that asks students to replicate the work of others or to engage in original research, such as quantitative research reports, case studies, and ethnographic analyses

- Writing that reflects common on-the-job communication tasks for members of a discipline, such as radio scripts, briefing notes, and informational reports

Many forms of writing in the social sciences call either explicitly or implicitly for argument (see Chapter 11). If you write an essay that reports on the results of a survey you developed about attitudes among students on your campus toward physician-assisted suicide, you will make an explicit argument about the significance of your data. But even with other forms of writing, such as summaries and book reports, you will implicitly argue that your description and analysis provide a clear, thorough overview of the text(s) you have read.

## Using style in the social sciences

Writing in the social sciences need not be dry and filled with jargon. While you need to understand the conventions, concepts, and habits of mind typical of a discipline, you can still write clear prose that engages readers.

When discussing research sources in a paper conforming to APA style, use the past tense or the present perfect tense (51e) for the verbs: *Raditch showed* or *Raditch has shown*. Make sure that any writing you do is as clear and grammatically correct as possible so that readers see you as capable and credible.

## Writing a literature review

Students of the social sciences carry out literature reviews to find out the most current thinking about a topic, to learn what research has already been carried out on that topic, to evaluate the work that has been done, and to set any research they will do in context. The following guidelines are designed to help you explore and question sources, looking for flaws or gaps. Such a critical review could then lead to a discussion of how your own research will avoid such flaws and advance knowledge.

- What is your topic or dependent variable (item or characteristic studied)?

- What is already known about this topic? What characteristics does the topic or dependent variable have? How have other researchers measured the item or characteristic being studied? What other factors are involved, and how are they related to each other and to your topic or variable? What theories are used to explain the way things are now?

- How has research been done so far? Who or what has been studied? How have measurements been taken?
- Has there been change over time? What has caused any changes?
- What problems do you find in the new research? What questions have not been answered? Have researchers drawn unwarranted conclusions?
- What gaps will your research fill? How is it new? What problems do you want to correct?

---

**EXERCISE 27.1**

Identify a literature review in a social-science field you are interested in (ask your instructor or a librarian for help in finding one), and read it carefully, noting how it addresses the questions above. Bring your notes to class for discussion.

---

## 27c  A student's psychology literature review

STUDENT WRITER
Tawnya Redding

Following is an excerpt from a psychology literature review by Tawnya Redding that adheres to the conventions for social science writing in this genre and follows the guidelines of APA style (see Chapter 19) to document sources. Note that an abstract is required only for papers prepared for publication in a journal, but a sample is included on page 415.

Page number appears flush right on first line of every page

1

Title (boldface), writer's name, department and school, course number and title, professor, and date centered and double-spaced

**Mood Music: Music Preference and the Risk for Depression and Suicide in Adolescents**

Tawnya Redding

School of Psychological Science, Oregon State University

PSY 480: Clinical Research Methods

Professor Ede

February 23, 2009

Annotations indicate effective choices or APA-style formatting.

2

## Mood Music: Music Preference and the Risk for Depression
## and Suicide in Adolescents

Full title boldface and centered

Music is a significant part of American culture. Since the explosion of rock and roll in the 1950s, there has been a concern for the effects that music may have on listeners, and especially on young people. The genres most likely to come under suspicion in recent decades have included heavy metal, country, and blues. These genres have been suspected of having adverse effects on the mood and behavior of young listeners. But can music really alter the disposition and create self-destructive behaviors in listeners? And if so, which genres and aspects of those genres are responsible? The following review of the literature will establish the correlation between potentially problematic genres of music such as heavy metal and country and depression and suicide risk. First, correlational studies concerning music preference and suicide risk will be discussed, followed by a discussion of the literature concerning the possible reasons for this link. Finally, studies concerning the effects of music on mood will be discussed. Despite the link between genres such as heavy metal and country and suicide risk, previous research has been unable to establish the causal nature of this link.

Background information about review supplied

Questions focus reader's attention

### The Correlation Between Music and Depression
### and Suicide Risk

Boldface headings help organize review

Studies over the past two decades have set out to answer this question by examining the correlation between youth music preference and risk for depression and suicide. A large portion of these studies have focused on heavy metal and country music as the main genre culprits associated with youth suicidality and depression (Lacourse et al., 2001; Scheel & Westefeld, 1999; Stack & Gundlach, 1992). Stack and Gundlach (1992) examined the radio airtime devoted to country music in 49 metropolitan areas and found that the higher the percentages of country music airtime, the higher the

Parenthetical references follow APA style

8

**References**

Baker, F., & Bor, W. (2008). Can music preference indicate mental
health status in young people? *Australasian Psychiatry, 16*(4),
284–288. https://doi.org/10.1080/10398560701879589

George, D., Stickle, K., Rachid, F., & Wopnford, A. (2007). The
association between types of music enjoyed and cognitive,
behavioral, and personality factors of those who listen.
*Psychomusicology, 19*(2), 32–56.

Lacourse, E., Claes, M., & Villeneuve, M. (2001). Heavy metal music
and adolescent suicidal risk. *Journal of Youth and Adolescence,
30*(3), 321–332.

Lai, Y.-M. (1999). Effects of music listening on depressed women in
Taiwan. *Issues in Mental Health Nursing, 20*(3), 229–246.
https://doi.org/10.1080/016128499248637

Martin, G., Clark, M., & Pearce, C. (1993). Adolescent suicide: Music
preference as an indicator of vulnerability. *Journal of the American
Academy of Child and Adolescent Psychiatry, 32*(3), 530–535.

Scheel, K., & Westefeld, J. (1999). Heavy metal music and
adolescent suicidality: An empirical investigation. *Adolescence,
34*(134), 253–273.

Siedliecki, S., & Good, M. (2006). Effect of music on power, pain,
depression and disability. *Journal of Advanced Nursing, 54*(5),
553–562. https://doi.org/10.1111/j.1365-2648.2006.03860.x

Smith, J. L., & Noon, J. (1998). Objective measurement of mood
change induced by contemporary music. *Journal of Psychiatric &
Mental Health Nursing, 5*(5), 403–408.

Stack, S. (2000). Blues fans and suicide acceptability. *Death Studies,
24*(3), 223–231.

Stack, S., & Gundlach, J. (1992). The effect of country music on suicide.
*Social Forces, 71*(1), 211–218. https://doi.org/10.2307/2579974

**References begin on new page; heading is centered and boldface**

**Print journal article**

**Journal article with DOI**

**Abstract and running head (for professional papers)**

MOOD MUSIC 2

### Abstract

There has long been concern for the effects that certain genres of music (such as heavy metal and country) have on youth. While a correlational link between these genres and increased risk for depression and suicide in adolescents has been established, researchers have been unable to pinpoint what is responsible for this link, and a causal relationship has not been determined. This paper will begin by discussing correlational literature concerning music preference and increased risk for depression and suicide, as well as the possible reasons for this link. Finally, studies concerning the effects of music on mood will be discussed. This examination of the literature on music and increased risk for depression and suicide points out the limitations of previous research and suggests the need for new research establishing a causal relationship for this link as well as research into the specific factors that may contribute to an increased risk for depression and suicide in adolescents.

*Keywords*: suicide, depression, music, adolescents

Running head (title shortened to 50 characters or fewer) in all capital letters on every page; heading centered and boldface

Abstract required for professional papers submitted for publication

Clear, straightforward description of literature under review

Text is double-spaced

Conclusions indicated

Keywords help readers find article online or in a database

## THINKING CRITICALLY ABOUT WRITING IN THE SOCIAL SCIENCES

### Reading with an eye for writing in the social sciences

Choose two readings from a social-science discipline, and read them with an eye toward issues of style. Does the use of disciplinary terms and concepts seem appropriate? In what ways do the texts attempt to engage readers and establish the authority of the writer? If the texts are not clear and understandable, how might they be improved?

### Thinking about your own writing in the social sciences

Choose a text you like that you have written for a social-science discipline. Then examine your style in this paper to see how well you have engaged your readers. Note variation in sentence length and type (do you, for example, use any questions?), number of active and passive verbs, use of concrete examples and everyday language, and so on. How would you rate your writing as a social scientist?

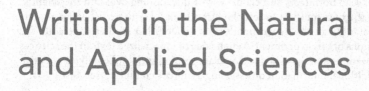

# CHAPTER 28

# Writing in the Natural and Applied Sciences

Natural sciences such as biology, chemistry, and physics study the natural world and its phenomena; applied sciences such as nanotechnology and the various fields of engineering apply knowledge from the natural sciences to practical problems. Whether you are working in the lab or the field, writing will play a key role in your courses in the natural and applied sciences.

## 28a Reading texts in the natural and applied sciences

Scientists and engineers work with evidence that can be observed, verified, and controlled. Though they cannot avoid interpretation, they still strive for objectivity by using the scientific method — observing or studying phenomena, formulating a hypothesis about the phenomena, and testing that hypothesis through controlled experiments and observations. Scientists and engineers aim to generate precise, replicable data; they develop experiments to account for extraneous factors. In this careful, precise way, scientists and engineers identify, test, and write persuasively about theoretical and real-world problems.

### Identifying argument

As you read in the sciences, try to become familiar with disciplinary terms, concepts, and formats, and practice reading — and listening — for detail. If you are reading a first-year biology textbook, you can draw upon general critical-reading strategies. In addition, charts, graphs, illustrations, models, and other visuals often play an important role in scientific writing, so your ability to read and comprehend these visual displays of knowledge is particularly important.

When you read a science or engineering textbook, you can assume that the information presented there is authoritative and as objective as possible. When you read specialized materials, however, recognize that although scholarly reports undergo significant peer review, they nevertheless represent arguments (see Chapter 11). The connection between facts and claims in the sciences, as in all subject areas, is created by the author rather than simply revealed by the data. So read both facts and claims with a questioning eye: Did the scientist choose the best method to test the hypothesis? Are there other reasonable interpretations of the experiment's results? Do other studies contradict the conclusions of this experiment? When you read specialized texts in the sciences with questions like these in mind, you are reading and thinking like a scientist. (For additional information on assessing a source's credibility, see 14d.)

## Recognizing conventional formats

As you advance in your course work, you will need to develop reading strategies for increasingly specialized texts as well as data and diagrams. Many scientific texts conform to the format and documentation style of the Council of Science Editors (CSE); for more on CSE style, see Chapter 21. (However, you should be prepared to follow an instructor's guidelines for citation and references if another style is used in your discipline or in a particular course.) In addition, articles often include standard features — an abstract that gives an overview of the findings, followed by an introduction, literature review, a materials and methods section, the results of the research, discussion, references, and tables of numerical data or other visuals.

An experienced reader in sciences and engineering might skim an abstract to see if an article warrants further reading. If it does — and this judgment is based on the reader's own research interest — he or she might then read the introduction to understand the rationale for the experiment and then skip to the results. A reader with a specific interest in the methods will read that section with particular care. You might expect, however, to read a journal article for a science or engineering course from start to finish, giving equal weight to each section.

### EXERCISE 28.1

Choose a respected journal in a discipline in the natural or applied sciences that interests you. (Ask your instructor or a reference librarian if you need help identifying a journal.) Then read quickly through two articles, taking notes on the authors' use of any headings and subheadings, specialized vocabulary, visuals, and evidence. Bring the results of your investigation to class for discussion.

## 28b Writing texts in the natural and applied sciences

In the sciences and engineering, you must be able to respond to a diverse range of writing and speaking tasks. Often, you must maintain lab or engineering notebooks that include careful records of experiments. You will also write memos, papers, project proposals and reports, literature reviews, and progress reports; in addition, you may develop print and web-based presentations for both technical and lay audiences (see Chapter 23). Particularly common writing assignments in the sciences are the literature review, research proposal, and research report.

## Understanding assignments

Writing a literature review enables you to keep up with and evaluate developments in your field. Literature reviews are an essential first step in any research effort, for they enable you to discover what research has already been completed and how you might build on earlier efforts. Successful literature reviews demonstrate your ability to identify relevant research on a topic and to summarize and in some instances evaluate that research.

Most scientists spend a great deal of time writing research or grant proposals aimed at securing funds to support their research. As an undergraduate, you may have an opportunity to make similar proposals to an office of undergraduate research or to a science-based firm that supports student research, for instance. Funding agencies often have guidelines for preparing a proposal. Proposals for research funding generally include the following sections: title page, introduction, purpose(s) and significance of the study, methods, timeline, budget, and references. You may also need to submit an abstract.

Research reports, another common writing form in the sciences, may include both literature reviews and discussions of primary research, most often experiments. Like journal articles, research reports generally follow this form: title, author(s), abstract, introduction, literature review, materials and methods, results, discussion, and references. Academic journals in many fields now expect work that they publish to follow this format, known by the shorthand "IMRAD" (for "Introduction, Methods, Results, and Discussion"). The focus of many IMRAD-format articles is on the introduction (which situates the research in the context of other work in the field) and on the discussion of the results. Many instructors will ask you to write lab reports (28c), which are briefer versions of research reports and may not include a literature review.

Today, most scientific writing is collaborative. As you move from introductory to advanced courses and then to the workplace, you will increasingly find yourself working as part of a team or group. Indeed, in such areas as engineering, collaborative projects are the norm (see Chapter 8).

## Using style in the natural and applied sciences

In general, use the present tense for most writing you do in the natural and applied sciences. Use the past tense, however, when you are describing research already carried out (by you or others) or published in the past.

As a writer in the sciences, you will need to produce complex figures, tables, images, and models and use software designed to analyze data or run computer simulations. In addition, you must present data carefully. If you create a graph, you should provide headings for columns, label axes with numbers or units, and identify data points. Caption figures and tables with a number and descriptive title. And avoid orphan data — data that you present in a figure or table but don't comment on in your text.

Finally, make sure that any writing you do is as clear, concise, and grammatically correct as possible to ensure that readers see you as capable and credible.

## 28c A student's chemistry lab report

STUDENT WRITER
Allyson Goldberg

Following is an excerpt from a lab report on a chemistry experiment by student Allyson Goldberg.

Goldberg 2

## Introduction

The purpose of this investigation was to experimentally determine
the value of the universal gas constant, R. To accomplish this goal, a
measured sample of magnesium (Mg) was allowed to react with an excess
of hydrochloric acid (HCl) at room temperature and pressure so that the
precise amount and volume of the product hydrogen gas ($H_2$) could be
determined and the value of R could be calculated using the ideal gas
equation, $PV=nRT$.

Introduction
explains
purpose of
lab and gives
overview of
results

## Materials & Methods

Two samples of room temperature water, one about 250mL and the
other about 400mL, were measured into a smaller and larger beaker,
respectively. 15.0mL of HCl was then transferred into a side arm flask
that was connected to the top of a buret (clamped to a ringstand)
through a 5/16" diameter flexible tube. (This "gas buret" was connected
to an adjacent "open buret," clamped to the other side of the ringstand
and left open to the atmosphere of the laboratory at its wide end, by
a 1/4" diameter flexible tube. These two burets were adjusted on the
ringstand so that they were vertically parallel and close together.) The
HCl sample was transferred to the flask such that none came in contact
with the inner surface of the neck of the flask. The flask was then
allowed to rest, in an almost horizontal position, in the smaller beaker.

Materials
and methods
section
explains lab
setup and
procedure

Passive voice
throughout
is typical
of writing
in natural
sciences

The open buret was adjusted on the ringstand such that its 20mL
mark was horizontally aligned with the 35mL mark on the gas buret.
Room temperature water was added to the open buret until the water
level of the gas buret was at about 34.00mL.

A piece of magnesium ribbon was obtained, weighed on an
analytical balance, and placed in the neck of the horizontal side arm
flask. Next, a screw cap was used to cap the flask and form an airtight
seal. This setup was then allowed to sit for 5 minutes in order to reach
thermal equilibrium.

After 5 minutes, the open buret was adjusted so that the menisci on
both burets were level with each other; the side arm flask was then tilted

Goldberg 3

vertically to let the magnesium ribbon react with the HCl. After the brisk reaction, the flask was placed into the larger beaker and allowed to sit for another 5 minutes.

Next, the flask was placed back into the smaller beaker, and the open buret was adjusted on the ringstand such that its meniscus was level with that of the gas buret. After the system sat for an additional 30 minutes, the open buret was again adjusted so that the menisci on both burets were level.

This procedure was repeated two more times, with the exception that HCl was not again added to the side arm flask, as it was already present in enough excess for all reactions from the first trial.

Results and calculations show measurements and calculations of final value of R

Results and Calculations

| Trial # | Lab Temp. (°C) | Lab Pressure (mbar) | Mass of Mg Ribbon Used (g) | Initial Buret Reading (mL) | Final Buret Reading (mL) |
|---|---|---|---|---|---|
| 1 | 24.4 | 1013 | 0.0147 | 32.66 | 19.60 |
| 2 | 24.3 | 1013 | 0.0155 | 33.59 | N/A* |
| 3 | 25.0 | 1013 | 0.0153 | 34.35 | 19.80 |

* See note in Discussion section.

| Trial # | Volume of $H_2$ (L) | Moles of $H_2$ Gas Produced | Lab Temp. (K) | Partial Pressure of $H_2$ (atm) | Value of R (L atm/ mol K) | Mean Value of R (L atm/ mol K) |
|---|---|---|---|---|---|---|
| 1 | 0.01306 | $6.05 \times 10^{-4}$ | 298 | 0.970 | 0.0704 | 0.0728 |
| 2 | N/A | N/A | N/A | N/A | N/A | |
| 3 | 0.01455 | $6.30 \times 10^{-4}$ | 298 | 0.968 | 0.0751 | |

Table 1 Experimental results

(Sample Calculations — see Table 1)

Volume of $H_2$ gas = final buret reading − initial buret reading

Volume of $H_2$ gas = 32.66mL − 19.60mL = 13.06mL = 0.01306 L

▼ ▼ ▼ ▼ ▼ ▼ ▼ ▼ ▼ ▼ ▼ ▼ ▼ ▼ ▼ ▼ ▼ ▼ ▼ ▼ ▼ ▼ ▼ ▼ ▼ ▼ ▼

THINKING CRITICALLY ABOUT WRITING FOR THE SCIENCES

### Reading with an eye for writing in the sciences

Identify one or more features of scientific texts, and consider their usefulness. Why, for instance, does an abstract precede the actual article? How do scientific nomenclatures, classification systems, and other features of scientific writing aid the work of scientists? Try to identify the functions that textual elements such as these play in the ongoing work of science.

### Thinking about your own writing in the sciences

Choose a piece of writing you did for a science class—a lab report, a research report, a proposal—and read it carefully. Note the format and headings you used, how you presented visual data, what kinds of evidence you used, and what citation system you used. Compare your piece of writing with a similar piece of writing published in a journal in the field. How well does your writing compare? What differences are most noticeable between your writing and that of the published piece?

CHAPTER 29

# Writing in Professional Settings

Today's professionals are part of a global economy that relies more than ever on clear written communication. Whether you are writing to get a job or writing on the job, keep in mind that texts you produce in professional settings will be more successful if you pay attention to your purpose and your audience and write in the genre that your readers expect.

## 29a Reading texts in professional settings

In business today, writers have almost unlimited access to information and to people whose expertise can be useful for a project. Somehow, you will need to negotiate and evaluate a huge stream of information.

General strategies for effective reading (Chapter 9) can help. One such strategy — keeping a clear purpose in mind when you read — is particularly important for work-related reading. Are you reading to solve a problem? to gather and synthesize information? to make a recommendation? Knowing why you are reading will increase your productivity. Time constraints and deadlines will also affect your decisions about what and how to read; the ability to identify important information quickly is a skill you should cultivate as a business reader; however, it's also important to know when *not* to skim and to attend carefully to an entire text or message.

## 29b Writing texts in professional settings

Writing assignments in business classes generally serve two related functions. While their immediate goal is to help you master the theory and practice of business, these assignments also prepare you for the kinds of writing that you will face in the workplace. For this reason, students in *every* discipline need to know how to write effective business documents such as memos, emails, letters, proposals, reports, and résumés.

Much writing in business today is collaborative in nature. You may find that your coworkers expect you to ask for or offer comments on drafts of important documents that will present your team's work to others in the company or to the public. For more on collaboration, see Chapter 8.

Professional writers tend to use conventional formats and academic written English. When you write to employers or prospective employers, stick to more formal communication unless you have a very good reason to do otherwise. Remember, too, that much or all of the writing you do at work is public writing as well, and that employers have easy access to — and in fact ownership of — email and other documents written by employees. As always, it's best to use discretion in all on-the-job communication.

## Writing a memo or email

Memos are a common form of communication sent within and between organizations. Today, memos are typically delivered as email messages; they tend to be brief and direct, often dealing with only one subject.

As with any writing, consider the audience for your memo carefully. Make sure to include everyone who might need the information, but be cautious about sharing it too widely, especially when the information in your document may be sensitive.

---

**QUICK HELP**

### Guidelines for writing effective memos and professional email

- Clearly identify the subject.
- Begin with the most important information: depending on the memo's purpose, you may have to provide background information, define the task or problem, or clarify the goal.
- Use your opening paragraph to focus on how the information you convey affects your readers.
- Focus each of your subsequent paragraphs on one idea pertaining to the subject.
- Relate your information concisely and in a way that is relevant to the reader.
- Emphasize exactly what you want readers to do and when.
- Use attachments for detailed supporting information.
- Adjust your style and tone to fit your audience.
- Attempt to build goodwill in your conclusion.

STUDENT WRITER
Michelle Abbott

STUDENT WRITER
Carina Abernathy

Following is a memo, written by student writers Michelle Abbott and Carina Abernathy, that presents an analysis and recommendation to help an employer make a decision.

## Memo

**TO:** ROSA DONAHUE, SALES MANAGER

**FROM:** MICHELLE ABBOTT & CARINA ABERNATHY

**SUBJECT:** TAYLOR NURSERY BID

*Opening provides background*

As you know, Taylor Nursery has requested bids on a 25,000-pound order of private-label fertilizer. Taylor Nursery is one of the largest distributors of our Fertikil product.

*Most important information put in bold*

**The total cost for manufacturing 25,000 pounds of the private-label brand for Taylor Nursery is $44,075.** This cost includes direct material, direct labor, and variable manufacturing overhead. Although our current equipment and facilities provide adequate capacity for processing this special order, the job will require overtime labor, which has been factored into our costs.

*Options presented*

The minimum price that Jenco could bid for this product without losing money is $44,075 (our cost). Applying our standard markup of 40% results in a price of $61,705. You could reasonably establish a price anywhere within that range.

*Final recommendation*

Taylor Nursery has requested bids from several competitors. One rival, Eclipse Fertilizers, is submitting a bid of $60,000 on this order. Therefore, our recommendation is to slightly underbid Eclipse with a price of $58,000, representing a markup of approximately 32%.

*Closing builds goodwill by offering further help*

Please let us know if we can be of further assistance in your decision on the bid.

## Writing a proposal

In businesses and the professions, writers are often called upon to write proposals that aim to evoke some action based on the proposal's recommendations. Writers in professional settings might have the need to propose a solution for a problem or propose a study of a problem. Often, proposals have a very specific purpose and audience. While the format can vary, almost all proposals will include the following parts, usually with subheadings to direct the reader:

- an abstract or summary that clarifies the purpose of the proposal
- a background section that includes a problem statement or statement of need
- a section on desired objectives or outcomes
- methods for achieving the outcomes
- a means of evaluating those outcomes
- information about how the results will be shared with others
- a budget

The following proposal excerpt begins by addressing the problem as the writer sees it and then by stating the major objective. Following this opening, the proposal goes on to include additional sections: Previous Research and Current Knowledge; Project Design; Statistical Analysis; Health and Safety Concerns; Implications for Fire Management, Firefighters, and Policymakers; and Budget.

Here is the opening of a proposal to conduct research to help reduce the smoke inhalation firefighters are exposed to.

---

### Wildland Firefighter Smoke Exposure

**Problem Statement**

Wildland firefighters work in a dynamic environment and are often

faced with a variety of hazards on any given day. One of the most                    Opening states a
                                                                                      problem
common, but often overlooked hazards is exposure to potentially

harmful levels of contaminants in wildland smoke. This may also

be one of the least understood risks of wildland firefighting. With

the increased information regarding the potential health effects

of vegetative smoke to respiratory and cardiovascular systems it

became apparent that more work needed to be done to measure the exposure experienced by firefighters during their work shift and by personnel at fire camps. Previous National Wildfire Coordination Group (NWCG)-sponsored smoke exposure studies indicated that employees were overexposed approximately 5% of the time at wildfires and 10% of the time at prescribed fires.[1]

Unlike their counterparts who fight structural fires, wildland firefighters do not wear respiratory protective equipment. Therefore it is essential that fire managers have a good understanding of the exposures their firefighters face under various conditions. In order to understand the potential effects of this exposure, managers must also be able to understand the exposure levels for critical time periods such as instantaneous exposures, short-term exposures, and longer-term exposures, including 24-hour exposure. In order to predict long-term effects of wildland smoke exposure, it will also be necessary to predict career-length exposures.

### Objective

Objective section explains the goals of the proposed research

The objective of this study is to expand the current state of knowledge on wildland firefighter smoke exposure. First, it will provide important information on the levels of irritants firefighters are exposed to. In order for fire managers and safety and health managers to develop safe exposure levels and mitigation measures to protect wildland firefighters, they must be able to understand the critical factors that influence exposure levels to firefighters. This research will measure the exposure levels of carbon monoxide (CO), particulate matter ($PM_4$), and crystalline silica ($SiO_2$) on wildland and prescribed fires in several geographic areas of the United States.

---

[1] Reinhardt, Timothy E.; Ottmar, Roger D. 2000. Smoke exposure at western wildfires. Res. Pap. PNW-RP-525. Portland, OR: U.S. Department of Agriculture, Forest Service, Pacific Northwest Research Station. 72 p.

## Writing a cover letter

A cover letter, which often accompanies a résumé, aims to demonstrate how the experiences and skills you outline in your résumé have prepared you for a particular job. Remember to focus, then, on how you can benefit the company, not how the company can help you. A well-written letter can help you stand out from a group of candidates, even if you are new to the field and don't yet have impressive qualifications, so craft your words carefully.

If you are posting a cover letter to accompany an online application, you will probably provide your contact information elsewhere, and you may not know the name or title of the person who will ultimately read the letter.

---

**QUICK HELP**

### Guidelines for effective professional communication

- Use a conventional format unless you have a specific reason to do otherwise.
- Whenever possible, write to a specific person (*Dear Mr. Robinson* **or** *Dear Ms. Otuteye*).
- Be polite—even if you have a complaint.
- Clearly state your reason for writing. Include whatever details will help your reader see your point and respond.
- If appropriate, make clear what you hope your reader will do.
- Express appreciation for your reader's attention.
- Make it easy for your reader to respond by including your contact information.

---

**STUDENT WRITER**
Nastassia Lopez

The following cover letter was written by student Nastassia Lopez.

## Cover letter

**Contact information**

**Nastassia Rose Lopez**
523 Brown Avenue
Stanford, CA 94305
650-326-5555 / nrl91@mail.com

February 1, 2019

**Inside address with full name, title, and address**

Mr. Price Hicks
Director of Educational Programs and Services
Academy of Arts and Sciences
5220 Lankersheim Blvd.
North Hollywood, CA 91601

**Salutation to specific person**

Dear Mr. Hicks:

**Opening provides information and lists major goals**

I am an enthusiastic student who believes that a Development Internship at the Academy of Arts and Sciences would greatly benefit both the Academy and me. A Los Angeles native in my first year at Stanford, I'm a serious student who is a hard worker. My current goal is to comprehend the full scope of the entertainment industry and to learn the ropes of the craft.

As an experienced writer, I am attracted to the Development Department because I am curious to learn the process of television production from paper to screen. In high school, I was enrolled in Advanced Placement Writing, and I voluntarily took a creative writing class. At Stanford, I received High Honors for maintaining an excellent grade-point average across all my classes, including several writing-intensive courses.

**Background information illustrates skills and strength of interest**

My passion for writing, producing, directing, and learning is real. If my application is accepted, I will bring my strong work ethic, proficiency, and creativity to the Academy.

Thank you very much for your time and consideration. My résumé is enclosed, and I look forward to hearing from you.

Sincerely yours,

**Four line spaces for signature**

*Nastassia Rose Lopez*

Nastassia Rose Lopez

## Writing a résumé

While a cover letter usually emphasizes specific parts of the résumé, telling how your background is suited to a particular job, a résumé summarizes your experience and qualifications and provides support for your letter. An effective résumé is brief, usually one or two pages. You should be aware, though, that conventions for résumés (or CVs) may differ from country to country. Job applicants for positions outside the United States, for example, will often report more personal information than is allowed in the U.S., along with a personal photo, information about family, and exam scores. In addition, they may use a narrative style as opposed to the lists (education, experience, publications, etc.) favored in the United States. If you are applying for a position in a country other than the U.S., be sure to look for examples of résumés used in that country.

Research shows that employers in the United States generally spend less than a minute reading a résumé. Since they are reading for the purpose of fulfilling *their* needs, they expect a résumé to be easy to read. Formatting your document neatly and using clear headings and adequate spacing will work in your favor.

A well-written résumé with a standard format and typefaces is still, in many cases, the best way to distinguish yourself, but in certain contexts, a creative résumé that includes media links, images, and other nontraditional content may help you succeed. As with any writing situation, consider your context and purpose.

Your résumé may be arranged chronologically (from most to least recent) or functionally (based on skill or expertise). Include the following information:

- **Name, address, phone number, email address.** You may also want to include links to a career profile page or personal website, and, if the content is professionally appropriate, to social media content such as a Twitter feed.
- **Educational background.** Include degrees, diplomas, majors, and special programs or courses that pertain to your field of interest.
- **Work experience.** Identify each job — whether a paying job, an internship, or military experience — with dates and names of organizations. Describe your duties by carefully selecting strong action verbs.
- **Skills, personal interests, activities, awards, and honors.**
- **References.** Most writers simply say that references are available on request.
- **Images.** Some applicants also include images in their résumés. Make choices that seem appropriate for your specific situation.

Job seekers today usually upload résumés to a company website when applying for a position. In such cases, take special care to make sure that you have caught any errors or typos before submitting the form.

**STUDENT WRITER**
Megan N. Lange

The following pages show student Megan N. Lange's résumé in two formats, one in traditional print style and the other in a creative format optimized for digital presentation. Like many recent college graduates, she is considering possible career paths, and having two very different résumés prepared allows her to present herself appropriately to either traditional or more creative potential employers.

## Standard résumé

**Megan N. Lange**

1234 Kingston Pike • Knoxville, TN 37919
Phone: 865.643.xxxx • Email: mlange1@utk.edu

Name in boldface and larger type size

Education

Exp. May 2018  **The University of Tennessee**, Knoxville. B.A. in Technical Writing and Business Editing, Classical Studies

May 2013  **Lenoir City High School**

Educational background

**Work Experience**

- **The Yankee Candle Company** – Store 433     August 2014 – present
  Sales Associate: assists guests in-store, answers phones, restocks floor, operates cash register

- **Holston Conference of the United Methodist Church**     June 2015 – August 2015
  Youth and Young Adult Intern: worked in-office with team, out-of-office with local youth workers, planned and facilitated youth retreats and events

- **Megan Lange Photography**     January 2015 – present
  Head Photographer: senior portraiture, weddings, maternity

Relevant work experience

**Relevant Courses**

- **Technical Writing 360**     Fall 2015
  Focused on proper formatting of different professional documents, teamwork, creative thinking

- **Technical Writing 460**     Spring 2016
  Proofreading and formatting of professional documents, email etiquette, international communication

Courses relevant to position being sought

**Affiliations/Memberships**

- **Society for Technical Communication**, East Tennessee Chapter     Spring 2016

**Other Experience**

- **Great Smoky Mountain Chrysalis Board**     August 2014 – present
- **University of Tennessee Singers**     August 2013 – May 2015
- **Cedar Springs Presbyterian Church Choir**     August 2015 – present

Affiliations and experience not listed above

*References available upon request.

Megan Lange uses this résumé to apply for most jobs. The clean, inviting, professional look presents the expected content in expected ways—her name and contact information, educational background, work experience, courses she has taken in the field she hopes to enter, and other information that may help prospective employers know more about the kind of person she is.

Creative résumé

# *Megan N. Lange*

megan@megannlange.com
megannlange.com
865.643.XXXX

## Education:

**B.A., Technical Writing**
University of Tennessee, Knoxville
Exp. graduation: May 2018

## Work Experience:

**Celeris Networks Consulting Group**     May 2017-Present
Email campaigns, graphic design for website & marketing,
website redesign (in-progress), social media, press releases

**EventBooking.com, LLC**     May 2016-Sept 2017
Email campaigns, maintain social media, client relations,
website redesign/maintenance, press releases, newsletter

## Other Experience:

**Photographer:** The International Biscuit Festival, May 2017
**Freelance Photographer:** University of Tennessee's **The Daily Beacon**, Fall 2017
**Media/Entertainment:** Sertoma Center's All That Jazz Dinner and Auction, 2015-2016
**Co-Chair/Entertainment:** Sertoma Center's All That Jazz Dinner and Auction, 2016-2017
**Event Chair:** Sertoma Center's All That Jazz Dinner and Auction, 2017-2018
**Fundraising Chair:** Artistic Spectrum, 2017-2018

## Social Media:

## Skillset:

Standard HTML Coding
Twitter Bootstrap Website Scaffolding
Adobe Photoshop/Illustrator
WordPress.org site management/basic development
Microsoft Word/Excel/PowerPoint
Photography (DSLR – manual shooting)
Zift.com/Contactology Email Clients

## Things I Like:

*Megan Lange uses this résumé to apply for positions for which her creativity would be an asset. The design is still easy to read, but reveals more of her personality. Icons under "Social Media" are live links to her feeds on various sites.*

▼ ▼ ▼ ▼ ▼ ▼ ▼ ▼ ▼ ▼ ▼ ▼ ▼ ▼ ▼ ▼ ▼ ▼ ▼ ▼ ▼ ▼ ▼ ▼ ▼ ▼ ▼ ▼ ▼ ▼

## THINKING CRITICALLY ABOUT PROFESSIONAL WRITING

### Reading with an eye for writing in professional situations

Monitor your mail, email, text messages, and targeted ads on social media sites for a few days, saving everything that tries to sell a product, provide a service, or solicit information or money. Then go through these pieces of professional writing and advertising, and choose the one you find most effective. What about the writing appeals to you or gets and holds your attention? What might lead you to buy the product, choose the service, or make a contribution? What might make the piece of writing even more effective? Bring the results of your investigation to class for discussion.

### Thinking about your own professional writing

Chances are, you have written a cover letter for a job, completed a résumé, or sent some business-related letters or email messages. Choose a piece of business-related writing that is important to you or that represents your best work, and then analyze it carefully. How clear is the writing? How well do you represent yourself in the writing? Do you follow the conventions for business letters, résumés, memos, and so on? Make notes on what you could do to improve this piece of writing.

## CHAPTER 30

# Essay Exams

The skills you need to perform well on a written exam can also serve you in your nonacademic life. Being prepared to present information effectively is always useful, such as when you are asked to submit a personal statement to accompany an application for insurance, an internship, or a loan.

## 30a Preparing for an essay exam

Nothing can take the place of knowing the subject well, so you can start preparing for an essay exam by taking careful notes on lectures and readings. You may want to outline a reading assignment, list its main points, list and define its key terms, or briefly summarize its argument. A particularly effective method is to divide your notes into two categories, labeling the left-hand side *Summaries and Quotations* and the right-hand side *Questions and Comments*. Then, as you read, use the left side to record summaries of major points and noteworthy quotations. On the right, record questions that your reading has not answered, puzzling ideas, and your own comments. This note-taking encourages active, critical reading and, combined with careful class notes, will do much to prepare you. Here are one student's notes:

| Summaries and Quotations | Questions and Comments |
|---|---|
| Rhetoric — "the art of discovering, in any particular case, all available means of persuasion." (Aristotle, on p. 3) | Maybe all language is persuasive, but if I greet people warmly, I don't consciously try to persuade them that I'm glad to see them. I just respond naturally. |
| All language is essentially argumentative — purpose is to persuade | |

In addition to taking careful, detailed notes, you can prepare by writing out essay answers to questions you think are likely to appear on the exam. Practicing ahead of time is much more effective than last-minute cramming. On the day of the exam, do ten to fifteen minutes of writing just before you go into the examination to warm up your thinking muscles.

---

> **EXERCISE 30.1**
>
> Create a question you think you might be likely to encounter on an essay exam in a class you are currently taking. Then write a paragraph or two about what you would need to know to write an exceptional answer.

---

## Analyzing essay questions

Before you begin writing, read the question carefully several times, and analyze what it asks you to do. Most essay exam questions contain two kinds of terms, strategy terms that describe your task in writing the essay and content terms that define the scope and limits of the topic.

| STRATEGY | CONTENT |
|---|---|
| Analyze | Jesus's Sermon on the Mount. |
| Describe | the major effects of Reconstruction. |
| Explain | the advantages of investing in government securities. |

Words like *analyze*, *describe*, and *explain* tell what logical strategy to use and often set the form your answer takes. Since not all terms mean the same thing in every discipline, be sure you understand exactly what the term means in the context of the material covered on the exam. In general, however, the most commonly used strategy terms have standard meanings. Don't hesitate to ask your instructor to clarify terms you're unsure of.

---

**QUICK HELP**

### Common strategy terms

- **Analyze:** Divide an event, idea, or theory into its component elements, and examine each one in turn.

  Analyze Milton Friedman's theory of permanent income.

- **Compare and/or contrast:** Demonstrate similarities or dissimilarities between two or more events or topics.

  Compare the portrayal of women in *Beloved* with that in *Their Eyes Were Watching God*.

- **Define:** Identify and state the essential traits or characteristics of something, differentiating it clearly from other things.

  Define *osmosis*.

- **Describe:** Tell about an event, person, or process in detail, creating a clear and vivid image of it.

  Describe the dress of a medieval knight.

▶

Common strategy terms, continued

- **Evaluate:** Assess the value or significance of the topic.

    Evaluate the contributions of jazz musicians to American music.

- **Explain:** Make a topic as clear and understandable as possible by offering reasons, examples, and so on.

    Explain the functioning of the circulatory system.

- **Summarize:** State the major points concisely and comprehensively. **(9e)**

    Summarize the major arguments against using animals in laboratory research.

If strategy terms are not explicitly stated in an essay question, you need to infer a strategy from the content terms. For example, a question that mentions two groups working toward the same goal may imply comparison and contrast, and a question referring to events in a given time period may imply summary.

## Thinking through your answer

You may be tempted to begin writing your essay exam at once. Time is precious — but so are organizing and planning. So spend some time (about 10 percent of the allotted time is a good rule of thumb) thinking through your answer.

Begin by deciding which major points you need to make and in what order to present them. Jot down support for each point. Craft a clear, succinct thesis that satisfies the strategy term of the exam question. In most writing situations, you start from a working thesis, but when writing under pressure you will probably find it more efficient to outline your ideas and craft your thesis from your outline. For example, if you were asked to define the three major components of personality according to Freud, you might write a brief informal outline as a framework for your answer.

Id

basic definition — what it is and is not
major characteristics
functions

Ego

basic definition — what it is and is not
major characteristics
functions

Superego

basic definition — what it is and is not
major characteristics
functions

From this outline, you can develop a thesis: *According to Freud, the human personality consists of three major and interconnected elements: the id, the ego, and the superego.*

# 30b Writing an essay exam response

Your goal in producing an essay exam answer is twofold: to demonstrate that you have mastered the course material and to communicate your ideas and information clearly, directly, and logically.

## Drafting

During the drafting stage, use your outline to keep yourself on track: if you depart from it, you will lose time and perhaps have trouble returning to the main discussion. As a general rule, develop each of your major points into at least one paragraph. Be sure to make clear the connections among your main points by using transitions. *The last element* of the human personality, according to Freud, is the superego.

Besides referring to your outline for guidance, pause and read what you have written before going on to a new point. Rereading may remind you of other ideas while you still have time to include them and should also help you establish a clear connection with whatever follows. If you are asked to write your essay on paper, write neatly, skip lines, and leave ample margins so that you have space for changes or additions when you revise. If you are writing your essay exam on a computer, use double spacing and paragraph indentations.

## Revising and editing

Leave enough time (a minimum of five minutes) to read through your essay answer carefully. Consider the following questions:

- Is the thesis clearly stated? Does it answer the question?
- Are all the major points covered?
- Are the major points adequately developed and supported?

- Is each sentence complete?
- Are spelling, punctuation, and syntax as correct as you can make them? Have you checked for missing words?
- Is the handwriting legible? If you are using a computer, take time to run your spell checker.

## 30c Writing take-home exams

You may sometimes be asked to do an essay exam at home. If so, make sure to clarify any guidelines about how much time you should spend working on the exam, how long your answer should be, and how you should submit the exam (for example, through email or your course platform).

You probably won't have as much time to write a take-home essay exam as you would a regular academic essay, so set a reasonable time line and stick to it. Be direct in your response, starting right in with your thesis, and use a straightforward beginning-middle-conclusion organizational sequence. Most important, as you plan for your take-home exam, bring in ways to show that you know the subject matter of the course and that you can provide concrete, detailed examples to support the main points you are making. As with any essay exam, look closely at the question itself and make sure that you are responding to the question in appropriate ways.

## 30d A student's essay exam response

A student in a first-year American history course had fifty-five minutes to answer two of three essay questions and three of five short-answer questions. She chose to answer the following question first:

> Between 1870 and 1920, African Americans and women both struggled to establish certain rights. What did each group want? Briefly analyze the strategies each group used, and indicate how successful they were.

This student began her exam with this question because she knew the most about this topic. With another essay and three short answers to write, she decided to devote no more than twenty minutes to this essay.

First, she analyzed what the question asked her to do, noting the strategy terms. She decided that the first sentence of the question strongly implied comparison and contrast of the two struggles. The second sentence asked for an explanation of the goals of each group, and in the third sentence, she took *analyze* and *indicate* to mean "explain what each group did and how well it succeeded." (As it turned out, this was a very shrewd reading of the question; the instructor later remarked that those who had included a comparison and contrast produced better answers than those who did not.) Note that, in this instance, the strategy the instructor expected is not stated explicitly in the question. Instead, class members were expected to read between the lines to infer the strategy.

The student identified content terms around which to develop her answer: the groups — African Americans and women — and their actions, goals, strategies, and degrees of success. Using these terms, she spent about three minutes producing the following informal outline:

Introduction

goals, strategies, degree of success

African Americans

want equality
two opposing strategies: DuBois and Washington
even with vote, great opposition

Women

many goals (economic, political, educational), but focus on vote
use men's arguments against them
use vote to achieve other goals

Conclusion

educational and economic differences between groups

From this outline, the student crafted the following thesis: *In the years between 1870 and 1920, African Americans and women were both fighting for equal rights but in significantly different ways.* She then wrote a brief answer that compared the strategies and successes of each group's struggle.

▼ ▼ ▼ ▼ ▼ ▼ ▼ ▼ ▼ ▼ ▼ ▼ ▼ ▼ ▼ ▼ ▼ ▼ ▼ ▼ ▼ ▼ ▼

## THINKING CRITICALLY ABOUT ESSAY EXAMS

Choose an essay exam that you have recently written. Use the guidelines in 30a to analyze what the exam question asked you to do. Then reread your answer carefully. Did you do what the question asked? If not, how should you have responded? Then, referring to 30b, reconstruct how you answered the question. How could you improve the content and presentation of your answer? Note any new strategies that might help you improve your success in taking essay exams.

# CHAPTER 31

# Portfolios

A portfolio is a selection of your work — whether for class, for a job, or for some other purpose — that you think shows off your skills to their best advantage. Many college writing classes require portfolios from students at the end of the course, but putting together a portfolio can also help you develop real-world skills. Applicants for jobs and internships in many fields can make an impact with a carefully chosen portfolio of work that shows off relevant expertise or training.

## 31a  Planning a portfolio

Depending on your purpose, audience, and the type of work that you plan to include, you may want to create a traditional paper portfolio in a folder or binder, an online portfolio, or some other specialized kind of portfolio. Your concept of what the portfolio should accomplish will ultimately affect the form it takes.

### Thinking about your purpose

Some possible purposes for a writing portfolio include fulfilling course require-ments, showing work to a prospective employer, entering a competition, and keeping a record of your college (or artistic) work. Each of these purposes will lead to different decisions about what to include in your portfolio, how to arrange the material, and whether to make work available online, in print, or in some other format.

### Considering your audience

Your audience will also affect what materials you include. If, for example, your audience is a writing instructor, you will need to demonstrate what you've learned; if it is a prospective employer, you may need to focus on what you can do. In some cases, the primary audience for a portfolio may be yourself.

## Organizing your work

Your audience and purpose should guide you in deciding how to organize the material. If you are presenting a portfolio as the final component of a course, your instructor may designate an organizational arrangement. If not, you may decide to arrange the portfolio in chronological order and comment on your progress throughout the course. Other methods of organization include arranging material by theme, by importance, or by some other category that makes sense for your work. If you are creating a digital portfolio, you can include a text in more than one category if it makes sense to do so.

## Creating an appealing design

Think carefully about how you want your portfolio to look. What impression do you want to give? Choose color, fonts, typefaces, images, and other graphic elements that will enhance the appeal of your portfolio and make the content inviting and accessible. Make sure the design is helpful for your audience, too, with clear navigation such as a table of contents. If you are creating a web portfolio, you may want to follow a template or model your portfolio on a site that works to show off the kinds of texts you will include. For more on design, see Chapter 22.

## Selecting contents

How many entries should you include in a portfolio? The answer depends on your purpose. If you are developing a personal portfolio to post online, for example, you may include materials in several categories — essays, audio recordings, photos, presentations, a résumé, or anything else that seems relevant — because those reviewing your portfolio will click on only those items that interest them. If you are developing a portfolio for a writing class, however, you should probably limit yourself to five to seven examples of your writing because readers will look at every item you include. Here are some kinds of texts — which may take either print or digital form — that you might include in a portfolio:

- an academic essay demonstrating your ability to argue a claim
- a personal essay that shows insight and demonstrates your ability to communicate vividly
- a piece of writing that reflects on your learning over the college years
- a brief report for a class or community project
- a writing project showing your ability to analyze and solve a problem
- your favorite piece of writing
- writing based on field research, library research, or both

- a piece of writing for a group, club, or campus publication
- an example of a collaboratively written text, accompanied by a description of how the team worked and what you contributed
- an example of your best writing on an essay exam
- correspondence, such as a letter of inquiry or a job application

You should also include the assignments for your work, whenever applicable. If your portfolio is for a writing course, you may be expected to include examples of your notes and early drafts as well as any responses you got from other readers.

One student who had done spoken-word performances throughout his college years decided to assemble a portfolio of those performances. To do so, he created a video compilation that he could distribute when applying for scholarships and for admission to graduate school — and that he could keep as a record of his writing and performing. Given his purpose and potential audiences, he organized the portfolio chronologically and made each piece easily accessible for future use.

### EXERCISE 31.1

Make a list of the times you have organized some of your work—to apply for a job, to create a record of your writing from middle through high school, or for some other reason. What spurred you on to carry out these tasks? Did you have an audience other than yourself in mind? What criteria did you use in choosing pieces? Bring your list to class to compare with those of other students.

## 31b Completing a portfolio

To complete a portfolio, you will need to prepare a reflective statement, assemble your material, obtain feedback from others, and prepare the final revised copy.

### Reflecting on your work

You should introduce a portfolio with a written statement that explains and reflects on your work. This statement might be in the form of a memo, cover letter, personal essay, or video, depending on what works best for your portfolio. Think carefully about the overall impression you want the portfolio to create, and make sure that the tone and style of your statement set the stage for the entire portfolio. The statement should include the following:

- **a description of what is in the portfolio:** What was the purpose of each work (or of the portfolio as a whole)?

- **an explanation of your choices:** How did you decide that these pieces represent your best work?

- **a reflection on your strengths and abilities:** What have you learned by completing the work for the portfolio? What problems have you encountered, and how have you solved them?

## Assembling the portfolio

For a print portfolio, number all pages in consecutive order, and prepare a table of contents. Label and date each piece of writing if you haven't done so previously. Put a cover sheet on top with your name and the date; if the portfolio is for a class, include the course title and number. Assemble everything in a folder.

For a digital portfolio, arrange the works in a way that makes sense to you and that allows your readers to find what they are looking for easily. Add any links that seem necessary to help users move from place to place within the portfolio or to external sites — and check that the links work.

## Getting responses

Once you have assembled your portfolio, seek responses to it from several classmates or friends and, if possible, from at least one instructor. (You may want to refer your reviewers to the guidelines on reviewing a draft in 6b.) Revise accordingly.

If this portfolio is part of your work in a course, ask your instructor whether a few corrections are acceptable. If you intend to use it as part of a job search, you should make each piece as final, professional, and functional as possible. Either way, the time and effort you spend revising and editing the contents of your portfolio will be time well spent.

# 31c  A student's portfolio home page

Jenny Ming composed the following home page for her digital portfolio in her senior year, because she was preparing to look for a job. She wanted to get her work out for others to see, and so she created an eye-catching graphic as a background for her name along with a menu of her work on the left side of the page. Her welcome text introduces herself clearly and simply and invites viewers to

take a look at her work and to contact her with comments or questions. Note that she includes a link to her résumé at the bottom of the page.

▼ ▼ ▼ ▼ ▼ ▼ ▼ ▼ ▼ ▼ ▼ ▼ ▼ ▼ ▼ ▼ ▼ ▼ ▼ ▼ ▼ ▼ ▼ ▼ ▼ ▼

## THINKING CRITICALLY ABOUT PORTFOLIOS

Choose a portfolio cover letter or home page that you have recently created. Ask first how your portfolio introduces your work to readers. How does the cover letter or home page represent your strengths as a communicator? How well do you present the portfolio physically? What could you change, add, or delete to make your portfolio more effective?

# CHAPTER 32

# Writing to Make Something Happen in the World

How do you define "good writing"? When researchers asked college students this question as part of a study, they expected fairly straightforward definitions like "writing that gets its message across," but the students kept coming back to one central idea: good writing "makes something happen in the world." The students felt particular pride in the writing they did for family and friends — and for many extracurricular activities that were meaningful to them. They produced newsletters for community action groups, nature guides for local parks, and websites for local emergency services; one student had even written an algorithm that helps to track sex traffickers on the web. Furthermore, once these students graduated from college, they continued to create and *value* these kinds of public writing. The writing that matters most to many students and citizens, then, is public writing that has an effect in the world: writing that gets up off the page or screen, puts on its working boots, and marches out to get something done!

## 32a Deciding what should happen

During and after your college years, you are likely to create writing that you do because you want to make a difference. You may already have found reasons for communicating with a public audience — perhaps you have

- invited others to an event you're hosting
- advertised your expertise
- reported on a project you were involved in
- advocated for a cause you believe in

Often the purpose for doing this kind of writing may seem obvious to you — you have a clear idea of *what* the writing needs to accomplish. Now take the time to consider *how* to get the results that you want. As with any writing, be sure to get feedback from friends and others who may be affected by your plan.

---

QUICK HELP

Characteristics of writing that makes something happen

- Public writing has a clear **purpose** (to promote a cause; to explain a problem; or to persuade others to act, for example). **(32a)**
- It is intended for a specific **audience** and addresses those people directly. **(32b)**
- It uses the **genre** most suited to its purpose and audience (a poster to alert people to an upcoming fund drive, a newsletter to inform members of a group, or a social media post to promote an upcoming performance). **(32b)**
- It appears in a **medium** (print, online, or both) where the intended audience will see it. **(32b)**
- It generally uses straightforward, everyday **language**.
- It generally uses **design** to get and hold the audience's attention.

## 32b Connecting with your audience

When you have clarified the actions you want your readers to take in response to your writing, think about the people you most want to reach — audiences today can be your immediate neighbors or like-minded people around the country or the globe. Who will be interested in the topic you are writing about? For example, if you want to encourage your elementary school to plant a garden, you might try to interest local parents, teachers, and PTA members; if you are planning to suggest a boycott of a particular national brand, you might start with social media followers.

With a target audience in mind, think carefully about where and how you are likely to find them, how you can get their attention, and what you can say to achieve your purpose.

### Appeals to an audience

What do you know about your audience's values and interests? Why should they appreciate what you want to communicate? If you want to convince neighbors to contribute resources to build a local playground, then you may have a head start: knowing the neighbors and their children, and understanding local concerns about safety, can help you think of effective appeals to get their attention and convince them to join in this project. However, if you want to create a flash mob to publicize ineffective security at chemical plants near your city, you will need to reach as many people as possible, most of whom you will not know. Finding ways to reach appropriate audiences and convince them to join your project may require you to do some research. (For more on emotional, ethical, and logical appeals, see 11i–k.)

### Genre and media

Even if you know the members of your audience, you still need to think about the genre and media that will be most likely to reach them. To get neighbors involved in a playground project, you might decide that a colorful print flyer delivered door to door and posted at neighborhood gathering places would work best, or you may put together a neighborhood Facebook page or email list in order to share information digitally. To gather a flash mob, an easily forwarded message — text, tweet, or email — will probably work best.

### Appropriate language

For all public writing, think carefully about the audience you *want* to reach — as well as unintended audiences your message *might* reach. Doing so can help you craft writing that will be persuasive without being offensive.

### Timing

When you want to make something happen, timing is crucial to the success of your project. If you want people to plan to attend an event, present your text to them two weeks ahead of time. If you are issuing a blog or newsletter, make sure that you create content frequently enough to keep people interested (but not so often that readers can't or won't bother to keep up). If you are reporting information based on something that has already happened, make it available as soon as possible so that your audience won't consider your report "old news."

## 32c Sample writing to make something happen in the world

On the following pages are some examples of the forms that public writing can take.

## Fundraising web page

PURPOSE  Student Justin Dart created a fundraising web page to crowd-source funding to help Jey, a young street vendor in Accra, Ghana, get a college education.

AUDIENCE  Justin, a marketing student at the University of Colorado, aimed this campaign, "Teach a Man: Wisdom," at friends and acquaintances.

GENRE  Using the Indiegogo template, Justin posted a video about the recipient's background and purpose of the fundraiser; a short description of the project, designed for easy reading; and a list of perks for donors at various levels. Other tabs offered updates that Justin posted over the course of the fundraising project, comments from donors, photos, and more.

DELIVERY  Justin delivered his text online and urged friends to share the campaign on other social media sites. He and his team ended up raising enough to pay for Jey's university tuition and housing.

**Web comic**

PURPOSE       Student Zack Karas worked with a team of classmates to do
              field research in a public space and then present a critical
              analysis of the environment they studied, a local coffee shop.

AUDIENCE      Zack and his team initially presented to their classmates.
              The secondary audience included blog readers who share
              Zack's interest in humor and online comics.

GENRE         Zack used his team's coffee shop experience as the basis for a
              comic, the final panels of which include a twist: his comic avatar
              fails to recognize that he, like many of the customers, is also a
              "post-ironic hipster … with facial hair, a hoodie, and an iPhone."

DELIVERY      After a traditional class presentation, Zack posted the
              comic on a blog created to host his artwork.

Pitch package

### AMERICA LOVES MUSICALS!!!

With hit shows like *Glee* and *Smash*, musicals are becoming a bigger phenomenon and more popular than ever. Now more gritty and raw, musicals are used to explore many different elements of life. *Strange Fruit* is no exception. Using the most popular musical art form today, hip-hop, *Strange Fruit* bravely goes into uncharted territory through innovative means. *Strange Fruit* is a film that digs up the deep roots of our American past, discovering how slavery affects interracial relationships today. It's a powerful and poignant film, full of music, drama, humor, and passion. It's aimed to be a musical sensation.

### SAMPLE BOX OFFICE GROSS COMPARISONS

| MOVIE | COST | GROSS |
|---|---|---|
| The Help | 25 million | 169 million |
| Dreamgirls | 70 million | 100 million |
| The Color Purple | 15 million | 98 million |
| Chicago | 45 million | 306 million |
| Back to the Future | 19 million | 350 million |
| Precious | 10 million | 47 million |

STRANGE FRUIT THE HIP-HOPERA

| | |
|---|---|
| PURPOSE | Deborah Jane and Jamie Burke collaborated to create a pitch package to encourage investment in a film based on Deborah's play *Strange Fruit: The Hip-Hopera*. |
| AUDIENCE | Local theater and film executives and enthusiasts |
| GENRE | The pitch package, a PDF, included a combination of traditional pages: a synopsis, cast list, character analyses, biographies of the production team, and a financial analysis — alongside the theater poster. |
| DELIVERY | The team assembled the pitch package digitally for easy email distribution. |

▼ ▼ ▼ ▼ ▼ ▼ ▼ ▼ ▼ ▼ ▼ ▼ ▼ ▼ ▼ ▼ ▼ ▼ ▼ ▼ ▼ ▼ ▼ ▼ ▼ ▼ ▼

## THINKING CRITICALLY ABOUT WRITING THAT MAKES SOMETHING HAPPEN IN THE WORLD

You have probably done quite a bit of writing to make something happen in the world, though you might not have thought of it as official "writing." Yet as this chapter shows, such writing is important to those who do it—and to those affected by it. Think about the groups you belong to—informal or formal, home- or community- or school-based—and choose a piece of writing you have done for the group, whether on your own or with others. Then look at it with a critical eye. Is its purpose clear? What audience does it address, and how well does it connect to that audience? Are the genre (newsletter, poster, flyer, brochure, report, etc.) and the medium (print, electronic) appropriate to achieving the purpose and reaching the audience? How might you revise this text to make it even more effective?

# PART 8
# Style: Effective Language

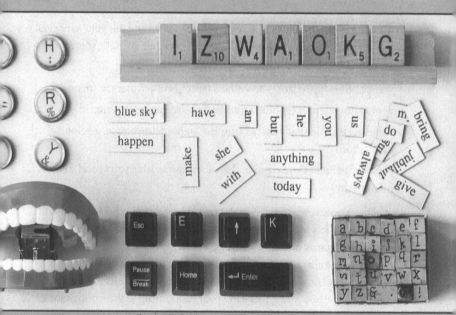

Photo by Mike Enright/www.menright.com. Photo styling by Barbara Lipp.

# CHAPTER 33

# Language and Identity

Draw a circle in the middle of a piece of paper or screen and put your name in it. Then add spokes pointing out from all around that circle and take some time to list words that identify you —

- your relationship to family and others (sister, brother, mentor, friend)
- your major interests (sports fan, athlete, reader, gardener, gamer)
- your background (nationality, birthplace or hometown, race, religion, sexual orientation)
- personal attributes you claim or that others use to label you (good student, friendly, shy)

Some of the words you've written are bits of language that help you to construct your identity. Others may be words that other people have used to identify you, words you may or may not agree with or accept.

*Identity* is a familiar word, but it's worth pausing to think a bit about what it means. Most scholars would define identity as a web of relationships built up through language: how you understand your relationship to the world around you and use that understanding to imagine possibilities for your future. And language is the scaffold we use to name these relationships.

Parts of your identity are stable — your age, for example, or your birthplace. But much of identity is constructed through social interactions with other people and with institutions and is thus flexible, subject to change and evolution. So identities can be multiple and shifting. They can also be imposed on you by other people or institutions that use language to label you in a way that is inappropriate, unfair, or unacceptable to you. In these ways, language works to construct who you are and who you can be.

## 33a Recognizing how the language of others can shape identity

Look back at the circle and spokes you drew and the words you attached to the spokes. Underline the ones that you think may be labels others would put on you. If you've found any words like "clumsy" or "bad at math" or "outsider" or "immigrant" or "top of the class," are these descriptors ones *you have chosen* as part of your identity? Research has shown that children who are put into groups labeled according to ability levels tend to simply adapt to that label. Mike Rose, now a professor at UCLA, has written about being placed in a non-college-bound track as a young person: "I lived down to expectations." In Rose's case, he was eventually able to resist and reject that label, with the help of a teacher. But until he did so, that label — *non-college-bound* — was a part of his identity.

It's worth taking time to ask how you use language (especially labels) to "identify" other people — those you know and those you don't know. While all people tend to categorize others as a way to understand them (she's a *sorority girl*; he's a *jock*), those labels may not be accurate or important to the other person's own understanding of themselves — and may indeed be oversimplifications or stereotypes. Open-minded, ethical college writers take care not to impose identities on others, just as they resist letting others impose identities on them.

## 33b Using language to shape your own identity

One of your main goals as a college writer is not only to be aware of how the language of other people and groups can shape your identity but also to resist such efforts by making sure that you are the person doing that shaping as much as possible. Professor Mike Rose had a chance to reject the label of lower-track student, but what's even more important is that he seized the opportunity to begin defining himself as a high-performing honors student who would eventually earn a PhD. Poet and artist Gloria Anzaldúa often asked her students "Who is the *you* you want to be in ten years?" because she knew that the language choices they were making were going to shape that distant identity.

In addition, college writers need to think about whose voices are heard and whose may be ignored in certain situations. For example, a student speaking or writing from the identity of a beginner or novice may not get the respect that one writing from an identity of expertise does. A student writing about mental health issues among college students, for example, might draw on her experience and expertise as an activist for mental health resources on campus, or as a double major in biology and psychology, or as a suicide attempt survivor. Or perhaps all of these aspects of her identity may help to establish her *ethos,* or her credibility (see also 11i). As a college writer, aim to be confident in your own identity, to communicate from an identity of your own choosing, and to imagine and pursue other identities you want to embrace.

▼ ▼ ▼ ▼ ▼ ▼ ▼ ▼ ▼ ▼ ▼ ▼ ▼ ▼ ▼ ▼ ▼ ▼ ▼ ▼ ▼ ▼ ▼ ▼ ▼

## THINKING CRITICALLY ABOUT LANGUAGE AND IDENTITY

Take a few minutes to jot down notes in response to these questions: How do I shape my own identity through language? How do other people and groups or institutions shape my identity through language? How do I use language that may be shaping the identities of others? Then write a paragraph describing how you would like to make changes to these identities or this use of language.

# CHAPTER 34

# Language Varieties

When Pulitzer Prize–winning author Junot Díaz spoke to a group of college students in California, he used one language variety — colloquial English — and Spanish, plus more than a few four-letter words, and the students loved every minute of it. When he was interviewed later on National Public Radio, however, Díaz addressed his nationwide audience in a second language variety — formal English. As a college student, you will need to think carefully about how to make appropriate choices. Since academic English is still expected for most of your classes, you will want to use it effectively. But you may also want to be open to using another language, a combination of languages, or one of the many rich varieties of English in your college writing. Strong writers understand how to mix languages and dialects or varieties of English as they use their entire language repertoire to create effective and compelling messages across a range of rhetorical situations.

## 34a Practicing language awareness

Recognizing the crucial role language plays in shaping identity has led some writers to conclude that "I am my language." Gloria Anzaldúa certainly makes that case when she says that she wants all of her languages to be recognized *and accepted* as part of her identity: the academic English and Spanish she has learned, working-class/slang English, the northern Mexican Spanish dialect, and Tex-Mex, the regional Spanish of Texas and New Mexico.

Think for a moment about the languages and dialects and varieties of languages that are part of your background and who you are. Today nearly 25 percent of people in the United States speak a language other than English at home. But even if you think of yourself as speaking only English, you probably also know and use a number of dialects. If you come from Boston, Minnesota, Appalachia, or many other regions of the country, you probably speak the regional dialect common to that area. In addition, you may be learning a professional dialect (like the specialized language of computer programmers) or using one associated with groups you belong to (surfers or political activists).

---

TALKING THE TALK | **WHAT DOES IT MEAN TO HAVE A *TRANSLINGUAL APPROACH* TO WRITING?**

As a way to further explain this approach, a group of scholars note the following characteristics:

- Understanding that languages are never fixed but rather flexible and changing across time and from genre to genre
- Having respect for differences within and across languages and dialects
- Paying careful attention to how writers use words, sentences, and stylistic features that push against boundaries and are experimental
- Understanding that "breaking" rules doesn't always indicate a mistake or an error: a one-word sentence fragment might create a desired special effect, for example

– adapted from Bruce Horner, Min-Zhan Lu, Jacqueline Royster, and John Trimbur, "Language Difference in Writing: Toward a Translingual Approach," *College English*, vol. 73, no. 3, Jan 2011, pp. 303–21.

---

The dialects and languages you have at your disposal allow you to communicate effectively and powerfully with a wide range of audiences.

Taking such a broad, inclusive, and accepting view of the rich varieties of language available to writers and speakers today is what scholars call having "translingual dispositions," or a "translingual approach" that views language varieties more open-mindedly than ever before.

## 34b Using academic English appropriately

How do writers decide when to mix languages or dialects? The key to answering this question is appropriateness — what is most effective and fitting for a writer's particular purpose and audience. Used appropriately and wisely, *all* varieties of English can help to get your messages across in compelling ways.

One variety of English, often referred to as "edited academic English," is taught in schools, represented in this and most other textbooks, used in much of the national media, and written and spoken widely by those holding social and economic power. As the language used in business and most public institutions, this variety of English is one you probably want to be completely familiar with. But even "edited academic English" is not static: like all language varieties, it encompasses a wide range of choices, from the formal style used in much of the writing you will do in college to the informal style characteristic of conversation.

Language varieties

You can use different languages and dialects to good effect for the following purposes:

- to repeat someone's exact words, precisely and respectfully
- to evoke a person, place, or activity
- to establish your credibility and build common ground
- to make a strong point
- to connect with an audience

## 34c Using varieties of English to evoke a place or community

Using the language of a local community is an effective way to evoke a character or place. See how author John Steinbeck uses dialect to let readers hear the language spoken by community members in his classic novel, *The Grapes of Wrath*:

> "Ever'body says words different," said Ivy. "Arkansas folks says 'em different from Oklahomy folks says 'em different. And we seen a lady from Massachusetts, an' she said 'em differentest of all. Couldn' hardly make out what she was sayin.'" —JOHN STEINBECK, *The Grapes of Wrath*

Weaving together regionalisms and more formal English can also be effective in creating a sense of place. Here, an anthropologist writing about one Carolina community chooses not to paraphrase; she takes care to let the residents speak their minds — and in their own words:

> For Roadville, schooling is something most folks have not gotten enough of, but everybody believes will do something toward helping an individual "get on." In the words of one oldtime resident, "Folks that ain't got no schooling don't get to be nobody nowadays." —SHIRLEY BRICE HEATH, *Ways with Words*

LANGUAGE, CULTURE, AND CONTEXT | **GLOBAL VARIETIES OF ENGLISH**

Like other world languages, English is used in many countries, so it has many global varieties. For example, British English differs somewhat from U.S. English in certain vocabulary (*bonnet* for hood of a car), syntax (*to hospital* rather than *to the hospital*), spelling (*centre* rather than *center*), and pronunciation. If you have learned a non-American variety of English, you will want to recognize, and to appreciate, the ways in which it differs from the variety widely used in U.S. academic settings.

## 34d Building credibility within a community

Whether you are Native American or trace your ancestry to Europe, Asia, Latin America, Africa, or elsewhere, your heritage probably lives on in the language you use.

See how one Hawaiian writer uses Hawaiian pidgin language to paint a picture of young teens hearing a "chicken skin" story from their grandmother.

> " — So, rather dan being rid of da shark, da people were stuck with many little ones, for dere mistake."
>
> Then Grandma Wong wen' pause, for dramatic effect, I guess, and she wen' add, "Dis is one of dose times. . . . Da time of da sharks."
>
> Those words ended another of Grandma's chicken skin stories. The stories she told us had been passed on to her by her grandmother, who had heard them from her grandmother. Always skipping a generation.
>
> —RODNEY MORALES, "When the Shark Bites"

Notice how the narrator of the story presents information necessary to the story line mostly in formal English while using terms characteristic of Hawaiian pidgin to represent spoken language. Mixing languages in this way demonstrates that the writer is a member of the community whose language he is representing and thus able to build credibility with others in the community.

Take care, however, in using the language of communities other than your own. When used inappropriately, such language can have an opposite effect, perhaps destroying credibility and alienating your audience.

### EXERCISE 34.1

Identify the purpose and audience for one of this chapter's examples of regional, ethnic, or communal varieties of English. Then rewrite the passage to remove all evidence of any variety of English other than the formal academic. Compare your revised version with the original and with those produced by some of your classmates. What differences do you notice in tone (is it more formal? more distant? something else?) and in overall impression? Which version seems most appropriate for the intended audience and purpose? Which do you prefer, and why?

## 34e Bringing in other languages

You might use a language other than English for the same reasons you might use different dialects of English: to represent the actual words of a speaker, to make a point, to connect with your audience, or to get their attention. See how Gerald Haslam uses Spanish to capture his great-grandmother's words and to make a point about his relationship to her.

"*Expectoran su sangre!*" exclaimed Great-grandma when I showed her the small horned toad I had removed from my breast pocket. I turned toward my mother, who translated: "They spit blood."

"*De los ojos*," Grandma added. "From their eyes," mother explained, herself uncomfortable in the presence of the small beast.

—GERALD HASLAM, *California Childhood*

And here, a student writer uses her native Spanish as she writes a literacy narrative about her experience growing up in Puerto Rico and learning English.

"Todo se ve bien . . ." my father would start and look at me with his right eyebrow raised. The same gesture I forced myself to learn, staring at a mirror for a month, just so I could prove to him that it didn't intimidate me. "¿Qué pasó con Inglés?" I would simply look away and shrug my shoulders, desperately avoiding the gaze of disappointment that his eyes would try to burn on me. After all, I was his firstborn, and there were a lot of expectations to meet. "¿Voy a ver un cambio para el próximo semestre, verdad?" And without glancing back at him, I would answer a soft, "Sí."

In elementary school, I got A's and B's in every course except one: English. As a young and naive mind, born and raised on a Spanish-speaking island, I never understood why I needed another language.

—Paola García-Muñiz

Note that García-Muñiz includes Spanish in her narrative without translating it. In this case, the student deliberately chose to include the phrases in Spanish because she wanted to represent her two worlds (two languages) in the essay so that "the audience would better understand what I was talking about: it wasn't about making it simpler or harder for readers to read, but allowing them to visualize the story exactly as it happened."

Another student describes how he combines multiple languages as part of his learning process. Taking notes in multiple languages, he says, "helps [him] save time."

[F]rom my personal experiences, I think that note-taking activities play a significant role in the retention of ideas in a systematic and efficient manner. Using multiple languages such as Hindi, Sanskrit, and English increases the speed of this activity and helps me retain knowledge of these languages for a long time. I mainly use Hindi to present my ideas briefly and Sanskrit to describe the actions of the subject. Suresh Canagarajah, in his chapter, "World Englishes as Code-Meshing," explains that code-meshing is a process of combining different languages to communicate an idea in a more efficient manner (273). When I do code-meshing, I use multiple languages because it helps me save time during note-taking, as well as retain knowledge about Hindi and Sanskrit languages.

Fig. 1 Sample of my note-taking activity during my Florida History class

09/07/15  प्राचीनिकथा Florida
- Spanish :- प्रथमः आगतः (1513)
- Florida - main port of entry (Sunshine state)
  ↳ गरमी नमी वायु
- Great Britain (19ᵗʰ century - controlled (18)
- Tribes, Apalachee, Calusa, Ais, Seminoles . . .
- Europeans ओर Americas
- Seminoles - आविष्कृत corn

Courtesy of Shravan Yandra

—Shravan Yandra

Like these students, you may want to bring other languages into your writing, using them to help you communicate more efficiently and effectively with your audiences.

▽ ▽ ▽ ▽ ▽ ▽ ▽ ▽ ▽ ▽ ▽ ▽ ▽ ▽ ▽ ▽ ▽ ▽ ▽ ▽ ▽ ▽ ▽ ▽ ▽

## THINKING CRITICALLY ABOUT LANGUAGE VARIETIES

The following description of a meal features English that is characteristic of the Florida backwoods in the 1930s. Using this passage as an example, write a description of a memorable event from your daily life. Try to include some informal dialogue. Then look at the language you used—do you use more than one variety of English? What effect does your use of language have on your description?

> Jody heard nothing; saw nothing but his plate. He had never been so hungry in his life, and after a lean winter and a slow spring . . . his mother had cooked a supper good enough for the preacher. There were poke-greens with bits of white bacon buried in them; sandbuggers made of potato and onion and the cooter he had found crawling yesterday; sour orange biscuits and at his mother's elbow the sweet potato pone. He was torn between his desire for more biscuits and another sandbugger and the knowledge, born of painful experience, that if he ate them, he would suddenly have no room for pone. The choice was plain.                    —MARJORIE KINNAN RAWLINGS, *The Yearling*

# CHAPTER 35

# Writing to the World

Writers today often communicate instantaneously across vast distances and cultures: students in Ohio take online classes in Canada or South Africa, and tweets from Buenos Aires find readers in Boston. You will almost certainly find yourself writing to (or with) others throughout the country and across the globe, and students in your classes may well come from many countries and cultures. When the whole world can be your potential audience, it's time to step back and think about how to communicate as effectively as possible with a diverse group — how to become a world writer.

## 35a Thinking about what seems "normal"

Your judgment on what's "normal" may be based on assumptions you are not even aware of. But remember: behavior that is considered out of place in one context may appear perfectly normal in another. What's considered "normal" in a text message would be anything but in a request for an internship with a law firm. If you want to communicate with people across cultures, try to learn something about the norms in those cultures and be aware of the norms that guide your own behavior.

---

**QUICK HELP**

**Communicating across cultures**

- Recognize what you consider "normal." Examine your own customary behaviors and assumptions with an open mind, and think about how they may affect what you think and say (and write). **(35a)**
- Listen closely to someone from another culture, and ask for clarification if necessary. Carefully define your terms. **(35b)**
- Think about your audience's expectations. How much authority should you have? What kind of evidence will count most with your audience? **(35c)**
- Organize your writing with your audience's expectations in mind. If in doubt, use formal style. **(35c)**

---

Like most people, you may tend to see your own way as the "normal" way to do things. How do your own values and assumptions guide your thinking and behavior? Keep in mind that if your ways seem inherently right, then — even without thinking about it — you may assume that other ways are somehow not right. These tips may help:

- Know that most ways of communicating are influenced by cultural contexts and differ widely from one culture to the next.
- Pay close attention to the ways that people from cultures other than your own communicate, and be flexible.
- Once you tune in to differences, keep an open mind: don't assume that all members of a community behave in the same way or value the same things.
- Remember that your audience may be made up of people from many backgrounds who have very different concepts about what is appropriate or "normal."

## 35b Clarifying meaning

When an instructor called for "originality" in his students' essays, what did he mean? A Filipina student thought *originality* meant going to an original source and explaining it; a student from Ohio thought *originality* meant coming up with an idea entirely on her own. The professor, however, expected students to read multiple sources and develop a critical point of their own about those sources. In subsequent classes, this professor defined *originality* as he was using it in his classes, and he gave examples of student work he judged original.

This brief example points to the challenges all writers face in trying to communicate across space, across languages, across cultures. While there are no foolproof rules, here are some tips for communicating with people from cultures other than your own:

- Listen carefully. Don't hesitate to ask people to explain or even repeat a point if you're not absolutely sure you understand.
- Take care to be explicit about the meanings of the words you use.
- Invite response — ask whether you're making yourself clear. This kind of back-and-forth is particularly easy (and necessary) in email and on social media.
- Remember that sometimes a picture is worth a thousand words. A visual may help make your meaning absolutely clear.

## 35c Meeting audience expectations

When you do your best to meet an audience's expectations about how a text should work, your writing is more likely to have the desired effect. In practice, figuring out what audiences want, need, or expect can be difficult — especially when you are writing in public spaces online and your audiences can be composed of anyone, anywhere. If you do know something about your readers' expectations, use what you know to present your work effectively. If you know little about your potential audiences, however, err on the side of caution and carefully examine your assumptions about your readers.

## Meeting expectations about your authority as a writer

In the United States, students are frequently asked to establish authority in their writing — by drawing on certain kinds of personal experience, by reporting on research they or others have conducted, or by taking a position for which they can offer strong evidence and support. But this expectation about writerly authority is by no means universal. Indeed, some cultures view student writers as novices whose job is to reflect what they learn from their teachers — those who hold the most important knowledge, wisdom, and, hence, authority. One Japanese student, for example, said he was taught that it's rude to challenge a teacher: "Are you ever so smart that you should challenge the wisdom of the ages?"

As this student's comment reveals, tone also depends on the relationship between a writer and readers or listeners. In this student's case, the valued relationship is one of respect and deference, of what one Indonesian student called "good modesty." As a world writer, you need to remember that those you're addressing may hold a wide range of attitudes about authority.

- Whom are you addressing, and what is your relationship to that person or group? (3d)
- What knowledge are you expected to have? Is it appropriate for or expected of you to demonstrate that knowledge — and, if so, how?
- What is your goal — to answer a question? to make a point? to agree? something else? (3b and c)
- What tone is appropriate? If in doubt, show respect: politeness is rarely if ever inappropriate. (6f)
- What level of control do you have over your writing? In a report, you may have the final say. But if you are writing on a wiki, where you share control with others, sensitivity to communal standards is key.

## Meeting expectations about persuasive evidence

How do you decide what evidence will best support your ideas? The answer depends, in large part, on the audience you want to persuade. Though research suggests that Americans make decisions based on emotions more often than logic, American academics generally give great weight to factual evidence.

Differing concepts of what counts as evidence can lead to arguments that go nowhere. Consider, for example, how rare it is for a believer in creationism to be persuaded by what the theory of evolution presents as evidence — or how rare for a supporter of evolutionary theory to be convinced by what creationists present as evidence. A person who regards biblical authority as the supreme evidence in any argument may never see eye to eye with a person who views religion and science as occupying separate spheres, each of which offers its own kind of truth. Think carefully about how you use evidence in writing, and pay attention to what counts as evidence to members of groups you are trying to persuade.

- Should you rely on facts? concrete examples? firsthand experience? religious or philosophical texts? other sources?

- Should you include the testimony of experts? Which experts are valued most, and why?

- Should you use analogies as support? How much will they count?

- When does evidence from unedited websites such as blogs offer credible support, and when should you question or reject it?

- Once you determine what counts as evidence in your own thinking and writing, think about where you learned to use and value this kind of evidence. You can ask these same questions about the use of evidence by members of other cultures.

## Meeting expectations about organization

As you make choices about how to organize your writing, remember that cultural influences are at work here as well: the patterns that you find pleasing are likely to be ones that are deeply embedded in your own culture. For example, the organizational pattern favored by engineers, highly explicit and leaving little or nothing unsaid or unexplained, is probably familiar to most U.S. students: introduction and thesis, necessary background, overview of the parts to follow, systematic presentation of evidence, consideration of other viewpoints, and conclusion. If a piece of writing follows this pattern, American readers ordinarily find it "well organized" or "coherent."

In the United States, many audiences (especially those in the academic and business worlds) expect a writer to get to the point as directly as possible and to take on the major responsibility of articulating that point efficiently and unambiguously. But not all audiences have such expectations. For instance, a Chinese student with an excellent command of English found herself struggling in her American classes. Her writing, U.S. teachers said, was "vague," with too much "beating around the bush." As it turned out, her teachers in China had prized this kind of indirectness, expecting audiences to read between the lines. To be more explicit could send the message that readers aren't capable of such intellectual work.

When writing for audiences who may not share your expectations, then, think about how you can organize material to get your message across effectively. There are no hard-and-fast rules to help you organize your writing for effectiveness across cultures, but here are a few options to consider:

- Determine when to state your thesis — at the beginning? at the end? somewhere else? not at all?

- Consider whether the addition of tangential topics, what U.S. writers may think of as digressions, is a good idea, a requirement, or best avoided with your intended audience.

- Remember that online communication may call for certain ways of organizing. In messages or postings, you need to place the most important information first and be as succinct as possible. Or you may need to follow a template, as in submitting a résumé online.

## Meeting expectations about style

As with beauty, good style is most definitely in the eye of the beholder — and thus is always affected by language, culture, and rhetorical tradition. In fact, what constitutes effective style varies broadly across cultures and depends on the rhetorical situation — purpose, audience, and so on (see Chapter 3). Even so, there is one important style question to consider when writing across cultures: what level of formality is most appropriate? In most writing to a general audience in the United States, a fairly informal style is often acceptable, even appreciated. Many cultures, however, tend to value a more formal approach. When in doubt, it may be wise to err on the side of formality in writing to people from other cultures, especially to elders or to those in authority.

- Take care to use proper titles:

  Dr. Faye Spencer Maor        Professor Jaime Mejía

- Be careful in using slang or informal structures such as fragments unless you are doing so for special effect and are certain your audience will understand your purpose.

- Do not use first names of people you do not know in correspondence (even in text messages) unless invited to do so. Note, however, that an invitation to use a first name could come indirectly; if someone signs a message to you with his or her first name, you are implicitly invited to use the first name as a term of address. (See 2g for more on effective digital communication.)

- For formal business correspondence, use complete sentences and words. Open with the salutation and the person's full name or title, if you know it ("Dear Sasha Vrebalov," "Dear Professor Otuteye").

Beyond formality, other stylistic preferences vary widely, and context matters. Long, complex sentences and ornate language may be exactly what some audiences are looking for. On Twitter, on the other hand, writers have to limit their character count — so using abbreviated words, symbols, and fragments is expected, even desirable, there.

World writers, then, should take very little about language for granted. To be an effective world writer, recognize and respect stylistic differences as you move from community to community, and meet expectations whenever you can.

▼ ▼ ▼ ▼ ▼ ▼ ▼ ▼ ▼ ▼ ▼ ▼ ▼ ▼ ▼ ▼ ▼ ▼ ▼ ▼ ▼ ▼ ▼ ▼ ▼ ▼ ▼

## THINKING CRITICALLY ABOUT ASSUMPTIONS IN YOUR WRITING

Choose a recent essay or assignment you have written for a class and then at least one piece of social media writing or a blog post. Examine each piece carefully, noting what you assume about what counts as persuasive evidence, good organization, and effective style. How do you represent yourself in relation to your audience? What assumptions do you make about the audience, and are such assumptions warranted? What other unstated assumptions about good writing can you identify?

# CHAPTER 36

# Language That Builds Common Ground

The words we select have power: they can praise, delight, inspire — and also hurt, offend, or even destroy. Words that offend prevent others from identifying with you and thus damage your credibility. Few absolute guidelines exist for using language that respects difference and builds common ground, but two general rules can help: consider the sensitivities and preferences of others, and watch for words that carry stereotypes and betray your assumptions, even though you have not directly stated them.

## 36a Avoiding stereotypes and generalizations

Unstated assumptions that enter into thinking and writing can destroy common ground by ignoring important differences between others and ourselves. For example, a student in a religion seminar who uses *we* to refer to Christians and *they* to refer to members of other religions had better be sure that everyone in the class identifies as Christian, or some may feel left out of the discussion.

At the same time, don't overgeneralize about or stereotype a group of people. Because stereotypes are often based on half-truths, misunderstandings, and hand-me-down prejudices, they can lead to intolerance, bias, and bigotry.

Sometimes stereotypes and assumptions lead writers to call special attention to a group affiliation when it is not relevant, as in *a woman plumber* or *a white basketball player*. Even positive stereotypes — for example, *Jewish doctors are the best* — or neutral ones — *all college students like pizza* — can hurt, for they ignore the uniqueness of an individual. Careful writers make sure their language doesn't stereotype any group or individual.

## 36b Examining assumptions about gender

Powerful gender-related words can subtly affect our thinking and our behavior. For instance, at one time many young women were discouraged from pursuing careers in medicine or engineering at least partially because speakers commonly referred to hypothetical doctors or engineers as *he* (and then labeled a woman who worked as a doctor *a woman doctor*, as if to say, "She's an exception; doctors are normally men"). Similarly, a label like *male nurse* may offend by reflecting stereotyped assumptions about proper roles for men. Equally problematic is the traditional use of *man* and *mankind* to refer to people of both sexes and the use of *he* and *him* to refer generally to any human being.

Today, some people reject the simple binary between male/female and do not wish to identify with either of those terms, being referred to not as *he* or *she* but as *they* (using *they* as singular) or as an alternative, neutral term such as *ze*.

## 36c Examining assumptions about race and ethnicity

Generalizations about racial and ethnic groups can result in especially harmful stereotyping. To build common ground, then, avoid language that ignores differences not only among individual members of a race or ethnic group but also among subgroups. Writers must be aware, for instance, of the diverse places from which Americans of Spanish-speaking ancestry have come.

When writing about an ethnic or racial group, how can you refer to that group in terms that its members actually desire? Doing so is sometimes not an easy task, for terms can change often and vary widely.

The word *colored*, for example, was once widely used in the United States to refer to Americans of African ancestry. By the 1950s, the preferred term had become *Negro*. This changed in the 1960s, however, as *black* came to be preferred by most, though certainly not all, members of that community. Since the late 1980s, both *black* — sometimes capitalized (*Black*) — and *African American* have been widely used.

Once widely preferred, the term *Native American* has been challenged by those who argue that the most appropriate way to refer to indigenous peoples is by the specific name of the tribe or pueblo, such as *Chippewa* or *Zuni*. Many people once referred to as *Eskimos* prefer *Inuit* or a specific term such as *Tlingit*. It has also become fairly common for tribal groups to refer to themselves as *American Indians*. In international contexts, the broader *indigenous peoples* is preferred.

The terms *Latino* and *Hispanic* are often interchanged. *Latino* and *Latina* (and the gender-neutral *Latinx*) are geographic references; these words describe people who trace their ancestry to any country in Latin America — that is, Mexico, Central America, South America, or the Caribbean. *Hispanic*, on the other hand, describes people who trace their ancestry to a Spanish-speaking country. For example, Native Brazilians, who speak Portuguese as their first language, are Latinx but not Hispanic.

Ethnic terminology changes often enough to challenge the most careful writers — including writers who belong to the groups they are writing about.

Consider your words carefully and seek information about ways members of groups refer to themselves (or ask about preferences), but don't expect one person to speak for all members of a group or expect unanimity on such terms.

---

**QUICK HELP**

**Editing to build common ground**

- What stereotypes and other assumptions might come between you and your readers? Look, for instance, for language implying approval or disapproval and for the ways you use *we*, *you*, and *they*. **(36a)**
- Avoid potentially sexist language, and omit irrelevant references to gender. Use gender-neutral pronouns and nouns when you may be referring to people of any gender (*firefighters* instead of *firemen*, for instance). **(36b)**
- Make sure your references to race, religion, gender, sexual orientation, physical ability, age, and so on are relevant or necessary to your discussion. **(36b–d)**
- Are the terms you use to refer to groups accurate and acceptable? Pay attention to the terms that members of the group prefer. **(36c and d)**

---

**EXERCISE 36.1**

The following excerpt is taken from the 1948 edition of Dr. Benjamin Spock's *Baby and Child Care*. Read it carefully, noting any language we might now consider sexist. Then try bringing it up-to-date by revising the passage, substituting nonsexist language as necessary.

> When you suggest something that doesn't appeal to your baby, he feels he *must* assert himself. His nature tells him to. He just says "no" in words or actions, even about things that he likes to do. The psychologists call it "negativism"; mothers call it "that terrible *no* stage." But stop and think what would happen to him if he never felt like saying "no." He'd become a robot, a mechanical man. You wouldn't be able to resist the temptation to boss him all the time, and he'd stop learning and developing. When he was old enough to go out into the world, to school and later to work, everybody else would take advantage of him, too. He'd never be good for anything.

---

## 36d Considering other kinds of difference

Gender, race, and ethnicity are among the most frequent challenges to a writer seeking to find common ground with readers, but you will face many others as well.

### Age

Mention age if it is relevant, but be aware that age-related terms can carry derogatory connotations (*matronly*, *well-preserved*, and so on). Although describing Mr. Fry as *elderly but still active* may sound polite to you, chances are Mr. Fry would prefer being called *an active seventy-eight-year-old* — or just *a seventy-eight-year-old*, which eliminates the unstated assumption of surprise that he is active at his age.

### Class

Take special care to examine your words for assumptions about class. In a *New York Times* column, for example, a young woman wrote about losing her high-paying professional job. Unable to find other "meaningful work," as she put it, she was forced to accept "absurd" jobs like cleaning houses and baby-sitting.

The column provoked a number of angry letters to the *Times,* including this one: "So the young and privileged are learning what we of the working classes have always understood too well: there is no entitlement in life. We have always taken the jobs you label 'absurd.' Our mothers are the women who clean your mothers' houses."

As a writer, then, do not assume that all your readers share your background or values — that your classmates all own or even want to own cars, for instance. And avoid using any words — *redneck, old money,* and the like — that might alienate members of an audience.

### Geography

Geography does not necessarily determine personality, politics, or lifestyle. New Englanders are not all thrifty and tight-lipped; people in "red states" may hold liberal social and political views; midwesterners are not always polite. Check your writing carefully to be sure it doesn't make such simplistic assumptions.

Check also that you use geographic terms accurately:

| | |
|---|---|
| **AMERICA, AMERICAN** | Although many people use these words to refer to the United States alone, such usage will not necessarily be acceptable to people from Canada, Mexico, and Central or South America. |
| **BRITISH, ENGLISH** | Use *British* to refer to the island of Great Britain, which includes England, Scotland, and Wales, or to the United Kingdom of Great Britain and Northern Ireland. In general, do not use *English* for these broader senses. |
| **ARAB** | This term refers only to people of Arabic-speaking descent. Note that Iran is not an Arab nation; its people speak Farsi, not Arabic. Note also that *Arab* is not synonymous with *Muslim* or *Moslem* (a believer in Islam). Most (but not all) Arabs are Muslims, but many Muslims (those in Pakistan, for example) are not Arab. |

*Physical ability or health*

When writing about a person with a serious illness or disability, ask yourself whether mentioning the disability is relevant to your discussion and whether the words you use carry negative connotations. You might choose, for example, to say someone *uses* a wheelchair rather than to say he or she is *confined to* one. Similarly, you might note a subtle but meaningful difference between calling someone *a person with cancer* rather than *a cancer victim*. Mentioning the person first and the disability second, such as referring to a *child with diabetes* rather than a *diabetic child* or a *diabetic*, is always appropriate. In addition, remember that people with disabilities may well resent the use of euphemisms like "physically challenged" because such terms can minimize the importance of a disability.

*Religion*

Religious stereotypes are very often inaccurate and unfair. For example, Roman Catholics hold a wide spectrum of views on abortion, Muslim women do not all wear veils, and many Baptists are not fundamentalists — so beware of making generalizations based on religion. In fact, many people do not believe in or practice a religion at all, so be careful of such assumptions. As in other cases, do not use religious labels at all unless they are relevant.

*Sexual orientation*

If you wish to build common ground, do not assume that readers all share one sexual orientation — that everyone is attracted to the opposite sex, for example. As with any label, reference to sexual orientation should be governed by context. Someone writing about Senator Tammy Baldwin's or former Federal Reserve chair Janet Yellen's economic views would probably have no reason to refer to either person's sexual orientation. On the other hand, someone writing about diversity in U.S. government might find it important to note that in 2012 Baldwin became the first openly gay person elected to the Senate or that Mayor Pete Buttigieg was the first openly gay person to seek the presidential nomination.

CONSIDERING DISABILITIES | **KNOWING YOUR READERS**

Government statistics indicate that in 2016, 20 percent of college undergraduates identified themselves as having one or more disabilities. As this figure suggests, living with a disability is more the norm than many previously thought. And the actual figure may well be higher, since many students with disabilities do not identify themselves in that way. Effective writers learn as much as possible about their readers so that they can find ways to build common ground.

▼ ▼ ▼ ▼ ▼ ▼ ▼ ▼ ▼ ▼ ▼ ▼ ▼ ▼ ▼ ▼ ▼ ▼ ▼ ▼ ▼ ▼ ▼ ▼ ▼ ▼ ▼ ▼

## THINKING CRITICALLY ABOUT HOW LANGUAGE CAN BUILD COMMON GROUND

Writer and filmmaker Ruth Ozeki has written widely on issues related to the environment. In this June 2009 posting from her blog, Ozeki appeals to readers to step back and cultivate silence as a necessary prelude to making difficult decisions. Who is the "we" that Ozeki addresses? What views and values do you think she expects her readers to share with her? Note the strategies the writer uses to establish common ground with readers in this paragraph.

> I'm more and more convinced that we need to cultivate mindful silence, and share it with others whenever possible, if we are going to be able to make the careful and difficult choices we will need to make in order to survive in a wired and warming world. This seems to me to be a key piece of activism and eco-pedagogy that we can all learn to cultivate.     —RUTH OZEKI, *Ozekiland* (blog)

# CHAPTER 37

# Words Matter!

Do words matter? Sometimes it may seem as if we are awash in words, rushing over us like a torrent but saying very little. And sometimes that is true. But you won't have to think long to remember when a word or words said a lot and mattered very much to you: a word of praise from a coach or trainer acknowledging your progress or performance; a put-down (or worse) on social media; the words of a very special song; a vow you have taken. As you write, it's useful to remember these powerful moments and the words that accompany them.

## 37a Choosing appropriate words for the context

For much of your writing in college, your style may be fairly formal, like the following passage from a report on the Global Climate Action Summit held in San Francisco during September 2018:

> Political and government leaders at all levels must bring society together to collectively and urgently address climate change and identify innovative measures to do so. They should set national, regional, sectoral, and city-level targets; put forward bold policies; and create the necessary frameworks to establish predictable economic and socially conscious environments.

For the report, the reporter chooses words appropriate for a major newspaper along with a fairly serious tone. Note the use of words that signal the importance of the message: *must, urgently, bold* stress the importance of the message, but without in any way going "over the top." Compare the passage above to the following speech excerpt, delivered by California Governor Jerry Brown at the same meeting:

> With science still under attack and the climate threat growing, we're launching our own damn satellite. . . . This groundbreaking initiative will help governments, businesses, and landowners pinpoint — and stop — destructive emissions with unprecedented precision, on a scale that's never been done before.

Brown is speaking to those in attendance at the climate summit. Known for his fiery speaking style and aware that he is facing a friendly audience, he opens with a very dramatic statement, using very informal language (including a curse) before shifting into a more formal, moderate style. But note too his use of vivid words: *attack, threat, groundbreaking, pinpoint,* and *destructive.* In his rhetorical situation and with this audience, he knows his words matter — and he chooses them carefully.

A writer's tone and level of formality vary with context. In an email or letter to a friend or close associate, informal language is often expected and appropriate. But when you are addressing people you do not know well, as in most academic and professional writing, more formal language is likely to have a better effect on your audience. Compare these responses to a request for information about a job candidate:

**EMAIL TO SOMEONE YOU KNOW WELL**

Maisha is great — hire her if you can!

**LETTER OF RECOMMENDATION TO SOMEONE YOU DO NOT KNOW**

I am pleased to recommend Maisha Fisher. She will bring good ideas and extraordinary energy to your organization.

In deciding on the right words to use in a particular piece of writing, a writer needs to be aware of the possibilities and pitfalls of different kinds of language, including slang and colloquial language; technical and occupational language; and pompous language, euphemisms, and doublespeak.

## Using slang and colloquial language

Slang, or extremely informal language, is often confined to a relatively small group and usually becomes obsolete rather quickly, though some slang gains wide use (*selfie, duh*). Colloquial language, such as *in a bind* or *snooze,* is slightly less informal, more widely used, and longer lasting than most slang.

The use of slang and colloquial language can be powerful ways to connect to audiences. But writers who use slang and colloquial language in the wrong context run the risk of not being understood or of not being taken seriously. If you are writing for a general audience about gun-control legislation and you use terms like *gat* or *Mac* to refer to weapons, some readers may not know what you mean, and others may be irritated by what they see as a frivolous reference to a serious subject.

### EXERCISE 37.1

Choose something or someone to describe—a favorite cousin, a stranger on the bus, an automobile, a musical instrument, whatever strikes your fancy. Describe your subject using colloquial language and slang. Then rewrite the description, this time using neither of these. Read the two passages aloud, and note what different effects each version creates.

## Using technical and occupational language

Those who work — or play — in particular fields sometimes create their own technical language. Businesspeople speak about *vertical integration* and *upside movement,* biologists about *nucleotides* and *immunodestruction,* and baseball fans about *fielder's choices* and *suicide bunts.* If you use any technical or occupation-specific language, make sure that your audience will understand your terms, and replace or define those that they will not. Technical and occupational language can be divided into two overlapping categories: neologisms and jargon.

### Neologisms

Defined as new words that have not yet found their way into dictionaries, neologisms are especially useful in rapidly changing fields, such as business and sciences. Terms like *nanotechnology* (coined in 1974 and popularized in the 1980s) and *vortal* (from "vertical portal"), for example, could not be easily replaced except by much more complex explanations. Some neologisms, however, do not meet a real need and are unlikely to have staying power. Before including a neologism in your writing, then, consider whether your audience will understand and appreciate it.

### Jargon

Jargon is the special vocabulary of a trade or profession, enabling members to speak and write concisely to one another. Reserve jargon for an audience that will understand your terms. The example that follows, from a blog about fonts and typefaces, uses jargon appropriately for an interested and knowledgeable audience.

The Modern typeface classification is usually associated with Didones and display faces that often have too much contrast for text use. The Ingeborg family was designed with the intent of producing a Modern face that was readable at any size. Its roots might well be historic, but its approach is very contemporary. The three text weights (Regular, Bold, and Heavy) are functional and discreet while the Display weights (Fat and Block) catch the reader's eye with a dynamic form and a whole lot of ink on the paper. The family includes a boatload of extras like unicase alternates, swash caps, and a lined fill. —FONTSHOP.COM blog

Depending on the needs of one's audience, jargon can be irritating and incomprehensible — or extremely helpful. Terms that begin as jargon for specialists (such as *asynchronous* or *vertical integration*) can quickly become part of the mainstream if they provide a useful shorthand for an otherwise-lengthy explanation. Before you use technical jargon, remember your readers: if they will not understand the terms, or if you don't know them well enough to judge, then say what you need to say in everyday language.

## Avoiding pompous language, euphemisms, and doublespeak

Stuffy or pompous language is unnecessarily formal for the purpose, audience, or topic. It gives writing an insincere or unintentionally humorous tone, making a writer's ideas seem insignificant or even unbelievable.

**POMPOUS**

Pursuant to the August 9 memorandum regarding petroleum pricing, it is incumbent upon us to endeavor to make maximal utilization of digital and alternate methods of communication in lieu of personal visitation.

**REVISED**

As the August 9 memo noted, gas costs are high, so please use email, texting, and phone calls rather than personal visits whenever possible.

As these examples illustrate, some writers use words in an attempt to sound expert or important, and these puffed-up words can easily backfire.

| INSTEAD OF | TRY USING |
|---|---|
| ascertain | find out |
| commence | begin |
| finalize | finish or complete |
| functionality | function |
| impact (as a verb) | affect |
| methodology | method |
| operationalize | start; put into operation |
| optimal | best |
| parameters | boundaries |
| peruse | look at |
| ramp up | increase |
| utilize | use |

Euphemisms are words and phrases that make unpleasant ideas seem less harsh. *Your position is being eliminated* seeks to soften the blow of being fired or laid off. Other euphemisms include *pass away* for *die* and *between jobs* for *unemployed.* Although euphemisms can sometimes show that the writer is considerate of people's feelings, such language can also sound insincere or evasive — or can unintentionally insult by implying that the term or idea being avoided is something shameful.

Unlike euphemisms, *doublespeak,* a word coined from the *Newspeak* and *doublethink* of George Orwell's novel *1984,* is language used deliberately to hide or distort the truth. During cutbacks in the business world, companies may speak of layoffs as *employee repositioning* or *proactive downsizing,* and of unpaid time off as a *furlough.* Nevertheless, most people — and particularly those who have lost jobs or taken pay cuts — recognize these terms as doublespeak.

### EXERCISE 37.2

Revise each of these sentences to use formal language consistently. Example:

> Although    be enthusiastic       as soon as
> I can ~~get all enthused~~ about writing, ~~but~~ I sit down to write, ~~and~~ my
>   ^         ^                ^
>               blank.
> mind goes ~~right to sleep.~~
>           ^

1. In Shakespeare's *Othello,* Desdemona just lies down like some kind of wimp and accepts her death as inevitable.

2. The budget office doesn't want to cough up the cash to replace the drafty windows, but cranking up the heat in the building all winter doesn't come cheap.

3. Finding all that bling in King Tut's tomb was one of the biggest archeological scores of the twentieth century.

4. In unfamiliar settings or with people he did not know well, Duncan often came off as kind of snooty, but in reality he was scared to death.

5. My family lived in Trinidad for the first ten years of my life, and we went through a lot of bad stuff there, but when we came to the United States, we thought we finally had it made.

### TALKING THE TALK | TEXTING ABBREVIATIONS

"Can I use text-message slang when I contact my teacher?" In a chat or text message, abbreviations such as *u* for *you* are conventional usage, but using such shortcuts when communicating with an instructor can be a serious mistake. At least some of your instructors are likely to view these informal shortcuts as disrespectful, unprofessional, or simply sloppy writing. Unless your instructor has invited you to use text-message lingo, keep to the conventions of standard English for your college writing — even in email.

LANGUAGE, CULTURE, | **AVOIDING FANCY LANGUAGE**
AND CONTEXT

In writing standard academic English, which is fairly formal, students are often tempted to use many "big words" instead of simple language. Although learning impressive words can be a good way to expand your vocabulary, it is usually best to avoid flowery or fancy language in college writing. Academic writing at U.S. universities tends to value clear, concise prose.

---

**QUICK HELP**

Editing for appropriate language

- Check to see that your language reflects the appropriate level of formality for your audience, purpose, and topic. **(37a)**
- Unless you are writing for a specialized audience that will understand jargon, either define technical terms or replace them with words that are easy to understand. **(37a)**
- Revise pompous language, inappropriate euphemisms, and doublespeak. **(37a)**
- Consider the connotations of words carefully. If you say someone is *pushy*, be sure you mean to be critical; otherwise, use a word like *assertive*. **(37b)**
- Use both general and specific words. If you are writing about the general category *beds*, for example, do you give enough concrete detail (*an antique four-poster bed*)? **(37c)**

## 37b Using words with appropriate connotations

Thinking of a stone tossed into a pool and ripples spreading out from it can help you understand the distinction between *denotation*, the dictionary meaning of a word (the stone), and *connotation*, the associations that accompany the word (the ripples).

Words with similar denotations may have connotations that vary widely. The words *enthusiasm, passion,* and *obsession,* for instance, all have roughly the same dictionary meaning. But the associations called up by each word are quite different: an *enthusiasm* is a pleasurable and absorbing interest; a *passion* has a strong emotional component and may affect someone positively or negatively; an *obsession* is an unhealthy attachment that excludes other interests. *Pushy* and *assertive* also have similar denotations but different connotations — one negative, the other neutral or positive.

Take special care to use words with the appropriate connotations for your intended meaning. Note the differences in connotation among the following three statements:

▶ **The group Students Against Racism erected a temporary barrier on the campus oval. Members say it symbolizes "the many barriers to those discriminated against by university policies."**

▶ **Left-wing agitators planted an eyesore right on the oval to try to stampede the university into giving in to their every demand.**

▶ **Supporters of human rights for all students challenged the university's investment in racism by erecting a protest barrier on campus.**

The first statement is neutral, merely stating facts (and quoting the assertion about university policy to represent it as someone's words rather than as facts); the second, by using words with negative connotations (*agitators, eyesore, stampede*), is strongly critical; the third, by using words with positive connotations (*supporters of human rights*) and presenting assertions as facts (*the university's investment in racism*), gives a favorable slant to the group's actions. Political parties use words with loaded connotations regularly: during the health care reform debate in 2009–2010, for example, anti-reform groups used the term *death panels* to describe legislation that would reimburse doctors for optional consultations with patients about hospice care, living wills, and similar services.

 **EXERCISE 37.3**

From the parentheses, choose the word with the denotation that makes most sense in the context of the sentence. Use a dictionary if necessary.

1. Sue listened (*apprehensively / attentively*) to the lecture and took notes.

2. The telemarketers were told to (*empathize / emphasize*) more expensive items.

3. The interns were (*conscientious / conscious*) workers who listened carefully and learned fast.

4. Franklin advised his readers to be frugal and (*industrial / industrious*).

5. All (*proceedings / proceeds*) from the bake sale went to the athletics program.

**EXERCISE 37.4**

Study the italicized words in each of the following passages, and decide what each word's connotations contribute to your understanding of the passage. Think of a synonym for each word, and see if you can decide what difference the new word would make on the effect of the passage.

1. If boxing is a sport, it is the most *tragic* of all sports because, more than any human activity, it consumes the very excellence it displays: Its very *drama* is this consumption. —JOYCE CAROL OATES, "On Boxing"

2. Then one evening Miss Glory told me to serve the ladies on the porch. After I set the tray down and turned toward the kitchen, one of the women asked, "What's your name, *girl*?" —MAYA ANGELOU, *I Know Why the Caged Bird Sings*

3. The Kiowas are a summer people; they *abide* the cold and keep to themselves; but when the season *turns* and the land becomes warm and *vital*, they cannot *hold still*. —N. SCOTT MOMADAY, "The Way to Rainy Mountain"

## 37c Balancing general and specific language

Effective writers move their prose along by balancing general words, which name or describe groups or classes of things, with specific words, which refer to individual items. Some general words are abstractions, referring to qualities or ideas, things that the five senses cannot perceive. Specific words are often concrete words, referring to things we can see, hear, touch, taste, or smell. We can seldom draw a clear-cut line between general or abstract words on the one hand and specific or concrete ones on the other. Instead, most words fall somewhere between these two extremes.

| GENERAL | LESS GENERAL | SPECIFIC | MORE SPECIFIC |
|---|---|---|---|
| book | dictionary | abridged dictionary | *The American Heritage College Dictionary* |

| ABSTRACT | LESS ABSTRACT | CONCRETE | MORE CONCRETE |
|---|---|---|---|
| culture | visual art | painting | van Gogh's *Starry Night* |

Passages that contain too many general terms or abstractions demand that readers supply the specific details with their imaginations, making such writing hard to read. But writing that is full of specifics can also be hard to follow if the main point is lost amid a flood of details. Strong writing usually provides readers both with a general idea or overall picture and with specific examples or concrete details to fill in that picture. In the following passage, the author might have simply made a general statement — *their breakfast was always liberal and good* — or simply described the breakfast. Instead, he is both general and specific.

> There would be a brisk fire crackling in the hearth, the old smoke-gold of morning and the smell of fog, the crisp cheerful voices of the people and their ruddy competent morning look, and the cheerful smells of breakfast, which was always liberal and good, the best meal that they had: kidneys and ham and eggs and sausages and toast and marmalade and tea. —THOMAS WOLFE, *Of Time and the River*

Here a student writer balances a general statement (*My next-door neighbor is a nuisance*) with specific details:

> My next-door neighbor is a nuisance, poking and prying into my life, constantly watching me as I enter and leave my house, complaining about the noise when I am having a good time, and telling my parents whenever she sees me kissing my date.

| LANGUAGE, CULTURE, AND CONTEXT | **MASTERING IDIOMS** |

Why do you wear a diamond *on* your finger but *in* your ear? (See 55a.)

---

**EXERCISE 37.5**

Rewrite each of the following sentences to be more specific and concrete.

1. The entryway of the building was dirty.
2. The sounds at dawn are memorable.
3. Our holiday dinner tasted good.
4. The attendant came toward my car.
5. I woke up.

---

# 37d Using figurative language

Figurative language, or figures of speech, can paint pictures in our minds, allowing us to "see" a point readily and clearly. For example, an economist might explain that if you earned one dollar per second, you would need nearly thirty-two years to become a billionaire. When scientists compare certain genetic variants to typographical errors, they too are giving us a picture to help us grasp a difficult concept. Far from being mere decoration, then, figurative language is crucial to understanding.

In important ways, all language is metaphoric, referring to something beyond the word itself for which the word is a symbol. Particularly helpful in building understanding are specific types of figurative language, including similes, metaphors, and analogies.

## Using similes

Similes use *like*, *as*, *as if*, or *as though* to make an explicit comparison between two things.

▶ **Rain slides slowly down the glass, as if the night is crying.**
—PATRICIA CORNWELL

▶ **You can tell the graphic-novels section in a bookstore from afar, by the young bodies sprawled around it like casualties of a localized disaster.**
—PETER SCHJELDAHL

## Using metaphors

Metaphors are implicit comparisons, omitting the *like, as, as if,* or *as though* of similes.

▶ **The dark web is an iceberg — only a small portion is visible to everyone.**
                                                                        —PATRICK NOHE

Often, metaphors are more elaborate.

▶ **Black women are called, in the folklore that so aptly identifies one's status in society, "the mule of the world," because we have been handed the burdens that everyone else — everyone else — refused to carry.**
                                            —ALICE WALKER, *In Search of Our Mothers' Gardens*

## Using analogies

Analogies compare similar features of two dissimilar things; they explain something unfamiliar by relating it to something familiar. Analogies are often several sentences or paragraphs in length. Here, the writer draws an analogy between corporate pricing strategies and nuclear war:

▶ **One way to establish that peace-preserving threat of mutual assured destruction is to commit yourself beforehand, which helps explain why so many retailers promise to match any competitor's advertised price. Consumers view these guarantees as conducive to lower prices. But in fact offering a price-matching guarantee should make it less likely that competitors will slash prices, since they know that any cuts they make will immediately be matched. It's the retail version of the doomsday machine.**
                                                                        —JAMES SUROWIECKI

Before you use an analogy, make sure that the two things you are comparing have enough points of similarity to justify the comparison.

## Avoiding clichés and mixed metaphors

Just as effective figurative language can create the right impression, ineffective figures of speech — such as clichés and mixed metaphors — may wind up boring, irritating, or unintentionally amusing readers.

A cliché is a frequently used expression such as *busy as a bee* or *children are the future.* By definition, we use clichés all the time, especially in speech, and many serve usefully as shorthand for familiar ideas. If you use too many clichés in your writing, however, readers may conclude that what you are saying is not very new or interesting — or true. For example, if you write that a group of schoolgirls looked *pretty as a picture,* this clichéd simile may sound false or insincere. A more original figure of speech, such as *pretty as brand-new red shoes,* might be more effective.

Since people don't always agree on what is a cliché and what is a fresh image, how can you check your writing for clichés? Here is a rule to follow: if you can predict exactly what the upcoming word(s) in a phrase will be, it is probably a cliché.

Mixed metaphors are comparisons that are not consistent. Instead of creating a clear impression, they confuse the reader by pitting one image against another.

▶ **The lectures were brilliant comets streaking through the night sky,**

~~showering~~ listeners with ~~a torrential rain~~ of insight.
  ^dazzling                      ^flashes

The images of streaking light and heavy precipitation are inconsistent; in the revised sentence, all of the images relate to light.

## Using allusions

Allusions are indirect references to cultural works, people, or events. When a sports commentator said, "If the Georgia Tech men have an Achilles heel, it is their inexperience, their youth," he alluded to the Greek myth in which the hero Achilles was fatally wounded in his single vulnerable spot, his heel.

You can draw allusions from history, literature, sacred texts, common wisdom, or current events. Many movies and popular songs are full of allusions. The *Simpsons* episode called "Eternal Moonshine of the Simpson Mind," for example, alludes to the film *Eternal Sunshine of the Spotless Mind*. Remember, however, that allusions work only if your audience recognizes them.

## Signifying

One distinctive use of figurative language found extensively in African American English is signifying, in which a speaker cleverly needles or insults the listener. In the following passage, two African American men (Grave Digger and Coffin Ed) signify on their white supervisor (Anderson), who ordered them to discover the originators of a riot:

> "I take it you've discovered who started the riot," Anderson said.
> "We knew who he was all along," Grave Digger said.
> "It's just nothing we can do to him," Coffin Ed echoed.
> "Why not, for God's sake?"
> "He's dead," Coffin Ed said.
> "Who?"
> "Lincoln," Grave Digger said.
> "He hadn't ought to have freed us if he didn't want to make provisions to feed us," Coffin Ed said. "Anyone could have told him that."
>
> —CHESTER HIMES, *Hot Day, Hot Night*

Coffin Ed and Grave Digger demonstrate the major characteristics of effective signifying: indirection, ironic humor, fluid rhythm — and a surprising twist, the revelation that Abraham Lincoln caused the riot by ending slavery. This twist leaves the supervisor speechless — and gives Grave Digger and Coffin Ed the last word.

▼ ▼ ▼ ▼ ▼ ▼ ▼ ▼ ▼ ▼ ▼ ▼ ▼ ▼ ▼ ▼ ▼ ▼ ▼ ▼ ▼ ▼ ▼ ▼ ▼ ▼ ▼

## THINKING CRITICALLY ABOUT WORD CHOICE

### Reflecting on word choice

Read the following brief passage. What dominant feeling or impression does the passage produce in you? Identify the specific words and phrases that help create that impression.

> She wore gray like rain clouds and wandered the red roads in bared feet. Calluses thick as boot leather. Hair caked with mud. Blackened nails as if she had scratched the slate of night. Her acres of legs carrying her, arms swaying like a loose screen. Her eyes the ink of sky, just before the storm.
>
> That is how Ruby walked when she lived in the splintered house that Papa Bell had built before he passed. When she dug into the East Texas soil under moonlight and wailed like a distant train. —CYNTHIA BOND, *Ruby*

### Thinking about your own word choice

Choose a description you have written. Note any words that carry strong connotations, and identify the concrete and abstract language as well as any use of figurative language. Revise any inappropriate language you find. What do you notice about the words you choose?

# PART 9
# Style: Effective Sentences

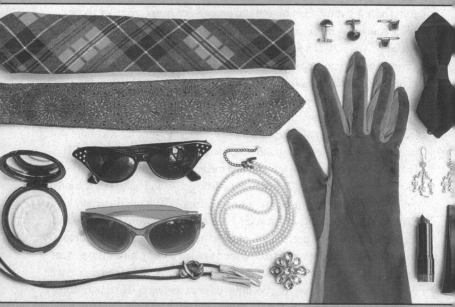

Photo by Mike Enright/www.menright.com. Photo styling by Barbara Lipp.

CHAPTER 38

# Concise Writing

If you have a Twitter account, and you probably do, you know a lot about being concise — that is, about getting messages across without wasting words. Recently, *New York Times* editor Bill Keller started a discussion by tweeting, "Twitter makes you stupid. Discuss." That little comment drew a large number of responses, including one from his wife that read, "I don't know if Twitter makes you stupid, but it's making you late for dinner. Come home."

But being concise is especially important today, when readers and writers face a daily onslaught of information and messages jostling for attention: which ones will you choose to skim, and which will you think carefully about? This fact of contemporary life is what has led media theorists Richard Lanham and Howard Rheingold to argue that being able to get — and hold — attention is the number-one problem facing communicators. What tools do writers have that will help them achieve that goal? Their answer, in a word, is *style*. Today, it's important that you present accurate and persuasive information, but to make sure that anyone will actually attend to what you say, it's also important to concentrate on how you present that information. And that's all about style: how clear and concise you can be; how you craft sentences that draw readers in and hold them; and how you make your messages memorable and compelling.

## 38a Eliminating unnecessary words

Sometimes writers say that something is large *in size* or red *in color* or that two ingredients should be combined *together*. The italicized words are unnecessarily repetitive; delete such redundant words.

▶ ~~Compulsory attendance~~ at assemblies is required.
  ^Attendance

▶ Many different forms of hazing occur, such as physical ~~abuse~~ and mental abuse.

490

## Deleting meaningless modifiers

Many modifiers are so overused that they have little meaning.

**MEANINGLESS MODIFIERS**

absolutely, awfully, definitely, fine, great, interesting, quite, really, very

## Replacing wordy phrases

Wordy phrases can be reduced to a word or two with no loss in meaning.

| WORDY | CONCISE |
|---|---|
| at that point in time | then |
| at the present time | now, today |
| due to the fact that | because |
| in order to | to |
| in spite of the fact that | although |
| in the event that | if |

---

**QUICK HELP**

Editing for conciseness

- Look for redundant words. If you are unsure about a word, read the sentence without it; if the meaning is not affected, leave the word out. (38a)
- Replace wordy phrases with a single word. Instead of *because of the fact that*, try *because*. (38a)
- Simplify grammatical structures whenever possible. For example, you might rewrite a sentence to make it more specific or combine two sentences that have the same subject or predicate. (38b)
- Identify all uses of *it is*, *there is*, and *there are*, and delete any that do not give your writing necessary emphasis. (38b)
- Note noun phrases whose meaning could be expressed by a verb, and try revising using the verb. (38b)
- Look for sentences that use the passive voice without a good reason. If the active voice would make the sentence livelier, clearer, or more concise, rewrite the sentence. (38c)

# 38b Simplifying sentence structure

Using simple grammatical structures can strengthen sentences and hold readers' attention.

▶ **Hurricane Dorian, ~~which was certainly~~ one of the most powerful**
**storms ever to hit the Bahamas, caused damage.** <sup>catastrophic</sup> ~~that amounted to a~~
~~catastrophe.~~

Deleting unnecessary words and replacing five words with one tightens the sentence and makes it easier to read.

▶ **When ~~she was~~ questioned about her previous job, Maria seemed**
**nervous,** <sup>and</sup> **~~Maria also~~ tried to change the subject.**

Combining two sentences produces one concise sentence.

## Avoiding unnecessary *there is, there are, it is, it seems* constructions

In general, do not use *there is, there are, it is, it seems,* or similar phrases unless you are introducing an idea to give it extra emphasis:

▶ **It is for us, the living, to ensure that We the People shall become the**
**powerful.** —JUNE JORDAN, "Inside America"

Here, *it is* slows down the opening of the sentence and sets up a formal rhythm that emphasizes what follows. Often, however, writers merely overuse expletives. Note how the following sentences are strengthened by deleting the expletives:

▶ <sup>Many</sup> **~~There are many~~ people ~~who~~ fear success because they do not believe**
**they deserve it.**

▶ <sup>Presidential</sup> **~~It is necessary for presidential~~ candidates ~~to~~** <sup>must</sup> **perform well on television.**

## Avoiding wordy noun forms

Forming nouns from verbs, a process sometimes called *nominalization,* can help make prose more concise — for example, using *abolition* instead of *the process of abolishing* — but it can also make a sentence wordy and hard to read. Using noun phrases when verbs will do can bury the action of a sentence and force the writer to use weak verbs and too many prepositional phrases. Too often, writers change verbs to nouns not to simplify a complex explanation but to make an idea sound more complex than it is.

▶ **The firm is now ~~engaged in an assessment of~~** <sup>assessing</sup> **its procedures for**
<sup>developing</sup> **~~the development of~~ new products.**

The original sentence sounds pretentious, and the noun phrases cloud the message. In contrast, the edited version is clear and forceful.

## 38c Using active and passive voice appropriately

In addition to choosing strong, precise verbs, you can help make your prose concise by using those verbs appropriately in active or passive voice (51g). Look at the <u>passive voice</u> in the following passage:

▶ [John F. Kennedy] died of a wound in the brain <u>caused</u> by a rifle bullet that <u>was fired</u> at him as he was riding through downtown Dallas in a motorcade.

Vice President Lyndon Baines Johnson, who was riding in the third car behind Mr. Kennedy's, <u>was sworn in</u> as the 36th President of the United States 99 minutes after Mr. Kennedy's death. —TOM WICKER, *New York Times*

As this passage indicates, the passive voice works effectively in certain situations: when the performer is unknown, unwilling to be identified, or less important than the recipient of the action. In general, however, try to use the active voice whenever possible. Because the passive voice diverts attention from the performer of an action and because it is usually wordier than the active voice, using it excessively makes for dull and difficult reading.

Edit an unnecessary passive construction to make it active.

      *his*          *Gower*
▶ In ~~Gower's~~ research, ~~it was~~ found that pythons often dwell in trees.

---

### EXERCISE 38.1

Look at the following sentences, which use the passive voice. Then rewrite each sentence in the active voice, and decide which version you prefer and why. Example:

  *I*            *you*
~~You are~~ hereby relieved of your duties. ~~by me.~~

1. Mistakes were made.
2. The candidate's speech was interrupted by hecklers.
3. Numerous reports of loud music from bars and shouting neighbors were taken by the city's new noise complaint hotline.
4. The violin solo was performed by an eight-year-old.
5. In a patient with celiac disease, intestinal damage can be caused by the body's immunological response to gluten.

**EXERCISE 38.2**

Revise the following paragraph to eliminate unnecessary words, nominalizations, expletives, and inappropriate use of the passive voice.

> As dogs became tamed and domesticated by humans over many thousands of years, the canine species underwent an evolution into hundreds of breeds designed to perform particular, specific tasks, such as pulling sleds and guarding sheep. Over time, there was a decreased need for many breeds. For example, as humans evolved from hunter-gatherers into farmers, it was no longer at all necessary for them to own hunting dogs. Later, as farming societies became industrialized, there was a disappearance of herd animals, and fewer shepherds watching sheep meant that there were fewer sheepdogs. But by this time humans had grown accustomed to dogs' companionship, and breeding continued. Today, most dogs are kept by their owners simply as companions, but some dogs still do the work they were intentionally bred for, such as following a scent, guarding a home, or leading the blind.

▼ ▼ ▼ ▼ ▼ ▼ ▼ ▼ ▼ ▼ ▼ ▼ ▼ ▼ ▼ ▼ ▼ ▼ ▼ ▼ ▼ ▼ ▼ ▼

## THINKING CRITICALLY ABOUT CONCISE WRITING

### Reading with an eye for conciseness

Bring two pieces of writing to class: one that is not just short, but concise—wasting no words but conveying its meaning clearly—and one that uses too many words to say too little. Compare both of your pieces with those chosen by your classmates.

### Thinking about your own writing

Find two or three paragraphs you have written recently, and study them with an eye for empty words. Using 38a for guidance, eliminate meaningless words such as *quite* and *very*. Compare notes with one or two classmates to see what empty words, if any, you tend to use. Finally, make a note of the empty words you use, and try to avoid them in the future.

# CHAPTER 39

# Coordination and Subordination

In speech, people tend to use *and* and *so* as all-purpose connectors.

> Leo enjoys psychology, and the course requires a lot of work.

The meaning of this sentence may be perfectly clear in speech, which provides clues through voice, facial expressions, and gestures. But in writing, the sentence could have multiple meanings, each of which suggests a different emphasis. Does the writer want to emphasize Leo's heavy workload or Leo's love of psychology?

> Although Leo enjoys psychology, the course requires a lot of work.

> Leo enjoys psychology even though the course requires a lot of work.

Coordinating conjunctions like *and* give ideas equal weight, whereas subordinating conjunctions like *although* emphasize one idea over another.

## 39a Relating equal ideas

When you want to give equal emphasis to different ideas in a sentence, link them with a <u>coordinating conjunction</u> (*and, but, for, nor, or, so, yet*) or a semicolon.

▶ **They acquired horses, <u>and</u> their ancient nomadic spirit was suddenly free of the ground.**   —N. SCOTT MOMADAY, *The Way to Rainy Mountain*

▶ **There is perfect freedom in the mountains, <u>but</u> it belongs to the eagle and the elk, the badger and the bear.**

   —N. SCOTT MOMADAY, *The Way to Rainy Mountain*

---

QUICK HELP

Editing for coordination and subordination

How do your ideas flow from one sentence to another? Do they connect smoothly and clearly? Are the more important ideas given more emphasis than the less important ones? These guidelines will help you edit with such questions in mind.

- Look for strings of short sentences that might be combined to join related ideas. (39a)

  ▶ The report was short/ ~~It was~~ persuasive/; ~~It~~ changed my mind.
  
  *but* ... *it*

- If you often link ideas with the conjunctions *and*, *but*, and *so*, are the linked ideas equally important? If not, edit to subordinate the less important ones. (39b)

- Are the most important ideas in independent clauses? If not, edit so that they are. (39b)

  ▶ ~~The~~ report was short, ~~even though~~ it changed my mind.
  
  *Even though the*

---

Coordination can help to make explicit the relationship between two separate ideas.

▶ Generations have now grown up with *The Simpsons*/; Bart, Lisa, and Maggie never get older, but today's college students may have been watching the show since before they could talk.

Connecting these two sentences with a semicolon strengthens the connection between two closely related ideas.

When you connect ideas in a sentence, make sure that the relationship between the ideas is clear.

▶ Surfing the Internet is a common way to spend leisure time, ~~and~~ it should not replace human contact.

*but*

What does being a common form of leisure have to do with replacing human contact? Changing *and* to *but* better relates the two ideas.

## Using coordination for special effect

Coordination can create special effects, as in a passage by Carl Sandburg describing the American reaction to Abraham Lincoln's assassination.

Men tried to talk about it and the words failed and they came back to silence.

To say nothing was best.

Lincoln was dead.

Was there anything more to say?

Yes, they would go through the motions of grief and they would take part in a national funeral and a ceremony of humiliation and abasement and tears.

But words were no help.

Lincoln was dead.            —CARL SANDBURG, *Abraham Lincoln: The War Years*

Everything in the passage is grammatically equal, flattened out by the pain and shock of the death. In this way, the sentence structure and grammar mirror the dazed state of the populace. The short sentences and independent clauses are almost like sobs that illustrate the thought of the first sentence, that "the words failed."

---

### EXERCISE 39.1

Using coordination to signal equal importance or to create special effects, combine and revise the following twelve short sentences into several longer and more effective ones. Add or delete words as necessary.

> The auditorium was filled with people. The sea of faces did not intimidate me. I had decided to appear in a musical with my local community theater group. There was no going back now. I reminded myself of how I had gotten here. It took hard work. I refused to doubt my abilities. Besides, the director and her staff had held auditions. I had read the heroine's part. I had sung a song. They had chosen me for the role. I was untrained. My skills as an actor would now be judged publicly. I felt ready to rise to the challenge.

---

## 39b Distinguishing main ideas

Subordination allows you to distinguish major points from minor points or to bring supporting details into a sentence. If, for instance, you put your main idea in an independent clause, you might then put any less significant ideas in dependent clauses, phrases, or even single words. The following sentence highlights the subordinated point:

▶ **Mrs. Viola Cullinan was a plump woman <u>who lived in a three-bedroom house somewhere behind the post office.</u>**

—MAYA ANGELOU, "My Name Is Margaret"

The dependent clause adds important information about Mrs. Cullinan, but it is subordinate to the independent clause.

Notice that the choice of what to subordinate rests with the writer and depends on the intended meaning. Angelou might have given the same basic information differently:

▶ **Mrs. Viola Cullinan, <u>a plump woman</u>, lived in a three-bedroom house somewhere behind the post office.**

Subordinating the information about Mrs. Cullinan's size to that about her house would suggest a slightly different meaning, of course. As a writer, you must think carefully about what you want to emphasize and must subordinate information accordingly.

Subordination also establishes logical relationships among different ideas. These relationships are often specified by subordinating conjunctions.

**SOME COMMON SUBORDINATING CONJUNCTIONS**

| | | |
|---|---|---|
| after | if | though |
| although | in order that | unless |
| as | once | until |
| as if | since | when |
| because | so that | where |
| before | than | while |
| even though | that | |

The following sentence highlights the subordinate clause and italicizes the subordinating word:

▶ **She usually rested her smile until late afternoon <u>*when* her women friends dropped in and Miss Glory, the cook, served them cold drinks on the closed-in porch.</u>** —MAYA ANGELOU, "My Name Is Margaret"

Using too many coordinate structures can be monotonous and can make it hard for readers to recognize the most important ideas. Subordinating lesser ideas can help highlight the main ideas.

▶ **Many people check email in the evening, and so they turn on the computer. ~~They~~ Though they may intend to respond only to urgent messages, a friend sends a link to a blog post, ~~and~~ which they decide to read ~~it~~ for just a short while./ Eventually, ~~and~~ they get engrossed in Instagram or Twitter, and they end up spending the whole evening in front of the screen.**

## Determining what to subordinate

Although our
▶ ~~Our~~ new boss can be difficult, ~~although~~ she has revived and maybe even
^

saved the division.

The editing puts the more important information — that the new boss has saved part of the company — in an independent clause and subordinates the rest.

## Avoiding excessive subordination

When too many subordinate clauses are strung together, readers may have trouble keeping track of the main idea expressed in the independent clause.

**TOO MUCH SUBORDINATION**

▶ Philip II sent the Spanish Armada to conquer England, which was ruled by Elizabeth, who had executed Mary because she was plotting to overthrow Elizabeth, who was a Protestant, whereas Mary and Philip were Roman Catholics.

**REVISED**

▶ Philip II sent the Spanish Armada to conquer England, which was ruled by Elizabeth, a Protestant. She had executed Mary, a Roman Catholic like Philip, because Mary was plotting to overthrow her.

Putting the facts about Elizabeth executing Mary into an independent clause makes key information easier to recognize.

You can employ a variety of grammatical structures — not merely dependent clauses — to subordinate a less important element within a sentence:

▶ The parks report was persuasively written. It contained five typed pages. [no subordination]

▶ The parks report, *which contained five typed pages*, was persuasively written. [dependent clause]

▶ The parks report, *containing five typed pages*, was persuasively written. [participial phrase]

▶ The *five-page* parks report was persuasively written. [adjective]

▶ The parks report, *five typed pages*, was persuasively written. [appositive]

▶ The parks report, *its five pages neatly typed*, was persuasively written. [absolute]

**EXERCISE 39.2**

Combine each of the following sets of sentences into one sentence that uses subordination to signal the relationships among ideas. Example:

> **I was looking through the cupboard.**
> **I noticed the cookies were gone.**
> **This snack is a favorite of my roommate.**
>
> *While I was looking through the cupboard, I noticed that the cookies, one of my roommate's favorite snacks, were gone.*

1. The original *Star Trek* television show ran from 1966 to 1969.
   It was critically acclaimed.
   It had low ratings and was canceled by the network.
2. Athena was the goddess of wisdom.
   Ancient Greeks relied on Athena to protect the city of Athens.
   Athens was named in Athena's honor.
3. Harry Potter is a fictional wizard.
   He turns eleven years old.
   He is taken to Hogwarts School of Witchcraft and Wizardry.
4. Flappers seemed rebellious to their parents' generation.
   They broke with 1920s social conventions.
   They cut their hair short and smoked in public.
5. Skateboarding originated in Venice, California.
   The time was the mid-seventies.
   There was a drought.
   The swimming pools were empty.

## Using subordination for special effect

Some particularly fine examples of subordination come from Martin Luther King Jr. In the following passage, he piles up dependent clauses beginning with *when* to build up suspense for his main statement, given in the independent clause at the end:

> Perhaps it is easy for those who have never felt the stinging darts of segregation to say, "Wait." But *when* you have seen vicious mobs lynch your mothers and fathers at will and drown your sisters and brothers at whim; *when* you have seen hate-filled policemen curse, kick, and even kill your black brothers and sisters; . . . *when* you have to concoct an answer for a five-year-old son who is asking: "Daddy, why do white people treat colored people so mean?"; *when* you take a cross-country drive and find it necessary

to sleep night after night in the uncomfortable corners of your automobile because no motel will accept you; . . . *when* your first name becomes "nigger," your middle name becomes "boy" (however old you are) and your last name becomes "John," and your wife and mother are never given the respected title "Mrs."; . . . *when* you are forever fighting a degenerating sense of "nobodiness" — then you will understand why we find it difficult to wait.

—MARTIN LUTHER KING JR., "Letter from Birmingham Jail"

A dependent clause can also create an ironic effect if it somehow undercuts the independent clause. A master of this technique, Mark Twain once opened a paragraph with this sentence:

▶ **Always obey your parents,** *when they are present.*

—MARK TWAIN, "Advice to Youth"

▼ ▼ ▼ ▼ ▼ ▼ ▼ ▼ ▼ ▼ ▼ ▼ ▼ ▼ ▼ ▼ ▼ ▼ ▼ ▼ ▼ ▼ ▼ ▼

## THINKING CRITICALLY ABOUT COORDINATION AND SUBORDINATION

### Reading with an eye for coordination and subordination

Read over the first draft of "All-Powerful Coke" (see 4g), paying special attention to the coordination and subordination. Do you notice any patterns—are there some of each? more of one than the other? Identify the coordination and subordination in one paragraph. Are they used appropriately? If not, revise the paragraph by following the guidelines in this chapter.

### Thinking about your own use of coordination and subordination

Analyze two paragraphs from one of your drafts. Do the independent clauses contain the main ideas? How many dependent clauses do you find? Should the ideas in the dependent clauses be subordinate to those in the independent clauses? Revise the paragraphs to use coordination and subordination effectively. What conclusions can you draw about your use of coordination and subordination?

# CHAPTER 40

# Sentence Variety

In one college classroom, a peer-response group worked on an essay for almost an hour, but its overall effect still seemed, well, boring. Finally, one student exclaimed, "These sentences all look the same!"

And they were: every sentence in the essay was about the same length, and every sentence started with the subject. The group went to work again, shortening some sentences and revising others to create new rhythms. With the resulting sentence variety, the essay took on new life; it flowed.

## 40a  Varying sentence length

Deciding how and when to vary sentence length is not always easy. Is there a "just right" length for a particular sentence or idea? The answer depends on, among other things, the writer's purpose, intended audience, and topic. A children's story, for instance, may call for mostly short sentences, whereas an article on nuclear disarmament may call for considerably longer ones.

Although a series of short or long sentences can sometimes be effective, alternating sentence length is usually the best approach in formal writing. For example, after one or more long sentences with complex ideas or images, the punch of a short sentence can be dramatic:

▶ **The fire of, I think, five machine-guns was pouring upon us, and there was a series of heavy crashes caused by the Fascists flinging bombs over their own parapet in the most idiotic manner. It was intensely dark.**

　　　　　　　　　　　　　　　　　　—GEORGE ORWELL, *Homage to Catalonia*

Similarly, try using a long sentence after several short ones.

▶ *Sith*. **What kind of a word is that? It sounds to me like the noise that emerges when you block one nostril and blow through the other, but to George Lucas it is a name that trumpets evil.**　　　　　—ANTHONY LANE

---

QUICK HELP

Editing for sentence variety

- Check sentence *length* by counting the words in each sentence. If the difference between the longest and the shortest sentences is fairly small—say, five words or fewer—try revising some sentences to create greater variety. Should two or more short sentences be combined because they deal with closely related ideas? Should a long sentence be split up because it contains too many important ideas? (**40a**)
- Look at sentence *openings*. If most sentences start with a subject, try recasting some to begin with a transition, a phrase, or a dependent clause. (**40b**)
- Vary types of sentences to make your writing more interesting. Do you use simple, compound, complex, and compound-complex sentences—or does one type predominate? Would a particular declarative sentence be more effective as a command or question or exclamation? Could you use a periodic or cumulative sentence for special effect? (**40c**)

---

◢ **EXERCISE 40.1**

The following paragraph can be improved by varying sentence length. Read it aloud to get a sense of how it sounds. Then revise it, creating some short, emphatic sentences and combining other sentences to create more effective long sentences. Add words or change punctuation as you need to.

Before planting a tree, a gardener needs to choose a good location and dig a deep enough hole. The location should have the right kind of soil, sufficient drainage, and enough light for the type of tree chosen. The hole should be slightly deeper than the root-ball and about twice as wide. The gardener must unwrap the root-ball, for even burlap, which is biodegradable, may be treated with chemicals that will eventually damage the roots. The roots may have grown into a compact ball if the tree has been in a pot for some time, and they should be separated or cut apart in this case. The gardener should set the root-ball into the hole and then begin to fill the hole with loose dirt. After filling the hole completely, the gardener should make sure to water the tree thoroughly. New plantings require extra water and extra care for about three years before they are well rooted.

---

# 40b Varying sentence openings

If sentence after sentence begins with a subject, a passage may become monotonous or even hard to read.

▶ **The way football and basketball are played is as interesting as the**
     *Because football*                                    *each*
**players. ~~Football~~ is a game of precision,/ ~~Each~~ play is diagrammed**
     ^                                          ^*however,*
**to accomplish a certain goal. Basketball, is a game of endurance.**
*In fact, a*                                          ^  *the*
**~~A~~ basketball game looks like a track meet,/ ~~The~~ team that drops of**
     ^                                                ^

**exhaustion first loses.**

The editing adds variety by using a subordinating word (*Because*) and transitions
(*however* and *In fact*) and by linking sentences. Varying sentence openings prevents
the passage from seeming to jerk or lurch along.

You can add variety to your sentence openings by using transitions, various
kinds of phrases, and introductory dependent clauses.

## Using transitional expressions for variety

See how transitions bring variety and clarity to this passage.

> In order to be alert Friday morning in New York, I planned to take the
> shuttle from Washington Thursday night. *On Thursday morning* it began to snow
> in Washington and to snow even harder in New York. *By mid-afternoon* I decided
> not to risk the shuttle and caught a train to New York. *Seven hours later* the train
> completed its three-hour trip. I arrived at Penn Station to find a city shut down
> by the worst blizzard since 1947.            —LINDA ELLERBEE, "And So It Goes"

Here the transitional words establish chronology as well as help carry readers
smoothly through the paragraph. (For more on transitions, see 5d.)

## Using phrases for variety

Prepositional, verbal, and absolute phrases can also provide variety in sentence
openings.

**PREPOSITIONAL PHRASES**

▶ <u>Before dawn</u>, tired commuters drink their first cups of coffee.

▶ <u>From a few scraps of wood in the Middle Ages to a precisely carved,
   electrified instrument in our times</u>, the guitar has gone through
   uncounted changes.

**VERBAL PHRASES**

▶ <u>Frustrated by the delays</u>, the driver shouted at his car radio.

▶ <u>To qualify for the finals</u>, a speller must win a regional championship.

ABSOLUTE PHRASES

▶ **<u>Our hopes for victory shattered</u>, we started home.**

In general, use a comma after such phrases whenever they open a sentence (56b).

## Using dependent clauses for variety

Dependent clauses are another way to open a sentence.

▶ **<u>While the boss sat on his tractor</u>, I was down in a ditch, pounding in stakes.**

▶ **<u>What they want</u> is a place to call home.**

In general, use a comma after adverb clauses whenever they open a sentence (56b).

# 40c Varying sentence types

In addition to using different lengths and openings, you can use different types of sentences. Sentences can be classified grammatically and functionally (as discussed in Chapter 49) as well as rhetorically.

## Varying grammatical types

Grammatically, sentences fall into four categories — simple, compound, complex, and compound-complex — based on the number of independent and dependent clauses they contain (49f). Varying your sentences among these grammatical types can help you create readable, effective prose.

## Varying functional types

In terms of function, sentences are declarative (making a statement), interrogative (asking a question), imperative (giving a command), or exclamatory (expressing strong feeling). Most sentences are declarative, but occasionally a command, a question, or an exclamation may be appropriate.

COMMAND

▶ **Coal-burning plants undoubtedly harm the environment in various ways; for example, they contribute to acid rain. <u>But consider the alternatives.</u>**

QUESTION

▶ **<u>Why would sixteen middle-aged people try to backpack forty-seven miles?</u> At this point, I was not at all sure.**

EXCLAMATION

▶ <u>Divorcés! They were everywhere!</u> Sometimes he felt like a new member of an enormous club, the Divorcés of America, that he had never before even heard of.

## Varying rhetorical types

By highlighting sentence endings and beginnings, periodic and cumulative sentences can create strong effects.

### Periodic sentences

Periodic sentences postpone the <u>main idea</u> (usually in an independent clause) until the very end of the sentence. They are especially useful for creating tension or building toward a climactic, surprise, or inspirational ending.

▶ **Even though large tracts of Europe and many old and famous states have fallen or may fall into the grasp of the Gestapo and all the odious apparatus of Nazi rule, <u>we shall not flag or fail</u>.** —WINSTON CHURCHILL

Look at the following sentence and its revision to see how periodic order can provide emphasis:

ORIGINAL SENTENCE

The nations of the world have no alternative but coexistence because another world war would be unwinnable and because total destruction would certainly occur.

REVISED AS A PERIODIC SENTENCE

Because another world war would be unwinnable and because total destruction would certainly occur, the nations of the world have no alternative but coexistence.

Nothing is really wrong with the first sentence. But to emphasize the idea in the independent clause — *no alternative but coexistence* — the writer chose to revise it using the periodic pattern.

### Cumulative sentences

Cumulative sentences, which begin with an independent clause and then add details in phrases and in dependent clauses (as does the preceding sentence labeled *original*), are far more common than periodic sentences. They are useful when you want to provide both immediate understanding of the <u>main idea</u> and a great deal of supporting detail.

▶ <u>**I can still see her**</u>, **a tiny nun with a sharp pink nose, confidently drawing a dead-straight horizontal line like a highway across the blackboard,**

**flourishing her chalk at the end of it, her veil flapping out behind her as
she turned back to class.** —KITTY BURNS FLOREY

 **EXERCISE 40.2**

Revise each of the following sentences twice, once as a periodic sentence and once
as a cumulative sentence.

1. Obviously not understanding reporters, the politician did not know their
   names, did not answer their questions, and did not read their stories.

2. Able to think only of my mother's surgery the next morning, I could not even
   eat my dinner, much less get any sleep, nor could I do my homework.

▼ ▼ ▼ ▼ ▼ ▼ ▼ ▼ ▼ ▼ ▼ ▼ ▼ ▼ ▼ ▼ ▼ ▼ ▼ ▼ ▼ ▼ ▼ ▼ ▼ ▼

## THINKING CRITICALLY ABOUT SENTENCE VARIETY

### Reading with an eye for sentence variety

Read something by an author you admire. Analyze two paragraphs for sentence
length, opening, and type. Compare the sentence variety in these paragraphs with
that in one of your paragraphs. What similarities or differences do you recognize,
and what conclusions can you draw about sentence variety?

### Thinking about your own sentence variety

Choose a piece of writing you have recently completed, and analyze two or three
pages for sentence variety. Note sentence length, opening, and type (grammatical,
functional, and rhetorical). Choose a passage you think can be improved for variety,
and make those revisions.

CHAPTER 41

# Memorable Prose

A student writer once asked me, "How can I make my sentences sing?" In answering, I pointed out that some writers seem to have a genius for choosing the perfect words, but with careful attention to style and good, solid practice, anyone can learn to write more memorable prose. When you notice a piece of writing that you admire — whether you find it in an advertisement, a blog post, a tweet, dialogue from a film, or a friend's social media status update — reflect on the writing style: what does it do well and how does it achieve its effects?

## 41a Writing emphatic sentences

When you speak, you achieve emphasis by raising your voice or stressing an important word or phrase. And much of the writing you see — in advertisements, on websites, in magazines — gains emphasis in similar fashion, with color or bold type, for instance. Even though academic writing can't always rely on such graphic devices, writers use other techniques to emphasize parts of their sentences.

---

**QUICK HELP**

Editing for memorable prose

- Identify the words you want to emphasize. If you've buried those words in the middle of a sentence, edit the sentence to change their position. The end and the beginning are generally the most emphatic. (**41a**)
- Note any sentences that include a series of words, phrases, or clauses. Arrange the items in the series in climactic order, with the most important item last. (**41a**)
- Underline all verbs, and look to see whether you rely too much on forms of *be*, *do*, and *have*. If so, try to substitute more specific verbs. (**41b**)

---

## Using closing and opening positions for emphasis

When you read a sentence, you usually remember the ending. This part of the sentence moves the writing forward by providing new information, as in the following example:

▶ **Employers today expect college graduates to have <u>excellent writing skills</u>.**

A less emphatic but still important position in a sentence is the opening, which often connects the new sentence with what has come before.

▶ **Today's employers want a college-educated workforce that can communicate well. <u>Excellent writing skills</u> are high on the list of qualifications.**

If you place relatively unimportant information in the memorable closing position of a sentence, you may undercut what you want to emphasize or give more emphasis to the closing words than you intend.

▶ ~~Last month, she~~                           $500,000.
**She gave $500,000 to the school capital campaign ~~last month~~.**

Moving *$500,000* to the end of the sentence emphasizes the amount.

## Using climactic order

Presenting ideas in climactic order means arranging them in order of increasing importance or drama so that your writing builds to a climax. By saving its most dramatic item for last, a sentence can make its point more forcefully.

▶ **After they've finished with the pantry, the medicine cabinet, and the attic, [neat people] will throw out the red geranium (too many leaves), sell the dog (too many fleas), and send the children off to boarding school (too many scuffmarks on the hardwood floors).**

—SUZANNE BRITT, "Neat People vs. Sloppy People"

"appetizer ribs" and "entrée ribs," with
▶ **The barbecue stand's menu offered "more ribs" for dessert**

~~after "appetizer ribs" and "entrée ribs."~~

The original version of the preceding sentence fails to achieve strong emphasis; the editing provides climactic order.

◢ **EXERCISE 41.1**

Revise each of the following sentences to highlight what you take to be the main or most important ideas. Example:

> His video soon went viral, bringing in increased advertising revenue, *accolades from subscribers to his YouTube channel,*
> *and*
> an offer to edit a feature film/. ~~and subscribers to his YouTube channel.~~

1. The president persuaded the American people, his staff, and Congress.

2. We can expect a decade of record-breaking tropical storms and hurricanes, if meteorologists are correct in their predictions.

3. From the sightseeing boat, we saw a whale dive toward us and then, before crashing its tail on the waves, lift itself out of the water.

4. I did not realize that living in the city would mean eating canned soup every night, selling my car, and losing half my closet space.

5. Jake experienced several side effects from the medication, including dizziness, severe abdominal pain, and dry mouth.

## 41b Choosing strong verbs

Verbs serve as the real workhorses of our language. Look, for instance, at the strong, precise verbs in the following passage:

> ▶ **A fire engine, out for a trial spin, <u>roared</u> past Emerson's house, hot with readiness for public duty. Over the barn roofs the martens <u>dipped</u> and <u>chittered</u>. A swarthy daughter of an asparagus grower, in culottes, shirt, and bandanna, <u>pedalled</u> past on her bicycle.** —E. B. WHITE, "Walden"

If White had used more general verbs — such as *drove, flew, called,* and *rode* — the passage would be much less effective. With White's verbs, however, readers can hear the roar of the fire engine, see the martens swooping downward and hear them chirping shrilly, and feel the young woman pushing on the pedals of her bicycle.

Some of the most commonly used verbs in English — especially *be, do,* and *have* — carry little or no sense of specific action. Try not to overuse them in situations where precise verbs would be more effective. Look at how much stronger the following sentences become when precise verbs are used:

> ▶ **Malnutrition** ~~is harmful to~~ *stunts and distorts* **children's development.**

▸   Sidewalk artists offered to ~~do~~ <sup>sketch</sup> my portrait in ten minutes.

▸   The young marines ~~had~~ <sup>sweated through</sup> basic training at Parris Island.

# 41c  Using special effects

Contemporary movies often succeed on the basis of their special effects. Similarly, special effects like repetition, antithesis, and inverted word order can animate your prose and help make it memorable.

## Using repetition for emphasis

Carefully used, repetition of sounds, words, phrases, or other grammatical constructions serves as a powerful stylistic device. Orators have long known its power. Here is a famous use of repetition from one of British prime minister Winston Churchill's addresses to the British people during World War II:

▸   <u>We shall</u> not flag or fail, <u>we shall</u> go on to the end. <u>We shall</u> fight in France, <u>we shall</u> fight on the seas and oceans, <u>we shall</u> fight with growing confidence and growing strength in the air, <u>we shall</u> defend our island, whatever the cost may be; <u>we shall</u> fight on the beaches, . . . <u>we shall</u> fight in the fields and in the streets, . . . <u>we shall</u> never surrender.    —WINSTON CHURCHILL

In this passage, Churchill uses the constant hammering of *we shall* accompanied by the repetition of *f* sounds (*flag, fail, fight, France, confidence, defend, fields*) to strengthen his listeners' resolve.

Though you may not be a prime minister, you can use repetition to equally good effect. Here is another example:

▸   So my dream date turned into a nightmare. Where was the quiet, considerate, caring guy I thought I had met? In his place appeared this jerk. He postured, he preened, he bragged, he bellowed. He practically brayed — just like the donkey he so much reminded me of.

Be careful, however, to use repetition only for a deliberate purpose.

## Using antithesis to emphasize contrast

Antithesis is the use of parallel structures to highlight contrast or opposition in writing (see Chapter 43). Like other uses of parallelism, antithesis provides a pleasing rhythm that calls readers' attention to the contrast, often in a startling or amusing way.

► Love is an ideal thing, marriage a real thing.

► The congregation didn't think much of the new preacher, and what the new preacher thought of the congregation she didn't wish to say.

► It is a sin to believe evil of others, but it is seldom a mistake.

—H. L. MENCKEN

### EXERCISE 41.2

Using one of the preceding examples as a guide, create a sentence of your own that uses antithesis. You might begin by thinking of opposites you could build on: hope / despair, good / evil, fire / ice. Or you might begin with a topic you want to write about: success, greed, generosity, and so on.

## Using inverted word order

Writers may invert the usual word order, such as putting the verb before the subject or the object before the subject and verb, to create surprise or to emphasize a particular word or phrase.

►  Out of the tree
   ~~Two dead birds~~ plummeted ~~out of the tree.~~  two dead birds.

   The inverted word order creates a more dramatic sentence by putting the emphasis at the end, on *two dead birds*.

As with any unusual sentence pattern, use inverted word order sparingly, only to create occasional special effects.

► Into this grey lake plopped the thought, I know this man, don't I?

—DORIS LESSING

► In a hole in the ground there lived a hobbit.      —J. R. R. TOLKIEN

### EXERCISE 41.3

Look at something you have written, and find a sentence that might be more effective with inverted word order. Experiment with the word order. Read the results aloud, and compare the effects.

▼ ▼ ▼ ▼ ▼ ▼ ▼ ▼ ▼ ▼ ▼ ▼ ▼ ▼ ▼ ▼ ▼ ▼ ▼ ▼ ▼ ▼ ▼ ▼ ▼ ▼

## THINKING CRITICALLY ABOUT PROSE STYLE

### Reading with an eye for prose style

One entertaining way to practice the elements of effective prose is to imitate them. Choose a writer you admire. Reread (or listen to) this writer's work, getting a feel for the rhythms, the structures, the special effects. Make a list of the elements that contribute to the distinctive style. Then choose a well-known story, and retell it in that writer's style. Following is the opening of "The Three Little Pigs" as one student imagined Edgar Allan Poe might have told it.

> It began as a mere infatuation. I admired them from afar, with a longing that only a wolf may know. Soon, these feelings turned to torment. Were I even to set eyes upon their porcine forms, the bowels of my soul raged, as if goaded by some festering poison. As the chilling winds of November howled, my gullet yearned for them. I soon feasted only upon an earnest and consuming desire for the moment of their decease.

## Thinking about your own prose style

Read over something you have written, looking for memorable sentences. If few sentences catch your eye, choose some that show promise — ones with strong verbs or a pleasing rhythm, perhaps. Using this chapter for guidance, try revising one or two sentences to make them more effective and memorable. Finally, note some ways in which your writing is effective and some strategies for making it more effective.

# PART 10
# Clarity

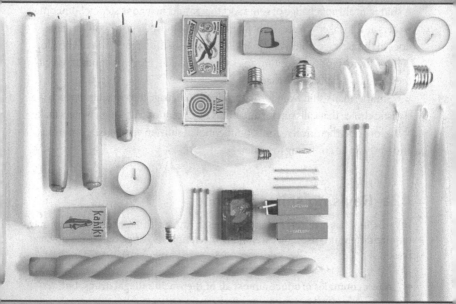

Photo by Mike Enright/www.menright.com. Photo styling by Barbara Lipp.

# CHAPTER 42

# Confusing Shifts

A shift is an abrupt change of some sort that results in inconsistency. Sometimes writers and speakers create deliberate shifts, as linguist Geneva Smitherman does in this passage from *Word from the Mother*: "In the larger realm of Hip Hop culture, there is cause for optimism as we witness Hip Hop younguns tryna git they political activist game togetha."

Smitherman's shift from formal academic language to vernacular speech is a stylistic choice that calls out for and holds our attention. Although writers make shifts for good rhetorical reasons, unintentional shifts in verb tenses, pronouns, and tone can be confusing to readers.

## 42a Revising shifts in tense

If verbs in a passage refer to actions occurring at different times, they may require different tenses. Be careful, however, not to change tenses for no clear reason.

▶ A few countries produce almost all of the world's illegal drugs, but
addiction ~~affected~~ *affects* many countries.

## 42b Revising shifts in mood

Be careful not to shift from one mood to another without good reason. The mood of a verb can be indicative (*he closes the door*), imperative (*close the door*), or subjunctive (*if the door were closed*). (See 51h.)

▶ Keep your eye on the ball, and ~~you should~~ bend your knees.

The writer's purpose is to give orders, but the original version shifts unnecessarily from the imperative to the indicative; the editing makes both verbs imperative.

## 42c Revising shifts in voice

Do not shift without reason between the active voice (*she sold it*) and the passive voice (*it was sold*). (See 51g.) Sometimes a shift in voice is justified, but often it only confuses readers.

▶ Two youths approached ~~me,~~ <sup>me</sup> and ~~I was~~ asked for directions.

The original sentence shifts from the active (*youths approached*) to the passive (*I was asked*), so it is unclear who asked for directions. Making both verbs active clears up the confusion.

## 42d Revising shifts in person and number

Unnecessary shifts in point of view between first person (*I, we*), second person (*you*), and third person (*he, she, it, one,* or *they*) or between singular and plural can be very confusing to readers.

▶ ~~One~~ <sup>You</sup> can do well on this job if you budget your time.

Is the writer making a general statement or giving advice to someone? Eliminating the shift eliminates this confusion.

## 42e Revising shifts between direct and indirect discourse

Multilingual

When you quote someone's exact words, you are using direct discourse: *Sue said, "I'm an editor."* When you report what someone says without repeating the exact words, you are using indirect discourse: *Sue said she was an editor.*

| | |
|---|---|
| DIRECT | Sue said, "My work *is* now complete." |
| INDIRECT | Sue *told* me that her work *was* now complete. |
| INDIRECT | Sue *tells* me that her work *is* now complete. |

In general, the verb introducing the indirect quotation (sometimes called the reporting verb) agrees in tense with the verb in the indirect quotation; there are, however, some exceptions. For example, if the reporting verb is in the past tense but the information that follows holds true in the present, shifting to a present-tense verb is acceptable.

▶ She *told* me that her work *is* as exciting as ever.

Shifting between direct and indirect discourse within the same sentence can cause problems, especially when the sentence is a question.

he
▶ **Viet asked what could ~~he~~ do to help?.**
        ^                              ^

The editing eliminates an awkward shift by reporting Viet's question indirectly. The sentence could also be edited to quote Viet directly: *Viet asked, "What can I do to help?"*

### ◢ EXERCISE 42.1

Revise the following sentences to eliminate unnecessary shifts in tense, mood, voice, or person and number and between direct and indirect discourse. Most of the items can be revised in more than one way. Examples:

**When a person goes to college, you face many new situations.**

**When people go to college, they face many new situations.**

Note: While the following revision is grammatically correct, it is increasingly thought to be a noninclusive revision:

**When a person goes to college, he or she faces many new situations.**

1. The greed of the 1980s gave way to the occupational insecurity of the 1990s, which in turn gives way to reinforced family ties in the early 2000s.

2. The building inspector suggested that we apply for a construction permit and that we should check in again when the plans are complete.

3. The instructor grabbed her coat, wondered why was the substitute late, and ran out of the room.

4. Suddenly, we heard an explosion of wings off to our right, and you could see a hundred or more ducks lifting off from the water.

5. In my previous job, I sold the most advertising spots and was given a sales excellence award.

6. A cloud of snow powder rose as skis and poles fly in every direction.

7. The flight attendant said, "Please turn off all electronic devices," but that we could use them again after takeoff.

8. The real estate market was softer than it had been for a decade, and a buyer could practically name their price.

9. When in Florence, be sure to see the city's famed cathedral, and many tourists also visit Michelangelo's statue *David*.

10. The freezing weather is threatening crops such as citrus fruits, which were sensitive to cold.

# 42f Revising shifts in tone and diction

Tone, a writer's attitude toward a topic or audience, is related to diction or word choice and to overall formality or informality. Watch out for tone or diction shifts that could confuse readers and leave them wondering what your real attitude is. (See 6f.)

**INCONSISTENT TONE**

The question of child care forces a society to make profound decisions about its economic values. Can most families with children actually live adequately on only one salary? If some conservatives had their way, June Cleaver would still be stuck in the kitchen baking cookies for Wally and the Beaver and waiting for Ward to bring home the bacon, except that with only one income, the Cleavers would be lucky to afford hot dogs.

In the preceding version, the first two sentences set a serious, formal tone as they discuss child care in fairly general, abstract terms. But in the third sentence, the writer shifts suddenly to sarcasm, to references to television characters of an earlier era, and to informal language like *stuck* and *bring home the bacon*. Readers cannot tell whether the writer is presenting a serious analysis or preparing for a humorous satire. The revision makes the tone consistently formal.

**REVISED**

The question of child care forces a society to make profound decisions about its economic values. Can most families with young children actually live adequately on only one salary? Some conservatives believe that women with young children should not work outside the home, but many mothers are forced to do so for financial reasons.

▼ ▼ ▼ ▼ ▼ ▼ ▼ ▼ ▼ ▼ ▼ ▼ ▼ ▼ ▼ ▼ ▼ ▼ ▼ ▼ ▼ ▼ ▼ ▼

THINKING CRITICALLY ABOUT SHIFTS

## Reading with an eye for shifts

The following paragraph includes several necessary shifts in person and number. Read the paragraph carefully, marking all such shifts. Notice how careful the author must be as he shifts back and forth among pronouns.

It has been one of the great errors of our time to think that by thinking about thinking, and then talking about it, we could possibly straighten out and tidy up our minds. There is no delusion more damaging than to get the idea in your head that you understand the functioning of your own brain. Once you acquire such a notion, you run the danger of moving in to take charge, guiding your thoughts, shepherding your mind from place to place, controlling it, making lists of regulations. The human mind is not meant to be governed, certainly not by any book of rules yet written; it is supposed to run itself, and we are obliged to follow it along, trying to keep up with it as best we can. It is all very well to be aware of your awareness, even proud of it, but never try to operate it. You are not up to the job. —LEWIS THOMAS, "The Attic of the Brain"

## Thinking about any shifts in your own writing

Find an article about a well-known person you admire. Then write a paragraph or two about that person, making a point of using both direct and indirect discourse. Using the information in 42e, check your writing for any inappropriate shifts between direct and indirect discourse, and revise as necessary.

# CHAPTER 43

# Parallelism

See how Jonathan Franzen uses parallelism in talking about a job:

> _Since_ I was paid better than the minimum wage, and _since_ I enjoyed topological packing puzzles, and _since_ the Geyers liked me and gave me lots of cake, it was remarkable _how_ fiercely I hated the job — _how_ I envied even those friends of mine who _manned_ the deep-fry station at Long John Silver's or _cleaned_ the oil traps at Kentucky Fried Chicken.

The parallelism indicated by the underscores brings a sense of orderliness to a long yet cohesive sentence. Making similar structures parallel will help clarify your writing.

## 43a Making items in a series parallel

All items in a series should be in parallel form — all nouns, all prepositional phrases, all adverb clauses, and so on. Such parallelism makes a series graceful and easy to follow.

▶ The quarter horse skipped, pranced, and ~~was sashaying.~~ sashayed.

▶ The children ran down the hill, raced over the lawn, and jumped into the swimming pool.

▶ The duties of the job include babysitting, housecleaning, and preparing ~~preparation of~~ meals.

Items in a list should be parallel.

▶ Kitchen rules: (1) Coffee to be made only by library staff. (2) Coffee service to be closed at 4:00 PM. (3) Doughnuts to be kept in cabinet. (4) Coffee materials not to be handled by faculty. ~~No faculty members should handle coffee materials.~~

Items on a formal outline and headings in a paper should be parallel. The headings in this chapter, for example, use parallel phrases.

---

**QUICK HELP**

Editing for parallelism

- Look for any series of three or more items, and make all of the items parallel in structure. If you want to emphasize one particular item, try putting it at the end of the series. **(43a and c)**
- Be sure items in lists and headings are parallel in form. **(43a)**
- Check for sentences that compare, contrast, or otherwise pair two ideas. Often these ideas will appear on either side of *and, but, or, nor, for, so,* or *yet* or after each part of *either . . . or, both . . . and, neither . . . nor, not only . . . but also, just as . . . so,* or *whether . . . or.* Edit to make the two ideas parallel in structure. **(43b)**
- Check all parallel structures to be sure you have included all necessary words—articles, prepositions, the *to* of the infinitive, and so on. **(43c)**

---

## 43b Using parallel structures to pair ideas

Parallel structures can help you pair two ideas effectively. The more nearly parallel the two structures are, the stronger the connection between the ideas will be. Parallel structures are especially appropriate when two ideas are compared or contrasted.

▶ <u>History became popular</u>, and <u>historians became alarmed.</u>  —WILL DURANT

▶ <u>I type in one place</u>, but <u>I write all over the house.</u>  —TONI MORRISON

To create an especially forceful impression, writers may construct a balanced sentence, one with two clauses that mirror each other.

▶ **Mankind must put an end to war, or war will put an end to mankind.**
—JOHN F. KENNEDY

*Using coordinating conjunctions*

When you link ideas with a coordinating conjunction — *and, but, or, nor, for, so, yet* — try to make the ideas parallel in structure.

▶ We performed <u>whenever folks would listen</u> and <u>wherever they would pay.</u>

▶ Consult a friend <sup>who is</sup> in your class or who is good at math.

*Using correlative conjunctions*

Always use the same structure after both parts of any correlative conjunction (48g) — *either . . . or, both . . . and, neither . . . nor, not . . . but, not only . . . but also, just as . . . so, whether . . . or.*

▶ **The organization provided both <u>scholarships for young artists</u> and <u>grants for established ones</u>.**

▶ **I wanted not only to go away to school but also to <sup>live in</sup> New England.**

The edited sentence is more balanced. Both parts of the correlative conjunction (*not only . . . but also*) precede a verb.

### EXERCISE 43.1

Complete the following sentences, using parallel words or phrases in each case. Example:

**The wise politician *promises the possible, faces the unavoidable,* and *accepts the inevitable.***

1. Before buying a used car, you should _____, _____, and _____.
2. Three activities I'd like to try are _____, _____, and _____.
3. Working in a restaurant taught me not only _____ but also _____.
4. We must either _____ or _____.
5. To pass the time in the waiting room, I _____, _____, and _____.

### EXERCISE 43.2

Revise the following sentences as necessary to eliminate any errors in parallel structure.

**I enjoy skiing, playing the guitar, and <sup>walking</sup> I walk on the beach in warm weather.**

1. I remember watching it for the first time, realizing I'd never seen anything like it, and immediately vowed never to miss even one episode of *The Daily Show*.
2. A crowd stood outside the school and were watching as the graduates paraded by.
3. An effective website is well designed, provides useful information, and links are given to other relevant sites.
4. It is impossible to watch *The Office* and not seeing a little of yourself in one of the characters.
5. Lila was the winner not only of the pie-eating contest but also won the yodeling competition.

# 43c Using parallel structures for emphasis and effect

Parallel structures can help a writer emphasize a point, as Joan Didion does in this passage about people living in California's San Bernardino Valley in the late 1960s:

> Here is where the hot wind blows and the old ways do not seem relevant, where the divorce rate is double the national average and where one person in every thirty-eight lives in a trailer. Here is the last stop for all those who come from somewhere else, for all those who drifted away from the cold and the past and the old ways. Here is where they are trying to find a new life style, trying to find it in the only places they know to look: the movies and the newspapers. —JOAN DIDION, "Some Dreamers of the Golden Dream"

The parallel phrases — *Here is, Here is* — introduce parallel details (*the hot wind* versus *the cold*; *the old ways* versus *a new life style*) that emphasize the emotional distance between *here* and the *somewhere else* that was once home for these new Californians.

▽ ▽ ▽ ▽ ▽ ▽ ▽ ▽ ▽ ▽ ▽ ▽ ▽ ▽ ▽ ▽ ▽ ▽ ▽ ▽ ▽ ▽ ▽ ▽ ▽

## THINKING CRITICALLY ABOUT PARALLELISM

### Reading with an eye for parallelism

Read the following paragraph about a bareback rider practicing her circus act, and identify all the parallel structures. Consider what effect they create on you as a reader, and try to decide why the author chose to put his ideas in such overtly parallel form. Try imitating the next-to-last sentence, the one beginning *In a week or two*.

> The richness of the scene was in its plainness, its natural condition—of horse, of ring, of girl, even to the girl's bare feet that gripped the bare back of her proud and ridiculous mount. The enchantment grew not out of anything that happened or was performed but out of something that seemed to go round and around and around with the girl, attending her, a steady gleam in the shape of a circle—a ring of ambition, of happiness, of youth. (And the positive pleasures of equilibrium under difficulties.) In a week or two, all would be changed, all (or almost all) lost: the girl would wear makeup, the horse would wear gold, the ring would be painted, the bark would be clean for the feet of the horse, the girl's feet would be clean for the slippers that she'd wear. All, all would be lost. —E. B. WHITE, "The Ring of Time"

### Thinking about your own use of parallelism

Read carefully several paragraphs from a draft you have recently written, noting any series of words, phrases, or clauses. Using the guidelines in this chapter, determine whether the series are parallel, and if not, revise them for parallelism. Then reread the paragraphs, looking for places where parallel structures would add emphasis or clarity, and revise accordingly. Can you draw any conclusions about your use of parallelism?

# CHAPTER 44

# Comma Splices and Fused Sentences

Writers sometimes use comma splices to create powerful special effects. In advertising and other slogans, comma splices can provide a catchy rhythm: *Dogs have owners, cats have staff.*

## 44a Identifying comma splices and fused sentences

A comma splice results from placing only a comma between two independent clauses, as in this tweet:

▶ **One thing is certain, girls everywhere need education.**

A related construction is a fused, or run-on, sentence, which results from joining two independent clauses with no punctuation or connecting word between them. As a fused sentence, the tweet above would read *One thing is certain girls everywhere need education.*

Using comma splices is increasingly common in writing that aims for a casual, informal feel, but comma splices and fused sentences in academic writing are likely to draw an instructor's criticism. If you use comma splices and fused sentences in formal writing, be sure your audience can tell that you are doing so for a special effect.

---

QUICK HELP

Editing for comma splices and fused sentences

If you find no punctuation between two of your independent clauses—groups of words that can stand alone as sentences—you have identified a fused sentence. If you find two such clauses joined only by a comma, you have identified a comma splice. Revise comma splices and fused sentences with one of these methods.

cs/fused

Editing for comma splices and fused sentences, continued

1. Separate the clauses into two sentences. **(44b)**

   ▶ Education is an elusive idea/. ~~it~~ means different things to different
     *It*
     people.

2. Link the clauses with a comma and a coordinating conjunction (*and, but, or, nor, for, so,* or *yet*). **(44c)**

   ▶ Education is an elusive idea, it means different things to different
     *for*
     people.

3. Link the clauses with a semicolon. **(44d)**

   ▶ Education is an elusive idea/; it means different things to different
     people.

   If the clauses are linked with only a comma and a conjunctive adverb—a
   word like *however, then, therefore*—add a semicolon.

   ▶ Education is an elusive idea/; it means different things to different
     *indeed,*
     people.

4. Recast the two clauses as one independent clause. **(44e)**

   ▶ ~~Education is an elusive idea, it~~ means different things to different
     *An elusive idea, education*
     people.

5. Recast one independent clause as a dependent clause. **(44f)**

   ▶ Education is an elusive idea/ it means different things to different
     *because*
     people.

6. In informal writing, link the clauses with a dash. **(44g)**

   ▶ Education is an elusive idea/—it means different things to
     different people.

## 44b Separating the clauses into two sentences

The simplest way to revise comma splices or fused sentences is to separate them into two sentences.

COMMA
SPLICE
My mother spends long hours every spring tilling the soil
This
and moving manure/. ~~this~~ part of gardening is nauseating.

FUSED
SENTENCE
My mother spends long hours every spring tilling the soil
This
and moving manure. ~~this~~ part of gardening is nauseating.

If the two clauses are very short, making them two sentences may sound abrupt and terse, so some other method of revision is probably preferable.

## 44c Linking the clauses with a comma and a coordinating conjunction

If the ideas in the two clauses are closely related and equally important, you can join them with a comma and a coordinating conjunction: *and, but, or, nor, for, so,* or *yet.* (See Chapter 56.) The conjunction helps indicate what kind of link exists between the two clauses. For instance, *but* and *yet* signal opposition or contrast; *for* and *so* signal cause-effect relationships.

COMMA
SPLICE
so
I got up feeling bad, I took some aspirin.

FUSED
SENTENCE
but
I should pay my tuition, I need a new car.

## 44d Linking the clauses with a semicolon

If the ideas in the two clauses are closely related and you want to give them equal emphasis, you can link them with a semicolon.

COMMA
SPLICE
This photograph is not at all realistic/; it uses dreamlike

images to convey its message.

FUSED
SENTENCE
The practice of journalism is changing dramatically;

advances in technology have sped up news cycles.

Be careful when you link clauses with either a conjunctive adverb or a transitional phrase. Precede such words and phrases with a semicolon (see Chapter 57), with a period, or with a comma combined with a coordinating conjunction (48g).

| COMMA SPLICE | Many developing countries have very high birthrates**;** therefore**,** most of their citizens are young. |
|---|---|
| FUSED SENTENCE | Many developing countries have very high birthrates**.** **T**herefore**,** most of their citizens are young. |
| FUSED SENTENCE | Many developing countries have very high birthrates**,** *and* therefore**,** most of their citizens are young. |

**SOME CONJUNCTIVE ADVERBS AND TRANSITIONAL PHRASES**

| | | |
|---|---|---|
| also | incidentally | nevertheless |
| anyway | in contrast | next |
| besides | indeed | otherwise |
| certainly | in fact | similarly |
| finally | instead | still |
| furthermore | likewise | then |
| however | meanwhile | therefore |
| in addition | moreover | undoubtedly |

---

**LANGUAGE, CULTURE, AND CONTEXT** | **SENTENCE LENGTH**

---

In U.S. academic contexts, readers sometimes find a series of short sentences "choppy" and undesirable. If you want to connect two independent clauses into one sentence, be sure to join them with a comma followed by a coordinating conjunction (*and, but, for, so, nor, or,* or *yet*) or with a semicolon. Doing so will help you avoid a comma splice, which is often considered an error in formal writing. Another useful tip for writing in American English is to avoid writing several very long sentences in a row. If you find this pattern in your writing, try breaking it up by including a shorter sentence occasionally. See the tips in Chapter 40 for altering the sentence lengths and patterns in your writing.

## 44e Recasting two clauses as one independent clause

Sometimes you can reduce two spliced or fused clauses to a single independent clause that is more direct and concise.

COMMA SPLICE

A large part of my mail is advertisements, *and* ~~most of the rest is~~ bills.

## 44f Recasting one independent clause as a dependent clause

When one independent clause is more important than the other, try converting the less important one to a dependent clause.

COMMA SPLICE

The arts and crafts movement, *which reacted against mass production,* called for handmade objects, ~~it reacted against mass production.~~

In the revision, the writer chooses to emphasize the first clause, the one describing what the movement advocated, and to make the second clause, the one describing what it reacted against, into a dependent clause.

FUSED SENTENCE

*Although* Zora Neale Hurston is regarded as one of America's major novelists, she died in obscurity.

In the revision, the writer chooses to emphasize the second clause and to make the first one into a dependent clause by adding the subordinating conjunction *although* (48g).

## 44g Linking two independent clauses with a dash

In informal writing, you can use a dash to join two independent clauses, especially when the second clause elaborates on the first.

COMMA SPLICE

Exercise trends come and go — this year yoga is hot.

### EXERCISE 44.1

Using two of the methods in this chapter, revise each item to correct its comma splice or fused sentence. Use each of the methods at least once. Example:

I had misgivings about the marriage, I did not attend the ceremony.

*Because*
I had misgivings about the marriage, I did not attend the ceremony.

1. Many motorists are unaware of the dangers of texting while driving, lawmakers have taken the matter into their own hands.

2. The tallest human on record was Robert Wadlow he reached an amazing height of eight feet, eleven inches.

3. Some employers provide on-site care for the children of their employees, others reimburse workers for day-care costs.

4. The number of vaccine manufacturers has plummeted the industry has been hit with a flood of lawsuits.

5. Most crustaceans live in the ocean, some also live on land or in freshwater habitats.

6. She inherited some tribal customs from her grandmother, she knows the sewing technique called Seminole patchwork.

7. Don't throw your soda cans in the trash recycle them.

8. My West Indian neighbor has lived in New England for years, nevertheless, she always feels betrayed by winter.

9. The Hope diamond in the Smithsonian Institution is impressive in fact, it looks even larger in person than online.

10. You signed up for the course now you'll have to do the work.

### EXERCISE 44.2

Revise the following paragraph, eliminating all comma splices by using a period or a semicolon. Then revise the paragraph again, this time using any of the other methods in this chapter. Comment on the two revisions. What differences in rhythm do you detect? Which version do you prefer, and why?

We may disagree on the causes of global warming, however, we cannot ignore that it is happening. Of course we still experience cold winters, on the other hand, average global temperatures have risen drastically for the last three decades. Polar ice caps are melting, as a result, sea levels are rising. Scientists predict more extreme weather in the coming decades, droughts will probably be more common, in addition, flooding and tropical storm activity may increase. Some experts fear that rising temperatures may cause large amounts of methane gases to be released, this could be disastrous for our atmosphere. Climate change might be a natural occurrence, more likely it is caused by human actions, nevertheless, we must find ways to save our planet.

▼ ▼ ▼ ▼ ▼ ▼ ▼ ▼ ▼ ▼ ▼ ▼ ▼ ▼ ▼ ▼ ▼ ▼ ▼ ▼ ▼ ▼ ▼ ▼ ▼ ▼

## THINKING CRITICALLY ABOUT COMMA SPLICES AND FUSED SENTENCES

### Reading with an eye for special effects

Roger Angell is known as a careful and correct stylist, yet he often deviates from the "correct" to create special effects, as in this passage about pitcher David Cone:

> And then he won. Next time out, on August 10th, handed a seven-run lead against the A's, he gave up two runs over six innings, with eight strike-outs. He had tempo, he had poise.  —ROGER ANGELL, "Before the Fall"

Angell uses a comma splice in the last sentence to emphasize parallel ideas; any conjunction, even *and*, would change the causal relationship he wishes to show. Because the splice is unexpected, it attracts just the attention that Angell wants for his statement.

Look through some stories or essays to find comma splices and fused sentences. Copy down one or two and enough of the surrounding text to show context, and comment in writing on the effects they create.

### Thinking about any comma splices and fused sentences in your own writing

Go through some essays you have written, checking for comma splices and fused sentences. Revise any you find, using one of the methods in this chapter. Comment on your chosen methods.

# CHAPTER 45

# Fragments

Sentence fragments are often used to make writing sound conversational, as in this Twitter post:

> 🐨 Realizing that there are no edible bagels in this part of Oregon.
> Sigh. #bagel

Fragments — groups of words that are punctuated as sentences but are not sentences — are often seen in intentionally informal writing and in public writing, such as advertising, that aims to attract attention or give a phrase special emphasis. Think carefully before using fragments in academic or professional writing, where some readers might regard them as errors.

## 45a Identifying fragments

A group of words must meet the following three criteria to form a complete sentence. If it does not meet all three, it is considered a fragment.

1. A sentence must have a subject. (49b)

2. A sentence must have a verb, not just a verbal. A verbal (such as the participle *singing*) needs a helping verb to function as a sentence's verb.

   **VERBAL**   The terrier *barking*.

   **VERB**   The terrier *is barking*.

3. Unless it is a question, a sentence must have at least one clause that does not begin with a subordinating conjunction such as *because, if, that,* or *when.* See 48g for a list of common subordinating conjunctions.

## 45b Revising phrase fragments

Phrases are groups of words that lack a subject, a verb, or both (49d). When phrases are punctuated like sentences, they become fragments. To revise such a fragment, either attach it to an independent clause or make it a separate sentence.

▶ NBC is broadcasting the debates~~,~~ ^with^ ~~With~~ discussions afterward.

> The word group *with discussions afterward* is a prepositional phrase, not a sentence. The editing combines the phrase with an independent clause.

▶ The town's growth is controlled by zoning laws~~,~~ ^a^ ~~A~~ strict set of regulations for builders and corporations.

> *A strict set of regulations for builders and corporations* is an appositive phrase renaming the noun *zoning laws.* The editing attaches the fragment to the sentence containing that noun.

▶ Kamika stayed out of school for three months after Linda was born.
^She wanted to^
~~To~~ recuperate and to take care of the baby.

> *To recuperate and to take care of the baby* includes verbals, not verbs. The revision — adding a subject (*she*) and a verb (*wanted*) — turns the fragment into a separate sentence.

## Avoiding fragments beginning with transitions

If you introduce an example or explanation with a transition, such as one of the following, be certain you write a sentence, not a fragment.

| | | |
|---|---|---|
| again | but | instead |
| also | finally | like |
| and | for example | or |
| as a result | for instance | such as |
| besides | however | that is |

▶ Barbara Ehrenreich has written on many subjects~~,~~ ^such^ ~~Such~~ as underemployment and positive psychology.

> In the original, the second word group is a phrase, not a sentence. The editing combines it with an independent clause.

# 45c Revising compound-predicate fragments

A compound predicate consists of two or more verbs, along with their modifiers and objects, that share the same subject. Fragments occur when one part of a compound predicate lacks a subject but is punctuated as a separate sentence.

These fragments usually begin with *and, but,* or *or.* You can revise them by attaching them to the independent clause that contains the rest of the predicate.

▶   They sold their house<sub>/</sub> <u>And</u> moved into an apartment.
                   *and*

### ◢ EXERCISE 45.1

Revise each of the following items to eliminate any sentence fragments, either by combining fragments with independent clauses or by rewriting them as separate sentences. Example:

                *Zoe looked close to tears.*
~~Zoe looked close to tears.~~ Standing with her head bowed<sub>/</sub>.

              *She was standing*
Zoe looked close to tears. ~~Standing~~ with her head bowed.

1.  Long stretches of white beaches and shady palm trees. Give tourists the impression of an island paradise.

2.  Forgetting to study for an exam. That is what many college students are afraid of.

3.  Much of New Orleans is below sea level. Making the city susceptible to flooding.

4.  Uncle Ron forgot to bring his clarinet to the party. Fortunately for us.

5.  Oscar night is an occasion for celebrating the film industry. And criticizing the fashion industry.

6.  Diners in Creole restaurants might try shrimp gumbo. Or order turtle soup.

7.  In the late 1940s, women began hosting Tupperware parties. Casual gatherings in which the hosts act as salespersons.

8.  Attempting to lose ten pounds in less than a week. I ate only cottage cheese and grapefruit.

9.  Our parents did not realize that we were hoarding our candy. Under our beds.

10. Thomas Edison was famous for his inventions. For example, the phonograph and the first practical lightbulb.

## 45d Revising dependent-clause fragments

Dependent clauses contain both a subject and a verb, but they cannot stand alone as sentences because they depend on an independent clause to complete their meaning. Dependent clauses usually begin with words such as *after, because, before, if, since, though, unless, until, when, where, while, who, which,* and *that* (48g and 49e). You can usually combine dependent-clause fragments with a nearby independent clause.

▶ The team had a dismal record, ~~Which~~ <sup>which</sup> spurred the owner to fire the

manager.

If you cannot smoothly attach a dependent clause to a nearby independent clause, try deleting the opening subordinating word and turning the dependent clause into a sentence.

▶ The majority of injuries in automobile accidents occur in two ways. ~~When an~~ <sup>An</sup> occupant either is hurt by something inside the car or is

thrown from the car.

---

### EXERCISE 45.2

Identify all the sentence fragments in the following items, and explain why each is grammatically incomplete. Then revise each one in at least two ways. Example:

Controlling my temper. ~~That~~ has been one of my goals this year.

<sup>One of my goals this year has been controlling</sup>
~~Controlling~~ my temper. ~~That has been one of my goals this year.~~

1. As soon as the seventy-five-year-old cellist walked onstage. The audience burst into applause.
2. The patient has only one intention. To smoke behind the doctor's back.
3. Some reality shows feature people working in dangerous situations. Such as fishing for Alaskan king crab or logging in swamps.
4. After writing and rewriting for almost three years. She finally felt that her novel was complete.
5. In the wake of the earthquake. Relief workers tried to provide food and shelter to victims.
6. Forster stopped writing novels after *A Passage to India*. Which is one of the greatest novels of the twentieth century.
7. Because only two students signed up. The class was canceled this semester.
8. I started running in April. And ran my first marathon in September.
9. We sat stunned as she delivered her monologue. A ten-minute speech about everything we had done to annoy her.
10. All primates have opposable thumbs. Which sets them apart from other mammals.

▼ ▼ ▼ ▼ ▼ ▼ ▼ ▼ ▼ ▼ ▼ ▼ ▼ ▼ ▼ ▼ ▼ ▼ ▼ ▼ ▼ ▼ ▼ ▼ ▼ ▼

## THINKING CRITICALLY ABOUT FRAGMENTS

### Reading with an eye for fragments

Identify the fragments in the following passage. What effect does the writer achieve by using fragments rather than complete sentences?

> On Sundays, for religion, we went up on the hill. Skipping along the hexagon-shaped tile in Colonial Park. Darting up the steps to Edgecomb Avenue. Stopping in the candy store on St. Nicholas to load up. Leaning forward for leverage to finish the climb up to the church. I was always impressed by this particular house of the Lord.
> —KEITH GILYARD, *Voices of the Self*

### Thinking about any fragments in your own writing

Read through some essays you have written. Using the guidelines in 45a, see whether you find any sentence fragments. If so, do you recognize any patterns? Do you write fragments when you're attempting to add emphasis? Are they all dependent clauses? phrases? Note any patterns you discover, and make a point of routinely checking your writing for fragments. Finally, revise any fragments to form complete sentences.

# CHAPTER 46

# Modifier Placement

Consider the following notice in a guidebook:

> Visit the old Dutch cemetery where early settlers are buried from noon to five daily.

Does the old cemetery really bury early settlers for five hours every day? Repositioning the modifier *from noon to five daily* eliminates the confusion and makes it clear when the cemetery is open: *From noon to five daily, visit the old Dutch cemetery where early settlers are buried.* To be effective, modifiers should refer clearly to the words they modify and be placed close to those words.

## 46a Revising misplaced modifiers

Misplaced modifiers cause confusion because they are not close enough to the words they modify or because they seem to modify more than one word in the sentence.

▶ She teaches a seminar this term ~~on voodoo~~ ^on voodoo^ at Skyline College.

The voodoo is not at the college; the seminar is.

▶ ~~Billowing from every window,~~ ^We^ saw clouds of smoke^billowing from every window.^

People cannot billow from windows.

▶ ^After he lost the 1962 race,^ Nixon said he would get out of politics. ~~after he lost the 1962 race.~~

The unedited sentence implies that Nixon planned to lose the race.

---

QUICK HELP

Editing for misplaced or dangling modifiers

1. Identify all the modifiers in each sentence, and draw an arrow from each modifier to the word it modifies.

2. If a modifier is far from the word it modifies, try to move the two closer together. **(46a)**

3. Does any modifier seem to refer to a word other than the one it is intended to modify? If so, move the modifier so that it refers clearly to only the intended word. **(46a and b)**

4. If you cannot find the word to which a modifier refers, revise the sentence: supply such a word, or revise the modifier itself so that it clearly refers to a word already in the sentence. **(46c)**

---

> **EXERCISE 46.1**

Revise each of the following sentences by moving any misplaced modifiers so that they clearly modify the words they should. Example:

*When they propose sensible plans, politicians*
~~Politicians~~ earn support from the people. ~~when they propose sensible plans.~~

1. The comedian had the audience doubled over with laughter relating stories in a deadpan voice.

2. News reports can increase a listener's irrational fears that emphasize random crime or rare diseases.

3. Studying legal documents and court records from hundreds of years ago, ordinary people in the Middle Ages teach us about everyday life at that time.

4. Risking their lives in war zones, civilians learn about the conflict from the firsthand accounts of journalists abroad.

5. Melena saw lions in the wild on a safari in Africa last spring.

6. Doctors recommend a new test for cancer, which is painless.

7. Every afternoon I find flyers for free pizza left on my windshield.

8. Screeching strings told the audience that the killer was coming after the opening credits.

9. The coach awarded a medal to the most valuable player made of solid brass.

10. Hanging on by a thread, the five-year-old finally lost her tooth.

---

## Using limiting modifiers

Be especially careful with the placement of limiting modifiers such as *almost, even, hardly, just, merely, nearly, only, scarcely,* and *simply.* In general, these modifiers should be placed right before or after the words they modify. Putting them in other positions may produce not just ambiguity but a completely different meaning.

| AMBIGUOUS | The court *only* hears civil cases on Tuesdays. |
| CLEAR | The court hears <u>only</u> civil cases on Tuesdays. |
| CLEAR | The court hears civil cases on Tuesdays <u>only</u>. |

In the first sentence, placing *only* before *hears* makes the meaning ambiguous. The revised versions clarify the meaning.

▶ The city ~~almost~~ <sup>almost</sup> spent $20 million on the new stadium.

The original sentence suggests the money was almost spent; moving *almost* makes clear that the amount spent was almost $20 million.

## Avoiding squinting modifiers

If a modifier can refer to *either* the word before it *or* the word after it, it is a squinting modifier. Put the modifier where it clearly relates to only a single word in the sentence.

| SQUINTING | Students who practice writing *often* will benefit. |

Does the writer mean that students often benefit from practice or that they benefit from practicing often?

| REVISED | Students who <u>often</u> practice writing will benefit. |
| REVISED | Students who practice writing will <u>often</u> benefit. |

### EXERCISE 46.2

Revise each of the following sentences in at least two ways. Move the limiting or squinting modifier so that it unambiguously modifies one word or phrase in the sentence. Example:

The course we hoped would engross us <sup>completely</sup> ~~completely~~ bored us.

The course we hoped would engross us ~~completely~~ bored us <sup>completely</sup>.

1. The division that profited most deserves the prize.
2. The soldier was apparently injured by friendly fire.
3. The collector who owned the painting originally planned to leave it to a museum.
4. Alcoholics who try to quit drinking on their own frequently tend to relapse.
5. Ever since I was a child, I have only liked green peas with ham.

## 46b Revising disruptive modifiers

Disruptive modifiers interrupt the connections between parts of a sentence, making it hard for readers to follow the progress of the thought. Most disruptive modifiers are adverbial clauses or phrases that appear between the parts of a verb phrase, between a subject and a verb, or between a verb and an object.

> If they are cooked too long, vegetables will
> ▶ ~~Vegetables will, if they are cooked too long,~~ lose most of their
>     ^
> nutritional value.

Separating the parts of the verb phrase, *will* and *lose*, disrupts the flow of the sentence.

>                    a secondhand car
> ▶ He bought with his first paycheck. ~~a secondhand car.~~
>          ^                            ^

Separating the verb *bought* from the object *a secondhand car* makes it hard to follow the thought.

### Splitting infinitives

A modifier placed between the *to* and verb of an infinitive (*to boldly go*) is known as a split infinitive. Once considered a serious writing error, split infinitives are no longer taboo. Few readers will object to a split infinitive in a clear and understandable sentence.

> ▶ Students need to *really* know the material to pass the exam.

Sometimes, however, split infinitives can be distracting to readers — especially when more than one word comes between the parts of the infinitive. In such cases, move the modifier before or after the infinitive, or reword the sentence, to remove the distracting interruption.

>                               surrender
> ▶ Hitler expected the British to fairly quickly. ~~surrender.~~
>                                 ^            ^

### ◢ EXERCISE 46.3

Revise each of the following sentences by moving the disruptive modifier so that the sentence reads smoothly. Example:

> During the recent economic depression, many
> **Many** unemployed college graduates ~~during the recent economic~~
>      ^
> ~~depression~~ attended graduate school.

1. Strong economic times have, statistics tell us, led to increases in the college dropout rate.

2. During finals an otherwise honest student, facing high levels of stress, may consider cheating to achieve a higher grade.

3. The director encouraged us to loudly and enthusiastically applaud after each scene.

4. Kobe Bryant earned, at the pinnacle of his career, roughly $30 million a year in endorsements.

5. The stock exchange became, because of the sudden trading, a chaotic circus.

## 46c Revising dangling modifiers

Dangling modifiers *seem* to modify something that is implied but not actually present in the sentence and can be distracting for readers. Dangling modifiers frequently appear at the beginnings or ends of sentences.

| | |
|---|---|
| DANGLING | Driving nonstop, Salishan Lodge is two hours from Portland. |
| REVISED | Driving nonstop from Portland, you can reach Salishan Lodge in two hours. |
| REVISED | If you drive nonstop, Salishan Lodge is two hours from Portland. |

The preceding revised sentences illustrate two ways to fix a dangling modifier. Often you need to add a subject that the modifier clearly refers to. Sometimes, however, you have to turn the dangling modifier itself into a phrase or clause.

▶ Reluctantly, the hound ~~was given away~~ our family gave to a neighbor.

In the original sentence, was the dog reluctant, or was someone else who is not mentioned reluctant?

▶ ~~As~~ When he was a young boy, his aunt told stories of her years as a country doctor.

His aunt was never a young boy.

▶ ~~Thumbing through the magazine, my~~ My eyes automatically noticed the perfume ads, as I was thumbing through the magazine.

Eyes cannot thumb through a magazine.

▶ Although a reserved and private man, he was everyone enjoyed his company.

The original clause does not refer to *everyone* or *his company*. It needs its own subject and verb.

◢ **EXERCISE 46.4**

Revise each of the following sentences to correct the dangling phrase. Example:

> *a viewer gets*
> **Watching television news, an impression is given of constant disaster.**
>                                    ^

1. No longer obsessed with being the first to report a story, information is now presented as entertainment.

2. Trying to attract younger viewers, news is blended with comedy on late-night talk shows.

3. Highlighting local events, important international news stories may get overlooked.

4. Chosen for their looks, the journalistic credentials of newscasters may be weak.

5. As an interactive medium, people can find information online that reinforces views they already hold.

▼ ▼ ▼ ▼ ▼ ▼ ▼ ▼ ▼ ▼ ▼ ▼ ▼ ▼ ▼ ▼ ▼ ▼ ▼ ▼ ▼ ▼ ▼ ▼ ▼ ▼

## THINKING CRITICALLY ABOUT MODIFIERS

### Reading with an eye for modifiers

Look at the limiting modifier italicized in the following passage. Identify which word or words it modifies. Then try moving the modifier to some other spot in the sentence, and consider how the meaning of the sentence changes as a result.

> It was, among other things, the sort of railroad you would occasionally ride *just* for the hell of it, a higher existence into which you would escape unconsciously and without hesitation.     —E. B. WHITE, "Progress and Change"

### Thinking about your own use of modifiers

As you examine two pages of a draft, check for clear and effective modifiers. Can you identify any misplaced, disruptive, or dangling modifiers? Using the guidelines in this chapter, revise as need be. Then look for patterns—in the kinds of modifiers you use and in any problems you have placing them. Make a note of what you find.

# CHAPTER 47

# Consistent and Complete Structures

You hear inconsistent and incomplete structures all the time in conversation. For instance, during an interview with journalist Bill Moyers, Jon Stewart discussed the supposed objectivity of news reporting:

> But news has never been objective. It's always . . . what does every newscast start with? "Our top stories tonight." That's a list. That's a subjective . . . some editor made a decision: "Here's our top stories. Number one: there's a fire in the Bronx."

Stewart is talking casually, so some of his sentences begin one way but then move in another direction. The mixed structures pose no problem for the listener, but sentences such as these can be confusing in writing. Because of social media, writing is getting more conversational — even academic writing. As a result, writers are free to develop a conversational and even experimental style. But in formal academic writing, it's still wise to stick with consistent and complete structures.

## 47a Revising faulty sentence structure

Faulty sentence structure poses problems for both writers and readers. A mixed structure results from beginning a sentence with one grammatical pattern and then switching to another one:

MIXED     The fact that I get up at 5:00 AM, a wake-up time that explains why I'm always tired in the evening.

The sentence starts out with a subject (*The fact*) followed by a dependent clause (*that I get up at 5:00 AM*). The sentence needs a predicate to complete the independent clause (49a), but instead it moves to another phrase (*a wake-up time*) followed by a dependent clause (*that explains why I'm always tired in the evening*), and what results is a fragment (Chapter 45).

REVISED     The fact that I get up at 5:00 AM explains why I'm always tired in the evening.

Deleting *a wake-up time that* changes the rest of the sentence into a predicate.

REVISED                I get up at 5:00 AM, a wake-up time that explains why
                       I'm always tired in the evening.

Deleting *The fact that* turns the beginning of the sentence into an independent clause.

Here is another example of a mixed structure:

▶ **Because hope was the only thing left when Pandora finally closed up the**

**mythical box, ~~explains why~~ even today we never lose hope.**

The dependent clause beginning with *Because* is followed by a predicate (beginning with *explains*) without a subject. Deleting *explains why* changes the predicate into an independent clause.

---

QUICK HELP

### Editing for consistency and completeness

- Check every confusing sentence to see whether it has a subject and a predicate. If not, revise as necessary. **(47a)** If you find both a subject and a predicate and you are still confused, see whether the subject and verb make sense together. If not, revise so that they do. **(47b)**
- Revise any *is when*, *is where*, and *the reason . . . is because* constructions. **(47b)**

  ▶ **Spamming is ~~where companies send~~ electronic junk mail.**
                      the practice of sending

- Check all comparisons for completeness. **(47c)**

  ▶ **We like Marian better than Margaret.**
                                    we like

## 47b Matching subjects and predicates

Another kind of faulty sentence structure, called faulty predication, occurs when a subject and predicate do not fit together grammatically or simply do not make sense together. Many cases of faulty predication result from using forms of *be* when another verb would be stronger.

▶ **~~A characteristic that~~ I admire ~~is~~ a generous person.**

A person is not a characteristic.

▶ **The rules of the corporation ~~expect~~ employees to be on time.**
                                  require

Rules cannot expect anything.

Constructions using *is when, is where,* and *the reason . . . is because* occur frequently in informal contexts, but they may be inappropriate in formal academic writing because they use an adverb clause rather than a noun as their subject complement (49a).

▶ A stereotype is ~~when someone characterizes~~ a group. ~~unfairly.~~
*an unfair characterization of*

▶ A confluence is where two rivers join to form one.
*a place*

▶ ~~The reason~~ I like to play soccer ~~is~~ because it provides aerobic exercise.

---

### EXERCISE 47.1

Revise each of the following sentences in two ways to make its structure consistent in grammar and meaning. Example:

> *Because*
> ~~The fact that~~ our room was cold, we put a heater between our beds.
>
> *led us to*
> The fact that our room was cold⟋ ~~we~~ put a heater between our beds.

1. To enroll in film school being my primary goal, so I am always saving my money and watching for scholarship opportunities.

2. The reason air-pollution standards should not be relaxed is because many people would suffer.

3. By turning off the water when you brush your teeth, saving up to eight gallons of water per day.

4. Irony is when you expect one thing and get something else.

5. The best meal I've ever eaten was sitting by a river eating bread and cheese from a farmers' market.

---

## 47c Completing elliptical constructions

Sometimes writers omit a word in a compound structure. They succeed with such an elliptical construction when the word omitted later in the compound is exactly the same as the word earlier in the compound.

▶ That bell belonged to the figure of Miss Duling as though it grew directly out of her right arm, as wings grew out of an angel or a tail [grew] out of the devil. —EUDORA WELTY, *One Writer's Beginnings*

The omitted word, *grew*, is exactly the same verb that follows *it* and *wings* in the earlier parts of the compound. You should not omit a word that does not exactly match the word used in the other part(s) of the compound.

▶ His skills are weak, and his performance only ^is^ average.

The verb *is* does not match the verb in the other part of the compound (*are*), so the writer needs to include it.

## 47d Checking for missing words

The best way to catch inadvertent omissions is to proofread carefully, reading each sentence slowly — and aloud.

▶ The new website makes it easier to look ^at^ and choose from the company's

inventory.

## 47e Making complete comparisons

When you compare two or more things, the comparison must be complete, logically consistent, and clear.

▶ I was embarrassed because my parents were so different/ ^from my friends' parents.^

Different from what? Adding *from my friends' parents* completes the comparison.

UNCLEAR        Aneil likes his brother more than his sister.

Does Aneil like his brother more than his sister does — or does he like his brother more than he likes his sister?

CLEAR          Aneil likes his brother more *than his sister does.*

CLEAR          Aneil likes his brother more *than he likes his sister.*

### ◢ EXERCISE 47.2

Revise each of the following sentences to eliminate any inappropriate elliptical constructions; to make comparisons complete, logically consistent, and clear; and to supply any other omitted words that are necessary for meaning. Example:

Most of the candidates are bright, and one ^is^ brilliant.

1. Convection ovens cook more quickly and with less power.
2. Argentina and Peru were colonized by Spain, and Brazil by Portugal.
3. She argued that children are even more important for men than women.
4. Do you think the barbecue sauce in Memphis is better than North Carolina?
5. The equipment in our new warehouse is guaranteed to last longer than our current facility.

▼ ▼ ▼ ▼ ▼ ▼ ▼ ▼ ▼ ▼ ▼ ▼ ▼ ▼ ▼ ▼ ▼ ▼ ▼ ▼ ▼ ▼ ▼ ▼ ▼ ▼ ▼ ▼

## THINKING CRITICALLY ABOUT CONSISTENCY AND COMPLETENESS

Read over three or four paragraphs from a draft or completed essay you have written recently. Check for mixed sentences and incomplete or missing structures. Revise the paragraphs to correct any problems you find. If you find any, do you recognize any patterns? If so, make a note of them for future reference.

# PART 11
# Grammar

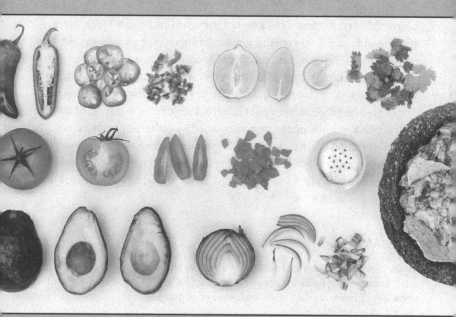

Photo by Mike Enright/www.menright.com. Photo styling by Barbara Lipp.

## CHAPTER 48

# Parts of Speech

Grammatical correctness is certainly not enough to ensure that a sentence is effective and artful — or even that it serves an appropriate purpose in your writing; to achieve these goals, you'll need to develop a powerful and persuasive style. Understanding grammatical structures can, however, help you produce sentences that are appropriate and effective as well as grammatically correct. The English language includes eight different categories of words called the *parts of speech* — verbs, nouns, pronouns, adjectives, adverbs, prepositions, conjunctions, and interjections. Many English words can function as more than one part of speech. When you *book an airplane flight*, the word *book* is a verb; when you *take a good book to the beach*, it is a noun; and when you have *book knowledge*, it is an adjective.

## 48a Verbs

Verbs move the meaning of sentences along by showing action (*glance, speculate*), occurrence (*become, happen*), or being (*be, seem*). Verbs change form to show *time, person, number, voice,* and *mood* (Chapter 51).

| TIME | we *work*, we *worked* |
|---|---|
| PERSON | I *work*, she *works* |
| NUMBER | one person *works*, two people *work* |
| VOICE | they *ask*, they *are* |
| MOOD | we *see*, if I *were* to *see* |

Helping verbs (also called *auxiliary verbs*) combine with main verbs to create verb phrases. Auxiliaries include the forms of *be, do,* and *have*, which are also used as main verbs, and *can, could, may, might, must, shall, should, will,* and *would* (51b).

▶ I <u>could have danced</u> all night.

▶ She <u>would prefer</u> to learn Italian rather than Spanish.

▶ When <u>do</u> you <u>need</u> the spreadsheet?

**EXERCISE 48.1**

Identify each verb or verb phrase in the following sentences. Example:

**Drivers <u>should expect</u> weather-related delays.**

1. The story was released to the press late on Friday evening.
2. Most athletes will be arriving well before the games.
3. Housing prices have fallen considerably in the past year.
4. No one spoke in the room where the students were taking the exam.
5. The suspect has been fingerprinted and is waiting for his lawyer.

## 48b Nouns

Nouns name persons (*aviator, child*), places (*lake, library*), things (*truck, suitcase*), or concepts (*happiness, balance*). Proper nouns, which are capitalized, name specific persons, places, things, or concepts: *Bill, Iowa, Supreme Court, Buddhism.* Collective nouns (52d) name groups: *flock, jury.*

Most nouns change from singular (one) to plural (more than one) when you add *-s* or *-es: horse, horses; kiss, kisses.* Some nouns, however, have irregular plural forms: *woman, women; mouse, mice; deer, deer.* Noncount nouns (50a) cannot be made plural because they name things that cannot easily be counted: *dust, peace, prosperity.*

The possessive form of a noun shows ownership. Possessive forms add an apostrophe plus *-s* to most singular nouns or just an apostrophe to most plural nouns: *the horse's owner, the boys' department.*

Nouns are often preceded by the article (or determiner) *a, an,* or *the: a rocket, an astronaut, the launch* (50c).

**EXERCISE 48.2**

Identify the nouns and the articles in each of the following sentences. Underline the nouns once and the articles twice. Example:

<u>The</u> <u>Puritans</u> hoped for <u>a</u> different <u>king</u>, but <u>Charles II</u> regained <u>the</u> <u>throne</u>.

1. After Halloween, the children got sick from eating too much candy.
2. Although June is technically the driest month, severe flooding has occurred in the late spring.
3. Baking is no longer a common activity in most households around the country.
4. A sudden frost turned the ground into a field of ice.
5. The cyclist swerved to avoid an oncoming car that had run a red light.

# Parts of Speech

See eight parts of speech in action in a single paragraph.

**1 Verbs show action, occurrence, or being. (48a)**

Anita and Trinh are running for school board, and maybe they will win. Hey, who knows? This could finally be their big chance and a win for the Asian community. Unlike the current board members, they actually reflect the population they will serve.

**2 Nouns name persons, places, things, or concepts. (48b)**

Anita and Trinh are running for school board, and maybe they will win. Hey, who knows? This could finally be their big chance and a win for the Asian community. Unlike the current board members, they actually reflect the population they will serve.

**3 Pronouns substitute for nouns. (48c)**

Anita and Trinh are running for school board, and maybe they will win. Hey, who knows? This could finally be their big chance and a win for the Asian community. Unlike the current board members, they actually reflect the population they will serve.

**4 Adjectives modify nouns or pronouns. (48d)**

Anita and Trinh are running for school board, and maybe they will win. Hey, who knows? This could finally be their big chance and a win for the Asian community. Unlike the current board members, they actually reflect the population they will serve.

**5 Adverbs modify verbs, adjectives, other adverbs, or entire clauses. (48e)**

Anita and Trinh are running for school board, and maybe they will win. Hey, who knows? This could finally be their big chance and a win for the Asian community. Unlike the current board members, they actually reflect the population they will serve.

6. **Prepositions express relationships between nouns or pronouns and other words. (48f)**

Anita and Trinh are running for school board, and maybe they will win. Hey, who knows? This could finally be their big chance and a win for the Asian community. Unlike the current board members, they actually reflect the population they will serve.

7. **Conjunctions join words or groups of words. (48g)**

Anita and Trinh are running for school board, and maybe they will win. Hey, who knows? This could finally be their big chance and a win for the Asian community. Unlike the current board members, they actually reflect the population they will serve.

8. **Interjections express surprise or emotion and do not relate grammatically to other parts of speech. (48h)**

Anita and Trinh are running for school board, and maybe they will win. Hey, who knows? This could finally be their big chance and a win for the Asian community. Unlike the current board members, they actually reflect the population they will serve.

---

LANGUAGE, CULTURE, | **COUNT AND NONCOUNT NOUNS**
AND CONTEXT |

Do people conduct *research* or *researches*? See 50a for a discussion of count and noncount nouns.

---

## 48c Pronouns

Pronouns often take the place of nouns or other words functioning as nouns so that you do not have to repeat words that have already been mentioned. A word or word group that a pronoun replaces or refers to is called the antecedent of the pronoun (53f).

ANTECEDENT                                    PRONOUN

▶  <u>Caitlin</u> refused the invitation even though <u>she</u> wanted to go.

Pronouns fall into several categories.

### Personal pronouns

Personal pronouns refer to specific persons or things. Each can take several forms (*I, me, my, mine*) depending on its function in the sentence (53a).

> *I, me, you, he, she, him, her, it, we, they, them*

▶  When Keisha saw the dogs again, <u>she</u> called <u>them</u>, and <u>they</u> ran to <u>her</u>.

**Note:** Some individuals use *they/them* for their personal pronouns instead of *he/him* or *she/her*. In the following example, *their list* refers to *Jordan's list*. See 53f and 53g.

▶  When Jordan chose classes for spring term, Spoken Word was at the top of their list.

### Possessive pronouns

Possessive pronouns are personal pronouns that indicate ownership (53a and 59b).

> *my, mine, your, yours, her, hers, his, its, our, ours, their, theirs*

▶  <u>My</u> roommate lost <u>her</u> keys.

### Reflexive pronouns

Reflexive pronouns refer to the subject of the sentence or clause in which they appear. They end in *-self* or *-selves*.

> *myself, yourself, himself, herself, itself, oneself, ourselves, yourselves, themselves*

▶  The seals sunned <u>themselves</u> on the warm rocks.

*Intensive pronouns*

Intensive pronouns have the same form as reflexive pronouns. They emphasize a noun or another pronoun.

▶ He decided to paint the apartment <u>himself</u>.

*Indefinite pronouns*

Indefinite pronouns do not refer to specific nouns, although they may refer to identifiable persons or things (52e and 53k). The following is a partial list:

> all, another, anybody, both, each, either, everything, few, many, most, neither, none, no one, nothing, one, some, something

▶ <u>Everybody</u> screamed, and <u>someone</u> fainted, when the lights went out.

*Demonstrative pronouns*

Demonstrative pronouns identify or point to specific nouns.

> this, that, these, those

▶ <u>These</u> are Peter's books.

*Interrogative pronouns*

Interrogative pronouns are used to ask questions.

> who, which, what

▶ <u>Who</u> can help set up the chairs for the meeting?

*Relative pronouns*

Relative pronouns introduce dependent clauses and relate the dependent clause to the rest of the sentence (49e). The interrogative pronoun *who* and the relative pronouns *who* and *whoever* have different forms depending on how they are used in a sentence (53b).

> who, which, that, what, whoever, whichever, whatever

▶ Maya, <u>who</u> hires interns, is the manager <u>whom</u> you should contact.

*Reciprocal pronouns*

Reciprocal pronouns refer to individual parts of a plural antecedent (48c).

> each other, one another

▶ The business failed because the partners distrusted <u>each other</u>.

◢ **EXERCISE 48.3**

Identify the pronouns and any antecedents in each of the following sentences, underlining the pronouns once and any antecedents twice. Example:

As identical <u>twins</u>, <u>they</u> really do understand <u>each other</u>.

1. He told the volunteers to help themselves to the leftovers.

2. There are two kinds of people: those who divide people into two kinds and those who don't.

3. Who is going to buy the jeans and wear them if the designer himself finds them uncomfortable?

4. Before an annual performance review, employees are asked to take a hard look at themselves and their work habits.

5. Forwarding an email warning about a computer virus to everyone in your address book is never a good idea.

# 48d Adjectives

Adjectives modify (limit the meaning of) nouns and pronouns, usually by describing, identifying, or quantifying those words (see Chapter 54). Adjectives that identify or quantify are sometimes called *determiners* (50b).

▶ The <u>red</u> Porsche ran off the road. [describes]

▶ <u>That</u> Porsche needs to be repaired. [identifies]

▶ We saw <u>several other</u> Porsches race by. [quantifies]

In addition to their basic forms, most descriptive adjectives have other forms that allow you to make comparisons: *small, smaller, smallest; foolish, more foolish, most foolish, less foolish, least foolish.*

▶ This year's attendance was <u>smaller</u> than last year's.

Adjectives usually precede the words they modify, though they may follow linking verbs: *The car was defective.* Many pronouns (48c) can function as identifying adjectives when they are followed by a noun.

▶ <u>That</u> is a dangerous intersection. [pronoun]

▶ <u>That</u> intersection is dangerous. [identifying adjective]

Other kinds of adjectives that identify or quantify are the articles *a, an,* and *the* (50c) and numbers (*three, sixty-fifth, five hundred*).

Proper adjectives, which are capitalized (62b), form from or relate to proper nouns (*Egyptian, Emersonian*).

## 48e Adverbs

Adverbs modify verbs, adjectives, other adverbs, or entire clauses (see Chapter 54). Many adverbs end in *-ly*, though some do not (*always, never, very, well*), and some words that end in *-ly* are not adverbs but adjectives (*friendly, lovely*). One of the most common adverbs is *not*.

▶ Business writers **frequently** communicate with strangers. [modifies the verb *communicate*]

▶ How can they attract customers in an **increasingly** difficult economy? [modifies the adjective *difficult*]

▶ They must work **especially** hard to avoid offending readers. [modifies the adverb *hard*]

▶ **Obviously**, they need to weigh their words with care. [modifies the independent clause that makes up the rest of the sentence]

Adverbs often answer the questions *when? where? why? how? to what extent?*

Many adverbs, like many adjectives, take different forms when making comparisons: *forcefully, more forcefully, most forcefully, less forcefully, least forcefully.*

▶ Of all the candidates, she speaks the **most forcefully**.

Conjunctive adverbs modify an entire clause, and they express the connection in meaning between that clause and the preceding clause (or sentence). More common conjunctive adverbs include *however, furthermore, therefore,* and *likewise.*

### EXERCISE 48.4

Identify the adjectives and adverbs in each of the following sentences, underlining the adjectives once and the adverbs twice. Remember that articles and some pronouns are used as adjectives. Example:

Inadvertently, the two agents misquoted their major client.

1. The small, frightened child firmly squeezed my hand and refused to take another step forward.
2. Meanwhile, she learned that the financial records had been completely false.
3. Koalas are generally quiet creatures that make loud grunting noises during mating season.
4. The huge red tomatoes looked lovely, but they tasted disappointingly like cardboard.
5. The youngest dancer in the troupe performed a brilliant solo.

# 48f Prepositions

Prepositions express relationships — in space, time, or other senses — between nouns or pronouns and other words in a sentence.

▸ We did not want to leave <u>during</u> the game.

▸ The contestants waited nervously <u>for</u> the announcement.

A prepositional phrase (see Chapter 55) begins with a preposition and ends with the noun or pronoun it connects to the rest of the sentence.

▸ Drive <u>across</u> the bridge and go <u>down</u> the avenue <u>past</u> three stoplights.

**SOME COMMON PREPOSITIONS**

| | | | |
|---|---|---|---|
| about | below | in | over |
| above | beside | inside | past |
| after | between | into | since |
| against | beyond | near | through |
| along | by | of | under |
| among | down | off | until |
| around | during | on | up |
| at | for | onto | with |
| before | from | out | |

**SOME COMPOUND PREPOSITIONS**

| | | |
|---|---|---|
| according to | in addition to | instead of |
| as well as | in front of | next to |
| because of | in place of | out of |
| except for | in spite of | with regard to |

Research for this book shows that many writers — including native speakers of English — have trouble choosing appropriate prepositions. If you are not sure which preposition to use, consult your dictionary.

#### ◢ EXERCISE 48.5

Identify the prepositions in the following sentences. Example:

<u>In</u> the dim interior <u>of</u> the hut crouched an old man.

1. The supervisor of the night shift requested that all available personnel work extra hours from October through December.

2. The hatchlings emerged from their shells, crawled across the sand, and swam into the sea.

3. Instead of creating a peaceful new beginning, the tribunal factions are constantly fighting among themselves.

4. After some hard thinking on a weeklong camping trip, I decided I would quit my job and join the Peace Corps for two years.

5. The nuclear power plant about ten miles from the city has the worst safety record of any plant in the country.

## 48g Conjunctions

Conjunctions connect words or groups of words to each other and tell something about the relationship between these words.

### Coordinating conjunctions

Coordinating conjunctions (39a) join equivalent structures, such as two or more nouns, pronouns, verbs, adjectives, adverbs, prepositions, conjunctions, phrases, or clauses.

▶ **A strong but warm breeze blew across the desert.**

▶ **Please print or type the information on the application form.**

▶ **Taiwo worked two shifts today, so she is tired tonight.**

COORDINATING CONJUNCTIONS

| and | but | for | nor | or | so | yet |
|-----|-----|-----|-----|-----|-----|-----|

### Correlative conjunctions

Correlative conjunctions join equal elements, and they come in pairs.

▶ **Both Bechtel and Kaiser submitted bids on the project.**

▶ **Maisha not only sent a card but also visited me in the hospital.**

CORRELATIVE CONJUNCTIONS

| both . . . and | just as . . . so | not only . . . but also |
|----------------|------------------|-------------------------|
| either . . . or | neither . . . nor | whether . . . or |

### Subordinating conjunctions

Subordinating conjunctions (39b) introduce adverb clauses and signal the relationship between the adverb clause and another clause, usually an independent clause. For instance, in the following sentence, the subordinating conjunction *while* signals a time relationship, letting us know that the two events in the sentence happened simultaneously:

▶ Sweat ran down my face <u>while</u> I frantically searched for my child.

SOME COMMON SUBORDINATING CONJUNCTIONS

| after | once | until |
|---|---|---|
| although | since | when |
| as | so that | where |
| because | than | whether |
| before | that | while |
| how | though | who |
| if | unless | why |

## Conjunctive adverbs

Conjunctive adverbs connect independent clauses and often act as transitional expressions (56f) that show how the second clause relates to the first clause. As their name suggests, conjunctive adverbs can act as both adverbs and conjunctions because they modify the second clause in addition to connecting it to the preceding clause. Like many other adverbs yet unlike other conjunctions, they can move to different positions in a clause.

▶ The cider tasted bitter; <u>however</u>, each of us drank a tall glass of it.

▶ The cider tasted bitter; each of us, <u>however</u>, drank a tall glass of it.

SOME CONJUNCTIVE ADVERBS

| also | instead | similarly |
|---|---|---|
| besides | meanwhile | still |
| certainly | moreover | then |
| finally | nevertheless | therefore |
| furthermore | next | thus |
| however | now | undoubtedly |
| indeed | otherwise | |

Independent clauses connected by a conjunctive adverb must be separated by a semicolon or a period, not just a comma (44d).

▶ Some of these problems could occur at any company; <u>still</u>, many could happen only here.

#### EXERCISE 48.6

Identify the coordinating, correlative, and subordinating conjunctions as well as the conjunctive adverbs in each of the following sentences. Example:

> We used sleeping bags, <u>even though</u> the cabin had sheets <u>and</u> blankets.

1. After waiting for an hour and a half, both Jenny and I were disgruntled, so we went home.

2. The facilities were not only uncomfortable but also dangerous.

3. I usually get a bonus each January; however, sales were down this year, so the company did not give us any extra money.

4. Although I had completed a six-week training regimen of running, swimming, and cycling, I did not feel ready, so I withdrew from the competition.

5. Enrique was not qualified for the job because he knew one of the programming languages but not the other; still, the interview encouraged him.

## 48h  Interjections and emojis

Interjections express surprise or emotion: *oh, ouch, hey*. Interjections often stand alone. Even when they are included in a sentence, they do not relate grammatically to the rest of the sentence.

▶   <u>Hey</u>, no one suggested that we would find an easy solution.

Today's digital messages — texts, posts, and to some extent email — are peppered with emojis, graphic representations of emotions and objects. Emojis often function as interjections. At times they serve to punctuate an idea in a visual way.

▶   I hadn't even thought of that possibility.

▶   The group will start work immediately on the petition

▼ ▼ ▼ ▼ ▼ ▼ ▼ ▼ ▼ ▼ ▼ ▼ ▼ ▼ ▼ ▼ ▼ ▼ ▼ ▼ ▼ ▼ ▼ ▼

### THINKING CRITICALLY ABOUT PARTS OF SPEECH

Some students in U.S. schools study parts of speech and other grammatical terms before college, and others don't. Jot down notes describing what you know about basic structures of English grammar and how you acquired this knowledge (from explicit instruction? from your own reading and intuition? somewhere else?). How confident are you that you understand English grammar? Do you think such knowledge is (or would be) useful? Why or why not?

# CHAPTER 49

# Parts of Sentences

The grammar of your first language comes to you almost automatically. Listen in on a conversation between two four-year-olds:

AUDREY: My new bike that Aunt A got me has a red basket and a loud horn, and I love it.

LILA: Can I ride it?

AUDREY: Yes, as soon as I take a turn.

This simple conversation features sophisticated grammar — the subordination of one clause to another, a compound object, and a number of adjectives — used effortlessly. If you are like many English speakers, you may never really have reflected on the details of how the language works. Paying close attention to how you put sentences together can help you understand the choices available to you whenever you write.

## 49a The basic grammar of sentences

A sentence is a grammatically complete group of words that expresses a thought. Words in a sentence can be identified by parts of speech (see Chapter 48), but you should also understand how words and phrases function in sentences.

### Recognizing subjects and predicates

To be grammatically complete, a sentence must contain both a subject, which identifies what the sentence is about, and a predicate, which says or asks something about the subject or tells the subject to do something.

| SUBJECT | PREDICATE |
| --- | --- |
| I | have a dream. |
| The rain in Spain | stays mainly in the plain. |
| Her skill as an archer | makes her a formidable opponent. |

Some sentences contain only a one-word predicate with an implied subject; for example, *Stop!* is a complete sentence, with the unspoken subject *you*. Most sentences, however, contain some words that expand upon the basic subject and predicate.

The central elements of subjects and predicates are <u>nouns</u> (48b) and <u>verbs</u> (48a).

```
┌──── SUBJECT ────┬──── PREDICATE ────┐
        NOUN        VERB
```
▶ A solitary **<u>figure</u> <u>waited</u>** on the platform.

```
┌──── SUBJECT ────┐ ┌──── PREDICATE ────────┐
      NOUN              VERB
```
▶ Her **<u>skill</u>** as an archer **<u>makes</u>** her a formidable opponent.

## Using conventional English word order

Multilingual

In general, subjects, verbs, and objects must all be placed in specific positions within a sentence.

SUBJECT VERB OBJECT ADVERB
▶ **Mario left Venice reluctantly.**

The only word in this sentence that you can move to different locations is the adverb *reluctantly* (*Mario reluctantly left Venice* or *Reluctantly, Mario left Venice*). The three key elements of subject, verb, and object rarely move out of their normal order.

## Recognizing sentence patterns

Knowing a word's part of speech (see Chapter 48) helps you understand how to use it, but you also have to look at the part it plays in a particular sentence. In the following sentences, the noun *description* plays different roles:

SUBJECT

▶ This **description** conveys the ecology of the Everglades.

DIRECT OBJECT

▶ I read a **description** of the ecology of the Everglades.

In the first sentence, *description* serves as the subject of the verb *conveys*, while in the second it serves as the direct object of the verb *read*.

---

**QUICK HELP**

Basic sentence patterns

1. Subject / verb
   ┌─ S ─┐ ┌─V─┐
   Babies drool.

2. Subject / verb / subject complement
   ┌─ S ─┐┌─V─┐┌─SC─┐
   Babies smell sweet.

3. Subject / verb / direct object
   ┌─ S ─┐┌─V─┐┌DO┐
   Babies drink milk.

4. Subject / verb / indirect object / direct object
   ┌─ S ─┐ ┌─V─┐ ┌──── IO ────┐ ┌── DO ──┐
   Babies give grandparents pleasure.

5. Subject / verb / direct object / object complement
   ┌─ S ─┐┌─V─┐ ┌─DO─┐ ┌─OC─┐
   Babies keep parents awake.

---

## 49b Subjects

The subject of a sentence identifies what the sentence is about. The simple subject consists of one or more nouns (48b) or pronouns (48c); the complete subject consists of the <u>simple subject</u> with all its modifiers.

▶ <u>Baseball</u> is a summer game.

   ┌──────── COMPLETE SUBJECT ────────┐
▶ Sailing over the fence, the <u>ball</u> crashed through Mr. Wilson's window.

   ┌──────── COMPLETE SUBJECT ────────┐
▶ <u>Those</u> who sit in the bleachers have the most fun.

A compound subject contains two or more <u>simple subjects</u> joined with a coordinating conjunction (*and, but, or*) or a correlative conjunction (*both . . . and, either . . . or, neither . . . nor, not only . . . but also*). (See 48g.)

▶ <u>Baseball</u> *and* <u>softball</u> developed from cricket.

▶ *Both* <u>baseball</u> *and* <u>softball</u> developed from cricket.

## Positioning subjects

The subject usually comes before the predicate (49a), but sometimes writers reverse this order to achieve a particular effect.

▶ **Up to the plate stepped <u>Casey</u>.**

In questions, the subject appears between the helping verb and the main verb.

▶ **Can <u>statistics</u> lie?**

▶ **How did the <u>manager</u> turn these players into a winning team?**

In sentences beginning with *there* or *here* followed by a form of the verb *be*, the subject always follows the verb. *There* and *here* are never the subject.

▶ **There was no <u>joy</u> in Mudville.**

## Using explicit subjects

Multilingual

While many languages can omit a sentence subject, English very rarely allows this. You might write *Responsible for analyzing data* on a résumé, but in most varieties of spoken and written English, you must state the subject explicitly. In fact, with only a few exceptions, all clauses in English must have an explicit subject.

▶ **They took the Acela Express to Boston because ^it was fast.**

English even requires a kind of "dummy" subject to fill the subject position in certain kinds of sentences.

▶ **It is raining.**

▶ **There is a strong wind.**

Imperative sentences (49f), which express requests or commands, are an exception to the rule of explicit subjects; the subject *you* is usually implied rather than stated.

▶ **<u>(You)</u> Keep your eye on the ball.**

### EXERCISE 49.1

Identify the complete subject and the simple subject in each sentence. Underline the complete subject once and the simple subject twice. Example:

The tall, powerful <u>woman</u> defiantly blocked the doorway.

1. That container of fried rice has spent six weeks in the back of the refrigerator.
2. Did the new tour guide remember to stop in the Ancient Greek gallery?
3. There was one student still taking the exam when the bell rang.

4. Japanese animation, with its cutting-edge graphics and futuristic plots, has earned many American admirers.

5. Sniffer dogs trained to detect drugs, blood, and explosives can help solve crimes and save lives.

## 49c Predicates

In addition to a subject, every sentence has a predicate, which asserts or asks something about the subject or tells the subject to do something. The key word of most predicates is a verb. The simple predicate of a sentence consists of the main verb and any auxiliaries; the complete predicate includes the simple predicate and any modifiers of the verb and any objects or complements (49a) and their modifiers.

▶ Both of us <u>are planning</u> to major in history.

    ─── COMPLETE PREDICATE ───

A compound predicate contains two or more verbs that have the same subject, usually joined by a coordinating or a correlative conjunction (48g).

▶ Omar <u>shut</u> the book, <u>put</u> it back on the shelf, *and* <u>sighed</u>.

On the basis of how they function in predicates, verbs can be divided into three categories: linking, transitive, and intransitive.

### Identifying linking verbs

A <u>linking verb</u> connects a subject with a subject complement (sc), a word or word group that identifies or describes the subject.

▶ Christine <u>is</u> an excellent teacher.
    S  V ─── SC ───

▶ She <u>is</u> patient.
    S  V  SC

A subject complement can be either a noun or pronoun (*teacher*) or an adjective (*patient*).

The forms of *be*, when used as main verbs, are common linking verbs. Other verbs, such as *appear, become, feel, grow, look, make, seem, smell*, and *sound*, can also function as linking verbs, depending on the sense of the sentence.

▶ The neighborhood <u>looked</u> prosperous.
  ─── S ───  V  SC

### Identifying transitive verbs

Multilingual

A <u>transitive verb</u> expresses action that is directed toward a noun or pronoun called the *direct object* (DO).

▶ He <u>peeled</u> all the rutabagas.
   S  V ─── DO ───

Here, the subject and verb do not express a complete thought. The direct object completes the thought by saying *what* he peeled.

A direct object may be followed by an object complement (OC), a word or word group that describes or identifies the direct object. Object complements may be adjectives, as in the first example below, or nouns, as in the second example.

```
  S   V  ┌─────────── DO ───────────┐┌──── OC ────┐
```
▶ **I find cell-phone conversations in restaurants very annoying.**

```
    S       V      DO       ┌──── OC ────┐
```
▶ **Alana considers Keyshawn her best friend.**

Some transitive verbs may also be followed by an indirect object (IO), which is the recipient of the direct object. The indirect object tells to whom or what, or for whom or what, the verb does its action.

```
┌──────── S ────────┐  V   IO  ┌──────── DO ────────┐
```
▶ **The sound of the traffic gave me a splitting headache.**

Transitive verbs typically require you to state the object explicitly. For example, you can't just say *Give!* even if it is clear that you mean *Give me the phone*.

## Identifying intransitive verbs

Multilingual

An intransitive verb does not have a direct object.

```
   ┌─ S ─┐    V
```
▶ **The Red Sox persevered.**

```
   ┌─ S ─┐   V
```
▶ **Their fans watched anxiously.**

The verb *persevered* has no object (it makes no sense to ask, *persevered what?*), and the verb *watched* is directed toward an object that is implied but not expressed.

Some verbs that express action can be only transitive or only intransitive, but most can be used either way, with or without a direct object.

```
   ┌─ S ─┐  V   ┌─ DO ─┐
```
▶ **The host opened the door.** [transitive]

```
   ┌─ S ─┐  V
```
▶ **The door opened silently.** [intransitive]

### EXERCISE 49.2

Identify the predicate in each of the following sentences. Label each verb as linking, transitive, or intransitive. Finally, label any subject complements, object complements, direct objects, and indirect objects. Example:

```
              TV        DO      OC
```
We considered city life unbearable.

1. He is proud of his heritage.
2. The horrifying news story made me angry.
3. The old house looks deserted.
4. Rock and roll will never die.
5. Chloe's boss offered her a promotion.

## 49d Phrases

A phrase is a group of words that lacks a subject or a predicate or both.

### Identifying noun phrases

Made up of a noun and all its modifiers, a <u>noun phrase</u> can function in a sentence as a subject, object, or complement.

>     SUBJECT
> ▶ **Delicious, gooey peanut butter is surprisingly healthful.**

>     OBJECT
> ▶ **I craved a green salad with plenty of fresh vegetables.**

>     COMPLEMENT
> ▶ **Soup is a popular lunch.**

### Identifying verb phrases

A main verb and its auxiliary verbs make up a <u>verb phrase</u>, which can function in a sentence only as a verb.

▶ **Frank can swim for a long time.**

▶ **His headaches might have been caused by tension.**

### Identifying prepositional phrases

A <u>prepositional phrase</u> begins with a preposition and includes a noun or pronoun (the object of the preposition) and any modifiers of the object. Prepositional phrases usually function as adjectives or adverbs.

>     ADJECTIVE
> ▶ **Our house in Maine was a cabin.**

>     ADVERB
> ▶ **From Cadillac Mountain, you can see the northern lights.**

### Identifying verbal phrases

Verbals look like verbs, but they function as nouns, adjectives, or adverbs. There are three kinds of verbals: participles, gerunds, and infinitives.

*Participles and participial phrases*

The present participle is the *-ing* form of a verb (*spinning*). The past participle of most verbs ends in *-ed* (*accepted*), but some verbs have an irregular past participle (*worn, frozen*). Participles function as adjectives (54a).

▶ A kiss awakened the dreaming princess.

▶ The cryptographers deciphered the hidden meaning in the message.

Participial phrases, which also act as adjectives, consist of a present or past participle and any modifiers, objects, or complements.

▶ Irritated by the delay, Luisa complained.

▶ A dog howling at the moon kept me awake.

*Gerunds and gerund phrases*

The gerund has the same *-ing* form as the present participle but functions as a noun.

SUBJECT
▶ Writing takes practice.

DIRECT OBJECT
▶ The organization promotes recycling.

Gerund phrases, which function as nouns, consist of a gerund and any modifiers, objects, or complements.

─── SUBJECT ───
▶ Opening their eyes to the problem was not easy.

─── DIRECT OBJECT ───
▶ They suddenly heard a loud wailing from the sandbox.

*Infinitives and infinitive phrases*

The infinitive is the *to* form of a verb (*to dream, to be*). An infinitive can function as a noun, an adjective, or an adverb.

┌ NOUN ┐
▶ She wanted to write.

ADJECTIVE
▶ They had no more time to waste.

┌ ADVERB ┐
▶ The corporation was ready to expand.

Infinitive phrases consist of an infinitive and any modifiers, objects, or complements. Like infinitives, they function as nouns, adjectives, or adverbs.

▶ My goal is <u>to be a biology teacher</u>. — NOUN

▶ A party <u>to end the semester</u> would be a good idea. — ADJECTIVE

▶ <u>To perfect a draft</u>, always proofread carefully. — ADVERB

---

**QUICK HELP**

Choosing between infinitives and gerunds  Multilingual

In general, infinitives indicate intentions, desires, or expectations, and gerunds indicate facts. Knowing whether to use an infinitive or a gerund in a sentence can be challenging.

**INFINITIVES TO STATE INTENTIONS**

▶ Kumar <u>expected to get</u> a good job after graduation.

▶ Last year, Fatima <u>decided to change</u> her major.

Verbs such as *expect* and *decide*, which indicate intentions, must always be followed by an infinitive.

**GERUNDS TO STATE FACTS**

▶ Jerzy <u>enjoys going</u> to the theater.

▶ Kim <u>appreciated getting</u> a card from Sean.

Verbs like *enjoy* and *appreciate*, which indicate that something has actually happened, can be followed by gerunds but not by infinitives.

**OTHER RULES AND GUIDELINES**

A few verbs can be followed by either an infinitive or a gerund. With some, such as *begin* and *continue*, the choice doesn't affect the meaning. With others, however, the difference is important.

▶ Carlos was working as a medical technician, but he <u>stopped to study</u> English.

The infinitive shows that Carlos quit because he intended to study English.

▶ When Carlos left the United States, he <u>stopped studying</u> English.

The gerund indicates that Carlos gave up his English studies when he left the United States.

▶

Choosing between infinitives and gerunds, *continued*

You can use only a gerund—never an infinitive—right after a preposition.

▶   This fruit is safe for ~~to eat~~. *eating.*

▶   This fruit is safe ~~for~~ to eat.

▶   This fruit is safe for *us* to eat.

Consult a learner's dictionary for more information on whether to follow a verb with an infinitive or a gerund.

## Identifying absolute phrases

An <u>absolute phrase</u> usually includes a noun or pronoun and a participle. It modifies an entire sentence rather than a particular word and is usually set off from the rest of the sentence with commas (56d).

▶   I stood on the deck, <u>the wind whipping my hair.</u>

▶   <u>My fears laid to rest,</u> I set off on my first solo flight.

When the participle is *being*, it is often omitted.

▶   The ambassador, <u>her head [being] high,</u> walked out of the room.

## Identifying appositive phrases

An <u>appositive phrase</u> is a noun phrase that renames the noun or pronoun that immediately precedes it (56d).

▶   The report, <u>a hefty three-volume work,</u> included more than ninety recommendations.

▶   We had a single desire, <u>to change the administration's policies.</u>

### ◢ EXERCISE 49.3

Read the following sentences, and identify all of the prepositional, verbal, absolute, and appositive phrases. Notice that one kind of phrase may appear within another kind. Example:

ABSOLUTE ┌──PREP──┐ PREP
His voice breaking with emotion, Ed thanked us for the award.

1. Chantelle, the motel clerk, hopes to be certified as a river guide.
2. Carpets made by hand are usually the most valuable.
3. My stomach doing flips, I answered the door.

4. Floating on my back, I ignored my practice requirements.

5. Driving across town during rush hour can take thirty minutes or more.

## 49e Clauses

A clause is a group of words containing a subject and a predicate. There are two kinds of clauses: independent and dependent. <u>Independent clauses</u> (also known as main clauses) can stand alone as complete sentences.

▶ **The window is open.**

Pairs of independent clauses may be joined with a coordinating conjunction and a comma (48g and 56c).

▶ **The window is open, so the room feels cool.**

Like independent clauses, <u>dependent clauses</u> (also referred to as subordinate clauses) contain a subject and a predicate. They cannot stand alone as complete sentences, however, for they begin with a subordinating word — a subordinating conjunction (48g) or a relative pronoun (48c) — that connects them to an independent clause.

▶ **Because the window is open, the room feels cool.**

The subordinating conjunction *because* transforms the independent clause *the window is open* into a dependent clause. In doing so, it indicates a causal relationship between the two clauses.

Dependent clauses function as nouns, adjectives, or adverbs.

### Identifying noun clauses

Multilingual

<u>Noun clauses</u> are always contained within another clause. They usually begin with a relative pronoun (*that, which, what, who, whom, whose, whatever, whoever, whomever, whichever*) or with *when, where, whether, why,* or *how.*

SUBJECT
▶ **What the archeologists found was startling.**

DIRECT OBJECT
▶ **She explained that the research was necessary.**

SUBJECT COMPLEMENT
▶ **The mystery was why the ancient city had been abandoned.**

OBJECT OF PREPOSITION
▶ **They were looking for whatever information was available.**

Like a noun, a noun clause is an integral part of the sentence; for example, in the second sentence the independent clause is not just *She explained* but *She explained that the research was necessary.* This complex sentence is built out of two sentences; one of them (*The research was necessary*) is embedded in the other (*She explained [something]*). The relative pronoun *that* introduces the noun clause that is the object of *explained.*

A *that* clause can serve as the subject of a sentence, but the effect is very formal:

> ──── SUBJECT ────
> **That the city had been abandoned was surprising.**

In less formal contexts, and in spoken English, a long noun clause is usually moved to the end of the sentence and replaced with the "dummy subject" *it.*

> ▶ *It* **was surprising that the city had been abandoned.**

## Identifying adjective clauses

Multilingual

Adjective clauses modify nouns and pronouns in another clause. Usually, they immediately follow the words they modify.

> ▶ The surgery, **which took three hours,** was a complete success.

> ▶ It was performed by the surgeon **who had developed the procedure.**

> ▶ The hospital was the one **where I was born.**

Sometimes the relative pronoun introducing an adjective clause may be omitted, as in the following examples:

> ▶ That is one book [that] I intend to read.

> ▶ The company [that] the family had invested in grew rapidly.

To see how the adjective clause fits into this sentence, rewrite it as two sentences: *The company grew rapidly. The family had invested in it.* To make the second sentence a relative clause, use a relative pronoun and move the words to the beginning of the clause: *The family had invested in it* becomes *that the family had invested in.* Then position the new clause after the word it describes (in this case, *company*): *The company that the family had invested in grew rapidly.*

In very formal writing, when the pronoun you are changing is the object of a preposition, select *which* (or *whom* for people, 53b) and move the whole prepositional phrase to the beginning of the clause: *The company in which the family had invested grew rapidly*. In many American English contexts, however, such constructions may sound too formal, so consider your audience carefully.

## Identifying adverb clauses

Adverb clauses modify verbs, adjectives, or other adverbs. They begin with a subordinating conjunction (48g). Like adverbs, they usually tell when, where, why, how, or to what extent.

▸　**We hiked <u>where few other hikers went</u>.**

▸　**My backpack felt heavier <u>than it ever had</u>.**

▸　**Climbers ascend Mount Everest <u>because it is there</u>.**

### EXERCISE 49.4

Identify the independent and dependent clauses and any subordinating conjunctions and relative pronouns in each of the following sentences. Example:

SC ┌────── DEPENDENT CLAUSE ──────┐ ┌────── INDEPENDENT CLAUSE ──────┐
Ⓘf I were going on a really long hike, I would carry a lightweight stove.

1. The hockey game was postponed because one of the players collapsed on the bench.
2. She eventually discovered the secret admirer who had been leaving notes in her locker.
3. After completing three advanced drawing classes, Jason was admitted into the fine arts program, and he immediately rented a small studio space.
4. The test was easier than I had expected.
5. I could tell that it was going to rain, so I tried to get home quickly.

### EXERCISE 49.5

Expand each of the following sentences by adding at least one dependent clause to it. Be prepared to explain how your addition improves the sentence. Example:

　　　　*As the earth continued to shake, the*
　　**T̶h̶e̶ books tumbled from the shelves.**
　　　　^

1. The economy gradually began to recover.
2. Simone waited nervously by the phone.
3. New school safety rules were instituted this fall.
4. Rob always borrowed money from friends.
5. The crowd grew louder and more disorderly.

# 49f Types of sentences

Like words, sentences can be categorized both grammatically and functionally.

## Identifying sentences by grammatical structure

Grammatically, sentences may be simple, compound, complex, or compound-complex.

### Simple sentences

A simple sentence consists of one <u>independent clause</u> and no dependent clause. The subject or the verb, or both, may be compound.

INDEPENDENT CLAUSE

▶ **The trailer is surrounded by a wooden deck.**

INDEPENDENT CLAUSE

▶ **Pompeii and Herculaneum disappeared under tons of lava and ash.**

### Compound sentences

A compound sentence consists of two or more <u>independent clauses</u> and no dependent clause. The clauses may be joined by a comma and a coordinating conjunction (48g) or by a semicolon.

INDEPENDENT CLAUSE     INDEPENDENT CLAUSE

▶ **Occasionally a car goes up the dirt trail, and dust flies everywhere.**

INDEPENDENT CLAUSE     INDEPENDENT CLAUSE

▶ **Alberto is obsessed with soccer; he eats, breathes, and lives the game.**

### Complex sentences

A complex sentence consists of one <u>independent clause</u> and at least one <u>dependent clause</u>.

INDEPENDENT CLAUSE     DEPENDENT CLAUSE

▶ **Many people believe that anyone can earn a living.**

DEPENDENT CLAUSE     INDEPENDENT CLAUSE

▶ **As I awaited my interview, I sat with another candidate**

DEPENDENT CLAUSE

**who smiled nervously.**

*Compound-complex sentences*

A compound-complex sentence consists of two or more independent clauses and at least one dependent clause.

INDEPENDENT CLAUSE ┌─── DEPENDENT CLAUSE ───┐    INDEPENDENT CLAUSE
▶  **I complimented Luis when he finished the job, and he seemed pleased.**

┌─── INDEPENDENT CLAUSE ───┐    ┌─── INDEPENDENT CLAUSE ───┐
▶  **The actors performed well, but the audience hated the play,**

┌─────── DEPENDENT CLAUSE ───────┐
**which was confusing and far too long.**

## Identifying sentences by function

In terms of function, sentences can be declarative (making a statement), interrogative (asking a question), imperative (giving a command), or exclamatory (expressing strong feeling).

| | |
|---|---|
| DECLARATIVE | He sings with the Grace Church Boys' Choir. |
| INTERROGATIVE | How long has he sung with them? |
| IMPERATIVE | Comb his hair before the performance starts. |
| EXCLAMATORY | What voices those boys have! |

### EXERCISE 49.6

Classify the following sentences as simple, compound, complex, or compound-complex. In addition, note any sentence that may be classified as interrogative, imperative, or exclamatory. Example:

COMPLEX
**I realized my mistake when I arrived.**

1. The boat rocked and lurched over the rough surf as the passengers groaned in agony.
2. Is this the coldest winter on record, or was last year even worse?
3. After waiting for over an hour, I was examined by the doctor for only three minutes!
4. Keeping in mind the terrain, the weather, and the length of the hike, decide what you need to take.
5. The former prisoner, who was cleared by DNA evidence, has lost six years of his life, and he needs a job right away.

▼ ▼ ▼ ▼ ▼ ▼ ▼ ▼ ▼ ▼ ▼ ▼ ▼ ▼ ▼ ▼ ▼ ▼ ▼ ▼ ▼ ▼ ▼ ▼ ▼

## THINKING CRITICALLY ABOUT SENTENCES

The following sentences come from the openings of well-known works. Identify the independent and dependent clauses in each sentence. Then choose one sentence, and write a sentence of your own imitating its structure, clause for clause and phrase for phrase. Example:

> When I wake up, the other side of the bed is cold.
> —SUZANNE COLLINS, *The Hunger Games*

Dependent clause: When I wake up
Independent clause: the other side of the bed is cold
Imitation: After I run, the bottom of my foot is sore.

1. We observe today not a victory of party but a celebration of freedom, symbolizing an end as well as a beginning, signifying renewal as well as change. —JOHN F. KENNEDY, *Inaugural Address*

2. Once in a long while, four times so far for me, my mother brings out the metal tube that holds her medical diploma.
—MAXINE HONG KINGSTON, "Photographs of My Parents"

CHAPTER 50

# Nouns and Noun Phrases

Multilingual

Although all languages have nouns, English nouns differ from those in some other languages in various ways, such as their division into count and noncount nouns and the use of plural forms, articles, and other modifiers.

## 50a Using count and noncount nouns

Multilingual

Nouns in English can be either count nouns or noncount nouns. Count nouns refer to distinct individuals or things that can be directly counted: *a doctor, an egg, a child; doctors, eggs, children.* Noncount nouns refer to masses, collections, or ideas without distinct parts: *milk, rice, courage.* You cannot count noncount nouns except with a preceding phrase: *a glass of milk, three grains of rice, a little courage.*

Count nouns usually have singular and plural forms: *tree, trees.* Noncount nouns usually have only a singular form: *grass.*

| COUNT | NONCOUNT |
|---|---|
| people (plural of person) | humanity |
| tables, chairs, beds | furniture |
| letters | mail |
| pebbles | gravel |
| suggestions | advice |

Some nouns can be either <u>count</u> or <u>noncount</u>, depending on their meaning.

| | |
|---|---|
| COUNT | Before video games, children played with <u>marbles</u>. |
| NONCOUNT | The palace floor was made of <u>marble</u>. |

When you learn a noun in English, you need to learn whether it is count, non-count, or both. Many dictionaries provide this information.

## 50b Using determiners

Determiners are words that identify or quantify a noun, such as _this study_, _all people_, _his suggestions_.

**COMMON DETERMINERS**

- the articles _a, an, the_
- _this, these, that, those_
- _my, our, your, his, her, its, their_
- possessive nouns and noun phrases (_Sheila's paper_, _my friend's book_)
- _whose, which, what_

| These determiners . . . | . . . can precede these noun types | Examples |
|---|---|---|
| _a, an, each, every_ | singular count nouns | _a_ book<br>_an_ American<br>_each_ word<br>_every_ Buddhist |
| _this, that_ | singular count nouns<br>noncount nouns | _this_ book<br>_that_ milk |
| (a) _little, much_ | noncount nouns | _a little_ milk<br>_much_ affection |
| _some, any, enough_ | noncount nouns<br><br>plural count nouns | _some_ milk<br>_any_ fruit<br>_enough_ trouble<br>_some_ books<br>_any_ questions<br>_enough_ problems |
| _the_ | singular count nouns<br>plural count nouns<br>noncount nouns | _the_ doctor<br>_the_ doctors<br>_the_ information |
| _these, those_,<br>(a) _few, many_,<br>_both, several_ | plural count nouns | _these_ books<br>_those_ plans<br>_a few_ ideas<br>_many_ students<br>_both_ hands<br>_several_ trees |

- *all, both, each, every, some, any, either, no, neither, many, much, (a) few, (a) little, several, enough*
- the numerals *one, two,* etc.

## Using determiners with singular count nouns

Every singular count noun must be preceded by a determiner. Place any adjectives between the determiner and the noun.

▶ *my*
 **sister**
 ^

▶ *the*
 **growing population**
 ^

▶ *that*
 **old neighborhood**
 ^

## Using determiners with plural nouns or noncount nouns

Noncount and plural nouns sometimes have determiners and sometimes do not. For example, *This research is important* and *Research is important* are both acceptable but have different meanings.

# 50c Using articles

Multilingual

Articles (*a, an,* and *the*) are a type of determiner. In English, choosing which article to use — or whether to use an article at all — can be challenging. Although there are exceptions, the following general guidelines can help.

## Using *a* or *an*

Use the indefinite articles *a* and *an* with singular count nouns. Use *a* before a consonant sound (*a car*) and *an* before a vowel sound (*an uncle*). Consider sound rather than spelling: *a house, an hour.*

A or *an* tells readers they do not have enough information to identify specifically what the noun refers to. Compare these sentences:

▶ **I need a new coat for the winter.**

▶ **I saw a coat that I liked at Dayton's, but it wasn't heavy enough.**

The coat in the first sentence is hypothetical rather than actual. Since it is indefinite to the writer and the reader, it is used with *a*, not *the*. The second sentence refers to an actual coat, but since the writer cannot expect the reader to know which one, it is used with *a* rather than *the*.

If you want to speak of an indefinite quantity rather than just one indefinite thing, use *some* or *any* with a noncount noun or a plural count noun. Use *any* in negative sentences and questions.

► This stew needs <u>some</u> more salt.

► I saw <u>some</u> plates that I liked at Gump's.

► This stew doesn't need <u>any</u> more salt.

## Using *the*

Use the definite article *the* with both count and noncount nouns whose identity is known or is about to be made known to readers. The necessary information for identification can come from the noun phrase itself, from elsewhere in the text, from context, from general knowledge, or from a superlative.

► Let's meet at ^the^ fountain in front of Dwinelle Hall.

The phrase *in front of Dwinelle Hall* identifies the specific fountain.

► Last Saturday, a fire that started in a restaurant spread to a nearby clothing store. ~~Store~~ ^The store^ was saved, although it suffered water damage.

The word *store* is preceded by *the*, which directs our attention to the information in the previous sentence, where the store is first identified.

► She asked him to shut ^the^ door when he left her office.

The context shows that she is referring to her office door.

► ~~Pope~~ ^The pope^ is expected to visit Africa in October.

There is only one living pope.

► Bill is now ^the^ best singer in the choir.

The superlative *best* identifies the noun *singer*.

## Using no article

Noncount and plural count nouns can be used without an article when making generalizations:

► In this world nothing is certain but death and taxes.

—BENJAMIN FRANKLIN

Franklin refers not to a particular death or specific taxes but to death and taxes in general, so no article is used with *death* or with *taxes*.

English differs from many other languages that use the definite article to make generalizations. In English, a sentence like *The ants live in colonies* can refer only to particular, identifiable ants, not to ants in general.

It is sometimes possible to make general statements with *the* or *a/an* and singular count nouns.

▶ *First-year college students* are confronted with many new experiences.

▶ *A first-year student* is confronted with many new experiences.

▶ *The first-year student* is confronted with many new experiences.

These sentences all make the same general statement, but the emphasis of each sentence is different. The first sentence refers to first-year students as a group, the second focuses on a hypothetical student taken at random, and the third sentence, which is characteristic of formal written style, projects the image of a typical student as representative of the whole class.

### EXERCISE 50.1

Each of the following sentences contains an error. Edit each sentence to correct the error. Example:

A hospital stay can often cause ~~an~~ anxiety.

1. Before a middle of the nineteenth century, surgery was usually a terrifying, painful ordeal.

2. Because anesthesia did not exist yet, only painkiller available for surgical patients was whiskey.

3. The pain of surgical procedures could be so severe that much people were willing to die rather than have surgery.

4. In 1846, one of the hospital in Boston gave ether to a patient before he had surgery.

5. The patient, who had a large on his neck tumor, slept peacefully as doctors removed it.

### EXERCISE 50.2

Rewrite the following passage from *The Silent Language*, by Edward T. Hall, inserting articles as necessary. Some blanks may not need an article.

Hollywood is famous for hiring _____ various experts to teach _____ people technically what most of us learn informally. _____ case in point is _____ story about _____ children of one movie couple who noticed _____ new child in _____ neighborhood climbing _____ tree. _____ children immediately wanted to be given _____ name of his instructor in _____ tree climbing.

# CHAPTER 51

# Verbs

Used skillfully, verbs can be the heartbeat of prose, moving it along, enlivening it, carrying its action: *As the little girl skipped in, she bounced a red rubber ball and smiled from ear to ear.*

## 51a Using appropriate verb forms

Except for *be*, all English verbs have five possible forms.

| BASE FORM | PAST TENSE | PAST PARTICIPLE | PRESENT PARTICIPLE | -S FORM |
|-----------|-----------|-----------------|--------------------|---------|
| talk | talked | talked | talking | talks |
| adore | adored | adored | adoring | adores |

### Using the base form

The base form is the one listed in the dictionary. For all verbs except *be*, use the base form to indicate an action or condition in the present when the subject is plural or when the subject is *I* or *you*.

▶ **During the ritual, the women <u>go</u> into trances.**

### Using the past-tense form

Use the past tense to indicate an action or condition that occurred entirely in the past. For most verbs, the past tense is formed by adding *-ed* or *-d* to the base form. Some verbs, however, have irregular past-tense forms. *Be* has two past-tense forms, *was* and *were*.

▶ **The Globe <u>was</u> the stage for many of Shakespeare's most famous works.**

▶ **In 1613, it <u>caught</u> fire and burned to the ground.**

### Using the past participle form

Use the past participle to form perfect tenses and the passive voice (51g). A past participle usually has the same form as the past tense, though some verbs have irregular past participles (51c).

▶ **She <u>had accomplished</u> the impossible.** [past perfect]

▶ **No one <u>was injured</u> in the explosion.** [passive voice]

## Using the present participle form

The present participle is constructed by adding *-ing* to the base form. Use it with auxiliary verbs to indicate a continuing action or condition.

▶ **Many students <u>are competing</u> in the race.** [continuing action]

Present participles sometimes function as adjectives or nouns (gerunds), and past participles can also serve as adjectives; in such cases they are not verbs but verbals (see 49d).

## Using the -s form

Except for *be* and *have*, the *-s* form consists of the base form plus *-s* or *-es*. This form indicates an action in the present for third-person singular subjects. All singular nouns; *he*, *she*, and *it*; and many other pronouns (such as *this* and *someone*) are third-person singular.

|  | SINGULAR | PLURAL |
|---|---|---|
| FIRST PERSON | I wish | we wish |
| SECOND PERSON | you wish | you wish |
| THIRD PERSON | he/she/it <u>wishes</u> | they wish |
|  | Joe <u>wishes</u> | children wish |
|  | someone <u>wishes</u> | many wish |

The third-person singular form of *have* is *has*.

---

**QUICK HELP**

Editing for *-s* and *-es* endings

If you tend to leave off or misuse the *-s* and *-es* verb endings in academic writing, check for them systematically.

1. Underline every verb, and then circle all of the verbs in the present tense.

2. Find the subject of every verb you circled.

3. If the subject is a singular noun; *he*, *she*, or *it*; or a singular indefinite pronoun, be sure the verb ends in *-s* or *-es*. If the subject is not third-person singular, the verb should not have an *-s* or *-es* ending.

4. Be careful with auxiliary verbs such as *can* or *may*. These auxiliaries are used with the base form, never with the *-s* or *-es* form (51b).

## Using forms of be

*Be* has three forms in the present tense (*am, is, are*) and two in the past tense (*was, were*).

*Present tense*

|  | SINGULAR | PLURAL |
|---|---|---|
| FIRST PERSON | I am | we are |
| SECOND PERSON | you are | you are |
| THIRD PERSON | he/she/it is | they are |
|  | Juan is | children are |
|  | somebody is | many are |

*Past tense*

|  | SINGULAR | PLURAL |
|---|---|---|
| FIRST PERSON | I was | we were |
| SECOND PERSON | you were | you were |
| THIRD PERSON | he/she/it was | they were |
|  | Juan was | children were |
|  | somebody was | many were |

---

TALKING ABOUT STYLE | **EVERYDAY USE OF *BE***

Spoken varieties of English may follow rules for the use of *be* that differ from the rules of most academic English. For instance, you may have heard speakers say, "She ain't here now" instead of "She isn't here now" or "He be at work every Saturday" instead of "He is at work every Saturday." (All of these are correct in dialects of English.) You may sometimes want to quote dialogue featuring such spoken usages when you write or to use what linguists refer to as "habitual *be*" in writing to particular audiences. In most academic and professional writing, however, you will want to follow the conventions of academic English. (For help with using varieties of English, see Chapter 34.)

---

## 51b Forming verb phrases

English sentences must have at least one verb or verb phrase that is not simply an infinitive (*to write*), a gerund (*writing*), or a participle (*written*) without any helping verbs. Use helping (also called *auxiliary*) verbs with a main verb — in its base form or in a present participle or past participle form — to create verb phrases.

The most common auxiliaries are forms of *be*, *have*, and *do*. *Have* is used to form perfect tenses that indicate completed action (51e); *be* is used with progressive forms that show continuing action (51e) and to form the passive voice (51g).

► The engineers <u>have considered</u> possible problems. [completed action]

► The college <u>is building</u> a new dormitory. [continuing action]

► The activists <u>were warned</u> to stay away. [passive voice]

As an auxiliary, *do* is used to show emphasis, to form questions, and to make negative statements.

► I <u>do respect</u> my opponent's viewpoint. [emphasis]

► <u>Do</u> you <u>know</u> the answer? [question]

► He <u>does</u> not <u>like</u> wearing a tie. [negative statement]

## Arranging helping (auxiliary) verbs

Multilingual

Verb phrases can be built up out of a main verb and one or more auxiliaries.

► Immigration figures <u>rise</u> every year.

► Immigration figures <u>are rising</u> every year.

► Immigration figures <u>have risen</u> every year.

► Immigration figures <u>have been rising</u> every year.

Verb phrases have strict rules of order. The only permissible change to word order is to form a question, moving the first auxiliary to the beginning of the sentence: *Have immigration figures been rising every year?*

When two or more auxiliaries appear in a verb phrase, they must follow a particular order based on the type of auxiliary:

1. A modal (*can, could, may, might, must, shall, should, will, would,* or *ought to*)

2. A form of *have* used to indicate a perfect tense (51e)

3. A form of *be* used to indicate a progressive tense (51e)

4. A form of *be* used to indicate the passive voice, followed by a past participle (51g)

► The invitation *must have been sent* through the mail.

## Using modals

Multilingual

The modal auxiliaries — *can, could, may, might, shall, should, will, would, must,* and *ought to* — indicate future action, possibility, necessity, or obligation.

▶ They <u>will explain</u> the procedure. [future action]
▶ You <u>can see</u> three states from the top of the mountain. [possibility]
▶ Students <u>must manage</u> their time wisely. [necessity]
▶ They <u>should examine</u> the results of the study. [obligation]

No verb phrase can include more than one modal.

▶ She will ~~can~~ speak Czech much better soon.
     *be able to*
          ^

### *Modals for requests or instructions*

Modals are often used in requests and instructions. If you use a modal such as *could* or *would,* you are politely acknowledging that the person you are talking to may be unable or unwilling to do what you ask.

▶ *Could* you bring me a pillow?

Modals appearing in instructions usually indicate whether an action is suggested or required:

1. You *can* / You *may* post your work online. [Posting online is allowed.]
2. You *should* submit your report electronically. [Posting online is recommended or required.]
3. You *must* / You *will* submit your report electronically. [Posting online is required.]

### *Modals to show doubt or certainty*

Modals can also indicate how confident the writer is about his or her claims. Using *may* or *might* results in a tentative suggestion, while *will* indicates complete confidence:

▶ The study <u>might help explain</u> the findings of previous research.
▶ The study <u>will help explain</u> the findings of previous research.

## Forming phrases with modals

Multilingual

Use the base form of a verb after a modal.

▶ Alice <u>can read</u> Latin.
▶ Sanjay <u>should have studied</u> for the test.
▶ They <u>must be going</u> to a fine school.

In many other languages, modals such as *can* and *must* are followed by an infinitive (*to* + base form). In English, only the base form follows a modal.

▶ **Alice can ~~to~~ read Latin.**

Notice that a modal auxiliary never changes form to agree with the subject.

For the most part, modals refer to present or future time. When you want to use a modal to refer to the past, you follow the modal with a perfect form of the main verb (see 51e).

▶ **If you have a fever, you <u>should see</u> a doctor.**

▶ **If you had a fever, you <u>should have seen</u> a doctor.**

The modal *must* is a special case. The past tense of *must* is *had to* or *needed to*.

▶ **You <u>must renew</u> your visa by the end of this week.**

▶ **You <u>had to renew</u> / You <u>needed to renew</u> your visa by last Friday.**

Note, too, the different meanings of the negative forms *must not* and *don't have to*.

▶ **You <u>must not go</u> to the party.** [You are forbidden to go.]

▶ **You <u>don't have to go</u> to the party.** [You are not required to go, but you may.]

## 51c Understanding regular and irregular verbs

A verb is regular when its past tense and past participle are formed by adding -*ed* or -*d* to the base form.

| BASE FORM | PAST TENSE | PAST PARTICIPLE |
|---|---|---|
| love | loved | loved |
| honor | honored | honored |
| obey | obeyed | obeyed |

---

QUICK HELP

Editing for -*ed* or -*d* endings

Speakers who delete the -*ed* or -*d* endings in conversation may forget to include them in academic writing. If you tend to drop these endings, make a point of checking for them when proofreading. Underline all the verbs, and then underline a second time any that are past tense or past participles. Check each of these for an -*ed* or -*d* ending. Unless the verb is irregular (see the following list), it should end in -*ed* or -*d*.

vf

A verb is irregular when it does not follow the *-ed* or *-d* pattern. If you are unsure about whether a verb is regular or irregular, or what the correct form is, consult the following list or a dictionary. Dictionaries list any irregular forms under the entry for the base form.

*Common irregular verbs*

| BASE FORM | PAST TENSE | PAST PARTICIPLE |
|---|---|---|
| arise | arose | arisen |
| be | was/were | been |
| bear | bore | borne, born |
| beat | beat | beaten |
| become | became | become |
| begin | began | begun |
| blow | blew | blown |
| break | broke | broken |
| bring | brought | brought |
| build | built | built |
| burn | burned, burnt | burned, burnt |
| buy | bought | bought |
| catch | caught | caught |
| choose | chose | chosen |
| come | came | come |
| cost | cost | cost |
| cut | cut | cut |
| dive | dived, dove | dived |
| do | did | done |
| dream | dreamed, dreamt | dreamed, dreamt |
| drink | drank | drunk |
| drive | drove | driven |
| eat | ate | eaten |
| fall | fell | fallen |
| feel | felt | felt |
| fight | fought | fought |
| find | found | found |
| fly | flew | flown |
| forget | forgot | forgotten, forgot |
| freeze | froze | frozen |
| get | got | gotten, got |

| BASE FORM | PAST TENSE | PAST PARTICIPLE |
|---|---|---|
| give | gave | given |
| go | went | gone |
| grow | grew | grown |
| hang (suspend)[1] | hung | hung |
| have | had | had |
| hear | heard | heard |
| hide | hid | hidden |
| keep | kept | kept |
| know | knew | known |
| lay | laid | laid |
| lead | led | led |
| leave | left | left |
| lend | lent | lent |
| let | let | let |
| lie (recline)[2] | lay | lain |
| lose | lost | lost |
| make | made | made |
| mean | meant | meant |
| meet | met | met |
| pay | paid | paid |
| prove | proved | proved, proven |
| read | read | read |
| ride | rode | ridden |
| rise | rose | risen |
| run | ran | run |
| say | said | said |
| see | saw | seen |
| send | sent | sent |
| shoot | shot | shot |
| show | showed | showed, shown |
| shrink | shrank | shrunk |
| sing | sang | sung |
| sit | sat | sat |

[1]*Hang* meaning "execute by hanging" is regular: *hang, hanged, hanged.*
[2]*Lie* meaning "tell a falsehood" is regular: *lie, lied, lied.*

| BASE FORM | PAST TENSE | PAST PARTICIPLE |
|-----------|------------|-----------------|
| sleep | slept | slept |
| speak | spoke | spoken |
| spend | spent | spent |
| spread | spread | spread |
| stand | stood | stood |
| steal | stole | stolen |
| strike | struck | struck, stricken |
| take | took | taken |
| teach | taught | taught |
| tear | tore | torn |
| think | thought | thought |
| throw | threw | thrown |
| wake | waked, woke | waked, woken |
| win | won | won |
| write | wrote | written |

### EXERCISE 51.1

Complete each of the following sentences by writing the past tense or past participle of the verb listed in parentheses. Example:

**They had already _eaten_ (eat) the entrée; later they _ate_ (eat) the dessert.**

1. The babysitter _____ (let) the children play with my schoolbooks, and before I _____ (come) home, they had _____ (tear) out several pages.

2. After they had _____ (review) the evidence, the jury _____ (find) the defendant not guilty.

3. Hypnosis _____ (work) only on willing participants.

4. My parents _____ (plant) a tree for me in the town where I was born, but I have never _____ (go) back to see it.

5. Some residents _____ (know) that the levee was leaking long before the storms, but authorities _____ (ignore) the complaints.

6. I _____ (paint) a picture from a photograph my sister had _____ (take) at the beach.

7. When the buzzer sounded, the racers _____ (spring) into the water and _____ (swim) toward the far end of the pool.

8. We had _____ (assume) for some time that surgery was a possibility, and we had _____ (find) an excellent facility.

9. Once the storm had _____ (pass), we could see that the old oak tree had _____ (fall).

10. Some high-level employees _____ (decide) to speak publicly about the cover-up before the company's official story had _____ (be) released to the media.

## 51d Using *lay* and *lie*, *sit* and *set*, *raise* and *rise*

*Lay* and *lie*, *sit* and *set*, and *raise* and *rise* cause problems for many writers because both verbs in each pair have similar-sounding forms and related meanings. In each pair, one of the verbs is transitive, meaning that it takes a direct object; the other is intransitive, meaning that it does not take an object. The best way to avoid confusing the two is to memorize their forms and meanings. All these verbs except *raise* are irregular.

| BASE FORM | PAST TENSE | PAST PARTICIPLE | PRESENT PARTICIPLE | -S FORM |
|---|---|---|---|---|
| lie (recline) | lay | lain | lying | lies |
| lay (put) | laid | laid | laying | lays |
| sit (be seated) | sat | sat | sitting | sits |
| set (put) | set | set | setting | sets |
| rise (get up) | rose | risen | rising | rises |
| raise (lift) | raised | raised | raising | raises |

*Lie* is intransitive and means "recline" or "be situated." *Lay* is transitive and means "put" or "place." This pair is especially confusing because *lay* is also the past-tense form of *lie*.

►   The doctor asked the patient to ~~lay~~ <sup>lie</sup> on his side.

►   Jason ~~sat~~ <sup>set</sup> the vase on the table.

►   Sami ~~raised~~ <sup>rose</sup> up in bed and glared at us.

### EXERCISE 51.2

Identify the appropriate verb form in each of the following sentences. Example:

The guests (<u>raised</u> / rose) their glasses to the happy couple.

1. That cat (*lies* / *lays*) on the sofa all morning.
2. The chef (*lay* / *laid*) his knives carefully on the counter.

3. The two-year-old walked carefully across the room and (*set / sat*) the glass vase on the table.

4. Grandpa used to love (*sitting / setting*) on the front porch and telling stories of his childhood.

5. Immediately, the dough (*sitting / setting*) by the oven began to (*raise / rise*).

---

# 51e Indicating verb tenses

Multilingual

Verb tenses show when the action takes place. The three simple tenses are the present tense, the past tense, and the future tense.

| | |
|---|---|
| **PRESENT TENSE** | I *ask*, I *write* |
| **PAST TENSE** | I *asked*, I *wrote* |
| **FUTURE TENSE** | I *will ask*, I *will write* |

More complex aspects of time are expressed through progressive, perfect, and perfect progressive forms of the simple tenses.

| | |
|---|---|
| **PRESENT PROGRESSIVE** | Sue *is asking*, Sue *is writing* |
| **PAST PROGRESSIVE** | Sue *was asking*, Sue *was writing* |
| **FUTURE PROGRESSIVE** | Sue *will be asking*, Sue *will be writing* |
| **PRESENT PERFECT** | Sue *has asked*, Sue *has written* |
| **PAST PERFECT** | Sue *had asked*, Sue *had written* |
| **FUTURE PERFECT** | Sue *will have asked*, Sue *will have written* |
| **PRESENT PERFECT PROGRESSIVE** | Sue *has been asking*, Sue *has been writing* |
| **PAST PERFECT PROGRESSIVE** | Sue *had been asking*, Sue *had been writing* |
| **FUTURE PERFECT PROGRESSIVE** | Sue *will have been asking*, Sue *will have been writing* |

The simple tenses locate an action only within the three basic time frames of present, past, and future. Progressive forms express continuing actions; perfect forms express actions completed before another action or time in the present, past, or future; perfect progressive forms express actions that continue up to some point in the present, past, or future.

## Using present-tense forms

### Simple present

The <u>simple present</u> tense indicates actions or conditions occurring now and those occurring habitually.

▶ **I <u>eat</u> breakfast every day at 8:00 AM.**

▶ **Love <u>conquers</u> all.**

Write about general truths or scientific facts in the simple present, even when the predicate of the sentence is in the past tense.

> makes
> Pasteur demonstrated that his boiling process ~~made~~ milk safe.

Use the simple present, not the past tense, when writing about action in literary works.

> realizes       is
> Ishmael slowly ~~realized~~ all that ~~was~~ at stake in the search for the white
>
> whale.

In general, use the simple present when you are quoting, summarizing, or paraphrasing someone else's writing.

> writes
> Keith Walters ~~wrote~~ that the "reputed consequences and promised
>
> blessings of literacy are legion."

But in an essay using APA (American Psychological Association) style (see Chapter 19), report your experiments or another researcher's work in the past tense (*wrote*, *noted*) or the present perfect (*has reported*).

> has noted
> Comer (1995) ~~notes~~ that protesters who deprive themselves of food are
>
> seen as "caring, sacrificing, even heroic" (p. 5).

*Present progressive*

Use the <u>present progressive</u> form when an action is in progress now. The present progressive uses a present form of *be* (*am*, *is*, *are*) and the *-ing* form of the main verb.

> He <u>is directing</u> a new film.

In contrast, use the simple present tense for actions that frequently occur during a period that might include the present, but that is not necessarily happening now.

> SIMPLE PRESENT       PRESENT PROGRESSIVE
> My sister <u>drives</u> a bus. She <u>is taking</u> a vacation now.

With an appropriate expression of time, you can use the present progressive to indicate a scheduled event in the future.

> We <u>are having</u> friends over for dinner tomorrow night.

Some verbs are rarely used in progressive forms in formal writing. These verbs are said to express unchanging conditions or mental states: *believe*, *belong*, *hate*, *know*, *like*, *love*, *need*, *own*, *resemble*, *understand*. However, in spoken and informal written English, progressive forms like *I'm loving this* and *You're not understanding me correctly* are becoming increasingly common.

### Present perfect

The <u>present perfect</u> tense indicates actions begun in the past and either completed at some unspecified time in the past or continuing into the present. To form the present perfect, use a present form of *have* (*has*, *have*) and a perfect participle such as *talked*.

▶ **Uncontrolled logging <u>has destroyed</u> many tropical forests.**

### Present perfect progressive

Use the <u>present perfect progressive</u> form to indicate continuous actions begun in the past and continuing into the present. To form the present perfect progressive, use the present perfect form of *be* (*have been*, *has been*) and the *-ing* form of the main verb.

▶ **The two sides <u>have been trying</u> to settle the case out of court.**

▶ **Since September, he <u>has been writing</u> a novel in his spare time.**

## Using past-tense forms

In the past tense, you can use simple past, past progressive, past perfect, and past perfect progressive forms.

### Simple past

Use the <u>simple past</u> to indicate actions or conditions that occurred at a specific time and do not extend into the present.

▶ **Germany <u>invaded</u> Poland on September 1, 1939.**

### Past progressive

Use the <u>past progressive</u> when an action was in progress in the past. It is used relatively infrequently in English, and it focuses on duration or calls attention to a past action that went on at the same time as something else. The present progressive uses a past form of *be* (*was*, *were*) and the *-ing* form of the main verb.

▶ **Lenin <u>was living</u> in exile in Zurich when the tsar was overthrown.**

### Past perfect

Use the <u>past perfect</u> to indicate actions or conditions completed by a specific time in the past or before some other past action occurred. To form the past perfect, use *had* and a perfect participle such as *talked*.

▶ **By the fourth century, Christianity <u>had become</u> the state religion.**

*Past perfect progressive*

Use the past perfect progressive form to indicate a continuing action or condition in the past that had already been happening when some other past action happened. (You will probably need the simple past tense for the other past action.) To form the past perfect progressive, use the past perfect form of *be* (*had been*) and the *-ing* form of the main verb.

▶ Carter **had been planning** a naval career until his father died.

## Using future-tense forms

The future tense includes simple, progressive, perfect, and perfect progressive forms.

*Simple future*

Use the simple future (*will* plus the base form of the verb) to indicate actions or conditions that have not yet begun.

▶ The exhibition **will come** to Washington in September.

*Future progressive*

Use the future progressive to indicate continuing actions or conditions in the future. The future progressive uses the future form of *be* (*will be*) and the *-ing* form of the main verb.

▶ The loans **will be coming** due over the next two years.

*Future perfect*

Use the future perfect to indicate actions or conditions that will be completed by or before some specified time in the future. To form the future perfect, use *will have* and a perfect participle such as *talked*.

▶ By next summer, she **will have published** the results of the research study.

*Future perfect progressive*

Use the future perfect progressive to indicate continuing actions or conditions that will be completed by some specified time in the future. To form the future perfect progressive, use the future perfect form of *be* (*will have been*) and the *-ing* form of the main verb.

▶ As of May 1, I **will have been living** in Tucson for five years.

**EXERCISE 51.3**

Complete each of the following sentences by writing an appropriate form of the verb listed in parentheses. Since more than one form will sometimes be possible, be prepared to explain the reasons for your choices. Example:

**The supply of a product _decreases_ (decrease) when the demand is great.**

1. History _____ (show) that crime usually decreases as the economy improves.

2. Ever since the first nuclear power plants were built, opponents _____ (fear) disaster.

3. Thousands of Irish peasants _____ (emigrate) to America after the potato famine of the 1840s.

4. The soap opera *General Hospital* _____ (be) on the air since 1963.

5. Olivia _____ (direct) the play next year.

6. While they _____ (eat) in a local restaurant, they saw a minor accident.

7. By this time next week, each of your clients _____ (receive) an invitation to the opening.

8. By the time a child born today enters first grade, that child _____ (watch) thousands of television commercials.

9. In one of the novel's most famous scenes, Huck _____ (express) his willingness to go to hell rather than report Jim as an escaped slave.

10. A cold typically _____ (last) for about a week and a half.

# 51f Sequencing verb tenses

Careful and accurate use of tenses is important to clear writing. Even the simplest narrative describes actions that take place at different times; when you use the appropriate tense for each action, readers can follow such time changes easily.

▶ **By the time he <u>offered</u> her the money, she <u>had declared</u> bankruptcy.**

QUICK HELP

Editing verb tenses

Errors in verb tenses take several forms. If you have trouble with verb tenses, check for common errors as you proofread.

• Errors of verb form: for example, writing *seen* for *saw*, which confuses the past-participle and past-tense forms (**51e**)

• Omitted auxiliary verbs: for example, using the simple past (*Uncle Charlie arrived*) when meaning requires the present perfect (*Uncle Charlie has arrived*) (**51b and e**)

▶

Editing verb tenses, continued

- Colloquial (informal) varieties of English in situations calling for academic English: for example, writing *they eat it all up* when the situation requires *they ate it all up* (**34b**)

The sequence of tenses shows the relationship between the tense of the verb in the independent clause of a sentence and the tense of a verb in a dependent clause or a verbal (Chapter 49).

## Using infinitives in sequences

Use the underline{infinitive} of a verb — *to* plus the base form (*to go, to be*) — to indicate actions occurring at the same time as or later than the action of the main verb in the clause.

▶ **The child waved to greet the passing trains.**

The waving and the greeting occurred at the same time in the past.

▶ **Each couple hopes to win the dance contest.**

The hoping is present; the winning is in the future.

Use *to have* plus the past participle (*to have asked*) to indicate that an action occurred before the action of the main verb.

▶ **He appeared to have left his wallet at home.**

The leaving of the wallet took place before the appearing.

## Using participles in sequences

Use the underline{present participle} (the base form plus *-ing*) to indicate actions occurring at the same time as the action of the main verb.

▶ **Seeking to relieve unemployment, Roosevelt established several public-works programs.**

Use *having* plus the underline{past participle} to indicate action occurring before that of the main verb.

▶ **Having changed his mind, he voted against the proposal.**

## Using habitual actions in sequences

In conversation, people often use *will* or *would* to describe habitual actions. In writing, however, stick to the present and past tenses for this purpose.

▶ **When I have a deadline, I ~~will~~ work all night.**

▶ **While we sat on the porch, the children ~~would play.~~** played.

◢ **EXERCISE 51.4**

Rewrite each of the following sentences to create the appropriate sequence of tenses. Example:

      *have sent*
**He needs to ~~send~~ in his application before today.**
        ∧

1. When she saw *Wonder Woman*, it had made her want to become an actress even more.

2. Leaving England in December, the settlers arrived in Virginia in May.

3. I hoped to make the football team, but injuries prevented me from trying out.

4. Working with great dedication as a summer intern at the magazine, Mohan called his former supervisor in the fall to ask about a permanent position.

5. As we waited for the bus, we would watch the taxis pass by.

# 51g Using active and passive voice

Voice tells whether the subject is acting (*he questions us*) or being acted upon (*he is questioned*). When the subject is acting, the verb is in the <u>active voice</u>; when the subject is being acted upon, the verb is in the <u>passive voice</u>.

    **ACTIVE VOICE**      The storm <u>uprooted</u> huge pine trees.

    **PASSIVE VOICE**   Huge pine trees <u>were uprooted</u> by the storm.

The passive voice uses the appropriate form of the auxiliary verb *be* followed by the past participle of the main verb: *he is being questioned, he was questioned, he will be questioned, he has been questioned.*

    While passive voice is appropriate and necessary in a lot of scientific writing, most contemporary writers use the active voice as much as possible because it livens up their prose. Passive-voice verbs often make a passage hard to understand and remember. In addition, writers sometimes use the passive voice to avoid taking responsibility for what they have written. A government official who admits that "mistakes were made" skirts the question: who made them?

    To shift a sentence from the passive to the active voice (42c), make the performer of the action the subject of the sentence, and make the recipient of the action an object.

        *My sister took the*
▶  **~~The~~ prizewinning photograph. ~~was taken by my sister.~~**
   ∧                  ∧

    The passive voice can work well in some situations. Journalists often use the passive voice when the performer of an action is unknown or less important than the recipient.

▶  **Colonel Muammar el-Qaddafi <u>was killed</u> during an uprising in his hometown of Surt.**

Much technical and scientific writing uses the passive voice to highlight what is being studied.

▶ **The volunteers' food intake <u>was</u> closely <u>monitored</u>.**

### EXERCISE 51.5

Convert each sentence from active to passive voice or from passive to active, and note the differences in emphasis these changes make. Example:

The                              is advised by Machiavelli
~~Machiavelli advises the~~ prince to gain the friendship of the people.
      ^                            ^

1. The surfers were informed by the lifeguard of a shark sighting.
2. The cartoonist sketched a picture of Sam with huge ears and a pointy chin.
3. The baby kangaroo is protected, fed, and taught how to survive by its mother.
4. The gifts were given out to the children by volunteers dressed as elves.
5. A new advertising company was chosen by the board members.

## 51h Using mood and forming conditional sentences

The mood of a verb indicates the attitude of the writer. The indicative mood states facts and opinions or asks questions. The imperative mood gives commands and instructions. The subjunctive mood (used mainly in clauses beginning with *that* or *if*) expresses wishes or conditions that are contrary to fact.

| | |
|---|---|
| INDICATIVE | I <u>did</u> the right thing. |
| IMPERATIVE | <u>Do</u> the right thing. |
| SUBJUNCTIVE | If I <u>had done</u> the right thing, I would not be in trouble now. |

### Forming subjunctives

The present subjunctive uses the base form, no matter what the subject of the verb is.

▶ **It is important that children <u>be</u> psychologically ready for a new sibling.**

The past subjunctive is the same as the simple past except for the verb *be*, which uses *were* for all subjects.

▶ **He spent money as if he <u>had</u> infinite credit.**

▶ **If the store <u>were</u> better located, it would attract more customers.**

## Using the subjunctive mood

Because the subjunctive can create a rather formal tone, many people today tend to substitute the indicative mood in informal conversation.

▶ **If I *was* a better swimmer, I would try out for the team.** [informal]

Nevertheless, formal writing still requires the use of the subjunctive in the following kinds of dependent clauses:

### Clauses expressing a wish

▶ **He wished that his mother <u>were</u> still living nearby.**

### As if and as though clauses

▶ **He started down the trail as if he <u>were</u> walking on ice.**

### That clauses expressing a request or demand

▶ **The job requires that the employee <u>be</u> in good physical condition.**

### If clauses expressing a condition that does not exist

▶ **If the sale of tobacco <u>were</u> banned, tobacco companies would suffer a great loss.**

One common error is to use *would* in both clauses. Use the subjunctive in the *if* clause and *would* in the main clause.

▶ **If I <s>would have</s> played harder, I would have won.**
  had

## Forming conditional sentences

Multilingual

Sentences that use an *if* clause don't always require subjunctive forms. Each of the following conditional sentences makes different assumptions about whether or not the *if* clause is true.

▶ **If you <u>practice</u> writing frequently, you <u>know</u> what your chief problems are.**

This sentence assumes that what is stated in the *if* clause is probably true. Any tense that is appropriate may be used in both the *if* clause and the main clause.

**mood**

▶ **If you practice writing for the rest of this term, you will understand the process better.**

This sentence makes a prediction. The main clause uses the future tense (*will understand*) or some other modal that can indicate future time (*may understand*). The *if* clause uses the present tense.

▶ **If you practiced writing every single day, it would eventually seem much easier to you.**

This sentence indicates doubt. In the *if* clause, the verb is past subjunctive, even though it refers to future time. The main clause contains *would* + the base form of the main verb.

▶ **If you practiced writing on Mars, you would find no one to read your work.**

This sentence imagines an impossible situation. The past subjunctive is used in the *if* clause, although past time is not being referred to, and *would* + the base form is used in the main clause.

▶ **If you had practiced writing in ancient Egypt, you would have used hieroglyphics.**

This sentence shifts the impossibility to the past; obviously, you aren't going to find yourself in ancient Egypt. But a past impossibility demands a form that is "more past": the past perfect in the *if* clause and *would* + the perfect form of the verb in the main clause.

---

◢ **EXERCISE 51.6**

Revise any of the following sentences that do not use the appropriate subjunctive verb forms required in formal writing. Example:

>                                *were*
> I saw how carefully he moved, as if he ~~was~~ holding an infant.
>                                     ^

1. Josh kept spending money as if he was still earning high commissions.
2. Marvina wished that she was able to take her daughter along on the business trip.
3. Protesters demanded that the senator resign from her post.
4. If the vaccine was more readily available, the county health department would recommend that everyone receive the shot.
5. It is critical that the liquid remains at room temperature for at least seven hours.

▼ ▼ ▼ ▼ ▼ ▼ ▼ ▼ ▼ ▼ ▼ ▼ ▼ ▼ ▼ ▼ ▼ ▼ ▼ ▼ ▼ ▼ ▼ ▼ ▼ ▼

## THINKING CRITICALLY ABOUT VERBS

### Reading with an eye for verbs

Take the time to study a newspaper with an eye for its verbs. Copy down several examples of strong verbs as well as a few examples of weak or overused verbs. For the weak ones, try to come up with better choices.

### Thinking about your own use of verbs

Writing that relies too heavily on the verbs *be, do,* and *have* almost always bores readers. Look at something you've written recently to see whether you rely too heavily on these verbs, and revise accordingly.

# CHAPTER 52

# Subject-Verb Agreement

In everyday terms, the word *agreement* refers to an accord of some sort: friends agree to go to a movie; an employer and a workers' union negotiate an agreement about higher wages. In most sentences, making subjects and verbs agree is fairly simple; only a few subject-verb constructions cause confusion.

## 52a Understanding subject-verb agreement

In academic varieties of English, verbs must agree with their subjects in number (singular or plural) and in person (first, second, or third).

To make a <u>verb</u> in the present tense agree with a third-person singular <u>subject</u>, add -*s* or -*es* to the base form.

▶ **A vegetarian <u>diet</u> <u>lowers</u> the risk of heart disease.**

To make a verb in the present tense agree with any other subject, use the base form of the verb.

▶ **<u>I</u> <u>miss</u> my family.**
▶ **<u>They</u> <u>live</u> in another state.**

The verbs *have* and *be* do not follow the -*s* or -*es* pattern with third-person singular subjects. *Have* changes to *has*; *be* has irregular forms in both the present and past tenses and in the first person as well as the third person. (See Chapter 51.)

▶ **<u>War</u> <u>is</u> hell.**
▶ **The <u>soldier</u> <u>was</u> brave beyond the call of duty.**

In some varieties of African American or regional English, third-person singular verb forms do not end with -*s* or -*es*: *She go to work every day*. In most academic writing, however, your audience will expect third-person singular verb forms to end in -*s* or -*es* (51a).

---

QUICK HELP

Editing for subject-verb agreement

- Identify the subject that goes with each verb. Cover up any words between the subject and the verb to identify agreement problems more easily. **(52b)**
- Check compound subjects. Those joined by *and* usually take a plural verb form. With those subjects joined by *or* or *nor*, however, the verb agrees with the part of the subject closest to the verb. **(52c)**
- Check collective-noun subjects. These nouns take a singular verb form when they refer to a group as a single unit but a plural form when they refer to the multiple members of a group. **(52d)**
- Check indefinite-pronoun subjects. Most take a singular verb form. *Both, few, many, others,* and *several* take a plural form; and *all, any, enough, more, most, none,* and *some* can be either singular or plural, depending on the noun they refer to. **(52e)**

---

## 52b  Making separated subjects and verbs agree

Make sure the <u>verb</u> agrees with the <u>subject</u> and not with another noun that falls in between.

▶ A <u>vase</u> of flowers <u>makes</u> a room attractive.

▶ Many books on the best-seller list ~~has~~ little literary value.
<sub>have</sub>

The simple subject is *books*, not *list*.

Be careful when you use phrases beginning with *as well as, along with, in addition to, together with,* or similar prepositions. They do not make a singular subject plural.

▶ A passenger, as well as the driver, ~~were~~ injured in the accident.
<sub>was</sub>

Though this sentence has a grammatically singular subject, it suggests the idea of a plural subject. The sentence makes better sense with a compound subject: *The driver and a passenger were injured in the accident.*

---

### EXERCISE 52.1

Identify the appropriate verb form in each of the following sentences. Example:

**The benefits of family planning (*is /are*) not apparent to many people.**

1. Soldiers who are injured while fighting for their country (*deserves / deserve*) complete medical coverage.

2. The dog, followed by his owner, (*races / race*) wildly down the street every afternoon.

3. Just when I think I can go home, another pile of invoices (*appears / appear*) on my desk.

4. The pattern of secrecy and lies (*needs / need*) to stop in order for counseling to be successful.

5. A substance abuser often (*hides / hide*) the truth to cover up his or her addiction.

6. The police chief, in addition to several soldiers and two civilians, (*was / were*) injured in the explosion.

7. Garlic's therapeutic value as well as its flavor (*comes / come*) from sulfur compounds.

8. The fiber content of cereal (*contributes / contribute*) to its nutritional value.

9. The graphics on this computer game often (*causes / cause*) my system to crash.

10. Current research on opioid addiction, in spite of the best efforts of hundreds of scientists, (*leaves / leave*) serious questions unanswered.

## 52c Making verbs agree with compound subjects

Two or more <u>subjects</u> joined by *and* generally require a plural <u>verb</u> form.

▶ <u>Tony and his friend</u> <u>commute</u> from Louisville.

▶ A backpack, a canteen, and a rifle ~~was~~ issued to each recruit.
  <sup>were</sup>

When subjects joined by *and* are considered a single unit or refer to the same person or thing, they take a singular verb form.

▶ <u>George W. Bush's older brother and political ally</u> <u>was</u> the governor of

Florida.

▶ Drinking and driving ~~remain~~ a major cause of highway fatalities.
  <sup>remains</sup>

  In this sentence, *drinking and driving* is considered a single activity, and a singular verb is used.

If the word *each* or *every* precedes subjects joined by *and*, the verb form is singular.

▶ <u>Each</u> <u>boy</u> and <u>girl</u> <u>chooses</u> one gift to take home.

With subjects joined by *or* or *nor*, the verb agrees with the part closest to the verb.

▶ **Neither my roommate nor my neighbors *like* my loud music.**

▶ **Either the witnesses or the defendant ~~are~~ lying.**
(is)

If you find this sentence awkward, put the plural noun closest to the verb: *Either the defendant or the witnesses <u>are</u> lying.*

## 52d Making verbs agree with collective nouns

Collective nouns — such as *family, team, audience, group, jury, crowd, band, class,* and *committee* — refer to a group. Collective nouns can take either singular or plural verb forms, depending on whether they refer to the group as a single unit or to the multiple members of the group. The meaning of a sentence as a whole is your guide to whether a collective noun refers to a unit or to the multiple parts of a unit.

▶ **After deliberating, the jury *reports* its verdict.**

The jury acts as a single unit.

▶ **The jury still *disagree* on a number of counts.**

The members of the jury act as multiple individuals.

▶ **The duck family ~~scatters~~ when the cat approaches.**
(scatter)

*Family* here refers to the many ducks; they cannot scatter as one.

Treat fractions that refer to singular nouns as singular and those that refer to plural nouns as plural.

SINGULAR     Two-thirds of the park *has* burned.
PLURAL         Two-thirds of the students *were* commuters.

Even though *eyeglasses, scissors, pants,* and other such words refer to single items, they take plural verbs because they are made up of pairs.

▶ **Where *are* my reading glasses?**

Treat phrases starting with *the number of* as singular and with *a number of* as plural.

SINGULAR     The number of applicants for the internship *was* unbelievable.
PLURAL         A number of applicants *were* put on the waiting list.

## 52e Making verbs agree with indefinite pronouns

Indefinite pronouns do not refer to specific persons or things. Most take singular verb forms.

**SOME COMMON INDEFINITE PRONOUNS**

| | | | |
|---|---|---|---|
| another | each | much | one |
| any | either | neither | other |
| anybody | everybody | nobody | somebody |
| anyone | everyone | no one | someone |
| anything | everything | nothing | something |

▶ Of the two jobs, <u>neither holds</u> much appeal.

▶ Each of the plays ~~depict~~ *depicts* a hero undone by a tragic flaw.

*Both, few, many, others,* and *several* are plural.

▶ Though <u>many apply</u>, <u>few are</u> chosen.

*All, any, enough, more, most, none,* and *some* can be singular or plural, depending on the noun they refer to.

▶ All of the cake *was* eaten.

▶ All of the candidates *promise* to improve the schools.

## 52f Making verbs agree with *who, which,* and *that*

When the relative pronouns *who, which,* and *that* are used as a subject, the verb agrees with the antecedent of the pronoun.

▶ Fear is an ingredient that *goes* into creating stereotypes.

▶ Guilt and fear are ingredients that *go* into creating stereotypes.

Problems often occur with the words *one of the.* In general, *one of the* takes a plural verb, while *only one of the* takes a singular verb.

▶ **Carla is one of the employees who always ~~works~~ overtime.**
  <sub>work</sub>

Some employees always work overtime. Carla is among them. Thus *who* refers to *employees*, and the verb is plural.

▶ **Ming is the only one of the employees who always ~~work~~ overtime.**
  <sub>works</sub>

Only one employee always works overtime, and that employee is Ming. Thus *one*, and not *employees*, is the antecedent of *who*, and the verb form is singular.

## 52g Making linking verbs agree with subjects

A linking verb should agree with its subject, which usually precedes the verb, not with the subject complement, which follows it (49a).

▶ **Three key treaties ~~is~~ the topic of my talk.**
  <sub>are</sub>

The subject is *treaties*, not *topic*.

▶ **Nero Wolfe's passion ~~were~~ orchids.**
  <sub>was</sub>

The subject is *passion*, not *orchids*.

## 52h Making verbs agree with subjects ending in -s

Some words that end in *-s* appear plural but are singular and thus take singular verb forms.

▶ **Measles still ~~strike~~ many Americans.**
  <sub>strikes</sub>

Some nouns of this kind (such as *statistics* and *politics*) may be either singular or plural, depending on context.

| | |
|---|---|
| SINGULAR | Statistics *is* a course I really dread. |
| PLURAL | The statistics in that study *are* highly questionable. |

## 52i Making verbs agree with following subjects

In English, verbs usually follow subjects. When this order is reversed, make the verb agree with the subject, not with a noun that happens to precede it.

▶ **Beside the barn ~~stands~~ silos filled with grain.**
  <sub>stand</sub>

The subject is *silos*; it is plural, so the verb must be *stand*.

In sentences beginning with *there is, there are, there was,* or *there were,* the word *there* serves only as a placeholder; the subject follows the verb.

▶ There <u>are</u> five basic <u>positions</u> in classical ballet.

The subject, *positions,* is plural, so the verb must also be plural.

## 52j Making verbs agree with titles and with words used as words

When the subject is the title of a book, film, or other work of art, the verb form is singular even if the title is plural in form.

▶ *One Writer's Beginnings* <u>describes</u> Eudora Welty's childhood.

Similarly, a word referred to as a word requires a singular verb form even if the word itself is plural.

▶ *Steroids* <u>is</u> a little word that packs a big punch in the world of sports.

### EXERCISE 52.2

Revise any of the following sentences as necessary to establish subject-verb agreement. (Some of the sentences do not require any change.) Example:

          darts
Into the shadows ~~dart~~ the frightened raccoon.

1. Room and board are the most expensive part of my college education.
2. *Goodfellas* tell the story of a boy growing up to be a mobster.
3. Hanging near the *Mona Lisa* is many more Renaissance paintings.
4. Most of the students oppose the shortened dining hall hours.
5. Each of the security workers are considered trained after viewing a twenty-minute videotape.
6. Neither his expensive clothes nor his charm were enough to get him the job.
7. The committee were expected to produce its annual report two weeks early.
8. My grandmother is the only one of my relatives who still goes to church.
9. Sweden was one of the few European countries that was neutral in 1943.
10. Economics involve the study of the distribution of goods and services.

▼ ▼ ▼ ▼ ▼ ▼ ▼ ▼ ▼ ▼ ▼ ▼ ▼ ▼ ▼ ▼ ▼ ▼ ▼ ▼ ▼ ▼ ▼ ▼

## THINKING CRITICALLY ABOUT SUBJECT-VERB AGREEMENT

### Reading with an eye for subject-verb agreement

The following passage, from a 1990 essay questioning a "traditional" view of marriage, includes several instances of complicated subject-verb agreement. Note the rules governing subject-verb agreement in each case.

> Marriage seems to me more conflict-ridden than ever, and the divorce rate—with or without new babies in the house—remains constant. The fabric of men-and-women-as-they-once-were is so thin in places no amount of patching can weave that cloth together again. The longing for connection may be strong, but even stronger is the growing perception that only people who are real to themselves can connect. Two shall be as one is over, no matter how lonely we get.
>
> —VIVIAN GORNICK, "Who Says We Haven't Made a Revolution?"

### Thinking about your own use of subject-verb agreement

*Visiting relatives is / are treacherous.* Either verb makes a grammatically acceptable sentence, yet the verbs result in two very different statements. Write a brief explanation of the two possible meanings. Then write a paragraph or two about visiting relatives. Using the information in this chapter, examine each subject and its verb. Do you maintain subject-verb agreement throughout? Revise to correct any errors you find. If you find any patterns, make a note to yourself of things to look for routinely as you revise your writing.

# CHAPTER 53

# Pronouns

These directions show one reason why it's important to use pronouns clearly:

> When you see a dirt road turning left off Winston Lane, follow it for two more miles.

The word *it* could mean either the dirt road or Winston Lane. Pronouns can improve understanding, but only when they're used carefully and accurately.

## 53a Understanding pronoun case

Most speakers of English know intuitively when to use *I*, *me*, or *my*. The choice reflects differences in case, the form a pronoun takes to indicate its function in a sentence. Pronouns functioning as subjects are in the subjective case; those functioning as objects are in the objective case; and those functioning as possessives are in the possessive case.

**SUBJECTIVE PRONOUNS**

| | | | | |
|---|---|---|---|---|
| I/we | you | he/she/it | they | who/whoever |

**OBJECTIVE PRONOUNS**

| | | | | |
|---|---|---|---|---|
| me/us | you | him/her/it | them | whom/whomever |

**POSSESSIVE PRONOUNS**

| | | | | |
|---|---|---|---|---|
| my/our | your | his/hers/its | their | whose |
| mine/ours | yours | his/hers/its | theirs | |

### Using pronouns as subjects

Use a <u>subjective pronoun</u> as a subject of a clause, a subject complement, or an appositive renaming a subject or subject complement (49a).

**SUBJECT OF A CLAUSE**

<u>They</u> could either fight or face certain death with the lions.

<u>Who</u> is your closest friend?

Pedro told the story to Lizzie, <u>who</u> told all her friends.

SUBJECT COMPLEMENT

The person in charge was <u>she</u>.

APPOSITIVE RENAMING A SUBJECT OR SUBJECT COMPLEMENT

Three colleagues — Peter, John, and <u>she</u> — worked on the program.

Americans often use the objective case for subject complements, especially in conversation: *Who's there? It's me.* However, expect to use the subjective case in formal writing. If you find the subjective case stilted or awkward, try rewriting the sentence using the pronoun as the subject.

▶ ~~The~~ first person to see Kishore after the awards. ~~was she.~~
    *She was the*

## Using pronouns as objects

Use an objective pronoun as a <u>direct or indirect object</u> (of a verb or verbal), an object of a preposition, an appositive renaming an object, or when the pronoun is followed by an infinitive (49a and c).

OBJECT OF A VERB OR VERBAL

The professor surprised <u>us</u> with a quiz. [direct object of *surprised*]

The grateful owner gave <u>them</u> a reward. [indirect object of *gave*]

The Parisians were always wonderful about helping <u>me</u>. [direct object of gerund]

OBJECT OF A PREPOSITION

Several friends went with <u>him</u>.

APPOSITIVE RENAMING AN OBJECT

The committee elected two representatives, Sach and <u>me</u>.

PRONOUN FOLLOWED BY AN INFINITIVE

The students convinced <u>him</u> to vote for the school bond.

## Using pronouns as possessives

Use a <u>possessive pronoun</u> to show possession or ownership. Notice that there are two forms of possessive pronouns: those that function as adjectives (*my, your, his, her, its, our, their, whose*) and those that take the place of a noun (*mine, yours, his, hers, its, ours, theirs, whose*).

**ADJECTIVE FORMS**

People were buying <u>their</u> tickets weeks in advance of the show.

<u>Whose</u> fault was the accident?

**NOUN FORMS**

The responsibility is <u>hers</u>.

<u>Whose</u> is this blue backpack?

When a pronoun appears before a verbal (49d) that ends in *-ing*, using a possessive pronoun leads to a different meaning than using an objective pronoun.

▶ **I remember *their* singing.**

The possessive pronoun *their* makes *singing* the object of *remember*.

▶ **I remember *them* singing.**

The pronoun *them* is the object of *remember*, and *singing* modifies *them*.

Choose the pronoun that makes sense for the meaning you want to convey.

## 53b Using *who, whoever, whom,* and *whomever*

A common problem with pronoun case is deciding whether to use *who* or *whom*. Even when traditional grammar requires *whom*, many Americans use *who* instead, especially in speech. Nevertheless, you should understand the difference between *who* and *whom* so that you can make informed choices in situations such as formal college writing that may call for the use of *whom* (or *whomever*) in the objective case.

Two particular situations lead to confusion with *who* and *whom*: when they begin a question and when they introduce a dependent clause.

## Choosing *who* or *whom* in questions

You can determine whether to use *who* or *whom* at the beginning of a question by answering the question using a personal pronoun. If the answer is *he, she,* or *they,* use *who*; if it is *him, her,* or *them,* use *whom*.

▶ ~~Whom~~ Who do you think wrote the story?

   I think *she* wrote the story. *She* is subjective, so *who* is correct.

▶ ~~Who~~ Whom did you visit?

   I visited *them. Them* is objective, so *whom* is correct.

## Using *who, whoever, whom,* and *whomever* in dependent clauses

The function a pronoun serves in a dependent clause determines whether you should choose *who* or *whom, whoever* or *whomever* — no matter how that clause functions in the sentence. If the pronoun acts as a subject or subject complement in the clause, use *who* or *whoever*. If the pronoun acts as an object, use *whom* or *whomever*.

▶ The center is open to ~~whomever~~ whoever wants to use it.

   *Whoever* is the subject of the clause *whoever wants to use it.* (The clause is the object of the preposition *to,* but the clause's function in the sentence does not affect the case of the pronoun.)

▶ The new president was not ~~who~~ whom she had expected.

   Here, *whom* is the object of the verb *had expected* in the clause *whom she had expected.*

If you are not sure which case to use, try separating the dependent clause from the rest of the sentence. Rewrite the clause as a new sentence, and substitute a personal pronoun for *who(ever)* or *whom(ever).* If the pronoun is in the subjective case, use *who* or *whoever*; if it is in the objective case, use *whom* or *whomever*.

▶ **The minister glared at (*whoever/whomever*) made any noise.**

Isolate the clause *whoever/whomever made any noise*. Substituting a personal pronoun gives you *they made any noise*. *They* is in the subjective case; therefore, *The minister glared at <u>whoever</u> made any noise.*

▶ **The minister glared at whoever ~~she thought~~ made any noise.**

Ignore such expressions as *he thinks* and *she says* when you isolate the clause.

---

### EXERCISE 53.1

Choose *who*, *whoever*, *whom*, or *whomever* to complete the blank in each of the following sentences. Example:

**Vrinda is someone \_\_\_\_who\_\_\_ will go far.**

1. _____ did you say was our most likely suspect?
2. _____ the audience chooses will move up to the next level.
3. The awards banquet will recognize _____ made the honor roll.
4. Professor Quiñones asked _____ we wanted to collaborate with.
5. _____ received the highest score?

---

## 53c Considering case in compound structures

When a pronoun is part of a compound structure, put it in the same case you would use if the pronoun were alone.

▶ **Come to the park with José and ~~I~~.** me.

Eliminating the other part of the compound, *José and*, leaves *Come to the park with me.*

▶ **When ~~him~~ and Zelda were first married, they lived in New York.** he

▶ **The boss invited ~~she~~ and her family to dinner.** her

▶ **This morning saw yet another conflict between my sister and ~~I~~.** me.

To decide whether to use the subjective or objective case in a compound structure, mentally delete the rest of the compound and try the pronoun alone.

▶ **Come to the park with Anh and I.**

Mentally deleting *Anh and* results in *Come to the park with I*. Rewrite as *Come to the park with Anh and me.*

## 53d  Considering case in elliptical constructions

In elliptical constructions, some words are left out but understood. A pronoun in an elliptical construction should be in the case it would be in if the construction were complete.

▶   **His brother has always been more athletic than** *he* [**is**]**.**

Sometimes the case depends on the meaning intended.

▶   **Willie likes Lily more than** *she* [**likes Lily**]**.**

> *She* is the subject of the implied clause *she likes Lily*.

▶   **Willie likes Lily more than** [**he likes**] *her***.**

> *Her* is the object of the verb *likes* in the implied clause *he likes her*.

## 53e  Using *we* or *us* before a noun

If you aren't sure whether to use *we* or *us* before a noun, recast the sentence without the noun. Use the pronoun that would be correct without the noun.

▶   **~~Us~~ fans never give up hope.** *(We)*

> *Fans* is the subject, so the pronoun should be subjective.

▶   **The Rangers depend on ~~we~~ fans.** *(us)*

> *Fans* is the object of a preposition, so the pronoun should be objective.

### ◢ EXERCISE 53.2

Identify the appropriate pronoun from the pair in parentheses in each of the following sentences. Example:

> **The possibility of (*their* / *them*) succeeding never occurred to me.**

1. Max has had more car accidents than Gabriella, but he still insists he is a better driver than (*she* / *her*).
2. Swimming with Hank and (*they* / *them*) reminded me of summers at the lake.
3. The coach gave honorable-mention ribbons to the two who didn't win any races—Aiden and (*I* / *me*).

4. There seemed to be no reason for (*them / their*) voluntarily studying on a Saturday night.

5. Tomorrow (*we / us*) recruits will have our first on-the-job test.

## 53f Making pronouns agree with antecedents

The antecedent of the pronoun is the word the pronoun refers to. The antecedent usually appears before the pronoun — earlier in the sentence or in a previous sentence. Pronouns and antecedents are said to agree when they match up in person, number, and gender.

▶ The **conductor** raised **her** baton, and the **boys** picked up **their** music.

### Using compound antecedents

Compound antecedents joined by *and* require plural pronouns.

▶ **My parents and I** tried to resolve **our** disagreement.

A compound antecedent preceded by *each* or *every*, however, takes a singular pronoun.

▶ **Every plant** and **animal** has **its** own ecological niche.

With a compound antecedent joined by *or* or *nor*, the pronoun agrees with the nearest antecedent. If the parts of the antecedent are of different genders or persons, however, this kind of sentence can be awkward, sexist, or noninclusive. The sentence might be improved by using singular *they* (53g).

| AWKWARD | Neither Annie nor Barry got *his* work done. |
|---------|----------------------------------------------|
| REVISED | Neither Annie nor Barry got *their* work done. |

When a compound antecedent contains both singular and plural parts, the sentence may sound awkward unless the plural part comes last.

        newspaper        radio stations      their
▶ Neither the ~~radio stations~~ nor the ~~newspaper~~ would reveal ~~its~~ sources.

### Using collective-noun antecedents

A collective-noun antecedent (*herd, team, audience*) that refers to a single unit requires a singular pronoun.

▶ The audience fixed *its* attention on center stage.

When such an antecedent refers to the multiple parts of the unit, however, it requires a plural pronoun.

▶ The director chose this cast because *they* had experience in their roles.

## Using indefinite-pronoun antecedents

Indefinite pronouns (52e) do not refer to specific persons or things. A pronoun whose antecedent is an indefinite pronoun should agree with it in number. Many indefinite pronouns are always singular (as with *one*); a few are always plural (as with *many*). Some can be singular or plural depending on the context.

▶ One of the ballerinas lost *her* balance.

▶ Many in the audience jumped to *their* feet.

▶ Some of the antique furniture was showing *its* age. [singular meaning for *some*]

▶ Some of the local farmers abandoned *their* land. [plural meaning for *some*]

---

**QUICK HELP**

Editing for pronoun-antecedent agreement

- Check all subjects joined by *and* or *or*. Rewrite any sentence in which agreement creates awkwardness.
- Check all uses of *anyone, each, everybody, many,* and other indefinite pronouns (see list in 52e) to be sure they are treated as singular or plural, as appropriate.
- If you find *he, his,* or *him* used to refer to persons of unknown gender or to persons who reject the binary distinction between *him* and *her,* rewrite the sentences altogether. Keep in mind that some individuals do not identify with *he* or *she;* see 53f and g to learn about uses of "singular *they.*"

---

# 53g Avoiding sexist and noninclusive pronouns

Indefinite pronouns often serve as antecedents. Writers used to use a masculine pronoun, known as the generic *he,* to refer to such indefinite pronouns. However, such wording ignores females and excludes individuals who do not identify as *he* or *she.*

When the antecedent is *anybody, each, everybody,* or *everyone,* some people avoid the generic *he* by using a plural pronoun — what some now call "singular *they.*"

▶ Each student should check *their* account by midnight tonight.

If you are writing for situations in which formal choices are expected, be aware that some people believe that it's a mistake to use the plural *their* with singular antecedents such as *anybody, each,* and *everyone.* However, you will hear such sentences in conversation and see them in more and more writing.

---

QUICK HELP

Editing for inclusion

*Everyone should know <u>his</u> legal rights.*

*Everyone should know <u>his or her</u> legal rights.*

Here are three ways to express the same idea without *his* (sexist) or *his or her* (noninclusive):

1. Revise to make the antecedent a plural noun.
   *All citizens should know <u>their</u> legal rights.*

2. Use *they* as a gender-neutral solution.
   *Everyone should know <u>their</u> legal rights.*

3. Revise the sentence altogether.
   *Everyone should have some knowledge of basic legal rights.*

---

⬛ **EXERCISE 53.3**

Revise the following sentences as needed to create pronoun-antecedent agreement and to eliminate the generic *he* and any awkward pronoun references. Some can be revised in more than one way. Examples:

>              a
> **Every graduate submitted ~~his~~ diploma card.**
>               ^

> All graduates          their         cards.
> **~~Every graduate~~ submitted ~~his~~ ~~diploma card~~.**
>  ^                   ^        ^

1. While shopping for a new computer for school, I noticed that a laptop costs much less than they used to.

2. Congress usually resists a president's attempt to encroach on what they consider their authority.

3. Marco and Ellen were each given a chance to voice their opinion.

4. An ER doctor needs to be swift; he also needs to be calm and careful.

5. Every dog and cat has their own personality.

---

# 53h Revising ambiguous pronoun references

If a pronoun can refer to more than one antecedent, revise the sentence to make the meaning clear.

>                           the bridge
> ▶ **The car went over the bridge just before ~~it~~ fell into the water.**
>                                                ^

What fell into the water — the car or the bridge? The revision makes the meaning clear by replacing the pronoun *it* with *the bridge*.

▶ Kerry told Ellen, ~~she~~ should be ready soon.

<sub>"I</sub> above ~~she~~, <sub>"</sub> after soon

Reporting Kerry's words directly, in quotation marks, eliminates the ambiguity.

---

**QUICK HELP**

Editing for clear pronoun reference

1. Identify a specific antecedent that each pronoun refers to. If you cannot find a specific antecedent, supply one. **(53h, i, and k)**

2. If the pronoun refers to more than one antecedent, revise the sentence. If the pronoun and its antecedent are so far apart that the reader cannot connect the two, replace the pronoun with the appropriate noun. **(53h)**

3. Be sure that any use of *you* refers to your specific reader or readers. **(53k)**

## 53i Revising vague use of *it*, *this*, *that*, and *which*

Writers often use *it*, *this*, *that*, or *which* as a shortcut for referring to something mentioned earlier. But such shortcuts can cause confusion. Make sure that these pronouns refer clearly to a specific antecedent.

▶ When the senators realized the bill would be defeated, they tried to

postpone the vote but failed. ~~It~~ was a fiasco.

*The entire effort* (above ~~It~~)

▶ Nancy just found out that she won the lottery, ~~which~~ explains her

*and her sudden wealth* (above ~~which~~)

resignation.

If a *that* or *which* clause refers to a specific noun, put the clause directly after the noun, if possible.

▶ We worked all night on the float ~~for the Rose Parade~~ that our club was

going to sponsor.

*for the Rose Parade.* (above sponsor)

Does *that* refer to the float or the parade? The editing here makes the meaning clear.

## 53j Using *who*, *which*, or *that* to refer to people

Use *who* to refer primarily to people or to animals with names. *Which* and *that* generally refer to animals or to things.

*who*

▶ The veterinarian ~~that~~ operated saved my dog's life.

*which*

▶ Cats, ~~who~~ are my favorite animals, often seem aloof.

## 53k Revising indefinite use of *you*, *it*, and *they*

In conversation, we frequently use *you*, *it*, and *they* in an indefinite sense in such expressions as *you never know*; *it said in the paper*; and *on television, they said*. In college writing, however, use *you* only to mean "you, the reader," and *they* only to refer to a clear antecedent.

▶ Commercials try to make ~~you~~ buy without thinking. [people]

▶ ~~On the~~ Weather Channel/ ~~it~~ reported that the earthquake devastated [The]

parts of Pakistan.

▶ ~~In France, they~~ allow dogs. ~~in most restaurants.~~ [Most restaurants in France]

## 53l Revising implied antecedents

Though an adjective or possessive may imply a noun antecedent, it does not serve as a clear antecedent.

▶ In ~~Alexa's~~ formal complaint, ~~she~~ showed why the test question was [her] [Alexa]

wrong.

### EXERCISE 53.4

Revise each of the following items to clarify pronoun reference. Most of the items can be revised in more than one way. If a pronoun refers ambiguously to more than one possible antecedent, revise the sentence to reflect each possible meaning. Examples:

~~After Jane left/.~~ Miranda found ~~her keys.~~ [Miranda found Jane's keys after]

~~After Jane left/.~~ Miranda found ~~her keys.~~ [Miranda found her own keys after]

1. All scholarship applicants must fill out a financial aid form, meet with the dean, and write a letter to the committee members. The deadline is October 24, so they should start the process as soon as possible.

2. Patients on medication may relate better to their therapists, be less vulnerable to what disturbs them, and be more responsive to them.

3. Ms. Dunbar wanted to speak to my mother before she spoke to me.

4. In Texas, you often hear about the influence of big oil corporations.

5. A small band of protestors picketed the new shopping center, which outraged many residents.

⬛ **EXERCISE 53.5**

Revise the following paragraph to establish a clear antecedent for every pronoun that needs one.

> In the summer of 2005, the NCAA banned the use of mascots that could be considered offensive to American Indians at any of their championship games. In order to understand this, it is important to consider that movies and television programs for years portrayed them as savage warriors that were feared and misunderstood. That is why some schools have chosen to use Indians as their mascot, a role typically played by wild animals or fictional beasts. You would not tolerate derogatory terms for other ethnic groups being used for school mascots. In the NCAA's new ruling, they ask schools to eliminate mascots that may be hurtful or offensive to America's indigenous population.

▽ ▽ ▽ ▽ ▽ ▽ ▽ ▽ ▽ ▽ ▽ ▽ ▽ ▽ ▽ ▽ ▽ ▽ ▽ ▽ ▽ ▽ ▽ ▽ ▽

## THINKING CRITICALLY ABOUT PRONOUNS

Turn to a recent piece of your writing (something at least four pages long), and analyze your use of pronouns. Look carefully at the pronoun case you tend to use most; if it is first person, ask whether *I* is used too much. And if you find that you rely heavily on any one case (*you*, for example), decide whether your writing seems monotonous as a result. Also take a look at whether you tend to use masculine pronouns exclusively to refer to people generally; if so, ask whether you would be more inclusive if you revised to use plural pronouns that are not marked as either masculine or feminine (such as *we* or *they*). Look at your work with this idea in mind: it's always best to use the pronouns people use for themselves, if you know what those are. Finally, check to make sure that your pronouns and their antecedents agree and that the pronouns refer clearly and directly to antecedents.

## CHAPTER 54

# Adjectives and Adverbs

As words that describe other words, adjectives and adverbs add liveliness and color to writing, helping writers show rather than just tell. In addition, adjectives and adverbs often provide indispensable meanings to the words they modify. In basketball, for example, there is an important difference between a *flagrant* foul and a *technical* foul, or an *angry* coach and an *abusively angry* coach. In each instance, the modifiers are crucial to accurate communication.

## 54a Understanding adjectives and adverbs

Adjectives modify nouns and pronouns, answering the question *which? how many?* or *what kind?* Adverbs modify verbs, adjectives, other adverbs, or entire clauses; they answer the question *how? when? where?* or *to what extent?* Many adverbs are formed by adding *-ly* to adjectives (*slight, slightly*), but many are not (*outdoors, very*). And some words that end in *-ly* are adjectives (*lovely, homely*). To tell adjectives and adverbs apart, identify the word's function in the sentence.

---

**QUICK HELP**

Editing adjectives and adverbs

- Scrutinize each adjective and adverb. Consider synonyms for each one to see whether you have chosen the best word possible.
- See if a more specific noun would eliminate the need for an adjective (*mansion* rather than *enormous house*, for instance); do the same with verbs and adverbs.
- Consider adding an adjective or adverb that might make your writing more vivid or specific.
- Make sure all adjectives modify nouns or pronouns and all adverbs modify verbs, adjectives, or other adverbs. Check especially for proper use of *good* and *well*, *bad* and *badly*, *real* and *really*. **(54c)**
- Make sure all comparisons are complete. **(54d)**
- If English is not your first language, check that adjectives are in the right order. **(54g)**

## 54b  Using adjectives after linking verbs

When adjectives come after linking verbs, they usually describe the subject: *I am patient*. Note that in specific sentences, some verbs may or may not act as linking verbs — *look, appear, sound, feel, smell, taste, grow*, and *prove*, for instance. When a word following one of these verbs modifies the subject, use an underline{adjective}; when the word modifies the verb, use an underline{adverb}.

ADJECTIVE        Fluffy looked angry.

ADVERB           Fluffy looked angrily at the poodle.

Linking verbs suggest a state of being, not an action. In the preceding examples, *looked angry* suggests the state of being angry; *looked angrily* suggests an angry action.

## 54c  Using adverbs

In everyday conversation, you will often hear (and perhaps use) adjectives in place of adverbs. When you write in standard academic English, however, use adverbs to modify verbs, adjectives, and other adverbs.

▶  You can feel the song's meter if you listen ~~careful.~~ carefully.

▶  The audience was ~~real~~ really disappointed by the show.

### Using *good* and *well, bad* and *badly*

The modifiers *good, well, bad*, and *badly* cause problems for many writers because the distinctions between *good* and *well* and between *bad* and *badly* are often not observed in conversation. Problems also arise because *well* can function as either an adjective or an adverb. *Good* and *bad* are always adjectives, and both can be used after a linking verb. In formal writing, do not use them to modify a verb, an adjective, or an adverb; use *well* or *badly* instead.

▶  The weather looks good today.

▶  He plays the trumpet ~~good~~ well and the trombone ~~bad.~~ badly.

*Badly* is an adverb and can modify a verb, an adjective, or another adverb. Do not use it after a linking verb in formal writing; use *bad* instead.

▶  I feel ~~badly~~ bad for the Cubs' fans.

As an adjective, *well* means "in good health"; as an adverb, it means "in a good manner" or "thoroughly."

| | |
|---|---|
| ADJECTIVE | After a week of rest, Julio felt <u>well</u> again. |
| ADVERB | She plays <u>well</u> enough to make the team. |

## Using regional modifiers (*right* smart, *wicked* fun)

Most regions have certain characteristic adjectives and adverbs. Some of the most colorful are intensifiers, adverbs meaning *very* or *absolutely*. In parts of the South, for example, and particularly in Appalachia, you are likely to hear the following: *He paid a right smart price for that car* or *She was plumb tuckered out*. In New England, you might hear *That party was wicked fun*. In each case, the adverb (*right, plumb, wicked*) acts to intensify the meaning of the adjective (*smart, tuckered out, fun*).

As with all language, use regional adjectives and adverbs to connect to an audience or to represent speech accurately — or for special effects (34d). In writing about a family member in Minnesota, for example, you might quote that person, bringing regional expressions or dialect into your writing.

### EXERCISE 54.1

Revise the following sentences to correct adverb and adjective use. Then identify each adjective or adverb you have revised and the word each modifies. Example:

The attorney delivered a ~~superb~~ superbly conceived summation.

1. Getting tickets at this late date is near impossible.
2. Derek apologized for behaving so immature on the football field.
3. Nora felt badly that the package would arrive one week later than promised.
4. It is real dangerous to hike those mountains in the winter.
5. He spoke confident about winning the race, but we doubted his abilities.
6. Paramedics rushed to help the victim, who was bleeding bad from the head.
7. The car ran good until the last two miles of the trip.
8. Arjun felt terrifically about his discussion with Professor Greene.
9. After we added cinnamon, the stew tasted really well.
10. Scientists measured the crater as accurate as possible.

## 54d Comparatives and superlatives

Most adjectives and adverbs have three forms: positive, comparative, and superlative.

| POSITIVE | COMPARATIVE | SUPERLATIVE |
| --- | --- | --- |
| large | larger | largest |
| early | earlier | earliest |
| careful | more careful | most careful |
| delicious | more delicious | most delicious |

▶ **Canada is larger than the United States.**

▶ **My son needs to be more careful with his money.**

▶ **This is the most delicious coffee we have tried.**

The comparative and superlative of most short (one-syllable and some two-syllable) adjectives are formed by adding *-er* and *-est*. With some two-syllable adjectives, longer adjectives, and most adverbs, use *more* and *most*: *scientific, more scientific, most scientific; elegantly, more elegantly, most elegantly*. If you are not sure whether a word has *-er* and *-est* forms, consult the dictionary entry for the simple form.

### Using irregular forms

A number of adjectives and adverbs have irregular comparative and superlative forms.

| POSITIVE | COMPARATIVE | SUPERLATIVE |
| --- | --- | --- |
| good, well | better | best |
| bad, badly, ill | worse | worst |
| little (quantity) | less | least |
| many, some, much | more | most |

## Choosing comparatives or superlatives

In academic writing, use the comparative to compare two things; use the superlative to compare three or more.

▶ **Rome is a much older city than New York.**

▶ **Damascus is one of the ~~older~~ cities in the world.**
  *oldest*

▶ **Which of the two candidates is the ~~strongest~~ for the job?**
  *stronger*

## Considering double comparatives and superlatives

Double comparatives and superlatives, used in some informal contexts, use both *more* or *most* and the *-er* or *-est* ending. Occasionally they can act to build a special emphasis, as in the title of Spike Lee's movie *Mo' Better Blues*. In college writing, however, double comparatives and superlatives may count against you. Make sure not to use *more* or *most* before adjectives or adverbs ending in *-er* or *-est* in formal situations.

▶ **Paris is the ~~most~~ loveliest city in the world.**

## Considering incomplete comparisons

Even if you think your audience will understand an implied comparison, you will be safer if you make sure that comparisons in formal writing are complete and clear (47e).

▶ **The patients taking the drug appeared healthier.**
  *than those receiving a placebo.*

## Considering absolute concepts

Some readers consider modifiers such as *perfect* and *unique* to be absolute concepts; according to this view, a construction such as *more unique* is illogical because a thing is either unique or it isn't, so modified forms of the concept don't make sense. However, many seemingly absolute words have multiple meanings, all of which are widely accepted as correct. For example, *unique* may mean *one of a kind* or *unequaled*, but it can also simply mean *distinctive* or *unusual*.

If you think your readers will object to a construction such as *more perfect* (which appears in the U.S. Constitution) or *somewhat unique*, then avoid such uses.

## Considering multiple negatives

One common type of repetition is to use more than one negative term in a negative statement. In *I can't hardly see you*, for example, both *can't* and *hardly* carry negative meanings. Emphatic double negatives — and triple, quadruple, and more — are especially common in the South and among speakers of some African American varieties of English, who may say, for example, *Don't none of my people come from up North*.

Multiple negatives have a long history in English (and in other languages) and can be found in the works of Chaucer and Shakespeare. In the eighteenth century, however, in an effort to make English more logical, double negatives came to be labeled as incorrect. In college writing, you may well have reason to quote passages that include them (whether from Shakespeare, Toni Morrison, or your grandmother), but it is safer to avoid other uses of double negatives in academic writing unless you are doing so to create a specific effect.

# 54e Using nouns as modifiers

Sometimes a noun can function as an adjective by modifying another noun, as in *chicken soup* or *money supply*. If noun modifiers pile up, however, they can make your writing harder to understand.

AWKWARD    The cold war–era Rosenberg espionage trial and execution continues to arouse controversy.

REVISED    The Rosenbergs' trial and execution for espionage during the cold war continues to arouse controversy.

### EXERCISE 54.2

Revise each of the following sentences to use modifiers correctly, clearly, and effectively. Many of the sentences can be revised in more than one way. Example:

bill to approve a financial plan for the
**He is sponsoring a housing project. ~~financial plan approval bill.~~**

1. Alicia speaks both Russian and German, but she speaks Russian best.

2. The summers are more rainier in New York than they are in Seattle.

3. He glanced at the menu and ordered the expensivest wine on the list.

4. Most of the elderly are women because women tend to live longer.

5. Minneapolis is the largest of the Twin Cities.

6. She came up with the most silliest plan for revenge.

7. Our theater company has produced several of the famousest classical Greek plays.

8. The student cafeteria is operated by a college food service system chain.

9. It is safer to jog in daylight.

10. Evan argued that subtitled films are boringer to watch than films dubbed in English.

---

## 54f Using adjectives ending in *-ed* and *-ing*

Multilingual

Many verbs refer to feelings — for example, *bore, confuse, excite, frighten, interest.* The present participles of such verbs, which end in *-ing,* and the past participles, which end in *-ed,* can be used as adjectives (48d).

Use the *-ed* (past participle) form to describe a person having the feeling.

▶   The *frightened* boy started to cry.

Use the *-ing* (present participle) form to describe the thing or person causing the feeling.

▶   The *frightening* movie gave him nightmares.

Be careful not to confuse the two types of adjectives.

▶   I am ~~interesting~~ in African literature.
    <sup>interested</sup> ^

▶   African literature seems ~~interested.~~
    <sup>Interesting.</sup> ^

## 54g Putting adjectives in order

Multilingual

Modifiers are words that give more information about a noun; that is, they *modify* the meaning of the noun in some way. Some modifiers precede the noun, and others follow it, as indicated in the chart in this section.

If there are two or more adjectives, their order is variable, but English has strong preferences, described below.

• Subjective adjectives (those that show the writer's <u>opinion</u>) go before objective adjectives (those that merely describe): *these <u>old-fashioned</u> kitchen tiles.*

• Adjectives of <u>size</u> generally come early: *these <u>large</u> old-fashioned kitchen tiles.*

• Adjectives of <u>color</u> generally come late: *these beautiful <u>blue</u> kitchen tiles.*

• Adjectives derived from <u>proper nouns</u> or from nouns that refer to <u>materials</u> generally come after color terms and right before noun modifiers: *these beautiful blue <u>Portuguese ceramic</u> kitchen tiles.*

• All other objective adjectives go in the middle, separated by commas (see 56e): *these decorative, heat-resistant, old-fashioned blue Portuguese ceramic kitchen tiles.*

| Modifier Type | Arrangement | Examples |
|---|---|---|
| determiners | at the beginning of the noun phrase | _these_ old-fashioned tiles |
| _all_ or _both_ | before any other determiners | _all_ these tiles |
| numbers | after any other determiners | these _six_ tiles |
| noun modifiers | directly before the noun | these _kitchen_ tiles |
| adjectives | between determiners and noun modifiers | these _old-fashioned_ kitchen tiles |
| phrases or clauses | after the noun | the tiles _on the wall_ the tiles _that we bought_ |

Of course, very long noun phrases are usually out of place in most kinds of writing. Academic and professional types of writing tend to avoid long strings of adjectives.

## 54h Avoiding overuse of adverbs and adjectives

In formal academic writing, expert writers tend to use adverbs and adjectives sparingly. So take a tip from the experts: using fewer modifiers can ensure that each adjective or adverb has a greater impact.

### Adverbs

In his memoir _On Writing_, novelist Stephen King says, "I believe the road to hell is paved in adverbs, and I will shout it from the rooftops." Note that he doesn't say he will shout it _loudly_, since readers already know that shouting is loud. Many adverbs are simply redundant:

▶ **Tourists meandered ~~aimlessly~~ in the garden.**

The verb _meandered_ means "wandered aimlessly," so _aimlessly_ is unnecessary.

In academic writing, avoid redundant adverbs, and omit adverbs that are so overused that they have little meaning anymore, such as _definitely_, _absolutely_, and _extremely_.

## Adjectives

Adjectives can also lead to redundancy. Ask yourself whether you need to say "the *large* mountain" or whether your readers will know that a mountain is large. When you overuse adjectives, you can simply bog down readers.

▶ The author responded to the ~~wonderful cheery~~ smiles lighting up all of the ~~happy, delighted~~ faces in the ~~listening~~ audience.

## Adjectives and adverbs in informal writing

As always, consider the context when deciding whether you are overusing adjectives and adverbs. Repetition that would be inappropriate in formal contexts can add effective emphasis in informal writing, as in the hashtag *#sosososcared* or a status update saying "I'm massively, insanely psyched for the show tonight."

▼ ▼ ▼ ▼ ▼ ▼ ▼ ▼ ▼ ▼ ▼ ▼ ▼ ▼ ▼ ▼ ▼ ▼ ▼ ▼ ▼ ▼ ▼

## THINKING CRITICALLY ABOUT ADJECTIVES AND ADVERBS

### Reading with an eye for adjectives and adverbs

> [Gwendolyn Brooks] describes the "graceful life" as one where people glide over floors in softly glowing rooms, smile correctly over trays of silver, cinnamon, and cream, and retire in quiet elegance.
> —MARY HELEN WASHINGTON, "Taming All That Anger Down"

Identify the adjectives and adverbs in the preceding passage, and comment on what they add to the writing. What would be lost if they were removed?

### Thinking about your own use of adjectives and adverbs

Take a few minutes to study something you can observe or examine closely. In a paragraph or two, describe your subject for someone who has never seen it. Using the guidelines in this chapter, check your use of adjectives and adverbs, and revise your paragraphs. How would you characterize your use of adjectives and adverbs?

# CHAPTER 55

# Prepositions and Prepositional Phrases

Multilingual

Words such as *to, from, over,* and *under* show the relations between other words; these words are prepositions, and they are one of the more challenging elements of English writing. You will need to decide which preposition to use for your intended meaning and understand how to use verbs that include prepositions, such as *take off, pick up,* and *put up with.*

## 55a  Using prepositions idiomatically

Multilingual

Each of the most common prepositions has a wide range of applications, and this range never coincides exactly from one language to another. See, for example, how *in* and *on* are used in English.

- ▶  **The peaches are <u>in</u> the refrigerator.**
- ▶  **The peaches are <u>on</u> the table.**
- ▶  **Is that a diamond ring <u>on</u> your finger?**

In some other languages (Spanish, for instance), these sentences might all use the same preposition. Be careful not to assume that what you know about prepositions in another language will help in English.

- ▶  **Is that a ruby ring i̶n̶ your finger?** *on*

There is no easy solution to the challenge of using English prepositions idiomatically. Search engines and online databases of English usage can, however, help you see how other writers have expressed a particular idiom. You can also try the strategies in the following Quick Help box.

---

QUICK HELP

Strategies for learning prepositions idiomatically

1. **Keep in mind typical examples of each preposition.**

    IN  The peaches are *in* the refrigerator.
        There are still some pickles *in* the jar.
        The book you are looking for is *in* the bookcase.

    Here the object of the preposition *in* is a container that encloses something.

    ON  The peaches are *on* the table.
        There are still some pickles *on* the plate.
        The book you are looking for is *on* the top shelf.

    Here the object of the preposition *on* is a horizontal surface that supports something with which it is in direct contact.

2. **Learn other examples that show some similarities and some differences in meaning.**

    IN  You shouldn't drive *in* a snowstorm.

    Here there is no container, but like a container, the falling snow surrounds the driver. The preposition *in* is used for other weather-related expressions as well: *in a tornado, in the sun, in the rain.*

    ON  Is that a diamond ring *on* your finger?

    The preposition *on* is used to describe things we wear: *the hat on his head, the shoes on her feet, the tattoo on his back.*

3. **Use your imagination to create mental images that can help you remember figurative uses of prepositions.**

    IN  Michael is *in* love.

    The preposition *in* is often used to describe a state of being: *in love, in pain, in a panic.* As a way to remember this, you might imagine the person immersed *in* this state of being.

4. **Try to learn prepositions not in isolation but as part of a system.** For example, in identifying the location of a place or an event, you can use the three prepositions *at, in,* and *on.*

    *At* specifies the exact point in space or time.

    AT  There will be a meeting tomorrow *at* 9:30 AM *at* 160 Main Street.

    Expanses of space or time within which a place is located or an event takes place might be seen as containers and so require *in.*

    IN  I arrived *in* the United States *in* January.                    ▶

> *On* must be used in two cases: with the names of streets (but not the exact address) and with days of the week or month.

> **ON**  The airline's office is *on* Fifth Avenue.
>
> I'll be moving to my new apartment *on* September 30.

---

### ◢ EXERCISE 55.1

Revise the following paragraph to include any needed prepositions.

The children's soccer game happened _____ 10:00 _____ Saturday morning. The families sat _____ blankets to watch the game. Everyone was _____ a good mood. When the game ended, both teams stood _____ a circle to cheer.

---

# 55b Using two-word verbs idiomatically

Multilingual

Some words that look like prepositions do not always function as prepositions. Consider the following two sentences:

▶  **The balloon rose *off* the ground.**

▶  **The plane took *off* without difficulty.**

In the first sentence, *off* is a preposition that introduces the prepositional phrase *off the ground*. In the second, *off* does not function as a preposition. Instead, it combines with *took* to form a two-word verb with its own meaning. Such a verb is called a phrasal verb, and the word *off*, when used this way, is called an adverbial particle. Many prepositions can function as particles to form phrasal verbs.

## Using phrasal verbs

The verb + particle combination that makes up a phrasal verb is a single entity that often cannot be torn apart.

> off
▶  **The plane took without difficulty. ~~off.~~**
         ^                          ^

However, when a phrasal verb takes a direct object (49a), the particle may sometimes be separated from the verb by the object.

▶  **I *picked up my baggage* at the terminal.**

▶  **I *picked my baggage up* at the terminal.**

If a personal pronoun (such as *it, her,* or *him*) is used as the direct object, that pronoun must separate the verb from its particle.

▶  **I *picked it up* at the terminal.**

## Using prepositional verbs

Some idiomatic two-word verbs are not phrasal verbs.

▶ **We *ran into* our neighbor on the train.**

Here, *into* is a preposition, and *our neighbor* is its object. You can't separate the verb from the preposition (*We ran our neighbor into on the train* does not make sense in English). Verbs like *run into* are called prepositional verbs.

Notice that *run into our neighbor* is different from a normal verb and prepositional phrase, such as *run into a room*. The combination *run + into* has a special meaning, "meet by chance," that you could not guess from the meanings of *run* and *into*.

English has many idiomatic prepositional verbs. Here is a small sample.

| PREPOSITIONAL VERB | MEANING |
|---|---|
| take after | resemble (usually a parent or older relative) |
| get over | recover from |
| count on | trust |

Other prepositional verbs have predictable meanings but require you to use a particular preposition that you should learn along with the verb: *depend on, look at, listen to, approve of*.

Finally, look out for phrasal-prepositional verbs such as these, which include a verb, a particle, and a preposition in a set order.

| PHRASAL-PREPOSITIONAL VERB | MEANING |
|---|---|
| put up with | tolerate |
| look forward to | anticipate with pleasure |
| get away with | avoid punishment for |

### EXERCISE 55.2

Each of the following sentences contains a two-word verb. In some sentences, the verb is used correctly; in others, it is used incorrectly. Identify each two-word verb, indicate whether it is a phrasal or prepositional verb, and rewrite any incorrect sentences correctly. Example:

I took time to <u>go over</u> my résumé carefully. *prepositional verb*

1. Soon after I was hired for my last job, I learned that the company might lay off me.

2. I was counting on the job to pay my way through school, so I was upset.

3. I decided to pick up a newspaper and see what other jobs were available.

4. As I looked the newspaper at, I was surprised to see that I was qualified for a job that paid much better than mine.

5. I gave my old job up and took the new one, which made attending school much easier.

# PART 12

# Punctuation and Mechanics

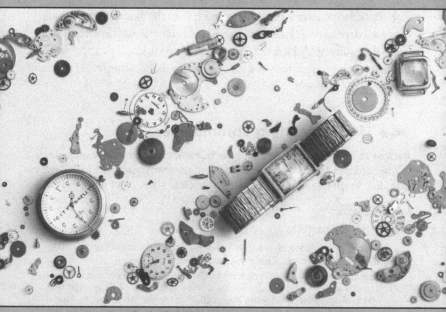

Photo by Mike Enright/www.menright.com. Photo styling by Barbara Lipp.

# CHAPTER 56

# Commas

Commas often play a crucial role in meaning. Even the directions for making hot cereal depend on the careful placement of a comma: *Add Cream of Wheat slowly, stirring constantly.* Here the comma tells the cook to *add the cereal slowly.* If the comma came before the word *slowly,* however, the cook might add the cereal all at once and *stir slowly.*

## 56a Understanding comma use

Because the comma can play many roles in a sentence, comma use often doesn't follow hard-and-fast rules. Using commas effectively requires you to make decisions that involve audience, purpose, rhythm, and style — not just grammar.

---

**QUICK HELP**

Editing for commas

Research for this book shows that five of the most common errors in college writing involve commas. Check your writing for these errors:

- Check every sentence that doesn't begin with the subject to see whether it opens with an introductory element (a word, phrase, or clause that tells when, where, how, or why the main action of the sentence occurs). Use a comma to separate the introductory material from the main part of the sentence. **(56b)**
- Look at every sentence that contains one of the conjunctions *and, but, for, nor, or, so,* or *yet.* If the groups of words before and after the conjunction both function as complete sentences, you have a compound sentence. Use a comma before the conjunction. **(56c)**
- Look at each adjective clause beginning with *which, who, whom, whose, when,* or *where,* and at each phrase and appositive. Decide whether the element is essential to the meaning of the sentence. If the rest of the sentence would be unclear without it, you should not set off the element with commas. **(56d)**
- Identify all adjective clauses beginning with *that,* and make sure they are not set off with commas. **(56d and 56k)**
- Do not use commas to set off restrictive elements; between subjects and verbs, verbs and objects or complements, or prepositions and objects; to separate parts of compound constructions other than compound sentences; or before the first or after the last item in a series. **(56k)**

# 56b Using commas after introductory elements

A comma usually follows an introductory word, expression, phrase, or clause.

▶ **However, the George Floyd demonstrations renewed the debate.**
         ^

▶ **In the end, only you can decide.**
         ^

▶ **Wearing new running shoes, Logan prepared for the race.**
                              ^

▶ **Pencil poised in anticipation, Audrey waited for the drawing contest to**
                                ^
   **begin.**

▶ **While her friends watched, Lila practiced her gymnastics routine.**
                            ^

Some writers omit the comma if the introductory element is short and does not seem to require a pause after it.

▶ *At the racetrack* **Henry lost nearly his entire paycheck.**

However, you will seldom be wrong if you use a comma after an introductory element. If the introductory element is followed by inverted word order, with the verb preceding the subject, do not use a comma unless misreading might occur.

▶ **From directly behind my seat/ came huge clouds of cigar smoke.**

▶ **Before he went, on came the rains.**
                 ^

### EXERCISE 56.1

Rewrite the following sentences to add any commas that are needed. Example:

**To find a good day-care provider, parents usually need both time and**
                                  ^
**money.**

1. After the concession speech the senator's supporters drifted out of the room.
2. To our surprise the charity auction raised enough money to build a new technology center.
3. Unaware that the microphone was on the candidate made an offensive comment.

4. Whenever someone rings the doorbell her dog goes berserk.

5. Therefore Sasha must take a summer course to receive her diploma.

6. With the fifth century came the fall of the Roman Empire.

7. A tray of shrimp in one hand and a pile of napkins in the other the waiter avoided me.

8. Toward the rapids floated an empty rubber raft.

9. When they woke up the exhausted campers no longer wanted to hike.

10. Tears in his eyes Keflezighi won the marathon.

## 56c Using commas in compound sentences

A comma usually precedes a coordinating conjunction (*and, but, for, nor, or, so,* or *yet*) that joins two independent clauses in a compound sentence.

▶ The title sounds impressive, but *administrative clerk* is just another word for *photocopier.*

▶ The show started at last, and the crowd grew quiet.

With very short clauses, writers sometimes omit the comma before *and* or *or.* You will never be wrong to include it, however.

▶ She saw her chance and she took it.

▶ She saw her chance, and she took it.

Always use the comma if there is any chance of misreading the sentence without it.

▶ The game ended in victory, and pandemonium erupted.

You may want to use a semicolon rather than a comma when the clauses are long and complex or contain their own commas.

▶ When these early migrations took place, the ice was still confined to the lands in the far north; but eight hundred thousand years ago, when man was already established in the temperate latitudes, the ice moved southward until it covered large parts of Europe and Asia.

—ROBERT JASTROW, *Until the Sun Dies*

Be careful not to use *only* a comma between independent clauses in formal writing. Doing so creates a comma splice (see Chapter 44). Either use a coordinating conjunction after the comma, or use a semicolon.

| COMMA SPLICE | Luck isn't the only thing responsible for your new job, give yourself the credit you deserve. |
| REVISED | Luck isn't the only thing responsible for your new job, so give yourself the credit you deserve. |
| REVISED | Luck isn't the only thing responsible for your new job; give yourself the credit you deserve. |

### EXERCISE 56.2

Use a comma and a coordinating conjunction (*and, but, for, nor, or, so,* or *yet*) to combine each of the following pairs of sentences into one sentence. Delete or rearrange words if necessary. Example:

I had finished studying for the test/, I went to bed.

*(so inserted above the comma)*

1. The chef did not want to serve a heavy dessert. She was planning to have a rich stew for the main course.

2. My mother rarely allowed us to eat sweets. Halloween was a special exception.

3. Scientists have mapped the human genome. They learn more every day about how genes affect an individual's health.

4. Perhaps I will change my name when I get married. Maybe I will keep my maiden name.

5. Penguins cannot fly. They cannot walk the way other birds do.

## 56d Using commas with nonrestrictive elements

Nonrestrictive elements are word groups that do not limit, or restrict, the meaning of the noun or pronoun they modify. Setting nonrestrictive elements off with commas shows your readers that the information is not essential to the meaning of the sentence. Restrictive elements, on the other hand, *are* essential to meaning and should *not* be set off with commas. The same sentence may mean different things with and without the commas:

▶ **The bus drivers rejecting the management offer remained on strike.**

▶ **The bus drivers, rejecting the management offer, remained on strike.**

The first sentence says that only *some* bus drivers, the ones rejecting the offer, remained on strike. The second says that *all* the drivers did.

Since the decision to include or omit commas influences how readers will interpret your sentence, you should think especially carefully about what you mean and use commas (or omit them) accordingly.

RESTRICTIVE    Drivers *who have been convicted of drunken driving* should lose their licenses.

In the preceding sentence, the clause *who have been convicted of drunken driving* is essential because it explains that only drivers who have been convicted of drunken driving should lose their licenses. Therefore, it is *not* set off with commas.

NONRESTRICTIVE    The two drivers involved in the accident, *who have been convicted of drunken driving,* should lose their licenses.

In this sentence, however, *who have been convicted of drunken driving* is nonrestrictive because it merely provides additional information about the particular drivers who were involved in the accident. Therefore, the clause *is* set off with commas.

To decide whether an element is restrictive or nonrestrictive, mentally delete the element, and see if the deletion changes the meaning of the rest of the sentence. If the deletion *does* change the meaning, you should probably not set the element off with commas. If it *does not* change the meaning, the element probably requires commas.

## Using commas with adjective and adverb clauses

An adjective clause that begins with *that* is always restrictive; do not set it off with commas. An adjective clause beginning with *which* may be either restrictive or nonrestrictive; however, some writers prefer to use *which* only for nonrestrictive clauses, which they set off with commas. (See 49e.)

RESTRICTIVE CLAUSES

▶ **The claim that men like seriously to battle one another to some sort of finish is a myth.**          —JOHN McMURTRY, "Kill 'Em! Crush 'Em! Eat 'Em Raw!"

The adjective clause is necessary to the meaning because it explains which claim is a myth; therefore, the clause is not set off with commas.

▶ **The man,/ who rescued Jana's puppy,/ won her eternal gratitude.**

The adjective clause is necessary to the meaning because it identifies the man, so it takes no commas.

NONRESTRICTIVE CLAUSES

▶ **I borrowed books from the rental library of Shakespeare and Company, which was the library and bookstore of Sylvia Beach at 12 rue de l'Odeon.**          —ERNEST HEMINGWAY, *A Moveable Feast*

The adjective clause is not necessary to the meaning of the independent clause and therefore is set off with a comma.

In general, set off an adverb clause that follows a main clause only if it begins with *although, even though, while,* or another subordinating conjunction expressing contrast.

▶ **The park became a popular gathering place, although nearby residents**

 **complained about the noise.**

The adverb clause expresses contrast; therefore, it is set off with a comma.

## Using commas with phrases

Participial <u>phrases</u> may be restrictive or nonrestrictive. Prepositional phrases are usually restrictive, but sometimes they are not essential to the meaning of a sentence and thus are set off with commas.

### NONRESTRICTIVE PHRASES

▶ **The singer's children, refusing to be ignored, interrupted the recital.**

Using commas around the participial phrase makes it nonrestrictive, telling us that all of the singer's children interrupted.

### RESTRICTIVE PHRASES

▶ **Wood <u>cut from living trees</u> does not burn as well as dead wood.**

The participial phrase *cut from living trees* is essential to the meaning.

▶ **The bodyguards were the men <u>in dark suits and matching ties</u>.**

The prepositional phrase *in dark suits and matching ties* is essential to the meaning.

## Using commas with appositives

An appositive is a noun or noun phrase that renames a nearby noun in a sentence. When an appositive is not essential to identify what it renames, it is set off with commas.

### NONRESTRICTIVE APPOSITIVES

▶ **Savion Glover, the award-winning dancer, taps like poetry in motion.**

Savion Glover's name identifies him; the appositive *the award-winning dancer* provides extra information.

### RESTRICTIVE APPOSITIVES

▶ **Mozart's opera/ *The Marriage of Figaro*/ was considered revolutionary.**

The phrase is restrictive because Mozart wrote more than one opera. Therefore, it is *not* set off with commas.

### EXERCISE 56.3

Use commas to set off nonrestrictive clauses, phrases, and appositives in any of the following sentences that contain such elements.

1. What can you buy for the person who has everything?
2. Embalming is a technique that preserves a cadaver.
3. The enormous new house which was the largest in the neighborhood had replaced a much smaller old home.
4. The rescue workers exhausted and discouraged stared ahead without speaking.
5. The new mall has the same stores and restaurants as all the other malls in town.
6. Viruses unlike bacteria can reproduce only by infecting live cells.
7. Napoléon was imprisoned after his defeat at the battle of Waterloo.
8. Hammurabi an ancient Babylonian king created laws that were carved on a stone for public display.
9. Birds' hearts have four chambers whereas reptiles' have three.
10. A female cheetah hisses and swats if another animal gets too close to her young.

## 56e Using commas to separate items in a series

Use a comma to separate items in a series of three or more words, phrases, or clauses.

▶ **He has plundered our seas, ravaged our coasts, burnt our towns, and destroyed the lives of our people.**

—THOMAS JEFFERSON, Declaration of Independence

You may see a series with no comma after the next-to-last item, particularly in newspaper writing. Occasionally, however, omitting the comma can cause confusion.

▶ **All the vegetables in the cafeteria — broccoli, green beans, peas, and**
                                                                      ^
 **carrots — were cooked to an unrecognizable mush.**

Without the comma after *peas*, you wouldn't know if the cafeteria offered three vegetables (the third being a *mixture* of peas and carrots) or four.

When the items in a series contain commas of their own or other punctuation, separate them with semicolons rather than commas (57b).

Coordinate adjectives, those that relate equally to the noun they modify, should be separated by commas.

▶ **The *long, twisting, muddy* road led to a shack in the woods.**

In a sentence like *The cracked bathroom mirror reflected his face*, however, *cracked* and *bathroom* are not coordinate because *bathroom mirror* is the equivalent of a single word, which is modified by *cracked*. Hence, they are *not* separated by commas.

You can usually determine whether adjectives are coordinate by inserting the word *and* between them. If the sentence still makes sense with the *and*, the adjectives are coordinate and should be separated by commas.

▶ **They are sincere *and* talented *and* inquisitive researchers.**

The sentence makes sense with the *and*s, so the adjectives should be separated by commas: *They are sincere, talented, inquisitive researchers.*

▶ **Byron carried an elegant ~~and~~ gold ~~and~~ pocket watch.**

The sentence does not make sense with the *and*s, so the adjectives should not be separated by commas: *Byron carried an elegant gold pocket watch.*

### EXERCISE 56.4

Revise any of the following sentences that require commas to set off words, phrases, or clauses in a series.

1. The students donated clothing school supplies and nonperishable food.
2. The hot humid weather did not stop the fans from flocking to the free outdoor concert.
3. The ball sailed over the fence across the yard and through the Wilsons' window.
4. Several art historians inspected the Chinese terra-cotta figures.
5. The young athletes' parents insist on calling every play judging every move and telling everyone within earshot exactly what is wrong with the team.

## 56f Using commas with parenthetical and transitional expressions

Parenthetical and transitional expressions often interrupt the flow of a sentence, so they are usually set off with commas. Parenthetical expressions (*in fact, by the way*) add comments. Transitional expressions (5d and e), including conjunctive adverbs (48g) such as *however* and *furthermore*, clarify how parts of sentences relate to what has come before them.

▶ **Roald Dahl's stories, it turns out, were often inspired by his own childhood.**
▶ **Ceiling fans are, moreover, less expensive than air conditioners.**

## 56g Using commas with contrasting elements, interjections, direct address, and tag questions

**CONTRASTING ELEMENTS**

▶ On official business it was she, not my father, one would usually hear on the phone or in stores.

—RICHARD RODRIGUEZ, "Aria: A Memoir of a Bilingual Childhood"

**INTERJECTIONS**

▶ My God, who wouldn't want a wife? —JUDY BRADY, "I Want a Wife"

**DIRECT ADDRESS**

▶ Remember, sir, that you are under oath.

**TAG QUESTIONS**

▶ The governor did not veto the unemployment bill, did she?

### EXERCISE 56.5

Revise each of the following sentences, using commas to set off parenthetical and transitional expressions, contrasting elements, interjections, words used in direct address, and tag questions.

1. One must consider the society as a whole not just its parts.
2. Drinking caffeinated beverages can in fact be good for your health.
3. You don't expect me to read this speech do you?
4. Coming in ahead of schedule and under budget it appears is the only way to keep this client happy.
5. Believe me Jenna I had no idea things would turn out this way.

## 56h Using commas with dates, addresses, titles, and numbers

*Dates*

Use a comma between the day of the week and the month, between the day of the month and the year, and between the year and the rest of the sentence, if any.

▶ The attacks on the morning of Tuesday, September 11, 2001, took the United States by surprise.

Do not use commas with dates in inverted order or with dates consisting of only the month and the year.

▶ She dated the letter <u>18 October 2014</u>.

▶ Thousands of Germans swarmed over the Berlin Wall in <u>November 1989</u>.

*Addresses and place-names*

Use a comma after each part of an address or place-name, including the state if no zip code is given. Do not precede a zip code with a comma.

▶ Forward my mail to the Department of English, The Ohio State

University, Columbus, Ohio 43210.

▶ Portland, Oregon, is much larger than Portland, Maine.

*Titles*

Use commas to set off a title such as *MD* or *PhD* from the name preceding it and from the rest of the sentence. The titles *Jr.* and *Sr.*, however, often appear without commas.

▶ Jaime Mejía, PhD, will speak about his ethnographic research.

▶ Martin Luther King Jr. was one of the twentieth century's greatest orators.

*Numbers*

In numerals of five digits or more, use a comma between each group of three digits, starting from the right.

▶ The city's population rose to 158,000 in the 2000 census.

The comma is optional in four-digit numerals but is never used in years.

▶ The college had an enrollment of 1,789 [or 1789] in the fall of 2006.

Do not use a comma in building numbers, zip codes, or page numbers.

▶ My parents live at 11311 Wimberly Drive, Richmond, Virginia 23233.

▶ Turn to page 1566.

◢ **EXERCISE 56.6**

Revise each of the following sentences, using commas appropriately with dates, addresses, place-names, titles, and numbers.

1. The city of Dublin Ireland has a population of over 500000.
2. I rode a total of almost 1200 miles on my bike in 2009.

3. New Delhi India and Islamabad Pakistan became the capitals of two independent nations at midnight on August 15 1947.

4. MLA headquarters are still located at 26 Broadway New York New York 10004.

5. I was convinced that the nameplate I. M. Well MD was one of my sister's pranks.

## 56i Using commas with quotations

Commas set off a quotation from words used to introduce or identify the source of the quotation. A comma following a quotation goes inside the closing quotation mark.

▶ **A German proverb warns, "Go to law for a sheep, and lose your cow."**

▶ **"All I know about grammar," said Joan Didion, "is its infinite power."**

Do not use a comma after a question mark or exclamation point.

▶ **"What's a thousand dollars?/" asks Groucho Marx in *The Cocoanuts*.**

 **"Mere chicken feed. A poultry matter."**

▶ **"Out, damned spot!/" cries Lady Macbeth.**

Do not use a comma to introduce a quotation with *that*.

▶ **The writer of Ecclesiastes concludes that/ "all is vanity."**

Do not use a comma with a quotation when the rest of the sentence does more than introduce or identify the source of the quotation.

▶ **People who say/ "Have a nice day" irritate me.**

▶ **He put off military service because he had/ "other priorities."**

Do not use a comma before an indirect quotation — one that does not use the speaker's exact words.

▶ **Patrick Henry declared/ that he wanted either liberty or death.**

◢ **EXERCISE 56.7**

Insert a comma in any of the following sentences that require one.

1. "The public be damned!" William Henry Vanderbilt was reported to have said. "I'm working for my stockholders."
2. My mother was fond of telling me "You'd make coffee nervous!"
3. I refuse to believe the old saying that "nice guys finish last."
4. "Learning without thought is labor lost; thought without learning is perilous" Confucius argued.
5. "Do you have any idea who I am?" the well-dressed young man asked belligerently.

# 56j Using commas for clarity

Use a comma if it will make a sentence easier to read or understand.

▶ **The members of the dance troupe strutted in, in matching costumes.**
                                                      ^

▶ **Before, I had planned to major in biology.**
          ^

# 56k Avoiding unnecessary commas

Excessive use of commas can spoil an otherwise fine sentence.

## Avoiding commas with restrictive elements

Do not use commas to set off restrictive elements — elements that limit, or define, the meaning of the words they modify or refer to (56d).

▶ **I don't let my children watch films / that are violent.**

▶ **A law / reforming campaign financing / was passed in 2002.**

▶ **The actor / Chiwetel Ejiofor / might win this award.**

## Avoiding commas between subjects and verbs, verbs and objects or complements, and prepositions and objects

Do not use a comma between a subject and its verb, a verb and its object or complement, or a preposition and its object — not even if the subject, object, or complement is a long phrase or clause. See the examples that follow.

▶ Watching old movies late at night / is a way for me to relax.

▶ Parents must decide / how much television their children should watch.

▶ The winner of / the community-service award stepped forward.

## Using commas in compound constructions

In compound constructions (other than compound sentences — see 56c), do not use a comma before or after a coordinating conjunction that joins the two parts.

▶ Designer Gloria Vanderbilt was born rich / and has used her money to

make even more money.

The *and* joins parts of the compound predicate *was born* and *has used*, which should not be separated by a comma.

▶ Ellen Johnson Sirleaf / and George Weah both claimed to have won the

election.

The *and* joins parts of a compound subject, which should not be separated by a comma.

## Using commas in a series

Do not use a comma before the first or after the last item in a series (56e).

▶ The auction included / furniture, paintings, and china.

▶ The swimmer took slow, powerful / strokes.

▼ ▼ ▼ ▼ ▼ ▼ ▼ ▼ ▼ ▼ ▼ ▼ ▼ ▼ ▼ ▼ ▼ ▼ ▼ ▼ ▼ ▼ ▼ ▼ ▼

THINKING CRITICALLY ABOUT COMMAS

### Reading with an eye for commas

The following poem uses commas to create rhythm and guide readers. Read the poem aloud, listening especially to the effect of the commas at the end of the first and fifth lines. Then read it again as if those commas were omitted, noting the difference. What is the effect of the poet's decision not to use a comma at the end of the third line?

> Some say the world will end in fire,
> Some say in ice.
> From what I've tasted of desire
> I hold with those who favor fire.
> But if it had to perish twice,
> I think I know enough of hate
> To say that for destruction ice
> Is also great
> And would suffice.
>
> —ROBERT FROST, "Fire and Ice"

### Thinking about your own use of commas

Choose a paragraph that you have written. Remove all of the commas, and read it aloud. What is the effect of leaving out the commas? Now, punctuate the passage with commas, consulting this chapter. Did you replace all of your original commas? Did you add any new ones? Explain why you added the commas you did.

# CHAPTER 57

# Semicolons

The following public service announcement, posted in New York City subway cars, reminds commuters what to do with a used newspaper at the end of the ride:

> Please put it in a trash can; that's good news for everyone.

The semicolon in the subway announcement separates two clauses that could have been written as separate sentences. Semicolons, which create a pause stronger than that of a comma but not as strong as the full pause of a period, show close connections between related ideas.

## 57a Using semicolons with independent clauses

You can join independent clauses in several ways: with a comma and a coordinating conjunction (56c), with a colon (61d), with a dash (61c), or with a semicolon. Semicolons provide writers with subtle ways of signaling closely related clauses. The clause following a semicolon often restates an idea expressed in the first clause; it can also expand on or present a contrast to the first.

▶ **Immigration acts were passed; newcomers had to prove, besides moral correctness and financial solvency, their ability to read.**
> —MARY GORDON, "More Than Just a Shrine"

In this example, Gordon uses a semicolon to lead to a clause that expands on the first one. The semicolon also gives the sentence an abrupt rhythm that suits the topic: laws that imposed strict requirements.

A semicolon should link independent clauses joined by conjunctive adverbs such as *therefore, however,* and *indeed* or transitional expressions such as *in a way, in fact, in addition,* and *for example* (44d).

▶ **The circus comes as close to being the world in microcosm as anything I know; in a way, it puts all the rest of show business in the shade.**
> —E. B. WHITE, "The Ring of Time"

If two independent clauses joined by a coordinating conjunction contain commas, you may use a semicolon instead of a comma before the conjunction to make the sentence easier to read.

▶ **Every year, whether the Republican or the Democratic Party is in office, more and more power drains away from the individual to feed vast reservoirs in far-off places; and we have less and less say about the shape of events which shape our future.**

—WILLIAM F. BUCKLEY JR., "Why Don't We Complain?"

---

**QUICK HELP**

Editing for semicolons

- Use semicolons only between independent clauses—groups of words that can stand alone as sentences **(57a)**—or between items in a series. **(57b)**
- If you find few or no semicolons in your writing, ask yourself whether closely related ideas in two sentences might be better expressed in one sentence with a semicolon.
- If you find too many semicolons in your writing, try deleting some of them. Would making some clauses into separate sentences make your writing smoother or less monotonous? **(57d)**

---

**EXERCISE 57.1**

Combine each of the following pairs of sentences into one sentence by using a semicolon. Example:

*meet*

Take the bus to Henderson Street/; ~~Meet~~ me under the clock at half past

three.

1. Abalone fishing in California is strictly regulated. A person is allowed to harvest only twenty-four of these large mollusks per year.

2. City life offers many advantages. In many ways, however, life in a small town is much more pleasant.

3. The door contains an inflatable slide to be used in an emergency. In addition, each seat can become a flotation device.

4. Most car accidents occur within twenty-five miles of the home. Therefore, you should wear a seat belt on every trip.

5. Involvement in team sports provides more than just health benefits for young girls. It also increases their self-confidence.

## 57b Using semicolons to separate items in a series

Ordinarily, commas separate items in a series (56e). But when the items themselves contain commas or other punctuation, using semicolons to separate the items will make the sentence clearer and easier to read.

▶ **Anthropology encompasses archaeology, the study of ancient civilizations through artifacts; linguistics, the study of the structure and development of language; and cultural anthropology, the study of customs, language, and behavior.**

## 57c Using semicolons with quotation marks

A semicolon goes *outside* closing quotation marks (60e).

▶ **Shirley Jackson's most famous story is "The Lottery"; its horrifying ending depicts a result of relying too heavily on tradition.**

## 57d Avoiding misused or overused semicolons

A comma, not a semicolon, should separate an independent clause from a dependent clause or a phrase.

▶ **The police found a set of fingerprints⫽, which they used to identify the thief.**

A colon, not a semicolon, should introduce a series.

▶ **The reunion tour includes the following bands⫽: Urban Waste, Murphy's Law, Rapid Deployment, and Ism.**

### ◢ EXERCISE 57.2

Revise the following passage, eliminating any misused or overused semicolons and, if necessary, replacing them with other punctuation.

Hosting your first dinner party can be very stressful; but careful planning and preparation can make it a success. The guest list must contain the right mix of people; everyone should feel comfortable; good talkers and good listeners are both important; while they don't need to agree on everything, you don't want them to have fistfights, either. Then you need to plan the menu; which should steer clear of problem areas; for vegans; no pork chops; for guests with shellfish allergies, no lobster; for nondrinkers; no tequila. In addition; make sure your home is clean and neat, and check that you have enough chairs; dishes; glasses; napkins; and silverware. Leave enough time to socialize with your guests; and save a little energy to clean up when it's over!

▼ ▼ ▼ ▼ ▼ ▼ ▼ ▼ ▼ ▼ ▼ ▼ ▼ ▼ ▼ ▼ ▼ ▼ ▼ ▼ ▼ ▼ ▼ ▼ ▼

## THINKING CRITICALLY ABOUT SEMICOLONS

### Reading with an eye for semicolons

Read the following paragraph, which describes a solar eclipse, with attention to the use of semicolons. What different effect would the paragraph have if the author had used periods instead of semicolons? What if she had used commas and coordinating conjunctions? What is the effect of all the semicolons?

> You see the wide world swaddled in darkness; you see a vast breadth of hilly land, and an enormous, distant, blackened valley; you see towns' lights, a river's path, and blurred portions of your hat and scarf; you see your husband's face looking like an early black-and-white film; and you see a sprawl of black sky and blue sky together, with unfamiliar stars in it, some barely visible bands of cloud, and over there, a small white ring. The ring is as small as one goose in a flock of migrating geese—if you happen to notice a flock of migrating geese. It is one 360th part of the visible sky. The sun we see is less than half the diameter of a dime held at arms' length.      —ANNIE DILLARD, "Total Eclipse"

### Thinking about your own use of semicolons

Think of something you might take five or ten minutes to observe—a football game, a brewing storm, an argument between friends—and write a paragraph describing your observations point by point and using semicolons to separate each point, as Annie Dillard does in the preceding paragraph. Then, look at the way you used semicolons. Are there places where a period or a comma and a coordinating conjunction would better serve your meaning? Revise appropriately. What can you conclude about effective ways of using semicolons?

# CHAPTER 58

# End Punctuation

Periods, question marks, and exclamation points often appear in advertising to create special effects or draw readers along from line to line.

> You have a choice to make.
> Where can you turn for advice?
> Ask our experts today!

End punctuation tells us how to read each sentence — as a matter-of-fact statement, a query, or an emphatic request. Making appropriate choices with end punctuation allows readers to understand exactly what you mean.

## 58a Using periods

Use a period to close sentences that make statements or give mild commands.

▶ **All books are either dreams or swords.**     —AMY LOWELL

▶ **Don't use a fancy word if a simpler word will do.**
                    —GEORGE ORWELL, "Politics and the English Language"

A period also closes indirect questions, which report rather than ask questions.

▶ **We all wonder who will win the election.**

Until recently, periods have been used with most abbreviations (see Chapter 63) in American English. However, more and more abbreviations are appearing without periods.

| | | |
|---|---|---|
| Mr. | MD | BC *or* B.C. |
| Ms. | PhD | BCE *or* B.C.E. |
| Mrs. | MBA | AD *or* A.D. |
| Dr. | RN | AM *or* a.m. |
| Jr. | Sen. | PM *or* p.m. |

Some abbreviations rarely if ever appear with periods. These include the postal abbreviations of state names, such as *FL* and *TN*, and most groups of initials (*MLA, CIA, AIDS, UNICEF*). If you are not sure whether a particular abbreviation should include periods, check a dictionary or follow the style guidelines (such as those of the Modern Language Association) you are using in a research project.

## 58b Using question marks

Use a question mark to close sentences that ask direct questions.

▶ **Have you finished the essay, or do you need more time?**

Question marks do not close *indirect* questions, which report rather than ask questions.

▶ **She asked whether I opposed his nomination?.**

Do not use a comma or a period immediately after a question mark that ends a direct quotation (60e).

▶ **"Am I my brother's keeper?/" Cain asked.**
▶ **Cain asked, "Am I my brother's keeper?"/**

Questions in a series may have question marks even when they are not separate sentences.

▶ **I often face a difficult choice: should I go to practice? finish my homework? spend time with my friends?**

## 58c Using exclamation points

Use an exclamation point to show surprise or strong emotion.

▶ **In those few moments of geologic time will be the story of all that has happened since we became a nation. And what a story it will be!**

—JAMES RETTIE, "But a Watch in the Night"

Today, we live in a world of excess exclamations, such as *Best Sale Ever!!!!!* But college writers will do well to use exclamation points sparingly in academic work because they can distract your readers or suggest that you are exaggerating. In general, try to create emphasis through diction and sentence structure rather than with exclamation points.

▶ This university is so large, so varied, that attempting to tell someone

everything about it would take three years!.

Do not use a comma or a period after an exclamation point that ends a direct quotation.

▶ On my last visit, I looked out the sliding glass doors and ran breathlessly

to Connor in the kitchen: "There's a *huge* black pig in the backyard!"

—ELLEN ASHDOWN, "Living by the Dead"

### EXERCISE 58.1

Revise each of the following sentences, adding appropriate punctuation and deleting any unnecessary punctuation you find. Example:

Jasmine asked the travel agent, "What is the air fare to Greece?"

1. Social scientists face difficult questions: should they use their knowledge to shape society, merely describe human behavior, or try to do both.
2. The court denied a New Jersey woman's petition to continue raising tigers in her backyard!
3. I screamed at Jamie, "You rat. You tricked me."
4. The reporter wondered whether anything more could have been done to save lives?
5. "Have you seen the new George Clooney film?," Mia asked.

## 58d Using end punctuation in informal writing

In informal writing, especially texts and tweets with character limits, writers today are increasingly likely to omit end punctuation entirely. In informal writing that does use end punctuation, research shows that ellipses (...), or "dots," are on the rise; they can be used to signal a trailing off of a thought, to raise questions about what is being left out, to leave open the possibility of further communication, or simply to indicate that the writer doesn't want or need to finish the sentence (61f). Exclamation marks can convey an excited or a chatty tone, so they are used more frequently in social media and other informal writing situations than in academic writing (where they tend to be rare). And some writers have argued that using a period at the end of a text or tweet rather than no punctuation at all can suggest that the writer is irritated or angry. The meaning of end punctuation is changing in informal contexts, so pay attention to how others communicate, and use what you learn in your own social writing.

▼ ▼ ▼ ▼ ▼ ▼ ▼ ▼ ▼ ▼ ▼ ▼ ▼ ▼ ▼ ▼ ▼ ▼ ▼ ▼ ▼ ▼ ▼ ▼ ▼ ▼ ▼ ▼ ▼

## THINKING CRITICALLY ABOUT END PUNCTUATION

### Reading with an eye for end punctuation

Consider the use of end punctuation in the following paragraph. Then experiment with the end punctuation. What would be the effect of deleting the exclamation point from the quotation by Cicero or of changing it to a question mark? What would be the effect of changing Cicero's question to a statement?

> To be admired and praised, especially by the young, is an autumnal pleasure enjoyed by the lucky ones (who are not always the most deserving). "What is more charming," Cicero observes in his famous essay *De Senectute*, "than an old age surrounded by the enthusiasm of youth! . . . Attentions which seem trivial and conventional are marks of honor—the morning call, being sought after, precedence, having people rise for you, being escorted to and from the forum. . . . What pleasures of the body can be compared to the prerogatives of influence?" But there are also pleasures of the body, or the mind, that are enjoyed by a greater number of older persons.
>
> —MALCOLM COWLEY, *The View from 80*

### Thinking about your own use of end punctuation

Look through something you have written recently, noting its end punctuation. Using the guidelines in this chapter, see if your use of end punctuation follows any patterns. Try revising the end punctuation in a paragraph or two to emphasize (or deemphasize) some point. What conclusions can you draw about ways of using end punctuation to draw attention to (or away from) a sentence?

## CHAPTER 59

# Apostrophes

The little apostrophe can make a big difference in meaning. The following sign at a neighborhood swimming pool, for instance, probably doesn't say quite what the writer intended:

> Please deposit your garbage (and your guests) in the trash receptacles before leaving the pool area.

Adding a single apostrophe would offer a more neighborly statement: *Please deposit your garbage (and your guests') in the trash receptacles before leaving the pool area* asks residents to remove the guests' garbage, not the guests themselves.

## 59a  Understanding apostrophes

Apostrophes are used for two main purposes: to show the possessive case and to show where a letter has been omitted from a contraction. Apostrophe placement can be confusing, especially today when smart devices put them in for you, and they are sometimes left out in informal writing. But they are still important in writing, so it's best to learn how to use them accurately.

---

**QUICK HELP**

### Editing for apostrophes

- Check each noun that ends in -s and shows ownership or possession. Then verify that the apostrophe is in the right place, either before or after the -s. **(59b)**
- Check the possessive form of each indefinite pronoun, such as *someone's*. Be sure an apostrophe comes before the -s. **(59b)**
- Check each possessive personal pronoun ending in -s (*yours, hers, his, its, ours, theirs*), and make sure that it does not include an apostrophe. **(59b)**
- Check each *its*. Does it show possession? If not, add an apostrophe before the -s. **(59c)**
- Check each *it's*. Does it mean "it is" or "it has"? If not, remove the apostrophe. **(59c)**

---

## 59b Using apostrophes to signal possessive case

The possessive case denotes ownership or possession of one thing by another (53a).

### Forming possessives of singular nouns and indefinite pronouns

Add an apostrophe and -*s* to form the possessive of most singular nouns, including those that end in -*s*, and of indefinite pronouns (52e).

▶ The <u>bus's</u> fumes overpowered her.

▶ *Star Wars* made <u>George Lucas's</u> fortune.

▶ <u>Anyone's</u> guess is as good as mine.

Apostrophes are never used with the possessive forms of personal pronouns: *yours, his, hers, its, ours, theirs.*

▶ His favorite movies have nothing in common with her/s.

### Forming possessives of plural nouns

For plural nouns that do not end in -*s*, add an apostrophe and -*s*.

▶ Most suits in the ~~mens'~~ men's department are appropriate business attire.

For plural nouns ending in -*s*, add only the apostrophe.

▶ The three ~~clowns's~~ clowns' costumes were bright green and orange.

### Forming possessives of compound words

For compound words, make the last word in the group possessive.

▶ The <u>secretary of state's</u> speech was televised.

▶ My <u>in-laws'</u> disapproval dampened our enthusiasm.

### Showing possession by more than one owner

To signal individual possession by two or more owners, make each noun possessive.

▶ The differences between <u>Ridley Scott's</u> and <u>Jerry Bruckheimer's</u> films are enormous.

Scott and Bruckheimer make different films.

To signal joint possession, make only the last noun possessive.

▶ **Wallace and Gromit's creator is Nick Park.**

Wallace and Gromit have the same creator.

### EXERCISE 59.1

Revise each of the following sentences to form the possessive case of the italicized words. Example:

> **A.J.'s older *brother's* name is Griffin.**

1. Grammar is not *everybody* favorite subject.
2. An *ibis* wingspan is about half as long as a *flamingo*.
3. *Prince William and Kate* first visit to Canada as a married couple included a meeting with the prime minister.
4. The long debate over *states* rights culminated in the Civil War.
5. *Tiger Woods* personal crisis once threatened to overshadow his athletic career.
6. She insists that her personal life is *nobody* business.
7. Parents often question their *children* choice of friends.
8. This dog has a *beagle* ears and a *St. Bernard* face.
9. The sidewalk smokers disregarded the *surgeon generals* warnings.
10. *Anna and Tobias* income dropped dramatically after Anna lost her job.

## 59c Using apostrophes to signal contractions

Contractions are two-word combinations formed by leaving out certain letters, which are indicated by an apostrophe.

| | |
|---|---|
| it is, it has/it's | do not/don't |
| was not/wasn't | does not/doesn't |
| I am/I'm | will not/won't |
| you will/you'll | let us/let's |
| I would, I had/I'd | cannot/can't |
| would not/wouldn't | |

Contractions are common in both conversation and informal writing. Some academic and professional work, however, calls for greater formality.

## Distinguishing *its* and *it's*

*Its* is the possessive form of *it*. *It's* is a contraction for *it is* or *it has*.

▶ **This disease is unusual; it's symptoms vary from person to person.**

▶ **It's a difficult disease to diagnose.**

## Signaling omissions

An apostrophe signals omissions in some common phrases:

| | | |
|---|---|---|
| ten of the clock | rock and roll | class of 2022 |
| ten o'clock | rock 'n' roll | class of '22 |

In addition, writers can use an apostrophe to signal omitted letters in approximating the sound of speech or a specific dialect.

▶ **You should'a seen 'em playin' together.**

# 59d Using guidelines for apostrophes with plurals

Many style guides advise against apostrophes for any plurals.

▶ **The gymnasts need scores of 8s and 9s to qualify for the finals.**

Others use an apostrophe and -*s* to form the plural of numbers, letters, symbols, and words referred to as terms.

▶ **The five *Shakespeare*'s in the essay were spelled five different ways.**

Check your instructor's preference. In any case, italicize numbers, letters, symbols, and terms but not the plural ending.

### ◢ EXERCISE 59.2

The following sentences, from which all apostrophes have been deleted, appear in Langston Hughes's "Salvation." Insert apostrophes where appropriate. Example:

> **"Sister Reed, what is this child's name?"**

1. There was a big revival at my Auntie Reeds church.
2. I heard the songs and the minister saying: "Why dont you come?"

3. Finally Westley said to me in a whisper: . . . "Im tired of sitting here. Lets get up and be saved."

4. So I decided that maybe to save further trouble, Id better lie. . . .

5. That night . . . I cried, in bed alone, and couldnt stop.

▼ ▼ ▼ ▼ ▼ ▼ ▼ ▼ ▼ ▼ ▼ ▼ ▼ ▼ ▼ ▼ ▼ ▼ ▼ ▼ ▼ ▼ ▼ ▼ ▼ ▼

## THINKING CRITICALLY ABOUT APOSTROPHES

Write a brief paragraph, beginning "I've always been amused by my neighbor's (or roommate's) _____." Then note every use of an apostrophe. Use the guidelines in this chapter to check that you have used apostrophes correctly.

# CHAPTER 60

# Quotation Marks

As a way of bringing other people's words into our own, quotation can be a powerful writing tool.

> Mrs. Macken urges parents to get books for their children, to read to them when they are "li'l," and when they start school to make certain they attend regularly. She holds herself up as an example of a "millhand's daughter who wanted to be a schoolteacher and did it through sheer hard work."
>
> —SHIRLEY BRICE HEATH, *Ways with Words*

The writer could have paraphrased, but by quoting, she lets her subject speak for herself — and lets readers hear that person's voice.

## 60a Using quotation marks to signal direct quotations

Use double quotation marks to signal a direct quotation.

▶ **The president asked Congress to "try common sense."**

▶ **She smiled and said, "Son, this is a day I will never forget."**

Single quotation marks enclose a quotation within a quotation. Open and close the quoted passage with double quotation marks, and change any quotation marks that appear *within* the quotation to single quotation marks.

▶ **James Baldwin says, "The title 'The Uses of the Blues' does not refer to music; I don't know anything about music."**

---

QUICK HELP

### Editing for quotation marks

- Use quotation marks around direct quotations and titles of short works. **(60a and b)**
- Do not use quotation marks around set-off quotations of more than four lines of prose or three lines of poetry or around titles of long works. **(60a and b)**

▶

**665**

Editing for quotation marks, continued

- Use quotation marks to signal irony and invented words, but do so sparingly. **(60c)**
- Never use quotation marks around indirect quotations. **(60d)**
- Do not use quotation marks to add emphasis to words. **(60d)**
- Check other punctuation used with closing quotation marks. **(60e)**
  Periods and commas should be *inside* the quotation marks.
  Colons, semicolons, and footnote numbers should be *outside*.
  Question marks, exclamation points, and dashes should be *inside* if they are part of the quoted material, *outside* if they are not.

## Quoting longer passages

If the prose passage you wish to quote exceeds four typed lines, set it off from the rest of the text by starting it on a new line and indenting it one inch from the left margin. This format, known as block quotation, does not require quotation marks.

> In "Suspended," Poet Laureate Joy Harjo tells of her first awareness of jazz as a child:
>
> > My rite of passage into the world of humanity occurred then, via jazz. The music made a startling bridge between the familiar and strange lands, an appropriate vehicle, for . . . we were there when jazz was born. I recognized it, that humid afternoon in my formative years, as a way to speak beyond the confines of ordinary language. I still hear it. (84)

This block quotation, including the ellipses and the page number in parentheses at the end, follows the style of the Modern Language Association (MLA). Other organizations, such as the American Psychological Association (APA) and the University of Chicago Press, have different guidelines for ellipses and block quotations. (See Chapters 18–21.)

## Quoting poetry

If the quotation is fewer than four lines, include it within your text, enclosed in double quotation marks. Separate the lines of the poem with slashes, each preceded and followed by a space, to tell the reader where one line of the poem ends and the next begins.

> In one of his best-known poems, Robert Frost remarks, "Two roads diverged in a wood, and I — / I took the one less traveled by, / And that has made all the difference" (lines 18–20).

To quote four or more lines of poetry, indent the block one inch from the left margin, and do not use quotation marks.

The duke in Robert Browning's "My Last Duchess" is clearly a jealous, vain person, whose own words illustrate his arrogance:

> She thanked men — good! but thanked
> Somehow — I know not how — as if she ranked
> My gift of a nine-hundred-years-old name
> With anybody's gift. (lines 31–34)

When you quote poetry, take care to follow the indentation, spacing, capitalization, punctuation, and other features of the original poem.

## Quoting dialogue

When you write dialogue or quote a conversation, enclose the words of each speaker in quotation marks, and mark each shift in speaker by beginning a new paragraph.

▶ **"I want no proof of their affection," said Elinor, "but of their engagement I do."**
**"I am perfectly satisfied of both."**
**"Yet not a syllable has been said to you on the subject, by either of them."**
—JANE AUSTEN, *Sense and Sensibility*

Because of the paragraph breaks in this example, we know when Elinor is speaking and when her mother is speaking without the author's having to repeat *said Elinor, her mother said,* and so on.

## 60b Using quotation marks to signal titles and definitions

Quotation marks are used to enclose the titles of short poems, short stories, articles, essays, songs, sections of books, and episodes of television and radio programs, as shown in the following examples.

▶ **"Dover Beach" moves from calm to sadness.** [poem]

▶ **Walker's " Everyday Use" is not just about quilts.** [short story]

▶ **The White Stripes released ten different versions of "The Denial Twist."** [song]

▶ **The *Atlantic* published an article titled "Illiberal Education."** [article]

▶ **In the chapter called "Complexion," Richard Rodriguez describes his sensitivity about his skin color.** [section of book]

▶ **The *Nature* episode "Echo of the Elephants" denounces ivory hunters.** [television series episode]

Use italics rather than quotation marks for the titles of television series, books, magazines, and other longer works (64a).

## 60c Using quotation marks to signal irony and invented words

To show readers that you are using a word or phrase ironically, or that you invented it, enclose it in quotation marks.

▶ **The "banquet" consisted mainly of dried-out chicken and canned vegetables.**

The quotation marks suggest that the meal was anything but a banquet.

▶ **Your whole first paragraph or first page may have to be guillotined in any case after your piece is finished: it is a kind of "forebirth."**
—JACQUES BARZUN, "A Writer's Discipline"

The writer made up the term *forebirth*.

### EXERCISE 60.1

Revise each of the following sentences, using quotation marks appropriately to signal titles, definitions, irony, or invented terms.

1. Stephen Colbert introduced Americans to the concept he calls truthiness on the first episode of *The Colbert Report*.

2. Margaret Talbot's article A Risky Proposal examined the constitutionality of state laws that banned gay marriage.

3. "The little that is known about gorillas certainly makes you want to know more," writes Alan Moorehead in his essay A Most Forgiving Ape.

4. My father's way of helping usually meant doing the whole project for me.

5. Should America the Beautiful replace The Star-Spangled Banner as the national anthem?

6. In the chapter called The Last to See Them Alive, Truman Capote shows the utterly ordinary life of the Kansas family.

7. *The Marvelous Mrs. Maisel* episode Kind of Bleu introduces homophobia, a heavy topic for a comedy series.

8. Several popular films, including *Mamma Mia!* and *Muriel's Wedding*, have used Abba hits such as Dancing Queen and Take a Chance on Me.

9. My dictionary defines *isolation* as the quality or state of being alone.

10. In his poem Harlem, Langston Hughes shows what can happen when people's dreams are consistently denied.

# 60d Avoiding misused quotation marks

Do not use quotation marks for *indirect* quotations — those that do not relay someone's exact words. (See 42e.)

▶ The teacher warned us that ⸝we could be expelled.⸜

Do not use quotation marks just to emphasize particular words or phrases.

▶ Much time was spent speculating about their ⸝relationship.⸜

Do not use quotation marks around slang or colloquial language; they create the impression that you are apologizing for using those words. Instead, try to express the idea in formal language. If you have a good reason to use a slang or colloquial term, use it without quotation marks (37a).

▶ After our twenty-mile hike, we were ready to ⸝turn in.⸜

# 60e Using quotation marks with other punctuation

Periods and commas go *inside* closing quotation marks.

▶ "Don't compromise yourself," said Janis Joplin. "You are all you've got."

*Exception*

When you use parenthetical documentation with a short quotation, place the period after the parentheses with source information (18c, 19c).

▶ In places, de Beauvoir "sees Marxists as believing in subjectivity" (Whitmarsh 63).

Colons, semicolons, and footnote numbers go *outside* closing quotation marks.

▶ **I felt only one emotion after reading "Eveline": sorrow.**

▶ **Everything is dark, and "a visionary light settles in her eyes"; this light is her salvation.**

▶ ***Tragedy* is defined by Aristotle as "an imitation of an action that is serious and of a certain magnitude."[1]**

Question marks, exclamation points, and dashes all go *inside* closing quotation marks if they are part of the quotation, *outside* if they are not.

PART OF THE QUOTATION

▶ **The cashier asked, "Would you like to super-size that?"**

▶ **"Jump!" one of the firefighters shouted.**

NOT PART OF THE QUOTATION

▶ **What is the theme of "A Good Man Is Hard to Find"?**

▶ **"Break a leg" — that phrase is supposed to bring good luck to a performer.**

For help using quotation marks in various documentation styles, see Chapters 18–21.

▼ ▼ ▼ ▼ ▼ ▼ ▼ ▼ ▼ ▼ ▼ ▼ ▼ ▼ ▼ ▼ ▼ ▼ ▼ ▼ ▼ ▼ ▼ ▼ ▼

## THINKING CRITICALLY ABOUT QUOTATION MARKS

### Reading with an eye for quotation marks

Read the following passage about the painter Georgia O'Keeffe, and pay particular attention to the use of quotation marks. What effect is created by the author's use of quotation marks with *hardness*, *crustiness*, and *crusty*? How do the quotations by O'Keeffe help support the author's description of her?

> "Hardness" has not been in our century a quality much admired in women, nor in the past twenty years has it even been in official favor for men. When hardness surfaces in the very old we tend to transform it into "crustiness" or eccentricity, some tonic pepperiness to be indulged at a distance. On the evidence of her work and what she has said about it, Georgia O'Keeffe is neither "crusty" nor eccentric. She is simply hard, a straight shooter, a woman clean of received wisdom and open to what she sees. This is a woman who could early on dismiss most of her contemporaries as "dreamy," and would later single out one she liked as "a very poor painter."     —JOAN DIDION, "Georgia O'Keeffe"

### Thinking about your own use of quotation marks

Choose a topic that is of interest on your campus, and interview one of your friends about it. On the basis of your notes from the interview, write two or three paragraphs about your friend's views, using several direct quotations that support the points you are making. Then see how closely you followed the conventions for quotation marks explained in this chapter. Note any usages that caused you problems.

# CHAPTER 61

# Other Punctuation Marks

Parentheses, brackets, dashes, colons, slashes, and ellipses are everywhere. Every URL includes colons and slashes, and dashes and ellipses are increasingly common in writing that expresses conversational informality.

You can also use these punctuation marks for more formal purposes: to signal relationships among parts of sentences, to create particular rhythms, and to help readers follow your thoughts.

## 61a Using parentheses

Parentheses enclose material of minor or secondary importance in a sentence — material that supplements, clarifies, comments on, or illustrates what precedes or follows it. Parentheses also enclose numbers or letters that precede items in a list, and sometimes they enclose source citations or publication information.

### Enclosing less important material

▶ **During my research, I found problems with the flat-rate income tax (a single-rate tax with no deductions).**

A period may be placed either inside or outside a closing parenthesis. If the parenthetical material is part of a larger sentence, put the period after the parentheses; if the entire sentence is in parentheses, put the period inside the parentheses. A comma, if needed, is always placed *outside* a closing parenthesis (and never before an opening one).

▶ **Gene Tunney's single defeat in an eleven-year career was to a flamboyant and dangerous fighter named Harry Greb ("The Human Windmill"), who seems to have been, judging from boxing literature, the dirtiest fighter in history.**                    —JOYCE CAROL OATES, "On Boxing"

If the material in parentheses is a question or an exclamation, use a question mark or exclamation point inside the closing parenthesis.

▶ **Our laughing (so deep was the pleasure!) became screaming.**
—RICHARD RODRIGUEZ, "Aria: A Memoir of a Bilingual Childhood"

In general, parentheses create more of an interruption than commas (Chapter 56) but less of an interruption than dashes (61c).

### Enclosing numbers or letters in a list

▶ **Five distinct styles can be distinguished: (1) Old New England, (2) Deep South, (3) Middle American, (4) Wild West, and (5) Far West or Californian.** —ALISON LURIE, *The Language of Clothes*

### Enclosing textual citations

The first of the following in-text citations shows the style of the American Psychological Association (see Chapter 19); the second shows the style of the Modern Language Association (see Chapter 18).

A recent study found that positive stereotypes of feminism bolster self-identification as feminist (Moore & Stathi, 2019).

Zamora notes that Kahlo referred to her first self-portrait, given to a close friend, as "your Botticelli" (110).

## 61b Using brackets

Use brackets to enclose parenthetical elements in material that is itself within parentheses and to enclose explanatory words or comments that you are inserting into a quotation.

### Setting off material within parentheses

▶ **The investigation examined the major agencies (including the National Security Agency [NSA]) that were conducting covert operations.**

### Inserting material within quotations

▶ **Massing notes that "on average, it [Fox News] attracts more than eight million people daily — more than double the number who watch CNN."**

The bracketed words clarify *it* in the original quotation.

In the quotation in the following sentence, the artist Gauguin's name is misspelled. The bracketed Latin word *sic*, which means "so," tells readers that the person being quoted — not the writer using the quotation — made the mistake.

▶ One admirer wrote, "She was the most striking woman I'd ever seen — a sort of wonderful combination of Mia Farrow and one of Gaugin's [*sic*] Polynesian nymphs."

### ◢ EXERCISE 61.1

Revise the following sentences, using parentheses and brackets correctly. Example:

She was in fourth grade (or was it third?) when she became blind.

1. The committee was presented with three options to pay for the new park: 1 increase vehicle registration fees, 2 install parking meters downtown, or 3 borrow money from the reserve fund.

2. The FISA statute authorizes government wiretapping only under certain circumstances for instance, the government has to obtain a warrant.

3. The health care expert informed readers that "as we progress through middle age, we experience intimations of our own morality *sic*."

4. Some hospitals train nurses in a pseudoscientific technique called therapeutic touch TT that has been discredited by many rigorous studies.

5. Because I was carrying an umbrella, which, as it turned out, wasn't even necessary, I was required to enter the stadium through the high-security gate.

## 61c Using dashes

In contrast to parentheses, dashes give more rather than less emphasis to the material they enclose. A typed dash is made with two hyphens (--) with *no* spaces before, between, or after.

### Inserting a comment

▶ The pleasures of reading itself — who doesn't remember? — were like those of Christmas cake, a sweet devouring.

— EUDORA WELTY, "A Sweet Devouring"

### Emphasizing explanatory material

▶ Indeed, several of modern India's greatest scholars — such as the Mughal historian Muzaffar Alam of the University of Chicago — are madrasa graduates.

— WILLIAM DALRYMPLE

## Emphasizing material at the end of a sentence

▶ Like you, he's black and from Harvard. Other than that, you know nothing — just the name, and it's an odd one.

—MICHELLE OBAMA, *Becoming*

## Marking a sudden change in tone

▶ New York is a catastrophe — but a magnificent catastrophe.

—LE CORBUSIER

### ◢ EXERCISE 61.2

Revise the following sentences to add dashes where appropriate. Example:

He is quick, violent, and mean — they don't call him Dirty Harry for

nothing — but appealing nonetheless.

1. Most people would say that Labradors are easy dogs to train but they never met our Millie.

2. Even if marijuana is dangerous an assertion disputed by many studies it is certainly no more harmful to human health than alcohol and cigarettes, which remain legal in every state.

3. If too much exposure to negative news stories makes you feel depressed or anxious and why wouldn't it? try going on a media fast.

4. Union Carbide's plant in Bhopal, India, sprang a leak that killed more than 2,000 people and injured an additional 200,000.

5. Refrigerators especially side-by-side models use up more energy than most people realize.

# 61d Using colons

Use a colon to introduce explanations, examples, lists, and sometimes quotations. In addition, follow conventions for using colons to separate some elements (such as titles and subtitles) from one another.

## Introducing an explanation or example

▶ The men may also wear the getup known as Sun Belt Cool: a pale beige suit, open-collared shirt (often in a darker shade than the suit), cream-colored loafers and aviator sunglasses.

—ALISON LURIE, *The Language of Clothes*

## Introducing a series, list, or quotation

▶ At the baby's one-month birthday party, Ah Po gave him the Four Valuable Things: ink, inkslab, paper, and brush.

—MAXINE HONG KINGSTON, *China Men*

▶ The teachers wondered: "Do boys and girls really learn differently? Do behavioral differences reflect socialization or biology?"

The preceding example could have used a comma instead of a colon before the quotation (56i). You can use a colon rather than a comma to introduce a quotation when the lead-in is a complete sentence on its own.

▶ The State of the Union address contained an unsurprising statement: "America is addicted to oil."

## Separating elements

SALUTATIONS IN FORMAL LETTERS

▶ Dear Dr. Mahiri:

RATIOS

▶ a ratio of 5:1

BIBLICAL CHAPTERS AND VERSES

▶ I Corinthians 3:3–5

TITLES AND SUBTITLES

▶ *Better: A Surgeon's Notes on Performance*

HOURS, MINUTES, AND SECONDS

▶ 4:59 PM

▶ 2:15:06

## Eliminating misused colons

Do not put a colon between a verb and its object or complement, unless the object is a quotation.

▶ Some natural fibers are: cotton, wool, silk, and linen.

Do not put a colon between a preposition and its object or after such expressions as *such as, especially,* or *including.*

▶ In poetry, additional power may come from devices such as: simile,

metaphor, and alliteration.

### ◢ EXERCISE 61.3

In the following items, insert a colon in any sentence that needs one and delete any unnecessary colons. Some sentences may be correct as written. Example:

*Images*: *My Life in Film* includes revealing material written by Ingmar

Bergman.

1. After discussing the case study, the class reached one main conclusion in any business, the most important asset is the customer.

2. Another example is taken from Psalm 139 16.

3. Roberto tried to make healthier choices, such as: eating organic food, walking to work, and getting plenty of rest.

4. A number of quotable movie lines come from *Casablanca*, including "Round up the usual suspects."

5. Sofi rushed to catch the 5 45 express but missed it and had to wait for the 6 19.

## 61e Using slashes

Use slashes to mark line divisions in poetry quoted within running text (60a). Whenever a slash separates lines of poetry, it should be preceded and followed by a space.

▶ **In "Digging," Seamus Heaney observes, "Between my finger and my thumb / The squat pen rests; snug as a gun."**

Slashes also separate parts of fractions and Internet addresses.

## 61f Using ellipses

Ellipses are three equally spaced dots. Ellipses usually indicate that something has been omitted from a quoted passage, but they can also signal a pause or hesitation in speech in the same way that a dash can. Today the use of ellipses in social media messages is rampant: too much of a good thing may not be so good after all!

### Indicating omissions

Just as you should carefully use quotation marks around any material that you quote directly from a source, so you should carefully use ellipses to indicate that you have left out part of a quotation that otherwise appears to be a complete sentence.

The ellipses in the following example indicate two omissions — one in the middle of the sentence and one at the end. When you omit the last part of a quoted sentence, add a period before the ellipses, for a total of four dots. Be sure a complete sentence comes before and after the four points. If you are adding your own ellipses to a quotation that already has other ellipses, enclose yours in brackets.

ORIGINAL TEXT

▶ **The quasi-official division of the population into three economic classes called high-, middle-, and low-income groups rather misses the point, because as a class indicator the amount of money is not as important as the source.** —PAUL FUSSELL, "Notes on Class"

WITH ELLIPSES

▶ **As Paul Fussell argues, "The quasi-official division of the population into three economic classes . . . rather misses the point. . . ."**

If your shortened quotation ends with a source (such as a page number, a name, or a title), follow these steps:

1. Use three ellipsis points but no period after the quotation.

2. Add the closing quotation mark, closed up following the third ellipsis point.

3. Add the source documentation in parentheses.

4. Use a period to indicate the end of the sentence.

▶ **Packer then argues, "The Administration is right to reconsider its strategy . . ." (34).**

## Indicating a pause or hesitation

Ellipses are becoming more common in informal communication, where many writers prefer them to a period at the end of a sentence.

▶ **Let me know where you want to meet tonight. . . .**

### EXERCISE 61.4

The following sentences use the punctuation marks presented in this chapter very effectively. Read the sentences carefully; then choose one, and use it as a model for writing a sentence of your own, making sure to use the punctuation marks in the same way in your sentence.

1. The dad was—how can you put this gracefully?—a real blimp, a wide load, and the white polyester stretch-pants only emphasized the cargo.
   —GARRISON KEILLOR, "Happy to Be Here"

2. Not only are the distinctions we draw between male nature and female nature largely arbitrary and often pure superstition: they are completely beside the point. —BRIGID BROPHY, "Women"

3. If no one, including you, liked the soup the first time round (and that's why you've got so much left over), there is no point in freezing it for some hopeful future date when, miraculously, it will taste delicious. But bagging leftovers—say, stews—in single portions can be useful for those evenings when you're eating alone.    —NIGELLA LAWSON, *How to Eat*

▼ ▼ ▼ ▼ ▼ ▼ ▼ ▼ ▼ ▼ ▼ ▼ ▼ ▼ ▼ ▼ ▼ ▼ ▼ ▼ ▼ ▼ ▼ ▼ ▼ ▼ ▼

## THINKING CRITICALLY ABOUT PUNCTUATION

### Reading with an eye for punctuation

In the following passage, Tom Wolfe uses dashes, parentheses, ellipses, and a colon to create rhythm and build momentum in a very long (178-word) sentence. The editorial comment inserted in brackets calls attention to the fact that the "right stuff" was, in the world Wolfe describes here, always male. Look carefully at how Wolfe and the editors use these punctuation marks, and then try writing a description of something that effectively uses as many of them as possible. Your description should be about the same length as Wolfe's passage, but it need not be all one sentence.

> Likewise, "hassling"—mock dogfighting—was strictly forbidden, and so naturally young fighter jocks could hardly wait to go up in, say, a pair of F-100s and start the duel by making a pass at each other at 800 miles an hour, the winner being the pilot who could slip in behind the other one and get locked in on his [never *her* or *his or her*!] tail ("wax his tail"), and it was not uncommon for some eager jock to try too tight an outside turn and have his engine flame out, whereupon, unable to restart it, he has to eject . . . and he shakes his fist at the victor as he floats down by parachute and his million-dollar aircraft goes *kaboom!* on the palmetto grass or the desert floor, and he starts thinking about how he can get together with the other guy back at the base in time for the two of them to get their stories straight before the investigation: "I don't know what happened, sir. I was pulling up after a target run, and it just flamed out on me."    —TOM WOLFE, *The Right Stuff*

### Thinking about your own use of punctuation

Look through a draft you have recently written or are working on, and check your use of parentheses, brackets, dashes, colons, slashes, and ellipses. Do you follow the conventions presented in this chapter? If not, revise accordingly. Check the material in parentheses to see if it could use more emphasis and thus be set off instead with dashes. Then check any material in dashes to see if it could do with less emphasis and thus be punctuated with commas or parentheses.

# CHAPTER 62

# Capital Letters

Capital letters are a key signal in everyday life. Look around any store to see their importance: you can shop for Levi's or *any* blue jeans, for Coca-Cola or *any* cola, for Kleenex or *any* tissue. As these examples show, one of the most common reasons for capitalizing a word is to indicate that it is part of a name or title — of a brand, person, article, or something else.

## 62a Capitalizing the first word of a sentence or line of poetry

Capitalize the first word of a sentence.

▶ **Posing relatives for photographs is a challenge.**

If you are quoting a full sentence, capitalize its first word.

▶ **Kennedy said, "Let us never negotiate out of fear."**

Capitalizing a sentence following a colon is optional.

▶ **Gould cites the work of Darwin: The [ *or* the] theory of natural selection incorporates the principle of evolutionary ties between all animals.**

Capitalize a sentence within parentheses unless the parenthetical sentence is inserted into another sentence.

▶ **Gould cites the work of Darwin. (Other researchers cite more recent evolutionary theorists.)**

▶ **Gould cites the work of Darwin (see page 150).**

When citing poetry, follow the capitalization of the original poem. Though most poets capitalize the first word of each line in a poem, some poets do not.

▶ **Morning sun heats up the young beech tree**
**leaves and almost lights them into fireflies**

—JUNE JORDAN, "Aftermath"

---

Editing for capitalization

- Capitalize the first word of each sentence. If you quote a poem, follow its original capitalization. **(62a)**
- Check to make sure you have appropriately capitalized proper nouns and proper adjectives. **(62b)**
- Review titles of people or of works to be sure you have capitalized them correctly. **(62b and c)**
- Double-check the capitalization of geographic directions (*north* or *North*?), family relationships (*dad* or *Dad*?), and seasons of the year (*winter*, not *Winter*). **(62d)**

## 62b Capitalizing proper nouns and proper adjectives

Capitalize proper nouns (those naming specific persons, places, and things) and most proper adjectives (those formed from proper nouns). All other nouns are common nouns and are not capitalized unless they begin a sentence or are used as part of a proper noun:

| PROPER NOUNS | COMMON NOUNS |
|---|---|
| **PEOPLE** | |
| Ang Lee | the film's director |
| Nixon | politician |
| **NATIONS, NATIONALITIES, ETHNIC GROUPS, AND LANGUAGES** | |
| Brazil, Brazilian | their native country, his citizenship |
| Italian American | an ethnic group |
| **PLACES** | |
| Pacific Ocean | an ocean |
| Hawaiian Islands | tropical islands |
| **STRUCTURES AND MONUMENTS** | |
| the Lincoln Memorial | a monument |
| the Eiffel Tower | a landmark |
| **SHIPS, TRAINS, AIRCRAFT, AND SPACECRAFT** | |
| the *Queen Mary* | a cruise ship |
| the *City of New Orleans* | the 6:00 train |

| PROPER NOUNS | COMMON NOUNS |
|---|---|
| **ORGANIZATIONS, BUSINESSES, AND GOVERNMENT INSTITUTIONS** | |
| United Auto Workers | a trade union |
| Library of Congress | a federal agency |
| **ACADEMIC INSTITUTIONS AND COURSES** | |
| University of Maryland | a state university |
| Political Science 102 | my political science course |
| **HISTORICAL EVENTS AND ERAS** | |
| the Easter Uprising | a revolt |
| the Renaissance | the fifteenth century |
| **RELIGIONS AND RELIGIOUS TERMS** | |
| God | a deity |
| the Qur'an | a holy book |
| Catholicism, Catholic | a religion, their religious affiliation |
| **TRADE NAMES** | |
| Nike | running shoes |
| Cheerios | cereal |

## Capitalizing product names

Some companies use capitals in the middle of their own or their product's names. Follow the style you see in company advertising or on the product itself — *eBay, FedEx, iPad.*

## Capitalizing titles before names

Capitalize titles used before a proper name. When used alone or following a proper name, most titles are not capitalized. One common exception is the word *president*, which many writers capitalize whenever it refers to the President of the United States.

| | |
|---|---|
| Chief Justice Roberts | John Roberts, the chief justice |
| Professor Lisa Ede | my English professor |
| Dr. Cheryl Gold | Cheryl Gold, our doctor |

---

LANGUAGE, CULTURE, | **ENGLISH CAPITALIZATION**
AND CONTEXT

Capitalization systems vary considerably among languages, and some languages (Arabic, Chinese, Hindi, and Hebrew, for example) do not use capital letters at all. English may be the only language to capitalize the first-person singular pronoun (*I*), but Dutch and German capitalize some forms of the second-person pronoun (*you*). German capitalizes all nouns; English used to capitalize more nouns than it does now (see, for instance, the Declaration of Independence).

## 62c Capitalizing titles of works

Capitalize most words in titles (of books, articles, plays, poems, songs, films, paintings, and so on). Do not capitalize an article (*a, an, the*), a preposition, a conjunction, or the *to* in an infinitive unless it is the first or last word in a title or subtitle.

| | |
|---|---|
| *Walt Whitman: A Life* | Declaration of Independence |
| "As Time Goes By" | *Charlie and the Chocolate Factory* |
| "Shooting an Elephant" | *Rebel without a Cause* |

 **EXERCISE 62.1**

Capitalize words as needed in the following sentences. Example:

>     T. S. Eliot,        *The Waste Land,*             Faber    Faber.
> ~~t. s. eliot,~~ who wrote ~~the waste land,~~ was an editor at ~~faber~~ and ~~faber.~~
>     ^               ^                        ^       ^

1. the town in the south where i was raised had a statue of a civil war soldier in the center of main street.

2. sarah palin, the former governor, frequently complained that the press had treated her harshly before she accepted a position as an analyst for fox news.

3. the corporation for public broadcasting relies on donations as well as on grants from the national endowment for the arts.

4. during the economic recession, companies such as starbucks had to close some of their stores; others, such as circuit city, went completely out of business.

5. most americans remember where they were when they heard about the 9/11 disaster.

# 62d Avoiding unnecessary capitalization

Do not capitalize a compass direction unless the word designates a specific geographic region.

▶ **Voters in the South and much of the West tend to favor socially conservative candidates.**

▶ **John Muir headed ~~West,~~** *west,* **motivated by the need to explore.**

Do not capitalize a word indicating a family relationship unless the word is used as part of the name or as a substitute for the name.

▶ **I could always tell when Mother was annoyed with Aunt Rose.**

▶ **When she was a child, my ~~Mother~~** *mother* **shared a room with my ~~Aunt.~~** *aunt.*

Do not capitalize seasons of the year and parts of the academic or financial year.

| | |
|---|---|
| spring | fall semester |
| winter | winter term |
| autumn | third-quarter earnings |

Capitalizing entire words and phrases in online writing gives them emphasis. On social media, writers may capitalize a few words or phrases for comic effect (*"I am shocked, SHOCKED to hear you say that!"*). But note that using all capital letters makes writing in digital environments feel like shouting. In email and professional writing, use italics, boldface, or underlining for emphasis.

### ◢ EXERCISE 62.2

Correct any unnecessary or missing capitalization in the following sentences. Some sentences may be correct as written. Example:

**A group of ~~Southern Governors~~** *southern governors* **meets annually in ~~washington,~~** *Washington,* **DC.**

1. The 2019 Walmart shootings in El Paso prompted yet another debate about Gun Control Laws in the United States.

2. Every Professor in the department of english has a degree in literature.

3. The Cast included several children, but only two of them had Speaking Roles.

4. Airport checkpoints are the responsibility of the Transportation Security Administration.

5. The price of oil has fluctuated this Winter.

▼ ▼ ▼ ▼ ▼ ▼ ▼ ▼ ▼ ▼ ▼ ▼ ▼ ▼ ▼ ▼ ▼ ▼ ▼ ▼ ▼ ▼ ▼ ▼ ▼

## THINKING CRITICALLY ABOUT CAPITALIZATION

The following poem uses unconventional capitalization. Read it over a few times, at least once aloud. What effect does the capitalization have? Why do you think the poet chose to use capitals as she did?

> A little Madness in the Spring
> Is wholesome even for the King,
> But God be with the Clown—
> Who ponders this tremendous scene—
> This whole Experiment of Green—
> As if it were his own!
> —EMILY DICKINSON

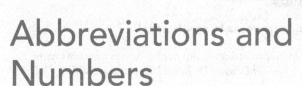

# CHAPTER 63

# Abbreviations and Numbers

Any time you look up an address, you see an abundance of abbreviations and numbers, as in the following movie theater listing from a Google map of Berkeley, California:

Oaks Theater, 1875 Solano Ave, Berkeley, CA

Abbreviations and numbers allow writers to present detailed information in a small amount of space. In academic writing, abbreviations and numbers follow conventions that vary from field to field.

## 63a Abbreviating titles and academic degrees

When used before or after a name, some personal and professional titles and academic degrees are abbreviated, even in academic writing.

| | |
|---|---|
| <u>Ms.</u> Siphiwe Ndlovu | Henry Louis Gates <u>Jr.</u> |
| <u>Mr.</u> Adam Banks | Gina Tartaglia, <u>MD</u> |
| <u>Dr.</u> Atma Vemulakonda | Bronwyn LaMay, <u>PhD</u> |

Most other titles — including any religious, military, academic, and governmental titles — should be spelled out in academic writing. In other writing, they may be abbreviated when they appear before a full name but should be spelled out when used with only a last name.

| | |
|---|---|
| Rev. Franklin Graham | Reverend Graham |
| Prof. Beverly Moss | Professor Moss |
| Gen. Colin Powell | General Powell |

Academic degrees may be abbreviated when used alone, but other titles used alone are never abbreviated.

▶ She received her <u>PhD</u> this year.

▶ He was a demanding ~~prof.~~ *professor,* and we worked hard.

Use either a title or an academic degree, but not both, with a person's name. Instead of *Dr. James Dillon, PhD,* write *Dr. James Dillon* or *James Dillon, PhD.*

## 63b Abbreviating years and hours

You can use the following abbreviations with numerals in formal academic writing. Notice that AD precedes the numeral; all other abbreviations follow the numeral. Today, BCE and CE are generally preferred over BC and AD, and periods in all four of these abbreviations are optional.

399 BCE ("before the common era") or 399 BC ("before Christ")

49 CE ("common era") or AD 49 (*anno Domini,* Latin for "year of our Lord")

11:15 AM (*or* a.m.)

9:00 PM (*or* p.m.)

## 63c Using acronyms and initial abbreviations

As long as you are sure your readers will understand them, it is acceptable to use common abbreviations such as NASA, DNA, and CIA. If the abbreviation may be unfamiliar to your readers, however, spell out the term the first time you use it, and give the abbreviation in parentheses. After that, you can use the abbreviation by itself.

▶ The U.S. Agency for International Development (USAID) fights poverty on a global scale.

## 63d Abbreviating company names

Use such abbreviations as *Co., Inc., Corp.,* and & if they are part of a company's official name. Do not, however, use these abbreviations in most other contexts.

▶ Sears, Roebuck & Co. was the only large ~~corp.~~ *corporation* in town.

## 63e Using Latin abbreviations

In general, avoid these Latin abbreviations except when citing sources:

|        |                              |      |                      |
|--------|------------------------------|------|----------------------|
| e.g.   | for example (*exempli gratia*) | i.e. | that is (*id est*)   |
| etc.   | and so forth (*et cetera*)     | n.b. | note well (*nota bene*) |

▶ Many firms have policies to help working parents — e.g., flexible hours,

     for example,

  parental leave, and day care.

▶ Before the conference began, Haivan unpacked the name tags,

  programs, pens, etc.
     and so forth.

## 63f Abbreviating reference information, geographic terms, and months

Though abbreviations for such words as *chapter* (ch.), *edition* (ed.), *page* (p.), or *pages* (pp.) are common in source citations, they are not appropriate in the body of a formal academic text.

▶ The 1851 ed. of *Twice-Told Tales* is now a valuable collectible.
          edition

Place-names and months of the year are often abbreviated in source citations, but they should almost always be written out within sentences.

▶ In Aug., I moved from Lodi, Calif., to L.A.
     August,              California,   Los Angeles.

Common exceptions are *Washington, DC,* and *U.S.* The latter is acceptable as an adjective but not as a noun.

▶ The U.S. delegation negotiated the treaty.

▶ The exchange student enjoyed the U.S.
                                United States.

## 63g Using symbols and units of measurement

In academic writing for English and the other humanities, symbols such as %, +, $, and = are acceptable in charts and graphs. Dollar signs are acceptable with figures: *$11* (but not with words: *eleven dollars*). Units of measurement can be abbreviated in charts and graphs (*4 in.*) but not in the body of a formal text (*four inches*). Check with your instructor about using a word or a figure with the word *percent*: some documentation styles, such as MLA, require a word (*ten percent*), while others, such as *Chicago*, require a figure whether the word (*10 percent*) or the symbol (*10%*) is used.

▶ **The ball sailed 425 ~~ft.~~ over the fence.**
   *feet*

Informal writing also has strong conventions for using certain symbols, such as the hashtag (#) for categorizing social media posts and the symbol @ for tagging Twitter users. Consider what symbols may be conventional in your context.

### EXERCISE 63.1

Revise each of the following sentences to eliminate any abbreviations that would be inappropriate in most academic writing. Example:

   *United States*
**The population of the ~~U.S.~~ grew considerably in the 1980s.**

1. Every Fri., my grandmother would walk a mi. to the P.O. and send a care package to her brother in Tenn.

2. The blue whale can grow to be 180 ft. long and can weigh up to 380,000 lbs.

3. Many a Mich.-based auto co., incl. GM, requested financial aid from the govt.

4. A large corp. like AT&T may help finance an employee's M.B.A.

5. Rosie began by saying, "If you want my two ¢," but she did not wait to see if listeners wanted it or not.

---

| LANGUAGE, CULTURE, AND CONTEXT | **THE TERM *HUNDRED*** |
|---|---|

The term *hundred* is used idiomatically in English. When it is linked with numbers like two, eight, and so on, the word *hundred* remains singular: *Eight <u>hundred</u> years have passed, and still old animosities run deep.* Add the plural *-s* to *hundred* only when no number precedes the term: <u>*Hundreds*</u> *of priceless books were lost in the fire.*

TALKING THE TALK | **ABBREVIATIONS AND NUMBERS IN DISCIPLINES**

Use of abbreviations and numbers varies in different fields. See a typical example from a biochemistry textbook:

> The energy of a green photon . . . is 57 kilocalories per mole (kcal/mol). An alternative unit of energy is the joule ( J), which is equal to 0.239 calorie; 1 kcal/mol is equal to 4.184 kJ/mol. — LUBERT STRYER, *Biochemistry*

These two sentences demonstrate how useful figures and abbreviations can be; reading the same sentences would be very difficult if the numbers and units of measurement had to be written out.

Be sure to use the appropriate system of measurement for the field you are discussing and for the audience you are addressing. Scientific fields generally use metric measurements, which are the standard in most nations other than the United States.

Become familiar with the conventions governing abbreviations and numbers in your field. The following reference books provide guidelines:

*MLA Handbook for Writers of Research Papers* for literature and the humanities

*Publication Manual of the American Psychological Association* for the social sciences

*Scientific Style and Format: The CSE Manual for Authors, Editors, and Publishers* for the natural sciences

*The Chicago Manual of Style* for the humanities

*AIP Style Manual* for physics and the applied sciences

## 63h Using numbers within sentences

In formal writing, if you can write out the number in one or two words, you should generally do so, and use figures for longer numbers.

▶ Her screams were heard by ~~38~~ thirty-eight people, but not one person called the

police.

▶ A baseball is held together by ~~two hundred sixteen~~ 216 red stitches.

If one of several numbers *of the same kind* in the same sentence requires a figure, use figures for all the numbers in that sentence.

▶ Our audio systems range in cost from ~~one hundred dollars~~ $100 to $2,599.

## 63i Using numbers to begin sentences

When a sentence begins with a number, either spell out the number or rewrite the sentence.

> *One hundred nineteen*
> ▶ ~~119~~ years of CIA labor cost taxpayers sixteen million dollars.
> ^

Most readers find it easier to read figures than three-word numbers; thus, the best solution may be to rewrite this sentence: *Taxpayers spent sixteen million dollars for 119 years of CIA labor.*

## 63j Following conventions for figures

| | |
|---|---|
| ADDRESSES | 23 Main Street; 175 Fifth Avenue |
| DATES | September 17, 1951; 4 BCE; the 1860s |
| DECIMALS AND FRACTIONS | 65.34; 8½ |
| PERCENTAGES | 77 percent (*or* 77%) |
| EXACT AMOUNTS OF MONEY | $7,348; $1.46 trillion; $2.50; thirty-five (*or* 35) cents |
| SCORES AND STATISTICS | an 8–3 Red Sox victory; a verbal score of 600; an average age of 22; a mean of 53 |
| TIME OF DAY | 6:00 AM (*or* a.m.) |

### ◢ EXERCISE 63.2

Revise the numbers in the following sentences as necessary for correctness and consistency. Some sentences may be correct as written. Example:

> *twenty-first*
> **Did the ~~21st~~ century begin in 2000 or 2001?**
> ^

1. In 2000, Al Gore won the popular presidential vote with 50,996,116 votes, but he was still short by 5 electoral votes.

2. 200,000 people may have perished in the 2010 Haitian earthquake.

3. The senator who voted against the measure received 6817 angry emails and only twelve in support of her decision.

4. Walker signed a three-year, $4.5-million contract.

5. In that age group, the risk is estimated to be about one in 2,500.

▼ ▼ ▼ ▼ ▼ ▼ ▼ ▼ ▼ ▼ ▼ ▼ ▼ ▼ ▼ ▼ ▼ ▼ ▼ ▼ ▼ ▼ ▼ ▼ ▼ ▼ ▼ ▼ ▼

## THINKING CRITICALLY ABOUT ABBREVIATIONS AND NUMBERS

### Reading with an eye for abbreviations and numbers

The paragraph by Roger Angell at the end of Chapter 64 follows the style of the *New Yorker* magazine, which often spells out numbers in situations where this chapter recommends using figures. Read the paragraph carefully, and then consider whether it would have been easier to read if figures had been used for some of the numbers. If so, which ones? Then consider how the paragraph would have been different if Angell had used *semi-professional* instead of *semi-pro*. What effect does the abbreviated form create?

### Thinking about your own use of abbreviations and numbers

Compare the way you have used abbreviations and numbers in a piece of formal writing for a class and in a sample of your informal writing. How are they different? Have you followed conventions for correctness, consistency, and appropriateness in both pieces of writing? If you discover a problem with abbreviations or numbers, make a note of it so that you can follow conventions appropriately in the future.

# CHAPTER 64

# Italics and Hyphens

The slanted type known as *italics* is more than just a pretty typeface. In the sentence "Many people read *People* on the subway every day," the italics (and the capital letter) tell us that *People* is a publication. Italics give words special meaning or emphasis. Hyphens, such as the one in "It's a well-liked publication," make sentences easier to read.

## 64a Using italics for titles

In general, use italics for titles of long works; use quotation marks for shorter works (60b and 62c).

| | |
|---|---|
| BOOKS | *Rise of the Black Panther* |
| CHOREOGRAPHIC WORKS | Agnes de Mille's *Rodeo* |
| FILMS AND VIDEOS | *Bohemian Rhapsody* |
| LONG MUSICAL WORKS | *Brandenburg Concertos* |
| LONG POEMS | *Bhagavad Gita* |
| MAGAZINES | *Ebony* |
| JOURNALS | the *New England Journal of Medicine* |
| NEWSPAPERS | the *Cleveland Plain Dealer* |
| PAINTINGS AND SCULPTURE | Kristen Visbal's *Fearless Girl* |
| PAMPHLETS | Thomas Paine's *Common Sense* |
| PLAYS | *Angels in America* |
| RADIO SERIES | *All Things Considered* |
| RECORDINGS | *Ladilikan* |
| SOFTWARE | *Final Cut Pro X* |
| TELEVISION SERIES | *Orange Is the New Black* |

Do not use italics for sacred books, such as the Bible and the Qur'an; for public documents, such as the Constitution and the Magna Carta; or for the titles of your own papers. With magazines and newspapers, do not italicize or capitalize an initial *the*, even if it's part of the official name.

## 64b Using italics for words, letters, and numbers referred to as terms

▶ One characteristic of some New York speech is the absence of postvocalic *r*, with some New Yorkers pronouncing *four* as "fouh."

▶ The first four orbitals are represented by the letters *s*, *p*, *d*, and *f*.

▶ On the back of his jersey was the famous *24*.

## 64c Using italics for non-English words and phrases

Italicize words and phrases from other languages unless they have become part of English, such as the Spanish "fiesta." If a word is in an English dictionary, it does not need italics.

▶ At last one of the phantom sleighs gliding along the street would come to a stop, and with gawky haste Mr. Burness in his fox-furred *shapka* would make for our door. —VLADIMIR NABOKOV, *Speak, Memory*

Always italicize Latin genus and species names.

▶ The caterpillars of *Hapalia*, when attacked by the wasp *Apanteles machaeralis*, drop suddenly from their leaves and suspend themselves in air by a silken thread. —STEPHEN JAY GOULD, "Nonmoral Nature"

## 64d Using italics for emphasis

Italics can help create emphasis in writing, but use them sparingly for this purpose. It is usually better to create emphasis with sentence structure and word choice.

▶ Great literature and a class of literate readers are nothing new in India. What is new is the emergence of a gifted generation of Indian writers *working in English*. —SALMAN RUSHDIE

### EXERCISE 64.1

In each of the following sentences, underline any words that should be italicized and circle any words that are italicized but should not be. Example:

The film Good Night, and Good Luck tells the story of a CBS newsman who helped to end the career of Senator Joseph McCarthy.

1. One critic claimed that few people listened to *The Velvet Underground and Nico* when the record was issued but that everyone who did formed a band.

2. Homemade *sushi* can be dangerous, but so can deviled eggs kept too long in a picnic basket.

3. The website Poisonous Plants and Animals lists tobacco (Nicotiana tabacum) as one of the most popular poisons in the world.

4. The monster in the Old English epic Beowulf got to tell his own side of the story in John Gardner's novel Grendel.

5. The 2009 film Star Trek imagines the youthful life of James T. Kirk and the crew of the Enterprise.

## 64e Using hyphens with compound words

Hyphen problems are now one of the twenty most common surface errors in student writing. The confusion is understandable. Over time, the conventions for hyphen use in a given word can change (*tomorrow* was once spelled *to-morrow*). New words, even compounds such as *firewall*, generally don't use hyphens, but style manuals still differ over whether to hyphenate *ebook* (or is it *e-book*?). And some words are hyphenated when they serve one kind of purpose in a sentence and not when they serve another.

Some compounds are one word (*rowboat*), some are separate words (*hard drive*), and some require hyphens (*sister-in-law*). You should consult a dictionary to be sure. However, the following conventions can help you decide when to use hyphens with compound words.

### Hyphenating compound adjectives

Hyphenate most compound adjectives that precede a noun but not those that follow a noun.

| | |
|---|---|
| a *well-liked* boss | My boss is *well liked*. |
| a *six-foot* plank | The plank is *six feet long*. |

In general, the reason for hyphenating most compound adjectives is to facilitate reading.

▶ **Designers often use potted plants as living-room dividers.**

Without the hyphen, *living* may seem to modify *room dividers*.

Commonly used compound adjectives, however, do not usually need to be hyphenated for clarity — *income tax reform* or *first class mail* would seldom if ever be misunderstood.

Never hyphenate an *-ly* adverb and an adjective.

▶ **They used a widely/distributed mailing list.**

Compound adjectives formed from compound proper nouns are hyphenated if the noun is hyphenated: *Austro-Hungarian history* but *Latin American literature*.

## Hyphenating coined compounds

You may need hyphens to link coined compounds, combinations of words that you are using in an unexpected way, especially as an adjective.

▶ **She gave me her I-told-you-so look before leaving the party.**

## Hyphenating fractions and compound numbers

Use a hyphen to write out fractions and to spell out compound numbers from twenty-one to ninety-nine, both when they stand alone and when they are part of larger numbers. (Usually such larger numbers should be written as numerals. See Chapter 63.)

| | |
|---|---|
| one-seventh | thirty-seven |
| two and seven-sixteenths | three hundred fifty-four thousand |

# 64f Using hyphens with prefixes and suffixes

Most words containing prefixes or suffixes are written without hyphens, such as *antiwar* or *Romanesque*. Here are some exceptions:

| | |
|---|---|
| **BEFORE CAPITALIZED BASE WORDS** | un-American, non-Catholic |
| **WITH FIGURES** | pre-1960, post-1945 |
| **WITH CERTAIN PREFIXES AND SUFFIXES** | all-state, ex-partner, self-possessed, quasi-legislative, mayor-elect, fifty-odd |
| **WITH COMPOUND BASE WORDS** | pre-high school, post-cold war |
| **FOR CLARITY OR EASE OF READING** | re-cover, anti-inflation, un-ionized |

*Re-cover* means "cover again"; the hyphen distinguishes it from *recover*, meaning "get well." In *anti-inflation* and *un-ionized*, the hyphens separate confusing clusters of vowels and consonants.

# 64g Avoiding unnecessary hyphens

Unnecessary hyphens are at least as common a problem as omitted ones. Do not hyphenate the parts of a two-word verb such as *depend on, turn off,* or *tune out* (55b).

▶ Players must pick/up a medical form before football tryouts.

> The words *pick up* act as a verb and should not be hyphenated.

However, be careful to check that the two words do indeed function as a verb in the sentence; if they function as an adjective, a hyphen may be needed (48a and d).

▶ Let's sign up for the early class.

> The verb *sign up* should not have a hyphen.

▶ Where is the sign-up sheet?

> The compound adjective *sign-up*, which modifies the noun *sheet*, needs a hyphen.

Do not hyphenate a subject complement — a word group that follows a linking verb (such as a form of *be* or *seem*) and describes the subject.

▶ Audrey is almost fifteen/years/old.

---

### ◢ EXERCISE 64.2

Insert or delete hyphens as necessary in the following sentences. Use your dictionary if you are not sure whether or where to hyphenate a word. Example:

> The governor-elect joked about the polls.

1. The group seeks volunteers to set-up chairs in the meeting room before the event.

2. Despite concerns about reliability, police line-ups are still frequently used to identify suspects.

3. I was ill-prepared for my first calculus exam, but I managed to pass anyway.

4. Some passengers were bumped from the over-sold flight.

5. Having an ignore the customer attitude may actually make a service-industry job less pleasant.

6. Both pro and antiState Department groups registered complaints.

7. At a yard sale, I found a 1964 pre CBS Fender Stratocaster in mint condition.

8. Applicants who are over fifty-years-old may face age discrimination.

9. Neil Armstrong, a selfproclaimed "nerdy engineer," was the first person to set foot on the moon.

10. Carefully-marketed children's safety products suggest to new parents that the more they spend, the safer their kids will be.

▼ ▼ ▼ ▼ ▼ ▼ ▼ ▼ ▼ ▼ ▼ ▼ ▼ ▼ ▼ ▼ ▼ ▼ ▼ ▼ ▼ ▼ ▼ ▼ ▼

## THINKING CRITICALLY ABOUT ITALICS AND HYPHENATION

### Reading with an eye for hyphenation

The following paragraph uses many hyphens. Read it carefully, and note how the hyphens make the paragraph easier to read. Why do you think *semi-pro* is hyphenated? Why is *minor-leaguers* hyphenated in the second sentence?

All semi-pro leagues, it should be understood, are self-sustaining, and have no farm affiliation or other connection with the twenty-six major-league clubs, or with the seventeen leagues and hundred and fifty-two teams . . . that make up the National Association—the minors, that is. There is no central body of semi-pro teams, and semi-pro players are not included among the six hundred and fifty major-leaguers, the twenty-five-hundred-odd minor-leaguers, plus all the managers, coaches, presidents, commissioners, front-office people, and scouts, who, taken together, constitute the great tent called organized ball.

—ROGER ANGELL, "In the Country"

### Thinking about your own use of italics

Write a paragraph or two describing the most eccentric person you know, italicizing some words for special emphasis. Read your passage aloud to hear the effect of the italics. Now explain each use of italics. If you find yourself unable to give a reason, ask yourself whether the word should be italicized at all. Then revise the passage to eliminate all but one use of italics. Try revising sentences and choosing more precise words to convey emphasis. Decide which version is more effective. Can you reach any conclusions about using italics for emphasis?

# GLOSSARY OF USAGE

Conventions of usage might be called the "good manners" of discourse. And just as manners vary from culture to culture and time to time, so do conventions of usage. Matters of usage, like other language choices you must make, depend on what your purpose is and on what is appropriate for a particular audience at a particular time.

**a, an** Use *a* with a word that begins with a consonant (*a book*), a consonant sound such as "y" or "w" (*a euphoric moment, a one-sided match*), or a sounded $\bar{h}$ (*a hemisphere*). Use *an* with a word that begins with a vowel (*an umbrella*), a vowel sound (*an X-ray*), or a silent *h* (*an honor*).

**accept, except** The verb *accept* means "receive" or "agree to." *Except* is usually a preposition that means "aside from" or "excluding." *All the plaintiffs except Mr. Kim decided to accept the settlement.*

**advice, advise** The noun *advice* means "opinion" or "suggestion"; the verb *advise* means "offer advice." *Doctors advise everyone not to smoke, but many people ignore the advice.*

**affect, effect** As a verb, *affect* means "influence" or "move the emotions of"; as a noun, it means "emotions" or "feelings." *Effect* is a noun meaning "result"; less commonly, it is a verb meaning "bring about." *The storm affected a large area. Its effects included widespread power failures. The drug effected a major change in the patient's affect.*

**all ready, already** *All ready* means "fully prepared." *Already* means "previously." *We were all ready for Lucy's party when we learned that she had already left.*

**all right, alright** Avoid the spelling *alright*.

**all together, altogether** *All together* means "all in a group" or "gathered in one place." *Altogether* means "completely" or "everything considered." *When the board members were all together, their mutual distrust was altogether obvious.*

**allude, elude** *Allude* means "refer indirectly." *Elude* means "avoid" or "escape from." *The candidate did not even allude to her opponent. The suspect eluded the police for several days.*

**allusion, illusion** An *allusion* is an indirect reference. An *illusion* is a false or misleading appearance. *The speaker's allusion to the Bible created an illusion of piety.*

**a lot** Avoid the spelling *alot*.

**already** See *all ready, already*.

**alright** See *all right, alright*.

**altogether** See *all together, altogether*.

**among, between** In referring to two things or people, use *between*. In referring to three or more, use *among*. *The relationship between the twins is different from that among the other three children.*

699

**amount, number** Use *amount* with quantities you cannot count; use *number* for quantities you can count. *A small number of volunteers cleared a large amount of brush.*

**an** See *a, an.*

**and/or** Avoid this term except in business or legal writing. Instead of *fat and/or protein,* write *fat, protein, or both.*

**any body, anybody, any one, anyone** *Anybody* and *anyone* are pronouns meaning "any person." *Anyone* [or *anybody*] *would enjoy this film. Any body* is an adjective modifying a noun. *Any body of water has its own ecology. Any one* is two adjectives or a pronoun modified by an adjective. *Customers could buy only two sale items at any one time. The winner could choose any one of the prizes.*

**anyplace** In academic and professional discourse, use *anywhere* instead.

**anyway, anyways** In writing, use *anyway,* not *anyways.*

**as** Avoid sentences in which it is not clear if *as* means "when" or "because." For example, does *Carl left town as his father was arriving* mean "at the same time as his father was arriving" or "because his father was arriving"?

**as, as if, like** In academic and professional writing, use *as* or *as if* instead of *like* to introduce a clause. *The dog howled as if* [not *like*] *it were in pain. She did as* [not *like*] *I suggested.*

**assure, ensure, insure** *Assure* means "convince" or "promise"; its direct object is usually a person or persons. *She assured voters she would not raise taxes. Ensure* and *insure* both mean "make certain," but *insure* usually refers specifically to protection against financial loss. *When the city rationed water to ensure that the supply would last, the Browns could no longer afford to insure their car-wash business.*

**as to** Do not use *as to* as a substitute for *about. Karen was unsure about* [not *as to*] *Bruce's intentions.*

**at, where** See *where.*

**awhile, a while** Always use *a while* after a preposition such as *for, in,* or *after. We drove awhile and then stopped for a while.*

**bad, badly** Use *bad* after a linking verb such as *be, feel,* or *seem.* Use *badly* to modify an action verb, an adjective, or another verb. *The hostess felt bad because the dinner was badly prepared.*

**because of, due to** Use *due to* when the effect, stated as a noun, appears before the verb *be. His illness was due to malnutrition.* (*Illness,* a noun, is the effect.) Use *because of* when the effect is stated as a clause. *He was sick because of malnutrition.* (*He was sick,* a clause, is the effect.)

**beside, besides** *Beside* is a preposition meaning "next to." *Besides* can be a preposition meaning "other than" or an adverb meaning "in addition." *No one besides Francesca would sit beside him.*

**between** See *among, between.*

**can, may** *Can* refers to ability and *may* to possibility or permission. *Since I can ski the slalom well, I may win the race.*

**censor, censure** *Censor* means "remove that which is considered offensive." *Censure* means "formally reprimand." *The newspaper censored stories that offended advertisers. The legislature censured the official for misconduct.*

**compare to, compare with** *Compare to* means "regard as similar." *Jamie compared the loss to a kick in the head. Compare with* means "examine to find differences or similarities." *Compare Tim Burton's films with David Lynch's.*

**complement, compliment** *Complement* means "go well with." *Compliment* means "praise." *Guests complimented her on how her earrings complemented her gown.*

**comprise, compose** *Comprise* means "contain." *Compose* means "make up." *The class comprises twenty students. Twenty students compose the class.*

**conscience, conscious** *Conscience* means "a sense of right and wrong." *Conscious* means "awake" or "aware." *Lisa was conscious of a guilty conscience.*

**consequently, subsequently** *Consequently* means "as a result"; *subsequently* means "then." *He quit, and subsequently his wife lost her job; consequently, they had to sell their house.*

**continual, continuous** *Continual* means "repeated at regular or frequent intervals." *Continuous* means "continuing or connected without a break." *The damage done by continuous erosion was increased by the continual storms.*

**could of** *Have*, not *of*, should follow *could, would, should,* or *might. We could have* [not *of*] *invited them.*

**criteria, criterion** *Criterion* means "standard of judgment" or "necessary qualification." *Criteria* is the plural form. *Image is the wrong criterion for choosing a president.*

**data** *Data* is the plural form of the Latin word *datum*, meaning "fact." Although *data* is used informally as either singular or plural, in academic or professional writing, treat *data* as plural. *These data indicate that fewer people are smoking.*

**different from, different than** *Different from* is generally preferred in academic and professional writing, although both of these phrases are widely used. *Her lab results were no different from* [not *than*] *his.*

**disinterested, uninterested** *Disinterested* means "unbiased." *Uninterested* means "indifferent." *Finding disinterested jurors was difficult. She was uninterested in the verdict.*

**distinct, distinctive** *Distinct* means "separate" or "well defined." *Distinctive* means "characteristic." *Germany includes many distinct regions, each with a distinctive accent.*

**doesn't, don't** *Doesn't* is the contraction for *does not*. Use it with *he, she, it*, and singular nouns. *Don't* stands for *do not*; use it with *I, you, we, they*, and plural nouns.

**due to** See *because of, due to*.

**each other, one another** Use *each other* in sentences involving two subjects and *one another* in sentences involving more than two.

**effect** See *affect, effect*.

**elude** See *allude, elude*.

**emigrate from, immigrate to** *Emigrate from* means "move away from one's country." *Immigrate to* means "move to another country." *We emigrated from Norway in 1999. We immigrated to the United States.*

**ensure** See *assure, ensure, insure*.

**every day, everyday** *Everyday* is an adjective meaning "ordinary." *Every day* is an adjective and a noun, meaning "each day." *I wore everyday clothes almost every day.*

**every one, everyone** *Everyone* is a pronoun. *Every one* is an adjective and a pronoun, referring to each member of a group. *Because he began after everyone else, David could not finish every one of the problems.*

**except** See *accept, except.*

**explicit, implicit** *Explicit* means "directly or openly expressed." *Implicit* means "indirectly expressed or implied." *The explicit message of the ad urged consumers to buy the product, while the implicit message promised popularity if they did so.*

**farther, further** *Farther* refers to physical distance. *How much farther is it to Munich? Further* refers to time or degree. *I want to avoid further delays.*

**fewer, less** Use *fewer* with nouns that can be counted. Use *less* with general amounts that you cannot count. *The world needs fewer bombs and less hostility.*

**firstly, secondly, etc.** *First, second,* etc., are more common in U.S. English.

**former, latter** *Former* refers to the first and *latter* to the second of two things previously mentioned. *Kathy and Anna are athletes; the former plays tennis, and the latter runs.*

**further** See *farther, further.*

**good, well** *Good* is an adjective and should not be used as a substitute for the adverb *well*. *Gabriel is a good host who cooks well.*

**good and** *Good and* is colloquial for "very"; avoid it in academic and professional writing.

**hanged, hung** *Hanged* refers to executions; *hung* is used for all other meanings.

**herself, himself, myself, yourself** Do not use these reflexive pronouns as subjects or as objects unless they are necessary. *Jane and I* [not *myself*] *agree. They invited John and me* [not *myself*].

**he/she, his/her** Better solutions for avoiding sexist and noninclusive language are to eliminate pronouns entirely or to make the subject plural. Instead of writing *Everyone should carry his/her driver's license,* try *Drivers should carry their licenses* or *Everyone should carry their driver's license.*

**himself** See *herself, himself, myself, yourself.*

**hisself** Use *himself* instead in academic or professional writing.

**hung** See *hanged, hung.*

**illusion** See *allusion, illusion.*

**immigrate to** See *emigrate from, immigrate to.*

**impact** Some readers object to the colloquial use of *impact* or *impact on* as a verb meaning "affect." *Population control may reduce* [not *impact*] *world hunger.*

**implicit** See *explicit, implicit.*

**imply, infer** To *imply* is to suggest indirectly. To *infer* is to guess or conclude on the basis of an indirect suggestion. *The note implied they were planning a small wedding; we inferred we would not be invited.*

**inside of, outside of** Use *inside* and *outside* instead. *The class regularly met outside* [not *outside of*] *the building.*

**insure** See *assure, ensure, insure.*

**interact, interface** *Interact* is a vague word meaning "do something that somehow involves another person." *Interface* is computer jargon; when used as a verb, it means "discuss" or "communicate." It is best to avoid both verbs in academic writing.

**irregardless, regardless** *Irregardless* is a double negative. Use *regardless*.

**is when, is where** These vague expressions are often incorrectly used in definitions. *Schizophrenia is a psychotic condition in which* [not *when* or *where*] *a person withdraws from reality.*

**its, it's** *Its* is the possessive form of *it*. *It's* is a contraction for *it is* or *it has*. *It's important to observe the rat before it eats its meal.*

**know, no** Use *know* to mean "understand." *No* is the opposite of *yes*.

**later, latter** *Later* means "after some time." *Latter* refers to the second of two items named. *Juan and Chad won all their early matches, but the latter was injured later in the season.*

**latter** See *former, latter* and *later, latter.*

**lay, lie** *Lay* means "place" or "put." Its main forms are *lay, laid, laid*. It generally has a direct object, specifying what has been placed. *She laid her books on the desk. Lie* means "recline" or "be positioned" and does not take a direct object. Its main forms are *lie, lay, lain. She lay awake until two.*

**leave, let** *Leave* means "go away." *Let* means "allow." *Leave alone* and *let alone* are interchangeable. *Let me leave now, and leave* [or *let*] *me alone from now on!*

**less** See *fewer, less.*

**let** See *leave, let.*

**lie** See *lay, lie.*

**like** See *as, as if, like.*

**literally** *Literally* means "actually" or "exactly as stated." Use it to stress the truth of a statement that might otherwise be understood as figurative. Do not use *literally* as an intensifier in a figurative statement. *Mirna was literally at the edge of her seat* may be accurate, but *Mirna is so hungry that she could literally eat a horse* is not.

**loose, lose** *Lose* is a verb meaning "misplace." *Loose* is an adjective that means "not securely attached." *Sew on that loose button before you lose it.*

**lots, lots of** Avoid these informal expressions meaning "much" or "many" in academic or professional discourse.

**man, mankind** Replace these terms with *people, humans, humankind*, or similar wording.

**may** See *can, may.*

**may be, maybe** *May be* is a verb phrase. *Maybe* is an adverb that means "perhaps." *He may be the head of the organization, but maybe someone else would handle a crisis better.*

**media** *Media* is the plural form of the noun *medium* and takes a plural verb. *The media are* [not *is*] *obsessed with scandals.*

**might of** See *could of.*

**moral, morale** A *moral* is a succinct lesson. *The moral of the story is that generosity is rewarded. Morale* means "spirit" or "mood." *Office morale was low.*

**myself** See *herself, himself, myself, yourself.*

**no** See *know, no.*

**nor, or** Use *either* with *or* and *neither* with *nor*.

**number** See *amount, number*.

**off of** Use *off* without *of*. *The spaghetti slipped off* [not *off of*] *the plate*.

**one another** See *each other, one another*.

**or** See *nor, or*.

**outside of** See *inside of, outside of*.

**passed, past** Use *passed* to mean "went by" or "received a passing grade": *The marching band passed the reviewing stand*. Use *past* to refer to a time before the present: *Historians study the past*.

**per** Use the Latin *per* only in standard technical phrases such as *miles per hour*. Otherwise, find English equivalents. *As mentioned in* [not *As per*] *the latest report, the country's average food consumption each day* [not *per day*] *is only 2,000 calories*.

**percent, percentage** Use *percent* with a specific number; use *percentage* with an adjective such as *large* or *small*. *Last year, 80 percent of the members were female. A large percentage of the members are women*.

**precede, proceed** *Precede* means "come before"; *proceed* means "go forward." *Despite the storm that preceded the ceremony, the wedding proceeded on schedule*.

**principal, principle** When used as a noun, *principal* refers to a head official or an amount of money; when used as an adjective, it means "most significant." *Principle* means "fundamental law or belief." *Albert went to the principal and defended himself with the principle of free speech*.

**proceed** See *precede, proceed*.

**quotation, quote** *Quote* is a verb, and *quotation* is a noun. *He quoted the president, and the quotation* [not *quote*] *was preserved in history books*.

**raise, rise** *Raise* means "lift" or "move upward." (Referring to children, it means "bring up.") It takes a direct object; someone raises something. *The guests raised their glasses to toast. Rise* means "go upward." It does not take a direct object; something rises by itself. *She saw the steam rise from the pan*.

**real, really** *Real* is an adjective, and *really* is an adverb. Do not substitute *real* for *really*. In academic and professional writing, do not use *real* or *really* to mean "very." *The old man walked very* [not *real* or *really*] *slowly*.

**reason is because** Use either *the reason is that* or *because*—not both. *The reason the copier stopped is that* [not *is because*] *the paper jammed*.

**reason why** Avoid this expression in formal writing. *The reason* [not *reason why*] *this book is short is market demand*.

**regardless** See *irregardless, regardless*.

**respectfully, respectively** *Respectfully* means "with respect." *Respectively* means "in the order given." *Karen and David are, respectively, a juggler and an acrobat. The children treated their grandparents respectfully*.

**rise** See *raise, rise*.

**set, sit** *Set* usually means "put" or "place" and takes a direct object. *Sit* refers to taking a seat and does not take an object. *Set your cup on the table, and sit down*.

**should of** See *could of*.

**since** Be careful not to use *since* ambiguously. In *Since I broke my leg, I've stayed home*, the word *since* might be understood to mean either "because" or "ever since."

**sit** See *set, sit*.

**so** In academic and professional writing, avoid using *so* alone to mean "very." Instead, follow *so* with *that* to show how the intensified condition leads to a result. *Aaron was so tired that he fell asleep at the wheel.*

**someplace** Use *somewhere* instead in academic and professional writing.

**some time, sometime, sometimes** *Some time* refers to a length of time. *Please leave me some time to dress. Sometime* means "at some indefinite later time." *Sometime I will take you to London. Sometimes* means "occasionally." *Sometimes I eat sushi.*

**subsequently** See *consequently, subsequently*.

**supposed to, used to** Be careful to include the final *-d* in these expressions. *He is supposed to attend.*

**sure, surely** Avoid using *sure* or *surely* as an intensifier. Instead, use *certainly*. *I was certainly glad to see you.*

**than, then** Use *than* in comparative statements. *The cat was bigger than the dog.* Use *then* when referring to a sequence of events. *I won, and then I cried.*

**that, which** A clause beginning with *that* singles out the item being described. *The book that is on the table is a good one* specifies the book on the table as opposed to some other book. A clause beginning with *which* may or

may not single out the item, although some writers use *which* clauses only to add more information about an item being described. *The book, which is on the table, is a good one* contains a *which* clause between the commas. The clause simply adds extra, nonessential information about the book; it does not specify which book.

**theirselves** Use *themselves* instead in academic and professional writing.

**then** See *than, then*.

**thorough, threw, through** *Thorough* means "complete": *After a thorough inspection, the restaurant reopened. Threw* is the past tense of *throw*, and *through* means "in one side and out the other": *He threw the ball through a window.*

**to, too, two** *To* generally shows direction. *Too* means "also." *Two* is the number. *We, too, are going to the meeting in two hours.* Avoid using *to* after *where*. *Where are you flying* [not *flying to*]?

**two** See *to, too, two*.

**uninterested** See *disinterested, uninterested*.

**unique** Some people argue that *unique* means "one and only" and object to usage that suggests it means merely "unusual." In formal writing, avoid constructions such as *quite unique*.

**used to** See *supposed to, used to*.

**very** Avoid using *very* to intensify a weak adjective or adverb; instead, replace the adjective or adverb with a stronger, more precise, or more colorful word. Instead of *very nice*, for example, use *kind, warm, sensitive, endearing*, or *friendly*.

**well** See *good, well*.

**where** Use *where* alone, not with words such as *at* and *to*. *Where are you going* [not *going to*]?

**which** See *that, which*.

**who, whom** Use *who* if the word is the subject of the clause and *whom* if the word is the object of the clause. *Monica, who smokes incessantly, is my godmother.* (*Who* is the subject of the clause; the verb is *smokes*.) *Monica, whom I saw last winter, lives in Tucson.* (*Whom* is the object of the verb *saw*.)

**who's, whose** *Who's* is a contraction for *who is* or *who has*. *Who's on the patio? Whose* is a possessive form. *Whose sculpture is in the garden? Whose is on the patio?*

**would of** See *could of*.

**your, you're** *Your* shows possession. *Bring your sleeping bag along. You're* is the contraction for *you are*. *You're in the wrong sleeping bag.*

**yourself** See *herself, himself, myself, yourself*.

# ANSWERS TO SELECTED EXERCISES

Here are answers to all the exercises that have specific answers. Partial and suggested answers are provided where appropriate, and exercises for which answers will vary are not covered here.

**EXERCISE 11.1: Suggested Answers**

1. Arguable
2. Not arguable
3. Arguable
4. Not arguable
5. Arguable
6. Not arguable, unless students want to discuss boiling temperatures at different air pressures
7. Arguable
8. Arguable, depending on the acceptance of statistical reports
9. Arguable
10. Arguable, although some studies continue to show correlations between reduced speed and lower accident rates. More readily verifiable is the correlation between speed limit and mortality rate.

**EXERCISE 11.3: Suggested Answers**

1. Immigration policy affects the U.S. economy in important ways. *Thesis:* While stricter immigration policies may protect American jobs in the short run, they will lower the level of innovation and scientific progress in the long run.
2. The public school system must do more to reverse bullying culture. *Thesis:* As part of a multitiered solution to the problem of bullying, school districts must educate teachers to be able to recognize and report what researchers call gateway behaviors among students.
3. College tuition is too expensive. *Thesis:* Lowering college tuition rates would benefit our entire society by allowing more people to become educated contributors to the country's economy.
4. The reinstatement of the U.S. military draft would force every citizen to consider whether a war would be worth their life, or the life of a family member. *Thesis:* Reinstating the draft would

help bring the reality of war home to the United States as it would force everyone, before they agreed to let the country go to war, to consider whether they themselves would be willing to fight.
5. Federal action on Internet privacy has been too weak. *Thesis:* The United States must strengthen legal protection of data gathered on social media platforms to prevent abusive targeting of individuals and groups.

**EXERCISE 11.7: Suggested Answers**

1. Marijuana is no more harmful than alcohol.
2. Women should not be exposed to a higher risk of death.
3. Only those who can talk can feel pain.

**EXERCISE 11.9: Suggested Answers**

1. Concern about students' health issues related to binge-drinking; concern about mental health issues that lead to binge-drinking; anger about campus sexual assaults and their tie to binge-drinking culture.
2. Fear of terrorist hijackings; concern over possible invasion of privacy; anger over failure of past security measures.
3. Relief that unwanted pregnancies can be prevented; fear that easy access will lead to promiscuity; anger that the burden lies primarily with women.
4. Anger that taxes will be raised; relief that everyone will have health insurance regardless of class; concern for the efficiency of a new system.
5. Gratitude for state and federal attention to a growing problem; fear for addicts' lives; anger about continued incarceration (as opposed to treatment) as a response.

## EXERCISE 16.1: Answers

1. Unacceptable; misstates the writer's intent
2. Acceptable
3. Unacceptable; wording is too similar to original
4. Unacceptable; wording is too similar to original, and the source is not credited
5. Acceptable

## EXERCISE 36.1: Suggested Answer

When you suggest something that doesn't appeal to them, they feel they *must* assert themselves. Their nature tells them to. They just say "no" in words or actions, even about things that they like to do. The psychologists call it "negativism"; many parents call it "that terrible *no* stage." But stop and think what would happen to children who never felt like saying "no." They'd become robots. You wouldn't be able to resist the temptation to boss them all the time, and they'd stop learning and developing. When they were old enough to go out into the world, to school, and later to work, everybody else would take advantage of them, too. They'd never be good for anything.

## CHAPTER 36—THINKING CRITICALLY ABOUT HOW LANGUAGE CAN BUILD COMMON GROUND: Suggested Answer

Ruth Ozeki appeals to a sense of community and thoughtfulness. By using the word *we* multiple times, she incorporates a feeling of togetherness. Ozeki urges understanding and patience as we assess the rapidly changing world. Her deliberate, calm tone underscores the urgency of environmental challenges that demand activist engagement. All of this, along with her description of human survival and compassion in the modern world, works to appeal to readers on an emotional level.

## EXERCISE 37.2: Suggested Answers

1. In Shakespeare's *Othello*, Desdemona simply lies down like a submissive victim and accepts her death as inevitable.
2. The budget office does not want to pay to replace the drafty windows, but the cost of heating the building should also be considered.
3. The discovery of the artifacts in King Tut's tomb was one of the most important archeological events of the twentieth century.
4. In unfamiliar settings or with people he did not know well, Duncan often appeared cold and distant, but in reality he was terrified.
5. My family lived in Trinidad for the first ten years of my life, and we experienced many hardships, but when we came to America, we thought our prospects were good.

## EXERCISE 37.3: Answers

1. attentively
2. emphasize
3. conscientious
4. industrious
5. proceeds

## EXERCISE 37.4: Suggested Answers

1. *tragic*: distressing, alarming, disturbing; *drama*: excitement, tension, vitality
2. *girl*: young lady, miss (The use of *girl*, in this context, is widely considered racist. Angelou uses the term to call attention to the racism she faced while working in a white woman's house in Arkansas in the 1930s.)
3. *abide*: tolerate; *turns*: changes; *vital*: alive; *hold still*: contain their energy

## EXERCISE 37.5: Suggested Answers

1. The entryway of the building looked like a garbage dump: paper was littered about, bottles lay shattered, and rotting cantaloupe and chicken parts gave off an unbearable odor.
2. The cheerful early morning sounds of birds outside my window make it easier to get up.
3. The feast at Mom's on Sunday was delicious as usual: roast chicken, garlic and sage stuffing, sweet garden peas, gravy, and half a fresh-baked apple pie each.
4. The valet stepped toward my Porsche with excitement in her eyes.
5. My alarm clock clamored insistently until I mustered the strength to get out of bed and turn it off.

## EXERCISE 38.1: Suggested Answers

1. We made mistakes. (The active voice implies that the speaker is taking responsibility in a mature way.)
2. Hecklers interrupted the candidate's speech. (The active voice emphasizes the hecklers' responsibility for their poor behavior, rather than its effect on others.)
3. The city's new noise complaint hotline took numerous reports about loud music from bars and shouting neighbors. (The active voice puts the focus on the new hotline.)
4. An eight-year-old performed the violin solo. (The active voice is more concise and dramatic.)
5. In a patient with celiac disease, the body's immunological response to gluten damages the intestine. (The original construction emphasizes the effects of celiac disease. The active voice highlights the irony of the body's hurting itself with its own defense mechanisms.)

## EXERCISE 38.2: Suggested Answer

As humans domesticated dogs over many thousands of years, the canine species evolved into hundreds of breeds designed to perform specific tasks such as pulling sleds and guarding sheep. Over time, as human civilization grew, the need for many breeds decreased. For example, as humans evolved from hunter-gatherers into farmers, they no longer needed hunting dogs. Later, as farming societies became industrialized, herd animals disappeared, and fewer shepherds meant fewer sheepdogs. But by this time, humans had grown accustomed to dogs' companionship, and breeding continued. Today, most owners keep dogs simply as companions, but some dogs still do the work they were intentionally bred for, such as following a scent, guarding a home, or leading the blind.

## EXERCISE 39.1: Suggested Answer

The auditorium was filled with people, but the sea of faces did not intimidate me. I had decided to appear in a musical with my local community theater group, and there was no going back now. I reminded myself that I had gotten here through hard work, and I refused to doubt my abilities. Besides, the director and her staff had held auditions, and after I had read the heroine's part and sung a song, they had chosen me for the role even though I was untrained. My skills as an actor would now be judged publicly, but I felt ready to rise to the challenge.

## EXERCISE 39.2: Suggested Answers

1. The original *Star Trek* television show, which ran from 1966 to 1969, had low ratings and was canceled by the network even though it was critically acclaimed.
2. Ancient Greeks relied on Athena, the goddess of wisdom, to protect the city of Athens, which was named in her honor.
3. When Harry Potter, a fictional wizard, turns eleven years old, he is taken to Hogwarts School of Witchcraft and Wizardry.
4. Flappers, who broke with 1920s social conventions by cutting their hair short and smoking in public, seemed rebellious to their parents' generation.
5. In the mid-seventies, skateboarding originated in Venice, California, where, because of a drought, the swimming pools were empty.

## EXERCISE 40.1: Suggested Answer

Before planting a tree, a gardener needs to choose a good location — one with the right kind of soil, sufficient drainage, and enough light for the type of tree chosen. The next step is to be sure to dig a deep enough hole. It should be deeper than the root-ball and about twice as wide. The gardener must unwrap the root-ball since the burlap, which is biodegradable, may be treated with chemicals that will eventually damage the roots if it is not removed. The roots may have grown into a compact ball if the tree has been in a pot for some time; they should be separated or cut apart. The gardener should set the root-ball into the hole and then begin to fill the hole with loose dirt. After filling the hole completely, the gardener should make sure to water the tree thoroughly, since new plantings require extra water and extra care. After about three years, they become well rooted.

## EXERCISE 40.2: Suggested Answers

1. *Periodic*: Not knowing their names, not answering their questions, and not reading their stories, the politician obviously did not understand reporters.
*Cumulative*: The politician obviously did not understand reporters, whose names he did not know, whose questions he did not answer, and whose stories he did not read.

2. *Periodic*: Unable to do my homework, eat dinner, or get any sleep, I could think only of my mother's surgery the next morning.
*Cumulative*: I could think only of my mother's surgery the next morning, so I was unable to do my homework, eat dinner, or get any sleep.

## EXERCISE 41.1: Suggested Answers

1. The president persuaded his staff, Congress, and the American people.

2. If meteorologists are correct in their predictions, we can expect a decade of record-breaking tropical storms and hurricanes.

3. From the sightseeing boat, we saw a whale dive toward us, lift itself out of the water, and crash its tail on the waves.

4. I did not realize that living in the city would mean selling my car, losing half my closet space, and eating canned soup every night.

5. Jake experienced several side effects from the medication, including dizziness, dry mouth, and severe abdominal pain.

## EXERCISE 42.1: Suggested Answers

1. The greed of the 1980s gave way to the occupational insecurity of the 1990s, which in turn gave way to reinforced family ties in the early 2000s.

2. The building inspector suggested that we apply for a construction permit and that we check in again when the plans are complete.

3. The instructor grabbed her coat, wondered why the substitute was late, and ran out of the room.

4. Suddenly, we heard an explosion of wings off to our right, and we could see a hundred or more ducks lifting off from the water.

5. In my previous job, I sold the most advertising spots and earned a sales excellence award.

6. A cloud of snow powder rose as skis and poles flew in every direction.

7. The flight attendant told us to turn off all electronic devices but mentioned that we could use them again after takeoff.

8. The real estate market was softer than it had been for a decade, and buyers could practically name their price.

9. When in Florence, be sure to see the city's famed cathedral as well as Michelangelo's statue *David*.

10. The freezing weather is threatening crops such as citrus fruits, which are sensitive to cold.

## CHAPTER 42—THINKING CRITICALLY ABOUT SHIFTS: Suggested Answers

third-person singular (*It has been . . .*) → first-person plural (*our time . . .*) → third-person singular (*There is no delusion . . .*) → second-person singular (*your head . . .*) → third-person singular (*The human mind . . .*) → first-person plural (*and we are obliged . . .*) → third-person singular (*It is all very well . . .*) → second-person singular (*your awareness . . .*)

(Note the shift in mood from the indicative to the imperative in the next-to-last sentence.)

## EXERCISE 43.1: Suggested Answers

1. Before buying a used car, you should note the mileage, take it for a test drive, and get it checked by a mechanic.

2. Three activities I'd like to try are mountain biking, cross-country skiing, and kayaking.

3. Working in a restaurant taught me not only the importance of service but also the art of small talk.

4. We must either walk quickly or drive slowly.

5. To pass the time in the waiting room, I read four magazines, texted all my friends, and stared at the clock.

## EXERCISE 43.2: Suggested Answers

1. I remember watching it the first time, realizing I'd never seen anything like it, and immediately vowing never to miss even one episode of *The Daily Show*.

2. A crowd stood outside the school and watched as the graduates paraded by.

3. An effective website is well designed, provides useful information, and gives links to other relevant sites.

4. It is impossible to watch *The Office* and not see a little of yourself in one of the characters.

5. Lila was the winner not only of the pie-eating contest but also of the yodeling competition.

Lila won not only the pie-eating contest but also the yodeling competition.

## CHAPTER 43—THINKING CRITICALLY ABOUT PARALLELISM: Suggested Answer

The richness of the scene was in *its plainness, its natural condition — of horse, of ring, of girl,* even to the girl's *bare feet* that gripped the *bare back* of her proud and ridiculous mount. The enchantment grew not *out of anything that happened or was performed* but *out of something that seemed to go round and around and around with the girl,* attending her, a steady gleam in the shape of a circle — a ring *of ambition, of happiness, of youth.* (And the positive pleasures of equilibrium under difficulties.) In a week or two, *all would be changed, all (or almost all) lost; the girl would wear makeup, the horse would wear gold, the ring would be painted, the bark would be clean for the feet of the horse, the girl's feet would be clean for the slippers that she'd wear.* All, all would be lost.

## EXERCISE 44.1: Suggested Answers

1. Many motorists are unaware of the dangers of texting while driving, so lawmakers have taken the matter into their own hands.

2. The tallest human on record was Robert Wadlow. He reached an amazing height of eight feet, eleven inches.

3. Some employers provide on-site care for the children of their employees; others reimburse workers for day-care costs.

4. The number of vaccine manufacturers has plummeted because the industry has been hit with a flood of lawsuits.

5. Although most crustaceans live in the ocean, some also live on land or in freshwater habitats.

6. She inherited some tribal customs from her grandmother, including the sewing technique called Seminole patchwork.

7. Don't throw your soda cans in the trash — recycle them.

8. Even though my West Indian neighbor has lived in New England for years, she always feels betrayed by winter.

9. The impressive Hope diamond in the Smithsonian Institution looks even larger in person than online.

10. You signed up for the course — now you'll have to do the work.

## EXERCISE 44.2: Suggested Answer

We may disagree on the causes of global warming; however, we cannot ignore that it is happening. Of course we still experience cold winters. On the other hand, average global temperatures have risen drastically for the last three decades. Polar ice caps are melting; as a result, sea levels are rising. Scientists predict more extreme weather in the coming decades. Droughts will probably be more common; in addition, flooding and tropical storm activity may increase. Some experts fear that rising temperatures may cause large amounts of methane gases to be released; this could be disastrous for our atmosphere. Climate change might be a natural occurrence; more likely it is caused by human actions. Nevertheless, we must find ways to save our planet.

## EXERCISE 45.1: Suggested Answers

1. Long stretches of white beaches and shady palm trees give tourists the impression of an island paradise.

2. Many college students are afraid of forgetting to study for an exam.

3. Much of New Orleans is below sea level, which makes it susceptible to flooding.

4. Fortunately for us, Uncle Ron forgot to bring his clarinet to the party.

5. Oscar night is an occasion for celebrating the film industry and criticizing the fashion industry.

6. Diners in Creole restaurants might try shrimp gumbo or turtle soup.

7. In the late 1940s, women began hosting Tupperware parties, casual gatherings in which the hosts act as salespersons.

8. I attempted to lose ten pounds in less than a week by eating only cottage cheese and grapefruit.
9. Our parents did not realize that we were hoarding our candy under our beds.
10. Thomas Edison was famous for such inventions as the phonograph and the first practical lightbulb.

## EXERCISE 45.2: Suggested Answers

1. *Dependent-clause fragment:* As soon as the seventy-five-year-old cellist walked onstage, the audience burst into applause.
2. *Phrase fragment:* The patient has only one intention, to smoke behind the doctor's back.
3. *Phrase fragment:* Some reality shows feature people working in dangerous situations, such as fishing for Alaskan king crab or logging in swamps.
4. *Dependent-clause fragment:* After writing and rewriting for almost three years, she finally felt that her novel was complete.
5. *Phrase fragment:* In the wake of the earthquake, relief workers tried to provide food and shelter to victims.
6. *Phrase fragment:* Forster stopped writing novels after *A Passage to India,* one of the greatest novels of the twentieth century.
7. *Dependent-clause fragment:* Because only two students signed up, the class was canceled this semester.
8. *Compound-predicate fragment:* I started running in April and ran my first marathon in September.
9. *Phrase fragment:* We sat stunned as she delivered her monologue, a ten-minute speech about everything we had done to annoy her.
10. *Dependent-clause fragment:* All primates have opposable thumbs, which sets them apart from other mammals.

## CHAPTER 45—THINKING CRITICALLY ABOUT FRAGMENTS: Answer

The sentence fragments are italicized.

On Sundays, for religion, we went up on the hill. *Skipping along the hexagon-shaped tile in Colonial Park. Darting up the steps to Edgecomb Avenue. Stopping in the candy store on St. Nicholas to load up. Leaning forward for leverage to finish the climb up to the church.* I was always impressed by this particular house of the Lord.

## EXERCISE 46.1: Suggested Answers

1. Relating stories in a deadpan voice, the comedian had the audience doubled over with laughter.
2. News reports that emphasize random crime or rare diseases can increase a listener's irrational fears.
3. Legal documents and court records can reveal the habits of ordinary people in the Middle Ages.
4. Civilians learn about the conflict from the firsthand accounts of journalists who risk their lives in war zones abroad.
5. On a safari in Africa last spring, Melena saw lions in the wild.
6. Doctors recommend a new, painless test for cancer.
7. Every afternoon I find my windshield covered with flyers for free pizza.
8. After the opening credits, screeching strings told the audience that the killer was coming.
9. The coach awarded a medal made of solid brass to the most valuable player.
10. The five-year-old finally lost her tooth, which was hanging on by a thread.

## EXERCISE 46.2: Suggested Answers

1. The division that most profited deserves the prize.
   The division that profited deserves the prize most.
2. Apparently, the soldier was injured by friendly fire.
   The soldier was injured, apparently by friendly fire.
3. The collector who originally owned the painting planned to leave it to a museum.
   Originally, the collector who owned the painting planned to leave it to a museum.
4. Alcoholics who frequently try to quit drinking on their own tend to relapse.
   Alcoholics who try to quit drinking on their own tend to relapse frequently.

5. Ever since I was a child, I have liked only green peas with ham.
Ever since I was a child, I have liked green peas only with ham.

## EXERCISE 46.3: Suggested Answers

1. Statistics tell us that strong economic times have led to increases in the college dropout rate.
2. Facing high levels of stress during finals, an otherwise honest student may consider cheating to achieve a higher grade.
3. The director encouraged us to applaud loudly and enthusiastically after each scene.
4. At the pinnacle of his career, Kobe Bryant earned roughly $30 million annually in endorsements.
5. Because of the sudden trading, the stock exchange became a chaotic circus.

## EXERCISE 46.4: Suggested Answers

1. No longer obsessed with being the first to report a story, news shows now focus on presenting information as entertainment.
2. Late-night talk shows blend news with comedy to attract younger viewers.
3. When news programs highlight local events, important international news stories may get overlooked.
4. Chosen for their looks, newscasters may have weak journalistic credentials.
5. As an interactive medium, the web offers online information that reinforces the views people already hold.

## EXERCISE 47.1: Suggested Answers

1. To enroll in film school being my primary goal, I am always saving my money and watching for scholarship opportunities.
To enroll in film school is my primary goal, so I am always saving my money and watching for scholarship opportunities.
2. Many people would suffer if air-pollution standards were relaxed.
The reason air-pollution standards should not be relaxed is that many people might suffer if they were.

3. By turning off the water when you brush your teeth, you can save up to eight gallons of water per day.
Turning off the water when you brush your teeth can save up to eight gallons of water per day.
4. Irony occurs when you expect one thing and get something else.
The experience of expecting one thing and getting another is irony.
5. I ate the best meal of my life, bread and cheese from a farmers' market, while sitting by a river.
By the side of a river, I ate the best meal of my life, which consisted of bread and cheese from a farmers' market.

## EXERCISE 47.2: Suggested Answers

1. Convection ovens cook more quickly and with less power than traditional ovens.
2. Argentina and Peru were colonized by Spain, while Brazil was colonized by Portugal.
3. She argued that children are even more important for men than they are for women.
4. Do you think the barbecue sauce in Memphis is better than it is in North Carolina?
5. The equipment in our new warehouse is guaranteed to last longer than the machines in our current facility.

## EXERCISE 48.1: Answers

1. was released
2. will be arriving
3. have fallen
4. spoke; were taking
5. has been fingerprinted; is waiting

## EXERCISE 48.2: Answers

Nouns are underlined once; articles are underlined twice.

1. Halloween; the; children; candy
2. June; the; month; flooding; the; spring
3. Baking; a; activity; households; the; country
4. A; frost; the; ground; a; field; ice
5. The; cyclist; an; car; a; light

## EXERCISE 48.3: Answers

Pronouns are underlined once; antecedents are underlined twice.

1. He, (not given); themselves, volunteers
2. those, who, people who divide; those, who, people who don't divide
3. Who, (interrogative); them, jeans; himself, designer; them, jeans
4. themselves, employees; their, employees'
5. everyone, (indefinite); your, address book

## EXERCISE 48.4: Answers

Adjectives are underlined once; adverbs are underlined twice.

1. The small; frightened; firmly; my; another; forward
2. Meanwhile; the financial; completely false
3. generally; quiet; loud; grunting; mating
4. The huge red; lovely; disappointingly
5. The youngest; the; a brilliant

## EXERCISE 48.5: Answers

1. of; from; through
2. from; across; into
3. Instead of; among
4. After; on; for
5. about; from; of; in

## EXERCISE 48.6: Answers

1. after; and; both . . . and; so
2. not only . . . but also
3. however; so
4. Although; so
5. because; but; still

## EXERCISE 49.1: Answers

Complete subjects are underlined once; simple subjects are underlined twice.

1. That container of fried rice
2. the new tour guide
3. One student
4. Japanese animation, with its cutting-edge graphics and futuristic plots
5. Sniffer dogs trained to detect drugs, blood, and explosives

## EXERCISE 49.2: Answers

Predicates are set in italics.

1. *is proud of his heritage*: LV — is; SC — proud

2. *made me angry*: TV — made; DO — me; OC — angry
3. *looks deserted*: LV — looks; SC — deserted
4. *will never die*: TV — will . . . die
5. *offered her a promotion*: TV — offered; IO — her; DO — promotion

## EXERCISE 49.3: Answers

1. APP — the motel clerk; VERBAL (INF) — to be certified as a river guide; PREP — as a river guide
2. VERBAL (PART) — made by hand; PREP — by hand
3. ABSO — my stomach doing flips; VERBAL (PART) — doing flips
4. ABSO, VERBAL (PART) — floating on my back; PREP — on my back
5. VERBAL (GER) — Driving across town during rush hour; PREP — across town; PREP — during rush hour

## EXERCISE 49.4: Answers

1. IND — The hockey game was postponed; DEP — because one of the players collapsed on the bench; SUB CONJ — because
2. IND — She eventually discovered the secret admirer; DEP — who had been leaving notes in her locker; REL — who
3. DEP — After completing three advanced drawing classes; SUB CONJ — after; IND — Jason was admitted into the fine arts program; IND — and he immediately rented a small studio space
4. IND — The test was easier; DEP — than I had expected; SUB — than
5. IND — I could tell that it was going to rain; DEP — that it was going to rain; REL — that; IND — I tried to get home quickly

## EXERCISE 49.5: Suggested Answers

1. The economy, which had been in a serious downturn, gradually began to recover.
2. After hearing of an insurgent attack near her husband's base station, Simone waited nervously by the phone.
3. Because some parents had complained about the lack of security on campus, new school safety rules were instituted this fall.
4. Rob, who frequently left his wallet at home, always borrowed money from friends.

5. When the police shut down the outdoor concert, the crowd grew louder and more disorderly.

## EXERCISE 49.6: Answers

1. complex
2. compound
3. complex
4. simple
5. compound-complex

## CHAPTER 49—THINKING CRITICALLY ABOUT SENTENCES: Suggested Answers

Independent clauses are set in boldface; dependent clauses are set in italics.

1. **We observe today not a victory of party but a celebration of freedom**, *symbolizing an end as well as a beginning, signifying renewal as well as change.* Imitation: I provided not a meal but a feast, feeding my guests' bodies and minds, satisfying their thirst for wine and company.
2. Once in a long while, four times so far for me, **my mother brings out the metal tube** *that holds her medical diploma.* Imitation: Sometimes when I yawn in class, when Alex is giving a long-winded answer, my professor gives me a look that tells me she understands.

## EXERCISE 50.1: Answers

1. Before the middle of the nineteenth century, surgery was usually a terrifying, painful ordeal.
2. Because anesthesia did not exist yet, the only painkiller available for surgical patients was whiskey.
3. The pain of surgical procedures could be so severe that many people were willing to die rather than have surgery.
4. In 1846, one of the hospitals in Boston gave ether to a patient before he had surgery.
5. The patient, who had a large tumor on his neck, slept peacefully as doctors removed it.

## EXERCISE 50.2: Answer

Hollywood is famous for hiring various experts to teach people technically what most of us learn informally. A case in point is *the* story about *the* children of one movie couple who noticed *a* new child in *the* neighborhood climbing *a* tree. *The* children immediately wanted to be given *the* name of his instructor in tree climbing.

## EXERCISE 51.1: Answers

1. let, came, torn
2. reviewed, found
3. works
4. planted, gone
5. knew, ignored
6. painted, taken
7. sprang, swam
8. assumed, found
9. passed, fallen
10. decided, been

## EXERCISE 51.2: Answers

1. lies
2. laid
3. set
4. sitting
5. sitting, rise

## EXERCISE 51.3: Answers

1. *shows/has shown* — present action; may be seen as having started in the past and still ongoing
2. *have feared/have been fearing* — action begun in the past continues
3. *emigrated* — completed action
4. *has been* — started in the past and still ongoing
5. *will direct/will be directing* — future (continuing) action
6. *ate/were eating* — past action, completed
7. *will have received* — future action completed by a certain time
8. *will have watched* — future action completed by a certain time
9. *expresses* — literary work
10. *lasts* — general truth

## EXERCISE 51.4: Answers

1. When she saw *Wonder Woman*, it *made* her want to become an actress.
2. *Having left* England in December, the settlers *arrived* in Virginia in May.
3. I *had hoped* to make the football team, but injuries prevented me from trying out.

4. *Having worked* with great dedication as a summer intern at the magazine, Mohan called his former supervisor in the fall to ask about a permanent position.
5. As we waited for the bus, we *watched* the taxis pass by.

## EXERCISE 51.5: Answers

1. The lifeguard *informed* the surfers of a shark sighting.
2. A picture of Sam with huge ears and a pointy chin *was sketched* by the cartoonist.
3. The mother kangaroo *protects* her baby, *feeds it*, and *teaches it* to survive.
4. Volunteers dressed as elves *gave* the gifts out to the children.
5. The board members *chose* a new advertising company.

## EXERCISE 51.6: Answers

1. was → were
2. was → were
3. (correct)
4. was → were
5. remains → remain

## EXERCISE 52.1: Answers

1. deserve
2. races
3. appears
4. needs
5. hides
6. was
7. comes
8. contributes
9. cause
10. leaves

## EXERCISE 52.2: Answers

1. are → is; *Room and board* is considered a singular unit
2. tell → tells; *Goodfellas* is singular, a title
3. is → are; the subject, *paintings*, is plural
4. (correct; *Most* refers to *students*)
5. are → is; the subject, *Each*, is singular
6. were → was; "neither/nor"
7. were → was; the subject, *committee*, is treated as singular
8. (correct; *who* refers to *one*)
9. was (second verb) → were; *that* refers to *countries*
10. involve → involves; the subject, *Economics*, is treated as singular

## CHAPTER 52—THINKING CRITICALLY ABOUT SUBJECT-VERB AGREEMENT: Suggested Answers

- "Marriage *seems* to me"; *Marriage* is singular
- "the divorce rate — with or without new babies in the house — *remains* constant"; *divorce rate* is singular
- "The fabric of men-and-women-as-they-once-were *is* so thin"; *fabric* is singular
- "no amount of patching *can weave* that cloth together"; *amount* is singular
- "but even stronger *is* the growing perception"; singular, subject is *perception*
- "that only people who *are* real to themselves"; plural, *who* refers to *people*
- "that only people who are real to themselves *can connect*"; *people* is plural
- "Two shall be as one *is* over"; singular, *Two shall be as one* is an expression that forms a singular subject
- "no matter how lonely we *get*"; *we* is plural

## EXERCISE 53.1: Answers

1. Who (subjective)
2. Whomever (direct object of *chooses*)
3. whoever (subject of the clause)
4. whom (object of preposition *with*)
5. Who (subjective)

## EXERCISE 53.2: Answers

1. she
2. them
3. me
4. their
5. we

## EXERCISE 53.3: Suggested Answers

1. While shopping for a new computer for school, I noticed that laptops cost much less than they used to.
2. Congress usually resists presidential attempts to encroach on what it considers congressional authority.
3. Marco and Ellen were each given a chance to voice an opinion.
4. ER doctors need to be swift; they also need to be calm and careful.
5. Every dog and cat has its own personality.

NOTE: Since it is increasingly acceptable to use the plural pronoun *they* to refer to a generic noun or to respect personal pronoun choices, sentences 3 and 4 could be labeled correct as written.

## EXERCISE 53.4: Suggested Answers

1. ... The deadline is October 24, so applicants should start the process as soon as possible.
    ... The deadline is October 24, so the committee members should start the process as soon as possible.
2. Patients on medication may relate better to their therapists and be more responsive to them; these patients may also be less vulnerable to what disturbs them.
    Patients on medication may be less vulnerable and more responsive to things that disturb them, and these patients may relate better to their therapists.
3. Ms. Dunbar wanted to speak to my mother before speaking to me.
    Ms. Dunbar wanted to speak to my mother before my mother spoke to me.
4. While you're in Texas, you'll often hear about the influence of big oil corporations.
    You often hear about the influence big oil corporations have in Texas.
5. Many residents were outraged by a small band of protestors picketing the new shopping center.
    The new shopping center, which outraged many residents, was picketed by a small band of protestors.

## EXERCISE 53.5: Suggested Answer

In the summer of 2005, the NCAA banned the use of mascots that could be considered offensive to American Indians at any NCAA-sponsored championship games. In order to understand why American Indians feel this issue is important, consider that, for years, movies and television programs portrayed members of Indian tribes as savage warriors who were feared and misunderstood. That stereotypical warrior image is what some schools have chosen to use as their mascot, a role typically played by wild animals or fictional beasts. Derogatory terms for other ethnic groups are never used for school mascots. In its new ruling, the NCAA asks schools to eliminate mascots that may be hurtful or offensive to America's indigenous population.

## EXERCISE 54.1: Answers

1. nearly → impossible
2. immaturely → behaving
3. bad → Nora
4. really → dangerous
5. confidently → spoke
6. badly → bleeding
7. well → ran
8. terrific → Arjun
9. good → stew
10. accurately → measured

## EXERCISE 54.2: Suggested Answers

1. Alicia speaks both Russian and German, but she speaks Russian better.
2. The summers are rainier in New York than they are in Seattle.
3. He glanced at the menu and ordered the most expensive wine on the list.
4. Women tend to live longer than men; hence, more of the elderly are women.
5. Minneapolis is the larger of the Twin Cities.
6. She came up with a very silly plan for revenge.
    She came up with the silliest plan for revenge that I had ever heard.
7. Our theater company has produced several of the most famous classical Greek plays.
8. The student cafeteria is operated by a college food service, which is part of a chain.
9. It is safer to jog in daylight than in the dark.
10. Evan argued that subtitled films are more boring to watch than films dubbed in English.

## CHAPTER 54 — THINKING CRITICALLY ABOUT ADJECTIVES AND ADVERBS: Answers

Adjectives are set in italics; adverbs are set in boldface.

*graceful*; **softly**; *glowing*; **correctly**; *quiet*

**EXERCISE 55.1: Answers**

The children's soccer game happened **at** 10:00 **on** Saturday morning. The families sat **on** blankets to watch the game. Everyone was **in** a good mood. When the game ended, both teams stood **in** a circle to cheer.

**EXERCISE 55.2: Suggested Answers**

1. *lay off:* phrasal verb
   Soon after I was hired for my last job, I learned the company may lay me off.
2. (correct) *count on:* prepositional verb
3. (correct) *pick up:* phrasal verb
4. *look at:* prepositional verb
   As I looked at the newspaper, I was surprised to see that I was qualified for a job that paid much better than mine.
5. (correct) *give up:* phrasal verb

**EXERCISE 56.1: Answers**

1. After the concession speech, the senator's supporters drifted out of the room.
2. To our surprise, the charity auction raised enough money to build a new technology center.
3. Unaware that the microphone was on, the candidate made an offensive comment.
4. Whenever someone rings the doorbell, her dog goes berserk.
5. Therefore, Sasha must take a summer course to receive her diploma.
6. (no comma needed)
7. A tray of shrimp in one hand and a pile of napkins in the other, the waiter avoided me.
8. (no comma needed)
9. When they woke up, the exhausted campers no longer wanted to hike.
10. Tears in his eyes, Keflezighi won the marathon.

**EXERCISE 56.2: Suggested Answers**

1. The chef did not want to serve a heavy dessert, *for* she was planning to have a rich stew for the main course.
2. My mother rarely allowed us to eat sweets, *but* Halloween was a special exception.
3. Scientists have mapped the human genome, *and* they learn more every day about how genes affect an individual's health.

4. Perhaps I will change my name when I get married, *or* maybe I will keep my maiden name.
5. Penguins cannot fly, *nor* can they walk the way other birds do.

**EXERCISE 56.3: Answers**

1. (no commas needed)
2. (no commas needed)
3. The enormous new house, which was the largest in the neighborhood, had replaced a much smaller old home.
4. The rescue workers, exhausted and discouraged, stared ahead without speaking.
5. (no commas needed)
6. Viruses, unlike bacteria, can reproduce only by infecting live cells.
7. (no commas needed)
8. Hammurabi, an ancient Babylonian king, created laws that were carved on a stone for public display.
9. Birds' hearts have four chambers, whereas reptiles' have three.
10. (no commas needed)

**EXERCISE 56.4: Answers**

1. The students donated clothing, school supplies, and nonperishable food.
2. The hot, humid weather did not stop the fans from flocking to the free outdoor concert.
3. The ball sailed over the fence, across the yard, and through the Wilsons' window.
4. (no commas needed)
5. The young athletes' parents insist on calling every play, judging every move, and telling everyone within earshot exactly what is wrong with the team.

**EXERCISE 56.5: Answers**

1. One must consider the society as a whole, not just its parts.
2. Drinking caffeinated beverages can, in fact, be good for your health.
3. You don't expect me to read this speech, do you?
4. Coming in ahead of schedule and under budget, it appears, is the only way to keep this client happy.
5. Believe me, Jenna, I had no idea things would turn out this way.

## EXERCISE 56.6: Answers

1. The city of Dublin, Ireland, has a population of over 500,000.
2. (no commas needed, but a comma is optional in *1,200*)
3. New Delhi, India, and Islamabad, Pakistan, became the capitals of two independent nations at midnight on August 15, 1947.
4. MLA headquarters are still located at 26 Broadway, New York, New York 10004.
5. I was convinced that the nameplate I. M. Well, MD, was one of my sister's pranks.

## EXERCISE 56.7: Answers

1. (no comma needed)
2. My mother was fond of telling me, "You'd make coffee nervous!"
3. (no comma needed)
4. "Learning without thought is labor lost; thought without learning is perilous," Confucius argued.
5. (no comma needed)

## EXERCISE 57.1: Answers

1. Abalone fishing in California is strictly regulated; a person is allowed to harvest only twenty-four of these large mollusks per year.
2. City life offers many advantages; in many ways, however, life in a small town is much more pleasant.
3. The door contains an inflatable slide to be used in an emergency; in addition, each seat can become a flotation device.
4. Most car accidents occur within twenty-five miles of the home; therefore, you should wear a seat belt on every trip.
5. Involvement in team sports provides more than just health benefits for young girls; it also increases their self-confidence.

## EXERCISE 57.2: Suggested Answer

Hosting your first dinner party can be very stressful, but careful planning and preparation can make it a success. The guest list must contain the right mix of people; everyone should feel comfortable. Good talkers and good listeners are both important, and while they don't need to agree on everything, you don't want them to have fistfights, either. Then you need to plan the menu, which should steer clear of problem areas: for vegans, no pork chops; for guests with shellfish allergies, no lobster; for nondrinkers, no tequila. In addition, make sure your home is clean and neat, and check that you have enough chairs, dishes, glasses, napkins, and silverware. Leave enough time to socialize with your guests — and save a little energy to clean up when it's over!

## EXERCISE 58.1: Suggested Answers

1. Social scientists face difficult questions: should they use their knowledge to shape society, merely describe human behavior, or try to do both?
2. The court denied a New Jersey woman's petition to continue raising tigers in her backyard.
3. I screamed at Jamie, "You rat! You tricked me!"
4. The reporter wondered whether anything more could have been done to save lives.
5. "Have you seen the new George Clooney film?" Mia asked.

## EXERCISE 59.1: Answers

1. Grammar is not *everybody's* favorite subject.
2. An *ibis's* wingspan is about half as long as a *flamingo's*.
3. *Prince William and Kate's* first visit to Canada as a married couple included a meeting with the prime minister.
4. The long debate over *states'* rights culminated in the Civil War.
5. *Tiger Woods's* personal crisis once threatened to overshadow his athletic career.
6. She insists that her personal life is *nobody's* business.
7. Parents often question their *children's* choice of friends.
8. This dog has a *beagle's* ears and a *St. Bernard's* face.
9. The sidewalk smokers disregarded the *surgeon general's* warnings.
10. *Anna and Tobias's* income dropped dramatically after Anna lost her job.

## EXERCISE 59.2: Answers

1. There was a big revival at my Auntie *Reed's* church.
2. I heard the songs and the minister saying: "Why *don't* you come?"
3. Finally Westley said to me in a whisper: . . . "*I'm* tired of sitting here. *Let's* get up and be saved."
4. So I decided that maybe to save further trouble, *I'd* better lie. . . .
5. That night . . . I cried, in bed alone, and *couldn't* stop.

## EXERCISE 60.1: Answers

1. Stephen Colbert introduced Americans to the concept he calls "truthiness" on the first episode of *The Colbert Report.*
2. Margaret Talbot's article "A Risky Proposal" examined the constitutionality of state laws that banned gay marriage.
3. "The little that is known about gorillas certainly makes you want to know more," writes Alan Moorehead in his essay, "A Most Forgiving Ape."
4. My father's way of "helping" usually meant doing the whole project for me.
5. Should "America the Beautiful" replace "The Star-Spangled Banner" as the national anthem?
6. In the chapter called "The Last to See Them Alive," Truman Capote shows the utterly ordinary life of the Kansas family.
7. *The Marvelous Mrs. Maisel* episode "Kind of Bleu" introduces homophobia, a heavy topic for a comedy series.
8. Several popular films, including *Mamma Mia!* and *Muriel's Wedding*, have used Abba hits such as "Dancing Queen" and "Take a Chance on Me."
9. My dictionary defines *isolation* as "the quality or state of being alone."
10. In his poem "Harlem," Langston Hughes shows what can happen when people's dreams are consistently denied.

## EXERCISE 61.1: Answers

1. The committee was presented with three options to pay for the new park: (1) increase vehicle registration fees, (2) install parking meters downtown, or (3) borrow money from the reserve fund.

2. The FISA statute authorizes government wiretapping only under certain circumstances (for instance, the government has to obtain a warrant).
3. The health care expert informed readers that "as we progress through middle age, we experience intimations of our own morality *[sic]*."
4. Some hospitals train nurses in a pseudoscientific technique called therapeutic touch (TT) that has been discredited by many rigorous studies.
5. Because I was carrying an umbrella (which, as it turned out, wasn't even necessary), I was required to enter the stadium through the high-security gate.

## EXERCISE 61.2: Answers

1. Most people would say that Labradors are easy dogs to train — but they never met our Millie.
2. Even if marijuana is dangerous — an assertion disputed by many studies — it is certainly no more harmful to human health than alcohol and cigarettes, which remain legal in every state.
3. If too much exposure to negative news stories makes you feel depressed or anxious — and why wouldn't it? — try going on a media fast.
4. Union Carbide's plant in Bhopal, India, sprang a leak — a leak that killed more than 2,000 people and injured an additional 200,000.
5. Refrigerators — especially side-by-side models — use up more energy than most people realize.

## EXERCISE 61.3: Answers

1. After discussing the case study, the class reached one main conclusion: in any business, the most important asset is the customer.
2. Another example is taken from Psalm 139:16.
3. Roberto tried to make healthier choices, such as eating organic food, walking to work, and getting plenty of rest.
4. (correct)
5. Sofi rushed to catch the 5:45 express but missed it and had to wait for the 6:19.

## EXERCISE 62.1: Answers

1. The town in the South where I was raised had a statue of a Civil War soldier in the center of Main Street.
2. Sarah Palin, the former governor, frequently complained that the press had treated her harshly before she accepted a position as an analyst for Fox News.
3. The Corporation for Public Broadcasting relies on donations as well as on grants from the National Endowment for the Arts.
4. During the economic recession, companies such as Starbucks had to close some of their stores; others, such as Circuit City, went completely out of business.
5. Most Americans remember where they were when they heard about the 9/11 disaster.

## EXERCISE 62.2: Answers

1. The 2019 Walmart shootings in El Paso prompted yet another debate about gun control laws in the United States.
2. Every professor in the Department of English has a degree in literature.
3. The cast included several children, but only two of them had speaking roles.
4. (correct)
5. The price of oil has fluctuated this winter.

## EXERCISE 63.1: Answers

1. Every Friday, my grandmother would walk a mile to the post office and send a care package to her brother in Tennessee.
2. The blue whale can grow to be 180 feet long and can weigh up to 380,000 pounds.
3. Many a Michigan-based auto company, including General Motors, requested financial aid from the government.
4. A large corporation like AT&T may help finance an employee's MBA.
5. Rosie began by saying, "If you want my two cents," but she did not wait to see if listeners wanted it or not.

## EXERCISE 63.2: Answers

1. In 2000, Al Gore won the popular vote with 50,996,116 votes, but he was still short by five electoral votes.
2. Two hundred thousand people may have perished in the 2010 Haitian earthquake.

As many as 200,000 people perished in the 2010 Haitian earthquake.
3. The senator who voted against the measure received 6,817 angry emails and only twelve in support of her decision.
4. (correct)
5. In that age group, the risk is estimated to be about 1 in 2,500.

## EXERCISE 64.1: Answers

1. One critic claimed that few people listened to *The Velvet Underground and Nico* when the record was issued but that everyone who did formed a band.
2. Homemade sushi can be dangerous, but so can deviled eggs kept too long in a picnic basket.
3. The website *Poisonous Plants and Animals* lists tobacco (*Nicotiana tobacum*) as one of the most popular poisons in the world.
4. The monster in the Old English epic *Beowulf* got to tell his own side of the story in John Gardner's novel *Grendel*.
5. The 2009 film *Star Trek* imagines the youthful life of James T. Kirk and the crew of the *Enterprise*.

## EXERCISE 64.2: Answers

1. The group seeks volunteers to set up chairs in the meeting room before the event.
2. Despite concerns about reliability, police lineups are still frequently used to identify suspects.
3. I was ill prepared for my first calculus exam, but I managed to pass anyway.
4. Some passengers were bumped from the oversold flight.
5. Having an ignore-the-customer attitude may actually make a service-industry job less pleasant.
6. Both pro- and anti-State Department groups registered complaints.
7. At a yard sale, I found a 1964 pre-CBS Fender Stratocaster in mint condition.
8. Applicants who are over fifty years old may face age discrimination.
9. Neil Armstrong, a self-proclaimed "nerdy engineer," was the first person to set foot on the moon.
10. Carefully marketed children's safety products suggest to new parents that the more they spend, the safer their kids will be.

# Acknowledgments

# INDEX
## with Glossary of Terms

Words in blue are followed by a definition. **Boldface** terms in definitions are themselves defined elsewhere in this index.

723

**730**    Index with Glossary of Terms

common errors, 2–11. *See also* Top Twenty
common ground, building, 15–16
  in arguments, 151
  language for, 461–62, 471–76
  Quick Help, 473
common knowledge, 219, 220
common nouns, 680–81
communicator, in rhetorical situation, 26–27
community, language evoking, 461–62
company names
  abbreviations of, 686
  capitalization of, 681
comparative, 627–29 The *-er* or *more* form of an **adjective** or **adverb** used to compare two things (*happier, more quickly*).
*compare to, compare with,* 701
comparison and contrast
  for essay exams, 437
  organizing with, 48
  for paragraph development, 65
comparisons
  complete, 546, 628
  transitions, 73
compass points, capitalization of, 683
*complement, compliment,* 701
complements. *See* object complements; subject complements
complete comparisons, 546, 628
complete predicates, 566
complete structures, 543–47
complete subjects, 564
complex sentences, 575
*compliment, complement,* 701
compliments, in peer review, 82
*compose, comprise,* 701
compound adjectives, 10, 694–95
compound antecedents, 618
compound-complex sentences, 576
compound nouns, 661, 694–95
compound numbers, 695
compound predicates, 533–34, 566
compound prepositions, 558
compound sentences, 5–6, 7, 575, 640–41
compound structures
  commas with, 650
  inconsistent, 545–46
  pronoun case in, 616
compound subjects, 564, 606–7

compound words
  apostrophes with, 661
  hyphens with, 694–95
  possessive, 661
  spell checkers and, 5
*comprise, compose,* 701
conciseness, 490–94 Using the fewest possible words to make a point effectively.
  in headings, 372
  in online texts, 371
  in presentations, 379–80
  Quick Help, 491
  in sentences, 490–94
conclusions
  of arguments, 155–56, 160–62
  of presentations, 378–79
  questions in, 76, 89, 231
  quotations in, 76, 89
  of research projects, 231–32
  revising, 89
  transitions for, 73
  vivid images in, 77, 89
  writing effective, 89
concrete words, in argument, 158
conditional sentences, 601–2
conjunction, 553, 559–61 A word or words joining words, **phrases,** or **clauses**. *See also* **coordinating conjunction; correlative conjunction; subordinating conjunction**
conjunctive adverb, 557, 560, 645 A word (such as *moreover* or *nevertheless*) that modifies an **independent clause** following another independent clause. A conjunctive adverb generally follows a semicolon and is followed by a comma: *Thoreau lived simply at Walden; however, he regularly joined his aunt for tea in Concord.*
  comma with, 645
  semicolon with, 528, 652–53
connotation, 92, 473–75, 482–83
*conscience, conscious,* 701
*consequently, subsequently,* 701
Considering Disabilities
  accessibility, 185, 374, 378, 390
  assistive technology, 55
  assumptions, 475
  audience, 32, 475
  collaborative projects, 105
  color, 370

**predicate** but can't stand alone as a **sentence** because it begins with either a **subordinating conjunction** (*because, although*) or a relative **pronoun** (*that, which*).

    in complex and compound-complex sentences, 575–76

    as sentence fragment, 534–35

    and sentence types, 575–76

    subordinating, 497–501, 505

description

    in emotional appeals (*pathos*), 158

    for essay examinations, 437

    for exploring a topic, 42

    for paragraph development, 64

design, 366–75. *See also* formatting; visuals and media

    for argument, 152–53, 163

    color, 370

    Considering Disabilities, 370, 378, 390

    critical reading and, 110, 113

    for digital texts, 367

    formats, 369–72

    genre and, 366–67

    headings, 372

    Language, Culture, and Context, 369

    margins, 370, 371

    planning, 367–69

    for portfolios, 443

    principles of, 367–69

    purpose and, 367

    for research projects, 228

    revising, 89

    spacing, 370

    templates for, 369, 443, 450

    type size and fonts, 371

    visuals and media, 366–67, 372–75

    white space, 370

detail. *See also* evidence

    in arguments, 158

    in paragraphs, 62–70

    revising, 88

    in visuals and media, 63

determiners, 551, 556, 579–80

development, of paragraphs, 60–77

diagrams, 373. *See also* visuals and media

dialects, regional, 461–62, 626

dialogue

    paragraphing, 667

    quotation marks for, 667

dictation, for notes, 178

diction. *See* word choice

difference, respecting, 465–66, 471–76

*different from, different than,* 701

digital texts. *See also* multimodal text; websites

    annotating, 208

    audience for, 31, 448–49, 465–70

    best practices for, 25

    blogs, 41, 225, 389

    chunking for, 371

    citing

        APA style, 295–96, 303, 306–9, 312

        *Chicago* style, 326–28, 331–44

        CSE style, 357–61

        MLA style, 246, 260–75

    collaborating on, 43, 102–6, 401

    cover letters for résumés, 429–30

    designing, 366–75

    discussion lists and forums, 225

    email, 25

    global communication, 465–70

    marking up, 81

    organizing, 53–54, 468–69

    permission for, 216

    podcasts, 390

    portfolios, 442–46

    presentations, 385–86

    print texts versus, 108–9, 367

    reading critically, 108–9

    research logs, 178

    résumés, 431

    rhetorical situation for, 33–34, 387–88

    sample student texts, 449–52

    social media, 19–20, 31, 225, 449

    streaming media, 390

    text messages, 225, 449, 469, 481

    Twitter and microblogs, 19–20, 390, 449, 470

    webcasts, 385

    wikis, 185, 390

direct address, 646

directions. *See* compass points, capitalization of; process analysis

directness, 21–22, 468–69

direct objects, 566–67, 635

direct questions, 657

direct quotations, 210, 665–67. *See also* quotations

possessive form, 551 The form of a **noun** or **pronoun** that shows possession. Personal pronouns in the possessive case

predicate, 544–45, 562–64, 566–67 The **verb** and related words in a **clause** or **sentence**. The predicate expresses what the **subject** does, experiences, or is. The simple predicate is the verb or **verb phrase**: *We have been living in the Atlanta area.* The complete predicate includes the simple predicate and its **modifiers**, **objects**, and complements: *We have been living in the Atlanta area.*

preposition, 558–59, 633–36 A word or word group that indicates the relationship of a **noun** or **pronoun** to another part of the **sentence**: *From the top of the ladder, we looked over the rooftops.*

# ADVICE FOR MULTILINGUAL WRITERS

Multilingual

*Look for the "Multilingual" icon to find advice of special interest to international students and others whose home language is not English. Numbers in parentheses refer to chapters in this book. Number-letter combinations refer to sections within chapters.*

## "Language, Culture, and Context" boxes

# REVISION SYMBOLS

*Some instructors use these symbols as a kind of shorthand to guide you in revision. The numbers refer to a chapter number or a section of a chapter.*

| | | | |
|---|---|---|---|
| abb | abbreviation (63a–f) | paraph | paraphrase (15c) |
| ad | adjective/adverb (54) | pass | inappropriate passive (38c, 51g) |
| agr | agreement (52, 53) | | |
| awk | awkward | ref | unclear pronoun reference (53h) |
| cap | capitalization (62) | | |
| case | case (53) | run-on | run-on (fused) sentence (44) |
| cliché | cliché (37d) | sexist | sexist language (36b, 53g) |
| cohere | coherence (5d) | shift | shift (42) |
| com | incomplete comparison (47e) | slang | slang (37) |
| concl | weak conclusion (5f, 6e, 17c) | sp | spelling |
| coord | coordination (39a) | subord | subordination (39b) |
| cs | comma splice (44) | sum | summarize (9e, 15d) |
| d | diction (37) | t | tone (6f, 37a, 42f) |
| def | define (5c) | trans | transition (5d–e) |
| dev | development needed (5c) | u | unity (5a, 5d) |
| dm | dangling modifier (46c) | verb | verb form (51a–d) |
| doc | documentation (18–21) | vs | verb sequence (51f) |
| emph | emphasis unclear (41a) | vt | verb tense (51e–h) |
| ex | example needed (4f, 5b) | wrdy | wordy (38) |
| frag | sentence fragment (45) | wv | weak verb (41b) |
| fs | fused sentence (44) | ww | wrong word (37) |
| hyph | hyphen (64e–g) | , | comma (56) |
| inc | incomplete construction (47) | ; | semicolon (57) |
| intro | weak introduction (5f, 6e, 17c) | . ? ! | period, question mark, exclamation point (58) |
| ital | italics (or underlining) (64a–d) | | |
| jarg | jargon (37) | , | apostrophe (59) |
| lc | lowercase letter (62) | " " | quotation marks (60) |
| log | logic (10f, 11j) | ( ) [ ] — | parentheses, brackets, dash (61) |
| lv | language variety (34) | | |
| mix | mixed construction (47a) | : / . . . | colon, slash, ellipses (61) |
| mm | misplaced modifier (46a) | ^ | insert |
| ms | manuscript form (18–21) | ~ | transpose |
| no , | no comma (56k) | ⌣ | close up |
| num | number (63g–j) | x | obvious error |
| org | organization (4e, 11m) | | |
| ¶ | paragraph (5) | | |
| // | faulty parallelism (43) | | |

# CONTENTS